# Zanzibar

## Pemba • Mafia

the Bradt Travel Guide

**Chris McIntyre**
**Susan Shand**

edition
6

www.bradtguides.com

Bradt Travel Guides Ltd, UK
The Globe Pequot Press Inc, USA

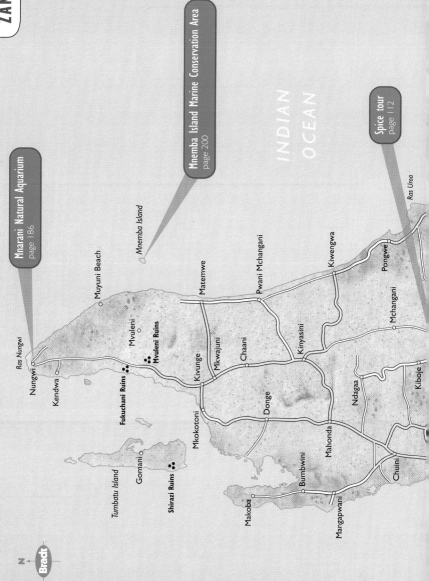

**Mnarani Natural Aquarium**
page 186

**Mnemba Island Marine Conservation Area**
page 200

**Spice tour**
page 112

INDIAN OCEAN

N

Bradt

Ras Nungwi

Muyuni Beach

Mnemba Island

Matemwe

Pwani Mchangani

Kiwengwa

Pongwe

Mchangani

Mvuleni
**Mvuleni Ruins**

**Fukuchani Ruins**

Nungwi

Kendwa

Kivunge

Mkwajuni

Chaani

Kinyasini

Ndagaa

Kiboje

Mkokotoni

Donge

Mahonda

Chuini

Tumbatu Island

Gomani

**Shirazi Ruins**

Makoba

Bumbwini

Mangapwani

Ras Uroa

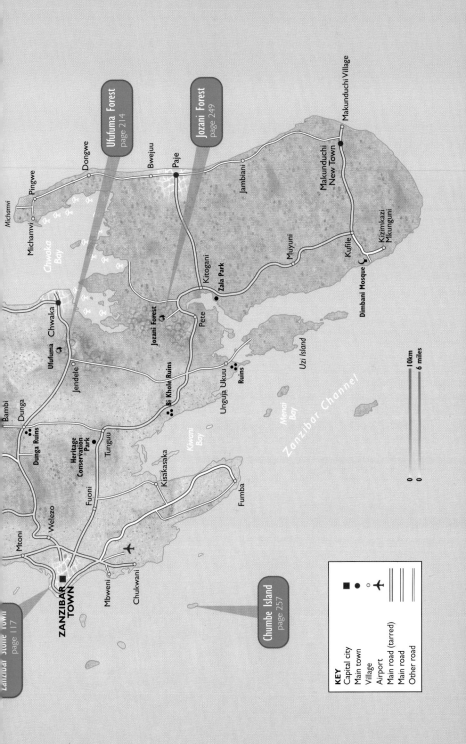

Zanzibar Stone Town
page 117

Ufufuma Forest
page 214

Jozani Forest
page 249

Chumbe Island
page 257

Michamvi
Pingwe
Michamvi
Dongwe
Bwejuu
Paje
Jambiani
Makunduchi Village
Makunduchi New Town
Kizimkazi Mkunguni
Kufile
Dimbani Mosque
Muyuni
Zala Park
Kitogani
Pete
Jozani Forest
Ruins
Unguja Ukuu
Uzi Island
Chwaka Bay
Chwaka
Ufufuma
Jendele
Bi Khole Ruins
Kiwani Bay
Kisakasaka
Tunguu
Fumba
Menai Bay
Zanzibar Channel
Dunga
Bambi
Dunga Ruins
Heritage Conservation Park
Fuoni
Welezo
Mtoni
Mbweni
Chukwani
ZANZIBAR TOWN

**KEY**

| | |
|---|---|
| ■ | Capital city |
| ● | Main town |
| ○ | Village |
| ✈ | Airport |
| | Main road (tarred) |
| | Main road |
| | Other road |

0    10km
0    6 miles

# Zanzibar
# Don't miss…

**Wildlife**
Kirk's red colobus
(AZ) page 251

**Beaches**
Nungwi West Beach
(SS) page 173

**Zanzibar Stone Town**
and House of Wonders
(AZ) page 147

**Diving & Snorkelling**
Moorish idol
with altheas
(RCC) page 93

**Culture**
Artist at work
(AZ) page 40

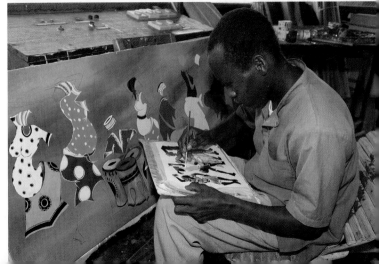

*opposite page* **Beach at Matemwe** (HT) page 195
*top* **Lionfish** (RCC)
*above left* **Soft coral** (RCC)
*above right* **Spotted eagle ray** (RCC)
*below* **Coral grouper** (RCC)

*top* **Flap-necked chameleon** *Chamaeleo dilepis* (AZ) page 51

*above left* **Giant coconut crab** *Birgus latro* (AZ) page 258

*above right* **Pineapple** (AZ) page 92

*below* **Suni antelope, Mnemba Island** (CM) page 200

top  Seaweed farming (AZ) page 225
above left  Cloves drying, Pemba (TH) page 48
above right  Clove bud (TH) page 48
below  Women gathering seaweed (KH) page 225

*above* **Men playing *bao*, Jambiani Village** (CM) page 42

*left* **Basket weaver** (AZ)

*below* **Children at play** (KH)

*above* **Fishing boat, Pemba**
(TH) page 272

*left* **Dhow building** (AZ) page 42

*below* **Traditional fishing basket,
Mafia** (TH) page 289

top right **The rooftops of Stone Town at sunrise** (CM) page 144

below left **On the way to Koran school, Stone Town** (AZ) page 144

below right **House of Wonders, Stone Town** (AZ) page 147

*above* **Market day, Stone Town** (AZ) page 145

*centre* **Child in Stone Town** (AZ) page 144

*right* **Slavery monument** (KH) page 11

_above_ **Walking inland from Matemwe Village** (CM) page 195

_centre_ _Dala-dala_, **Jambiani post office** (CM) page 236

_below_ **Maharubi Palace** (AZ) page 161

*above* **Tingatinga paintings and curios on sale in Nungwi** (SS) page 173

*below* **Ox and cart, Vumawimbi Beach, Pemba** (TH) page 285

*above* **Sailing dhows** (AZ) page 295
*below* **Dhow at sunset, Fukuchani** (AZ) page 192

# Authors and Contributors

**Chris McIntyre** went to Africa in 1987, after reading physics at Queen's College, Oxford. He taught with VSO in Zimbabwe for almost three years and travelled extensively, before co-authoring the UK's first guide to Namibia and Botswana for Bradt Travel Guides. He now writes the Bradt guides to Namibia, Botswana and Zambia, and updates them with months of travel and research every year.

Chris is also the managing director of Expert Africa – a leading African tour operator. When not travelling, he works with his specialist team to organise individual trips and honeymoons to southern and eastern Africa – including the islands of Zanzibar and Mafia.

He is a Fellow of the Royal Geographical Society, and occasionally writes and photographs for the media. Based in West London, he lives with his fiancée, Susan Shand, and can be contacted by email on chris.mcintyre@expertafrica.com.

**Susan Shand** spent her formative years living in Zambia and Saudi Arabia, which gave her a tremendous enthusiasm for travel. After returning to the UK to attend university, Susan spent a further year globetrotting before joining the travel industry in a professional capacity in 1999. Having created communications strategies for tourist boards, hotels and tour operators, Susan sought a career in African travel, the area about which she is most passionate. Susan has acted as a consultant for Expert Africa and now manages the media and public relations for Classic Representation – a collection of some of southern Africa's finest independent safari camps and boutique hotels.

Susan spends several months each year in Africa with Chris McIntyre, and many more encouraging the press and public to visit; she can be contacted by email on susan.shand@blueyonder.co.uk.

**Philip Briggs** provided information for the *Southern Tanzania Safaris* chapter and many additional facts and figures. He is the author of the Bradt guides to Tanzania, Uganda, Ethiopia, Malawi, Mozambique and Ghana, and co-author of their guide to Rwanda. He also contributes regular travel and wildlife features to *Travel Africa*, *Africa Geographic* and *Africa Birds & Birding* magazines.

**Sarah Chanter** wrote the original *History* section and many of the historical items for early editions of this book. She has a keen interest in the history and culture of Zanzibar, has worked as a teacher in Kenya, and has travelled extensively throughout east and southern Africa. Her enthusiasm has been contagious and invaluable.

**Said el-Gheithy** lives and works in both Zanzibar and London. As director of the Centre for African Language Learning (London) and the Princess Salme Institute (Zanzibar/London), he kindly provided information for the *Language* and *History* sections in previous editions of this book.

**David Else** is a professional travel writer. He first reached Zanzibar in 1985, sailing by dhow from Dar es Salaam. Over the next two decades (and using more comfortable transport) he visited Zanzibar regularly and wrote the first five editions of this guidebook. David has also travelled in other parts of Africa, from Cairo to Cape Town, from Senegal's Atlantic shore to the Indian Ocean beaches of Kenya and Tanzania, via most of the bits in between. When not in Africa, David lives in the north of England – a long way indeed from a tropical coastline.

**Jeff Fleisher** is an archaeological researcher in the Department of Anthropology at the University of Virginia, and provided valuable information for the historical and cultural sections of this book.

**Tricia and Bob Hayne** updated the section on Pemba for this edition. As editorial director of Bradt Travel Guides, Tricia is only too familiar with the minutiae of putting together a guidebook, and enjoys seeing it from the other side of the fence. She and Bob have also helped to update Chris's guides to Namibia, Botswana and Zambia, as well as writing their own Bradt guide to the Cayman Islands. In researching obscure corners of the globe, they can both indulge their interest in outdoor pursuits and the environment.

**Penny Hooper** updated the *Mafia Archipelago* chapter and helped with the Zanzibar research. She taught in China, and travelled throughout southeast Asia and South America, before reading English and European Literature at Warwick University. Since then she's fallen in love with Africa, and led many tours through Morocco, Djibouti and South Africa. She now concentrates on organising trips to Tanzania at Expert Africa.

**Dudley Iles** is a keen ornithologist and conservationist, and provided information on the wildlife of Zanzibar. From 1993 to 1995 he worked for the Commission for Lands and Environment in Zanzibar, helping to set up environmental clubs and train conservation officers.

**Christine Osborne** wrote the original text on which this book's *Mafia Archipelago* chapter is based. Born in Australia, she has travelled widely through Africa and the

Indian Ocean islands as a writer and photographer. Christine now runs the multi-faith and travel image libraries www.worldreligions.co.uk and www.copix.co.uk. She is a member of the British Guild of Travel Writers & Photographers.

**Gemma Pitcher** is a travel writer who lived and worked on Zanzibar, and travelled widely throughout eastern and southern Africa. She provided sections on various aspects of the people and culture of Zanzibar for this book; some of the text originally appeared in *Zanzibar Style* which was written by Gemma, with photographs by Javed Jafferji, published by Gallery Publications, and is reproduced with permission.

**Dr Matthew Richmond** is a marine science and fisheries expert who has lived and worked on Zanzibar and around the western Indian Ocean since 1989. Matt is involved in numerous marine education and biodiversity projects in the region, is the author of *A Guide to the Seashores of Eastern Africa and the Western Indian Ocean Islands*, and provided the text on marine wildlife for this book.

## THE NEXT EDITION

Our readers play a vital role in updating books for the next edition. If you have found changes, or new and exciting places, or have a story to share, do write. Email the authors on chris.mcintyre@expertafrica.com or susan.shand@blueyonder.co.uk, or write to: 'Zanzibar', Bradt Travel Guides Ltd, 23 High St, Chalfont St Peter, Bucks SL9 9QE, UK; ✆ +44 (0)1753 893444; **e** info@bradtguides.com; www.bradtguides.com.

The first Bradt travel guide was written in 1974 by George and Hilary Bradt on a river barge floating down a tributary of the Amazon. In the 1980s and '90s the focus shifted away from hiking to broader-based guides covering new destinations – usually the first to be published about these places. In the 21st century Bradt continues to publish such ground-breaking guides, as well as others to established holiday destinations, incorporating in-depth information on culture and natural history with the nuts and bolts of where to stay and what to see.

Bradt authors support responsible travel, and provide advice not only on minimum impact but also on how to give something back through local charities. In this way a true synergy is achieved between the traveller and local communities.

My association with Zanzibar goes back to 1976 when the newly 'Africanised' and socialist government of the island was hostile to foreign visitors. I have since returned many times as lecturer on board expedition ships and have relished the changes I have seen. The beaches are still superb, and while Stone Town still has the intimacy and total otherness that I loved, the buildings have been renovated and tourists now receive a warm welcome. On my last visit I escaped my group and wandered the narrow streets away from the tourist centre, stopping to watch a small child play with a toy car made from wire and bottle tops. His father, seeing my interest, came forward with a broad grin and asked me to photograph the two of them. That brief encounter epitomised all that I love about Zanzibar.

Chris McIntyre's talent at knowing what Bradt readers are looking for has made him one of our most praised writers on Africa. His extensive revision, with Susan Shand, of one of our most successful guides will be welcomed by his many fans.

**Reprinted April 2008** Sixth edition June 2006 First published 1993

Bradt Travel Guides Ltd
23 High Street, Chalfont St Peter, Bucks SL9 9QE, England; www.bradtguides.com
Published in the USA by The Globe Pequot Press Inc, 246 Goose Lane,
PO Box 480, Guilford, Connecticut 06475-0480

Text copyright © 2006 Chris McIntyre
Maps copyright © 2006 Bradt Travel Guides Ltd
Illustrations © 2006 individual photographers and artists

British Library Cataloguing in Publication Data
A catalogue record for this book is available from the British Library
ISBN-10: 1 84162 157 9  ISBN-13: 978 1 84162 157 9

**Photographs** Chris McIntyre (CM), Ariadne Van Zandbergen (AZ), Russell & Cindy Campbell (RCC; russandcindy@oceansense.net), Tricia Hayne (TH), Keith Hern (KH), Susan Shand (SS), Heather Tyrrell (HT)
*Front cover* Leaving a sandbar (CM)
*Back cover* Colourful Zanzibar painting (AZ)
*Title page* Dhow (AZ), Girl at traditional Zanzibar door (AZ), Fabric stall, Stone Town (KH)
**Illustrations** Annabel Milne, Carole Vincer  **Maps** Steve Munns, Terence Crump

Typeset from the authors' disc by Wakewing
Printed and bound in India by Nutech Photolithographers

# Acknowledgements

Chris McIntyre and Susan Shand have extensively updated and rewritten the guide for this sixth edition, building on the firm base left by David Else. Thanks are due to the many people who have helped with advice, information and contributions throughout the book's many years of life.

Some are already listed as *Major contributors* (page II) and others are named in the text. Of the rest, special thanks go to Peter Bennett, who helped research and gather information for four editions of this book. Further help has come from many others, including Javed Jafferji, John da Silva and Balkishna Gorolay (who greatly benefited our *History* section), and Fiona Clark and Jim Boggs (for input on wildlife and culture). For wildlife contributions, particular thanks to Rob Wild, Dr Nadia Corp, Lorna Slade, Dudley Iles, Dr Per Berggren; and to Matt Richmond PhD for extensive information on Zanzibar's marine wildlife. Thanks also to Toufiq Juma Toufiq, Ali Addurahim, and Ali Khamis Mohammed for local insights; and to Jeff Fleisher and Adria LaViolette for historical, archaeological and anthropological input. Hildegard Kiel and Yusuf Mahmoud helped with the *Music and dance* section; as did Michael Sweeney and Roger Gook with travel information.

For this sixth edition we're very grateful also to all those who have helped us so much. They include Salim Abdullah, William Ackroyd, Therese Allan, Anna Asheshov, Patrizia Barresi, Dr Per Berggren, Janice Booth, Amanda Botha, Peter Byrne, Janet Carroll, Maura Cavallo, Max Cheli, Jan Christiaens & Leen Charle, Nicola Colangelo, A Cotcher, Lara Cowan & Jamie Hendriksen, Jason Dalrymple, Simonetta di Barbora, Raihana Ehsanullah, Andrea Funkhouser, James Gillies, Chris Goodwin, N F Green, Gwen Griffiths, Andy Hamilton and Vivien Hicks, J P Krejci, Farhat 'Raf' Jah, Massimo Lancellotti, Alex Liambey, Peter and Amy Lumley-Wood, Maggie Mattock, Saori Miura, Elly M'langa, Dr Aviti J Mmochi, Nicola Moody, Mustafa Mukame, Ali Mwinyi, Georges Noel, Sandy Orton, Tamsin Pearce & Edward Scarr, Natalie Pope, Sue Pryde, Marilyn Reynolds, Klaus Richter, Susan Robinson, Rochelle le Roux, Anne Rutter, Adam Sachs, Peter & Tonya Siebert, Helen Simmans, Paul Shepherd, Abdul Simai, Christian Steer, Petra Sutila, Jacky Sutton, Maurice Turner, Agnes Viellard, Jean de Villiers, Laura Wade and Samantha Witman and Chris & Robin Watson.

Last but by no means least, our thanks also to the many Zanzibaris who openly shared with us impressions, opinions and knowledge of their country, and thus contributed to this and previous editions.

# Contents

# Introduction

An artist could find genial occupation for years; but your matter-of-fact … tourist would vote the place slow, of course, see nothing in it, and sigh for a future of broad streets and civilisation, broad-cloth, bottled beer and blacking; and from such revilers of the picturesque I trust a kindly Providence may long deliver the quaint, queer, rambling old Arab town of Zanzibar.

J F Elton, *Travels and Researches among the Lakes and Mountains of Eastern and Central Africa* (1879)

Zanzibar is one of those magical African names, like Timbuktu, Casablanca and Kilimanjaro. For many travellers, the name itself is often reason enough to come. Yet although expectations run high, awareness of the reality on Zanzibar and its neighbouring islands is often rather hazy.

Like many visitors, we discovered the islands only recently. We both had friends who had sailed from the mainland Tanzania to Zanzibar, and returned eulogising about the intoxicating aroma of spices, the amazing beaches, and just how cheap it was – but somehow neither of us made it there.

When we eventually visited in the early 2000s, stylish lodges were starting to flourish alongside backpackers' beach hideaways, and flights around the islands were becoming easier. On that first trip we also discovered Mafia – a smaller and quieter archipelago to the south, with fewer visitors, spectacular diving, and a more recent accessibility.

It's now five years, and many trips, since our first encounters, but the magic remains. It's impossible not to smile as you approach from the air, looking down on sparkling turquoise waters, darkened only by patch reefs, and punctuated by the billowing triangular white sails of passing dhows. Then, as you step off the plane, Zanzibar's blend of warmth, humidity and aromatic spices envelops you in the exotic.

Palm-lined stretches of powder-white coral sand line the coast for miles. Below the waves, iridescent fish flit amongst brightly coloured coral gardens, overshadowed by the occasional pelagic looming out of the blue from the depths of the Indian Ocean. From the turtles that nest here, to the whale sharks seen annually off Mafia, there is always something unexpected awaiting the diver and snorkeller.

On land, too, take the time to look beyond the gaze of most visitors. It may not always be easy, but it's worth it. While researching this guidebook, one particular day started off in much the same way as any other: we'd progressed slowly along the coast, wishing for the time to take a dip in the sea, but instead stopping at every hotel from backpackers' dives to exclusive lodges. Some were good and some bad. On leaving one that was just plain ugly, a man on the back of a scooter shouted to us, 'Are you the guidebook authors?'

We stopped to talk, and as we listened the situation became clear. Mr Mustafa was a village elder who had had worked as a driver for the government around

Zanzibar Town. Several years before, he'd set up a small project to preserve an area of native forest: Ufufuma Forest Reserve. Prior to arriving for this trip, we had tried to contact him about the project, but we'd heard nothing and so given up on him. Meanwhile he'd waited patiently for us to come and see him on the island. When we didn't arrive, he had eventually persuaded a friend to drive with him and help scour the coast for us.

We took that next afternoon off, away from the beach lodges, to visit his beloved reserve. Clambering through Ufufuma Forest that day, we saw why he had been so passionate about it. We followed him, and his fellow guides, through the forest, finding Kirk's red colobus monkeys, identifying trees used for local medicines, and stopping to explore several sacred caves that are used for local ceremonies. Mr Mustafa explained why it was so important to let the world know about Ufufuma Forest. His village had a history and a culture that was bound to the forest. It was vital to protect this, and if visitors could only come and see it, they hoped that it would bring in some much-needed cash to their economy – and stop others from cutting down the trees for firewood. Like many rural Zanzibaris, the villagers at Ufufuma were not rich; yet we felt both privileged and humbled to spend time with them. Their enthusiasm and warmth was infectious, and made this one of our favourite days on Zanzibar.

The message is clear: for some of the best experiences, get off the beaten track, perhaps with some of the islands' residents. Backpackers might feel the pull towards the popular low-budget haunts around Kendwa and Nungwi, but there are also some great (and equally inexpensive) places to stay on Zanzibar's east coast – which don't throng with budget travellers, and where your welcome will be all the more genuine.

Don't discount the less well-known areas of Zanzibar, Pemba Island or the Mafia Archipelago. The stunning new Fumba Beach Lodge in southwest Zanzibar is trail-blazing a new part of Zanzibar in some style; ecologically sound places like Chumbe Island demand a close look, and on Pemba – where tourism is scarcely in its infancy – an altogether slower pace of life beckons. While for those who want to escape to simple, small lodges with great diving and snorkelling, the handful of lodges on Mafia are already becoming firm favourites.

These islands now receive more than 100,000 visitors every year; about one in every fifty is likely to have a copy of this guide. We hope it helps you to get there, to choose the right places to stay, and to make the most of your time on the islands. But more than that, we hope that it will give you the confidence to venture off on your own, away from the lodges that we've so carefully described, to explore and to meet people like Mr Mustafa, and his community at Ufufuma – for their sake, as well as for the good of your holiday.

# Part One

## GENERAL INFORMATION

## ZANZIBAR AT A GLANCE

**Islands** Zanzibar Island (Unguja), Pemba Island, and surrounding islands

**Location** About 40km off the coast of east Africa, in the Indian Ocean, about 6°S of Equator

**Size** Zanzibar 1,660km², Pemba 985km²

**Climate** Wet season mid-Mar to end May; short rains Nov; rest of year generally dry. Average temperature 26–28°C

**Status** Separate state within United Republic of Tanzania, governed by Revolutionary Council and House of Representatives

**Population** 984,625 (2002)

**Life expectancy** 48

**Main town** Zanzibar Town, population 205,870 (2002)

**Economy** Fishing, agriculture, tourism

**Languages** Swahili (official), also Arabic

**Religion** Islam

**Currency** Tanzanian shilling (TSh)

**Exchange rate** £1 = TSh2,340, US$1 = TSh1,240, €1 = TSh1,584 (May 2006)

**International telephone code** +255

**Time** GMT +3

**Electrical voltage** 230v 50Hz; round or square three-pin 'British-style' plugs

**Weights and measures** Metric

**Flag** Green triangle top left, light blue triangle lower right, divided diagonally by yellow stripe with black edging

**National anthem** *Mungu ibariki Afrika* (God Bless Africa)

**Public holidays** 1 January, 12 January, 26 April, 1 May, 7 July, 9 December, 25 December (see also page 69)

# History, Politics and Economy

HISTORY *Sarah Chanter, with additional contributions by Jeff Fleisher*

The monsoons that blow across the Indian Ocean have allowed contact between Persia, Arabia, India and the coast of east Africa (including the islands of Zanzibar) for over 2,000 years. The first European arrivals were Portuguese 'navigators' looking for a trade route to India. They reached Zanzibar at the end of the 15th century and established a trading station here and at other points on the east African coast.

At the end of the 17th century the Portuguese were ousted by the Omani Arabs. During this period, Zanzibar became a major slaving centre. In 1840, the Omani Sultan Said moved his court from Muscat to Zanzibar, and the island became an Arab state and an important centre of trade and politics in the region. Many European explorers, including Livingstone and Stanley, began their expeditions into the interior of Africa from Zanzibar during the second half of the 19th century.

Zanzibar was a British protectorate from 1890 until 1963, when the state gained independence. In 1964, the sultan and the government were overthrown in a revolution. In the same year, Zanzibar and the newly independent country of Tanganyika combined to form the United Republic of Tanzania.

**FIRST INHABITANTS AND EARLY VISITORS** The first human beings, *Homo erectus*, evolved in the East African Rift Valley, within a thousand miles of Zanzibar, about 1.5 million years ago. They migrated throughout Africa and later Asia and beyond, becoming hunter-gatherers. Near rivers and coasts these people developed fishing techniques, and it is possible that Zanzibar's first human inhabitants were fishermen who crossed from the African mainland in dugout canoes sometime during the 1st millennium BC.

At around the same time, or even earlier, the east African coast (including the islands of Zanzibar) may have received visitors from many parts of the ancient world, such as Mesopotamia (present-day Iraq) and Egypt. The Egyptian pharaohs sent expeditions to the land they called Punt (present-day Somalia) in around 3000BC and again in 1492BC; these possibly continued southwards down the east African coast. This theory is supported by carvings on temple walls at Luxor showing sailing boats with slaves unloading gold, ivory tusks, leopard skins and trees of frankincense.

Other visitors may have included Phoenicians, a seafaring people from the eastern shores of the Mediterranean. Around 600BC, a Phoenician fleet sailed south along the coast, past Zanzibar, and is believed to have circumnavigated Africa before returning to the Mediterranean three years later.

By the 1st century AD Greek and Roman ships were sailing from the Red Sea down the east African coast, searching for valuable trade goods such as tortoiseshell, ebony and ivory. Around AD60, a Greek merchant from Alexandria wrote a guide for

3

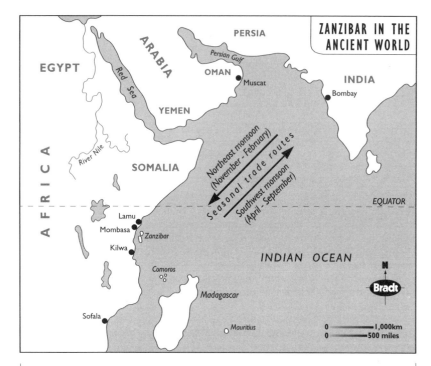

ships in the Indian Ocean called *The Periplus of the Erythaean Sea*. This is the first recorded eyewitness account of the east African coast, and describes 'the Island of Menouthesias' (most likely the present-day island of Unguja, also called Zanzibar Island) as 'flat and wooded' with 'many rivers' and 'small sewn boats used for fishing'. Another Alexandrine Greek, Claudius Ptolemaeus (usually called Ptolemy), also mentioned Menouthesias in his book *Geographike*, written about AD150.

At about the same time, it is thought that Arab and Persian trading ships from the Persian Gulf were also sailing down the coast of east Africa. They sailed south on the northeast monsoon between November and February, carrying beads and cloth, and even Chinese porcelain that had come via India. Then, between March and September, after the winds changed direction, they returned north on the southwest monsoon, carrying the same tortoiseshell, ebony and ivory that had attracted the Greeks and Romans, plus mangrove poles for timber and other goods. The Arabs and Persians traded with the local inhabitants but they remained visitors and, at this stage, did not settle.

During the 3rd and 4th centuries AD, other groups of migrating peoples started to arrive on the east coast of Africa. These people were Bantu (the name comes from the term used to define their group of languages); they originated from the area around present-day Cameroon in the centre of the continent, then spread throughout eastern and southern Africa. On the east African coast, they established settlements, which slowly grew into towns, and eventually became the major trading cities such as Kilwa, Lamu and Mombasa on the mainland, and Unguja Ukuu on the island of Unguja (Zanzibar Island). These coastal settlers traded with the Arabs, exporting ivory, rhino-horn, tortoiseshell and palm oil, and importing metal tools and weapons, wine and wheat.

The Arab traders called the east African coast 'Zinj el Barr', meaning 'land of the black people', from where the modern name Zanzibar is derived. 'Zinj' comes from *zang*, the Persian word for 'black', and *barr* is the Arabic word for 'land'. The Arabs may also have derived the word from Zayn za'l barr, meaning 'Fair is this land'. Zanzibar remained the name of the whole coast, including the islands of Unguja and Pemba (which together make up the present-day state of Zanzibar), until the late 15th century.

**EARLY ARAB SETTLERS** The 7th century AD saw the rise of Islam in Arabia. At the same time wars in this area, and subsequent unrest in Persia, caused a small number of people from these regions to escape to the east African coast, where they settled permanently, bringing the new Islamic religion with them.

There are several accounts of emigrations from Arabia to east Africa. (The history of this period is largely based on stories handed down by word of mouth through generations, which are difficult to separate from myth and legend.) One story tells of two Arab chiefs from Oman who arrived in east Africa with their families around the end of the 7th century, and settled on the island of Pate, near Lamu. Another story tells of an emigration from Shiraz, in Persia, some time between the 8th and 10th centuries. The Sultan of Shiraz and his six sons migrated with their followers in seven boats. One of the sons stopped at Pemba, while others settled in Mombasa and Kilwa. The 9th-century Arab tale of Sinbad the Sailor, one of the stories in *The Arabian Nights*, was most probably inspired by accounts of journeys by Arab sailors to east Africa and southeast Asia.

**THE RISE OF THE SWAHILI** During the second half of the first millennium, the coastal Bantu people developed a language and culture (in fact, a whole civilisation) which became known as Swahili. This name came from the Arabic word *sahil* meaning 'coast'. Their language, Kiswahili, although Bantu in origin, contained many Arabic words. It also included some Persian words, mainly nautical terms. There was some intermarriage, and the Swahili adopted many Arab customs and traditions, including the Islamic religion. On Unguja (Zanzibar Island), Shirazi settlers are believed to have married into the family of the island's Swahili king. Several centuries later, the Mwinyi Mkuu ('The Great Lord'), the traditional ruler of Unguja, continued to claim descent from a Shirazi prince.

By the 7th century, the Swahili people were trading regularly with Arab and Persian merchants. In the same way, Swahili dhows (traditional ships based on an Arab design) also became involved in the trade and sailed regularly to and from the Persian Gulf, carrying gold, ivory, rhino-horn, leopard skins, tortoiseshell, and ambergris from whales. African slaves were also carried to the Persian Gulf, probably to work in the marshlands of Mesopotamia.

Over the following centuries the trade between Africa and Arabia increased, as did trading links between east Africa and Asia. Ivory was exported to India, and later China, while Indian cloth and Chinese porcelain and silk were imported to Arabia and Zanzibar. At around this time, Indonesian sailors from Java and Sumatra are thought to have reached east Africa and Madagascar, possibly introducing coconuts and bananas.

From this period (7th to 10th centuries) archaeologists have discovered a very distinctive kind of local pottery, known as Tana Tradition, which looks the same at sites along the whole east African coast, from northern Kenya to southern Tanzania, and out to the Comoros Islands. The similarity of this pottery over such a large area shows how closely linked the people of the coast were, and also shows – for the first time – a sense of commonality and shared experience. Imported ceramics, called Sassian Islamic, from the Persian Gulf have also been discovered.

Archaeological, linguistic and historical research conducted since the early 1980s has also led to a shift in the way that the early history of the coast is interpreted, rejecting some of the ideas put forward by scholars working during the 1950s, 1960s and 1970s. In essence, this research suggests that at its core – its foundation – Swahili culture and history are an African phenomenon. Until recently, archaeologists had proposed that the large towns of the east African coast (such as Kilwa, Lamu, Mombasa and Unguja Ukuu) had been built by Persian or Arab settlers, and the local Bantu people had then intermarried and 'Africanised' the Arabs, thus resulting in the Swahili people. But, through extensive excavations at many of these towns, it is now known that they were founded by people from the interior of Africa and, instead of simply starting as grand towns, were actually built up slowly over time by these same people.

Unquestionably, the links to the Indian Ocean trade were some of the most important for these towns, but there is little evidence of large-scale migrations from Arabia or Persia to the coast of east Africa until the middle of the second millennium.

**ZANZIBAR ENTERS THE SECOND MILLENNIUM** On Unguja, one of the earliest remaining examples of permanent settlement from Persia is a mosque at Kizimkazi, on the southern part of the island. It contains an inscription dated AH500 (Anno Hegirae), which corresponds to the Christian year AD1107, making this the oldest-known Islamic building on the east African coast. From the end of the 12th century, Omani immigrants also settled in Pemba. At around the same time, the settlement that was to become Zanzibar Town also began to grow.

As the trade between Africa, Arabia and the rest of the Indian Ocean continued to expand, Zanzibar became an increasingly powerful and important commercial centre. Major imports included cotton cloth, porcelain and copper from Dabhol, a port on the west coast of India, and exports included iron from Sofala (in present-day Mozambique). By the 13th century, Zanzibar was minting its own coins, and stone buildings were starting to replace more basic mud dwellings. In 1295, the Venetian traveller Marco Polo wrote of Zanzibar: 'The people have a king … elephants in plenty … and whales in large numbers', although he never visited the island. Other writers of the time noted that the kings and queens of Zanzibar and Pemba dressed in fine silks and cottons, wore gold jewellery, and lived in stone houses decorated with Persian carpets and Chinese porcelain.

Many Chinese imports had come to Zanzibar via India, but in the early 15th century the ports on the coast of east Africa were trading directly with China. Gold, ivory and rhino-horn were transported to the East, as well as a small number of slaves. In 1414, a dhow from the city of Malindi (in present-day Kenya) carried a giraffe to China, as a present for the emperor. The trade came to an abrupt end in 1443 when the new Ming emperor banned Chinese merchants from going abroad, but the demand for ivory remained, supplied by Arab dhows via markets in India.

By the mid 15th century the islands of Zanzibar, along with Mombasa, Malindi, Lamu and Kilwa, formed a chain of thriving Swahili Islamic city states, each with its own sultan, spread along the east African coast. These cities had close trading links with Arabia, Persia, India and southeast Asia. Commerce between Africa and the Indian Ocean had become very profitable, and it seems that the sultans of Zanzibar and the other city states were more than happy for their territories to remain as gateways or conduits for it. At the end of the 15th century, though, the situation was severely disrupted by the arrival of the Portuguese on the coast of east Africa.

**PORTUGUESE RULE** By the mid 15th century, Prince Henry 'the Navigator' of Portugal was encouraging voyages of exploration around the African coast. He hoped to find a sea route to the East, as well as the Christian kingdom of the legendary Prester John (or 'Priest-king') of Abyssinia. With the rise of the Ottoman Empire in 1453, all goods from the East, including the increasingly valuable spices, now reached Portugal via potentially hostile Muslim countries.

In 1487, Prince Henry's successor, King John II, despatched two expeditions to the East led by Bartholomew Dias and Pedro da Covilhan: one by sea around the southern tip of Africa, the other overland through Egypt. In 1497, another Portuguese navigator, Vasco da Gama, encouraged by the reports of Dias and da Covilhan, rounded the Cape of Good Hope and sailed northwards up the coast of east Africa, on the way to India. He passed Zanzibar and landed at Mombasa, where he received a hostile reception from the sultan. But he got a warm welcome in Malindi, an old enemy of Mombasa. Da Gama built a pillar of friendship on the shore at Malindi and employed an Omani navigator called Ahmed bin Majid to guide him across the Indian Ocean. On his return from India in 1499 he moored for a day off Unguja.

More Portuguese ships followed in the wake of da Covilhan and da Gama. They needed safe provisioning and repair bases for their voyages to and from the Far East, and so garrisons were established in the harbours of Unguja, Pemba and Mombasa.

Any early friendship was soon forgotten when the Portuguese took control of Unguja in 1503. A ship commanded by Rui Lorenco Ravasco moored off the southern end of the island while Portuguese sailors captured over 20 Swahili dhows and shot about 35 islanders. The Mwinyi Mkuu (king of Zanzibar) was forced to become a subject of Portugal, and agreed to allow Portuguese ships free access to Zanzibar. Additionally, he was required to pay an annual tribute to the Portuguese crown.

Portuguese domination of the region continued. In 1505 they took control of Mombasa, and in 1506 Pemba. Between 1507 and 1511 the Portuguese also occupied territories in the Arabian Gulf, including Muscat and the island of Hormuz.

By 1510 Unguja's tribute had fallen short and the people of Pemba had also become hostile to the Portuguese. Under Duarte de Lemos, the Portuguese looted and set fire to settlements on Unguja, then plundered the town of Pujini in Pemba. They soon regained both islands and by 1525 the whole east African coast, from Lamu to Sofala, was under Portuguese control. Gold, ivory, ebony and slaves from the interior were carried to Portuguese colonies in India or back to Portugal. Iron ore and garnets from Sofala, and coconut fibre and gum-copal (a tree resin) from the islands were also exported. Cloth, beads, porcelain and metal tools were imported to the east African coast from Oman and Portugal.

Around 1560 the Portuguese built a church and small trading settlement on a western peninsula of Unguja. This was to become Zanzibar Town. But although the Portuguese occupied Unguja, and forced the local people to trade under their supervision, the islanders continued to pay allegiance to the Mwinyi Mkuu, their own king.

Portugal was not the only European power with interests in the Indian Ocean. In November 1591 the *Edward Bonaventura*, captained by Sir James Lancaster, became the first English ship to call at Zanzibar. It was supplied with fresh food and water by the Mwinyi Mkuu. Soon, more European ships were calling at Zanzibar on their way to and from the Indian subcontinent and islands of the East Indies.

John Henderson, a Scottish sailor from one English ship, was reportedly held captive on Zanzibar in 1625. He later escaped, but not until he had fallen in love with a Zanzibari princess who escaped with him back to Scotland. Today, their portraits are in the collection of the Scottish National Portrait Gallery in Edinburgh.

With the advent of English ships in the Indian Ocean, the Portuguese needed to strengthen their position on the coast. In 1594 they built a fort at Chake Chake in

Pemba, and from 1593 to 1595 Fort Jesus in Mombasa was constructed. Settlers arrived from Portugal, and a Portuguese garrison was established in Fort Jesus, brutally suppressing the local population. Mombasa became known as *Mvita*, 'the place of war', and the Portuguese governor as *Afriti*, 'the devil'.

Despite these fortifications, however, the Portuguese position in east Africa began to weaken. In Arabia, Hormuz was regained by the Persians in 1622, and in January 1650 Muscat was regained by the Omani Arabs. Following this victory, the Sultan of Oman's navy sailed to Zanzibar to help the Mwinyi Mkuu, Queen Mwana Mwema. The Omanis raided the Portuguese settlement on Unguja, killing many people and imprisoning about 400 in the church. They also attacked and burnt the Portuguese settlement on Pemba. By 1668, virtually the entire coastal area was in Omani hands. The only garrisons still held by the Portuguese were at Fort Jesus in Mombasa, and on the western peninsula of Unguja.

In 1682 the Portuguese persuaded the Queen of Pemba, who was living in Goa, to return, but this attempt to install a friendly ruler in Pemba was frustrated when her own subjects drove her out. The last Portuguese inhabitants were expelled in 1695.

By this time, Queen Mwana Mwema of Unguja had been succeeded by her son, Yusuf. After his death, towards the end of the 17th century, the island was divided between his two children, Bakari and Fatuma. King Bakari ruled the southern part of the island, with Kizimkazi as his capital, while his sister, Queen Fatuma, ruled the northern part. Fatuma supported the Portuguese, so her capital was built near the garrison on the western peninsula which later became the site of Zanzibar Town.

When the Omani fleet arrived at Mombasa and laid siege to Fort Jesus in March 1696, Queen Fatuma sent three dhows full of food to help the Portuguese defenders. The dhows were captured and burnt by the Omanis, who then attacked Zanzibar itself, forcing Queen Fatuma and her followers to flee into the interior of the island.

The siege of Mombasa lasted until December 1698, when the Omani forces took Fort Jesus and installed an Omani governor. Once again, the Omanis attacked Zanzibar. They drove out the last of the Portuguese settlers, captured Queen Fatuma and took her to Oman, where she spent the next 12 years in exile before returning to resume her rule. While she was away, her son Hassan took the title Mwinyi Mkuu, but paid allegiance to Oman.

Thus the Portuguese were finally ousted from the whole east African coast, and the Omanis were firmly in control of the entire region as far south as present-day Mozambique (which remained in Portuguese hands until 1972).

## OMANI RULE

**Early sultans and the rise of the slave trade** From 1698 the Sultan of Oman ruled the islands of Zanzibar from Muscat, his capital, through appointed governors and occasional armed raids to put down minor rebellions. To consolidate his grip on the islands, a fort was built in Zanzibar Town, on the site of the Portuguese church, and by 1710 about 50 Omani soldiers were garrisoned there.

By this time, Oman had become a major trading nation. One of its major exports was dates, and the expansion of date plantations created a demand for cheap slave labour. The rules of Islam forbade the enslavement of Muslims, so Africans were imported in large numbers, many of them transported through Zanzibar. It is estimated that there were about 5,000 African slaves in Oman at the beginning of the 18th century, with about 500 new slaves arriving each year. Although most slaves were used on the plantations, others were employed as domestic workers or concubines, and some were re-exported to Persia or India.

In 1744, in Oman, the ruling Yaa'rubi dynasty (which had been in power since 1624) came to an end after a long civil war. It was succeeded by the new Busaidi dynasty led by Ahmed bin Said al Busaidi, an Omani merchant and shipowner. Ahmed was made Sultan of Oman and the east African coast; one of his first moves was to install a new governor in Zanzibar.

At this time, the governors of the east African city states paid allegiance to Oman, but in practice they enjoyed a great deal of autonomy. Zanzibar, Pemba, Lamu and Kilwa were all ruled by members of the Busaidi family, but Mombasa was controlled by a rival Omani family, the Mazrui. In 1746 the Mazruis declared Mombasa independent of Oman, and overthrew the Busaidi force on Pemba. In 1753 they tried to capture Zanzibar, but the governor here remained loyal to Oman and repelled the attack.

During this period, the Mwinyi Mkuu, King Hassan, had died and been succeeded by his son, named Sultan, who in turn was succeeded by his son Ahmed, and then by his grandson Hassan II.

Zanzibar was now a major commercial centre and had also become very important strategically. From the middle of the 18th century there was a flourishing trade in slaves from Zanzibar and Kilwa to the Mascarenes (present-day Mauritius and Réunion). By the 1770s these numbered about 3,000 slaves a year. In the same period Dutch ships came to Zanzibar in search of slaves to work on plantations in the East Indies.

Until this time African slave traders had brought captured slaves to the coast, but by the end of the 18th century the demand for slaves had increased to such an extent that Arab and Swahili traders from the coast and islands were penetrating the African interior. By the 1770s caravan traders had already travelled inland as far as Lake Nyasa (present-day Lake Malawi). For more details, see the *East African slave trade* box, on pages 150–1.

**Sultan bin Ahmed and British involvement** In Oman a new sultan, Sultan bin Ahmed, came to power in 1792. He needed a strong ally to help him combat the Mazrui of Mombasa and also to keep the Persians out of Oman. He found this ally in Britain, by this time a powerful maritime nation with an empire expanding all over the world. In the late 18th century, Britain was at war with France and knew that the French emperor, Napoleon Bonaparte, was planning to march through Persia and capture Muscat, on his way to invade India. In 1798 Britain and Oman agreed a Treaty of Commerce and Navigation. Sultan bin Ahmed pledged himself to British interests in India, and his territories became out of bounds to the French. He allowed the British East India Company to establish a trading station in the Persian Gulf, and a British consul was posted to Muscat.

As well as defeating Bonaparte, the British had another motive for the treaty with Oman: they wanted to put pressure on the sultan to end slavery, which had been declared illegal in England in 1772. At this time, the trade from Africa to Oman was still buoyant.

At the same time, Zanzibar's position as an important trade centre was bolstered further when the supply of ivory from Mozambique to India collapsed because of excessive Portuguese export duties. The traders simply shipped their ivory through Zanzibar instead.

**Sultan Said and the birth of the spice trade** In 1804 Sultan bin Ahmed of Oman was killed in battle, and his sons Salim and Said (aged 15 and 13) jointly inherited his kingdom with their cousin Bedr acting as regent. Two years later the young Said killed Bedr, who he believed was plotting to kill him; in 1806 he was proclaimed Sultan of Oman and the east African coast.

Said ruled his kingdom from Muscat and did not visit his African territories for several years. He maintained good relations with Britain because, like his father, he hoped for British help against the Persians and the Mazruis. During this period, wars and drought had drained Oman's economy, and many Omani merchants migrated to Zanzibar to participate in coastal trading and the caravans to the interior.

Meanwhile, in Europe, a campaign led by William Wilberforce resulted in the abolition of the slave trade within the British Empire in 1807. The USA passed a law against slave trading in 1808; the French and Germans did the same a few years later.

In east Africa, however, about 8,000 slaves were brought from the mainland to Zanzibar every year, many of them carrying ivory. The resultant surplus of slaves was addressed in 1812, when a Muscat-born Arab called Saleh bin Haramil al Abray introduced clove trees into Zanzibar from the island of Bourbon (now Réunion). The slaves were diverted to work on clove plantations and demand increased once again.

As the demand for slaves and ivory continued to expand, Arab traders from the coast pushed further inland. In 1820, they established a trading centre at Kazeh (near present-day Tabora, in Tanzania), over 800km (500 miles) from the coast. From Kazeh, trade routes branched north to the shores of present-day Lake Victoria, northwest to Buganda (now Uganda), and southwest to the southern end of Lake Tanganyika. (See *Zanzibar and the slave trade* map, opposite.)

**Early British anti-slaving attempts** To combat this expansion in slavery the British consul in Muscat continued to put pressure on Sultan Said to end the slave trade. In September 1822 Said signed an anti-slavery treaty with the British Captain Fairfax Moresby which prohibited slave transport south and east of the 'Moresby Line' drawn from Cape Delgado, the southern limit of the sultan's domain in Africa, to Diu Head on the coast of India. (See *Zanzibar and the slave trade* map opposite.)

This treaty meant that the transport of slaves from Zanzibar to the Mascarenes and India was banned, but still permitted between Zanzibar and Oman. The sultan was also banned from selling slaves to Christians, which included the French for their Indian Ocean islands. British warships gained the right to confiscate any dhows found carrying slaves in forbidden waters. Ironically, British prohibition of the slave trade to the Mascarenes only led to an increased development of the slave trade in Zanzibar itself. Sultan Said lost the revenue he would have received as duty on all slaves sold, so to make up the shortfall he encouraged the development of more clove plantations.

Meanwhile, Sultan Said continued to attempt to oust the Mazrui Sultan of Mombasa. In 1823 the sultan asked for British protection against Oman. Captain William Owen of HMS *Leven* saw that he could use this local dispute to Britain's advantage: he sailed to Muscat and informed Sultan Said that he intended to grant

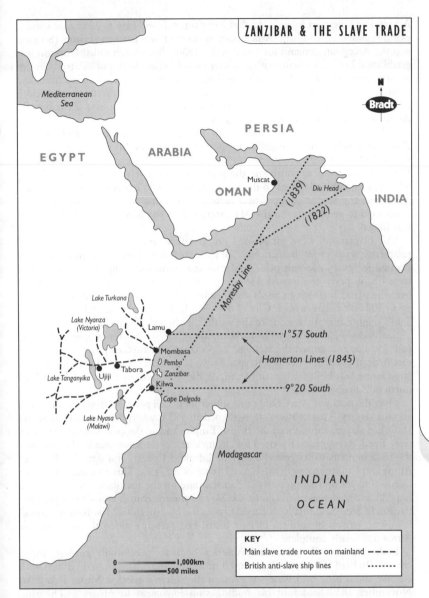

Mediterranean Sea

PERSIA

EGYPT

ARABIA

OMAN

Muscat

*(1839)*

Diu Head

INDIA

*(1822)*

Moresby Line

Lake Turkana

Lake Nyanza (Victoria)

Lamu

1°57 South

Mombasa

Pemba

Hamerton Lines (1845)

Tabora

Zanzibar

Lake Tanganyika

Ujiji

Kilwa

9°20 South

Lake Nyasa (Malawi)

Cape Delgado

Madagascar

INDIAN

OCEAN

**KEY**
Main slave trade routes on mainland – – – –
British anti-slave ship lines ·········

0 ————— 1,000km
0 ————— 500 miles

the Mazrui request for British protection unless Said agreed to end the slave trade. Said refused to do this, so Owen declared Mombasa a British Protectorate, along with the coastline from Malindi to Pangani, on condition that the Mazrui sultan agreed to abolish the slave trade. The sultan agreed, but within a few years, the Mazrui reverted to slave trading, and the British Protectorate was lifted in July 1826.

**Sultan Said in Zanzibar** In 1827, Sultan Said sailed from Muscat to Zanzibar to inspect his far-flung territory. Here he met one Edmund Roberts, an American merchant from Portsmouth, New Hampshire, who suggested a commercial treaty between Said and America. Soon Zanzibar was supplying large amounts of ivory to

America and western Europe. African ivory was soft and easy to carve into combs, piano keys and billiard balls. Asian ivory, in contrast, was hard and brittle. (So great was the American demand for ivory in the 1830s that a town called Ivoryton was established in Connecticut, with a factory making piano keys and billiard balls out of ivory imported from Zanzibar.) The Americans also purchased animal hides and gum-copal, a tree resin used in the manufacture of varnish. In return, cotton cloth (called 'Amerikani'), guns and gunpowder were imported into Zanzibar for distribution along the coast and to Arabia.

Sultan Said realised that trade with Europe and America would increase Zanzibar's wealth and strength, and thereby consolidate his own position, so at the end of the 1820s he decided to develop Zanzibar's clove industry further. His first move was to confiscate the plantations of Saleh bin Haramil al Abray, who had introduced cloves to the island in 1812. Said's reason for this was that Saleh was the leader of a political faction competing for power, and had also continued to send slaves to the Mascarenes after the Moresby treaty had made this illegal.

Vast plantations were established on Zanzibar and Pemba, and the islands' prosperity soon grew dramatically. Said decreed that three clove trees must be planted for every coconut palm, and that any landowner failing to do so would have his property confiscated. He became the owner of 45 plantations scattered over the island, with about 50 slaves working as labourers on the smaller plots and up to 500 on the larger ones. Cloves fetched a high price abroad and by the end of Said's reign Zanzibar was one of the world's leading clove producers.

Said valued Zanzibar's large harbour, abundant freshwater supply and fertile soil. He also recognised the strategic importance of a Busaidi power base on the east African coast, and decided to spend several months on the island each year. A large house was built for him at Mtoni, on the west coast of the island about 5km north of Zanzibar Town.

Over the next few years, Said came under increased pressure from the British to abolish slavery. This call was strengthened in 1833, when the Emancipation Act abolished slavery throughout the British Empire and all slaves in British territories were freed. Recognising the need for strong allies, in the same year Said formalised the trade agreement suggested earlier by Edmund Roberts and signed a Treaty of Amity and Commerce with the United States of America. This gave the Americans freedom to set up trading posts at Zanzibar and on the mainland. In return, Said hoped for armed assistance against the Mazrui and for British anti-slavery pressure to ease. In 1837 Said finally managed to oust the Mazrui from Mombasa and install his own garrison of soldiers in Fort Jesus. His presence along the coast of east Africa was finally complete.

Links between Zanzibar and America became increasingly cordial, and a consul, Richard Waters, was appointed in March 1837. Said presented him with a horse and a boat, and Waters was often the sultan's guest at Mtoni Palace. In November 1839 Said sent his trading ship *El-Sultani* to America. The ship arrived in New York in May 1840, the first Arab boat ever to visit an American port, and returned to Zanzibar with a cargo of arms and ammunition, china, beads and 'Amerikani' cloth.

## Zanzibar becomes the capital of Oman

In December 1840 Sultan Said established his capital in Zanzibar, transferring it 3,000 miles from Muscat. He made this move at a time when Zanzibar's prosperity was increasing rapidly, and Oman's was in decline. Said also believed that the dual powerbase of Zanzibar and Oman would help safeguard his territories on the African mainland and maintain his dominance over Indian Ocean trade. Many of Oman's most influential merchants were already based in Zanzibar, and more followed him in the move from Muscat.

Said's title was now Sultan of Zanzibar and Oman. He ruled Zanzibar directly while his eldest surviving son, Thuwaini, remained in Muscat as governor of Oman. Zanzibar's own king, the Mwinyi Mkuu, presided over local matters but Said's government took control of trade and international affairs. Zanzibar Town began to expand: when Said had first arrived in the 1820s the buildings were mostly huts of mud thatched with coconut fronds, but by the 1850s many impressive stone buildings had been constructed by the new immigrants from Oman.

Said was also followed to Zanzibar by Captain Atkins Hamerton, who had originally been installed in Muscat to act as British Consul. In December 1841 he became the first British consul in Zanzibar. France also established diplomatic relations with Zanzibar: a French consulate was opened in 1844.

Meanwhile, despite the restrictions imposed by the Moresby Treaty, the slave trade continued to expand. In 1841 Arab traders had established a trading colony at Ujiji on Lake Tanganyika, almost 1,600km (1,000 miles) from the coast, and in 1843 the first Arab caravans had reached Buganda (now Uganda) on the shores of present-day Lake Victoria. By the end of the 1840s, Arab traders had gone even further, reaching the Upper Congo (now eastern DRC), the Central Highland area around Mount Kenya, the Rift Valley lakes of Baringo and Turkana, and southern Ethiopia. About 13,000 slaves a year were arriving in Zanzibar from the mainland. (See *Zanzibar and the slave trade* map, page 11.)

**Britain's opposition to the slave trade** Sultan Said became increasingly concerned that British attempts to abolish the slave trade would weaken his power in the region. In 1842 he sent his envoy Ali bin Nasur to London on the ship *El-Sultani* to plead his case. Said's gifts for Queen Victoria included emeralds, cashmere shawls, pearl necklaces and ten Arab horses.

In reply, the British government told the Zanzibari ruler that it wished to abolish the slave trade to Arabia, Oman, Persia and the Red Sea. To soften the blow Queen Victoria gave Said a state coach and a silver-gilt tea service. (The state coach arrived in pieces and had to be assembled. It was still unused a year later, as Zanzibar had no roads. The tea service was considered too ornate to use and was taken to the British consulate for safe keeping.)

Britain continued putting restrictions on the slave trade. In October 1845 Said was virtually forced by Captain Hamerton to sign another anti-slavery treaty, which allowed slave transport only between lines of latitude 1° 57" S and 9° 20" S (between Lamu and Kilwa, the northern and southern limits of Said's dominions on the coast). This meant slaves could still be imported into Zanzibar but could no longer be exported to Oman.

Ships from the British navy were employed to help enforce the treaty by capturing any dhows carrying slaves. When a dhow was captured, it was set on fire and the slaves were taken to Aden, India, or a free-slave community on the mainland coast, such as English Point in Mombasa. However, with only four ships to patrol a huge area of sea, the British navy found it hard to enforce the treaty, so the slave dhows continued to sail. Ships from France, Germany, Spain, Portugal and America also continued to carry slaves, as there were still huge profits to be made. And on the mainland slave traders continued to push further into the interior.

**Early European explorers** In the 1840s, European missionaries and explorers began to venture into the east African interior. In Britain, an Association for Promoting the Discovery of the Interior Parts of Africa had been formed as early as 1788, and had since merged with the Royal Geographical Society (RGS). In the following years it would play a leading role in the search for the source of the River Nile.

Zanzibar became the usual starting point for journeys into the interior. Here, the European missionaries and explorers paid their respects to Sultan Said, who 'owned' most of the land they would pass through. They equipped their expeditions with supplies and porters, before sailing to Bagamoyo on the mainland. Many explorers followed the established slaving routes into the interior, often employing slave traders to act as guides.

In 1844, the English Church Missionary Society, unable to find any British recruits, sent the German Johann Krapf to east Africa in an early attempt to convert the local people to Christianity. He was joined by his missionary colleague, Johann Rebmann, who arrived in Zanzibar two years later. They travelled widely across the areas now known as southern Kenya and northern Tanzania. In May 1848 Rebmann became the first European to see Kilimanjaro and in December 1849 Krapf was the first European to see Mount Kenya. (See *Exploration in east Africa* map opposite.)

Meanwhile on Zanzibar the slave trade continued. By the 1850s about 14,000 to 15,000 slaves a year were being imported into Zanzibar from the mainland, providing Sultan Said with a large income from duties. Zanzibar traders pushed even deeper into the interior, reaching what is now northern Zambia. In 1852 a caravan reached Benguela (in present-day Angola) having completely traversed the continent from east to west, while the following year another group reached Linyanti, in the present-day Caprivi Strip of Namibia.

Through the slave caravans Said had become the nominal ruler of a vast commercial empire stretching along the coast from Mozambique to the Somali ports, and inland to the Great Lakes of Nyasa (Malawi), Tanganyika, Nyanza (Victoria) and Turkana. By the end of his reign Zanzibar's empire covered about 2.5 million km$^2$ (1 million square miles), or 10% of the African continent, including the whole of present-day Tanzania, plus sizeable parts of Malawi, Zambia, DRC, Uganda and Kenya. The Arabs had a saying: 'When the flute plays in Zanzibar, they dance on the lakes.' But it was an empire in name only and Said never attempted to conquer or develop the area.

**The end of Said's reign** Sultan Said made periodic visits to Muscat, leaving his son Khaled as governor of Zanzibar in his absence. Khaled had a predilection for French goods and called his principal country estate Marseilles, after the French Mediterranean port. When Khaled died of tuberculosis in November 1854, an order came from Said in Muscat appointing another son, the 20-year-old Majid, as governor.

In September 1856 Said sailed for Zanzibar again in his boat *Kitorie*. He travelled with his family, including his son Barghash, now 19 years old. Said ordered some loose planks of wood to be loaded onto the ship, saying that if anyone should die on board, the body must not be buried at sea according to Muslim custom, but embalmed and taken to Zanzibar in a coffin. Said seemed to know it was he who was about to die: he began to suffer severe pains from an old wound in his thigh followed by an attack of dysentery. On 19 October 1856 he died on board the ship. He was 65 years old.

Barghash put his father's body in the coffin and took command of the fleet. He knew his elder brother Majid would succeed his father as the new Sultan of Zanzibar, but he also realised that Majid would be unaware of their father's death. On the night of his arrival at Zanzibar, Barghash came ashore secretly and tried to take control of the palace at Mtoni and the Fort in Zanzibar Town, but he was unable to muster enough supporters and his attempt was thwarted.

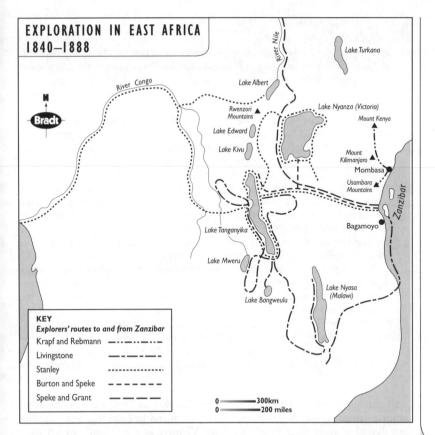

## EXPLORATION IN EAST AFRICA 1840–1888

**Bradt**

Lake Turkana

River Nile

River Congo

Lake Albert

Lake Nyanza (Victoria)

Rwenzori Mountains ▲

Mount Kenya ▲

Lake Edward

Lake Kivu

Mount Kilimanjaro ▲

Mombasa

Usambara Mountains ▲

Zanzibar

Lake Tanganyika

Bagamoyo

Lake Mweru

Lake Nyasa (Malawi)

Lake Bangweulu

**KEY**
*Explorers' routes to and from Zanzibar*

Krapf and Rebmann  —··—··—··—

Livingstone  — —  — —

Stanley  ···············

Burton and Speke  – – – – – –

Speke and Grant  —  —  —  —

0 ———300km
0 ———200 miles

On 28 October 1856 Majid bin Said was proclaimed Sultan of Zanzibar. A ship was sent to Oman with the news, but Said's eldest son Thuwaini refused to acknowledge Majid as sultan, believing that he was the legitimate successor. Majid agreed to pay Thuwaini 40,000 Maria Theresa dollars annually as compensation, but after a year the payment ceased.

**Later European explorers** By this time, the reports of early explorers like Rebmann and Krapf encouraged the British Royal Geographical Society to send an expedition to east Africa to search for the source of the White Nile. The leaders were Lieutenant (later Sir) Richard Francis Burton and Lieutenant John Hanning Speke.

In December 1856, on the last day of mourning for Sultan Said, Burton and Speke arrived in Zanzibar. They sailed for Bagamoyo and followed the slave route towards Lake Tanganyika, which they hoped was the source of the Nile. When they arrived, in January 1858, local Arab traders told them that a river at the northern end of the lake flowed into the lake (not out of it). Burton and Speke were unable to reach the point where the river met the lake.

Bitterly disappointed, they began to return eastwards to Zanzibar. Burton became ill, and was forced to stop, so Speke struck out northwards on his own, and became the first European to see the great *nyanza* (meaning 'lake') which he named Lake Victoria, certain it was the source of the White Nile – although he was unable to prove it at the time. Speke and Burton returned to Zanzibar in March 1859, and then separately to London.

In October 1859 Barghash was plotting to overthrow his brother, Majid, who was Sultan of Zanzibar. Barghash was living in a house in Zanzibar Town, close to the palace of Beit el Sahel, with his sister Meyye and 11-year-old brother Abdil Aziz. Two more sisters, Salme and Khole, and two of his nieces, the princesses Shembua and Farashuu, all supported Barghash and wanted Majid overthrown.

Majid, aware that his brother was plotting against him, arranged to have their houses watched and ordered Barghash's house to be blockaded. Several hundred soldiers were posted outside the front of the house with strict orders to shoot any suspicious person and cut off all communications. But Barghash had plenty of provisions, and his fellow conspirators smuggled water to him through the back of the house.

Meanwhile, at the fortified plantation of Marseilles, in the centre of the island, the conspirators stored arms, ammunition and food supplies in preparation for a siege. (The plantation had been named Marseilles by another brother, Khalid, who had a predilection for all things French.) Princess Salme played an important part in the preparations because she could write, and prepared secret messages to be carried between the other conspirators. She later referred to herself as 'secretary to the alliance of rebels'.

At midnight on 8 October 1859 Salme and Khole went to Barghash's house with a large escort including Shembua and Farashuu. Bluffing their way past the soldiers on duty (Arab women did not normally speak to strange men), they were allowed to pay the prisoner a short visit. They brought women's robes and veils and Barghash wrapped himself in a voluminous black robe, which left only his eyes free. The tallest women walked alongside him to make his height less conspicuous, and the guards on the door made way respectfully for the royal party when they left the building.

Once outside the town Barghash threw off his disguise and headed for Marseilles with

---

To verify his theory, Speke returned to Zanzibar in 1860 with the Scottish explorer James Grant. Together they travelled inland to Lake Victoria, and this time found a great river emptying Lake Victoria at a waterfall, which they named the Ripon Falls after the president of the Royal Geographical Society. Although they were still unable to prove without doubt that this river was the Nile, it was the closest any explorer had got to settling the great geographical question of the age.

**The division of Oman and Zanzibar** Meanwhile, back on Zanzibar, a power struggle was developing between the Omani rulers. Sultan Thuwaini of Oman planned to overthrow Sultan Majid of Zanzibar, as his promised tribute had not been paid. In February 1859 Thuwaini sailed southwards but was intercepted by a British cruiser at the eastern tip of Arabia. The British government wanted to keep control of the sea route to India, and did not want a civil war to develop in this area. Captain Hamerton, the British consul, had died, but Thuwaini was persuaded to submit his claims to the arbitration of Lord Canning, the Governor-General of India. Thuwaini agreed and returned to Muscat.

But Majid was in danger from another member of the family. His brother Barghash was still plotting to overthrow him and proclaim himself Sultan of Zanzibar. Majid learnt of the plot but Barghash escaped to the Marseilles plantation. He was finally captured and exiled to India for two years. (For more details see *The escape to Marseilles* box above.)

In April 1861 Lord Canning declared that Oman and Zanzibar should be completely separate states. The annual tribute from Zanzibar to Oman was reinstated and in March 1862 Britain and France signed an Anglo-French his supporters, while his sisters returned to Zanzibar Town. Majid soon heard news of Barghash's escape, and mustered 5,000 soldiers, while the British consul, Sir Christopher Rigby, provided nine soldiers and a gun from the British warship HMS *Assaye*.

Majid marched to Marseilles and started to bombard the house, but Barghash's supporters emerged from their fortifications, and fought off Majid's troops until sunset. Several hundred lives were lost. Majid retreated for the night but, as he and his army slept, Barghash and his supporters slipped back into town. On the morning of 16 October, Majid re-advanced on Marseilles and smashed open the gates, only to find it abandoned.

By this time, Barghash had returned to his house. Realising that his plans were thwarted, he remained concealed, refusing even to go to the window. Rigby arranged for HMS *Assaye* to be anchored just offshore, and a detachment of marines landed and marched to the front of Barghash's house, calling on Barghash to surrender. When there was no answer, the marines started to fire their guns at the front of the house. Khole, calling from her house across the street, persuaded her brother to surrender. Contemporary reports describe how cries of '*Aman!*' ('Peace!') were heard from inside the house and how, after the firing had stopped, Rigby rapped on the door with his walking stick and demanded immediate surrender. When Barghash emerged, Rigby arrested him and put him on board the Assaye. He was taken to India, where he lived in exile for two years. Abdil Aziz insisted on accompanying his elder brother and stayed in India after Barghash's return in 1861.

Princess Salme was rejected by her family, and in 1866 met a German trader called Heinrich Ruete. They became lovers and moved to Germany, where Salme changed her name to Emily and later wrote a book about her life at the court of Zanzibar. (For more details see the *Princess Salme* box, pages 164–5.)

declaration which recognised Majid as Sultan of Zanzibar and his territories as an independent sovereignty.

Although the Mwinyi Mkuu still lived in the palace at Dunga, his power was now negligible. Hassan II was succeeded by Mohammed, who died in 1865, aged 80. He was succeeded by his son, Ahmed, who died of smallpox in March 1873, leaving no male heir. The line of the Mwinyi Mkuu of Zanzibar had come to an end, and its passing was hardly noticed.

In 1866, in Oman, Thuwaini was murdered in his sleep by his son, Salim, who succeeded him. Majid discontinued the payment of the tribute on the grounds that Salim was a usurper, and Oman withdrew into isolation. (This isolation lasted for over a hundred years, until the accession of Sultan Qaboos bin Said in 1970.)

**DAVID LIVINGSTONE AND 'STINKIBAR'** In 1866 the Scottish missionary and explorer David Livingstone arrived in Zanzibar. He had already travelled across much of central and southern Africa, and written at great length about the horrors of the slave trade. He wanted to introduce what he regarded as essential elements of civilisation – commerce and Christianity – to Africa as a way of defeating the slave trade. He had also been asked by the Royal Geographical Society to clarify the pattern of the watersheds in the area of Lake Nyasa and Lake Tanganyika and their relation to the source of the White Nile – still an unsolved problem for the geographers of the day.

By this period, Zanzibar's increasing trade and growing population had created its own problems and Livingstone did not enjoy his stay:

No-one can truly enjoy good health here. The stench from... two square miles of exposed sea-beach, which is the general depository of the filth of the town, is quite horrible. At night, it is so gross and crass, one might cut a slice and manure the garden with it. It might be called 'Stinkibar' rather than Zanzibar.

During the same period, other European visitors arriving by ship claimed they could smell Zanzibar before they could see it. In the town itself, the freshwater springs were not particularly fresh. Dr James Christie, an English physician who arrived in Zanzibar in 1869, reported that the springs consisted of the 'diluted drainage of dunghills and graveyards'. Not surprisingly, this led to frequent bouts of dysentery and epidemics of smallpox and cholera. Malaria and bilharzia were also problems. Cholera epidemics had occurred in 1821 and 1836, and smallpox in 1858. Later cholera epidemics in 1858 and 1869–70 killed one-sixth of the population of Zanzibar Town, and 35,000 people throughout the island.

At this time, slavery had still not been abolished on Zanzibar. In the early 1860s an average 15,000 slaves a year were being imported into Zanzibar from mainland Africa, and by 1866 this had grown to 20,000 a year. The slave population had reached its peak and clove production entered a phase of overproduction and stagnation, so prices dropped.

As a result of the declining profitability of clove production, there was a greater interest in the production of coconut and sesame seed oils, mainly for export to France. There was also a revival of sugar production, and rubber plantations were established along the coast.

### LIVINGSTONE, STANLEY AND THE RELIEF EXPEDITIONS David Livingstone had left
Zanzibar in March 1866. Lack of news in the outside world led to speculation on his whereabouts, and in January 1871 the American journalist Henry Morton Stanley arrived in Zanzibar, having been commissioned by the *New York Herald* to search for the 'lost explorer'. In November the same year Stanley arrived at Ujiji, where he found Livingstone and greeted him with the now immortal phrase, 'Doctor Livingstone, I presume?' (For more details on the explorations of Livingstone see the *David Livingstone* box, page 153, and the *Henry Morton Stanley* box opposite.)

After Stanley had found Livingstone, and returned alone to Zanzibar, Livingstone stayed at Kazeh until August 1872, then set off southwards on another expedition to find the source of the Nile, which he thought would take no more than a few months. (He had already been in the interior for six years at this stage.)

Meanwhile the RGS in London was unaware of Stanley's 'find' so in February 1872 the Livingstone Search and Relief Expedition, led by Lieutenant Llewellyn Dawson, was dispatched to Zanzibar in the steamship *Abydos*. Two months later, the expedition arrived in Zanzibar, where their ship was caught in the freak hurricane of 14 April. Every ship and dhow in the harbour was driven ashore except the *Abydos*. The town was wrecked, many people were killed, and over two-thirds of the coconut and clove trees on the island were uprooted.

A few weeks after the hurricane, in May 1872, Stanley arrived at Bagamoyo, where he met Dawson and told him that Livingstone was safe and would be arriving after a few more months. Dawson cancelled the Search and Relief Expedition and returned to London. But by the end of 1872 Livingstone had still not arrived back at Zanzibar as expected, so in February 1873 a second Relief Expedition, led by Lieutenant Verney Lovett Cameron, set out from Zanzibar to find him.

Unknown to Cameron, and the rest of the world, Livingstone had grown ill, with a recurrence of dysentery. On 2 May 1873 he died in the village of Chitambo, near Lake Bangweulu (in present-day Zambia), 800km (500 miles) south of Ujiji, and even further from the actual source of the Nile. Two of his companions carried his body back towards Zanzibar. In August 1873 they reached Kazeh, where they met Cameron.

The man known to the world as Henry Morton Stanley was born John Rowland on 29 January 1841 at Denbigh in Wales. He spent nine years in a workhouse and two years as a farmhand, before joining a ship from Liverpool to New Orleans, which he reached in 1858. In New Orleans he was adopted by his employer, a cotton merchant, from whom he took his new name, Henry Stanley. 'Morton' was added later.

By 1869 Stanley was a correspondent for the *New York Herald*. The manager of the newspaper, James Gordon Bennett, despatched him to Africa with orders to cover the inauguration of the Suez Canal, and then find Livingstone if he was alive, or bring back his bones if he was dead.

Stanley arrived in Zanzibar on 6 January 1871. He borrowed a top hat from the American consul, John Francis Webb, and went to visit Sultan Barghash who gave him letters of recommendation to show his agents in the interior. Stanley set off from Zanzibar in March that year, just two days before the start of the rainy season. His provisions included American cloth, beads of glass, coral and china for trading, plus two silver goblets and a bottle of champagne for the day he met Livingstone.

Stanley finally met Livingstone at Ujiji, on the eastern shore of Lake Tanganyika, on 10 November 1871. According to Stanley's own description of the meeting, Stanley took off his hat, held out his hand, and said, 'Doctor Livingstone, I presume?' When Livingstone answered, 'Yes,' Stanley continued with, 'I thank God that I have been permitted to see you,' to which Livingstone gravely replied, 'I feel thankful that I am here to welcome you.'

After these traditional English niceties, and the seemingly mundane phrase that was to dog Stanley for the rest of his life, Stanley and Livingstone travelled in the area together for some time, but Livingstone was still determined to discover the source of the Nile and pressed on southwards alone. Stanley returned to Zanzibar on 7 May 1872, before travelling to London.

Two years later, Stanley gave up journalism to return to Africa as an explorer. He reached Zanzibar again in September 1874, and left for the mainland in November the same year. On this expedition he rounded the southern shore of Lake Victoria, went through Buganda (now Uganda), and followed the Congo River (through present-day DRC) to the Atlantic Ocean, which he reached on 12 August 1877, thus crossing Africa in 999 days.

From 1879 to 1884, Stanley returned to the Congo for King Leopold II of Belgium. He established and governed the Congo Free State (which was to become Zaire, now renamed the Democratic Republic of Congo), and the town of Stanleyville (now Kisangani) was named after him.

After another expedition from 1887 to 1889, Stanley returned to Britain a celebrity. He was married in Westminster Abbey in 1890, elected to parliament as a Liberal Unionist for North Lambeth in 1895, and knighted in 1899. He died in London on 10 May 1904.

Cameron decided to march on to Ujiji which he reached in February 1874 and where he found Livingstone's papers. From Ujiji, Cameron continued westwards, eventually reaching the Atlantic coast in November 1875, thereby becoming the first European to travel across this part of Africa from east to west.

**SULTAN BARGHASH AND JOHN KIRK** By this time, on Zanzibar, Sultan Majid had died, aged 36. His only child was a daughter so his brother Barghash (who had twice already tried to seize the throne and had returned to Zanzibar from exile in India in 1861) finally succeeded to the throne, and was proclaimed sultan on 7 October

1870. In the same year, Dr John Kirk (who had originally come to Zanzibar as a medical officer on Livingstone's expedition) was made acting British consul.

After the hurricane of April 1872, Sultan Barghash had announced plans to grow new plantations, and the slave trade picked up once again. By late 1872 around 16,000 slaves had been imported into Zanzibar. (The hurricane hit only the southern tip of Pemba, leaving most of the clove trees on that island untouched. By the 1880s Pemba was producing about 80% of the total clove harvest from Zanzibar and Pemba.)

At the same time, the anti-slavery movement continued to grow, fuelled in America by the publication of *Uncle Tom's Cabin*. In January 1873 Sir Bartle Frere, a special envoy from Queen Victoria, arrived in Zanzibar to negotiate a treaty which he hoped would finally put an end to the Arab slave trade. Sultan Barghash was naturally reluctant to end slavery and Frere sailed for England at the beginning of March 1873 without a treaty. Almost immediately the British navy began a blockade of every slave port on the mainland. The number of slaves passing through the Customs House in Zanzibar Town between January and March dropped to 21, compared with 4,000 in the same period the previous year.

In June 1873 Sir John Kirk informed Sultan Barghash that a total blockade of Zanzibar Island was imminent. Reluctantly Barghash signed the Anglo-Zanzibari treaty which provided for the complete abolition of the slave trade in Barghash's territories, the closing of all slave markets and the protection of all liberated slaves. Transport of slaves was forbidden, and slaves could no longer be exported from mainland Africa to Zanzibar and Pemba, except for domestic purposes.

The large slave market in Zanzibar Town was closed immediately. The site was bought by missionaries of the Universities Mission in Central Africa (UMCA), and work started on the cathedral which can still be seen in Zanzibar Town today (see *Chapter 6*).

One of the main effects of the treaty, now that slavery was illegal, was to push up the price of slaves and the trade continued in a clandestine manner. Through the 1870s smugglers were estimated to be exporting between 10,000 and 12,000 slaves a year.

In 1875 Kirk brought Sultan Barghash an official invitation to visit Britain to ratify the Anglo-Zanzibari treaty. In June the same year Barghash and Kirk arrived in London where Barghash received the Freedom of the City at the Guildhall and attended a state banquet at Mansion House. While Barghash was in London, his sister Salme had come from Germany (see the *Princess Salme* box, pages 164–5) hoping to be reconciled with her brother, but Barghash refused to meet her. After four weeks of intensive sightseeing and entertainment, Barghash and his party returned to Zanzibar via Paris and Marseilles, arriving home in September.

For the British, Zanzibar was no longer a distant, obscure island, and links between the two countries became even more firmly established. In 1869 the Suez Canal had opened, making the sea voyage between Britain and the coast of east Africa much shorter and simpler. In 1872 the British India Steamship Navigation Company started a monthly mail service between Zanzibar and Aden. It brought the first scheduled passenger and cargo service to Zanzibar, which allowed merchandise to be exported quickly. Communication was again improved in 1879, when the Eastern Telegraph Company completed their cable from Zanzibar to Europe via Aden, and a telegraphic link with Europe was established.

Inspired by his visit to Europe, Barghash decided to make many changes on Zanzibar. Advised by John Kirk (now firmly installed as the power behind the throne), he appointed Lieutenant William Lloyd Mathews (see *William Lloyd Mathews* box, page 170) to reorganise his army and enforce his sovereignty over the interior.

During his exile in India, Barghash had seen the opulent wealth of the Indian palaces and he tried to emulate them on Zanzibar. Many luxurious palaces were

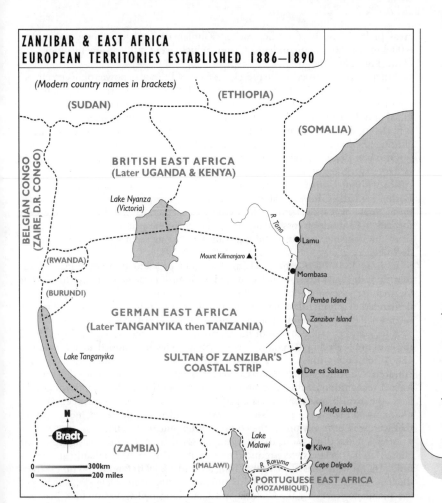

**ZANZIBAR & EAST AFRICA**
**EUROPEAN TERRITORIES ESTABLISHED 1886–1890**

*(Modern country names in brackets)*

(SUDAN)

(ETHIOPIA)

(SOMALIA)

BELGIAN CONGO
(ZAIRE, D.R. CONGO)

**BRITISH EAST AFRICA**
(Later **UGANDA & KENYA**)

Lake Nyanza
(Victoria)

R Tana

Lamu

(RWANDA)

Mount Kilimanjaro ▲

Mombasa

(BURUNDI)

Pemba Island

**GERMAN EAST AFRICA**
(Later **TANGANYIKA** then **TANZANIA**)

Zanzibar Island

Lake Tanganyika

**SULTAN OF ZANZIBAR'S**
**COASTAL STRIP**

Dar es Salaam

Mafia Island

N

**Bradt**

(ZAMBIA)

Lake
Malawi

Kilwa

0 ——— 300km
0 ——— 200 miles

(MALAWI)

R Rovuma

Cape Delgado

**PORTUGUESE EAST AFRICA**
(MOZAMBIQUE)

built, including Chukwani, to the south of Zanzibar Town, and Maruhubi Palace, to the north, for his harem. Another palace, in the town, became known as the Beit el Ajaib, or House of Wonders, as it was the first building on Zanzibar to have electric lighting. In all his palaces, Barghash upgraded the dinner services from silver to gold. Divan coverings of goat and camel hair were replaced by silks and taffetas, and French carpets covered the floors.

Barghash introduced Zanzibar's first clean water system to replace supplies from local wells and rainwater: aqueducts and conduits brought pure water from a spring at Bububu into Zanzibar Town, a distance of some 6km. Other developments introduced by Barghash included a police force, an ice-making factory, electric street lighting, and telephones to connect his city and country palaces. Barghash also built and improved the roads on the island, and every year he provided one of his private steamships for Muslims wishing to make the pilgrimage to Mecca.

**THE SCRAMBLE FOR AFRICA** In 1884 Dr Karl Peters, founder of the Society for German Colonisation, arrived in Zanzibar, then sailed for the mainland where he made 'treaties of eternal friendship' with the local African chiefs in return for large areas of land. By the time he reached Kilimanjaro he had annexed more than 6,000km² (2,500 square miles) of land, which were still nominally under the control of Sultan Barghash.

Britain was concerned at the presence of a rival European power on its patch, but was distracted by events elsewhere. In January 1885 Khartoum, the capital of Anglo-Egyptian Sudan, fell to the forces of the Mahdi. The British General Gordon was killed and the British governor of Equatoria Province, south of Khartoum, was cut off. (Ironically, the governor was actually a German called Eduard Schnitzer, although he had adopted the name Emin Pasha and was working for the British.)

Otto von Bismark, the German chancellor, saw the Mahdi's victory as a sign of Britain's weakness and believed that Germany could consolidate its claims in east Africa without British opposition. In February the same year the General Act of Berlin, signed by Kaiser Wilhelm of Germany, officially proclaimed a German protectorate over the territories annexed by Karl Peters. Sultan Barghash was only formally told about his loss of land in April of the same year. He hoped for support from the British, but Britain did not want to make an enemy of Germany, and so declined.

In June 1885 the Germans claimed another protectorate over Witu and the mouth of the Tana River, near Lamu, and in August the same year five ships of the German navy, commanded by Carl Paschen, arrived in Zanzibar harbour. Paschen demanded that Sultan Barghash recognise the German protectorates. Kirk on the recommendations of the British government persuaded Barghash to submit.

A few days after the arrival of the German fleet, another German ship entered the harbour, carrying Barghash's sister Salme (who had eloped to Germany in 1866). She was with her son Said-Rudolph, now 16 years old, and two other children. On Kirk's advice, Barghash tolerated Salme's presence. Barghash sent his formal recognition of the German protectorate to Carl Paschen and two months later, the British government arranged for a joint commission between Britain, Germany and France to establish their own boundaries in the mainland territories that were still officially under the control of the Sultan of Zanzibar.

After lengthy discussions the first Anglo-German agreement was signed in late 1886. Barghash's lands were reduced to Zanzibar, Pemba, Mafia, Lamu and a ten-mile (16km) wide coastal strip stretching around 1,200km (about 750 miles) from the Tana River, near Lamu, to the Rovuma River, near Cape Delgado. The rest of the mainland, east of Lake Victoria and Lake Tanganyika, was divided between Britain and Germany. Britain took the northern portion, between the Tana and Umba rivers, which became British East Africa, later Kenya. Germany took the southern portion, between the Umba and Rovuma rivers. This became German East Africa, later Tanganyika. (See *Zanzibar and east Africa* map, page 21.)

Given no option, Barghash agreed to this treaty in December 1886 and the French government signed it a few days later. In June 1887 Barghash leased the northern section of his coastal strip (between the Tana and Umba rivers) to the British East African Association (BEAA), which had been formed by William Mackinnon in May the same year. Meanwhile the Germans and Portuguese met in Barghash's absence to discuss their own border, and Portugal gained more of Barghash's land in the south.

In February 1888 Barghash sailed to Muscat, to recuperate from tuberculosis and elephantiasis at the healing Bushire Springs on the Persian coast. He returned to Zanzibar on 26 March, but died five hours after his arrival, aged 51.

On 29 March 1888 Barghash's brother Khalifa bin Said was proclaimed sultan. In April the same year, the British East African Association became the Imperial British East Africa Company (IBEA), with its capital at Mombasa, which was beginning to take Zanzibar's place as the commercial centre for Africa.

**A BRITISH PROTECTORATE** In September 1889 Khalifa signed an agreement with the British government agreeing to abolish slavery in his territories. Anybody who entered the sultan's realms, and any children born, would be free. Britain and Germany were awarded a permanent right to search for slaves in Zanzibar's waters. As a sign of Britain's appreciation, Khalifa was knighted, but less than a month later he died, aged 36.

Khalifa's brother, Ali bin Said was the fourth and last of Said's sons to become Sultan of Zanzibar. On 1 August 1890 Ali signed an anti-slavery treaty forbidding the purchase and sale of slaves. With the end of the slave trade, the only viable export from the interior was ivory, by now a rapidly waning asset.

Meanwhile in the interior Karl Peters entered Uganda in February 1890 and claimed the territory for Germany, just ahead of Sir Frederick Jackson from England. The British politician Lord Robert Salisbury realised that control of the Upper Nile could lead indirectly to the control of the Suez Canal and thus the trade route to India. Germany was persuaded to renounce any claims over Uganda in return for British support of the Kaiser against the major European powers of the day, France and Russia.

By the second Anglo-German agreement (the Treaty of Zanzibar) of 1 July 1890, Germany agreed to recognise a British protectorate over the Sultanate of Zanzibar, and to abandon any claim to Witu and the country inland as far as the Upper Nile. Germany also abandoned any claim to the west of Lake Nyasa but, in return, gained sovereignty over the coast of German East Africa, later to become Tanganyika. The British–German border was continued westwards across Lake Victoria to the boundary of the Belgian territory of Congo, thus securing Uganda for Britain. The British coastal strip (which still belonged to the Sultan of Zanzibar) was removed from the control of the British East Africa Company and administered by the British East Africa Protectorate, later to become Kenya and Uganda.

In exchange for the thousands of square miles of east African territory, including the islands of Zanzibar (Unguja and Pemba) which it gave up to British control, Germany gained Heligoland, a strategically important small island off the German coast which lay near the mouth of the Kiel Canal.

In 1891 a constitutional government was established in Zanzibar, with General Sir Lloyd Mathews as first minister. But although Zanzibar enjoyed the status of a British protectorate, the island's importance as a commercial centre was declining further in favour of Mombasa.

The British now controlled Zanzibar, so when Sultan Ali died in March 1893, without making a will, they proclaimed Hamad, son of Thuwaini (the former sultan of Oman), as sultan.

During Hamad's reign, in November 1895, Zanzibar issued its first stamps (from about 1875 the island had been using Indian stamps with 'Zanzibar' overprinted). Then a newspaper, the *Gazette for Zanzibar and East Africa,* was produced. It was followed by others in English, Arabic, Swahili and Urdu.

**THE LAST YEARS OF THE 19TH CENTURY** When Sultan Hamad died in August 1896, the British recommended his cousin Hamoud as sultan. But Barghash's son, Khaled, who had already tried to seize power from Hamad, made a second attempt at snatching the throne. He was briefly successful this time but was ousted by the British, after 'the shortest war in history' (see *The shortest war in history* box, page 25).

On 27 August 1896 Hamoud was conducted into the Customs House and proclaimed Sultan of Zanzibar, amidst the salute of the ships. The new sultan supported the British government and on 5 April 1897 he signed a treaty to abolish the legal status of slavery in Zanzibar and Pemba. Shortly after this Queen Victoria awarded him the Grand Cross of the Most Distinguished Order of St Michael and

St George. Hamoud sent his son Ali to school at Harrow in England where he represented his father at the coronation of King Edward VII.

Sultan Hamoud died on 18 July 1902 and the British proclaimed the 18-year-old Ali as the new sultan. From his school days he spoke English fluently, and continued to travel in Europe during his reign. In May 1911 Ali attended the coronation of King George V in England. While in Europe his health deteriorated and he abdicated in December 1911. He spent the last seven years of his life in Europe, and died in Paris in December 1918. Khalifa bin Harub, a cousin of Ali, became Sultan Khalifa II on 16 December 1911.

**ZANZIBAR ENTERS THE 20TH CENTURY** Sultan Khalifa bin Harub proved to be a moderate but influential ruler, and proceeded to guide Zanzibar through the first half of the turbulent 20th century with skill and diplomacy.

Soon after Khalifa gained power, changes were made to the British way of overseeing their interests in Zanzibar. In July 1913 responsibility for Zanzibar was transferred from the Foreign Office to the Colonial Office. The post of British consul became British Resident, subject to the control of the governor of the British East Africa Protectorate. At the same time a Protectorate Council was established. This was an advisory body with the sultan as president and the British Resident as vice-president.

During World War I the German and British armies, with conscripted African soldiers, were involved in several campaigns on the mainland. The war did not affect Zanzibar directly except for one incident when the British ship *Pegasus* was bombarded and sunk by the German ship *Königsberg* in Zanzibar Town harbour. (Graves marking the bodies of sailors killed in this incident can still be seen on Grave Island.)

Towards the end of the war, in 1917, the British army drove the Germans out of their territory and marched into Dar es Salaam. Khaled, who had tried to seize the throne of Zanzibar during 'the shortest war' in 1896, was still there and was captured. He was exiled to the Seychelles, then allowed to return to Mombasa in 1925 where he lived quietly until 1927.

After the war, the German East African territory was administered by Britain under a League of Nations mandate and called Tanganyika. Later, in 1920, the British East Africa Protectorate became known as the Kenya Colony.

In 1925 the British Resident on Zanzibar was made directly responsible to the Colonial Office in London, and a new Legislative Council was established. The ten-mile (16km) wide strip of land along the coast of Kenya, including Mombasa, which had been leased to Kenya in 1895 was still technically 'owned' by the Sultan of Zanzibar and the new Kenya government continued to pay the lease of £11,000 per year.

During World War II, Zanzibar was not involved in any military action. The war's main effect was to interrupt the supply of rice, a staple food for the Asian and African people, that had until then been imported from Burma.

**THE ROAD TO INDEPENDENCE** After World War II Britain gradually allowed the local people of Zanzibar to become involved in the island's government. Several local political parties were formed and Zanzibar's first elections were held in July 1957. The Afro-Shirazi Union (which later became the Afro-Shirazi Party – ASP) defeated the Zanzibar Nationalist Party (ZNP). Broadly speaking, the ASP was dominated by Africans, the ZNP by Arabs.

In October 1960 Sultan Khalifa died, after ruling for 49 years, and was succeeded by his only son, Abdullah. In November the same year Zanzibar was granted a new constitution which allowed for the elections of the members of the

Sultan Hamad died on 25 August 1896 while the British consul, Arthur Hardinge, was on leave in England. The acting British consul, Basil Cave, recommended that Hamoud (Hamad's cousin) be appointed sultan, but when Cave and Sir Lloyd Mathews reached the palace of Beit el Sahel in Zanzibar Town they found the doors barred. Khaled, the son of Barghash (and another cousin of Hamoud), had arrived before them with about 60 armed men, entered the palace by climbing through a broken window, and been quickly joined by more than 2,000 supporters.

Khaled proclaimed himself sultan, and raised the red flag of Zanzibar on the palace roof. But Basil Cave refused to recognise his claim: British ships in the harbour landed guards of marines, which were posted at the British consulate (where the British women sought refuge), the Customs House, and elsewhere around the town. Many foreigners gathered on the roof of the English Club, where they had a clear view of the harbour and the palace.

On the morning of 26 August the three British ships were reinforced by the timely arrival of two others, and the following day, at dawn, the British fleet under Rear-Admiral Harry Holdsworth Rawson delivered an ultimatum: Khaled was to surrender, disarm, evacuate the palace and be at the Customs House by 09.00, or the British ships would open fire. At 08.00 Khaled sent an envoy to Cave, asking for a chance to discuss peace, but his request was refused.

The palace clock struck three (09.00 British time) and at 09.02 the bombardment started. In half an hour Beit el Sahel and the adjoining palace of Beit el Hukm were badly damaged. The lighthouse outside the palace was in flames and the nearby House of Wonders was also hit a few times. Many of Khaled's supporters had fled, leaving 500 dead and wounded lying about the palace grounds.

At 09.40 Khaled surrendered. He lowered the flag, the firing ceased and the war was over. This dispute over the succession is listed in the *Guinness Book of Records* as the shortest war in history.

Khaled escaped through the narrow streets and fled to the German consulate, where he was given asylum. As the steps of the consulate led onto the beach, Khaled was able to board the German warship *Seeadler* without risking arrest. Khaled was taken to Dar es Salaam where he lived in exile. He died in Mombasa in 1927, aged 53.

History, Politics and Economy **HISTORY**

Legislative Council. Elections took place in January 1961, producing no clear result, and again in June 1961, but these were marked by serious inter-racial rioting. Nevertheless the ZNP, along with the aligned Zanzibar and Pemba People's Party, won 13 of the seats on the council, while the ASP won ten.

Britain realised that internal self-government for Zanzibar was inevitable, and this was finally granted in June 1963. In July that year Sultan Abdullah died. Throughout his short reign he had suffered from severe pains in his legs, which were eventually amputated. Abdullah was succeeded by his eldest son Jamshid.

On 10 December 1963 Zanzibar became an independent sultanate, and the coastal strip was finally ceded to Kenya, which became independent two days later. Zanzibar was made a full member of the British Commonwealth and on 16 December became a member of the United Nations. But the new sultanate was short-lived: on 12 January 1964 the Zanzibari government was overthrown in a violent revolution.

**REVOLUTIONARY ZANZIBAR** The leader of Zanzibar's revolution was a Ugandan called John Okello who had been living in Pemba. The local African population supported Okello with great enthusiasm, and went on a rampage through the islands, during which more than 17,000 Arabs and Indians were killed in one night. The leader of the Afro-Shirazi Party, Sheik Abied Amani Karume, was installed as president of the newly proclaimed People's Republic of Zanzibar, which included the islands of Unguja and Pemba.

Karume and other prominent ASP members formed the Revolutionary Government of Zanzibar (Serikali ya Mapinduzi ya Zanzibar, or SMZ). Most of Zanzibar's Asian and Indian people left the islands; their property was confiscated and their land nationalised. (On the mainland Sultan Jamshid was given temporary asylum in Dar es Salaam, then went to Britain where he lived in exile.)

Meanwhile, Tanganyika had also become independent in December 1961, with Julius Nyerere elected as president the following year. Nyerere had known and supported Karume since the mid-1950s but the Zanzibar Revolution created problems in Tanganyika, inspiring an attempted coup in Dar es Salaam only a few days later. (To suppress this coup Nyerere received help from Britain in the form of a battalion of commandos.)

Once Nyerere had regained control he approached Karume to discuss a political union, and on 24 April 1964 the two countries joined to form the United Republic of Tanganyika and Zanzibar. In October the same year the country was renamed Tanzania (from 'Tan' in Tanganyika and 'Zan' in Zanzibar). Nyerere became the president of the new state while Karume became vice-president. The SMZ was to control all local affairs on the islands of Unguja and Pemba, while foreign affairs would be handled by the Tanzanian government.

(During the negotiations John Okello had gone to the mainland to meet Nyerere. On his return to Zanzibar in March 1964 he was sent back to Dar es Salaam. He made no further public appearances.)

Despite the so-called union Karume kept Zanzibar separate from the rest of Tanzania in many respects. The clove plantations on Unguja and Pemba were developed and the earnings from exports continued to increase, but this revenue was not shared with mainland Tanzania.

After the revolution almost all the European and Asian residents had left Zanzibar. To fill the vacuum caused by the departure of these skilled people Karume attracted technical and military assistance from Cuba, China and the then Eastern bloc countries of East Germany, Bulgaria and the Soviet Union. Engineers from East Germany designed and built new blocks of flats in Zanzibar Town, and in 'new towns' elsewhere on the islands of Unguja and Pemba. In 1970 Karume's government was accused of human rights violations against political opponents.

On 7 April 1972 Karume was assassinated while playing cards in the ASP headquarters in Zanzibar Town. Aboud Jumbe Mwinyi, who had been a member of the ASP since before independence, became the new leader of the Revolutionary Government. Mwinyi was less hardline than Karume and introduced several reforms. He was also more sympathetic towards Nyerere and mainland Tanzania. In February 1977 the ASP united with Nyerere's party, the Tanzania African National Union (TANU), to form the Chama Cha Mapinduzi (Party of the Revolution).

After this unification, both leaders began to relax some of their policies on nationalised industries and state financial control. Relations with some Western nations, including Britain, slowly improved. In July 1979, as a sign that Tanzania was regaining some international respect, Queen Elizabeth II of the UK visited Zanzibar. Then, in 1980, the first presidential elections took place, and Aboud Jumbe Mwinyi was officially elected as president of Zanzibar.

Zanzibar forms a separate state within the United Republic of Tanzania. It is governed by a Revolutionary Council and House of Representatives, whose members are elected or appointed. The president of Zanzibar is also the vice-president of Tanzania.

Zanzibar has seen many changes on the political front since the early 1990s. Along with the rest of Tanzania, Zanzibar ceased to be a one-party state in 1992. For the first time in almost 20 years Chama Cha Mapinduzi (CCM) was faced with several new opposition groups, which quickly coalesced into parties. The Civic United Front (CUF), led by Seif Sherif Hamad from Pemba, became the major opposition party for Zanzibar. Elections were planned for October 1995, as all parties agreed that a gradual transition to a multi-party political system would be beneficial. Salmin Amour remained Zanzibar's president and CCM leader, while on the mainland the CCM chose a new president, Benjamin Mkapa, in July 1995. This followed the resignation of Julius Nyerere, the 'father of the nation' who had ruled since independence, although he remained an important figure behind the scenes.

Elections were duly held in Zanzibar on 22 October 1995, a week before the mainland vote. It was a simple two-horse race between Salmin Amour and Seif Sherif Hamad for president of Zanzibar, and between CCM and CUF candidates in the islands' parliament. There was a very high turnout (over 95% of registered voters) and voting passed peacefully, but the counting took three days for just over 300,000 votes.

Although the ruling party's control of the government structure gave it an in-built advantage, it soon transpired that the CUF was polling strongly. Complaints by the CCM that the election process was flawed were withdrawn when it transpired that Amour had won with 50.2% of the vote, but then the CUF picked up the claim of unfair procedures. International observers agreed that there was evidence of serious irregularities, but the nominally independent Zanzibar Electoral Commission refused to hold a recount or to compare their figures with some of those recorded by the UN. On the mainland, a divided opposition and an even more shambolic election, not to mention the possibility of vote-rigging, meant that the CCM and President Mkapa stayed in power. The CUF brought a high-profile legal case against the CCM on the grounds that the results and the whole election process were not representative of the wishes of the people, but this was bogged down in the courts and finally dismissed in 1998.

In the lead-up to elections in late 2000, Amour rocked the boat by announcing he would stand for a third (and unconstitutional) term as president. The instant response among the people of Zanzibar was a sharp swing in support for the CUF. An equally quick response from CCM high command meant Amour was relieved of his post, and Amani Karume, son of President Karume who had been assassinated in the 1960s, was ushered in as Zanzibar's new CCM leader and presidential candidate.

At a grassroots level, there was still considerable support for the CUF, but the strong Pemba following this party enjoyed meant that ostensibly political differences stood in danger of degenerating into inter-island (or 'tribal') conflicts. This sense of grievance also translated into separatist aspirations; since the end of the 1990s, the desire of many Zanzibaris to be independent of mainland Tanzania has been stronger than it has been for many years. The urge for separation is also partly due to the death in 1999 of Julius Nyerere.

When elections were held in October 2000, President Mpika and the CCM romped home with huge and increased majorities. The people of mainland Tanzania seemed happy (in fact, many seemed indifferent) about the result, and international observers agreed that voting had been free and fair. On Zanzibar, however, it was a different story. In the period leading up to the election, fist-fights erupted on several occasions between CUF and CCM supporters, local party offices were attacked or burned, and CUF demonstrations were broken up by the police and army. On election day, things were so bad in 16 constituencies that the whole process was cancelled, and a re-run vote arranged for 5 November. CUF demonstrations turned into violent protests, especially in Zanzibar Town, to be met with police tear gas, rubber bullets and even live ammunition. In disgust, the CUF pulled out of the election process, leaving the November re-runs to be easily won by CCM candidates. In response, the CUF announced its continued boycott of procedures in the House of Representatives.

In one of his first moves as newly elected president of Zanzibar, Amani Karume called for peace and reconciliation between the two sides, which he backed up by releasing from prison the group of CUF leaders who'd been held on charges of treason since 1998. Hopes for peace were dashed shortly afterwards when a series of bombs exploded in Zanzibar. The trouble simmered on, with more CUF street protests in January 2001. This time the police used even stronger tactics to break things up: in a single day, between 20 and 70 demonstrators were shot, one policeman was killed, and many more were injured. The events were reported in media around the world, the USA and the donor nations of Europe expressed concern, and aid money which had been frozen following the discrepancies of the 1995 election remained firmly out of reach.

In March 2001, at the direct behest of President Mkapa, leaders from the CCM and the CUF tentatively started to discuss their differences, and in October that year, after a long series of negotiations, the two sides signed an accord to end their dispute over the election results. By 2002, the islands had returned to their traditional calm and peaceful atmosphere, and Zanzibar was fully open for business once again.

The most recent elections were held in October 2005. Once again, the CCM and the CUF were vying for power, with rallies held across the island throughout the summer of 2005. Although there seemed to be little in the way of party manifestos, and despite claims by the CUF of vote rigging and other irregularities, this time the election passed off comparatively peacefully. With a 90% turnout of the electorate, the CCM retained control, with the CUF polling 46% of the total votes, and Amani Karume retaining the presidency.

## ECONOMY

For the people of Zanzibar, fishing and farming are the main economic activities. From the beginning of the 19th century to the mid-1970s Zanzibar exported a large proportion of the world's supply of cloves, and the islands' economy was based largely on this commodity. Some diversification has occurred since then as the world market price for cloves fell dramatically in the 1980s, but cloves are still a major export, along with coconut products and other spices. In recent years, seaweed has also become an important export commodity. The potential for tourism to be a major earner of foreign currency has been recognised and this is being developed.

**SEAWEED FARMING** In 1989, seaweed farming was introduced on the east coast of Unguja (Zanzibar Island) and has since become a vital source of income for coastal villagers. The seaweed is planted and tended on beach areas between the high- and low-water marks (see *Sustainable seaweed farming* box, page 225). It is harvested and dried, collected in Zanzibar Town, and then exported to several countries in Europe and Asia for use as a food thickener or stabiliser. Seaweed is now a valuable

## HISTORY OF ZANZIBARI AGRICULTURE

The earliest peoples on Zanzibar are thought to have been hunter-gatherers who made little impact on the natural vegetation. However, the first Bantu settlers, who probably arrived some time in the 3rd or 4th centuries AD, started to clear patches of natural forest to plant crops such as millet and sorghum.

At some stage, plants such as bananas, coconut palms and yams were introduced, possibly by peoples from Madagascar who in turn had originally migrated from the islands of Indonesia. As these crops became more popular, more indigenous forest was cleared.

In the 16th century, Portuguese traders established bases along the east African coast, including those on Zanzibar and Pemba, and introduced plants such as cassava and maize from their colonies in South America. More forest was felled as local people cleared the land required to grow these crops.

After the Omani Arabs gained control of the islands in the early 18th century, and the trade in ivory and slaves expanded, Zanzibar became an important import and export centre. Cassava was used for feeding the vast numbers of slaves who passed through the island's infamous market. Another major export at this time was copra (produced from coconuts) which meant more land was cleared for coconut palm plantations.

At the turn of the 19th century, cloves were introduced from other islands in the Indian Ocean, and they soon became a major export crop. Other spices, such as vanilla and cardamom, were also grown and yet more forest was cleared for plantations.

Throughout the 19th century, the powerful nations of Europe put pressure on the sultans of Zanzibar to restrict the trade in slaves. As this was reduced, the trade in cloves and other spices became even more important. During the colonial period, plantations continued to be developed and the natural forest continued to be reduced. A department of forestry was established to exploit the forests' timber supplies, but apparently it was not until the 1950s that it came to the attention of the Forestry Department that there was very little indigenous forest left on the island of Zanzibar. The largest remaining area, Jozani Forest, to the southeast of Zanzibar Town, was purchased from an Arab landowner by the department and the felling of trees was restricted. In 1960, Jozani was declared a protected nature reserve.

addition to Zanzibar's traditional exports of coconuts, cloves and other spices. (For details on cloves and coconuts see boxes, pages 48 and 47.)

Despite the success with seaweed, exports are limited, and Zanzibar imports many basic foodstuffs, including rice (from Pakistan, Thailand, Vietnam, Indonesia, India, China and the USA), maize (from mainland Tanzania), cooking oil (from Kenya, Tanzania, Singapore and Dubai), sugar (from Brazil), plus wheat and flour (from France, Germany and the USA). Other imports include mineral water (from the Gulf states) and beer (from Denmark).

**TOURISM** The first half of the 1990s saw a dramatic increase in the development of tourism. The Zanzibar Commission for Tourism was founded in 1987 to promote Zanzibar as a tourist destination, and in 1992 the Zanzibar Investment Promotion Agency was created to encourage overseas investment, particularly in tourism projects.

In 1995, over 56,000 visitors were arriving in Zanzibar each year – contributing an estimated US$1,971 million to the economy. By the end of 2005, numbers had exceeded 100,000 visitors per year for the first time. Tourist arrivals to Pemba and the Mafia Archipelago remain insignificant by comparison.

While far below the figures recorded by countries like Kenya, these figures show that Zanzibar's tourism industry has changed gear since the early 1980s. Tourism currently represents about 20% of Zanzibar's gross domestic product (GDP), which contrasts with cloves, which account for around 45% of GDP. Whilst export earnings from this traditional commodity fall (for more details see the *Cloves* box in the *Flora* section on page 48), the income from tourism is rising to plug the gap. Some observers expect it to be Zanzibar's largest generator of foreign exchange within about a decade.

It's not all good news though. Although tourism has obvious financial benefits, it isn't always managed sustainably. For years beach sand was used for construction, leading to problems of erosion. Mangrove poles used in new buildings are seldom sustainably harvested, resulting in a reduction in mangroves and an acceleration of coastal erosion.

Fresh water is very precious on low-lying islands like these, and there is evidence of groundwater depletion; water levels in wells used by villagers for generations have dropped. One survey claimed that on average, tourists use 180 litres of water per day (this of course includes all use – washing, laundry, hotel cleaning, etc) compared with the average local Zanzibari's consumption of less than 40 litres. There is also concern about over-fishing, particularly for crab, lobster, squid and octopus, to supply a growing number of restaurants catering for tourists.

Most pragmatic observers agree that it's not tourism which is the problem per se; it's the sustainability of those tourism developments. It's all about how responsible the tourism enterprises are with the resources and culture of the islands. This issue of 'sustainability' and 'responsible tourism' is moving up the agenda, as witnessed by consciously responsible lodges like Chumbe Island and Mafia's Chole Mjini, but there's a long way to go before all of the hotels and lodges match the high standards set by these.

Officially, the government recognises this problem, and back in 1992 introduced a National Environmental Policy for Zanzibar, stressing that the quality of life of the Zanzibaris should not be harmed by the destruction of their environment, and that cultural and biological diversity should be preserved. In the words of President Salmin Amour, 'unchecked development could soon become unsustainable for our people and our small islands'.

There are certainly more checks on developments than there used to be. For example, a developer needs to apply for specific permission to take any sand for any reason – even to use small amounts to lay beside a swimming pool. We must hope that environmental restrictions like this gather momentum, while as visitors we can do our best to act as responsibly towards Zanzibar's environment and cultures.

# Zanzibar Excursions

is a comprehensive resource for researching, planning and booking your holiday on Zanzibar. We have great pleasure in introducing our company to you or your organization in connection with specialised excursions such as Spice tours, City tours, Jozani forest, Dolphin tours, East coast visits Jeep tours, Safari blue and hotel reservations all over Zanzibar. We also arrange competitively priced safaris on mainland Tanzania.

For more information, please drop into our office in the Old Fort or visit us online at www.zanzibarexcursions.com

Tel/Fax: 255 23 2237281
Mobile: +255 777410414/ (0) 741 591064
Email: info@zanzibarexcursions.com

# 2

# People and Culture

## PEOPLE

**POPULATION AND SETTLEMENT** The population of Zanzibar was 984,625 in 2002, the date of the last census, with an annual growth rate of 3.1%, which has remained fairly steady for some years. Of this, around two-thirds of the people – 622,459 – live on Zanzibar Island (Unguja), with the greatest proportion settled in the densely populated west. Zanzibar's largest settlement is Zanzibar Town (sometimes called Zanzibar City), on Zanzibar Island, with 205,870 inhabitants. Other towns on Zanzibar Island include Chaani, Bambi, Mahonda and Makunduchi, but these are small. Outside these towns, most people live in small villages and are engaged in farming or fishing.

On Pemba the overall settlement pattern is similar. The largest town is Chake Chake, with a population of 19,283; other smaller towns are Wete and Mkoani. Mafia's total population was 40,801.

There is considerable disparity in the standard of living between the inhabitants of Pemba and Unguja and between urban and rural populations, which are split roughly equally. The average annual income of just US$250 hides the fact that about half the population lives below the poverty line. Despite a relatively high standard of primary health care and education, infant mortality is still 83 in 1,000 live births, and it is estimated that malnutrition affects one in three of the islands' people; life expectancy at birth is 48. While the incidence of HIV/AIDS is considerably less in Zanzibar than in Tanzania as a whole (0.6% of the population, as against the national average of around 8%), it is a growing problem.

**ORIGINS** It is thought that Zanzibar's original inhabitants came from the African mainland around 3,000 to 4,000 years ago, although this is not certain and no descendants of these early people remain, having been completely absorbed by later arrivals.

Over the last 2,000 years, the records have become a little clearer. Historians know that Bantu-speaking people migrated from central Africa and settled across east and southern Africa during the 1st millennium AD. (For more details see *History* in *Chapter 1*.) Those who settled on the east African coast and offshore islands, including Zanzibar, came into contact with Arab traders who had sailed southwards from the Red Sea region. The Bantu adopted some customs of the Arabs and gradually established a language and culture which became known as Swahili.

From the 10th century, small groups of immigrants from Shiraz (Persia) also settled at various places along the east African coast, and especially in Zanzibar, and mingled with the local people. Over the following centuries, small groups of Arab and Persian peoples continued to settle here and intermarried with the Swahili and Shirazi. The largest influx occurred in the 18th and 19th centuries, when Omani Arabs settled on Zanzibar as rulers and landowners, forming an elite group. At about the same time, Indian settlers formed a merchant class.

Today, most of the people in Zanzibar are Shirazi or Swahili, although clear distinctions are not always possible. They fall into three groups: the Wahadimu (mainly in the southern and central parts of Zanzibar Island), the Watumbatu (on Tumbatu Island and in the northern part of Zanzibar Island), and the Wapemba (on Pemba Island), although again distinctions are hard to draw, and in fact, often not made by the people of Zanzibar themselves. The islands' long history of receiving (if not always welcoming) immigrants from Africa and Arabia has created a more relaxed attitude to matters of tribe or clan than is found in some parts of Africa.

Zanzibar is also home to groups of people of African origin who are descendants of freed slaves, dating from the 18th and 19th centuries. In more recent times, a large number of Africans have immigrated from mainland Tanzania. Additionally, some Arabs who were expelled after the 1964 Revolution have returned to Zanzibar.

Other people on Zanzibar include small populations from Goa, India and Pakistan, mainly involved in trade or tourism, and a growing number of European expatriates and volunteers, many working in the tour industry, with others employed as teachers, doctors and engineers.

## LANGUAGE with thanks to Said el-Gheithy

The indigenous language spoken throughout Zanzibar is Swahili (called Kiswahili locally). This language is also spoken as a first language by Swahili people along the east African coast, particularly in Kenya and mainland Tanzania, and as a second or third language by many other people throughout east Africa (including Kenya, Tanzania and Uganda, and in parts of several other countries such as Rwanda, Mozambique and Congo), making Swahili the common tongue of the region. Although there are many forms and dialects found in different areas, visitors with a basic grasp of Swahili will be understood anywhere.

Swahili is an African language, and includes many words and phrases of Arabic origin, plus words from other languages such as Persian, English and Portuguese. Over the centuries Swahili has developed into a rich language, lending itself especially to poetry. Zanzibar is regarded as the home of Swahili – it is spoken in its purest form here and in pockets on the coast of Tanzania and Kenya. In fact in these areas, tradition dictates that ordinary conversation should approximate the elegance of poetry. Generally, as you travel further inland on the east African mainland, the Swahili becomes increasingly more basic and simplified.

For visitors, English and several other European languages, such as French and Italian, are spoken in Zanzibar Town and most tourist areas. However, if you get off the beaten track a few words of Swahili will be useful to ask directions, to greet people or even to begin a simple conversation. Even in the tourist areas, using a few Swahili words (for example, to ask the price of a souvenir, or order a meal in a restaurant) can add to the enjoyment of your visit. Arabic is also spoken. For basic words and phrases, see *Appendix 1.*

## RELIGION

Most of the people in Zanzibar are Muslims (followers of the Islamic faith) and all towns and villages on Zanzibar Island and Pemba have mosques. Visitors to Zanzibar Town cannot fail to hear the evocative sound of the muezzins calling people to prayer from the minarets, especially for the evening session at sunset. And visitors cannot fail to notice the effects of the holy month of Ramadan, when most people fast during the day, and the pace of life slows down considerably. (See also *Public holidays*, page 69.) There are also small populations of Christians and Hindus.

**ISLAM** Islam was founded by the Prophet Mohammed, who was born around AD570 in Arabia. He received messages from God during solitary vigils on Mount Hira, outside his home town of Mecca. When driven out of Mecca by his enemies, he migrated to Medina. Here, at the age of about 53, he started to convert the world to Islam, and his message spread rapidly through the Arab world and beyond.

Mohammed died in AD632, but fired by evangelist zeal Arab Muslims had conquered all of northern Africa by the early 8th century, and introduced the new religion there. By AD1100 Islam had spread from Arabia and the Horn of Africa along the east African coast, through the current countries of Kenya and Tanzania, all the way down to Sofala (in present-day Mozambique). Today, Islam is the dominant religion of these coastal areas, which include the islands of Zanzibar.

The five main tenets of Islam are prayer (five times a day), testimony of the faith, fasting (the period of Ramadan), almsgiving, and the pilgrimage to Mecca (the Haj). The Muslim calendar dates from the Hejira, the flight of Mohammed from Mecca to Medina, which corresponds to 16 July AD622 in the Christian calendar. The Muslim year consists of 12 lunar months of 29 or 30 days each, making 354 days. Eleven times in every cycle of 30 years a day is added to the year. This means that Muslim festivals fall 11 or 12 days earlier every year, according to the Western calendar.

**OTHER RELIGIONS** There are small populations of Christians and Hindus living on the islands. The two most notable churches are the Anglican Cathedral Church of Christ and the Catholic Church of St Joseph in Zanzibar Town; Hindu temples are also present to serve the local community.

Alongside the established world faiths, traditional African beliefs are still held by most local people, and there is often considerable cross-over between aspects of Islam and local customs. See *The Shetani of Zanzibar* box overleaf for more details.

## CULTURE

### ARTS AND CRAFTS
**Music and dance**  *Hildegard Kiel, Yusuf Mahmoud*
As you wander around Zanzibar Town, you will hear calls to prayer from the many mosques as well as the sounds of American rap music and Jamaican reggae. Around the next corner, however, you are also likely to hear film music from India or the latest chart-toppers from Egypt and the Gulf States. Thankfully the islands have not entirely lost their own cultural traditions, and equally popular in Zanzibar are local musical forms, in particular the style known as *taarab*.

**Taarab**  Zanzibar has been at the crossroads of trade routes for thousands of years as peoples of Africa, India, Iran, China and other parts of Asia and the Arab world have all played their parts in influencing the music, architecture, food and culture of the region. In its origins, taarab was court music, played in the palace of Sultan Barghash. The sounds of Arabic musical traditions and those from India, Indonesia and other countries of the 'Dhow region' (the Indian Ocean basin) are clearly distinguishable even today, mingling to form a unique flavour and providing the frame for the Swahili poetry which makes up the heart of taarab music.

Currently, two major taarab groups exist in Zanzibar: Nadi Ikhwan Safaa and Mila na Utamaduni (also called Culture Musical Club, or just Culture). Of the two, Culture are the more professional and have become quite well known internationally, not only through CD releases such as *Spices of Zanzibar* or the more recent *Bashraf* albums, but also because they have successfully toured Belgium, France, Germany, Switzerland, the Arab Emirates, Réunion and many other

*Gemma Pitcher*

Throughout the centuries Zanzibar Island (Unguja) and, to a greater extent, Pemba Island have been famous as centres of traditional religion and witchcraft, alongside their better-known role as centres of the spice and slave trades. Today the cult of the *shetani* (meaning a spirit or spirits, the word is singular or plural) is still going strong in Zanzibar and Pemba – a dark undercurrent unseen and unknown by the majority of visitors.

According to local traditional beliefs, *shetani* are creatures from another world, living on earth alongside animals and humans, but invisible most of the time and generally ill-intentioned. Many of the ebony carvings on sale in Zanzibar's curio shops depict the various forms a *shetani* can take – for example, a hunched and hideously twisted old woman, a man-dog hybrid, or a young girl with the legs of a donkey.

There is no real way, say the locals, of protecting yourself from the possibility of being haunted or attacked by a *shetani*. The best thing is simply to keep out of their way and try to make sure they keep out of yours – for example by hanging a piece of paper, inscribed with special Arabic verses, from the ceiling of the house. Almost every home or shop in Zanzibar has one of these brown, mottled scraps, attached to a roof beam by a piece of cotton.

Should the worst happen in spite of these precautions and a *shetani* decide to take up residence in your home – or even, in the worst-case scenario, your body – the only thing to do is to visit a *mganga* (sorcerer). To be a *mganga* is a trade that generally runs in families, with secrets and charms passed on from father to son or mother to daughter. Waganga (plural of *mganga*) meet periodically in large numbers to discuss their business (patients must pay handsomely for their services) and initiate new recruits. A committee of elderly, experienced practitioners will vet a younger, untested *mganga* before declaring him or her fit to practise.

Each *mganga* is in contact with ten or so *shetani*, who can be instructed to drive out other *shetani* from someone who is possessed, or to work their power in favour of the customer. The waganga are also herbalists, preparing healing medicines where spirit possession is not indicated, or combining both physical and occult treatment in severe cases.

But there are some *shetani*, goes the current thinking, which even a *mganga* cannot control. The latest and most famous of these was (or is) Popo Bawa – a phenomenon of far greater significance than just a run-of-the-mill *shetani*, which gripped Zanzibar's population in a wave of mass hysteria in 1995.

Popo Bawa (the name comes from the Swahili words for 'bat' and 'wing') began on

countries. Nadi Ikhwaan Safaa, affectionately known by local people as Malindi Music Club, are Zanzibar's oldest group, who trace their roots back to 1905. The group plays a style of taarab in which the distant Middle Eastern origins are still very much to the fore.

Different theories abound about the real origins of taarab in Zanzibar. Legend has it that in the 1870s Sultan Bargash sent a Zanzibari to Cairo to learn to play the *qanun*, a kind of zither, common to the Arab-speaking world. Among the first singers to record taarab music in the Swahili language was the legendary Siti binti Saad, who was taken to India by a film director. Siti stopped performing in the 1940s, but her records – solo and in duet with Sheikh Mbaruk – continued to be issued on 78rpm throughout the 1950s and are still much in demand. Besides the qanun, other instruments that came to feature in the taarab groups (or orchestras) include the oud, violins, ney, accordion, cello and a variety of percussion. Hence much of the traditional taarab music sounds like a more the island of Pemba, where he terrorised the local population to such an extent that they called upon their most powerful sorcerers to drive him across the sea to Zanzibar. There the reign of terror of the 'shetani-above-all-shetani' continued.

The experiences of those who claimed to be visited by the demon were terrifying. They awoke in the middle of the night to find themselves paralysed and with the feeling of being suffocated. They then saw a squat, winged figure, around 1m tall, or slightly smaller, and with a single eye in the middle of its forehead, approaching the bed. Helpless, they were powerless to move or cry out as the demon raped them, men and women alike. Only when Popo Bawa had departed were they able to raise the alarm.

During the height of the Popo Bawa hysteria, people took to the rooftops and village squares, following a rumour that safety could only be had by those who slept outside, in a group. Despite precautions like these, tales of the demon's progress around the island spread, until the government was forced to broadcast announcements on the radio pleading for calm. Despite this, a helpless, mentally handicapped young man was beaten to death by a mob that had become convinced he was the demon. This seemed to be the climax of the whole affair – after that, the hysteria abated somewhat and Popo Bawa retreated. He is widely expected to return, however, and when local people talk of him, it's with a nervous laugh.

American psychologists came to Zanzibar to study the events and write papers, and stated that the case of Popo Bawa is simply a Zanzibari version of a phenomenon known as a 'waking dream'. One of the characteristics of such a dream is a feeling of being weighted down or even paralysed. Other characteristics include extreme vividness of the dream and bizarre or terrifying content. It is this same phenomenon that is used by sceptics in the USA to explain the stories of those who claim to have been abducted by aliens.

Nevertheless, to the people of Zanzibar, Popo Bawa was very real and proof that shetani exist. Of course, they are not all as horrific as Popo Bawa; the lesser shetani come in all shapes, sizes and colours – beautiful Arabic women, hideous Ethiopian hags, or tall, handsome white men. Shetani can be forced to work for humans, but it's a risky business. Some successful businessmen are said to keep a whole room of shetani in their houses to promote material success and make mischief on their adversaries. But the price of such supernatural intervention is high – a goat, a chicken or a cow must be sacrificed regularly and its blood sprinkled in the four corners of the room. If this sacrifice is not faithfully and regularly made, the shetani will take a terrible substitute – it will demand instead one of its master's male children…

Africanised version of some of the great Egyptian popular classical orchestras that played alongside singers like Oum Kulthoum, who is still played on Radio Zanzibar to this day.

The best way to experience taarab is at a local concert, but visitors to Zanzibar are also welcome at the orchestras' rehearsals in Malindi or at Vuga Clubhouse in the evening. What Andy Morgan (*Roots* magazine) says in an article on Zanzibari music definitely holds true: 'There's hardly anything in the whole of Africa as uplifting as the swelling sounds of a full taarab orchestra in full sail.'

**Kidumbak** The suburb of Ng'ambo – the 'other side' of Zanzibar Town, where the lower-class living areas spread out and where poorer families and more recent arrivals to the city live – is the home of *kidumbak*. This music style, which is less refined and more upbeat than taarab, could be located musically somewhere between Stone Town big-orchestra taarab and the rural *ngoma* music. It is most

A description of the music of Zanzibar would not be complete without mentioning Bi Kidude – now well into her 90s, and still one of the island's most famous singers. She used to perform with Siti bint Saad, has toured the world and has sold thousands of cassettes. When she is performing, she claims to feel like a 14-year-old, and for once, seeing is believing. Her voice is raw and unfiltered, and her singing and drumming with a large drum strapped to her hips is an exhibition of sheer energy. With the agility of a teenager and the sly wisdom of a thoroughly experienced performer, her stage presence is absolute and intense. She is most famous for her performance of *unyago ngoma*, which is played at all-female initiation rituals for brides to prepare them for their wedding night, featuring explicit lyrics as well as movements.

often performed at weddings and other celebrations and is closely related to taarab. In fact, contemporary kidumbak often makes use of the latest taarab hit songs and is sometimes called '*kitaarab*', which means 'a diminutive type of taarab' or 'derived from taarab'. Historical evidence suggests that Swahili taarab was originally performed in a very similar way to kidumbak and only later changed to resemble court orchestra music.

The kidumbak ensemble consists of a single melodic instrument, customarily a violin (played in frantic fiddle-style), a *sanduku*, or tea-chest-bass, two small clay drums (*ki-dumbak*), which form the rhythmic core of every such ensemble, and other rhythm instruments, such as *cherewa*, a kind of maracas manufactured from coconut shells filled with seeds, or *mkwasa*, short wooden sticks played like claves. In contrast to taarab, kidumbak is much more rhythmic and the lyrics more drastic than the poetic settings of the taarab songs, often criticising other people's social behaviour. At wedding performances, the singer has to be able to string together a well-timed medley of ngoma songs, and she or he must have the ability to compose lyrics on the spot. At a Zanzibar wedding, one kidumbak set usually lasts for an hour; as one song joins the next, the intensity heats up, with the main attraction being the interplay between the music and song of the players and the dancing and chorus response of the wedding guests.

**Beni** This brass band music originated around the end the 19th century as a mockery of colonial style military bands. It was soon incorporated in the competitive song-and-dance exchanges so popular on the Swahili coast and spread from there all over east Africa. Beni (from English 'band') is a popular wedding entertainment with a strong focus on rhythm and dance, and audience participation.

Beni borrows choruses from the latest taarab hits and arranges them in extended medleys with the female wedding audience joining in for the chorus and as dancers. It is funny music, vivacious, raucous and lively. If you can imagine a deranged military marching band playing as loud as possible on half-broken trumpets, trombones, drums – only vaguely in tune with each other, but having a great time – then you will get the idea!

In Zanzibar, beni is performed both as a street parade and, stationary, for a wedding dance. The band Beni ya Kingi usually kicks off the opening parade for the Festival of the Dhow Countries (see *Festivals* on page 44), which winds its way slowly through the narrow streets of Stone Town before reaching Forodhani Gardens at the waterfront with a great crowd which then turns into a wild and lively party.

**Ngoma** Ngoma literally translated means 'drum' and is a term used to encompass all local African traditional forms of dancing, drumming and singing. There are literally hundreds of different ngoma styles throughout Tanzania, variations often being so slight that untrained eyes and ears can hardly notice the difference. A number of these originate from Zanzibar and Pemba and all are spectacular to watch. The often-elaborate native costumes emphasise the unity of the dancers' steps and the rhythm section which usually consists of several handmade drums and percussion instruments (such as oil tins beaten with a stick). *Ngoma ya kibati* from Pemba, for example, consists of a very rapid declamatory style of singing which is an improvised dialogue to drum accompaniment with singers/dancers coming in for a chorus every so often. Even if you can't follow a single word of the firework-like exchange between the two main singers, kibati is hilariously funny; if you understand all the references and hints implied, it is of course even more so. Another example is *msewe*, supporting the rhythm section, and named after the material which is strapped to the ankles of the male dancers.

Each ngoma style has its own special costume. In *kyaso*, men dance dressed in shirts and *kikois* (special woven cloth from the east African coast) with a long, narrow stick in their hand, all movements beautifully co-ordinated. In *ndege* women in colourful dresses all hold bright umbrellas, moving forwards with slightly rotating steps and movements of the hips. In *bomu*, the women dress up like men and in other funny costumes and dance around in a circle.

The variations are endless and performances are never dull. According to Abdalla R Mdoe, choreographer for Imani Ngoma Troupe, a privately initiated performance ensemble that specialises in all kinds of ngoma, three different types can be differentiated: ceremonial ngomas, which are performed at weddings, circumcision and other festivities; ritual ngomas (eg: *kisomali* to cure a sick person, or *pungwa* to avert evil); and religious ngomas, which in Zanzibar are closely related to the Muslim festivities of Zikri, Duffu, Maulidi and Hom.

### VENUES AND RECORDINGS

To get a flavour of the unique experience of Zanzibar music, recommended recordings are listed below. For an unforgettable live experience, your best option is the Festival of the Dhow Countries around the beginning of July each year (see page 44). You can also stop by the Dhow Countries Music Academy, Zanzibar's first music school, which opened in the old Customs House on the waterfront of Stone Town in 2002. The school provides music lessons as well as instruments at minimal cost to anyone interested in studying music from the Dhow region or acquiring mastery of an instrument. Particular emphasis is on teaching traditional Zanzibar music styles, with most of the teachers coming from Zanzibar. It is a great place to meet local musicians and get further information on Zanzibar music and cultural events.

*The Music of Zanzibar*, vols 1–4 (Globestyle Recordings, 1988)
*Mila na Utamaduni – Spices of Zanzibar* (Network Medien GmbH, 1996)
*Kidumbak Kalcha: Ng'ambo – The other side of Zanzibar* (Dizim, 1997)
*Zanzibar: Music for Celebration* (Topic Records, 2000)
*Bashraf: Taarab Instrumentals from Zanzibar* (Dizim, 2000)
*Beni ya Kingi – Brass Band Music of Zanzibar* (Dizim Records, 2003)
*Waridi : Scents of Zanzibar – Culture Musical Club* (Virgin France, 2004)
*Spices of Zanzibar – Culture Musical Club* (Network, 2004)

**Modern taarab** Undoubtedly a pop-phenomenon (and therefore ephemeral) is a modern style of taarab, called *rusha roho*, which translates literally 'to make the spirit fly' and has some untranslatable meaning approximating to 'upsetting someone' or 'making the other one jealous'. Modern taarab is also the first style of taarab that's designed to be danced to, and features direct lyrics, bypassing the unwritten laws of lyrical subtlety of the older groups. Much of modern taarab music is composed and played on keyboards, increasing portability; hence the group is much smaller in number than 'real taarab' orchestras and therefore more readily available to tour and play shows throughout the region. This fact has led to enormous popularity in Zanzibar, boosted by the prolific output of cassette recordings, which, though not up to European studio quality standards, still outsell tapes by any other artist local or international.

## Visual arts

**Tingatinga paintings** Among the visual arts, by far the best-known contemporary Zanzibari style is Tingatinga (or tinga-tinga). Paintings in this distinctive style can be found for sale at souvenir stalls and shops all over Zanzibar, as well as at tourist centres on the Tanzanian mainland, and in Kenya. The subjects of Tingatinga paintings are usually African animals, especially elephants, leopards, hippos, crocodiles and gazelles, as well as guineafowl, hornbills and other birds. The main characteristics of the style include images which are both simplified and fantastical, bold colours, solid outlines and the frequent use of dots and small circles in the design.

The style was founded by Edward Saidi Tingatinga, who was born in southern Tanzania in 1937 and came to Dar es Salaam looking for work in the 1950s. After doing various jobs, in the early 1960s Tingatinga became unemployed and looked

### ZANZIBAR DOORS

Around Zanzibar and particularly in Stone Town, you'll come across massive, carved and decorated doorways, some on imposing frontages and others tucked incongruously down narrow alleys.

When a house was built in Zanzibar, the door was traditionally the first part to be erected. The greater the wealth and status of the house's owner, the larger and more elaborately carved his front door. Symbolic designs and quotations from the Koran were added to exert a benign influence: a kind of hand-crafted insurance policy. Waves of the sea climbing up the doorpost represent the livelihood of the Arab merchant to whom the house belonged, while frankincense and date-palms symbolise wealth and plenty. From a darker side of history, chains carved at the side indicate that slaves were held in the house. Some designs are thought to pre-date the Koran: the stylised lotuses could relate to Egyptian fertility symbols, and the fish may possibly represent the protective Syrian goddess Atargatis or the ancient Egyptian fish-god.

Many doors are studded with brass spikes and bosses, which may stem from the Indian practice of studding doors of medieval castles with sharp iron spikes to prevent their being battered in by war elephants. In AD915, an Arab traveller recorded that Zanzibar Island abounded in elephants, and around 1295 Marco Polo wrote that Zanzibar had 'elephants in plenty'. But they must have been extinct long before the Arabs built houses in Stone Town, and the studs and bosses seen today are purely decorative.

The oldest carved door in Zanzibar, which dates from AD1694, is now the front door of the Peace Memorial Museum.

*Gemma Pitcher*

*Baraza* benches, often simply called *barazas*, have been a focal point of community life in Zanzibar for centuries. These thick benches of solid stone are built into the walls around courtyards or flank the heavy doors of distinctive Arab-style townhouses. The houses which line the long, narrow streets of Stone Town often have barazas outside – and you will also see barazas on the verandas outside traditional Swahili homes, while in the villages a palm-leaf shelter, flanked by wooden seats, fulfils the same function.

Barazas evolved as a way for Islamic men to receive visitors in their homes without compromising the privacy of their womenfolk. Coffee and sweetmeats would be served on the baraza to anyone who arrived, with only the closest friends or family members being invited into the house. The Omani sultans held public meetings, also known as barazas, outside their palaces to receive petitioners or give visiting dignitaries a public audience.

Today, barazas are still a meeting point for all sections of Zanzibari society. Every urban baraza area is lined with people lolling on the warm, smooth cement benches, gossiping, playing games of bao or cards, drinking sweet, thick Arabic coffee or simply idling away a long afternoon with a nap. Draughts boards are scratched in chalk on the stone surfaces, ladies sit comfortably to plait each other's hair, and for traders with no market stall of their own, a baraza provides a flat surface on which to pile their tiny pyramids of oranges, tomatoes and mangoes.

In the rainy season, when torrents of water, sometimes laced with rubbish, make walking down the streets of Stone Town uncomfortable and even hazardous, the barazas outside the houses provide a useful elevated pavement, and pedestrians jump from one to the next in an attempt to keep their feet dry.

The baraza as an architectural feature is an idea that seems to have caught on in a big way among the designers of Zanzibar's smarter hotels; almost every courtyard, nook and cranny – and even bathroom – now boasts its own baraza bench, often whitewashed to match the coral walls or inlaid with mosaic tiles.

around for a way to earn money. At that time, carvers and sculptors, notably Makonde people, were producing some indigenous work, but most local painters favoured pictures based on European representational styles or Congolese styles from central Africa. (In fact, in the 1950s and 1960s many painters from Congo and Zaire (now the DRC) came to Kenya and Tanzania to sell their work to tourists and well-off residents.) Legend has it that Saidi Tingatinga decided he could do what the Congo artists did – paint pictures and sell them for money.

With no training, he produced pictures that were initially simple and straightforward. Subjects were the animals and people he remembered from his home in southern Tanzania. He used just four or five different colours (actually house paint – and the only colours available) and painted on wooden boards. But despite this humble beginning, Tingatinga quickly sold his early paintings, mainly to local European residents who admired the original, 'naïve' style.

Within a few months, Tingatinga's paintings were in high demand. He couldn't keep up with the orders which flooded in, so he employed several fellow painters to help him produce more. There was no concept of copyright, and Tingatinga encouraged his colleagues to base their works on his style. As their success grew, soon the artists were able to afford to use bright enamel paints (the type used for touching up paintwork on cars and bicycles) and painted on canvas so tourists could take home pictures more easily. By the end of the 1960s, Tingatinga painting had become recognised as truly original contemporary African art.

In 1972 Saidi Tingatinga died, but the artists he'd encouraged formed a group named in his honour, and continued to produce and sell works in his style. Today, demand from tourists is still high, and vast numbers of Tingatinga artists produce paintings on cloth, wooden boards and other objects such as trays, plates and model wooden cars. There's even an aeroplane at Zanzibar Airport with its tail decorated in Tingatinga style.

With so many Tingatinga paintings available in Zanzibar and around east Africa, the quality of the work varies considerably; many pictures for sale in the streets have been bashed out quickly with little care or attention to detail. But if you search hard among the dross, or visit a shop where the trader has an interest in stocking better-quality stuff, you can often find real works of art (and still at reasonable prices) which do justice to the memory of Saidi Tingatinga – the founder of a fascinating, entertaining and quintessentially African style.

## Traditional games *Gemma Pitcher*

Stroll casually around any village or town on the islands of Zanzibar, and eventually you'll be sure to come across two hunched, intent figures seated on a *baraza* bench – their grunts of satisfaction or derision accompanied by the click of counters on wood. Sometimes a crowd of spectators will have gathered, pointing and shouting garbled instructions. Look closer and you'll make out the object of all this excitement – a flat wooden board, 32 little round holes, and a lot of brown polished seeds. This is *bao* – Zanzibar's favourite pastime.

Games of bao – the name simply means 'wood' in Swahili – can go on for hours or even days at a time. Experienced players develop little flourishes, scattering the counters (known as *kete* – usually seeds, or pebbles or shells) expertly into holes or slapping handfuls down triumphantly at the end of a turn. Bao is played, under

### DHOWS OF THE SWAHILI COAST

*Philip Briggs*

The word dhow, commonly applied by Europeans to any traditional seafaring vessel used off the coast of east Africa, is generally assumed to be Arabic in origin. There is, however, no historical evidence to back up this notion, nor does it appear to be an established Swahili name for any specific type of boat. Caroline Sassoon, writing in *Tanganyika Notes & Records* in 1970, suggests that the word 'dhow' is a corruption of *não*, used by the first Portuguese navigators in the Indian Ocean to refer to any small local seafaring vessel, or of the Swahili *kidau*, a specific type of small boat.

The largest traditional sailing vessel in wide use off the coast of East Africa is the *jahazi*, which measures up to 20m long and whose large billowing sails are a characteristic sight off Zanzibar and other traditional ports. With a capacity of about a hundred passengers, the *jahazi* is used mainly for transporting cargo and passengers over relatively long distances or in open water, for instance between Dar es Salaam and Zanzibar. Minor modifications in the Portuguese and Omani eras notwithstanding, the design of the modern *jahazi* is pretty much identical to that of similar seafaring vessels used in medieval times and before. The name *jahazi* is generally applied to boats with cutaway bows and square sterns built on Zanzibar and nearby parts of the mainland. Similar boats built in Lamu and nearby ports in Kenya are called *jalbut* (possibly derived from the English 'jolly boat' or Indian 'gallevat') and have a vertical bow and wineglass-shaped stern. Smaller but essentially similar in design, the *mashua* measures up to 10m long, has a capacity of about 25 passengers, and is mostly used for fishing close to the shore or as local transport.

various different names and with many rule variations, across Africa, western India and the Caribbean. Swahili people are proud of their version, known as 'king' bao, and claim it as the original and purest form of the game. Tournaments are held periodically in Zanzibar and on the coast of the mainland – as in chess, one grandmaster eventually emerges.

The object of the game is simple: to secure as many of your opponent's counters as possible. Bao masters (usually old men) are said to be able to think strategically five to seven moves ahead, a level comparable to professional chess players. Children learn bao as soon as they can count, scratching little holes in the ground in lieu of a board and using chips of wood or stones as counters.

The African love of carving has produced a proliferation of bao boards of many different sizes, shapes and forms – the board can be represented as resting on the back of a mythical beast, grows human heads from either end, or is smoothed into the shape of a fish. Bao boards make excellent souvenirs and are sold in almost every curio shop, often along with a badly photocopied set of printed instructions that are guaranteed to bamboozle even a maths professor. Far better to find a friendly local to teach you – the game is actually surprisingly simple to pick up.

*Keram* is the second most popular game in Zanzibar, and probably first arrived here from India. It's a fast-paced, raucous game played on a piece of wood carefully shaped into a small, square snooker table with cloth pockets at each corner. The game is similar to pool, with nine black disks, nine white disks, one red 'queen' disk and one larger white striker. Players flick the striker from their side of the board in an effort to get their own-colour disks into the pockets. Boards are kept smooth and speedy by liberal applications of talcum powder.

Bao and keram, like their Western equivalents chess and pool, have very different characters. While bao is traditionally a daytime game, played in shady village squares by elderly, dignified men, keram is popularly played at night in bars, often in the midst of a noisy and tipsy crowd of jack-the-lads.

The most rudimentary and smallest type of boat used on the Swahili Coast is the *mtumbwi*, which is basically a dugout canoe made by hollowing out the trunk of a large tree – the mango tree is favoured today – and used for fishing in mangrove creeks and other still water environments. The *mtumbwi* is certainly the oldest type of boat used in east Africa, and its simple design probably replicates that of the very first boats crafted by humans. A more elaborate and distinctive variation on the *mtumbwi* is the *ngalawa*, a 5–6m-long dugout supported by a narrow outrigger on each side, making it sufficiently stable to be propelled by a sail. The *ngalawa* is generally used for fishing close to shore as well as for transporting passengers across protected channels such as the one between Mafia and Chole islands in the Mafia Archipelago.

The largest traditional boats of the Indian Ocean, the ocean-going dhows that were once used to transport cargo between east Africa, Asia and Arabia, have become increasingly scarce in recent decades due to the advent of foreign ships and other, faster modes of intercontinental transport. Several distinct types of ocean-going dhow are recognised, ranging from the 60-ton *sambuk* from Persia to 250-ton boats originating from India. Oddly, one of the larger of these vessels, the Indian *dengiya*, is thought to be the root of the English word 'dinghy'. Although a few large dhows still ply the old maritime trade routes of the Indian Ocean, they are now powered almost exclusively with motors rather than by sails.

There's an excellent small exhibition on boats in the Pemba Museum in Chake Chake, and in the House of Wonders in Zanzibar Town. Don't miss the fascinating examples of traditional 'stitched dhows', with their timbers 'sewn' tightly together.

## FESTIVALS

**Festival of the Dhow Countries** Without a doubt, the highlight of Zanzibar's artistic and cultural calendar is the Festival of the Dhow Countries – a 16-day event usually held in early July every year, and touted as east Africa's premier cultural event and among the most significant cultural events in all of Africa. The 'dhow countries' are those of Africa and the Indian Ocean basin, and so include east and southern Africa, northern east Africa, west and central Africa, the Horn of Africa, Arabia, Iraq, Iran, the subcontinent of India, Madagascar and the Indian Ocean Islands, plus what the organisers call 'their global diaspora'.

The festival has grown from strength to strength since its humble beginnings at the Zanzibar International Film Festival (ZIFF) back in 1998, and now includes theatre, performances of traditional and contemporary music and dance, plus exhibitions of paintings, sculptures, craftwork and photography. However, the central part of this event is still the film festival, with its large, interesting and eclectic mix of films from all the dhow countries and places further afield. Several film-makers are also present, there are prestigious awards for new films (short and long features, and documentaries) and the festival also includes workshops, talks and discussions, as well as an energetic series of entertainments called the Children's Panorama.

On the more serious side, film and media-related workshops have included Women Film-makers, Making Current Affairs Programmes for African Audiences, Constructing African History in the Cinema, and Creative Journalism.

The main venue for the festival is the open-air theatre at the Arab Fort, with films and performances on the main stage of the amphitheatre and live music in the adjoining Mambo Club, while other events are held at the Palace Museum, the House of Wonders and the Old Dispensary (Stone Town Cultural Centre). The Old Customs House, which became the home of the Dhow Countries Music Academy in 2002, is the venue for musical master classes. There's also a series of free shows in Forodhani Gardens, just outside the Fort.

Many events are free and admission charges are kept to a minimum (around US$0.50 for Tanzanian residents, US$5 for non-residents) to encourage local participation. There's also an ambitious (but highly successful) programme of 'Village Events', which transports a selection of everything the festival offers in Zanzibar Town (film, music, theatre, women's workshops, children's shows, etc) out to the rural areas of Unguja and Pemba islands. The Festival of the Dhow Countries' organisers are keen to promote July as 'culture month' on Zanzibar, and this is undoubtedly an excellent time to visit the islands, although of course it's likely to be busy at this time. You can get more information from ZIFF, the festival organisers, who are based at the Old Fort in Zanzibar Stone Town (*PO Box 3032, Zanzibar;* ↘ *0 747 411499;* f *0747 419955;* e *ziff@ziff.or.tz; www.ziff.or.tz*).

**Mwaka Kogwa** In a very different vein, the festival of Mwaka Kogwa is held every year in several villages around Zanzibar, but most famously and most flamboyantly at the village of Makunduchi, in the south of Zanzibar Island. The traditional festival originated in Persia and celebrates the arrival of the New Year according to the Shirazi calendar. This one-day festival normally occurs during July, but it would be better to check the dates locally as changes are possible. For more details on the festival itself see the box on page 241.

# 3

# Natural Environment

## PHYSICAL ENVIRONMENT

This place, for the goodness of the harbour and watering and plentiful refreshing with fish, and for sending sorts of fruits of the country, as cows ... and oxen and hens, is carefully to be sought for by such of all ships as shall hereafter pass that way.

James Lancaster, captain of the *Edward Bonaventure*,
first English ship to visit Zanzibar (1592)

**LOCATION AND SIZE** Zanzibar consists of two large islands, plus several smaller ones, about 40km off the coast of east Africa, in the Indian Ocean, about 6° S of the Equator. The two large islands are Unguja (usually called Zanzibar Island) and Pemba. Zanzibar Island is about 85km long and between 20km and 30km wide, with an area of 1,660km². The smaller Pemba Island, at around 985km², is some 67km long and between 15km and 20km wide.

The islands are generally flat and low lying, surrounded by coasts of rocky inlets or sandy beaches, with lagoons and mangrove swamps, and coral reefs beyond the shoreline. The western and central parts of Zanzibar Island have some low hills, where the highest point is about 120m above sea level. Pemba Island has a central ridge, cut by several small valleys, and appears more hilly than Zanzibar Island, although the highest point on Pemba is only 95m above sea level.

### CLIMATE

February 19th. We anchored off Zanzibar at dawn. A day of fierce heat. The island is said to enjoy a cool season. I have never struck it. An hour's stroll ashore sufficed to revive old memories, then I retired to the ship for a cold bath and an afternoon under the electric fans.

Evelyn Waugh, *Tourist in Africa* (1959)

The climate of Zanzibar is dominated by the movements of the Indian Ocean monsoons, and characterised by wet and dry seasons. The northeast monsoon winds (known locally as the *kaskazi*) blow from November/December to February/March, and the southwest monsoon winds (the *kusi*) blow from June to September/October. The main rains (the *masika*) fall from mid-March to the end of May, and there is a short rainy season (the *vuli*) in November.

Throughout the year, humidity is generally quite high (less so in the rainy season), although this can be relieved by winds and sea breezes. Temperatures do not vary greatly throughout the year, with daytime averages around 26°C (80°F) on Zanzibar Island from June to October, and around 28°C from December to February, although in this latter period the humidity is often higher, so temperatures feel hotter. Pemba tends to be cooler and get slightly more rain than Zanzibar Island.

Unlike on the African mainland, there are no large wild animals on Zanzibar. Forest areas are inhabited by monkeys and small antelopes, while civets and various species of mongoose are found all over the islands. Birdlife is varied and interesting, with over 100 species being recorded, although bird populations are not as high as in other parts of the east African region. The marine wildlife, in the coral reefs that surround the islands, is particularly rich.

**FLORA** The islands of Pemba and Unguja (usually called Zanzibar Island) were originally forested, but human habitation has resulted in widespread clearing, although a few isolated pockets of indigenous forest remain. Formed about 27 million years ago and seven million years ago respectively, both islands were originally coral reefs which became exposed as sea levels dropped, so the main rock type is a coralline limestone, known locally as 'coral rag'.

On the eastern side of Zanzibar Island, and in parts of the northern and southern areas, the landscape is very flat where coralline rock is exposed or covered by a thin layer of a calcareous sandstone soil, which supports low scrubby bush, known as coral rag thicket, quite dense in some areas. The western and central parts of the island are slightly more undulating, with a deeper soil cover: red, iron-rich and more fertile. Additionally, the western sides receive more rain than the eastern sides of the islands. Thus the western parts of Zanzibar Island were once covered in forest, similar in most respects to the low coastal forest which existed on the east African mainland, but today very little of Zanzibar's indigenous natural forest remains, as it has mostly been cleared and used for agriculture. Local people grow crops on a subsistence basis, and this area is also where most of Zanzibar Island's commercial farms and spice and fruit plantations have been established.

The only significant areas of natural forest remaining in Zanzibar are at Jozani, a forest reserve on the south-central part of Zanzibar Island, and at Ngezi, a forest reserve in the north of Pemba Island, although smaller patches do exist elsewhere. The water table around Jozani is particularly high (during the rainy season the water can be over 1m above the ground) and the trees are mainly moisture-loving species.

**Trees and deforestation** Despite the establishment of forest reserves such as Jozani and Ngezi, Zanzibar's forests continue to be cut down at an unsustainable rate. Timber is used for boatbuilding and furniture-making, and as fuel, both for domestic purposes and to burn coral to produce lime for building construction. (This last use has grown particularly quickly as the number of hotels in Zanzibar has increased.)

Mangrove wood from coastal areas is also being cut at an unsustainable rate. Forestry Department figures show that in 1992 about ten million poles were cut in Chwaka Bay Forest, compared with 2.5 million in 1990. This wood is used for fuel and furniture, and in the construction and repair of buildings, but unfortunately the cutting of poles in the mangrove swamps leads to beach erosion and the destruction of habitats for fish and other marine life.

To replace some of the disappearing forest, through the 1990s, the Zanzibar Forestry Department planted acacia, casuarina and eucalyptus trees in Unguja and Pemba, as well as orange, coffee and cinnamon plants in Pemba. Another scheme, called the Zanzibar Cash Crop Farming System Project (ZCCFSP), discouraged farmers from cutting clove trees for firewood. All logging, and even the removal of dead wood, has officially been stopped in the Jozani and Ngezi reserves, although how carefully this new rule will be policed remains to be seen.

Coconuts are the second most important crop on Zanzibar after cloves. They grow on a certain species of palm tree which is generally planted where clove trees cannot survive, although as diversification is encouraged it is not uncommon today to see coconut palms and clove trees on the same plantation.

Coconuts are picked throughout the year, and large quantities are consumed locally as food, with the milk used for cooking. The pickers skilfully climb up the palm trunks using only a short loop of rope, then drop the nuts to the ground. The outer husks of the coconuts are removed by striking them on a sharp stick or metal bar fixed in the ground.

Coconut products – mainly the 'kernel' (the white edible parts) – are also exported. The process involves splitting the coconuts in two and leaving them to dry so that the white fleshy kernels can be easily removed from the shells. The kernels are then dried for a few more days in the sun or in a special kiln. Gangs of workers separating the husks and kernels, and small coconut kilns, can be seen in the plantation areas outside Zanzibar Town.

When the kernels are properly dried, the resulting substance is called 'copra', which is widely used in the food industry as a flavouring, or for decoration. Copra is also processed into an oil that is used in some foods and in the production of soap, candles and hair oils. In the days before aerosol foam, copra was particularly good for making shaving soap as it helped produce a good lather.

The coconut husks are not wasted: they are buried under sand on the beach for several months, which helps to soften the fibres and make them separate from the rest of the husk. They are periodically dug up and beaten on rocks to help this process, and then buried again for another few months. The fibre is called 'coir', and is used for mats and rope-making. In the areas outside the towns you will often see local women working with coir in this way.

A new project outside Zanzibar Town is engaged in the use of timber from coconut palm trees, which are found all over Zanzibar and Pemba islands. Traditionally, palm has not been used as a timber because it is very hard to cut or plane. However, modern high-quality joinery tools mean coconut wood can now be turned into beautiful furniture and fittings such as doors and window frames. The aim of the project is to use the local palm trees after they have come to the end of their natural fruit-producing life. By using this local source of timber, it is hoped that other trees will not be cut down or imported to Zanzibar from the mainland. Several of the hotels and tour companies around Zanzibar are now using coconut-wood items.

Other trees occurring on Zanzibar include mango (mwembe), which is used for its fruit and as timber for boatbuilding, and kapok (capoc), *Bombax rhodographalon*, which is used in light construction, and also produces a substance similar to cotton, traditionally used to make stuffing for mattresses and pillows. Other fruit-producing trees, grown in plantations or singly around local villages, include guava, breadfruit, orange and pomegranate.

**Spice trees and food plants** The main crops grown in Zanzibar are coconuts and cloves. Bananas, citrus fruits and other spices are also grown commercially. As well as the famous clove trees, other spice plants found on Zanzibar and Pemba include black pepper, cinnamon, cardamom, jasmine, chilli and henna, whose small leaves are dried, ground and mixed with lemon to give the paste familiar to Eastern beauticians. The main crops grown by local people for their own consumption

Cloves are the buds of a tree which, when dried, produce a unique flavour and aroma that is beloved of chefs the world over. The name comes from the French word 'clou' meaning 'nail', which the buds resemble.

Cloves were introduced to Zanzibar from the end of the 18th century from the French colonies of Seychelles, Ile de France (now Mauritius) and Réunion, where they had earlier been introduced from the Moluccas in Indonesia by French sailors. Sultan Said (sultan from 1804 to 1856) recognised their value and encouraged the setting up of plantations on Zanzibar and Pemba. When the plantations were established, it was found that growing conditions on Pemba Island were superior to those on Zanzibar, and the bulk of the clove crop actually came from there.

At the height of the clove trade, in the second half of the 19th century and the early 20th century, the islands of Zanzibar produced more than 90% of the world's supply of cloves, and the power and wealth of Zanzibar were based largely on this trade. Today, about 75% of the islands' total produce comes from Pemba.

Clove trees (*Eugenia aromatica* or *Eugenia caryophyllata*) grow to a height of around 10–15m and can produce crops for over 50 years. In the first eight years of growth the buds are left to turn into colourful pink flowers. When a tree reaches maturity, however, the buds are painstakingly picked by hand before they open, when they are still white, then separated from their stems. Buds and stems are dried in the sun on palm-leaf mats or on a special stone platform called a *sakufu*, during which time they turn brown. During the harvest season, between July and January, with a break during the November rainy season, the scent of cloves is carried on the breeze right across Pemba in particular, where you can often see sacks of cloves being loaded at Mkoani for shipping to Zanzibar Island. Here, they are offloaded at the port, or on the beach near the Tembo Hotel, and carried by truck to the nearby distillery.

All cloves in Zanzibar have to be sold to the government, which buys at fixed rates, then sells on at market rates to the users and producers. So important is the crop that, on Pemba, vehicles have to stop as they pass police checkpoints to give the opportunity for vehicles to be checked for smuggled cloves. Sometimes, however, the government rates paid to the clove growers are so low that a harvest is not economically viable, and the cloves are left on the trees. As a result, some plantations have been completely abandoned in recent years, creating anger and resentment among the local farmers.

Most of the cloves that are harvested are processed into oil at the distillery on Zanzibar Island. This oil is used mainly as a flavouring device in foods such as cakes, pickles, cooked meats and ready-made mixes. It is also used in some antiseptic solutions, such as mouthwashes, and in mild painkillers for toothache. Its other major use is in cosmetics, where it gives a sweet-spicy note to many different kinds of perfumes.

The best-quality dried buds are kept separate and used whole in cooking, pickling or the making of spiced wines and liqueurs. These buds are also distilled into a high-grade oil for use in particularly fine perfumes. In the cosmetics industry the oil from good Zanzibar clove buds is reckoned to be the best in the world.

Today, Zanzibar is still a major exporter of cloves and clove products, representing about 70% of foreign-exchange earnings – although these are highly dependent on the fluctuating world market price. Agriculture's contribution to Zanzibar's gross domestic product (GDP) currently stands at around 34%, although this has been falling over recent years.

include maize, cassava, yams, bananas and pumpkins. See box *History of Zanzibari agriculture* on page 29.

**MAMMALS** As described above, much of Zanzibar's indigenous forested area has been cleared, so natural habitats for all wild animals are severely restricted. Probably the best places to see indigenous mammals are the Jozani Forest Reserve on Zanzibar Island and the Ngezi Forest Reserve on Pemba.

In this section, scientific names of species are given according to information provided by Jozani Forest Reserve and Ngezi Forest Reserve. Other authorities disagree on some classifications and nomenclature, especially regarding subspecies, but this is unlikely to be important for most visitors.

Jozani Forest Reserve is well known for its population of **red colobus monkeys** (see colour section). This animal is found elsewhere in Africa, but those on Zanzibar form a distinct species, called Zanzibar red colobus or Kirk's red colobus (*Procolobus kirkii*), endemic to the island and one of the rarest primates in Africa.

Although hard to see in the forest canopy, one group of red colobus in Jozani is partly habituated to human presence, so you are quite likely to spot some if you visit. These monkeys are mainly reddish-brown in colour, with a darker back and 'cap', and a paler forehead patch, but their most striking and unusual feature is the male's white crest on the forehead. On closer inspection, particularly of facial areas, you will notice that each monkey has slightly different coat patterns and colourings.

In Jozani and some other patches of forest you are likely to see the **blue monkey**, also called Sykes' monkey, mitis monkey or the Zanzibar white-throated guenon (*Cercopithecus mitis albgularis*), which on Zanzibar is bluish-grey, or even a greenish-grey, with a distinct white throat-patch. Although the two types of monkey compete for some food items, they are often seen foraging peacefully in mixed groups. The Swahili word for monkey is *kima*. On Zanzibar, the blue monkey is more commonly given this name. When distinguishing between the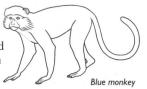

Blue monkey

two, the blue monkey is called *kima mweusi*, and the red colobus *kima punju* – 'poison monkey' (probably because the colobus has a stronger smell than other monkeys, and is reputed to have an evil influence on trees where it feeds).

A local subspecies of **vervet monkey** (*Cercopithecus aethiops nesiotes*) occurs on Pemba, but it is thought not on Zanzibar Island. This monkey is smaller than the red colobus and the blue monkey, generally greyish with a dark, rusty-brown back and black feet.

Other mammals found on Zanzibar, mainly in forested areas, include **bush pig** (*Potamochoerus porcus*), although its numbers are reported to be greatly reduced; **Zanzibar tree hyrax** (*Dendrohyrax arboreus neumanni*), a rodent-like animal the size of a rabbit (this subspecies is endemic), with hoofed feet and rounded ears, and a loud piercing scream when threatened; **Ader's duiker** (*Cephalophus adersi*), a species of small antelope found only on Zanzibar and, until recently, the Kenyan coast; and **Zanzibar suni** (*Nesotragus moschatus moschatus*), another endemic subspecies of antelope which is even smaller than the duiker. The endemic **Pemba blue duiker** (*Cephalophus monticola pembae*) occurs at Ngezi Forest. All these animals are nocturnal or extremely shy and are unlikely to be seen.

*Ader's duiker*

The Zanzibar leopard, *Panthera pardus adersi*, is a local subspecies. Two different types have been recorded: the *kisutu*, which is similar to the mainland leopard, but with a more compact spot pattern and lighter background; and the *konge*, which is larger than the kisutu with dark fur and faint spot pattern.

Leopard tend to be shy, and mainly active at night. Perhaps because of their elusive, nocturnal habits, they have traditionally been considered unlucky by local people, and are often associated with witchcraft, so have been actively hunted. They are also hunted because they are seen as vermin by farmers, and for their skins which can be sold to dealers. The leopard has been further pushed to the edge of extinction by an ever-growing loss of suitable habitat, as forest areas are cleared, and by a loss of prey, as Zanzibar's small antelopes are also hunted unsustainably.

By the 1980s the leopard was believed to be extinct in Zanzibar, but in 1994 an American researcher called Scott Marshall found evidence of three leopards on Unguja (Zanzibar Island), including prints, droppings and a suspected den near Chwaka. In his report, Marshall suggested that these leopards were trapped and 'domesticated' at a young age, to be used in ceremonies by local witchdoctors or traditional healers. He also suggested that there may be several more leopards similarly kept in captivity at other villages in Zanzibar, although this assumption was based on local anecdotal evidence, rather than on positive sightings.

However, in 1998, the South African wildlife experts Chris and Tilde Stuart published a report describing their exhaustive methods to locate any signs of leopard on Zanzibar Island, and concluded that none existed in a wild state. They also looked into the possibility of a few 'kept' leopards remaining in existence but found no hard evidence. They further concluded that even if a small number of 'kept' leopards were being held in secret, there was no hope at all for long-term survival of this species on Zanzibar.

**Leopard** (*Panthera pardus adersi*, or *chui* in Swahili) have been recorded in Jozani, and elsewhere in Zanzibar. Again, this is an endemic subspecies, smaller than the mainland version and with finer markings, and also very unlikely to be sighted. Recent studies have concluded that this animal is now extinct on Zanzibar. For more details see the *Leopards in Zanzibar* box above.

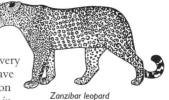

Zanzibar leopard

The small-eared **greater galago** or **bushbaby** (*Otolemur garnettii*) and the Zanzibar **lesser galago** (*Galagoides zanzibaricus*) both occur in Zanzibar, the latter listed as vulnerable by the IUCN. The small-eared galago (*komba* in Swahili) is about the size of a rabbit, generally brown, with very distinctive large ears and eyes, and a large bushy tail. The Zanzibar galago (*komba ndogo*) also has large eyes and ears, but it is smaller (about half the size of the greater galago) and grey in colour. Both animals are nocturnal, especially active at dawn and dusk, and have distinctive cries – sometimes like a child crying (hence their name), other times loud and shrill, and positively spine-chilling. They are known to be inquisitive and will forage around huts and villages at night. They are attracted to bowls of locally brewed palm wine, and often get captured when intoxicated and incapable of escape. A local saying, '*mlevi kama komba*', means 'as drunk as a bushbaby'!

Also found in Zanzibar is the **African civet** (*Viverra civetta schwarzi, orngawa* in Swahili); it looks like a very large cat with a stocky body, thick tail, and black, white and grey markings which form rough stripes. The **Javan civet** (*Viverricula indica rasse*) occurs on Pemba and Unguja, probably introduced by southeast Asian traders.

Smaller mammals include the **Zanzibar slender mongoose** (*Herpestes sanguineus rufescens*), most often seen running across roads with its tail vertical, and the **bushy-tailed mongoose** (*Bdeogale crassicauda tenuis*) – rarely seen anywhere. The **marsh mongoose** (*Atilax paludinosus rubescens*) occurs only on Pemba and may be seen at Ngezi Forest. The **banded mongoose** is a non-indigenous species, introduced to Zanzibar Island.

Populations of rats, mice and shrews (plus 14 species of bat) occur on both Zanzibar and Pemba islands. Those worthy of note include the **Zanzibar four-toed elephant shrew** (*Petrodromus tetradactylus zanzibaricus*) with distinctive long slender legs and a trunk-like snout for eating insects, and the **Pemba flying fox** (*Pteropus voeltzkowi*), a large fruit bat with distinctive rufous colouring and fox-like face, found only on Pemba Island. For more details, see page 262.

## REPTILES, AMPHIBIANS AND INVERTEBRATES

Of all the reptiles on Zanzibar, undoubtedly the easiest to spot are the **giant tortoise** (*Geochelone gigantea*) that inhabit Prison Island, a few kilometres offshore from Zanzibar Town. They were introduced here from the island of Aldabra, in the Seychelles archipelago, in the 18th century.

If you visit Jozani, you'll probably see some of the forest's population of tiny black and gold **frogs**. In the rainy season, when the ground floods, you'll see their tadpoles too. **Chameleons** can also be seen in Jozani and other parts of the island. Like the mongoose they are often seen crossing roads, but often very slowly, and very precariously. Other reptiles include snakes (rarely seen) and geckos (frequently seen on the inside walls of buildings – particularly the budget hotels in Zanzibar Town – although this is no cause for worry as they're small, timid and harmless).

The long black millipedes which you'll see on paths, especially after rains, are also harmless, and will curl up in a ball if you disturb them. Smaller still, though much more dangerous, is the mosquito. These are relatively common on Zanzibar, so see the section on *Malaria prevention* on pages 76–8 before you arrive.

One of the best places to see some of Zanzibar's reptiles (among other animals) is at the Zanzibar Land Animals Park (ZALA) a few kilometres west of Jozani Forest on the road to Kizimkazi. For more details see pages 252–3.

## BIRDS Dudley Iles

Zanzibar is not noted as a major birdwatching area, but over 200 species of bird have been recorded on the islands of the archipelago. The avifauna of Zanzibar includes the resident birds, plus visitors – migrants and seabirds. For any keen birdwatcher travelling on the east African mainland, polishing off the holiday with at least a few days on Zanzibar can make the trip-list even more impressive – the islands boast several species and races which are unique. Even for the more casual birdwatcher, Zanzibar provides some fine opportunities. Knowing the name of the bird that flew over the beach, or sings from a bush in your hotel garden, will make your time in Zanzibar even more rewarding and enjoyable.

**Overview** Like the majority of offshore islands, Unguja and Pemba have a smaller avifauna than the mainland of east Africa. Unguja can claim about 220 species, and Pemba slightly fewer. Of these, about 35 have been added since 1994, an indication of increasing tourist interest and observations. On Zanzibar, visitors are able to

*from information provided by Dudley Iles, updated by Helen de Jode,
Zanzibar Ecotourism Association*

The Indian house crow (*Corvus splendens*) was introduced to Zanzibar in 1891. The bird is a scavenger and 50 crows were sent by the Indian government to help clear domestic waste building up in Stone Town at the time. Although the Indian house crow did consume some of this rubbish, it is by nature an aggressive bird and it began to attack many of the island's small birds and their eggs. As early as 1917 it was realised that the crows had become a pest, and they were subject to various control efforts including trapping, shooting and poisoning, but to little effect. By the 1940s the Indian house crow had spread throughout Zanzibar Island, and by the 1970s their population had increased to such an extent in Zanzibar Town that many small bird species were rarely seen.

The crow population continued to grow and by 1990 their impact on the indigenous bird population was considerable, with the town becoming virtually devoid of all other species. In addition the Indian house crow was affecting agricultural and livestock production: feeding on germinating maize, sorghum and soft fruits, eating young chicks and ducklings and attacking calves and sometimes even cattle.

Between 1990 and 1995 the Finnish International Development Agency funded a control programme organised by wildlife expert Tony Archer and a team from the Zanzibar Commission for Lands and Environment. They used firstly a Malaysian-designed crow trap, and later a poison which was developed in the USA to control starlings as agricultural pests. The trapping and poisoning strategies were combined with a bounty on the collection of Indian house crow eggs and chicks during the breeding season. According to a report issued by Tony Archer, almost 45,000 crows were killed between 1993 and 1995. An estimated 95% of the crow population was killed in Stone Town and 75% across the island as a whole, allowing the small bird populations to return.

Unfortunately, since 1995, as funding dried up, there has been little continued effort to control the numbers of crows in Zanzibar. Increasing amounts of rubbish generated by a growing human population in Zanzibar Town, and a growth in tourism in coastal areas, are partly to blame for the rise in the number of crows. Current levels are having a serious impact on the indigenous bird population and are becoming an environmental health hazard.

In Dar es Salaam, where a similar crow problem exists, the Wildlife Conservation Society of Tanzania (WCST) has succeeded in killing over 43,000 crows using crow traps paid for by hotel owners and with some limited funding from the Canadian Fund for Local Initiatives.

In Zanzibar, a small voluntary organisation, registered as the Zanzibar Ecotourism Association or ZEA (e ecotourism-znz@twiga.com), has since 1999 been encouraging hotels to become part of a similar sustainable programme for Zanzibar, but lacks financial support. Under ZEA co-ordination several hotels and individuals around Unguja have now established their own crow traps, but many more are needed if the island is to be rid of the Indian house crow.

make a larger contribution to natural history records than on the mainland, since there have been fewer observers until recently.

Although Unguja and Pemba are similar in size, geography and position, they provide an interesting avifauna comparison. Unguja has woodpeckers, shrikes, cuckoo-shrikes and bulbuls, while Pemba has none of these. But Pemba has its own species of green pigeon, scops owl, white-eye and sunbird found nowhere else in the world.

As well as the resident birds, migrants from Eurasia, the Middle East and southern Africa pass through or remain to winter on the islands. Those from the north arrive in September/October and leave again in February/March. For European visitors it is a delight to see a familiar spotted flycatcher in the hotel garden, or hear the sound of a curlew calling from the shore at low tide.

**Habitats** The main bird habitats on Zanzibar, and some of the species found there, are described below. If the name of a bird is singular (eg: golden weaver), it refers to one species. If the name is plural (eg: bee-eaters, kingfishers), it refers to several species of the same or similar genus.

*Parks and gardens* Perhaps surprisingly, some of the best places to see birds are the parks and public gardens of Zanzibar Town, or the gardens of the many hotels situated along the coasts of Unguja and Pemba. The seed- and fruit-bearing trees, and the insects they attract, in turn attract many mannikins, warblers, coucals, sunbirds and swifts.

A bird you cannot miss in towns and around the big hotels on the coast is the Indian house crow – see the box opposite for more information.

*Farmland* The more fertile areas of Zanzibar, mostly the centre and west of Unguja and much of Pemba, are occupied by the majority of the rural population. Over the centuries natural coastal scrub and forest have been cleared and turned over to agriculture, either for small-scale subsistence farming, or for commercial plantations growing fruit and spices. The plentiful supplies of seeds, fruits and insects here attract many birds, including the beautiful long-tailed paradise flycatcher and parties of golden weaver (the only widespread weaver in Zanzibar). You may also see green wood-hoopoe, crested guineafowl (although these are now rare) and the diminutive emerald-spotted wood dove.

The telegraph wires along the roads provide vantage points for lilac-breasted roller and occasionally for the rufous-coloured broad-billed roller, and in winter for the blue-cheeked bee-eater.

Lesser-striped swallow hunt for flying insects over the countryside, and visit pools to collect mud for nest building. In areas where there are coconut palms you will see palm swift.

*Freshwater ponds and grasslands* Some farming areas consist of grassland, grazed by cattle, and often flooded after rain. Some of these wet areas are used to grow rice. Here you will see black-winged bishop, a small bright red weaver, plus herons and egrets, especially cattle egret, and maybe even a goshawk or harrier.

Where undisturbed, ponds and marshes support breeding jacana (or lilytrotter) and black crake, and possibly Allen's gallinule. You may also see small parties of pygmy goose, white-faced whistling duck and occasionally the rare white-backed duck. In winter months, purple heron and yellow wagtails (from Eurasia) feed in the rushes along pond edges.

Other birds seen in these areas include little grebe, red-billed teal and moorhen.

*Bush* Many areas of Zanzibar, especially the north and east of Unguja (Zanzibar Island), are not fertile and have not been cleared. They are covered in low scrubby vegetation called coral rag bush. It grows on well-drained rock which was once a coral reef, but was exposed when sea levels dropped many millions of years ago.

The poor vegetation here does not attract great numbers of birds, but a few exciting species can be seen, especially in the early morning or late evening, including the pale-eyed sombre bulbul, eastern bearded scrub robin, crowned hornbill and collared sunbird. You might also see birds of prey such as African goshawk or black kite, plus rollers and shrikes. With luck a Gabon nightjar may rise suddenly from near your feet.

**Forests and woodland** Only a small percentage of Zanzibar's indigenous forest remains, following centuries of clearing for farms and plantations. The main areas are Jozani Forest on Unguja and Ngezi Forest and Kiyuu Forest on Pemba, characterised by tall trees with buttressed roots and a convergent canopy, interspersed with ferns and smaller bushes. Masingini Forest near Bububu north of Zanzibar Town can also be rewarding. The forest birds of Zanzibar are shy and hard to spot, but your chances are better in the early morning, when you might see Fischer's turaco, wood owl, crested guineafowl or tambourine dove, plus swifts, hornbills, woodpeckers and weavers.

In patches of woodland, on the edge of areas which have been cleared for farming, you may see more weavers, plus coucals, sunbirds, flycatchers and bulbuls.

**Mangroves** Mangroves occur on small offshore islands or around estuaries, in or near areas which are covered by water at high tide. Individual mangroves can grow to 5m in height, and close together, which creates a forest-like atmosphere. (The mangrove vegetation of Zanzibar is discussed in the *Seas and shores of Zanzibar* section that follows.) This habitat is rich in marine life, which is exploited by humans as well as resident and migrant shore birds including herons and kingfishers. Other species you are likely to see include mouse-coloured sunbird and blue-cheeked bee-eater.

**Seashore and sandbars** Naturally, as a group of islands, Zanzibar is surrounded by seashores, made up of beaches, low cliffs, creeks and tidal coral-mud flats. On the beaches you will find various wading birds, including plovers, whimbrels and sandpipers; many of these will be familiar to European naturalists, as Zanzibar becomes an increasingly important wintering ground for these northern species.

Also look out for the greater sand plover (which comes from central Asia) and the striking crab plover, which breeds along the Somali coast. Another notable shore bird is the dimorphic heron, which feeds along the tide line: about 49% of these birds is mouse grey, and another 49% is pure white, while the rest show intermediate plumages. Perhaps the most striking seashore bird is the African fish eagle, which may be seen in some areas.

On the numerous sandbars off the west coast of Zanzibar you can see more waders, plus flocks of terns, gulls and cormorants. The sooty gull often seen here is a visitor from the Red Sea.

**Open sea** Some birds spend most of their time at sea, in (or above) deeper water, and rarely come to the shore. You will see these only if you are out on a boat, possibly diving or fishing, or crossing to Zanzibar Town on a ship from Pemba or Dar es Salaam. Oceanic birds are rare, but you may occasionally see frigatebirds or a roseate tern, or a masked booby from the breeding colony on Latham Island, south of Zanzibar.

**Birdwatching areas** There are many places where you can watch birds on Zanzibar, and we list just a few recommended areas here.

**The People's Gardens** In Zanzibar Town, formerly known as Victoria Gardens (see pages 154–5), this small park has flowers and flowering trees and attracts a good range of birds. Here you might see scarlet-breasted sunbird, the Indian race of house sparrow, bronze mannikin, black and white mannikin, and the neat but skulking green-backed camaroptera, a complex name for Zanzibar's only widespread resident warbler. Overhead, parties of little swift hawk for insects.

**Mbweni Ruins Hotel garden** On the outskirts of Zanzibar Town (see page 161), this good hotel has a beautiful garden, and is an excellent birdwatching area. You don't have to be a guest to come here for lunch and a walk around their nature trail. At least 50 species have been recorded here by the hotel management who are very knowledgeable on local wildlife, and can advise on good birdwatching places on Zanzibar. The hotel's dining veranda overlooks a beach, where many shore birds, including oystercatchers, whimbrels, sooty gull and lesser crested tern, await the retreat of the tide. Nearby is an area of mangrove. In the hotel gardens you'll see bronze mannikin, mangrove kingfisher, little swift and scarlet-chested sunbird, plus Eurasian golden oriole and blue-cheeked bee-eater in winter. During the heat of the day, the hotel pond is beloved by black-breasted glossy starling, dark-capped bulbul (more widely known as common, black-eyed or yellow-vented bulbul), golden weaver and as many as 50 Java sparrows (introduced around 1857, but now resident).

**Bwawani Marsh** Situated near the port, on the edge of Zanzibar Town, this is the largest reed swamp on Unguja, although it was formed by accident when the Bwawani Hotel was built. Some 20% of Unguja's birds have been recorded here including a few, like the hottentot teal and purple gallinule, which have not been recorded elsewhere on the island.

Other species to look out for are lesser swamp warbler, Allen's gallinule, jacana, wood sandpiper, night heron, purple heron and the African race of the little bittern. The best viewing spots are on the Bububu road and on the smaller road leading to the hotel. Unfortunately, the swamp has become a dumping ground for local rubbish. Beware!

**Jozani Forest** A good area for keen birders, particularly if you visit early or late in the day, is Jozani Forest Reserve, although the birds here typically hide themselves in the undergrowth or high canopies. The area south of Jozani Forest itself, on the other side of the main road, where the semi-habituated monkeys are found, is also good for birding. (For more details see page 252.) Birds occurring here include the olive sunbird, the little greenbul (a racial endemic), dark-backed weaver, paradise flycatcher, east coast batis (a neat black-and-white flycatcher), crowned hornbill and cardinal woodpecker. Local specials include the east coast akalat and Fischer's turaco. At dawn or dusk you may also see African wood owl.

In the nearby mangrove forest, where a walkway has been constructed, you can see mangrove kingfisher, mouse-coloured sunbird and maybe tropical boubou.

**Chwaka Bay** This is the largest and most complex area of mud and sand on Zanzibar. It is an important area for local fishing, seaweed production, and for wintering shore birds, most notably the **crab plover**. Much of the east coast, from Chwaka to Nungwe, can offer good birdwatching along the shore – and even beyond the reef at low tide. Birds occurring here include **waders**, **terns** and **gulls**, plus herons such as the **green-backed heron** and **dimorphic heron**.

**Matemwe** This is a small village about halfway between Chwaka and Nungwe – with typical east coast conditions. There is a wide beach here, backed by palm groves and coral rag bush, and each habitat attracts typical species. The Matemwe Bungalows gardens are typical of many carefully planted and well-watered lodge gardens; they attract sombre greenbul, collared sunbird and paradise flycatcher, among others.

**Chumbe Island** This small island lies off the west coast, within easy reach of Zanzibar Town. About 63 bird species have been recorded here since 1992, but these are mostly sea and shore birds. The resident land birds are limited to about six common species, including African reed warbler, and most notably the small colony of mouse-coloured sunbird. Perhaps Chumbe's main avian interest lies in the vagrants which occasionally appear, such as a wood warbler (only the third recorded sighting in all Tanzania) and, in 1999, a peregrine falcon. In 1994 around 750 pairs of roseate tern bred on two islets off Chumbe but, although some 500 young were reared, the birds have not returned. House crows, fish eagles, rats (now eliminated) and bad weather were the probable reasons for their staying away.

**Misali and Panza islands** Misali Island lies close to Pemba Island while Panza Island lies off Unguja. Each has coastal forest and typical shore habitats. Like all small islands they are limited in bird species but are attractive for migrants. Misali is noted for a small population of Fischer's turaco, while on Panza brown-necked parrot occur. Panza also has large colonies of fruit bat and white-winged bat which attract bat hawks.

**Ngezi Forest** On Pemba Island, Ngezi Forest is a good birding destination. Birds recorded here include palm-nut vulture, African goshawk, and four endemics: Pemba scops owl, Pemba white-eye, Pemba green pigeon and Pemba violet-breasted sunbird. Ngezi is also home to a good population of fruit bats.

# THE SEAS AND SHORES OF ZANZIBAR Matt Richmond PhD

For anyone visiting the islands of Zanzibar, Mafia Island or the coast of mainland Tanzania, the diversity of marine life in the surrounding shallow waters may not be immediately obvious. However, the main marine habitats (mangroves, coral reefs and seagrass beds) are part of an extremely diverse, productive and vitally important marine ecosystem. Other marine habitats are the beaches and cliffs fringing the shore, and the vast areas of open water. The species of plants and animals which make up these habitats around Zanzibar and off mainland Tanzania are mostly the same as those found elsewhere in the western Indian Ocean (eg: Mozambique, Madagascar, Mauritius and Seychelles), though slightly different from those in similar habitats as far away as southeast Asia, Australia and the South Pacific islands. Some species of fish and other creatures do, however, span this entire Indo-Pacific region.

## MARINE HABITATS

**Beaches and cliffs** Around the main islands of Zanzibar (that is, Unguja and Pemba), many shores are fringed by either coconut-lined coral-sand beaches, where ghost crabs scamper, or rocky limestone cliffs – remains of ancient reefs once below the sea (over 100,000 million years ago), then exposed as sea levels dropped, now undercut and battered by high-tide waves. The cliffs provide a home to the brilliant red-yellow grapsid rock crabs and the bizarre eight-plated chiton snail, plus numerous other small snails, rock oysters and rock-skipper fish.

**Mangroves** In sheltered bays and inlets, where wave action is reduced, mangrove stands and forests are commonplace. Mangrove trees are specially adapted to survive in the sea, and all ten species found in the western Indian Ocean occur in Zanzibar. At high tide mangroves attract numerous species of fish, crabs and shrimps which depend on the forests as nursery grounds for their young. At low tide, red-clawed **fiddler crabs** carry out their formal challenges when not sifting the mud for food, while **mud-skippers** flip from pool to pool, or from branch to branch when the tide is in. One of the best places to experience these fascinating marine forests is the mangrove boardwalk at Jozani Forest – especially when the tide is in. You can also snorkel around a mangrove forest on Misali Island, off Pemba, or in many other inlets around the main islands.

**Seagrass beds and lagoons** The intertidal areas or zones lie between the high- and low-tide marks. Where beaches slope sharply, this is a narrow strip. Where old coral beds slope imperceptibly and are almost flat, this area may extend 2km or more. Intertidal zones provide a habitat for thousands of molluscs, crabs, sea-cucumbers, seaweeds and several species of seagrasses, which are themselves food for fish at high tide.

*Seagrass Thalassodendron ciliatum*

*Seagrass Cymodocea rotundata*

Along the east coast of Unguja (and the east coasts of the other islands and the mainland) shallow lagoons occur, extending to the reef crest. The lagoons support assorted coral, seagrass and seaweed communities and often great selections of **starfish** and beautiful **nudibranch** (sea hares and their relatives).

*Blue starfish*

**Coral reefs** Corals are not plants, but animals belonging to the *Coelenterata* group (which also includes sea anemones and jellyfish). Corals exist in clean, clear, shallow, warm water, and so are only found in the tropical regions. A coral begins life as a soft many-tentacled 'polyp' around 1mm in size, and then produces a hard calcium carbonate skeleton around itself for protection. These types of coral are called '**hard corals**'. A coral colony develops from a single polyp by a process called 'budding' (where a new polyp grows out of an existing one). When

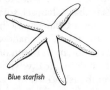

*Crown-of-thorns starfish feeding on brain coral*

3

polyps die, their hard skeletons remain, and the colony expands as new polyps form on the skeletons of old dead polyps. In this way colonies grow, and the growth rate varies from about 1cm to 5cm per year depending on species, depth and water conditions. Groups of colonies together make up the coral reefs found fringing the islands. Different types of hard coral form their colonies in different shapes; the commonly known varieties include stag-horn coral, plate coral, mushroom coral, table corals and brain corals – all abundant in shallow water.

*Staghorn coral*

Coral also uses a form of sexual reproduction where sperm and eggs are mixed (either internally with a coral embryo or larvae later being released, or by 'spawning' where eggs and sperm are released by polyps to mix in the water). In both ways the corals can colonise new areas.

Within the polyps exist microscopic algae-type organisms called *zooxanthellae*, which trap the sunlight needed to power the chemical reactions which produce the coral's hard calcium skeleton. It is the *zooxanthellae* which give the coral its colour – usually pink or pale brown in a variety of shades – as the coral polyps themselves are virtually transparent. Thus when coral is picked, and taken out of the water, the corals and the *zooxanthellae* die and lose colour, leaving only the pale 'bleached' chalky-white skeletons.

During daylight hours, the coral colonies use sunlight in much the same way as plants do, but at night-time on a reef, most hard coral species are busy, with polyps extending their tentacles to catch planktonic foods.

**Soft corals**, on the other hand, do not have a hard external skeleton and do not form reefs. They are far more colourful than hard corals, although they also require light to build the tiny crystal fibres embedded in their soft pink, lilac or cream-coloured tissues. The daytime feeding of the eight-tentacled polyps, a feature of this group, is clearly visible on soft corals which can, in places, dominate underwater scenes.

On the east coasts of Unguja and Pemba typical fringing reefs are marked by a continuous line of surf resulting from Indian Ocean swells. At low tide the reef crest dries out revealing pink algal-rock and boulders – the coral itself usually only becoming prolific on the seaward slope below 5m. On Unguja, the coral-covered reef slopes dip down to about 20m, after which a fairly bare sandy seabed continues down a further 4km to the ocean bottom. On the more sheltered west coasts of the Zanzibar Channel smaller, isolated patch reefs with sandbars, and island reefs (around Chapwani, Changuu, Bawe and Chumbi islands), provide coral gardens in the relatively shallow waters. In contrast, parts of the reef around Pemba Island drop down over 50m or more offering spectacular vertical coral walls. Some of the most dramatic dive sites along the Tanzanian coast are found on the steep slopes of Pemba Island.

On any of these coral reefs you will immediately note the amazing variety of colourful fish of all sizes and shapes, incredible in their patterns and forms: butterflyfish, parrotfish, surgeonfish, damselfish, emperors, goatfish, pufferfish, angelfish, triggerfish, groupers and grunts to name a few. Most of these typical coral reef fish are territorial and reside over small areas of reef, rarely leaving their patch and aggressively protecting it from others of their own species. Some,

*Emperor fish*

like the butterflyfish, pair up for life and occupy a patch the size of a tennis court; others, such as the blue-lined yellow snappers, roam around the reefs *Grouper* in schools of a few hundred.

Because of the rich diversity of life forms, coral reefs have been compared to tropical rainforests. With Zanzibar's waters containing more than 700 fish species associated with coral reefs, over 100 species of hard corals, 150-odd species of seaweed and 300-plus species of seashells, to mention just a few of the more obvious sea creatures, the comparison is certainly a valid one. Then there are sponges, anemones, brittlestars, sea cucumbers, sea-squirts, feather-stars and crustaceans, all forming a seemingly chaotic, mind-boggling complexity which has fascinated scientists since Darwin's time.

The loss of the microscopic *zooxanthellae* from the coral, resulting in bleaching, was a major feature of the reefs around Zanzibar and elsewhere in the tropics in 1998, as the region experienced increased seawater temperatures (up to 32°C) associated with a severe, and much-publicised, shift in global climate conditions called El Niño. Although coral bleaching had occurred in the past, this event was on a scale not witnessed before. Much coral (both hard and soft) bleached and failed to regain its *zooxanthellae*. Within about five months vast areas of previously rich and diverse coral communities died. In many reef areas since then, new, small colonies have begun to emerge from settlement of coral larvae, and the coral component of these reefs is beginning to return to that prior to 1998. In other areas, total recovery to pre-1998 conditions may take decades or centuries. For reasons that are still unclear, much more coral around Pemba eventually died, whereas on Unguja corals recovered after bleaching.

**Open waters** The open waters, though mostly empty at first glance, can be very busy at times. They are home to vast schools of small, plankton-feeding, pelagic fish species such as sardines, silver-sides and Indian mackerel, continuously on the move and relentlessly pursued by larger pelagic fish, like skipjack, yellowfin tuna, kingfish, sailfish and marlin. Out at sea, in the Pemba Channel or off the east coast, flocks of hundreds of white terns identify tuna feeding frenzies as they dart into the shoals of small pelagic fish forced up to the surface by the tuna below.

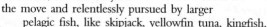

Sailfish

Yellowfin tuna

Also feeding out at sea for most of their lives are **turtles**, coming into shallow waters when looking for a mate. Green and hawksbill turtles are the most common; for more details, see pages 62–4.

Both the friendly bottlenose dolphin and the less bold humpback dolphin can be seen in small groups, or pods, quite close to the shore. (See the *Kizimkazi dolphins* box, page 247.) Around Unguja there appear to be a few pods of 10–15 members, each with its own territory. One area where they are commonly seen is off Kizimkazi in southwest Unguja (viewing is easily arranged with a local boat), or around Mnemba Island in the northeast, or, with a bit of luck, even off Zanzibar Town. (Watching dolphins is especially enjoyable if you're also sipping a cool beer on Africa House Hotel terrace at sunset.) At Kizimkazi and Mnemba it's also sometimes possible to see groups of hundreds of spinner dolphins, providing an unforgettable memory.

Less common are **whales**, though humpback whales have been spotted several times around October–November in the Zanzibar Channel and off Nungwi in the north, leading their recently born young back to the summer feeding grounds in Antarctica.

**TIDES AND WEATHER** Tides, the daily rise and fall of sea level, are a noticeable feature along the east coast of Africa. They are dictated mostly by the moon (and to a lesser extent the sun) and there are two main types. The smaller tides, known as neap tides, occur during the half-moon phases and result in a tidal range (the difference between high and low water) of only 1.5m. From this period onwards the tidal range increases, until a full or new moon (ie: every two weeks), when spring tides occur. These result in the largest tidal range, of about 4m between high tide and low tide. Spring tide low water always occurs at around 10.00–11.00, for about three days, twice every lunar cycle (at full moon and new moon). Through the rest of the lunar cycle, the time of each tide changes from one day to the next by an average of 50 minutes (about 30 minutes during spring). So if high tide is at 15.00 on one day it will be about 15.50 on the following day.

During spring low tides the low-water mark can be a couple of kilometres out and these days are ideal for walking out on the inter-tidal flats and reef crest to explore the kaleidoscope of life. Take care to avoid trampling on living coral and on sea urchins or blue-spotted stingrays. Good footwear (trainers, plastic sandals or neoprene booties) is strongly recommended. Even the tiniest cut or graze can flare up into a nasty tropical ulcer which will keep you out of the sea for days recovering. Be aware, also, of the speed with which the tide comes in and don't be caught out on the reef crest of the east coast with the incoming tide around your waist – you'll have an exhausting swim back to the beach if you do. And remember, tidal currents are strongest during spring tides so be careful not to swim too far out, or into tidal channels.

*Needle spine urchin*

Prevailing weather also greatly influences sea conditions and travellers should be aware of the main seasons. These are described in more detail under *When to visit* in *Chapter 4*.

**LOCAL PEOPLE AND MARINE LIFE** It won't take you long to realise that a great number of Zanzibaris are dependent on the surrounding seas and shallows for their variety of foods. Various fishing methods are used to catch this vital source of protein which contributes over 70% of the needs of the local population. On dark new-moon nights in the Zanzibar Channel, sardine boats with lights attract and net vast shoals; on the same nights gill-netting boats, with 15cm-mesh nets, are after the large pelagic species (tuna, kingfish and billfish) in the southern Pemba Channel, operating mostly from Nungwi. Conventional hook-and-line fishing and passive fish-trapping using baited basket-traps (*madema*) are still practised all around the islands.

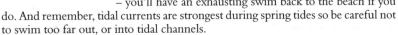

*Kingfish*

During the low spring tides thousands of women and children collect octopus, shells, sea-cucumbers and moray eels from the intertidal flats, whilst other women tend to their seaweed (*mwani*) farm patches in the lagoons on the east coast. The lines of sticks protruding out of the water at low tide can't be missed (for details see the box on *Sustainable seaweed farming*, page 225).

*Octopus*

Mangroves are also harvested: the wood has been used for building poles for centuries, because of its resistance to rotting and insect infestation. However, the rapid increase in demand over the last few years, with overcutting in places, has led to deterioration of the forests and the marine life which relies on them. Recently, the felling of planted casuarina (Australian pine, though not actually a true pine) has produced, so far, acceptable insect-resistant poles, easing some of the pressure on the mangroves.

**CONSERVATION** Due to the rapid increase in population (at present doubling every 20 years), the availability of new fishing materials, the development of a number of destructive fishing methods and the inability of the government to enforce fisheries regulations, the delicate balance of life in the shallow seas (and therefore this vital source of food) is beginning to be destroyed. Spear-fishing is on the increase and due to its effectiveness can quickly strip the reefs of the larger fish, and even of small species such as butterflyfish. Not only does it reduce fish numbers and make them wary of snorkellers, such as around the shallow reefs close to Zanzibar Town or in the lagoon on the east, but by removing these vital predators the balance within the ecosystem is being lost. Netting around reefs, and the type of fishing known locally as *Kigumi* where corals are broken deliberately to force fish out into the surrounding net, are also practised and extremely destructive. Dynamite-fishing is also very destructive, but mostly restricted to the mainland coast. Also restricted to the mainland and Mafia coasts, fortunately for Zanzibar, is the collecting of shallow live coral (mainly of the genus *Porites*) for baking on open kilns into lime. On Unguja at least, quarried coral rock is used instead.

Careless anchoring of boats on coral reefs can also, over a short time, cause considerable localised damage. In 1994 a project funded by the Dutch Embassy of Dar es Salaam through the Institute of Marine Sciences established, in conjunction with the tourist boat operators who use the reefs, 15 permanent moorings for the islands and reefs close to Zanzibar Town, thus reducing tourism-related damage. Although these have since deteriorated and are no longer functional, the project did serve to increase the awareness of the importance and needs of living coral reefs, and in general boat operators around Zanzibar Town are careful when dropping anchor, attempting to set it in sand or rubble. Perhaps in the future the shallow coral gardens around Bawe Island and the sandbanks off Stone Town will come under some form of management to conserve their productivity and attractiveness to visitors. The main threat to these shallow coral reefs, some of which have superb hard coral communities, remain the Kigumi fishermen.

The local demand for marine curios (shells, dead coral and turtle products) has increased with the growing number of tourists, further adding to the over-exploitation of the marine resources. The collection of large, colourful, attractive mollusc shells like the giant triton (*Charonia tritonis*) and the bull-mouth helmet shell (*Cypraecassis rufa*) have secondary effects which are not that obvious. These feed on the crown-of-thorns starfish (*Acanthaster planci*) and sea-urchins respectively. Absence of the molluscs again upsets the balance, and populations of these echinoderms can increase alarmingly, furthering the destruction of the coral reefs. Collection of live hard corals is, of course, extremely damaging to the reef ecosystem. A colony the size of a football can take over 20 years to grow and the implications of mass removal for sale to tourists or export need no further explanation. Don't buy the stuff!

*Giant triton shell*

crimson-red

*Bull-mouth helmet shell*

Some steps are being taken to try and address the problems. With the involvement of donor organisations, and conservation bodies such as the Worldwide Fund for Nature, private enterprise, the Institute of Marine Sciences, and the Zanzibar authorities (Department of Fisheries, Commission of Environment and Department of Tourism), plans to create marine protected areas have made some progress. On Pemba the only marine protected area is Misali Island Conservation Area which involves local fishermen in conservation and charges fees to visiting divers and snorkellers. On Unguja, a few miles south of Zanzibar Town, Chumbe Island Coral Park (CHICOP), a private investment, includes a protected forest and coral reef on its western shores. Chumbe (see page 257) can be visited for a day, or you can stay overnight, and funds generated contribute to raising awareness of marine issues through the educational centre used by local school pupils. Further south the Menai Bay Conservation Area brings fisheries and mangrove issues to local community groups supported by the government in an attempt to manage the resources for the long term. The only other marine protected area is a zone 200m wide around Mnemba Island, an exclusive private island resort off the northeast coast. However, the spectacular turquoise waters around Mnemba Island extend beyond this boundary and the 20km of fringing reefs are accessible to divers and snorkellers from several beach hotels operating from the north and east coasts of Unguja.

Tourism development, now a rapidly growing industry, also has a role to play in marine conservation. By acknowledging that the marine resources on which it depends are finite and also vital to the neighbouring coastal villages, and by attempting to come up with methods which assist all the users, tourism can contribute to a healthy future for all concerned. Survival of both may be in the balance.

So, when bobbing around over a coral garden, or simply sitting on the seabed, 10m down, watching the coral reef world around you, or wading through the dark mud in a mangrove forest, think about it ... and enjoy it. There's a whole lot going on: between individuals, between species, between habitats and between the ecosystem and the people who use it. This section has touched on some of the more salient issues and examples of life in the seas and on the shores of Zanzibar. Many more exist to be discovered and pondered upon; while doing so, the following are a few points to remember:

- Don't touch living coral. There's no need to and it is more sensitive than it looks. Be careful when reef walking and snorkelling or diving. Be aware of what your flippers are doing and avoid landing on coral when entering into the water. Maintain good buoyancy control at all times.
- Help prevent anchor damage. Insist on the use of permanent moorings, if available, or anchor only in sand.
- Don't buy shells, turtle products or corals.
- Spread the word. Explain what you now know about the local marine ecosystems to other visitors and locals.

**SEA TURTLES** *Original text by Fiona Clark, updated by Lorna Slade, ecologist, Zanzibar Sea Turtle Survival Project*

Five types of sea turtle occur in the western Indian Ocean: the **green turtle** (*Chelonia mydas*), the **hawksbill turtle** (*Eretmochelys imbricata*), the **loggerhead turtle** (*Caretta caretta*), the **olive ridley turtle** (*Lepidochelys olivacea*) and the **leatherback turtle** (*Dermochhelys coriacea*). All are endangered species. The most commonly found turtle in Zanzibar is the green turtle, followed by the hawksbill. Both nest in Zanzibar. Leatherback and loggerhead are sometimes seen, but don't nest. There have been no records for the olive ridley since 1975.

Zanzibar is not a major turtle nesting site, but appears to be a feeding ground for sea turtles from other areas; nesting is more prolific on Pemba. Conservationists have recovered tags from captured turtles showing that green turtles come to Zanzibar from Aldabra Island, in the Seychelles, and from Europa and Tromelin islands. Loggerheads that nest in KwaZulu-Natal (South Africa) also feed in Tanzania – one loggerhead was captured in Tanzania just 66 days after being tagged in South Africa.

**The bad news** The sea turtle population is decreasing in Zanzibar. This is bad because turtles are part of a food web which includes sea-grasses, sponges, jellyfish and tiger sharks, and also because living turtles are attractive to tourists and (like dolphins) can sometimes be a way for local people to earn money.

The number of nesting sites has been reduced dramatically, and turtles are hunted and trapped by more efficient means than previously. Local fishermen tell how, 20 or 30 years ago, some beaches would contain 100 or more turtle nests every year. But these days the same beaches contain only two or three nests. Places where nests can still be found include Mnemba Island, the beaches north of Matemwe Bungalows, and around Kizimkazi. Pemba is home to the most important nesting beaches; turtles nest on Misali Island, at Ras Kiuyu and on the beaches near Ngezi Forest – especially Vumawimbi. Unfortunately, except for the island sites, few of these nests are successful: many eggs are taken by people, while others are lost to the sea when erosion has formed steps on some beaches forcing turtles to nest in places that are vulnerable to the high tide.

The burgeoning tourist industry also has its costs. In the last ten years many hotels have been built on turtle-nesting beaches. Buildings often extend right to the beach, vegetation is cleared and the beach lit up at night, disturbing any turtles coming up to nest and disorienting any hatchlings. For example, Kiwengwa Beach on the east coast of Unguja (Zanzibar Island) is now wall-to-wall hotel with no space or peace for turtles.

Turtle hunting in Zanzibar only became illegal in October 1993. Although penalties are quite severe (a large fine, or two years in prison, or both) enforcement of the new law is unlikely. The Fisheries Department is under-resourced and has many other problems to deal with (such as dynamite-fishing).

Turtles are usually captured with gill nets, which are set on the sea bed, while others are caught with spear guns. They are brought ashore and have their flippers and shell removed, often while still alive. The number of turtles caught increased dramatically in the 1960s when gill nets, snorkelling gear and spear guns were introduced. Some local fishermen claim that their increased catch proves the population is increasing too, but the same fishermen also agree that nesting turtles have all but disappeared. Uroa on the east coast of Unguja is a renowned area for turtle hunting and the beach sometimes looks like a turtle graveyard.

In March 1996 there were two incidents of poisoning in Pemba through the consumption of turtlemeat, resulting in the death of 37 people. Hawksbill turtles, in particular, are known on occasion to harbour toxins thought to originate from toxic algae in the food chain. These toxins do not harm the turtle, but have disastrous effects on any humans eating the meat. These unfortunate incidents helped reduce turtle slaughter, but apparently only for a short while.

**The good news** Since 1992, there have been several small-scale turtle protection projects run with volunteer help through the government of Zanzibar's Department of the Environment. These include the following:

- A Swahili-language education package for schools and other youth groups, emphasising the plight of sea turtles, and their need to be protected. A poster carrying the same message has also been produced both in English, aimed at visitors, and in Swahili, aimed at locals.
- A nest protection scheme, run by Matemwe Bungalows, a hotel on the east coast. Local villagers are paid a small fee if they report an intact nest, and a further bonus for each successful hatching. To avoid the problems of beach erosion, some nests are moved to safer sites.
- A survey and protection scheme carried out by the management of the exclusive lodge on the private Mnemba Island. This is an ideal site for turtles, with safe beaches (no local fishermen are allowed to land) and deep-water access.

- A nest protection and monitoring scheme on the protected Misali Island, off Pemba, now a marine conservation area, patrolled by local rangers. (Misali is one of the best turtle-nesting areas in Zanzibar, with over 65 nests recorded in 1999.)
- From 1995 to 1998 there was a community education and nest-recording programme in both Pemba and Unguja, including the successful production of an educational drama and video.
- Mnarani Aquarium at Nungwi, a local initiative set up by a group of local fishermen, in a large tidal-fed rock pool. The pool has been stocked with several species of fish and around ten green and hawksbill turtles. The Department of the Environment has allowed this group (only) to keep a maximum of eight turtles for educational purposes and any excess brought in by fishermen are periodically tagged and released. Although generally keeping turtles in captivity is not to be encouraged, in this case the local community benefit, and the educational value to locals (school children are allowed in free) and tourists is judged to be worth it. The aquarium does not keep mature female turtles.

**Turtle-shell products** Zanzibar used to be a major centre for turtle-shell, usually called 'tortoiseshell', and at the height of the trade (the early 20th century) some 3,300kg were exported every year from the islands and nearby mainland coast. Demand dropped, but has recently been revived by the growth of tourism. A survey showed that the amount of turtle-shell jewellery went up five times between early 1993 and late 1994. Less than half the tourists who bought turtle-shell items knew what it was, or that turtles were endangered. However, local conservationists and aware tourists complained to such a degree that many shops now refuse to stock turtle-shell products. Tourists are asked by conservation organisations to boycott any shops that continue to sell turtle products.

Local police and customs officials are now also aware that turtle-shell products are illegal. In 1995, a tourist who bought a whole shell from a hawker on the east coast was stopped at a road block on the way back to Zanzibar Town after hotel staff tipped off the police. The tourist was reprimanded, and the shell was confiscated.

**Local perspectives** Lest we get too self-righteous about all this, we should perhaps remember that Zanzibar is a poor country and that a large sea turtle is worth about a month's wages for an office worker, and considerably more than that to a fisherman or farmer. Turtle meat is also held traditionally to have healing properties. Stopping the local people from catching turtles will inevitably make some of them poorer, yet if the turtle hunting continues there will soon be none left anyway. But many Zanzibaris can't afford the luxury of thinking ahead. Life is hand to mouth and the 'If I don't catch it someone else will' attitude is of course understandable.

Having said that, there does need to be a halt to turtle killing as populations are in danger of extinction. In addition to finding alternative food and income sources for local communities, it is also essential that continued education, improved law enforcement and government protection for important nesting beaches are maintained, to ensure that the turtle has a place in Zanzibar's future.

# 4

# Planning and Preparation

Truly prepossessing was our first view ... of Zanzibar. Earth, sea and sky all seemed wrapped in a soft and sensuous repose ... The sea of purest sapphire ... lay basking ... under a blaze of sunshine.

Richard Burton, British explorer (1856)

## WHEN TO VISIT

The best time to visit these islands is during the dry seasons: December to February and June to October. Generally speaking, from December to February any wind comes from the northeast, so beaches on the southern and western parts of the islands are more sheltered. Conversely, from June to October it tends to come from the southwest, so northern and eastern coasts are best. Ultimately, however, these islands are at the mercy of the ocean, and their weather patterns can be unpredictable at any time of year. Even during the 'dry' seasons, afternoon showers are not unknown, although they tend to be short and pleasantly cooling. For more details, see the *Climate chart*, below.

It is also possible to visit the islands during the rainy season. Then there are fewer visitors and you are more likely to get good bargains for accommodation and trips. The rain can be heavy, but is not usually constant; the sunsets can be particularly magnificent; and pineapples are in season! Travel can be more difficult at this time, with roads damaged and buses delayed, but you'll get there eventually.

At holiday times, such as Christmas and Easter, the islands are popular with expatriate workers from Dar es Salaam and Nairobi as well as overseas visitors. Expect full flights and higher hotel rates. Conversely, during the Islamic fasting period of Ramadan (see page 69), many restaurants and shops are closed during the day, and life runs at a generally slower pace.

If you're going scuba diving or game fishing, see the *Zanzibar diving and fishing seasons* box, page 95. If local festivals appeal, then see page 44. Sports fans may like to tie in their visit with the Zanzibar International Marathon, held every year in early November.

| CLIMATE CHART | | | | | | | | | | | | |
|---|---|---|---|---|---|---|---|---|---|---|---|---|
| | Jan | Feb | Mar | Apr | May | Jun | Jul | Aug | Sep | Oct | Nov | Dec |
| Temp (°C): av min | 25 | 25 | 24 | 23 | 22 | 20 | 19 | 19 | 19 | 21 | 22 | 24 |
| av max | 31 | 31 | 31 | 30 | 29 | 29 | 28 | 28 | 28 | 29 | 30 | 31 |
| Hrs of sun/day | 8 | 8 | 7 | 5 | 6 | 8 | 7 | 8 | 8 | 8 | 8 | 8 |
| Rainfall (mm) | 80 | 70 | 140 | 390 | 250 | 60 | 45 | 40 | 50 | 90 | 220 | 160 |
| Av days of rain | 7 | 6 | 12 | 19 | 14 | 4 | 5 | 6 | 6 | 7 | 14 | 12 |

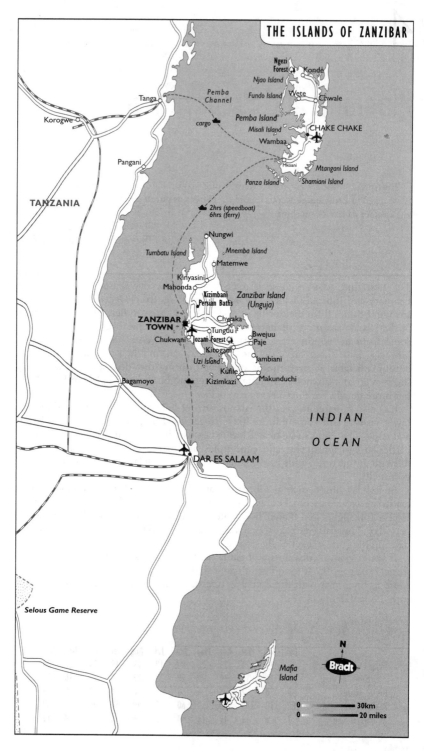

Ngezi
Forest
Konde

Njao Island

Fundo Island
Wete

Chwale

Tanga

Pemba
Channel

Korogwe

cargo

Pemba Island

CHAKE CHAKE

Misali Island

Wambaa

Pangani

Mkoani

Mtangani Island

Panza Island

Shamiani Island

TANZANIA

2hrs (speedboat)
6hrs (ferry)

Nungwi

Mnemba Island

Tumbatu Island

Matemwe

Kinyasini

Mahonda

Kizimbani
Persian Baths

Zanzibar Island
(Unguja)

ZANZIBAR
TOWN

Chwaka

Tungdu

Chukwani

Jozani Forest

Bwejuu

Paje

Kitogani

Jambiani

Uzi Island

Kufile

Bagamoyo

Kizimkazi

Makunduchi

INDIAN

OCEAN

DAR ES SALAAM

Selous Game Reserve

N

Mafia
Island

Bradt

0 ——— 30km
0 ——— 20 miles

Read this book's introduction to understand why we think the real highlights of these islands are often away from the resorts and obvious places – and in the unscheduled interactions with the local people that you meet, and the unspoilt areas you stumble across whilst exploring. That said, we recognise that a little initial direction can help to make the best of a trip so we'll try to give you a few pointers here.

**WHERE TO STAY** The choice of places to stay is endless – but a few really stand out. Top of the list, and most budgets, is **Mnemba Island** (pages 200–2). It's very expensive, but it's also exceedingly good. We approached it fully expecting to comment that it was over-priced, but the reality is that it is in a different league to the other places in this guide. It's very polished, yet also very simple.

For small, high-quality beach lodges with more reasonable price tags, our top tips would be the spacious Arab splendour of **The Sultan Palace** (pages 221–2), the more relaxed **Matemwe Bungalows** (pages 196–7), or the new, stylish **Fumba Beach Lodge** (page 225) in the quiet southwest of Zanzibar.

Whilst looking at these, compare them with the three main lodges on Mafia Island: **Pole Pole** (pages 296–7), **Kinasi** (page 297) and **Chole Mjini** (pages 306–7). Mafia doesn't offer the extensive beaches of Zanzibar, but it's much quieter and in many ways gives a great deal of exclusivity for your money, with the added bonus of some superb diving and snorkelling. It's a great favourite of ours, and very under-valued.

For small, secluded beach retreats which cost even less, have a look at **Pongwe Beach Hotel** (page 210) and the excellent **Sunrise Hotel and Restaurant** (pages 230–1) – which unquestionably serves some of Zanzibar's best food. In the Nungwi area, **Flame Tree Cottages** (page 178) offers a great-value place to stay a few minutes' walk from the buzzing heart of town, and a little further away **Mnarani Beach Bungalows** (pages 179–80) has space and some of the island's best views.

Budget travellers might want to keep an eye on the **Sunset Bungalows** in Kendwa (pages 189–90), which offers particularly good value, and perhaps on developments at **Bellevue Bungalows** (page 229) north of Bwejuu, on the Michamvi Peninsula, which look very promising. Meanwhile, **Santa Maria Coral Reef** (page 210) is a small and simple place in a coconut grove beside a sweeping bay; it's proof that you can still find magical places to match tight budgets.

If you're taking a family, lack mobility, or are simply seeking the facilities of a larger resort, then look first at the new **La Gemma dell'Est** (pages 190–1) in Kendwa – we feel it's a step above most of the island's other big resort offerings (albeit very new and shiny when we visited).

For something completely different, those interested in ecology or conservation shouldn't miss a few days at **Chumbe Island** (pages 257–9) for a terrific all-round experience!

The places in Stone Town change quite fast, but currently **Beyt al Chai** (page 122) is the rising star amongst the upmarket, boutique guesthouses, whilst the large and efficient Serena Hotel (page 123) remains the undisputed best hotel in town.

**THINGS TO SEE AND DO** Whilst lazing on the beach can be very relaxing, you potentially miss out on a lot if this is the limit of your activities. At least accept the offer of a local beach masseuse if there is one; they can be surprisingly good.

The highlights of many people's trips to Zanzibar and Mafia is the **diving**, which is good at many places around these islands. The best diving spots would certainly include the reef around Mnemba Island, and those around Mafia. The less aquatic might prefer to go **snorkelling**, and if so they should add Chumbe Island to this short list of reefs. Chumbe has world-class, pristine coral and no diving is allowed there. Chumbe's also worth visiting for its guided **forest and inter-tidal walks**, which are both attractions in their own right, especially for nocturnal sightings of huge coconut crabs.

A sunset show cruise can be magical and romantic, but better still is a **dhow trip to a remote sandbar**, organised from Mafia; where else can you lie on the beach, or snorkel on a reef, with nothing but a tropical ocean all around you?

If you're in the Nungwi area, then do wander along to see the turtles at the **Mnarani Natural Aquarium** (page 186). It's a great conservation project and a rare chance to see hatchling turtles at very close quarters.

More generally, any trip to Zanzibar Island should include a **spice tour**. The idea may seem clichéd, but plucking everyday spices from what seems like a tangled bit of unruly forest can be fascinating. If you can combine this with a visit to the colobus colony in **Jozani Forest** (pages 249–52), then do so. Meanwhile, those in search of a much more original, albeit less predictable, experience should consider visiting the community beside **Ufufuma Forest** (pages 214–17).

No trip to Zanzibar is really complete without a night or two in **Stone Town**. Whilst here, take a walk around the narrow alleys, venture into the amazing market on Creek Road, and treat yourself to a roof-top meal on a balmy evening.

**WHERE TO EAT** If you enjoy good food, then Zanzibar can be a great place to visit – though choose your lodges carefully. Most of the top lodges have good food and you can expect to eat well; but only a few stand out. The costly **Ras Nungwi Beach Hotel** (page 181) didn't make our line-up of the best-value lodges, but it does come right at the top of the menu for its cuisine. It shares this spot with the vastly cheaper **Sunrise Hotel and Restaurant** (pages 230–1): a superb restaurant in an implausibly simple and inexpensive hotel.

For up-to-date advice on Stone Town's best restaurants, we'd always suggest that you ask someone locally. Things change fast in this game and our recommendations here are likely to be out of date sooner than they're printed. However, favourites must include the reliable **terrace at the Serena Hotel** (page 123), **Monsoon** (page 132), **Rendezvous Le Spices** (page 132) and **The Livingstone Beach** (page 131).

An important part of your preparation for a visit is learning about the history, geography and culture of Zanzibar before you arrive. If textbooks and encyclopaedias put you off, read a few novels or travelogues to get yourself in the mood, or dip into some of the early explorers' accounts (see the books listed in *Appendix 2*). Also, scan the foreign pages of newspapers, or magazines specialising in developing countries, to familiarise yourself with politics and current affairs. You should certainly try to learn a few phrases of Swahili. All this will make your trip much more rewarding.

## TOURIST INFORMATION

**Tanzania Tourist Board** Tanzania Trade Centre, 78–80 Borough High St, London SE1; ↘ 020 7407 0566; f 020 7403 2003; www.tanzaniatouristboard.com

## PUBLIC HOLIDAYS

The islands share most public holidays with the rest of Tanzania. Offices and businesses are usually closed on these days, although some tour companies remain open. Public holidays include:

| | |
|---|---|
| 12 January | Mapinduzi (Revolution) Day |
| 26 April | Union Day |
| 1 May | Workers' Day |
| 7 July | Peasants' and Farmers' Day (called Saba Saba – Seven Seven) |
| 9 December | Independence Day |

Christmas Day, New Year's Day and Easter are also public holidays, although many tour companies stay open, and celebrations are low-key on this largely Muslim island.

The Muslim feasts of Idd il Fitri – the end of Ramadan – and Idd il Maulidi (also called Maulidi ya Mfunguo Sita) – Mohammed's birthday – are celebrated by many people and are effectively public holidays. Dates of these holidays depend on the lunar calendar, and fall 11 or 12 days earlier every year. Approximate dates for Ramadan for the next few years are as follows:

| | |
|---|---|
| 2006 | 24 September to 24 October |
| 2007 | 13 September to 13 October |
| 2008 | 2 September to 2 October |

On Revolution Day (12 January), don't be surprised if you hear gunfire (live) from the army barracks or even heavy anti-aircraft artillery (also live) from warships moored off Zanzibar Town, particularly at night (when the tracer makes a nice arc through the sky). It's just the military celebrating – not another revolution.

## RED TAPE

Most foreigners entering the country need a visa for Tanzania or a visitor's pass, depending on their own nationality. Currently, most visas can be obtained on arrival in Tanzania – although the airport queues can be long and so it's often best to get them in advance. A visa will often take several weeks to issue, so apply well in advance of your trip. The charge for issuing a visa ranges from US$20 to US$50, depending on your nationality.

If you are planning to come via Nairobi or Mombasa, you may also need a visa or visitor's pass for Kenya. You may also need a return ticket out of Tanzania or Kenya, or be required to show that you have sufficient funds to cover your stay. (For other currency matters, see page 88.)

Whether you first arrive in Dar or Zanzibar, you will be asked how long you want to stay. Up to three months is usually not a problem, and you'll receive a stamp in your passport. If you haven't obtained a visa in advance, this can be done upon arrival, though it must be paid for in hard currency cash.

You are not allowed to import or export Tanzanian shillings, unless you are travelling to or from mainland Tanzania. There are no other currency regulations at present, which means you can import or export as much foreign ('hard') currency as you like.

There is no longer any legal requirement for a yellow fever vaccination certificate unless you have come from a country where yellow fever is endemic. That said, the vaccination is strongly advised (see pages 75–6). In theory you might also be asked for a cholera-exemption certificate; in practice we've never experienced this.

If you intend hiring a car or motorbike, then it's best to bring an International Driving Permit (IDP), which is easy to obtain from your national motoring association (in Britain contact the AA or RAC). The cost is minimal, but you need two passport photos. Entry regulations do change, so double-check the above with your nearest Tanzanian embassy, high commission or tourist office before you leave.

# Ⓔ EMBASSIES AND CONSULATES

## TANZANIAN EMBASSIES ABROAD

**UK** 3 Stratford Place, Bond St, London W1C 1AS; ✆/f 020 7569 1470; www.tanzania-online.gov.uk. You can download a visa application form from this website, and send it off to the High Commission along with your passport, the visa fee (currently £38 for a single-entry visa), two passport photos, and an SAE for return. The process takes up to 10 days by post. If you want to visit the high commission in London in person, you need to pay in cash; cards, cheques or postal orders are not accepted.
**USA** 2139 R St, NW, Washington, DC 20008; ✆ 202 939 6125; www.tanzaniaembassy-us.org

**Belgium** 363 Av Louise, 1050 Brussels; ✆ (32 2) 640 6500; direct line: 647 6749; f 646 8026
**Canada** 50 Range Rd, Ottawa, Ontario K1N 8J4; ✆ 613 232 1500/1509; f 612 232 5184
**Germany** Botschaft der Vereinigte Republik von Tansania, Eschenallee 11, Charlottenburg, Westend, 14050 Berlin; ✆ 030 3030800; f 030 30308020; www.tanzania-gov.de
**South Africa** 822 George Av, Arcadia 0083; ✆ +27 12 342 4371; www.tanzania.org.za

**FOREIGN CONSULATES IN ZANZIBAR** Most countries have embassies or high commissions in Dar es Salaam or Nairobi, and some – including Britain, the USA and Germany – also have limited diplomatic representation on Zanzibar:

**UK** British Consular Correspondent, Mr Carl Salisbury at ZanAir (see *Regional and local air companies*, pages 104 and 140).
**USA** American Warden, Mr Emerson Skeens, at

Emerson & Green Hotel (see page 122).
**Germany** Honorary Consul, Mrs Angelica Sapetu, at the International School, ✆ 024 2233691, 024 2234062, 0747 410045.

They are generally unable to assist with visas or with simple problems such as illness or theft of belongings, but they will try to help in more serious cases such as wrongful arrest or imprisonment.

If you lose your passport, you can get an Emergency Travel Document from the Ministry of the Interior in Zanzibar. This will allow you to leave Zanzibar, and either go directly back to your own country, or reach Dar where most countries have representation and you should be able to get a replacement.

## ✈ BY AIR

Most visitors to these islands fly first into Tanzania, usually to Dar es Salaam (which is on the mainland, near Zanzibar), and then take a regional service from Dar to Zanzibar. There are a few direct flights from Europe into Zanzibar which are generally charter flights – mostly run by Italian, French and Spanish mass-market tour operators.

If you do arrive into Dar, then small Tanzanian carriers (particularly Coastal Airways and ZanAir) offer reliable flights that tie in with the international arrivals (see page 104), and this is by far the best way to reach the islands using scheduled flights.

### From Europe

*Scheduled flights* The main international scheduled airlines serving Dar es Salaam are:

**British Airways** www.ba.com. From London, direct to Dar, 3 flights a week.
**KLM** www.klm.com. From Amsterdam, direct to Dar daily, via Kilimanjaro International Airport.
**Kenya Airways** www.kenya-airways.com. At least 2 flights daily between Nairobi and Dar, with good connections to Europe and around Africa.
**Emirates** www.emirates.com. From London, via Dubai, to Dar daily.
**Ethiopian Airlines** www.flyethiopian.com. From Addis Ababa daily except Thu, with connections to most European and several American cities.
**South African Airlines** www.saa.co.za. To Dar from Johannesburg daily, with good connections to Zanzibar; new for 2006 are direct flights between Johannesburg and Zanzibar three times per week.
**Air Tanzania** www.airtanzania.com. To Dar from Johannesburg daily, with good connections to Zanzibar as well as numerous other cities internationally.

Britain is one of the cheapest places in Europe to buy scheduled flights to Zanzibar, Dar, Mombasa or Nairobi. Specialist African agencies can also arrange regional flights to/from Zanzibar, and make other arrangements if you need them, such as hotel and tour bookings. The cheapest direct flights from London to Zanzibar start from around £400 (US$700) in the low season, and rise to around £750 (US$1,300) in the high season – plus about £120 in airport and departure taxes.

The best deals are usually found by buying a long time (9–12 months) in advance; tickets for travel in the near future usually command a premium.

To buy just flights, you should talk to the 'seat-only' travel agents. To find them, look through the advertisements in the travel supplements of the Sunday newspapers. Be prepared to shop around, and to find that many of the bargain fares offered in ads are unavailable when you phone.

Flights bought as part of a whole trip which includes accommodation (known as 'Inclusive Tour fares', or 'IT fares' in the jargon) will usually be the lowest. To buy an IT fare as part of a whole trip, seek out a tour operator who specialises in Africa, perhaps starting with the list of specialist tour operators, on pages 73–5.

*Charter flights* For visitors from mainland Europe, another option to consider may be holiday charter flights. Increasing numbers of charter flights from Europe (and particularly Italy, France and Spain) fly direct to Zanzibar; currently there are none from the UK. These are usually sold only as part of a week or two-week package visiting one of Zanzibar's larger 'resorts'. However, if the planes are not full then tour operators will sometimes sell 'flight only' deals, which are good value. Again, see adverts in national newspapers.

**From the USA** There are no direct flights to any of the islands, or even to Dar es Salaam, from the USA. You must fly to Europe or another African capital such as Johannesburg, Nairobi or Addis Ababa, and then connect through to Dar es Salaam or Zanzibar

**From Kenya** Air Kenya and Precision Air fly between Nairobi and Zanzibar at least once on most days; the fare is about US$250 one-way, including taxes, and the flight takes 60–90 minutes. Agents in Nairobi or Mombasa can arrange these flights. More details of airlines are given under *Local services* in *Chapter 6*.

**From South Africa and elsewhere** From South Africa, Air Tanzania and South African Airways run a combined flight between Johannesburg and Dar es Salaam daily, with a direct connection to Zanzibar (at no extra cost if you book through Air Tanzania). South African Airways has also started direct flights between Johannesburg and Dar, flying three times a week.

If you want to reach Zanzibar from somewhere else in the world other than the countries mentioned above, it is usual to fly to Europe, Nairobi, or the Gulf states and pick up a connecting flight from there. For example, from many parts of Asia you could fly on Gulf Air to Muscat then take another plane to Dar es Salaam.

**Departure taxes** There is a departure tax in US dollars (currently US$20) when flying out of Tanzania or Zanzibar airport on international flights. This is payable in US dollars, either in cash or, increasingly, included in the cost of pre-paid airline tickets. If you do need to pay in cash, then travellers' cheques, other currencies and even Tanzanian shillings are not accepted for this; you must have US dollars. You can change whatever you have into US dollars at an airport bureau de change, but often the exchange rates given are very poor. However you carry your money, it's always worth carrying some dollars cash to cover costs like this. For domestic flights, the airport tax is TSh6,000.

Before you pay anything, especially if you've come to Zanzibar on an international return flight, check that the departure tax isn't already included in your ticket price (even better, check what taxes are included when you buy your ticket). If you are flying to Dar to pick up an international flight, you need only pay the international departure tax once (probably at Dar), although you will still pay the domestic flight rate at Zanzibar.

Even ship passengers cannot escape departure tax! Tourists leaving by boat from Zanzibar are charged a US$5 'seaport departure service charge'. This also is payable in dollars only, but many of the ship companies include this tax in the ticket price. Check this carefully to avoid paying twice.

**Organised tours** If you're staying on a low budget (eg: US$20-per-night bungalows) or want to travel without a fixed schedule, then you'll probably do best to arrange your own accommodation and flights, booking things as you go, pre-arranging very little, and just travelling as the mood takes you.

The advantages of such a trip hinge around the freedom that you have to make and change your arrangements on the hoof, which can give a great sense of freedom, as well as from the increased choice of lower-budget options available to you (few tour operators will deal with low-budget accommodation). The disadvantages mainly arise from the problems you may have when places are full, and you are forced to spend time and energy finding somewhere different to stay.

However, if you're planning to book your trip in advance, and you want to stay in more comfortable places (eg: US$75 per night or more), then you're likely to find it easier and cheaper to arrange your trip through a specialist tour operator. Some tour operators offer scheduled trips (ie: you join a group on fixed dates and with a predetermined itinerary), while most work on a tailor-made basis (they design a trip for you, around your dates and what you want to do).

The advantages of such trips include their largely all-inclusive nature, as you pay one price up-front which includes most things; the relaxation that comes from sitting back to enjoy the trip, knowing you don't need to worry about where you're staying; and, if you use a specialist who knows the islands well, then you'll have planned your trip with the benefit of the operator's experience, and you're much more likely to be staying at places that will really suit you well. If you're visiting top-end lodges and camps, then it's almost certainly cheaper to book your trip through a good specialist than it would be to arrange the trip for yourself.

The main disadvantage is the fixed itinerary: you cannot change your plans to spend more or less time at a particular place.

The best way to find a trip that suits your own interest and pocket is to phone the tour operators direct. Ask for their brochure, and look at their website, and then discuss your ideas with them. As with the seat-only agents, you'll often find tour operators advertising in the Sunday travel supplements.

**Tour operators** Finding a good tour operator for a trip to Zanzibar and the islands isn't always easy. Endless operators can send you, but you will get the best trip if you work with an operator who really knows the area and has visited all of the islands and lodges.

Don't let anyone convince you that there are only half-a-dozen decent beach lodges here: it's simply not true. If the operator that you're speaking to doesn't know most of the places in this book and offer a wide choice to suit you – then use one that does.

Here I (Chris McIntyre) must admit a personal interest in the tour operating business. I run the specialist UK tour operator Expert Africa (❤ *020 8232 9777; f 020 8758 4718; e info@expertafrica.com; www.expertafrica.com*). We organise trips to Tanzania and its islands for travellers from all over the world. Booking your trip with us will always cost you the same as or less than if you had contacted the safari camps and beach lodges directly.

We advise our travellers from personal experience, and then allow them to make up their own minds. None of our team works on commission – so unlike many companies, we'll never push you into buying anything. Similarly, we have no financial ties to anywhere in Africa, so can offer truly independent advice on the full range of the choices available. Our only aim in advising you is to arrive at a trip that suits you perfectly.

Our trips are completely flexible, and they start at about US$1,750/£1,000 per person for a week, including flights from London, accommodation and meals. I believe that Expert Africa has the best-value programme to Zanzibar and the islands – and will happily send you a detailed colour brochure to demonstrate this. However, for a fair comparison, some of the better specialist African tour operators who also feature Zanzibar and the islands include:

## In the UK

**Aardvark Safaris** RBL House, Ordnance Rd, Tidworth, Hants SP9 7QD; ❤ 01980 849160; f 01980 849161; e mail@aardvarksafaris.com; www.aardvarksafaris.com. Small, reliable upmarket safari specialist to Africa and Madagascar.

**Abercrombie & Kent** St George's House, Ambrose St, Cheltenham, Glos GL50 3LG; ❤ 01242 547700; f 01242 547707; www.abercrombiekent.co.uk. Worldwide holidays for groups and individuals to upmarket destinations with upmarket price tags.

**Acacia Expeditions** 23a Craven Terrace, London W2 3QH; ✆ 020 7706 4700; f 020 7706 4686: www.acacia-africa.com. Adventure holidays and overland/camping safaris throughout Africa.

**Africa Archipelago** ✆ 020 7471 8780; f 020 7384 9549; www.africaarchipelago.com. Also known as Tanzania Odyssey, this tiny, largely web-based tour operator offers tailor-made trips throughout Africa.

**Africa Travel Centre** ✆ 0845 450 1520; f 020 7387 7512; e africatravel@easynet.co.uk; www.africatravel.co.uk. Long-standing seat-only outlet now offering trips throughout Africa and the Americas.

**Africa Travel Resource** ✆ 01306 880770; f 01306 887655; e info@africatravelresource.com; www.africatravelresource.com. Relatively new web-based tour operator with a Zanzibar programme.

**Cazenove & Loyd** 9 Imperial Studios, 3–11 Imperial Rd, London SW6 2AG; ✆ 020 7384 2332; f 020 7384 2399; www.caz-loyd.com. Top-end tailor-made specialists to Africa, Indian Ocean Islands, Latin America and the Indian subcontinent.

**Expert Africa** (formerly Sunvil Africa) 9 & 10 Upper Sq, Old Isleworth, Middx TW7 7BJ; ✆ 020 8232 9777; f 020 8758 4718; www.expertafrica.com. Specialist team including Chris McIntyre, this book's co-author, and Penny Hooper, a major contributor, offer comprehensive tailor-made island choices.

**Gane & Marshall** 7th floor, Northway House, 1379 High Rd, London N20 9LP; ✆ 020 8445 6000; f 020 8441 7376; e holidays@ganeandmarshall.co.uk; www.ganeandmarshall.co.uk. Worldwide operator with a Zanzibar programme.

**Hartley Safaris** The Old Chapel, Chapel Lane, Hackthorn, Lincs LN2 3PN; ✆ 01673 861600; f 01673 861666; www.hartleys-safaris.co.uk. Long-established tailor-made specialists to east and southern Africa and Indian Ocean islands.

**Imagine Africa** 1a Salcott Rd, London SW11 6DQ; ✆ 020 7228 5655; e info@imagineafrica.co.uk; www.imagineafrica.co.uk. New tour operator offering all Africa plus the Indian Ocean.

**Okavango Tours & Safaris** Marlborough House, 298 Regents Park Rd, London N3 2TJ; ✆ 020 8343 3283; e info@okavango.com; www.okavango.com.

Tailor-made specialists to Africa and Indian Ocean islands, with a good knowledge of Tanzania.

**Pulse Africa** ✆ 020 8995 5909; e info@pulseafrica.com; www.pulseafrica.com. Specialist operator featuring Egypt, Gabon, and southern and east Africa, including Zanzibar.

**Rainbow Tours** 305 Upper Street, London N1 2TU; ✆ 020 7226 1004; f 020 7226 2621; e info@rainbowtours.co.uk; www.rainbowtours.co.uk. Established specialists to South Africa, with a northern Tanzania programme and extensions to the islands.

**Safari Consultants** Orchard House, Upper Rd, Little Cornard, Suffolk CO10 0NZ; ✆ 01787 228494; f 01787 228096; www.safari-consultants.co.uk. Long-established tailor-made specialists to east and southern Africa, and Indian Ocean islands

**Scott Dunn World** Fovant Mews, 12 Noyna Rd, London SW17 7PH; ✆ 020 8682 5020; f 020 8682 5090; www.scottdunn.com. Worldwide coverage (everywhere except North America), with a tailor-made programme to Tanzania.

**Simply Tanzania** 54 Cotesbach Rd, London, E5 9QJ; ✆/f +44 20 8986 0615; www.simplytanzania.co.uk. Tiny but very responsible operator featuring Tanzania, Kenya and northern Mozambique.

**Steppes Travel** (formerly Art of Travel) 51 Castle St, Cirencester, Glos GL7 1QD; ✆ 01285 650011; f 01285 885888; www.steppestravel.co.uk. Upmarket tailor-made specialists to Latin America, Asia, Africa, and the Indian Ocean islands.

**Tim Best Travel** 68 Old Brompton Rd, London SW7 3LQ; ✆ 020 7591 0300; f 020 7591 0301; www.timbesttravel.com. Upmarket holidays to Africa, the Indian Ocean islands and Latin America.

**Tribes Travel** 12 The Business Centre, Earl Soham, Woodbridge, Suffolk IP13 7SA; ✆ 01728 685971; f 01728 685973; www.tribes.co.uk. Small, award-winning operator, particularly strong on cultural trips, offering holidays worldwide on fair-trade principles.

**Zanzibar Travel** Reynards House, Selkirk Gdns, Cheltenham, Glos GL52 5LY; ✆/f 01242 222027; e info@zanzibartravel.co.uk; www.zanzibartravel.co.uk. Small operator concentrating on Kenya, Tanzania and Tanzania's islands.

## In France

**Wild Spirit Safari** ✆/f +33 1 45 74 11 14, +33 1 47 49 91 50; e infos@wild-spirit-safari.com; www.wild-spirit-safari.com. Kenya and Tanzania

specialists offering add-on trips to Zanzibar, with offices in Paris and Arusha.

## In South Africa

**Unusual Destinations** ✆ 011 706 1991; f 011 463 1469; e info@unusualdestinations.com;

www.unusualdestinations.com. Respected trips to east Africa and the Indian Ocean islands.

**Dive specialists** If you're looking for a pure diving trip, perhaps including a live-aboard (see page 96), then you should consider one of the UK's specialist diving operators:

**Aquatours** ☎ 020 8398 0505; e info@
aquatours.com; www.aquatours.com
**Dive Tours** ☎ 01244 401177; e info@
divetours.co.uk; www.divetours.co.uk

**Dive Worldwide** ☎ 0845 130 6980; e info@
diveworldwide.com; www.diveworldwide.com
**Scubasnacks Diving** ☎ 0870 746 1266; e info@
scubasnacks.co.uk; www.scuba-diving-safaris.co.uk

## BY SEA

**From Kenya** We're not aware of any passenger ships currently running between Zanzibar and Mombasa. Dhows taking tourists from Kenya to Zanzibar Island are very rare; they're more frequent between Mombasa and Pemba (see page 263) but do read the warnings in *Chapter 5* carefully before deciding on this form of transport. If you ask around in the old port area of Mombasa you can usually find a boat going about twice a week to Wete or Mkoani on Pemba, although times and days are variable. A one-way trip costs about US$10 to US$15, payable in Kenyan shillings or hard currency.

**From mainland Tanzania** Several large passenger ships run daily between Dar es Salaam, Zanzibar and Pemba, and less frequently to other points on the mainland. For details of these see pages 104–6 in *Chapter 5*.

## HEALTH with Dr Felicity Nicholson and Dr Jane Wilson-Howarth

### BEFORE YOU GO
### Immunisations

All visitors to Tanzania (including Zanzibar) should be vaccinated against yellow fever provided that it is deemed suitable. If the vaccine is contraindicated then you are advised to carry an exemption certificate, which can be obtained from a travel clinic. You may not always be required to show a yellow fever certificate (or exemption certificate) when you enter the country, but it's important to be prepared. The certificate is not valid until ten days after your vaccination, but then lasts for ten years. Vaccinations for typhoid, tetanus, diphtheria, polio and hepatitis A are also generally recommended.

Most travellers are advised to have immunisation against hepatitis A with hepatitis A vaccine (eg: Havrix Monodose, Avaxim). One dose of vaccine lasts for one year and can be boosted to give protection for up to 20 years. The course of two injections costs about £100. It is now felt that the vaccine can be used even close to the time of departure and has replaced the old-fashioned gamma globulin. The newer typhoid vaccines last for three years and are about 85% effective. They should be encouraged unless the traveller is leaving within a few days for a trip of a week or less when the vaccine would not be effective in time.

Meningitis vaccine (containing strains ACW and Y) is also recommended, especially for trips of more than four weeks, or for shorter trips if you are working with children (see *Meningitis*, page 80).

Immunisation against cholera is considered ineffective in the UK, but a cholera exemption certificate is in theory mandatory for Zanzibar, and should be obtained before departure (you do not have a vaccination for this). Vaccinations for rabies are advised for travellers visiting more remote areas (see *Rabies*, pages 80–1). Hepatitis B vaccination should be considered for longer trips (two months or more) or for those working in situations where the chance of contact with blood is increased, or with children. Three injections are preferred and can be given over a

*Dr Jane Wilson-Howarth*

Long-haul air travel increases the risk of a deep vein thrombosis (DVT). Although recent research has suggested that many of us develop clots when immobilised, most resolve without us ever having been aware of them. In certain susceptible individuals, though, large clots form and these can break away and lodge in the lungs. This is dangerous but happens in a tiny minority of passengers.

Studies have shown that flights of over five-and-a-half-hours are significant, and that people who take lots of shorter flights over a short space of time form clots. People at highest risk are:

- Those who have had a clot before – unless they are now taking warfarin
- People over 80 years of age
- Anyone who has recently undergone a major operation or surgery for varicose veins
- Someone who has had a hip or knee replacement in the last three months
- Cancer sufferers
- Those who have ever had a stroke
- People with heart disease
- Those with a close blood relative who has had a clot

Those with a slightly increased risk:

- People over 40
- Women who are pregnant or have had a baby in the last couple of weeks
- People taking female hormones or other oestrogen therapy
- Heavy smokers
- Those who have very severe varicose veins
- The very obese
- People who are very tall (over 6ft/1.8m) or short (under 5ft/1.5m)

21-day period (Engerix only) prior to travel. Longer schedules are preferred if you go to your doctor in plenty of time. A BCG vaccination against tuberculosis (TB) may be advised for trips of two months or more if you have not had one before, although this recommendation is becoming less common. Ideally, then, you should visit your own doctor or a specialist travel clinic (see below) to discuss your requirements about eight weeks before you plan to travel.

**Malaria prevention** There is no vaccine against malaria, but using prophylactic drugs and preventing mosquito bites will considerably reduce the risk of contracting it. Seek professional advice for the best anti-malarial drugs to take. Mefloquine (Lariam) is still the most effective prophylactic agent for Tanzania and Zanzibar. If this drug is suggested and you have never tried it before then you should start at least two and a half weeks before departure to check that it suits you. Stop immediately if it seems to cause depression or anxiety, visual or hearing disturbances, severe headaches or changes in heart rhythm. Anyone who has been treated for depression or psychiatric problems, has diabetes controlled by oral therapy, or who is epileptic (or who has suffered fits in the past) or has a close blood relative who is epileptic should not take mefloquine. Divers should also be aware that some dive operators may refuse to go down with someone taking mefloquine, so do check this in advance or, better still, opt for an alternative. Mefloquine may be recommended in the second or third trimester of pregnancy if the risk of taking no prophylactic drugs or something less effective outweighs the risk of contracting malaria.

A deep vein thrombosis is a blood clot that forms in the deep leg veins. This is very different from irritating but harmless superficial phlebitis. DVT causes swelling and redness of one leg, usually with heat and pain in one calf and sometimes the thigh. A DVT is only dangerous if a clot breaks away and travels to the lungs (pulmonary embolus). Symptoms of a pulmonary embolus (PE) include chest pain that is worse on breathing in deeply, shortness of breath, and sometimes coughing up small amounts of blood. The symptoms commonly start three to ten days after a long flight. Anyone who thinks that they might have a DVT needs to see a doctor immediately who will arrange a scan. Warfarin tablets (to thin the blood) are then taken for at least six months.

**PREVENTION OF DVT** Several conditions make the problem more likely. Immobility is the key, and factors like reduced oxygen in cabin air and dehydration may also contribute. To reduce the risk of thrombosis on a long journey:

- Exercise before and after the flight
- Keep mobile before and during the flight; move around every couple of hours
- During the flight drink plenty of water or juices
- Avoid taking sleeping pills and excessive tea, coffee and alcohol
- Perform exercises that mimic walking and tense the calf muscles
- Consider wearing flight socks or support stockings (see www.legshealth.com)
- Taking a meal of oily fish (mackerel, trout, salmon, sardines, etc) in the 24 hours before departure reduces blood clotability and thus DVT risk
- The jury is still out on whether it is worth taking an aspirin before flying, but this can be discussed with your GP.

If you think you are at increased risk of a clot, ask your doctor if it is safe to travel.

Malarone (proguanil and atovaquone) is now considered as effective as mefloquine. It has the advantage of having few side effects and need only be continued for one week after returning. However, it is expensive and because of this tends to be reserved for shorter trips, even though it can be used for around three months. Malarone may not be suitable for everybody so advice should be taken from a doctor. Paediatric Malarone is also now available and is prescribed on a weight basis for children weighing 11kg or more. The antibiotic doxycycline (100mg daily) should be considered when either mefloquine or Malarone is not considered suitable for whatever reason. Like Malarone, it need only be started one–two days before arrival. It may also be used by travellers with epilepsy, unlike mefloquine, although the anti-epileptic therapy may make it less effective. Users must be warned about the possibility of allergic skin reactions developing in sunlight which can occur in about 1–3% of people. The drug should be stopped if this happens. Women using the oral contraceptive should use an additional method of protection for the first four weeks when using doxycycline.

Chloroquine and proguanil are no longer considered to be very effective for this area. However, they may still be recommended if no other regime is suitable. All prophylactic agents should be taken with or after the evening meal, washed down with plenty of fluid and, with the exception of Malarone (see above), continued for four weeks after leaving Tanzania/Zanzibar.

Travellers to remote parts may wish to consider carrying a course of malaria treatment. At present Malarone or Co-artemether is the favoured regime but check for up-to-date advice on the current recommended treatment. Self-treatment is not without risks and diagnosing malaria may not be easy which is why consulting a doctor as soon as possible is important. Assume that any high fever lasting more than a few hours is malaria regardless of any other symptoms. And remember malaria may occur anything from seven days into the trip to up to one year after leaving Africa. Zanzibar's hospitals and medical centres are listed in *Chapter 6*, pages 142–3.

It's a good idea to have a dental check-up before you go, as local dentists can be painful, expensive, or both.

**Travel clinics and health information** A full list of current travel clinic websites worldwide is available from the International Society of Travel Medicine on www.istm.org. For other journey preparation information, consult www.tripprep.com. Information about various medications may be found on www.emedicine.com.

## UK

**Berkeley Travel Clinic** 32 Berkeley St, London W1J 8EL (near Green Park tube station); \ 020 7629 6233
**British Airways Travel Clinic and Immunisation Service** 213 Piccadilly, London W1J 9HQ; \ 0845 600 2236; www.ba.com/travelclinics. Walk-in service (no appointment necessary) Mon, Tue, Wed, Fri 08.45–18.15, Thu 08.45–20.00, Sat 09.30–17.00. As well as providing inoculations and malaria prevention, they sell a variety of health-related goods.
**Cambridge Travel Clinic** 48a Mill Rd, Cambridge CB1 2AS; \ 01223 367362; e enquiries@cambridgetravelclinic.co.uk; www.cambridgetravelclinic.co.uk. Open Tue–Fri 12.00–19.00, Sat 10.00–16.00.
**Edinburgh Travel Clinic** Regional Infectious Diseases Unit, Ward 41 OPD, Western General Hospital, Crewe Rd South, Edinburgh EH4 2UX; \ 0131 537 2822; www.link.med.ed.ac.uk/ridu. Travel helpline (0906 589 0380) open weekdays 09.00–12.00. Provides inoculations and antimalarial prophylaxis and advises on travel-related health risks.
**Fleet Street Travel Clinic** 29 Fleet St, London EC4Y 1AA; \ 020 7353 5678; www.fleetstreetclinic.com. Vaccinations, travel products and latest advice.
**Hospital for Tropical Diseases Travel Clinic** Mortimer Market Building, Capper St (off Tottenham Ct Rd), London WC1E 6AU; \ 020 7388 9600; www.thehtd.org. Offers consultations and advice, and is able to provide all necessary drugs and vaccines for travellers. Runs a healthline (0906 133 7733) for country-specific information and health hazards. Also stocks nets, water purification equipt and personal protection measures.
**Interhealth Worldwide** Partnership House, 157 Waterloo Rd, London SE1 8US; \ 020 7902 9000;

www.interhealth.org.uk. Competitively priced, one-stop travel health service. All profits go to their affiliated company, InterHealth, which provides health care for overseas workers on Christian projects.
**MASTA** (Medical Advisory Service for Travellers Abroad) London School of Hygiene and Tropical Medicine, Keppel St, London WC1 7HT; \ 0906 550 1402; www.masta.org. Individually tailored health briefs available for a fee, with up-to-date information on how to stay healthy, inoculations and what to bring. There are currently 30 MASTA pre-travel clinics in Britain. Call 0870 241 6843 or check online for the nearest. Clinics also sell malaria prophylaxis memory cards, treatment kits, bednets, net treatment kits.
**NHS travel website** www.fitfortravel.scot.nhs.uk. Provides country-by-country advice on immunisation and malaria, plus details of recent developments, and a list of relevant health organisations.
**Nomad Travel Store/Clinic** 3–4 Wellington Terrace, Turnpike Lane, London N8 0PX; \ 020 8889 7014; travel-health line (office hours only) 0906 863 3414; e sales@nomadtravel.co.uk; www.nomadtravel.co.uk. Also at 40 Bernard St, London WC1N 1LJ; \ 020 7833 4114; 52 Grosvenor Gardens, London SW1W 0AG; \ 020 7823 5823; and 43 Queens Rd, Bristol BS8 1QH; \ 0117 922 6567. For health advice, equipt such as mosquito nets and other anti-bug devices, and an excellent range of adventure travel gear.
**Trailfinders Travel Clinic** 194 Kensington High St, London W8 7RG; \ 020 7938 3999; www.trailfinders.com/clinic.htm
**Travelpharm** The Travelpharm website, www.travelpharm.com, offers up-to-date guidance on travel-related health and has a range of medications available through their online mini-pharmacy.

## Irish Republic

**Tropical Medical Bureau** Grafton Street Medical Centre, Grafton Buildings, 34 Grafton St, Dublin 2; ⟍ 1 671 9200; www.tmb.ie. A useful website specific to tropical destinations. Also check website for other bureaux locations throughout Ireland.

## USA

**Centers for Disease Control** 1600 Clifton Rd, Atlanta, GA 30333; ⟍ 800 311 3435; travellers' health hotline 888 232 3299; www.cdc.gov/travel. The central source of travel information in the USA. The invaluable Health Information for International Travel, published annually, is available from the Division of Quarantine at this address.

**Connaught Laboratories** PO Box 187, Swiftwater, PA 18370; ⟍ 800 822 2463. They will send a free list of specialist tropical-medicine physicians in your state.

**IAMAT** (International Association for Medical Assistance to Travelers) 1623 Military Rd, 279, Niagara Falls, NY 14304-1745; ⟍ 716 754 4883; e info@iamat.org; www.iamat.org. A non-profit organisation that provides lists of English-speaking doctors abroad.

**International Medicine Center** 920 Frostwood Drive, Suite 670, Houston, TX 77024; ⟍ 713 550 2000; www.traveldoc.com

## Canada

**IAMAT** Suite 1, 1287 St Clair Av W, Toronto, Ontario M6E 1B8; ⟍ 416 652 0137; www.iamat.org

**TMVC** Suite 314, 1030 W Georgia St, Vancouver BC V6E 2Y3; tel: 1 888 288 8682; www.tmvc.com

## Australia, New Zealand, Singapore

**TMVC** ⟍ 1300 65 88 44; www.tmvc.com.au. 31 clinics in Australia, New Zealand and Singapore including:

*Auckland* Canterbury Arcade, 170 Queen St, Auckland; ⟍ 9 373 3531

*Brisbane* 6th floor, 247 Adelaide St, Brisbane, QLD 4000; ⟍ 7 3221 9066

*Melbourne* 393 Little Bourke St, 2nd floor, Melbourne, VIC 3000; ⟍ 3 9602 5788

*Sydney* Dymocks Bldg, 7th floor, 428 George St, Sydney, NSW 2000; ⟍ 2 9221 7133

**IAMAT** PO Box 5049, Christchurch 5, New Zealand; www.iamat.org

## South Africa and Namibia

**SAA-Netcare Travel Clinics** P Bag X34, Benmore 2010; www.travelclinic.co.za. Clinics throughout South Africa.

**TMVC** 113 D F Malan Drive, Roosevelt Park, Johannesburg; ⟍ 011 888 7488; www.tmvc.com.au. Consult website for details of 9 other clinics in South Africa and Namibia.

## Switzerland

**IAMAT** 57 Chemin des Voirets, 1212 Grand Lancy, Geneva; www.iamat.org

**COMMON MEDICAL PROBLEMS** When travelling around Zanzibar or east Africa, the different climatic and social conditions mean visitors are exposed to diseases not normally encountered at home. Although you will have received all the vaccinations recommended in the *Before you go* section, this does not mean you will be free of all illness during your travels: certain precautions still have to be taken.

You should read a good book on travel medicine (see *Appendix 2*) and be aware of the causes, symptoms and treatments of the more serious diseases. But don't let these colourful descriptions put you off – with a little care and attention most of these illnesses can be avoided.

## Travellers' diarrhoea

What with bad water and worse liquor, the Briton finds it hard to live on Zanzibar.

Richard Burton, British explorer (1857)

At least half of those travelling to the tropics will suffer from a bout of travellers' diarrhoea during their trip; the newer you are to exotic travel, the more likely you will be to suffer. By taking precautions against travellers' diarrhoea you will also avoid typhoid, cholera, dysentery, worms, etc. Travellers' diarrhoea and the other faeco-oral diseases come from getting other people's faeces in your mouth. This most often happens from cooks not washing their hands after a trip to the toilet. Even if the restaurant cook does not understand basic hygiene you will be safe if your food has been properly cooked and arrives piping hot. The maxim to remind you what you can safely eat is:

PEEL IT, BOIL IT, COOK IT OR FORGET IT.

This means that fruit you have washed and peeled yourself, and hot foods, should be safe, but raw foods, cold cooked foods, salads, fruit salads which have been prepared by others, ice cream, and ice are all risky. Foods kept lukewarm in hotel buffets are usually dangerous. It is also important to maintain a high standard of personal hygiene: wash your hands after going to the toilet and before eating. It is a good idea to carry antiseptic wipes for the times when water or soap are hard to find.

## OTHER MEDICAL PROBLEMS

**Meningitis** This is a particularly nasty disease as it can kill within hours of the first symptoms appearing. The telltale symptoms are a combination of a blinding headache (light sensitivity), a blotchy rash and a high fever. Immunisation protects against the most serious bacterial form of meningitis and the tetravalent vaccine (ACWY) is recommended for Tanzania and Zanzibar. Other forms of meningitis exist (usually viral) but there are no vaccines for these. Local papers normally report outbreaks. If you show symptoms go immediately to a doctor.

**Rabies** Rabies is carried by all mammals (beware the village dogs and small monkeys that are used to being fed in the parks) and is passed on to humans through a bite, scratch or a lick of an open wound. You must always assume any animal is rabid (unless personally known to you) and seek medical help as soon as possible.

In the interim, scrub the wound with soap and bottled/boiled water then pour on a strong iodine or alcohol solution. This helps stop the rabies virus entering the body and will guard against wound infections including tetanus.

### TREATING TRAVELLERS' DIARRHOEA

It is dehydration that makes you feel awful during a bout of diarrhoea and the most important part of treatment is drinking lots of clear fluids. Sachets of oral rehydration salts give the perfect biochemical mix to replace all that is pouring out of your bottom! However, any dilute mixture of sugar and salt in water will do you good, so if you like Coke or orange squash, drink that with a three-finger pinch of salt added to each glass. Otherwise make a solution of a four-finger scoop of sugar with a three-finger pinch of salt in a glass of water. Alternatively add eight level teaspoons of sugar (18g) and one level teaspoon of salt (3g) to one litre (5 cups) of safe water. A squeeze of lemon or orange juice improves the taste and adds potassium, which is also lost during a bout of diarrhoea. Drink two large glasses after every bowel action and more if you are thirsty. You need to drink three litres a day plus whatever is pouring into the toilet.

It is best to avoid food for 24 hours then eat bland, non-fatty foods for the next two or three days. Also avoid the use of blocking agents such as Lomotil or Imodium, unless you have no access to toilet facilities.

If the diarrhoea is bad, or you are passing blood or slime, or you have a fever, you will probably need antibiotics in addition to the fluid replacement. Try to seek medical advice before starting antibiotics. If this is not possible then a single dose of ciprofloxacin (500mg) repeated after 12 hours may be appropriate. If the diarrhoea is greasy and bulky and is accompanied by sulphurous (eggy) burps the likely cause is giardia. This is best treated with tinidazole (2g in one dose repeated seven days later if symptoms persist).

It is less common to get sick from drinking contaminated water but it happens, so try to drink from safe sources. At good hotels, clean drinking water will always be available. You can now buy bottled water widely throughout these islands, although if you venture very far from the beaten track, then supplies are not always reliable so carry bottles with you.

When buying bottled water, check the seal as it is not unknown for discarded bottles to be filled with tap water and sold again. That said, don't become nervous and avoid drinking altogether; such scams are very rare. It is vital to keep up your liquid intake in the hot climate to avoid dehydration.

If heading far from civilisation, then prepare to purify your own water with tablets (or iodine solution), which are available from outdoor/camping shops. Bring these with you; you may not be able to buy them here. These will work more effectively if you filter out any larger, suspended particles from the water before adding them. Several manufacturers in Europe and USA produce filter pumps designed to do this whole process quickly and easily.

If you intend to have contact with animals and/or are likely to be more than 24 hours away from medical help, then pre-exposure vaccination is advised. Ideally three doses should be taken over a minimum of 21 days. Contrary to popular belief, these vaccinations are relatively painless!

If you are exposed as described, then treatment should be given as soon as possible, but it is never too late to seek help as the incubation period for rabies can be very long. Those who have not been immunised will need a full course of injections together with rabies immunoglobulin (RIG), but this product is expensive (around US$800) and may be hard to come by. Another reason why pre-exposure vaccination should be encouraged in travellers who are planning to visit more remote areas!

Tell the doctor if you have had pre-exposure vaccine, as this will change the treatment you receive. Remember if you contract rabies, mortality is 100% and death from rabies is probably one of the worst ways to go.

**Malaria** As anti-malaria drugs do not provide complete protection, you should also take steps to avoid being bitten by a mosquito: wear long-sleeved shirts and long trousers, covering wrists and ankles, in the evening when mosquitoes are active. Most hotels have mosquito nets and these should always be used. In cheaper hotels some nets may be broken, so a needle and thread for quick repairs is useful. Or carry your own (see *What to take*, pages 85–8). The nets should also be impregnated with permethrin – if in doubt carry an impregnation kit bought before you leave.

Insect sprays and mosquito coils, which burn slowly through the night, can be bought in shops in Zanzibar Town, but the tubes of repellent to rub on your skin which tend to be very effective (eg: the Repel range containing 50% DEET) are not available. If you need medical attention, there are several hospitals and medical centres in Zanzibar Town. These are listed in *Chapter 6*.

**Dengue fever** This mosquito-borne disease may mimic malaria but there is no prophylactic available to deal with it. The mosquitoes that carry this virus bite during the daytime, so it is worth applying repellent if you see them around. Symptoms include strong headaches, rashes and excruciating joint and muscle pains and high fever. Dengue fever lasts for only a week or so and is not usually fatal. Complete rest and paracetamol are the usual treatments. Plenty of fluids also help. Some patients are given an intravenous drip to keep them from dehydrating.

*Gordon Rattray*

With crowded markets and narrow, often bumpy streets, Zanzibar sounds like the last place you'd want to venture to if you have difficulties walking. Wheelchairs and sandy beaches just don't agree, and to cap it all, Zanzibar's island status provides more logistical problems, forcing you to ask if the getting there is actually worth it.

It is. A Zanzibar experience is unique, and with some preparation, patience, and the innate helpfulness of the local people, you will be surprised by just how possible it is.

**GETTING THERE AND AWAY** The ferries from Dar es Salaam are not an easy option. Boarding on Zanzibar is via a gangplank, which is steep at low tide and can be difficult even for able-bodied people with luggage. On board there are various decks with stairways between them and there are no facilities to make mobility easier.

A quicker, more comfortable and more practical (albeit more expensive) option is to fly. The airport staff reportedly cope well with disabled passengers, although you will need to be manually lifted in and out of the small 13-seater planes which are used for many flights from Dar to Zanzibar.

**TRANSPORT** Buses and *dala dalas* are cramped, with no facilities for wheelchairs, and getting off and on can be a hectic affair. Therefore, unless you can walk at least to some degree then taxi is going to be your only easy way of getting around. Drivers will be happy to assist with transfers, but are obviously not experienced in this skill so you must be assertive and explain clearly what help you need. Tour companies often use minibuses – higher than taxis – for spice-farm visits and other excursions. This means you may need help from two people to transfer. It is always advisable for people prone to skin damage to sit on their wheelchair cushion in the vehicle as it may be old, meaning the seating won't give as much support as it once did.

**ACCOMMODATION** Put simply, I know of no completely wheelchair-friendly accommodation on Zanzibar. Most buildings' entrances are at least one step up from street level, and cheaper hotels are often small. However, there are many establishments throughout the island that can be construed as accessible, depending on your abilities and your willingness to compromise. The more upmarket the hotel is, the greater the chance that

**Bilharzia** Bilharzia or schistosomiasis is a common debilitating disease afflicting perhaps 200 million people worldwide. Those most affected are the rural poor of the tropics who repeatedly acquire infections. Infected travellers and expatriates generally suffer fewer problems because symptoms will encourage them to seek prompt treatment and they are also exposed to fewer parasites. But it is still an unpleasant problem, and worth avoiding.

When someone with bilharzia excretes into fresh water, the eggs hatch and swim off to find a pond snail to infest. They develop inside the snail to emerge as torpedo-shaped cercariae, barely visible to the naked eye but able to digest their way through human or animal skin. This is the stage at which it attacks people as they wade, bathe or shower in infested water. The snails which harbour bilharzia are a centimetre or more long and live in still or slow-moving fresh water which is well oxygenated and contains edible vegetation (water-weed, reeds). The risk is greatest where local people use the water, bearing in mind that wind can disperse cercariae a few hundred metres from where they entered the water. Wading in slow-moving, reed-fringed water near a village thus carries a very high risk of acquiring bilharzia, while swimming in a rocky pool below a waterfall in a forest carries a negligible one.

the rooms and bathrooms will be spacious, and that conveniences like bedside telephones will be present.

Unless you are going to have the time and energy to look for accommodation on arrival, the best advice is to research your options in advance. Specialist tour operators will normally take time to listen to your needs, or if you prefer, many hotels can be found directly on the internet. If photos aren't available, the owners are easily contacted and can describe their facilities by email.

**RESTAURANTS** Many eateries are on the ground floor, with one or two steps at the entrance. The proprietors will want your custom, so if you fancy eating there, you can be sure they will quickly organise a couple of waiters to help you in.

**HEALTH** Doctors will know about 'everyday' illnesses, but you must understand and be able to explain your own particular medical requirements. African hospitals are often basic, so if possible, take all necessary medication and equipment with you. It is advisable to pack this in your hand luggage during flights in case your main luggage gets lost.

Zanzibar is hot all year. If this is a problem for you, a plant-spray bottle is an ideal cooling aid.

**SECURITY** The usual advice applies to all travellers, but it is worthwhile remembering that, as a disabled person, you are more vulnerable. Stay aware of who is around you and where your bags are, especially during car transfers and similar. These activities often draw a crowd, and the confusion creates easy pickings for an opportunist thief.

**ACTIVITIES** Stone Town tours, spice-farm visits and many other excursions are certainly possible. Inform your guide or tour company in advance of what you can and cannot do and they will make an appropriate itinerary. For some visitors, many of the older buildings will prove impenetrable. For instance, there is a ramp up to the Palace Museum but then staircases inside with no lifts.

Beaches will always be naturally difficult for wheelchair users. I've still not heard of anyone on Zanzibar using a beach wheelchair (wheelchair with massive tyres to ride on soft sand), but I have no doubt this will come. Until then, we'll need to be content with sipping a cool drink in the shade with a good book. Is that so bad?

Water that has been filtered or stored snail-free for two days is safe, as is water that has been boiled or treated with Cresol or Dettol. Some protection is afforded by applying an oily insect repellent like DEET to your skin before swimming or paddling.

Cercariae live for up to 30 hours after they have been shed by snails, but the older they are, the less vigorous they are, and the less capable they are of penetrating skin. Cercariae are shed in the greatest numbers between 11.00 and 15.00 hours. If water to be used for bathing is pumped early in the morning from deep in the lake (cercariae are sun-loving) or from a site far from where people excrete there will be less risk of infestation. Swimming in the afternoon is riskier than in the early morning. Since cercariae take perhaps ten to 15 minutes to penetrate, a quick shower or a splash across a river followed by thorough drying with a towel should be safe. Even if you are in risky water longer, towelling off vigorously after bathing will kill any cercariae in the process of penetrating your skin. Only a proportion of those cercariae which penetrate the skin survive to cause disease. The absence of early symptoms does not necessarily mean there is no infection, but symptoms usually appear two or more weeks after penetration:

typically a fever and wheezy cough. A blood test, which should be taken six weeks or more after likely exposure, will determine whether or not parasites are going to cause problems. Treatment is generally effective, but failures occur and re-treatment is often necessary for reasons that aren't fully understood, but which may imply some drug resistance. Since bilharzia can be a nasty illness, avoidance is better than waiting to be cured and it is wise to avoid bathing in high-risk areas.

**Jiggers or sandfleas** These latch on if you walk barefoot in contaminated places, and set up home under the skin of the foot, usually at the side of a toenail, where they cause a painful, boil-like swelling. They need picking out by a local expert; if the distended flea bursts during eviction, the wound should be dowsed in spirit, alcohol or kerosene, or more jiggers will infest you.

## CRIME AND SAFETY

As in most countries, crime in these islands is gradually on the increase. Similarly, problems tend to occur more in the cities than in the rural areas. Perhaps inevitably, the juxtaposition of relatively wealthy tourists and a high density of relatively poor local people causes envy and leads to the occasional crime.

Zanzibar Town is notable for the opportunist pickpocket operating, and occasionally tourists do have bags and cameras snatched while walking around the narrow streets of the Old Town. (For more specific details on places to be careful, see the *Zanzibar Town* chapter.) There have also been robberies on some of the beaches around Zanzibar Town; it is better not to go there alone, especially at night. The authors have yet to hear of any crime problems on Mafia Island – but then this is a small, rural island with a low population density.

You can reduce the chances of having anything stolen by not displaying your wealth. Don't bring valuable jewellery to these islands; leave it at home. Keep your valuables secure, out of sight and preferably back in the safe at your hotel. Keep most of your money there too, and do not peel off notes from a huge wad for every small purchase. Wandering around the town with a camera or personal stereo casually slung over your shoulder is insensitive and simply asking for trouble. A simple, dull-looking bag is much safer than something smart or fashionable.

Theft from hotel rooms is unusual. Most hotels have safes, where valuables can be stored, although reports of stuff disappearing from the safes of small hotels are not unknown. For more details see the *Zanzibar Town* chapter, page 120.

In contrast to the comments above, there have been several very serious incidents in recent years where an organised, armed gang attacks and robs a remote beach lodge or resort. These incidents are thankfully rare – but they do happen. In response, some of the more upmarket resorts now have armed security teams or armed policemen patrolling at night. Whist these cannot guarantee the safety of visitors, it does give some reassurance that such serious crime is being tackled by the Zanzibari police.

**TERRORISM** On 7 August 1998 al-Qaeda bombed the US embassies in Nairobi and Dar es Salaam; they killed about 224 people (of whom only 12 were Americans) and injured more than 5,000. Ever since then, some travellers have looked nervously towards east Africa, citing Islamic influences, porous borders, long coastlines, and a relative availability of arms as reasons to be wary of terrorism there.

The truth is that there are large Islamic communities on the islands, especially on Pemba and Zanzibar. These communities may also have their extremist elements; very much like the extremists who live in communities in the UK,

Europe and the USA. So whilst Zanzibar (and, to a lesser extent, Pemba) has many factors which add up to the British Foreign and Commonwealth Office rating it as having a 'high threat from terrorism', at the time of writing nobody has been injured in any terrorist attacks here.

## WHAT TO TAKE

**CLOTHING** You are unlikely to experience great extremes of temperature on Zanzibar, although days can be very warm and some nights chilly. Clothing should be light and loose-fitting for daytime, and you may need something slightly more substantial for evenings. Even in the dry seasons, a rain jacket is a good idea (though you may not need it). Umbrellas (should you need them) are available locally. You'll need a good pair of shoes for sightseeing, and a pair of sandals for relaxing. A hat to keep off sun and rain completes the outfit.

Plastic beach shoes, rafting sandals, or something similar to avoid the spiky sea-urchins, are useful for walking out into the sea across old coral beds. (Remember, though, never to tread on live coral. In a few seconds you can break off chunks which will take several decades to re-grow.)

Dress codes are very relaxed, even in the smartest hotels and restaurants, so you won't need black tie or ball gown. However, it's important to be sensitive towards local customs. When wandering around towns and villages you should be aware of local Muslim sensibilities: dress modestly and do not expose too much bare flesh. Remember that a woman walking around a Zanzibar town with bare shoulders and a short skirt, or a man without a shirt, is as unacceptable as someone parading naked in your local high street.

Of course, tourists don't need to don robes, veils and turbans, but around town it is important for women to have knees and shoulders covered. This is recommended for men, too. Therefore, for men and women, long trousers are better than shorts, although baggy surf-shorts or culottes are acceptable. Many women find skirts more comfortable than trousers. For men and women, long-sleeved shirts and blouses are better than vests and skimpy T-shirts. For the beach, normal swimming gear is fine, although going into local fishing villages in briefs or bikinis shows a complete lack of sensitivity.

**EQUIPMENT** If you're planning to base yourself in one place during your stay, or have all your transfers arranged, then carrying your stuff in a suitcase or kitbag is absolutely fine. If you're likely to have to carry your own luggage, particularly if you're travelling around and visiting the islands as part of a longer trip, then it is usually easier to carry all your clothing and equipment in a rucksack.

Most new rucksacks have internal frames, whilst some turn neatly into travel bags, with a zipped flap to enclose the straps and waist-belt. Both are fine, although if the straps can be zipped away then they are less likely to be damaged on bus roof-racks or airport carousels.

If you're staying in the cheaper hotels, sheets are not always very clean, so a light sheet sleeping bag is useful. It's unlikely you'll need a full sleeping bag; if you do hit the islands in a cold snap, most smaller hotels provide blankets. The better hotels and lodges have good facilities including towels and clean bed linen.

To avoid getting malaria, it is important to protect yourself from mosquitoes. Most hotels provide nets over the beds, but in the smaller cheaper hotels these are often in bad condition and riddled with holes. Either take your own mosquito net (visit a good camping shop before you travel), or take a needle and cotton to make running repairs. For added protection, bring a roll-on insect repellent and use

*Ariadne Van Zandbergen*

Zanzibar doesn't offer the possibilities for wildlife photography that exist on mainland Tanzania (although the red colobus monkeys at Jozani Forest can be an excellent subject), but the Swahili culture combined with the idyllic Indian Ocean beach scenes create some stunning photographic opportunities.

**EQUIPMENT** Although with some thought and an eye for composition you can take reasonable photos with a 'point-and-shoot' camera, you need an SLR camera if you are at all serious about photography. Modern SLRs tend to be very clever, with automatic programmes for almost every possible situation, but remember that these programmes are limited in the sense that the camera cannot think, but only make calculations. Every starting amateur photographer should read a photographic manual for beginners and get to grips with such basics as the relationship between aperture and shutter speed.

Always buy the best lens you can afford. The lens determines the quality of your photo more than the camera body. Fixed fast lenses are ideal, but very costly. A zoom lens makes it easier to change composition without changing lenses the whole time. If you carry only one lens, a 28–70mm (digital 17–55mm) or similar zoom should be ideal. For a second lens, a lightweight 80–200mm or 70–300mm (digital 55–200mm) or similar will be excellent for candid shots and varying your composition. Wildlife photography will be very frustrating if you don't have at least a 300mm lens. For a small loss of quality, tele-converters are a cheap and compact way to increase magnification: a 300 lens with a 1.4x converter becomes 420mm, and with a 2x it becomes 600mm. Note, however, that 1.4x and 2x tele-converters reduce the speed of your lens by 1.4 and 2 stops respectively.

For wildlife photography from a safari vehicle, a solid beanbag, which you can make yourself very cheaply, will be necessary to avoid blurred images, and is more useful than a tripod. A clamp with a tripod head screwed on to it can be attached to the vehicle as well. Modern dedicated flash units are easy to use; aside from the obvious need to flash when you photograph at night, you can improve a lot of photos in difficult 'high contrast' or very dull light with some fill-in flash. It pays to have a proper flash unit as opposed to a built-in camera flash.

**DIGITAL/FILM** Digital photography is now the preference of most amateur and professional photographers, with the resolution of digital cameras improving the whole time. For ordinary prints a 6 megapixel camera is fine. For better results and the possibility to enlarge images and for professional reproduction, higher resolution is available up to 16 megapixels.

Memory space is important. The number of pictures you can fit on a memory card depends on the quality you choose. Calculate in advance how many pictures you can fit on a card and either take enough cards to last for your trip, or take a storage drive onto which you can download the content. A laptop gives the advantage that you can see your

mosquito coils (available locally) in your room at night. Remember: it takes only one mosquito to give you malaria.

Camping on the islands is not really an option, so it's probably not worth bringing a tent. There are no official campsites and security for campers would be very difficult; fortunately, hotels can be cheap.

Personal items include toiletries, lipsalve, sun protection cream and sunglasses. Soap, toothpaste and medicines can be bought locally if you run out. Suncream is also available in some hotel shops, but it's expensive, so bring all pictures properly at the end of each day and edit and delete rejects, but a storage device is lighter and less bulky. These drives come in different capacities up to 80GB.

Bear in mind that digital camera batteries, computers and other storage devices need charging, so make sure you have all the chargers, cables and converters with you. Most hotels have charging points, but do enquire about this in advance. When camping you might have to rely on charging from the car battery; a spare battery is invaluable.

If you are shooting film, 100 to 200 ISO print film and 50 to 100 ISO slide film are ideal. Low ISO film is slow but fine grained and gives the best colour saturation, but will need more light, so support in the form of a tripod or monopod is important. You can also bring a few 'fast' 400 ISO films for low-light situations where a tripod or flash is no option.

**DUST AND HEAT** Dust and heat are often a problem. Keep your equipment in a sealed bag, stow films in an airtight container (eg: a small cooler bag) and avoid exposing equipment and film to the sun. Digital cameras are prone to collecting dust particles on the sensor which results in spots on the image. The dirt mostly enters the camera when changing lenses, so be careful when doing this. To some extent photos can be 'cleaned' up afterwards in Photoshop, but this is time-consuming. You can have your camera sensor professionally cleaned, or you can do this yourself with special brushes and swabs made for the purpose, but note that touching the sensor might cause damage and should only be done with the greatest care.

**LIGHT** The most striking outdoor photographs are often taken during the hour or two of 'golden light' after dawn and before sunset. Shooting in low light may enforce the use of very low shutter speeds, in which case a tripod will be required to avoid camera shake.

With careful handling, side lighting and back lighting can produce stunning effects, especially in soft light and at sunrise or sunset. Generally, however, it is best to shoot with the sun behind you. When photographing animals or people in the harsh midday sun, images taken in light but even shade are likely to be more effective than those taken in direct sunlight or patchy shade, since the latter conditions create too much contrast.

**PROTOCOL** In some countries, it is unacceptable to photograph local people without permission, and many people will refuse to pose or will ask for a donation. In such circumstances, don't try to sneak photographs as you might get yourself into trouble. Even the most willing subject will often pose stiffly when a camera is pointed at them; relax them by making a joke, and take a few shots in quick succession to improve the odds of capturing a natural pose.

*Ariadne Van Zandbergen is a professional travel and wildlife photographer specialising in Africa. She runs the Africa Image Library. For photo requests, visit www.africaimagelibrary.co.za or contact her on ariadne@hixnet.co.za.*

you need. All but the cheapest hotels provide towels.

You'll almost certainly be bringing a camera. Make sure you bring spare batteries and enough film (although basic print film can be bought in Zanzibar Town, and from some hotels and beach lodges). For more information on cameras and photography, see box above.

A first-aid and medical kit is recommended, but what you need depends on your type of holiday, the amount of travel, and how far you plan to get off the beaten track. Whatever, you should include the basics:

- sticking plasters (some waterproof)
- antiseptic cream
- antihistamine tablets and cream (good for insect bites)
- tubigrip bandages
- aspirin or paracetamol
- anti-diarrhoea pills
- adequate supplies of any personal medication you may need

More elaborate medicines, if you need them, are available from the private hospitals in Zanzibar (see pages 142–3). A few travellers also carry an 'anti-AIDS' kit (a pack of needles, syringes and other items which come into contact with blood) for use in an emergency. Your doctor or a vaccination centre can provide more information.

If you're staying in the smaller, cheaper hotels, the following items will be useful:

- **Torch/flashlight** Power cuts are not infrequent in the towns, and the smaller beach hotels have generators that run for only a few hours each night.
- **Water bottle and purification tablets** Water supplies in the most remote areas may not always be drinkable.
- **Universal sink plug** Plugs always seem to be missing from the more basic hotels.
- **Snorkelling gear** If you're keen on snorkelling it is worth taking your own snorkelling mask and fins. Hiring these is usually easy and cheap, but hired kit often fits poorly, spoiling the whole experience.

# $ MONEY AND BANKING

**CURRENCY** Tanzania's unit of currency, used throughout these islands, is the Tanzania shilling (TSh). However, as non-Tanzanians have to pay for some items, such as flights, ferry tickets and hotels, in foreign currency, the US dollar has effectively become an unofficial second currency. The prices of many other items, such as tours or rental cars, are also often quoted in dollars, although these may be paid in TSh at the current rate. Prices in TSh, and exchange rates against hard currencies, are likely to vary considerably in the future, but prices in US dollars tend to remain more constant. Both currencies are quoted in this book.

In May 2006, the rate of exchange was as follows:

US$1   = TSh1,240
£1     = TSh2,340
€1     = TSh1,584

For visitors to the islands, the most convenient currency to use is US dollars. Ideally, it should be carried in cash, in a mix of high and low denominations; this is handy as it can be used almost anywhere. Although travellers' cheques are a more secure form of money to carry (as they can be replaced if stolen), here they attract very poor rates of exchange and are simply not accepted by some hotels. Hence unless you're bringing a great deal, cash is much easier to carry.

**CHANGING MONEY** On the islands, the easiest place to change money is Zanzibar Town, where there are banks and many bureaux de change (see *Chapter 6*). It is also possible to change money in Chake Chake on Pemba (see page 268). Around Zanzibar Island, money can also be changed at most large and medium-sized hotels – although often the rates are poor. Several tour companies are also licensed to change money. For those travelling via Dar es Salaam Airport, there are a couple of convenient bureaux de change just outside the international terminal; the domestic terminal has no change facility.

Both banks and bureaux de change offer tourists 'free market rates', which means the rates are not artificially fixed (and therefore usually good for tourists). Generally, the banks offer better rates for travellers' cheques and the private bureaux offer better rates for cash, particularly for large denomination bills. The change bureaux also tend to have a faster service. Banks and bureaux accept most foreign currencies, but staff are most familiar with US dollars, and these get relatively higher rates than other hard currencies.

Try not to change more than you will need into Tanzanian shillings (TSh); it can be difficult changing this back into hard currency. The bank often just refuses to do it, and private change bureaux may offer poor rates or not have foreign currency available. When calculating the amount of money you need to change into TSh, remember that many items, such as the larger hotels, car hire and air tickets, are payable in hard currency only (usually US dollars). Many other items, such as bike hire, boat trips and souvenirs, can also be paid for with US dollars.

**CREDIT CARDS** You can pay for many items such as tours, better hotels and air tickets with a credit card (or debit card), but you may be charged a high commission. This can be as much as 10–20%. Drawing cash may also be possible through hotels and tour companies, but once again high commissions are charged, or poor rates given. The official explanation for these charges is that the islands are not hooked up to any international electronic card validation process, and staff have to make telephone calls (sometimes to the card's country of origin) to get authorisation before the card can be accepted. In reality, it's because plastic is still pretty new on Zanzibar, and most people still prefer to deal in tangible cash! (More information on credit and debit cards is given under *Payments and reservations* in *Accommodation*, page 91). For Visa cardholders there's an Assistance Point at the office of Coastal Travels and Mtoni Marine Centre near the Serena Hotel in Zanzibar Town. This is not a bank or bureau, though: it issues only relatively small amounts of cash against a card in cases of emergency, and the exchange rates are still poor compared with cash or travellers' cheques.

**COSTS AND BUDGETING** The cost of a visit to the islands depends very much on your standard of travel. Zanzibar Town has the most choice and, in many ways, the lowest prices for the quality that you get. At the bottom line, the cheapest hotels cost between US$10 and US$20 a night, per person. If you have meals in local eating-houses and small restaurants (snacks US$2–3; curry US$4–5; grilled seafood US$4–9; pizza US$5–6), supplemented by lunches of fruit and bread from the market, plus tea or soft drinks (US$1–3) or the occasional alcoholic sundowner (US$3–4), then food and drink will cost another US$15 to US$20 a day. Hotels in the expansive middle range cost between about US$75 and US$150 for a double, and meals in smarter restaurants cost the equivalent of around US$15 per person. Towards the top of the range, good-quality hotels are US$150–300 for a double, with meals in the best establishments from around US$25.

Outside of Zanzibar Town, most places are beach lodges. The cheapest of these, supplying little more than a (sometimes clean) room, will again be around US$10–20 per person per night. Pay between about US$40–75 per person per night and you can find clean and pleasant places by the dozen. US$75–150 per person per night buys you somewhere smart – usually places that need booking in advance, whilst you can pay up to US$880 per person sharing for the exclusive delight of Mnemba – but then this can lay claim to be one of east Africa's top beach destinations.

You also need to take into account the costs of getting around. Buses are very cheap, costing the equivalent of only a few dollars to cross the island. For independent travel, you can hire bicycles for around US$5 per day, motor-scooters for US$25 or cars from around US$40.

Organised tours of the spice plantations, Jozani Forest or boat trips out to the smaller islands start from about US$25 per person for a small group. If you want a vehicle or boat to yourself, this can go up to about US$75 for a day's outing. Snorkelling trips are around US$30 whilst a single dive to local reefs starts at US$35; both activities command a supplement for Mnemba Island which ranges from US$15 to US$60. PADI Open Water dive certification courses range from US$300 to US$500; centres are now obliged to sell the teaching material (around US$50) for these courses, but this is usually included in the price. Game-fishing trips are notoriously costly with a half day coming in at US$450. Entry to most of the historical sites and ruins on the island is free, as is lying on the beach!

#  ACCOMMODATION

For visitors to Zanzibar, the accommodation and food available are amongst the most important aspects of a visit. This section describes briefly what you can expect, but these things do change with time and you should be ready for this.

## HOTELS AND GUESTHOUSES

**Zanzibar Town** At the upper end of the range, Zanzibar Town's only large, international-standard hotel is the Serena Inn, part of a chain with other properties in Tanzania and Kenya. Double rooms cost around US$265. There is currently nothing in Stone Town of the same quality and size, although several grand old buildings have been renovated and opened as smaller, boutique hotels. They combine good quality with local flavour and often some style, although they lack some of the extensive facilities of the Serena. Prices range from US$125 to US$200 for a double room.

Zanzibar Town has a wide choice of mid-range hotels, costing between US$50 and US$120 for a double, where rooms are en suite, clean and comfortable, but are unlikely to be air conditioned.

At the lower end of the price range there are several small hotels and guesthouses which offer a basic room for US$10–20 per person. Rooms may not be spotless, and are not usually en suite, but these are generally friendly places and popular with budget travellers.

All hotels in Zanzibar include breakfast in the room price, unless otherwise stated.

**Zanzibar Island** Around Zanzibar Island, away from Zanzibar Town, nearly all the hotels and guesthouses are built on, or very near, idyllic tropical beaches, complete with palm trees, white sand and warm blue waters. Some travellers come here for a couple of days, just to relax; others linger for weeks. Places to stay range from large hotels and resorts with many facilities, through small but comfortable lodges and bungalows, to local-style guesthouses which are very basic.

At the top end are a dozen or so fairly stylish, **smaller beach lodges** which cater to individual visitors, usually on prearranged trips. Typically they'll have between about ten and 30 rooms. Staying here you can expect good food, very comfortable accommodation and a fairly exclusive atmosphere. Expect to pay around US$75–150 per person per night for somewhere smart – or considerably more in the case of Mnemba.

Next there are a number of **large beach resorts**, with upwards of 50 rooms each. These are generally used by pre-booked package tourists who fly in and spend most or all of their time on Zanzibar within the resort. Some focus so clearly on packages bought overseas that their rates are in euro and they do not even accept 'walk-in' guests.

At the **bottom end of the market**, US$10–60 will give you a night at one of a diverse range of places. These have little in common except that they normally deal largely with walk-in guests. (At the better places, reservations are recommended during the busy season.) There's a huge choice, ranging from places that are aspiring to be the next exclusive beach lodge, down to basic bungalows beside a beach where even if you could reserve a room (if they had a phone, and if it was working), it would be a very unusual thing to do.

As the number of tourists visiting Zanzibar continues to grow (in 2005 it passed the 100,000 per year mark!), the number of places on Zanzibar's coast – and the range of places – increases also. Expect to find more new places when you arrive, and expect a few old places to have disappeared or been renamed.

**Pemba and Mafia** Visitor numbers to Pemba and Mafia are absolutely minuscule compared with Zanzibar, and so these islands have far less choice than Zanzibar. Mafia's clutch of small lodges represent particularly good value if you value a fairly high degree of exclusivity, without wanting anything that is too luxurious or expensive. Pemba has only two real beach lodges, both very differently priced.

**SELF-CATERING** Cooking for yourself is not usually possible at any of the larger, more expensive hotels in Zanzibar Town or on the coast, as Western-style self-catering apartments are not available. At some of the bottom-end hotels and guesthouses, you may be allowed to use the kitchen, but this would be unusual. Where places do allow self-catering this is mentioned in the various hotel listings.

**CAMPING** As yet, there are no official campsites in Zanzibar. Camping is permitted in the grounds of some budget hotels on the coast, but this is not usual as the hotels are so cheap anyway. On the most popular beaches, there have been occasional incidents of theft from unoccupied tents.

**PAYMENTS AND RESERVATIONS** Officially, all non-Tanzanian visitors must pay hotel bills in hard currency, usually US dollars, so all prices are quoted in this currency. Residents and citizens are charged lower rates (between 50% and 80% of the visitor rate), and can usually pay in Tanzanian shillings (TSh). In many places foreigners can also pay in TSh – at the current rate of exchange so it makes no difference to the price – but dollars are usually easier to carry and deal with. Smaller hotels accept only cash. In larger hotels you can pay with US dollar travellers' cheques, although the hotel will usually make a surcharge (to cover its own bank charges). Some of the hotels, mostly in the US$50-per-night-plus bracket, accept credit cards – but surcharges of between 5% and 20% are still common. To save any surprises, check their policy on credit cards before reserving a room. Despite ambitious claims made in some tourist promotional literature about the ease of using credit cards, Zanzibar is still essentially a cash economy.

Low-season prices are often 25% to 50% lower than high-season prices, and there may be additional premiums (over and above the high-season rates) over Christmas and the New Year. At any time of year, rates may be negotiable if you're in a small group (more than about four or five people), or plan to stay for a long time (more than about five or six nights); this is especially true of the smaller, lower-budget lodges and hotels.

Between December and March is the main mango time on Zanzibar, and the markets are full of these tasty green-to-yellow fruits. From March to mid-June it's the wet season (*Masika*), when pineapples are plentiful, and July to September is when oranges are in abundance.

If you intend staying in one of the cheaper places it is usually possible simply to arrive and get a room on the spot. However, advance reservations are wise at the smarter hotels, and during the busier periods. Communications by phone, fax and email are all possible, but allow between three and five weeks for a reply by normal mail!

# ✖ FOOD AND DRINK

**RESTAURANTS** In Zanzibar Town, there are several good restaurants catering specifically for the tourist trade, specialising in local dishes, seafood or curries (remember that Zanzibar is on the shores of the Indian Ocean). Meals in such places usually cost between US$7 and US$20 per person. There are also smarter restaurants, and restaurants attached to large hotels, where prices are higher.

Zanzibar Town also has restaurants where meals and snacks are less elaborate and prices are around US$5. There are also some small eating-houses catering mainly for local people where you can eat for around US$2. They usually only have one or two types of food available, such as stew and rice, but they also serve chapattis, samosas and other snacks.

**Outside Zanzibar Town**, in the smaller towns and villages on Zanzibar, Pemba and Mafia, there are relatively few places to eat. Local people tend to eat in their own houses and there are not enough tourists around yet to create a market for cafés and restaurants. On the coast, hotels and guesthouses usually have restaurants attached, where food and service generally reflect the overall standard of the accommodation. A few small restaurants have opened by the most popular beaches, catering for the growing influx of visitors.

**CAFÉS AND BARS** In Zanzibar Town, many places serve drinks as well as food, although at busy times you may be required to buy a meal rather than have a drink on its own. You can buy international and Tanzanian brands of fizzy drink, plus local and imported beers. Prices vary greatly according to where you drink: a bottle of Coke from a shop or small backstreet café costs US$0.25, and may cost four times this in a smarter café or restaurant. A bottle of local beer (including Safari, Tusker or Kilimanjaro) costs US$1 in a local bar, and at least double this in smarter places.

At larger hotels and restaurants in Zanzibar Town or on the coast you can also buy imported beers, wines (mostly from South Africa) and spirits.

**SELF-CATERING** If you plan to provide for yourself, in Zanzibar Town there are several shops selling locally produced bread and cakes, plus a reasonable choice of food in tins and packets imported from Kenya or other parts of the world. Zanzibar Town has a very good market where you can buy all sorts of fruit and vegetables, plus fresh meat and fish if you have a means of cooking it. Other towns on Zanzibar and Pemba also have small markets where you can buy meat, fish, fruit and vegetables, and shops with a limited but adequate supply of tinned food.

These islands have some superb destinations for divers, fishermen (and women) and watersports enthusiasts, and even if you're only a casual snorkeller or angler, there's plenty to attract you. Some diving and fishing companies are based in Zanzibar Town, but most operate from the coastal hotels around the islands. For details on the best seasons for diving and fishing, see the box on page 95.

**DIVING** Diving is an important element of an increasing number of people's trips, and so here are some general comments on the various areas for diving around the islands. See individual sections for more details.

**Dive sites** The seas around these islands offer some of the best diving conditions in the Indian Ocean. As well as coral reefs, the marine life is also a major attraction. All around the islands you'll find coral and colourful reef fish, while encounters with larger fish such as groupers, barracudas, sharks, rays and mantas, plus turtles, dolphins and even whales, are possible at the better dive sites.

**Off the west coast of Zanzibar Island**, and within easy reach of Zanzibar Town, are numerous small islands, sandbanks and reefs where divers can experience good corals with slopes and drop-offs. There are also some good sites for experienced divers, including a couple of wrecks. (There are no wrecks on the east coast.)

**Off the north coast** and northern part of the east coast are many more reefs. There's also Mnemba Island (sometimes more fancifully termed Mnemba Atoll). This tiny island stands on the edge of a much larger circular coral reef upon which you'll find some of the finest dive sites of this stretch of the east African coast. These days it is popular though, and so you'll find many dive boats floating above different sites on this reef – and coming from all around Nungwi and the northeast cost of Zanzibar. Tumbatu Island also has some good reefs, used by one or two of the operations in Kendwa and Nungwi.

One long barrier reef runs along virtually the whole of the **east coast of Zanzibar Island**. Although this is seldom quite as colourful as the Mnemba reef, it does offer good variation between its different sites, and many are good. You are much more likely to be on your own here, especially towards the south, than anywhere around the northern tip of Zanzibar.

**Southwest Zanzibar** is much more of an unknown quantity, although initial reports sound promising. We'll know more when the scuba centre at Fumba Beach opens, and the area starts to be dived regularly by the team there.

**Pemba Island**, and the numerous smaller islands nearby, has some spectacular diving spots. A number of Pemba's wall and drift dives are notable for variable and strong currents, and so are really more suitable for very experienced divers – hence the island is a favourite amongst live-aboard operations.

**Mafia Island**, by contrast, has a real mix. Inside Chole Bay is generally sheltered and shallow; an ideal place for novice divers to learn with some lovely, gentle diving. Outside the bay is more dramatic fare, capable of surprising even experienced divers with big ocean fish and breathtaking sights, including a particularly spectacular ocean-facing coral wall.

**Dive companies** The main diving seasons are outlined in the box on page 95, but it's worth noting that at any time of year the east coast areas are exposed to the Indian Ocean swell, while the west coast tends to be more sheltered.

The many diving operators are listed below, grouped by location, with more details provided in the relevant area chapters. Prices for dives vary slightly between them.

PADI International recognises that there can be issues with some unlicensed dive centres and instructors passing themselves off as registered centres, particularly in remote locations. Their advice to all divers is 'don't take anything at face value – certificates, flags and branding can be forged and obtained outside official channels'. In a bid to combat these unscrupulous operations and individuals, PADI has recently set up a searchable database of licensed members and resorts so that divers can access reliable, up-to-date information – www.padi.com/english/common/search/dcnr. It is equally possible to search by location for instructors and companies that are under investigation or have been suspended. It may be wise to check both before donning any sub-aqua kit.

With all dive centres, PADI registered or not, divers are well advised to talk with the staff (and management where possible) to ascertain their commitment to providing a quality service. Are they eager to listen? Do they understand the kind of dive experience sought? Are they willing, perhaps even eager, to prove their credentials? Are they willing to demonstrate the quality of their equipment before requiring a commitment to hire or dive with it? Can they demonstrate that the air in the cylinders is from a reputable source, and is recently certified as clean (air quality should be sampled and checked quarterly)? Is there a sense of pride among the staff that they are working for a trustworthy and reputable company?

There are many operations on Zanzibar, Pemba and Mafia offering safe, enjoyable diving, with well-maintained modern equipment, clean air and a keen eye on customer service, but asking questions and getting a feel for an operation is critical before taking the decision to venture underwater.

Diving is a dangerous sport and some of the better operators will insist on rusty divers doing a 'refresher course' before diving with them; treat this as a valuable re-introduction, and it's a sensible precaution.

Nearly all the dive centres on the islands are based at hotels and beach lodges, and can be contacted either directly or through the hotel/lodge. You do not need to be staying at a hotel to use the dive centre facilities, although some places give a discount to guests.

## Zanzibar Town

**Zanzibar Dive Centre** One Ocean Ltd, PO Box 608, Zanzibar; ☎/f 024 2238374/0742 750161; e oneocean@zanlink.com; www.zanzibaroneocean.com. Based near the beach to the west of Forodhani Gardens, at the junction of Shangani and Kenyatta roads, this is the only PADI 5-star instructor development centre in Zanzibar, with efficient management, modern gear and keen staff. The base is open 08.00 to 18.30 daily. Most of the diving is done on the islands, reefs and wrecks off Zanzibar Town, using traditional dhows fitted with diesel engines, but they also have faster boats so that some of the more distant and rarely visited sites, such as Boribu Reef, can also be reached. Sgl dives are US$40, dbl dives US$70 (a day trip, inc lunch). 4 dives are US$130, and night dives US$45. A Discover Scuba for total beginners is US$50, an Open Water course (over 4 or 5 days) is US$320 and an advanced course is US$240. A 10% discount is given if you have your own gear. Confined water training is done in the Serena swimming pool. Snorkelling trips and dhow cruises are also arranged from Zanzibar Town. This company also has bases on the east coast of Zanzibar Island at Matemwe Beach Bungalows and at Bluebay Beach Resort, which gives divers access to the reefs in this area, which includes Mnemba Island. Diving tours to Pemba can also be arranged.

**Bahari Divers** PO Box 204, Zanzibar; ☎ 0742 750293; e baharidivers@hotmail.com; www.zanzibar-diving.com. This small, friendly and well-organised operation has an office near the northern end of Kenyatta Road. The main dive sites are Bawe Island, Fungu Reef and Pange Sandbank, all within easy reach of Zanzibar Town. 1 dive is US$40, 2 dives

US$70 (inc lunch) and 4 dives US$120. Night dives are US$45. A discovery dive for complete beginners is US$50, and a 4-day Open Water course is US$320.

## Northern Zanzibar

**Spanish Dancer Dive Centre** PO Box 3486, Stone Town, Zanzibar; ☎ 024 2240091/0777 417717/0777 430005; e spanishdancerznz@hotmail.com; www.spanishdancerdivers.com (✪ SPANDA 5°43.891'S; 39°17.473'E). Family-run, Spanish operation based on Nungwi's South Beach. See page 183, *Nungwi.*

**Sensation Divers** PO Box 3528, Zanzibar; ☎ 0746 442203; e sensationdivers@yahoo.com/ info@sensationdivers.com; www.sensationdivers.com (✪ SENSAT 5°43.795'S; 39°17.484'E). PADI centre located on the 'Nungwi Strip', offering Nitrox diving and a range of sub-aqua toys. See page 183, *Nungwi.*

**East Africa Diving & Watersport Centre** PO Box 2750, Nungwi, Zanzibar; ☎ 0777 416425/420588; e EADC@zitec.org; www.diving-zanzibar.com (✪ EADIVE 5°43.602'S; 39°17.535'E). Long-established

PADI operation with good, efficient staff, on Nungwi's West Beach. See page 183, *Nungwi.*

**Divemaxx** PO Box 4200, Zanzibar; ☎/f 024 2240014/0741 324744; e info@sazanibeach.com; www.sazanibeach.com (✪ SAZANI 5°43.775'S; 39°18.669'E). No resident dive instructor, but experienced divers can rent equipt. See page 183, *Nungwi.*

**Ras Nungwi Beach Hotel Dive Centre** PO Box 1784, Zanzibar; ☎ 024 2233767/2232512; f 024 2233098; e watersports@rasnungwi.com; www.rasnungwi.com/diving/ (✪ RASNUN 5°43.809'S; 39°18.691'E). Excellent Gold Palm 5-Star PADI Instructor Development Centre, based at Ras Nungwi Beach Hotel. See page 181, *Nungwi.*

**Scuba Do Diving** PO Box 3546, Stone Town, Zanzibar; ☎ 0777 417157/0748 415179/UK +44 (0)1326 250773; e info@scubado.demon.co.uk/do-scuba@scuba-do-zanzibar.com; www.scubado.demon.co.uk/www.scuba-do-zanzibar.com (✪ SCUBAD 5°45.071'S; 39°17.387'E). Excellent, British-owned and -run centre in the heart of Kendwa Beach. See page 191, *Kendwa.*

---

## ZANZIBAR DIVING AND FISHING SEASONS

If you are coming to Zanzibar specifically for scuba diving, there are some points you need to know. Diving is possible at any time of year, and divers visit different parts of the archipelago according to conditions. Having said that, most people avoid the main rainy season from March/April to May, even though during this period there can be some very good days. The weather is especially changeable at this time, and in less than an hour can switch from beautifully calm and sunny conditions to a full-blown tropical rainstorm, reducing visibility on the surface to a few hundred metres and churning up the water.

Generally speaking, from June/July to October, when the winds come from the south, the northern coasts of Zanzibar Island and Pemba Island are better, although during August some days can offer perfect conditions, while on other days the sea may be rough. September–December is usually the calmest time, and from November to February/March, the southern coasts are preferred, as the winds come from the north. Pemba enjoys some of the best visibility of the year in February.

At any time of year the western sides are more sheltered, while the eastern sides (the ocean side) are more prone to swells and rough days. As in many other parts of the world, the weather and sea conditions on Zanzibar are unpredictable and there's always a chance of a bad day during the 'good' times, and perfect conditions at the heart of the 'bad' times.

If you're seriously into game fishing, the best time is August–March, although conditions are also reasonable from July to September. August–November boasts excellent sport fishing for yellowfin tuna, sailfish and marlin, The latter are even more prevalent between November–March during the billfish season, when striped marlin are positively prolific (schools up to ten recorded) and blue and black marlin are common.

## Northeast Zanzibar

**Mnemba Island Lodge Dive Centre** PO Box 3107, Zanzibar; ☎ 0777 438656; f 0741 326575; e jnb@ccafrica.com; www.ccafrica.com (⊕ MNEMBA 5°49.2'S; 39°22.978'E). Fabulous Belgian-run dive centre on Mnemba, for resident use only. See page 201, *Mnemba Island*.

**One Ocean – Ocean Paradise** PO Box 608, Zanzibar; ☎ 0777 453892/024 2238374; f 024 2234877; e oneocean@zanlink.com; www.zanzibaroneocean.com (⊕ OCEANP 5°56.231'S; 39°21.635'E). Reliable PADI dive centre with Ocean Paradise resort. See page 205, *Pwani Mchangani*.

**One Ocean Bluebay** PO Box 607, Zanzibar; ☎ 024 2240244/0777 414332; e oneocean@zanlink.com; www.zanzibaroneocean.com (⊕ BLUEBA 5°58.676'S; 39°22.48'E). Well-equipped PADI dive centre at Bluebay Resort, sharing boats with its Ocean Paradise branch. See page 208, *Kiwengwa*.

## Southeast Zanzibar

**Kaskazi Sports Centre** PO Box 71, Pingwe, Zanzibar; ☎ 0777 415447; f 0741 325670; e zanzibarsurf@yahoo.com; www.kaskazi.net. PADI centre at Karafuu Hotel offering diving and host of other watersports. See page 226, *Michamvi Peninsula*.

**Rising Sun Dive Centre** PO Box 479, Zanzibar; ☎ 0777 440883/84/85/88; f 0741 333151; e bookings@risingsun-zanzibar.com; www.risingsun-zanzibar.com (⊕ BREEZE 6°11.717'S; 39°31.968'E). Smart, English-run PADI centre on the beach at Breezes Beach Club, with good underwater photography knowledge and kit. See page 224, *Michamvi Peninsula*.

**Paje Dive Centre** Based in Paje village and receiving mixed safety reports. See page 236, *Paje*.

**Big Ocean Divers** PO Box 1520, Zanzibar; ☎ 0777 875515; e bigoceandivers@yahoo.com (⊕ BIGOCE 6°15.571'S; 39°32.148'E). Next door to Paje Ndame and concentrating on local reef dives. See page 236, *Paje*.

## Southwest Zanzibar

**Fumba Beach Lodge Dive Centre** PO Box 3075, Stone Town, Zanzibar; ☎ 0777 860504/878025; e reservations@fumbabeachlodge.co.tz/ info@fumbabeachlodge.co.tz;

www.fumbabeachlodge.com (⊕ FUMBAB 6°18.898'S; 39°16.501'E). New dive centre opening here in Jun 2006.

## Pemba

See pages 270–1.

## Mafia

See page 300.

## Live-aboards

**Dive 'n' Sail Zanzibar** ☎ 0777 420 770; e info@dive-n-sail.com/ sales@gourmetzanzibar.com; www.dive-n-sail.com. 50ft Admiral catamaran, *Julia*, moored off Nungwi offering live-aboard dive trips to Pemba and Mafia. See under *Nungwi*.

**SY Aristos** ☎ +254 (0)720 441487/(0)733 825718/(0)723 110031; e info@divingsailing.com; www.divingsailing.com. 17m ketch operates diving and sailing trips out of Kalifi in Kenya, visiting Zanzibar Island, Pemba and Mafia Island. See page 271, *Pemba*.

**Floating Beach Resort** ☎ 0747 414177; book through Italian agents such as Albatros (www.albatros.com) or Viaggiland (www.viaggiland.it). 15 rooms and dive centre on board 32m former hydrofoil moored off the south coast near Mkoani. See page 271, *Mkoani*.

**SY Jambo** PO Box 82234, Mombasa, Kenya; ☎ 0741 320025; f +254 41 471771–2/473969/+254 733 619965; e info@oneearthsafaris.com; www.mantareeflodge.com/www.onearthsafaris.com. The twin-masted 23m *Jambo* operates out of Shimoni, down the west coast of Pemba to Ras Nungwi on Zanzibar Island. See page 271, *Pemba*.

**Pemba Afloat** ☎ 0748 400748/341459; e pembaafloat@zanlink.com/ pembaafloat@pembaisland.com; www.pembaisland.com. Bookings on the island can be made through Wacom in Chake Chake. Pemba Afloat consists of 3 20m ketches, one of which has 12 cabins, permanently moored in the calm waters of Njao Lagoon. See page 271, *Pemba*.

**Sahil Reis** ☎ 024 2452786; f 024 2452768; e swahilidivers@intafrica.com; www.swahilidivers.com. New live-aboard should be ready around the end of 2006. See page 271, *Pemba*.

**SNORKELLING** Most of the dive centres mentioned above will also cater for snorkellers, by hiring out snorkels and fins. You'll have to take a boat from virtually all the lodges and hotels throughout the islands in order to reach decent reefs for snorkelling. Some places will offer excursions of an hour, at other places snorkelling is a half-day trip and you'll share the boat with divers.

**Off the west coast of Zanzibar Island,** Chumbe Island stands out as having some of the best preserved and most easily accessible coral in the region; it really is in pristine condition, outshining any of the coral gardens known elsewhere near the islands.

**Off the northeast coast,** the house reef close to the shore on the western side of Mnemba Island is used by many lodges from Nungwi and the northeast coast. Residents of Mnemba have the relaxing luxury of being able to walk into the water rather than sail for several hours to get there, but they share the same reef. Further south, on **Zanzibar's southeast coast,** snorkelling is along the main barrier reef.

The **southwest of Zanzibar** has been explored relatively little compared with most of Zanzibar's other areas, although it's perhaps worth noting that the team from Safari Blue (see page 256) offer snorkelling on the tiny islands south of Fumba.

The place most often used for snorkelling off **Pemba** is known as Misali Island. After a speedboat ride here from Fundu Lagoon, you can snorkel from the beach (often while the boat takes divers elsewhere here to dive). Live-aboards obviously have more scope, although they tend to concentrate on the diving rather than snorkelling.

From the lodges on **Mafia Island,** snorkelling is usually an hour or two's dhow ride away. The reefs around the mouth of Chole Bay are interesting and quite tidal; the sand-banks exposed by the ocean around low tide are idyllic – magical empty places to laze around, beachcomb and snorkel from the beach.

◄ **FISHING** The waters around Zanzibar and Pemba islands offer some of the best fishing in the world, especially the Pemba Channel, between Zanzibar and Pemba islands, or around Mafia Island, south of Zanzibar. Big-game fish include barracuda, kingfish, sailfish, billfish, wahoo, dorado and blue marlin.

**Fishing companies** There are several fishing companies based on Zanzibar, but note that while most are experienced and reputable, some others seem less so. When making bookings or enquiries you should ask about the equipment they use: What type is it? How suitable is it for big game fishing? How old is it? How often is it serviced? Ask about safety equipment too: Are the boats fitted with radios? Do they carry spare outboard motors, lifejackets and so on?

**Ras Nungwi Fishing** PO Box 1784, Zanzibar; ☎ 024 2233767/2232512; **f** 024 2233098; **e** info@rasnungwi.com; www.rasnungwi.com (✣ RASNUN 5°43.809'S; 39°18.691'E). One of the best game-fishing operations on Zanzibar. Based out of Ras Nungwi Beach Hotel, operating its own professional sportfishing boat in the rich waters between Zanzibar and Pemba. See page 181, Nungwi.

**Fishing Zanzibar** **e** gerry@fishingzanzibar.com/ info@fishingzanzibar.com; www.fishingzanzibar.com. Also operating out of Nungwi, this 30ft fly-bridge, sport-fishing boat takes small charter groups to Leven Bank and the Pemba Channel.

Some of the diving centres listed above also organise fishing trips on request. Mtoni Marine Centre (listed under Hotels in the *Zanzibar Town* chapter, on page 168) can also put you in touch with game-fishing operators on the north coast and east coast.

## THINGS TO BUY

If you're looking for souvenirs, collectables or gifts to take home, then the islands have a lot to offer. Most of the shops and stalls are in Zanzibar Town (see *Shopping,* in *Chapter 6,* pages 137–9), but you can also buy things at many of the lodges and hotels elsewhere.

Zanzibar Town market is particularly good for the aromatic spices that make Zanzibar so famous. Wander around the Old Town to find endless shops and stalls selling wooden carvings; paintings in the Tingatinga (see pages 40–2) style and others; jewellery in stone, gold and silver; models or mobiles made from coconut shells; and a plethora of other souvenirs. Carved boxes inlaid with shells, or decorated with hammered brass, are very popular.

Several curio shops here sell antiques, original hand-crafted pieces, and lots of genuine junk. Some antiques have been brought to the islands by Arab or Indian traders in the last couple of centuries; most are now reproductions. The Zanzibar clocks, originally used by Zanzibari merchants, are unique. Carpets, rugs and mats, made in the Persian or Arab style, are easy to carry home. Traditional Zanzibar furniture, such as tables, beds and wardrobes decorated with stained glass and mirrors, can be found but these are less easy to get back!

Some shops still sell shells and coral, taken from the reefs and beaches around the islands. They wouldn't do this if thoughtless visitors didn't buy them. This trade encourages people to catch and collect live molluscs, and to break off live coral. Reefs take decades to grow, and if you buy these items, then you are helping to degrade, and eventually destroy, the islands' fascinating marine life.

You may also see turtle-shells, or items made from turtle-shell such as bracelets or earrings. Again, turtles are an endangered species in Zanzibar and you should not buy these things. (For more details, see the *Sea turtles* section on pages 62–4.) Similarly, in this part of the world anything made from ivory is likely to have come from a poached elephant; avoid it.

## MEDIA AND COMMUNICATIONS

**MEDIA** Unlike mainland Tanzania's vibrant media scene, Zanzibar's independent press has had a rough ride. In November 2003, *Dira,* the island's first post-revolution, independent newspaper, was forced to cease publication after the Zanzibar government alleged that it had violated registration procedures and professional ethics. The popular private paper had been previously almost bankrupted by a huge libel fine of TSh660 million (about US$500,000) following the publication of 'false and harmful' reports about the Zanzibar President's family: namely two articles that accused his children of using their father's influence to buy up state-owned companies.

Following this, a period ensued where, in spite of international pressure to allow free expression, the media scene was wholly government run; private broadcasters and newspaper publishers were banned. Then, at the end of 2005, 13 new private publications were granted licences, including four newspapers: *Zanzibar Wiki Hii, Marhaba, ZIFF* and *Fahari*. However, it must be noted that their content is far from independent and impartial. State-operated TV Zanzibar and its radio counterpart, Voice of Tanzania-Zanzibar, still dominate, and continue to act as a channel for government opinion, with little, if any, room for political criticism of those in power. The current media environment may be private but it is far from independent.

International media rights organisation Reporters Without Borders, who campaign for global press freedom and the right to be informed, maintain that there is 'no press freedom in Zanzibar'. However, many locals can in fact receive mainland (independent) broadcast channels and satellite television is increasingly widespread. The BBC World Service is also available on FM in both Zanzibar and Pemba.

Looking to the future, it is possible that the combination of allowing private press to operate, and the creation of a revised Freedom of Information Act, will eventually lead to increased press freedom on the island.

**POST** Most towns and large villages on these islands have post offices, but it's best to send all your mail from Zanzibar Town. The main poste restante service for Zanzibar is also in Zanzibar Town (see page 141). The post service is reliable, with letters taking about a week to ten days to reach destinations in Europe and North America (Australia takes a bit longer). Letters to destinations inside Tanzania cost about US$0.20, while postcards to countries outside Africa are about US$0.50 (slightly more for letters).

**TELEPHONE AND FAX** The best place on the islands for calling from a landline is the public call office, next to the old post office in Zanzibar Town. There are several private phone bureaux around here also. International calls to Europe or the USA cost between US$2.50 and US$5 per minute, depending on where you go. Note that most places charge per full minute; go over by one second and you might as well speak for the next 59. More details are given in the *Zanzibar Town* chapter, on pages 141–2. Elsewhere on the islands the better hotels and lodges will usually allow guests to make international calls, although rates are high.

There are now a handful of mobile phone (cell phone) networks. These work around Zanzibar Town, in many parts of Zanzibar Island, in and around Chake Chake and Mkoani on Pemba Island, and even around the lodges on Mafia Island.

If you're bringing a mobile phone from home, those with GSM capability should work here; check with your own service provider before you depart.

**INTERNET** Most of the phone bureaux in Zanzibar Town also offer internet services, and there are also many dedicated internet bureaux. More details are given in the *Zanzibar Town* chapter, on page 142.

## BUSINESS HOURS

Most shops and travel company offices in Zanzibar Town are open every day, although some close on Fridays, the Muslim holy day, or on Sundays, the official day off. Normal business hours are from between 08.00 and 09.00 until noon, then from 13.00 or 14.00 until 17.00 or 18.00. Some private shops and tour agencies take a longer break at midday and stay open later in the evening. In the low season, some souvenir shops stay closed, while others open mornings only. Government offices and banks are closed on Saturdays and Sundays. Post offices are closed on Saturday afternoons and Sundays. Opening hours on Pemba and Mafia are similar, but less predictable.

## TRAVELLING RESPONSIBLY

### CULTURAL ETIQUETTE

- Dress and act sensitively: locals consider revealing clothing or public displays of affection offensive. Keep swimwear for the beach, and in towns or villages keep your upper legs and shoulders covered. Sporting bare chests or bikini tops as you stroll around the market is the height of rudeness and arrogance.
- Support locally owned, small-scale shops and businesses. This is the best way for your money to benefit the grassroots economy.
- Buy locally made crafts, but avoid wildlife products, such as ivory, skins, coral, shells from turtles or any other kind of marine animal, and even wooden carvings, unless the material comes from a sustainable renewable source.
- Always ask permission before photographing local people. And accept refusals.
- Non-Muslims should not enter mosques without permission.

4

Changes to telephone codes are a frequent occurrence in Tanzania, Zanzibar and the other archipelago islands. Every effort has been made to ensure this book is accurate; however, further numeric variations are inevitable in the future. The key dialling codes and most significant recent changes are detailed here.

**CALLS TO ZANZIBAR** The area code for all of Zanzibar (Zanzibar Island and Pemba Island) is 024, if you are calling from elsewhere in Tanzania, Kenya or Uganda. For calls from other countries, individual numbers must be prefixed with the international code for Tanzania +255, then 24 for Zanzibar (minus the first 0).

**CALLS WITHIN ZANZIBAR** Calling within Zanzibar, you simply dial the number you want, without the 024 area code. Some literature will be out of date, so note that individual numbers on Zanzibar Island and Pemba all changed in January 2000 – becoming six digits instead of five – and then altered again in 2002, when they increased to seven digits.

For emergency calls dial 112 (replacing 999), and for directory enquiries dial 118 (replacing 991).

**CALLS FROM ZANZIBAR** Phoning out of Zanzibar to mainland Tanzania, Kenya or Uganda you will need the city or area code (see changes below), followed by the individual number. For all other countries, it is necessary to dial the international access code (000), plus the country code (eg: 1 for USA, 44 for Britain, 27 for South Africa), followed by the city or area code (minus the first 0), then the individual number.

Area codes on the Tanzanian mainland that have changed include:

| Area | Old code | New code | Area | Old code | New code |
|------|----------|----------|------|----------|----------|
| Dar es Salaam | 051 | 022 | Mtwara | 059 | 023 |
| Tanga | 053 | 027 | Dodoma | 061 | 026 |
| Arusha | 057 | 027 | Tabora | 062 | 026 |
| Kilimanjaro | 055 | 027 | Mwanza | 068 | 028 |

**MOBILE TELEPHONE NUMBERS** Zanzibari mobile phones currently have six-digit numbers, but this is set to change with the introduction of seven-digit numbers and new operator codes. It is essential to prefix any mobile number with a code, wherever you're phoning from.

In line with the Tanzania Communications Regulatory Authority's national numbering plan, the new mobile phone codes, many of which have already been introduced, must be fully operational by 30 June 2006. Zantel has already made the switch, altering the former 0747 code to 0777, and all other service providers will follow shortly. The new codes will follow this pattern:

| Service Provider | Old format | New format |
|------------------|------------|------------|
| Celtel | +255 748 xxxxxx | +255 78 xxxxxx |
| Celtel | +255 749 xxxxxx | +255 78 xxxxxx |
| MIC | +255 741 xxxxxx | +255 71 xxxxxx |
| Vodacom | +255 744 xxxxxx | +255 74 xxxxxx |
| Vodacom | +255 745 xxxxxx | +255 74 xxxxxx |
| Zantel | +255 747 xxxxxx | +255 77 xxxxxx |

- During the holy month of Ramadan, local people fast, and you can show understanding for this tradition by not eating or drinking in public places. (Eating in tourist restaurants is fine.)

**GIVING SOMETHING BACK** During our research, we contacted a number of local NGOs in Zanzibar who seem to be doing excellent work there. However, we know from experience that they're not always good at responding to enquiries – perhaps partly due to the pressures that they're under and partly due to the limitations of their communications.

However, one NGO stood out as not only doing some great work but also being easy to contact. They have a clear website which can accept donations and arrange child sponsorship. They're trying to provide as normal an environment as possible for their children. This precludes impromptu visits from curious visitors, although existing sponsors are warmly welcomed.

**SOS Children's Village** Zanzibar www.soschildrensvillages.org.uk. The Zanzibar SOS Children's Village was built in 1988, in a residential district near the airport. Eleven family houses are now home to 120 orphaned and abandoned children, providing them with a safe place to live, a 'mother', love and care. The construction of a nursery school, primary and secondary school, health-care centre, sports fields and mosque, have led the Village to become a real neighbourhood centre, serving the local community as well as the orphans. Away from the village, three youth houses are home to older children and young people taking their first steps towards independence. The orphanage is doing excellent work but it relies on the continued charity of many people: for financial donations to fund school books, desks, a generator, construction and renovation; gifts from footballs to pens; and child sponsorship. If you are interested in helping, visit their website.

# 5

# Zanzibar Island Essentials

## GETTING TO ZANZIBAR

International flights to Tanzania are covered in *Chapter 4*, page 71. From mainland Tanzania, there are two main ways of reaching Zanzibar. The gruelling and slightly cheaper option is by sea, using one of several boat services that cross daily between Zanzibar and Dar es Salaam.

However, the vast majority of people arrive by air on one of the many direct daily flights from Dar es Salaam, Arusha or Kilimanjaro International Airport (the latter lies roughly midway along the 80km road connecting the towns of Arusha and Moshi). Light aircraft flights (often via Dar) also link Zanzibar to Pemba and Mafia, as well as the more popular national parks and game reserves in northern and southern Tanzania.

**ZANZIBAR'S PORT AND AIRPORT** Zanzibar's main port is beside Zanzibar Town; its airport is about 7km inland. The island's customs and immigration officials used to have a reputation for toughness; today they're usually polite, if sometimes disorganised. In any case, most people arriving from Europe, Kenya or elsewhere will fly via Dar – and clear customs and immigration there.

If you are leaving Zanzibar on a large international flight (as is the case with most charters to Europe), then, even though there is a large departure hall behind the check-in desks, you may well be required to queue outside under the African sun. Queues are long and check-in can be slow, so come with a cool hat, some water and lots of patience.

If you have arranged a tailor-made trip with a good tour company, then they will usually arrange for a member of staff to guide you through the check-in and often help you to circumvent any long queues for charter planes.

**✈ BY AIR** Dar es Salaam's domestic terminal is a short drive from the international terminal. (Take a taxi for a few dollars!) There is no bureau de change here, but a small souvenir shop has a good range of books. Here – and for all internal flights – you will be asked to pay a departure tax of US$6 – made up of US$5 'safety tax', and a further US$1 port tax.

**Scheduled flights** There are a number of scheduled flights from Dar es Salaam to Zanzibar, and although airfares vary slightly you'll be looking at around US$50–60 one-way from Dar es Salaam. Flights between Zanzibar and Pemba are US$80; Zanzibar and Mafia around US$150; Zanzibar and Selous are US$140 – and then flights to Ruaha, Zanzibar and Arusha are US$200 – which gives access from there to the parks of the northern circuit.

The main carriers on these routes are:

**Air Tanzania** (ATC) ATC Building, Ohio St, Dar es Salaam; ✆ 022 211 8411/2; e airtanres@airtanzania.com; www.airtanzania.com. Flies daily between Dar es Salaam and Zanzibar, with same-day connection to flights to and from Johannesburg.

**Coastal Aviation** ✆ Dar es Salaam 022 211 7959 or (airport) 284 3293; f 022 211 8647; e aviation@coastal.cc; www.coastal.cc. A reliable small operator with a good network of scheduled flights connecting Zanzibar daily to Dar es Salaam, Arusha, Tanga, Pemba, Selous Game Reserve, Ruaha National Park, Mwanza, Serengeti, Ngorongoro and Manyara.

**Precision Air** Flight Services ✆ 022 223 4520; e info@precisionairtz.com/precision-

dar@twiga.com; www.precisionairtz.com. This company has a few daily flights between Zanzibar and Dar, as well as connections to several other destinations in east Africa.

**ZanAir** PO Box 2113; main office: Malawi Rd, Zanzibar Town; ✆ 024 223 3670/3768; branch office, Zanzibar Airport; ✆ 024 2232993/0747 413240; e reservations@zanair.com; wwwzanair.com. This is based on Zanzibar – with offices in Zanzibar Town and at the airport. There are at least 3 services from Dar es Salaam to Zanzibar daily, and these usually tie in with the timetables of long-haul flights to/from Europe. There are also connecting flights to Arusha and Pemba.

**Private charter flights** If you're in a hurry, or need to connect to another flight at a difficult time, then you can charter your own aircraft to get from Zanzibar to almost anywhere in east Africa. The charter planes are small, from three to eight seats, and best arranged well in advance. Private charters can be arranged with Precision, Coastal or ZanAir (listed above).

If you're on Zanzibar Island and need to fly to the mainland, more details on air services are given in *Chapter 6* (page 140).

**BY SEA** Several large passenger ships run daily between Dar es Salaam, Zanzibar and Pemba, and – more rarely – to other points on the mainland. As the number of flights between Dar and Zanzibar has increased, and their airfares have become more competitive, the number of passenger boat services has declined.

Ships that are used by occasional tourists are listed below. In both Dar es Salaam and Zanzibar Town, all the ship booking offices are at the main passenger port, very near the city centre. Schedules and prices are chalked up on boards outside each office, and you can easily buy tickets on the spot. Reservations are not essential but if you are on the spot a day or two (or even an hour or two) before you want to travel, you should buy a ticket in advance to make sure. Non-Tanzanians usually have to pay in US dollars and prices are quoted in this currency. Tanzanian residents enjoy cheaper rates, and can pay in Tanzanian shillings.

Note that all non-Tanzanian passengers leaving Dar must pay a port departure tax of US$5. The departure tax office is near the ship booking offices, and tickets are carefully checked before you board. Most of the shipping companies include this charge in the ticket price, so check very carefully whether this is included to avoid paying again unnecessarily at the port tax office.

In Zanzibar particularly, many touts and hustlers hang around the boat ticket offices, encouraging you to go to one company instead of another. This can be disconcerting, and as an alternative you can buy your ticket through one of the tour companies listed on pages 111–14. This will often save time and hassle, and it usually does not cost you any more money (the tour company gets a commission from the shipping company). Some tour companies do charge extra for this service, however, so check before you make arrangements. At Dar es Salaam, there are fewer hustlers, but still it's best to decline assistance politely.

Travellers at the port have also reported problems from over-zealous porters. If you drive into the port by taxi, you might want to ask your taxi driver to carry your bags for an extra tip, simply to avoid hassle.

Some shoestring travellers have been approached by baggage porters at the ferry port, and been tempted into buying ferry tickets at the (cheaper) residents' rate, rather than the foreigners' rate. The porter offers to buy the ticket for you, then accompanies you onto the boat, explaining to 'their friend' the ticket collector about your temporary residential status. Then, once you're on board the porter asks for (or demands) a tip – which is often more than the foreigners' ticket price. If you resist, you get reported to the no-longer-friendly ticket collector, who demands that you pay a costly fine. Resist that, and they'll call the police, who will no doubt be keen to extract their own, even more costly, fine. So you end up paying the porter more than the normal ferry price, and feeling cheap and embarrassed into the bargain.

Now it's our turn for a tip: always pay the correct fare.

Traditional dhows do still run between Dar es Salaam, Zanzibar and the ports along the Swahili coast, but – following a spate of incidents in which tourists drowned – the government has imposed strict safety standards on any dhows wanting to carry tourists. (They need to have radios, lifejackets, and various other fairly standard pieces of marine safety equipment – which are notably lacking from most dhows!)

We advise strongly against travelling illegally on any dhow unless the captain is very clearly aware of these regulations, and working within them. Not only is it illegal, but many 'normal' working dhows are dangerously overloaded, and quite frightening and unpleasant vessels in which to cross a busy stretch of open ocean.

**Passenger ships and ferries** The main passenger ships used by visitors between Dar es Salaam and Zanzibar are:

**Sea Bus I and Sea Bus II** ☎ 024 2231655 (Zanzibar)/022 212 3324 (Dar); m 0747 334347; e azam@cats-net.com; www.azam-marine.com. Highly recommended, these are 2 large Australian-built high-speed boats, owned by Azam Marine both running once daily in either direction between Zanzibar and Dar, taking about 2hrs to make the crossing. *Sea Bus I* departs from Dar es Salaam at 10.30 and starts the return trip from Zanzibar at 13.00. *Sea Bus II* departs from Zanzibar at 10.00 and starts the return trip from Dar es Salaam at 16.00. *First-class tickets cost US$40, second-class US$35, children US$20, inc tax.*

**Sea Star** ☎ 024 223 4768; m 0747 411505. This large catamaran is also among the most efficient services between Dar es Salaam and Zanzibar. It departs from Dar es Salaam at around 14.00, arriving at Zanzibar at around 15.45, then turning back more or less immediately to reach Dar between 17.30 and 18.00. *US$30 plus tax.*

**MV Sepideh** ☎ 024 223 2423; m 0747 303308. This nippy daily service between Dar es Salaam and Zanzibar also continues on to Pemba, taking around 2hrs for each leg. The daily timetable starts in Dar es Salaam at 07.00, departs from Zanzibar at 10.00, turning around in Pemba at 13.00, then leaving Zanzibar at 16.00, arriving back in Dar at around 18.30. *US$35 per leg inc port taxes.*

**Sea Express** ☎ 024 223 3002 (Zanzibar)/022 213 7049 (Dar); m 0744 278692; e zpd@cats-net.com. A large hydrofoil with a capacity of 150 passengers, this travels between Dar and Zanzibar once daily in each direction. The journey takes 90 minutes. Departures from Dar are at 16.00, from Zanzibar 07.00. This boat is reported to be unsteady in rough seas, and seasick-bags are not provided! There is no deck-space either. *US$35 inc tax.*

**Flying Horse** ☎ 024 223 3031 (Zanzibar)/022 212 4507 (Dar); m 0741 610884. This large catamaran, run by the African Shipping Corporation, has a capacity of more than 400 passengers. The daytime service from Dar to Zanzibar departs at 12.30 daily and arrives at 15.30. The trip from Zanzibar departs at 22.00 daily and arrives in Dar at 06.00 – the boat runs deliberately slowly on this overnight journey so passengers don't have to board or leave the boat in the middle of the night. The seating areas are air conditioned, and an 'in-flight' video is usually shown. The ship also has a small bar and restaurant. It's possible to travel on the deck, which has a few seats and an awning to keep off the sun, but little else. However, it is a very pleasant way to travel, especially when you come into Zanzibar port at sunset. *Tickets US$20 inc tax, inc mattress for overnight service.*

**Aziza I and Aziza II** Pride of the fleet is *Aziza I*, which together with *Aziza II* sails daily between Dar and Zanzibar, leaving at the same times as *Flying Horse*. Going the other way it's an overnight trip. The journey time is 5–8 hrs. *Dar–Zanzibar US$20, Zanzibar–Dar US$20, Zanzibar–Pemba US$20; all inc port tax.*

**Mapinduzi** ☏ 024 2230302/ 2857. Zanzibar Shipping Corporation (ZSC), the state-owned line, runs the *Mapinduzi* ('Revolution'), an old cargo–passenger ship, between Dar and Zanzibar, and also between Zanzibar and Pemba, and Dar and Mtwara on the southern coast of mainland Tanzania. These services are used by local people because they are cheap, and some travellers on a tight budget also travel this way. Although the boats are slow, the cabins are quite airy and comfortable, and this is a pleasant way to travel if you're in no hurry. The official schedule follows a 2-week pattern, although it is notoriously unreliable. *Around US$5 for a place on the deck, US$10 for a bed in a shared cabin, and US$12 for a bed in a private cabin.*

**SES II** ☏ 022 2137049. A new speedboat owned by Fast Ferries Ltd commenced operations between Dar, Zanzibar Island and Pemba in Nov 2005. Schedules are similar to those of the Sepideh, but the journey is around 30 mins faster. *Dar–Zanzibar US$35 1-way.*

## GETTING AROUND ZANZIBAR ISLAND

You can travel around Zanzibar Island in several different ways: by hire-car, motorbike, scooter, bicycle, tourist minibus, *dala-dala*, bus, taxi, organised tour, walking, hitchhiking, or a combination of all of these. Outside Zanzibar Town, the main roads are often tarred, whilst the rest are dirt or graded gravel. All are highly variable in quality, from smooth, newly resurfaced tar to appallingly rutted gravel, where travel can be slow and uncomfortable.

As in the rest of east and southern Africa, traffic drives on the left in Zanzibar.

### HIRED VEHICLES

🚗 **Car hire** Car hire is possible on Zanzibar Island, although whether it's wise for most visitors is a real question. Driving standards are not good on the islands and roads are often in poor condition, so accidents are frequent. We do not recommend visitors to hire cars here, but if you choose to then exercise great caution. You should *never* drive at night; it can be exceedingly dangerous.

If you do want a car, it's probably best arranged through one of the tour companies listed under *Organised tours* (pages 110–14). A few have their own vehicles, while others will make arrangements on your behalf. Rates vary but are generally between US$50 and US$60 per day for a small car (eg: a Suzuki 'jeep') and around US$100 per day for a larger car (eg: a Toyota Land Cruiser). However, quality is more variable than price, and standards on Zanzibar are often low; check your car very carefully for defects and even go for a short test drive before accepting it. The price usually includes unlimited distance, but you pay for the fuel.

Insurance is normally included in the rental, although some companies are vague about this. It's always important to check your exact legal position should you be unfortunate enough to have an accident involving another car or person. Get this in writing. A deposit and proof of identity are usually asked for. Make sure you have a valid IDP or local driving permit. (See *Driving licences*, page 109.)

🛵 **Motorbike and scooter hire** It is possible to hire motorbikes (almost all are Honda 125cc or 250cc trail bikes or similar) or scooters (mostly Vespas and Piaggios) from many of the tour companies listed under *Organised tours* (pages 110–14). Prices vary, but are generally around US$25–30 per day for a scooter, US$35–40 per day for a motorbike.

For a cheaper deal, try Nasor Aly Mussa's Scooter Service, usually shortened to Fundi Nasor, a small garage just off New Mkunazini Road in Zanzibar Town, near the Anglican Cathedral. As with cars, you should take your scooter for a test drive to make sure everything works before agreeing to hire.

Some tourists to Zanzibar hire scooters, imagining them to be similar to Greek-island-style mopeds. However, scooters have larger engines and are harder to handle than mopeds, and there have been a number of accidents and injuries. You should not hire a scooter if you have never ridden one before; the dirt tracks and pot-holed roads of Zanzibar are not ideal places to start learning.

Check beforehand that your travel insurance policy covers you for using this type of transport, as not all do.

**Bicycle hire** For getting around Zanzibar Town, or going further afield around the island, fit and adventurous visitors will find bicycles ideal. Most bikes are heavy steel Chinese-built roadsters, so you shouldn't plan on covering too many miles (it's too hot to cycle fast anyway). You can also hire mountain bikes, but most of these are pretty basic all-steel models, and only slightly lighter than the Chinese roadsters. They do have gears though, which makes them easier to ride.

Bikes can be hired through several of the tour companies listed under *Organised tours* (pages 110–14). Daily rates start at US$10 for the Chinese roadsters, and US$15 for mountain bikes. Take your bike for a short test ride before hiring to make sure everything works. Unless you plan extensive off-road forays, make sure your tyres are pumped up fairly hard, especially on the mountain bikes where semi-flat fat tyres can make for hard going. Your bike should come with a puncture outfit and pump, but if it doesn't these can be bought from the bicycle fundi (mechanic) in the market in Zanzibar Town.

Roads can be rough, but are generally flat, and traffic is very light once you get away from Zanzibar Town. If you get tired, you can put your bike on top of a bus or *dala-dala* and come home the easy way.

Keen cyclists might like to contact Mreh Tours (listed on page 112) – the only company as far as we know to offer specific cycle tours of Zanzibar.

**Taxis** The saloon car taxis which are available around Zanzibar Town can be hired to take you further afield, but some drivers do not like to go off the tar roads as the rocky dirt roads are liable to damage the undersides of their beloved vehicles (the minibuses have higher clearance, or at least the drivers seem not to worry).

A short ride through town will cost just over US$1, a trip further afield to Mbweni Ruins or Mtoni Marine Centre around US$5–7 (one way), and an airport transfer to/from Zanzibar Town US$10–15. A taxi to Jozani Forest is US$20–25 one-way, or around US$30–35 return, possibly more if you plan to spend all day in the forest. To Nungwi or Bwejuu is around US$30 one-way. If you're going this far, then it's probably best to arrange for a proper minibus and guide to take you.

**Tourist minibuses** On Zanzibar Island, most travellers will get between Zanzibar Town and one of the beaches using a minibus. These can be arranged by the *papaasi* (touts – see box on page 118) who lurk at budget hotels looking for custom. A ride in one of these vehicles can cost as little as US$3–5, although often the papaasi will have their own favourite beach places, which pay them a commission for each visitor who stays; make sure you are very clear about your destination, the timings and the cost before getting on board.

If haggling with the papaasi is not for you, then most local travel agents can arrange a reliable private minibus from Zanzibar Town to any beach lodge for about US$50 per vehicle.

Alternatively, if you know which lodge you want to go to, call them and ask them to arrange a minibus for you; they will often do this through a reliable travel agent with whom they work.

If you have pre-arranged your trip, then you'll probably be met at the airport by a driver and vehicle who will transfer you to your chosen lodge. Sometimes it's easy to incorporate a visit to a spice farm on the way, as part of these transfers.

## PUBLIC TRANSPORT
### Buses

It is possible to reach many parts of Zanzibar Island by public bus, although few visitors use their services. (Most use tourist minibuses or *dala-dalas*.) All buses leave from the market area, or from Darajani Bus Station, both on Creek Road in Zanzibar Town. Fares are very cheap: for example, it costs about only US$1 to travel half the length of the island between Zanzibar Town and Bwejuu. Note, however, that prices can rise suddenly if there is a fuel shortage.

On most routes, especially the longer ones, there is only one bus each day. They usually leave Zanzibar Town around midday to take people back to their villages after visiting the market. They reach their destinations in the evening, and 'sleep' there before returning to Zanzibar Town very early in the morning (between 02.00 and 04.00) in time for the start of that day's market. Some of the longer journeys can be very slow. For example, Zanzibar Town to Nungwi takes three to five hours, Zanzibar Town to Makunduchi between four and eight hours.

The bus route numbers and destinations are:

**Route No 1**, to Mkokotoni, on the west coast, north of Zanzibar Town, occasionally continuing to Nungwi, on the north coast

**Route No 2**, to Bumbwini and Makoba, on the west coast, north of Zanzibar Town, via Mangapwani

**Route No 3**, to Kidichi and Kizimbani, an area of plantations to the northeast of Zanzibar Town, via Welezo

**Route No 4**, to Mchangani, in the centre of the island, northeast of Zanzibar Town, via Dunga, Bambi and Uzini (some buses also go to Umbuji)

**Route No 5**, to Ndagaa, in the centre of the island, northeast of Zanzibar Town, via Kiboje

**Route No 6**, to Chwaka, about halfway down the east coast (some buses continue to Uroa and Pongwe)

**Route No 7**, to Fumba, at the end of a peninsula south of Zanzibar Town, via Kombeni

**Route No 8**, to Unguja Ukuu, about halfway down the southwest coast, opposite Uzi Island

**Route No 9**, to Paje, on the east coast, and sometimes to Bwejuu and Jambiani

**Route No 10**, to Makunduchi, at the southern end of the east coast, via Tunguu, Pete and Munyuni

**Route No 11**, to Fuoni, about 7km east of Zanzibar Town, via Tungu and Binguni

**Route No 13**, to Dunga (on the east coast road) then north to Bambi

**Route No 14**, to Uroa on the east coast, north of Chwaka

**Route No 16**, to Nungwi, via Mahonda, Kiniasini and Chaani

**Route No 17**, to Kiwengwa, on the east coast, north of Uroa

**Route No 18**, to Matemwe, on the northern part of the east coast.

Buses do not always go to their final destination. For example, bus No 1 (the route for Nungwi) may only go as far as Mkokotoni. Therefore, always check that the bus is going to the destination you think it should be.

Some of the bus routes listed above are also covered by public minibuses or *dala-dalas*, which fill the gaps in the bus service 'timetables'. These are usually slightly more expensive than the buses, but also tend to be quicker.

**Public minibuses and dala-dalas** For independent travellers, local minibuses and small converted trucks called *dala-dalas* cover many routes around Zanzibar Island. On Pemba, minibuses and *dala-dalas* link Chake Chake to the towns of Wete and

Mkoani, and also serve outlying villages. Minibuses and *dala-dalas* are faster than buses, and gradually replacing them on the roads. Fares are cheap: typically around US$0.35 around Zanzibar Town and US$1 to cross the island.

Buses and *dalas-dalas* from outlying villages heading for Zanzibar Town tend to leave very early in the morning but, apart from that, there are no fixed timetables: most vehicles simply leave when they're full. At any bus or *dala-dala* station, don't expect an information board: you will need to ask around to find the transport you need.

## HITCHHIKING

Hitching around Zanzibar Island is possible, but traffic can be light so you will need patience. However, a combination of public transport, walking and hitching is sometimes the only way to travel – and simply a mater of taking the first vehicle which will give you a lift. You should usually expect to pay a few dollars for a lift.

## PRACTICALITIES

**Driving licences** Unlike mainland Tanzania, you need an International Driving Permit (IDP) or a 'local driving permit' to drive either cars or motorcycles legally on Zanzibar.

An IDP is easy to obtain from your national motoring association (eg: in Britain contact the AA), provided that you have a standard driving licence at home. If applying by post, the process takes time so order one well in advance of your trip.

The alternative is a local driving permit, which can be issued for you in Zanzibar. The rental company can usually organise this for you with minimal fuss for about US$10.

It is essential that you have either this or an IDP if you drive a car or a motorcycle on the islands; your own national driving licence is not enough. Enforcing this, the traffic police on Zanzibar routinely stop any tourist they see behind a wheel. (There are several checkpoints on the roads between Zanzibar Town and the north and east coasts.) If you do not have either an IDP or a local driving permit then you'll have repeatedly to pay small bribes or a heftier official fine.

Beware of eager tour companies who are keen to rent you a car and say that IDPs are not essential. Also watch out for a scam where local papaasi rent you a motorbike claiming that an IDP is not needed, before informing the police, who then find and fine you.

**Petrol and diesel** Petrol is available (usually, but not with total reliability) in Zanzibar Town, and at Kiniasini, on the road to Nungwi, and at Kitogoni, near the junction where the road turns off to Paje.

Petrol costs about US$0.90 per litre (Tsh1,050/litre), and diesel is very slightly cheaper (Tsh1,020/litre). Occasional fuel shortages in outlying parts of the island mean it is generally worth filling up in Zanzibar Town, though in an emergency it is normally possible to locate 'black market' fuel at about 20% above the standard pump price.

**Maps** A straightforward tourist map of Zanzibar Town and Zanzibar Island is available from the Zanzibar Tourist Corporation offices, and from some bookshops and hotels in the town. It costs around US$2. Better than this is the excellent hand-drawn map of Zanzibar Stone Town and Zanzibar Island produced by local artist Giovanni, which is widely available. The Zanzibar Island map on the reverse is at a scale of about 1:100,000. This is part of a wider series of maps, including many of the national parks and mountains of mainland Tanzania.

The *Gallery Map of Zanzibar* is available in the bookshop of the same name. The map of Zanzibar Island is not as clear to read as the Giovanni map, but the map of Stone Town is clear and useful.

A map called *Pemba: The Clove Island* is available in some book and gift shops, and is well researched at a scale of 1:100,000. There are two versions however: one from 1992, and a better one from 1995. The date is on the back cover.

Most commercially produced maps of Tanzania also include Zanzibar. One of the best is the *Tanzania Travellers Map* published by Macmillan, which shows the mainland at a scale of 1:2,000,000 and has more detailed maps of Zanzibar Island (1:500,000) and Pemba Island (1:830,000) on the back, although even these contain a few errors.

Good-quality maps of Zanzibar and Pemba islands (produced by the British Directorate of Overseas Surveys at scales of 1:50,000 and 1:10,000) are available in Zanzibar Town from the Map Office in the Commission of Lands and Planning, part of the Ministry of Environment, near the People's Bank of Zanzibar and the Fort. Maps cost about US$2.

## ORGANISED TOURS

In Zanzibar Town, it seems that every other shop or office is a tour company, and it's always easy to find someone to arrange/organise tours within Zanzibar. The problem is finding a good tour company, and the following section should help you locate something suitable.

The most popular tours organised from Zanzibar Town are boat excursions to Prison Island and the trips around the plantations called 'spice tours'. (see the *Spices and spice tours* box, pages 112–13). Most companies also arrange tours to Jozani-Chwaka Bay National Park to see the colobus monkeys (page 251), trips to Kizimkazi to see the dolphins (page 247), and visits to old palaces and other ruins in the Zanzibar Town area (page 161–3) or elsewhere on the island. You can also usually arrange transport to the beaches on the north or east coasts and other parts of Zanzibar with a tour company.

Many companies can also make hotel and ship reservations, flight bookings, car hire arrangements, and so on. Check the arrangement before organising this: some make no charge for the service (instead getting commission from the transport company or hotel), whilst others charge a small fee. Watch out for those charging a hefty fee for the service, which can sometimes be no more than a couple of phone calls on your behalf.

Tour prices are usually quoted in US dollars (although they can be paid for in TSh or other currencies), and tend to vary considerably between the different companies. A lot depends on the quality you're looking for. At one end of the scale, budget outfits offer cheap and cheerful tours, where you'll be sharing a basic minibus or *dala-dala* with several other tourists, and the quality or knowledge of your guide may be poor. At the other end of the scale, you can arrange a private tour for just a couple of people, in a good-quality vehicle, often with air conditioning, and a knowledgeable guide. Good companies can provide guides who speak English, French, German, Italian and some other languages.

This is not to knock the cheaper outfits: many tourists go on budget tours and have an excellent time. In the same way, some of the so-called upmarket companies may rest on their laurels a bit and not be up to scratch. It is therefore worth comparing a few tour companies before finally arranging your tour, and when comparing prices it is also very important to compare exactly what you get for your money. Your best source of recommendations (good or bad) is always other tourists and travellers, so talk to some of them if you can before signing up for anything.

All the companies listed here have been recommended by the authors or readers of previous editions of this book.

To get an idea of prices, companies running tours which you share with other people (4–8) offer the following rates:

| | | | |
|---|---|---|---|
| Prison Island Tour | US$20 | Dolphin Tour | US$30–40 |
| Spice Tour | US$15–20 | Jozani Forest Tour | US$20–25 |
| City Tour | US$15 | | |

All these rates are per person, but for the tour only, and do not include extras like entrance fees (for the Palace Museum this is US$2, for Prison Island US$4, for Jozani Forest US$4).

If you want a private tour, with a mid-range or top-quality tour company, the rates are more likely to be around: Prison Island US$35; City Tour US$20; Jozani Forest US$35; Spice Tour US$30–55; Dolphin Tour US$65; Nungwi US$50–65. These prices are per person, for a minimum of two passengers, and usually include all entrance fees, although you should check this when booking or comparing prices.

While in Zanzibar you can also use tour companies to set you up with tours to Pemba, the Tanzanian mainland, Kenya and even further afield. In recent years there's been significant growth in the number of companies offering fly-in safaris to the national parks of Selous and Ruaha in southern Tanzania. Logistically it's easier to get there than to the northern parks of Serengeti and Ngorongoro, although many companies offer this option, too.

All tour companies have to be licensed by the government of Zanzibar and, if you have a reason to be dissatisfied, you can complain to the Ministry of Tourism who may take action against the company on your behalf. In reality, there's little control but it's still best to use only registered companies. If you decide to use unofficial operators, take care. We heard of a group of travellers who arranged things with a company which turned out to be bogus, and were then attacked and robbed when their minibus was on a remote stretch of road. The whole thing appeared to be a scam set up between the driver and the robbers, but don't let it worry you too much – it was an isolated event.

Most of the companies listed here can arrange tours on the spot (or with a day's notice), but you can also make prior arrangements by phoning, faxing or emailing in advance.

**TOUR COMPANIES** Recommended tour companies based in Zanzibar Town include the following (listed alphabetically):

**Eco & Culture Tours** ✆ 024 36808; e ecoculture@gmx.net; www.ecoculture-zanzibar.org. Relatively new on the scene, this tour company (situated on Hurumzi St opposite Emerson & Green Hotel) is deliberately not trying to do what all the other companies do. For example, instead of the ubiquitous 'standard' spice tour, it takes guests to plantations and gardens guided by a local herbalist, and as well as a visit to Jozani Forest, walks in the community forest at Ufufuma are arranged. Village tours are another option – a good opportunity to meet local people, whereas dolphin trips are avoided. Trips are slightly more expensive than those arranged by some other tour companies in Zanzibar but they are refreshingly different. The eventual plan is for profits from tours to be put back into various community schemes around the island.

**Fernandes Tours & Safaris** PO Box 647; ✆ 024 2230666; e fts@zanlink.com. This small, friendly and well-connected company on Vuga Rd used to work mainly with incoming tour groups from Britain, South Africa and elsewhere, but is now branching out to provide good-quality tailor-made trips around Zanzibar for groups and individuals in the mid-range price bracket. You can arrange things on the spot, or in advance.

5

*Gemma Pitcher*

Sooner or later every visitor to Zanzibar Island (Unguja) will be offered a 'spice tour' – a trip to the farmlands just outside Stone Town to see aromatic plants and herbs growing wild or cultivated in kitchen-gardens. Even if you decline a tour, the array of spices on offer in the souvenir shops or heaped in baskets in the local markets will tell you that spice is central to Zanzibar's history and economy.

The history of spices in Zanzibar begins early in the 16th century, when the 'spice race' between the major European powers to control the lucrative trading routes to the Far East was at its height. Portuguese traders gained a toe-hold on Zanzibar as part of their plan to rule the coast of east Africa and imported various plants, including spices, from their colonies in South America and India. Some land was cleared for plantations, but the Portuguese never really developed their presence on Zanzibar beyond a military one.

It was left to the Omani Arabs, who ruled Zanzibar from the early 19th century, to develop Zanzibar economically as a spice-producing entity. Sultan Seyyid Said, the first Omani sultan to govern Zanzibar, quickly realised the potential of his new dominion, with its hot climate and regular rainfall, as a location for spice farming. With the demise of the slave trade in the late 19th century, spices became Zanzibar's main source of income.

When the era of the sultans ended and the long arm of the British Empire reached Zanzibar, the island's new colonial administrators encouraged the farming of spices and other useful plants, bringing European scientists to establish experimental agricultural

**Fisherman Tours** ✎ 024 2238791–2, 0777 412996–7; f 024 228790; e reservation@fishermantours.net; www.fishermantours.net. This well-established and experienced company on Vuga Rd has skilled and efficient staff, and caters for overseas tour groups, as well as individuals and small parties, offering a complete guide and escort service. They have their own fleet of vehicles, and most drivers are equipped with mobile phones. Other services include the organisation of wildlife safaris on mainland Tanzania, as well as the usual tours around Zanzibar, plus car hire, hotel bookings, ground transfers and so on. In 1999, Fisherman Tours received quality awards from 2 business organisations based in Europe and America. The office is near Air Tanzania and they have full credit card facilities.

**Madeira Tours** ✎/f 024 2230406; e madeira@zanzinet.com. All the usual tours are offered by this switched-on and efficient company situated opposite Baghani House Hotel, plus air ticket reservations, safaris on the mainland, and car, motorbike and bicycle hire.

**Mreh Tours** ✎ 024 2233476; e mrehtours@zanzinet.com. This company offers all the usual tours, and is especially keen on bicycle hire and tours by bike. One itinerary is a 9-day

cycling trip around the island (no doddle even on Zanzibar's flat roads, as the bikes are the traditional steel Chinese models, not tip-top lightweight jobs), though shorter, more manageable variations are possible. Costs are around US$50 a day inc bike, food, drink and back-up vehicle. Basically, if you have the slightest interest in cycling, call in at their office on Baghani St, near the Chavda Hotel, and discuss the options with Saleh Mreh Salum, the energetic and friendly owner.

**Sama Tours** ✎/f 024 2233543; ✎ 0741 608576/0777 430385/0777 431665; e samatours@zitec.org; www.samatours.com. As well as spice tours, boat trips and all the usual services, the friendly and helpful team at Sama Tours on Gizenga St arranges cultural tours, giving visitors an opportunity to meet local people: recommended by clients as a great opportunity for photos. Guides speak English, French, German and Italian. Sama Tours also offers 'special' spice tours, organised by one of the knowledgeable, multi-lingual owners, Salim Abdullah. Sama Tours caters for both groups (anything from cruise ships to overland trucks) and individuals seeking tailor-made tours, airport and port collection, hotels, excursions, transfers, car hire, and so on. Prices depend on the length of the tour, the services required and the number in the group.

stations and government farms such as those at Kizimbani and Kindichi. Today these areas still contain spice plantations controlled by the modern Tanzanian government.

But spices in Zanzibar today are by no means simply the preserve of governments keen to produce cash-rich export products or a useful tourist attraction. For the ordinary people of Zanzibar, spices and useful plants are a vital part of everyday life and a rich element in the island's strong and vibrant culture. The spices grown in village kitchen-gardens give their flavour to the distinctive cuisine of Zanzibar, provide innumerable cures for everyday ailments, and yield the dyes and cosmetic products needed to celebrate weddings and festivals.

A spice tour is probably the best way of seeing the countryside around Stone Town and meeting rural communities. Guides take you on a walking tour of the villages and plantations at Kizimbani or Kindichi, picking bunches of leaves, fruit and twigs from bushes and inviting you to smell or taste them to guess what they are. Pretty much all the ingredients of the average kitchen spice rack are represented – cinnamon, turmeric, ginger, garlic, chillies, black pepper, nutmeg and vanilla among many others. Local children follow you all the way round, making baskets of palm leaves and filling them with flowers to give to you. At lunchtime, you'll stop in a local house for a meal of pilau rice and curry, followed by sweet Arabic coffee and perhaps a slice of lemongrass cake. Many spice tours include a visit to the Persian baths built by Sultan Said for his harem, and stop at Fuji or Mangapwani beaches just outside Stone Town for a swim on the way back.

All in all, even if horticulture isn't one of your interests, a spice tour is still an excellent way of gaining an insight into one of the most important aspects of rural life in Zanzibar.

This company has an office on Gizenga St, behind the House of Wonders.

**Sun N Fun Safaris** ☎ 024 2237381/024 2237665/0741 600206;
e zanzibarsun@hotmail.com. In the same building as the waterfront Sea View Indian Restaurant, and with the same enthusiastic management, this company can set you up with absolutely anything, usually at a very reasonable price. It runs tours of Zanzibar Town and the island, provides transfer services to the airport or east coast, and can help with general tourist information on the island and beyond. It can also assist with visas, car and bike hire, boat trips, flight tickets and bus tickets, in Zanzibar and on the mainland. The office sells postcards, stamps (it has a mailbox), maps and souvenirs of the 'I love Zanzibar' sticker variety.

**Suna Tours** ☎ 024 2237344. Suna is run by the formidable Naila Majid Jiddawi, a former Zanzibari MP and bastion of Zanzibar tourism promotion. The company represents some mid-range hotels on the east coast and can assist with reservations for any other hotel on the coast, as well as arranging transport, good-quality spice tours and trips to the islands. The company office is in a small white building at the end of Forodhani Gardens, near the Arab Fort, and the staff here are very happy to

provide general tourist information, even if you don't take one of their tours.

**Tropical Tours** ☎ 024 2230868/0777 413454; e tropicalts@hotmail.com. From a small but highly efficient office, this straightforward and friendly budget company has been recommended by several travellers, and offers the usual range of tours (a spice tour, dolphins, Jozani Forest, Nungwi and Prison Island trips), plus car hire, and ferry and air ticket reservations. It's on Kenyatta Rd, opposite Mazson's Hotel.

**ZanTours** ☎/f 024 2233042/3116; ☎ 0777 417279; e zantoursinfo@zitec.org; www.zantours.com. This company confidently entered the tourist scene in 1997, and is now one of the largest operators in Zanzibar, if not the largest. It has a smart office in the Malindi area, trained efficient staff, a fleet of modern vehicles and an impressive range of tours, transfers, excursions and safaris. They cater for groups of any size (from several hundred to just a few) inc individuals wanting tailor-made services. You can walk in and they'll set something up on the spot, although most of their clients arrange things in advance by email. ZanTours is closely allied to ZanAir (see page 104) and some tours utilise their fleet of planes. One of their most popular tours is a short fly-in excursion from Zanzibar direct to the Selous

National Park in southern Tanzania, which many other agents sell. For more details see *Chapter 14*, page 315.

**Zanzibar Excursions** ☏ 024 2237281; m 0777 410414; e info@zanzibarexcursions.com; www.zanzibarexcursions.com. Situated in the Old Fort, this responsive and long-serving company offers a wide selection of tours around the island, as well as organising vehicle hire, transfers, hotel reservations, air tickets, and safaris to the mainland.

**Zenith Tours** ☏ 024 2232320/0777 413084; f 024 2233973; e zenithtours@zitec.com; www.zenithtours.net. This very professional and efficient organisation, situated behind the Old Fort, offers transfers, accommodation and excursions in the mid-range price bracket, inc safaris to the mainland.

**INDEPENDENT GUIDES** If you prefer not to use a tour company, it is possible to arrange a tour of the spice plantations, a boat trip to the islands or transport to the east coast with an independent guide. Many double as taxi drivers; in fact many are taxi drivers first, and guides second. One driver, a Mr Mitu, has been doing these tours for many years and has been recommended by many visitors, although sometimes he subcontracts work to other drivers. These days he's so popular that instead of Mr Mitu in his taxi you might find yourself joining a large group touring the island in a fleet of minibuses. He's even got his own office (☏ *024 2234636;* m *0777 418098*) – a tiny room tucked away behind the Ciné Afrique with the walls covered in photos. Mr Mitu's tours leave from outside the Ciné Afrique every morning at 09.30, returning about 15.00, cost US$10 per person and are still highly recommended by those who have been.

There are several other taxi drivers who also organise their own spice tours. Most will undercut the tour companies (about US$30 for the car seems average), although you may not get the same degree of information that you'd get with a specialist guide.

You are almost certain to meet some of the local independent 'guides' who are in fact just hustlers (see the *Guides and the papaasi* box, page 118) who tout for business outside hotels and restaurants, or along the streets of Stone Town. For spice tours, papaasi prices are often cheaper than those offered by regular companies; but the tours are usually shorter, the vehicles out of condition, and without a proper guide, which usually makes the whole thing pointless unless you are a fairly skilled botanist.

For boat trips to the island it doesn't usually make much difference if you go with the papaasi or a regular company, although if you deal with the papaasi and things go wrong, it is very difficult to complain or get your money back.

# Part Two

## THE GUIDE

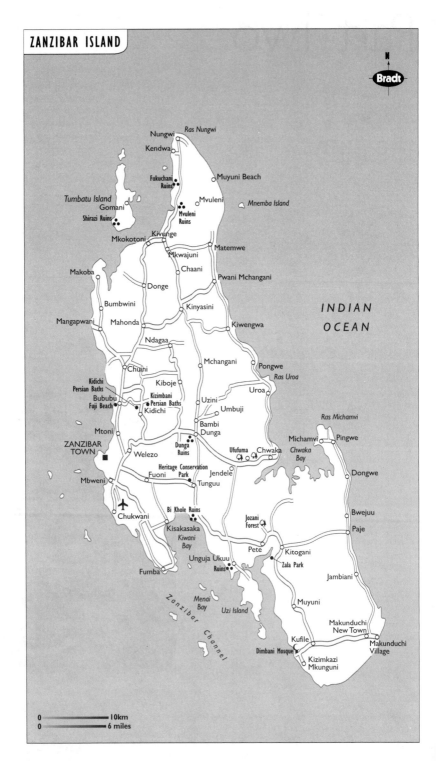

ZANZIBAR ISLAND

N
**Bradt**

Nungwi
Ras Nungwi
Kendwa
Fukuchani
Ruins
Muyuni Beach
Tumbatu Island
Gomani
Shirazi Ruins
Mvuleni
Mvuleni
Ruins
Mnemba Island
Mkokotoni
Kivunge
Mkwajuni
Matemwe
Chaani
Makoba
Pwani Mchangani
Donge
Bumbwini
Kinyasini
Mangapwani
Mahonda
Kiwengwa
Ndagaa
INDIAN
OCEAN
Mchangani
Pongwe
Chuini
Ras Uroa
Kiboje
Uroa
Kidichi
Persian Baths
Kizimbani
Persian Baths
Uzini
Bububu
Fuji Beach
Kidichi
Umbuji
Mtoni
Bambi
Dunga
Ras Michamvi
Michamvi
Pingwe
ZANZIBAR
TOWN
Dunga
Ruins
Ufufuma
Chwaka
Chwaka
Bay
Welezo
Heritage Conservation
Park
Jendele
Dongwe
Fuoni
Mbweni
Tunguu
Bwejuu
Bi Khole Ruins
Chukwani
Jozani
Forest
Paje
Kisakasaka
Kiwani
Bay
Pete
Kitogani
Zala Park
Unguja Ukuu
Ruins
Jambiani
Fumba
Menai
Bay
Muyuni
Uzi Island
Makunduchi
New Town
Kufile
Makunduchi
Village
Dimbani Mosque
Kizimkazi
Mkunguni

0 ——— 10km
0 ——— 6 miles

# 6

# Zanzibar Town

The streets are, as they should be under such a sky, deep and winding alleys, hardly twenty feet broad, and travellers compare them to the threads of a tangled skein.

Richard Burton, British explorer (1857)

Zanzibar Town, sometimes called Zanzibar City, is situated about halfway along the west coast of Zanzibar Island. It has a population estimated at 205,870 in the 2002 national census, which makes it by far the largest settlement on the islands of Zanzibar, and the sixth largest in Tanzania. During the colonial period, before the development of towns such as Dar es Salaam, Nairobi and Mombasa, Zanzibar Town was the largest settlement in the whole of east Africa.

Zanzibar Town is divided into two sections by Creek Road, though the creek itself has now been reclaimed. On the west side is the 'heart' of Zanzibar Town: the evocative old quarter, usually called Stone Town. This is the most interesting section for visitors: many of the buildings here were constructed during the 19th century (although some date from before this time), when Zanzibar was a major trading centre and at the height of its power. The trade created wealth which in turn led to the construction of palaces, mosques and many fine houses. Discovering the architectural gems hidden along the tortuous maze of narrow streets and alleyways that wind though Stone Town is part of the town's magic and mystery for many visitors. Aside from the souvenir tinga-tinga painting and beaded jewellery, it's a scene virtually unchanged since the mid-19th century, when it was described by Burton in this chapter's epigraph.

On the east side of Creek Road is Michenzani, or the 'New City', though this part of town used to be called Ng'ambo (literally 'the other side') and is still often referred to by its unofficial name. It's a sprawling area of mainly single-storey houses, local shops and offices, covering a much wider area than Stone Town. This used to be where the poorer African and Swahili people lived, while wealthier Arabs, Indians and Europeans lived in Stone Town. To a large extent this rich–poor division still exists today. Some attempt has been made to 'modernise' this area: at the centre of Michenzani are some dreary, uninviting blocks of flats (apartment buildings) which were built in the late 1960s by East German engineers as part of an international aid scheme. Few visitors go to this eastern part of Zanzibar Town, as there is little in the way of 'sights', though a visit certainly helps to broaden your perception if you realise that outside the tourist areas of Stone Town is a place where many thousands of real people live and work in much less exotic, but no less authentic, surroundings.

The best way to explore Stone Town is on foot, but the maze of lanes and alleys can be very disorientating. To help you get your bearings, it is useful to think of Stone Town as a triangle, bounded on two sides by sea, and along the third by Creek Road (see the *Zanzibar Stone Town* map on pages 128–30). If you get lost, it is always possible to aim in one direction until you reach the outer edge of the town where you should find a recognisable landmark.

Nearly all tourists who come to Zanzibar Town use the services of a guide at some stage during their visit. If you come on an organised tour arranged at home, this will of course include the services of a guide. Even if you arrange something simple through a tour company on the spot, like a trip to the spice plantations, the price always includes a guide to show you around. Guides from reputable companies have to be registered with the Tourism Commission, and will carry identity cards.

There are also many other guides in Zanzibar who are not registered. Most of these are not really guides at all, but touts and hustlers who make their money showing tourists to hotels and souvenir shops, arranging transport or getting groups together to share boat rides. These touts are known locally as beach-boys or *papaasi* – literally meaning 'ticks', ie: parasites or irritating blood-suckers.

When a ship comes into Zanzibar from Dar es Salaam, there is usually a group of *papaasi* on the dockside. Some can be quite aggressive, but a few are not too unpleasant and will help you find a place to stay (which may be useful, as the labyrinth of alleys in Stone Town is disorientating at first). Tell them exactly what you want in terms of standard and price. It should not cost you any more money (the *papaasi* get a commission from the hotel) and could save you a lot of walking.

Unfortunately, this plan does not always work, as some hotels pay more commission than others, and some do not pay at all, so the *papaasi* will only take you to the places where they get a decent cut. We have heard from several travellers who arrived on Zanzibar, aiming to stay in a certain hotel only to be told by the welcome party of *papaasi* that it was 'full', 'closed' or even 'burnt down'. If you're in any doubt, it is best to be polite but firm (or simply ignore them completely), and find your own hotel. Even better, make a phone call or send an email to reserve a room in advance; some hotels even give discounts for advance bookings.

After arranging your hotel, most *papaasi* will want to be your 'guide', offering to show you around the sights or souvenir shops of Stone Town, find companions for dive trips or boat excursions, or arrange transport to the east coast. Use these services if you need them but be prepared to pay if necessary, or be aware that the owners of the souvenir shops, boats and dive centres will have to pay commission to the *papaasi*, a charge which will of course be passed on to you.

Some *papaasi* are outright crooks, and involved in robberies and other crimes like drug dealing. Others are con-men, and some travellers have been stung arranging budget hire cars where a *papaasi* has taken a deposit then simply disappeared. Changing money is another potentially expensive operation, where initially tempting good rates precede sleight-of-hand tricks or simply snatch and run theft. Budget travellers have also reported having drugs planted on them by *papaasi* they befriended, who then reported them to the police; any fines (official or unofficial) paid out included a kickback to the informant.

If you deal only with reputable tour companies (whether low or high budget) you'll have none of these problems. Although trustworthy guides have identity cards, some *papaasi* have managed to get some too (they could be fakes, or simply stolen – it's hard to tell). This of course is confusing for tourists. There is a need for legitimate guides on Zanzibar, who can help tourists without hassling them, and it is hoped that the government department responsible for tourism will apply itself to this matter in the near future.

Although most of the thoroughfares in Stone Town are too narrow for cars, when walking you should watch out for bikes and scooters being ridden around at breakneck speed! It's also useful to realise that thoroughfares wide enough for cars are usually called roads while narrower ones are generally referred to as streets. Hence, you can drive along New Mkunazini Road or Kenyatta Road, but to visit a place on Kiponda Street or Mkunazini Street you have to walk. When looking for hotels or places of interest, you should also note that most areas of Stone Town are named after the main street in that area: the area being referred to as Kiponda Street or Malindi Street, instead of simply Kiponda or Malindi. This can be confusing, as you may not be on the street of that name. But don't worry: at least you're near!

## TRAVEL AROUND ZANZIBAR TOWN

Most visitors and locals get around the town on foot, and in Stone Town this is the best and often only way, but there are other means of transport available.

**TAXI** Private taxis for hire wait at taxi ranks around town; they do not usually cruise for business, although if you see a taxi in the street it is always possible to flag it down. The main taxi ranks are near the BP petrol station on Creek Road, outside the ZanAir office just east of the Port Gates, beside the House of Wonders, in front of the Serena Inn, and at the northern end of Kenyatta Road.

There are no meters. Wherever you go, you should check the fare with the driver *before* starting your journey. A short ride through town costs US$1.50 to US$2. All the way across town costs US$2 to US$3. A longer ride, from town out to Mtoni Marine Centre or Mbweni Ruins Hotel will be about US$3–5. From town to the airport is around US$10, and it should be the same the other way, but from the airport into town, taxi drivers may quote fares of US$20 or higher.

One last thing to remember: if there is a petrol shortage, taxi fares go up.

**DALA-DALA** Converted small lorries with two rows of wooden seats at the back, called *dala-dalas* (or dalas for short) carry passengers on local runs around town and to outlying suburbs. There are several routes, all starting at the Darajani Bus Station on Creek Road. The most useful routes for visitors are:

**Route A**, to Amaani Stadium and the eastern part of the New Town, via the Main Post Office;
**Route B**, along the coast road north of Zanzibar Town, to Bububu, near Fuji Beach;
**Route U**, along the main road south of Zanzibar Town, to the airport (Uwanje ya Ndege).

If you go the whole way, *dala-dala* fares are about US$0.20 on Route A, and about US$0.25 on Routes B and U. If you travel only part of the route, the fare is slightly cheaper.

**BICYCLE** For getting around Zanzibar Town and the surrounding area, a bike is very handy. Bikes can be hired from several of the tour companies listed in this chapter. They are either sturdy steel Chinese-made models, or more modern looking (though almost as heavy) mountain bikes. Prices for Chinese bikes are about US$10 per day. Mountain bikes are US$15 per day. A deposit of around US$50 may be required.

**CAR AND MOTORBIKE** A car or motorbike is not really necessary or practical for getting around Zanzibar Town as distances are short and parking is often difficult. However, both can be hired from various tour companies listed in *Chapter 5* (see

Theft from hotel rooms is very unusual, but we've heard from some readers of a scam played by staff in one of the less reputable hotels in Zanzibar Town. Apparently, the guests left a small bag of valuables (passport, air tickets, money, etc) in the hotel safe, only to find items missing when they returned to collect it. It seems that a member of staff had a duplicate key to the safe and removed a few US$20 bills in the hope that the theft wouldn't be noticed. The only way to prevent this happening to you is to store your valuables in a lockable bag or pouch, to prevent tampering when it's out of your hands, or count and write down everything you have in the presence of the receptionist (although this can be embarrassing and possibly a bit too tempting). This is not a problem at hotels in the middle and upper price ranges, because most offer individual safe deposit boxes, either at reception or in the rooms, and several of the budget hotels in Zanzibar Town now run an organised system with a book for guests to write in exactly what they leave.

More serious robberies (sometimes with violence) have occurred on some of the beaches in and around Zanzibar Town. You should not walk here alone, particularly after dark. Other notorious parts of town include the port, and the area around the Garage Club and the Bashasha Bar, especially late at night when drunken youths wander the streets looking for kicks (just as they do in many other parts of the world). Another time to be wary is the hour or two just after sunset during the period of Ramadan, when everybody is inside breaking their fast, and the streets are absolutely deserted.

pages 111–14). Prices vary, but are generally around US$25 to US$30 per day for a scooter, US$35 to US$40 per day for a motorbike, between US$50 and US$60 per day for a small car (eg: a Suzuki 'jeep') and around US$100 per day for a larger car (eg: a Toyota Land Cruiser). Petrol costs about US$1 per litre, and diesel is only slightly cheaper. For more details on car and motorbike hire see page 106.

# WHERE TO STAY IN ZANZIBAR TOWN

The following section is a selection of places to stay in and around Zanzibar Town. The list is not absolute, as new places keep opening and there are frequent name and location changes, but indicates the range of accommodation available and the best in each price bracket.

If you are coming from the airport (or elsewhere on the island) by taxi, and don't have a reservation, be firm about which hotel you want to go to, otherwise the driver may take you to wherever offers him the best commission. Also, remember that many hotels in the older part of Zanzibar Town cannot be reached by vehicle, and you may have to walk some distance through the narrow streets. If the driver shows you the way (and he'll also probably help with your luggage), it's usual to give a fair tip for this extra service.

Much of the accommodation is in, or very near, Stone Town, which is the best area for atmosphere and ease of getting around. Several of the places do not have exact street addresses, or if they do these are not used, as many lanes and house numbers, even if they exist, are often unmarked. Most are marked on the *Zanzibar Stone Town* map, pages 128–30.

**CATEGORIES** We have divided the list into the following five categories, which broadly correspond to price brackets and are based on the cost of a standard double room:

| Exclusive | US$125 upwards | Budget | US$30–50 |
|---|---|---|---|
| Upmarket | US$US$80–120 | Shoestring | Below US$30 |
| Mid-range | US US$50–80 | | |

## Exclusive

🏠 **Africa House Hotel** (15 rooms) PO Box 3246, Zanzibar; ☎ 0777 432340; f 0777 439340; e theafricahouse@zanlink.com; www.theafricahouse-zanzibar.com. Re-opened in 2003 following extensive restoration, this sea-facing hotel, which served as the English Club from 1888 until the end of the colonial era, now ranks among the most characterful places to stay in Zanzibar. Situated along the Shangani waterfront, Africa House is perhaps best known for its balcony bar, which formed a popular sundowner venue even when the hotel itself was non-functional and still offers a winning combination of reasonably priced (albeit not cheap) drinks, a great view and good bar food. It also displays some interesting 'before' and 'after' photographs documenting the restoration. The otherwise stylish traditional décor of the spacious en-suite rooms is undermined somewhat by an incongruously tiled floor, and supplemented by satellite TV, AC, bath and minibar. *US$125–200 dbl, b&b; substantial low-season discounts Apr–Jun.*

## MEMORIES OF THE ENGLISH CLUB

We received these reminiscences from a former member of the English Club (now the Africa House Hotel) who served in the colonial government before Zanzibar's independence:

The English Club, Zanzibar, was the oldest expatriate club in East Africa. The Rules and Regulations of 1888 – the year of its foundation – state that 'it is established for the association of an unlimited number of English Residents, together with officers of the Royal Navy stationed in these waters'. At this date the RN officers from no fewer than six warships outnumbered the other members.

By the 1950s eligibility for membership was widened to include 'any British subject or American citizen of European extraction'. Extraordinary members could also be elected from other residents such as the representatives of European trading companies. Honorary membership was extended to resident members of the Universities Mission to Central Africa, the Catholic Mission to Zanzibar, Armed Forces officers, officers of any British Cable or Merchant Ship or Civil Aircraft, and so on. There was also reciprocity with similar clubs in Nairobi, Dar es Salaam and Mombasa, which was a bonus when travelling in East Africa.

Bedrooms were available for visitors, and for use by members when departing or arriving from home leave. A Dining Room provided meals for single members, if required, and was popular for entertaining. After garages were built at ground level, their roof formed an attractive terrace – which remained one of the most popular meeting spots in Zanzibar Town, especially for drinks at sunset. There was a Billiard Room and a quite extensive Library. Sporting facilities were available at a separate site at the far end of Mnazi Mmoja Road, where tennis and golf were popular, together with squash, cricket and hockey.

In the latter years of the Club's existence, the fancy dress dance on New Year's Eve was a well-attended event. Among the other communities it was known that the *wazungu* (Europeans) would be walking through Stone Town, or arriving by car at the Club about 8.00pm, dressed in weird costumes, and there was always a sizeable gathering of local people to look with amusement at these strange antics.

The reader may be of the opinion that this all smacked of a monopoly of club life, but this was not so. There were Goan, Parsee, Bohora, Hindu, Ismaili, Ithnashery and other clubs, each used by a single community, whilst preserving an easy-going and relaxed contact among the various communities resident in the Island.

🏠 **Beyt al Chai** (6 rooms) PO Box 4236, Kelele Sq, Stone Town, Zanzibar; ☎ 0777 444111; f 0777 444112; e reservations@stonetowninn.com; www.stonetowninn.com. Behind thick walls and antique shuttered windows, Beyt al Chai is a relaxed and peaceful haven. Standing across Kelele Sq from the Serena, it was originally built by an Arab merchant and its name, literally meaning 'house of tea', bears testament to its past use as a place where the local nobility came to indulge in the house speciality, spiced tea. Until its recent opening as a boutique hotel, the building had always been someone's home, and its French manageress, Agnes Viellard, and her friendly team continue to offer relaxed hospitality and home comforts. There are 6 en-suite rooms – 5 dbls, 1 twin – spread over 3 floors and each with an individual name and style. The rooms are large and full of character with high ceilings, authentic Zanzibari furniture and vibrant silk and organza fabrics covering the windows and beds. Although all lovely, the 3 room categories, sultan, prince and princess, are distinguished largely by the size and opulence of the rooms, with only the last also having no view over the square. On the first floor, a large landing area leads out onto a small courtyard and b/fast area, whilst the corner of the house boasts a bright and airy lounge filled with stylish antique furniture covered in sumptuous, azure and gold-thread cushions. An honesty bar (local and imported alcohol), self-service stereo, and views on 2 sides into the square and sea beyond, make this a wonderfully chilled place to read, write, chat, snooze and watch the world go by. Only b/fast is served, but with such a convenient location, it's easy to wander to any of the town's restaurants or bars, and Agnes will happily recommend the current culinary hot spots. *Sultan rooms US$250 dbl, b&b; prince rooms US$170 dbl, b&b; princess room US$100 dbl, b&b. Reduce rates by US$25 for sgl occupancy; add US$65 for extra bed. Children under 2 stay free – cot available. Payment in local or international currency. Cash preferred; 5% credit card surcharge.*

🏠 **Emerson & Green Hotel** (16 rooms) PO Box 3417, Zanzibar; ☎ 024 223 0171; m 0777 423266; f 024 223 1038;

e emerson&green@zitec.com; www.emerson-green.com. An offshoot of the defunct Emerson's House, Emerson & Green Hotel sprawls across two venerable buildings dating from 1840–70, one of which was originally the home of the prominent Ismaili Indian merchant Tharia Topan (who also built the Old Dispensary, see page 146). The house has been completely restored and tastefully decorated with antique Zanzibar furniture and carpets, and has a peaceful and slightly bohemian atmosphere. Each of the 16 rooms is different in character, inc the vast Ball Room and the airy island South Room – reached by a small bridge! Each room, very deliberately, has no phone, no TV and no fridge. Some rooms have AC, others rely on natural cooling – shutters, shades, deep balconies and a sea breeze. B/fast is taken in the hotel's Tower Top Restaurant, the second-highest building in Zanzibar Town, with some of the finest views on the whole island. Dinners are also served here; you don't have to be resident to eat, but reservations are essential (for more details see page 131). *US$165–200 dbl, b&b; tpls for families on request.*

🏠 **Zanzibar Serena Inn** (51 rooms) PO Box 4151, Zanzibar; ☎ 024 223 2306; f 024 223 3019; e zserena@zanzinet.com; www.serenahotels.com. Part of the internationally renowned Serena chain, which has lodges all over east Africa, this large hotel is in the Shangani area of Stone Town, overlooking the sea. The hotel has been converted from two historic buildings, and restored at great expense (see box opposite). All rooms are en-suite and air conditioned, with all the facilities visitors expect of an international-class hotel, inc a large swimming pool, fine restaurant and coffee shop. If you happen not to be on holiday here, there's a business centre with fax, photocopying and email services (although rates are high), and conference facilities. In addition to its standard rooms, the hotel also has state, executive, honeymoon and business rooms. Generous discounts are available in the low season and sometimes also during quiet midweek periods. Cheaper rates are also sometimes available if you book through a tour operator rather than direct. *US$210/265 sgl/dbl; US$25 seaview suppt; US$20/35 HB/FB suppt*

## Upmarket

🏠 **Chavda Hotel** (40 rooms) PO Box 540, Zanzibar; ☎ 024 2232115; fax 2231931; e chavda@zanlink.com. Situated in Baghani St, just off Kenyatta Rd in the Shangani area, this fairly new hotel is decorated with lots of antique-style Indian

furniture and Persian carpets, but it's still a little dark and uninspiring. Rooms are fine, although some are a bit small, but all have a large en-suite bathroom, and some dbls have a separate lounge. Upstairs is a restaurant and a very pleasant rooftop

The Zanzibar Serena Inn is in the Shangani part of Stone Town. The main building was originally the External Communications ('Extelcoms') headquarters, built in the early 20th century by the British colonial administration. The next-door house is much older and was originally known as the Chinese Doctor's Residence. The explorer David Livingstone stayed here before one of his journeys to the African mainland. It later became the private home of the British consul.

The Extelcoms building had been empty for many years, and the Chinese Doctor's Residence had fallen into a bad state of repair, before restoration began. Their conversion into today's Serena Inn hotel was sensitively handled, the design reflecting Zanzibar's Indian, Arabic and colonial heritage. The regeneration was completed in 1997, and the architects and local craftsmen must be congratulated on the quality of their work and the retention of the building's original character. The walls of the hotel are decorated with historic prints and contemporary paintings, but perhaps the most interesting 'decorations' are the old telecommunications equipment that was discovered in the basement. Abandoned and forgotten by the colonial staff 100 years before, most of the apparatus was handmade in wood and brass. Several items have now been restored to their original condition.

The Serena's restoration goes beyond façades and decorations. It is the first hotel in Zanzibar to install a sewage plant, so that waste discharges are treated to international standards. (Most other waste from Stone Town gets pumped out to sea in its raw state.) Although dumping sewage at sea, in whatever state, is never an ideal solution, the hotel owners should be congratulated for this positive step.

bar. Free collections from the port or airport are available for guests. *US$80/100 sgl/dbl; US$120 with balcony.*

🏠 **Dhow Palace Hotel** (28 rooms) PO Box 3974, Zanzibar; ✆ 024 223 3012; f 024 223 3008; e dhowpalace@zanlink.net; www.tembohotel.com. In the Shangani area, just off Kenyatta Rd, this is an excellent and frequently recommended renovated old house built around a cool central courtyard, complete with tinkling fountain. Rooms all have en-suite bathroom (complete with Persian baths) and lead off long balconies which overlook the courtyard. The hotel is furnished with real antiques and antique-style items (apart from the incongruous TV in the lounge and the table football upstairs, both of which are hardly used). The whole place is spotlessly clean and the atmosphere is very peaceful and tranquil. It lacks only a sea view, although if it had this the rates would be higher, so you get comfort at a very fair price. B/fast and other meals are served in the lovely rooftop restaurant. Guests from the Dhow Palace can use the swimming pool at the Tembo Hotel free of charge – ask for a voucher at reception. *US$60/90 sgl/dbl.*

🏠 **Mazsons Hotel** (36 rooms) PO Box 3367, Zanzibar; ✆ 024 2233062/2233694/0741 340042; f 2233695; e mazsons@zanlink.com;

www.mazsonshotel.com. This hotel on Kenyatta Rd in the Shangani area has an interesting history: old records show it was built in the mid 19th century by Said bin Dhanin, who is thought to have settled here about the time that Sultan Said moved his court to Zanzibar from Muscat. Ownership changed hands several times, and during the early part of the 20th century the building was a Greek-run hotel before becoming a private dwelling once again. After the revolution, the house, along with many others, fell into disrepair. Today, it is once more a hotel. Most rooms are self-contained, air conditioned and well-appointed, but all are a little soulless. The hotel has a good restaurant, satellite TV, a business centre and bureau de change. Although power supplies are pretty good on Zanzibar these days, this hotel has its own large generator in case of cuts – in fact, it's so big it supplies many surrounding buildings as well. *'Moderate' sgl US$50. Standard rooms US$70/90 sgl/dbl.*

🏠 **Tembo Hotel** (36 rooms) PO Box 3974, Zanzibar; ✆ 024 223 3005/2069; f 024 223 3777; e tembo@zitec.org; www.tembohotel.com. This hotel has a great location on Shangani Rd, just west of Forodhani Gardens. Part of the hotel was a grand old house, and there's a more recent extension, so that the hotel now has a new wing and old wing, both overlooking the ocean and decorated in a mixture of traditional and modern styles. A notable feature is the upstairs landing separated from a balcony by a huge stained-glass window which fills the room with coloured light. All rooms are en-suite, with AC, fridge, telephone and TV. Most have a sea view, or overlook the large swimming pool, but some don't — so choose carefully, or specify a view when booking. It's worth noting that alcohol is not served. Non-guests can use the pool for US$3. US$85 sgl, US$95–105 dbl. Deluxe rooms with seafront balconies US$125–150. US$25/US$40 HB/FB suppt.

## Mid range

🏠 **Abuso Inn** (12 rooms) PO Box 465, Zanzibar; 📞 024 2235886; m 0777 425565. Newly opened in early 2005, this convenient small hotel in the busy Shangani quarter offers a selection of large, bright en-suite rooms with wooden floors, AC, fans, nets, hot water and attractive traditional Zanzibari furnishings. One of the best deals in this range. US$50/65/75 sgl/dbl/tpl.

🏠 **Baghani House Hotel** (8 rooms) PO Box 609, Zanzibar; 📞 024 2235654; f 2233030; e baghani@zanzinet.com. In the Shangani area, almost next door to the Dhow Palace Hotel, this is a friendly place, immaculately kept, with just 8 rooms — all simple but with a pleasant décor, TV, AC and big, clean, spacious bathrooms. Rates include full b/fast served in a small open-air courtyard (there's no restaurant) and — a nice touch — afternoon tea. US$40/45–60 sgl/dbl.

🏠 **Clove Hotel** (8 rooms) PO Box 1117, Zanzibar; 📞 0777 484567; clovehotel@zanlink.com; www.zanzibar.nl. This old stalwart, which stands about halfway along Hurumzi St, had become rather rundown prior to being bought, renovated and re-opened by a new Dutch owner-manager in 2004. En-suite rooms are small but stylishly decorated with a large dbl bed, fan and netting. The residents-only rooftop bar offers a great view over the town, and the hotel is very close to the waterfront. US$35/50 sgl/dbl.

🏠 **Coco de Mer Hotel** (13 rooms) PO Box 2363, Zanzibar; 📞 024 2230852; m 0777 433550; e cocodemer_znz@yahoo.com. In Shangani, off Kenyatta Rd, this is a straightforward but clean and friendly place with en-suite rooms set around a very pleasant airy courtyard, decorated with potted plants. The rooms downstairs are a bit dark, but those upstairs are bright and cheerful. The restaurant does tasty good-value food. A good choice in this range. The ground-floor bar is one of the few bespoke drinking holes in Stone Town, and it serves a variety of snacks and sandwiches. US$35 sgl; US$50 dbl; US$60 tpl.

🏠 **Hotel International** (21 rooms) PO Box 3784, Zanzibar; 📞 024 2233182; f 2236248; e hotelinter@zanlink.com; www.zanzibar.net/hotelinternational. In the Ukatani area, this hotel is a large old house, built around a central roofed courtyard. Although the rooms are all spacious and well-equipped (AC and completely self-contained with a bathroom, dining area, fridge, satellite TV and video), they all seem a bit dilapidated and uncared-for, which makes the hotel rather soulless and uninspiring. Additionally, rooms on the lower floors have no view, so are worth avoiding, while the upstairs rooms are better, although the very steep stairs might put some people off going up further than they need to. Credit cards are accepted, and the hotel has an efficient bureau de change. At the front is a shady café serving pizzas for US$3, local dishes for US$3.50 and other meals from US$4, and upstairs is a restaurant serving meals around US$7.50. US$45/60/80 sgl/dbl/tpl.

🏠 **Hotel Marine** (24 rooms) PO Box 4063, Zanzibar; 📞 024 2232088/2233055, 0777 411102; f 233082; e hotelmarine@zanlink.com; www.zanzibar.co.tz. This hotel is in a large old renovated house overlooking the roundabout on Mizingani Rd, near the port gates. Inside, a grand staircase winds around an inner courtyard to the rooms on two upper floors, but the potential has been totally wasted, with threadbare purple carpets and dark-brown paint on the walls making the whole place very gloomy. The rooms are all en-suite, and fair quality, furnished with Zanzibar beds, but they feel a bit rundown and assumed essentials such as fridge and TV make things cramped. Bathrooms are tiny (having a shower without falling down the loo is tricky) and feel rather overpriced. On the plus side, the staff are great, and free transfers to/from the port or airport are available. US$40/50/60 sgl/dbl/tpl.

🏠 **Shangani Hotel** PO Box 4222, Zanzibar; 📞/f 024 2236363; f 024 2233688; m 0777 411703; e shanganihotel@hotmail.com; www.shanganihotel.com. On busy Kenyatta Rd, near the old post office, this hotel is an adequate choice in the middle range. The en-suite rooms have AC, fridge, telephone and satellite TV. B/fast and other meals are taken in the rooftop restaurant. A good internet café is attached. US$50/65 sgl/dbl.

## Budget

⌂ **Bwawani Hotel** (78 rooms) m 0777 486487. This 4-storey government-owned monolith on the outskirts of town is a drab monstrosity on the outside and abysmally dreary inside, with an institutional feel more appropriate to a prison than a hotel. The large en-suite rooms all cost the same, and, while this rate is just about acceptable for those rooms that have been renovated, it ranks as spectacularly bad value for those that haven't. It's probably best avoided, though the sheer number of rooms might count in its favour if you have difficulty finding accommodation in the high season. Unverifiable rumours have long circulated that the hotel will one day be privatised and rebuilt by an international hotel chain. *US$35/52 sgl/dbl.*

⌂ **Garden Lodge** (18 rooms) PO Box 3413, Zanzibar; ✆ 024 2233298; e gardenlodge@zanlink.com. Situated on Kaunda Rd near the People's Gardens and the main hospital, this place is simple but neat and friendly, and good value in this range. Upstairs rooms are clean and bright and airy; downstairs they're still spacious and adequate but darker and a little musty. All rooms have en-suite bathroom, the showers are warm, the b/fast is filling and there's a nice little garden terrace out the front. When choosing a room, try to get one at the back as those overlooking Kaunda Rd are noisy. *Downstairs with cold shower US$15/25 sgl/dbl, upstairs with hot shower US$25/40 sgl/dbl.*

⌂ **Island View Hotel** (18 rooms) PO Box 6, Zanzibar; ✆ 024 2234605, 2235222; e islandview@africamail.com. About 2km south of Zanzibar Town, at Kilimani, this is a small and welcoming B&B, run by the friendly Mitha family. All rooms are spacious, clean and tidy, with dbl/twin bed, mosquito net, en-suite bathroom, fan, TV, fridge and telephone. Meals can be ordered, tea or coffee is available all day free of charge, and there's internet access. This hotel is very handy for the airport, and only a few mins' drive from town (transport can be provided). *US$20/30/40 sgl/dbl/tpl. AC is an extra US$3.*

⌂ **Karibu Inn** (22 rooms) PO Box 3428, Zanzibar; ✆/f 024 2233058; e karibuinn@zanzinet.com. On a narrow street, parallel with Kenyatta Rd, in the Shangani part of town, this very simple, hostel-like place caters mainly for backpackers, budget tour groups or people travelling on overland trucks. The friendly and helpful management can set you up with budget tours, and also run a very well organised safe-deposit scheme. Clean but basic sgl/dbl en-suite rooms are available, as are dormitories, each of which sleeps between 4 and 7 people and has an en-suite bathroom. *Rooms US$20/30/40 sgl/dbl/tpl; dormitory US$10 pp.*

⌂ **Kiponda Hotel** (14 rooms) PO Box 3446, Zanzibar; ✆ 024 2233052; f 022 2233020; e hotelkiponda@email.com. On Nyumba ya Moto St in the Kiponda area, not far from the main seafront, this is a small, quiet hotel in a building which used to house part of a sultan's harem. It has been renovated in local style and still has an original carved wooden entrance door. The Dutch–Australian–Zanzibari management team give the place a relaxed and friendly atmosphere, and although it's a touch more expensive than the budget hotels to which it is sometimes compared, it is also a lot cleaner, quieter and much better value. All prices are discountable for long stays and for groups, with extra reductions in low season. There's a rooftop restaurant specialising in Zanzibari and seafood dishes. The hotel also has good connections with the local Kenya Airways office and can help with flights and reservations. *US$18/35/45 sgl/dbl/tpl; en-suite rooms US$45/55 sgl/dbl.*

⌂ **Mauwani Inn** (7 rooms) PO Box 3752, Zanzibar; ✆ 024 2238949; m 0777 475748; e reservations@mauwaniinn.com. www.mauwaniinn.com. Another new hotel, situated just off Kenyatta Rd behind the Rendezvous Les Spices Restaurant, this offers cramped but very clean en-suite rooms with tiled floor, fan, net and in some cases AC — it looks to be good value! *US$25/40/50 sgl/dbl/tpl.*

⌂ **Malindi Guesthouse** (14 rooms) PO Box 609, Zanzibar; ✆ 024 2230165; e malindi@zanzinet.com; www.zanzibarhotels.net/malindi. In the northern part of Stone Town, near the port, this place has been consistently popular with travellers for many years. It's clean and nicely decorated, with a lot of character and a fine collection of old photographs from Arab-ruled, British colonial times and the early years of independence. There's also a bar and restaurant. *Room with shared facilities US$20/30 sgl/dbl; en-suite room US$25/40 sgl/dbl; 6-person room US$60.*

⌂ **Narrow Street Hotel** (8 rooms) ✆ 024 2232620; e narrow22@yahoo.com. In an interesting bit of town, this old hotel on Malindi St is recently renovated. The rooms are all neat and tidy, but quite small, so ideally you should know your roommate well. The en-suite bathrooms are also small and simple but clean. The staff are a bit sleepy, but this is a fair choice in the low-to-middle range. *US$15/20/35 sgl/dbl/tpl; US$5/room suppt for AC.*

⌂ **St Monica's Hostel** (15 rooms) ☏ 024 2235348; f 2236772; e monicaszanzibar@hotmail.com; www.stmonicahostelzanzibar.s5.com. Very near the Anglican Cathedral, on Sultan Ahmed Mugheiri Rd (which everyone still calls New Mkunazini Rd), this hostel is mainly for church guests, but it is also open to the public. The hostel was built in the 1890s and formerly housed teachers and nurses working at the UMCA mission. The reverential atmosphere remains but this place really has an aura, with thick walls, wide staircases, sweeping arches and rooms with balconies (some have views of the cathedral). Rooms are simple and very clean. In the same building is a restaurant, with simple good-value meals. No alcohol is allowed. On the lower floor is a small art workshop where you can buy paintings and hand-printed T-shirts. *Room with shared facilities US$12 pp; en-suite room US$28/32 sgl/dbl.*

## Shoestring

⌂ **Bandari Lodge** (16 rooms) PO Box 1063, Malindi, Zanzibar; ☏ 024 223 7969; m 0777 423638; e bandarilodge@hotmail.com. One of the newer additions to the assortment of affordable hotels in Malindi, just 100m from the port, this pleasant place offers good-value accommodation in airy clean rooms with net and fan. Facilities include a common lounge area and paperback book swap service. *US$12 pp*

⌂ **Bottoms Up Guesthouse** Named after the attached disreputable bar, this place is hard to find in the narrow alleys between the Spice Inn and the House of Wonders, and was closed for renovation in late 2005. In its previous incarnation the facilities were basic, the bathrooms were dilapidated and the atmosphere at night was not pleasant, but it's possible that this will change when it re-opens in 2006 with rooms in the US$10–20 range. An enduring attraction is the roof terrace where guests used to relax, sunbathe and swap travel tales.

⌂ **Flamingo Guesthouse** (18 rooms) PO Box 4279, Zanzibar; ☏ 024 2232850; f 024 2233144; m 0777 491252; e flamingoguesthouse@ hotmail.com. Although the surrounding area is a bit noisy, this no-frills place on Mkunazini St is popular with budget travellers for its friendly atmosphere and simple but clean rooms with net and fan. Facilities include TV and video lounge, book-swap service and sale of cold drinks. From the terrace

⌂ **Safari Lodge** (28 rooms) PO Box 3231, Zanzibar; ☏ 024 223 6523/0748 606177; f 022 2124507; e asc@raha.com; www.safarilodgetz.com. This new hotel in the Malindi quarter, though somewhat bland and soulless, is good value for money. The neat and spacious en-suite rooms have large beds and cable TV, and larger suites are also available. It has a convenient location for exploring the old town and a decent rooftop restaurant is attached. *Standard room US$20/30 sgl/dbl; suite USSUS$35/40 sgl/dbl.*

⌂ **Warere Town House** (10 rooms) PO Box 1298, Zanzibar; ☏ 024 223 3835; m 0741 509368; e warere_townhouse@hotmail.com; www.wareretownhouse.com. Situated in an early 20th-century homestead, in the northern part of Stone Town, very near the port, this 3-storey lodge has been popular for many years with travellers on a tight budget. It now offers even better value following a major renovation a couple of years back. The comfortable and airy en-suite rooms come with a 4-poster bed, TV, fan and attractive period furnishing. *US$25/40 sgl/dbl.*

upstairs you get great views of the Anglican Cathedral. *Room with shared facilities US$8 pp; en-suite room US$10 pp.*

⌂ **Haven Lodge** (9 rooms) PO Box 3746, Zanzibar; ☏ 024 2235677; m 0777 413660/437132; e thehaven2008@yahoo.com;. This is a very friendly and good-value place, in the southern part of Stone Town between Soko Muhugo St and Vuga Rd, and many budget travellers have written to recommend it. Makame the manager knows what backpackers want, and offers very simple but clean bedrooms and bathrooms, hot water, and a big b/fast with as much tea and coffee as you like. There's a generator in case of power cuts, an organised safe-deposit system, luggage storage, a kitchen for self-catering (free) and travel information boards about Tanzania and other parts of east Africa. The staff can arrange cheap transfers to the coast, boat trips and tours, and they also have bikes for hire. *US$10 pp.*

⌂ **Jambo Guesthouse** (9 rooms) PO Box 635, Zanzibar; ☏ 024 2233779; m 0777 496571; e jamboguest@hotmail.com. In a quiet and peaceful quarter of the Mkunazini area, near the Anglican Cathedral and opposite the Green Garden Restaurant, this straightforward little hotel has a range of rooms. It's a good budget place, which has been justifiably popular with backpackers for many years. The rooms are simple and bright but can get a bit hot, in spite of all having AC or a fan. The shared bathrooms are

Zanzibar Town gets occasional cuts in the electrical supply. To overcome this, most of the larger hotels have generators, but some of the small budget places don't, which can mean no lights and no fans. If the lights go out, kerosene lamps may be provided but it's best to have a torch or candles handy just in case. When the fans stop working there's not much that can be done, and inside rooms can get unbearable during Zanzibar's hot season. Bear this in mind when choosing a place to stay. Hotels that have been built recently rely on a constant electrical supply to work the fans or AC, whilst older hotels were built to withstand the hot weather using designs that date from before the invention of electricity. If you can't find a genuinely old hotel, at least look for one built in traditional style: large windows, thick walls, high ceilings, courtyards, wide verandas and even a double roof, not just a pseudo-oriental façade!

OK. Book in advance to arrange a pick-up from the port. Free tea and coffee available throughout the day, and the on-site internet café charges US$1/hr. *US$15/20/30 sgl/dbl/tpl.*

🏠 **Kokoni's Hotel** (14 rooms) PO Box 3257, Zanzibar; ☎ 024 223 0239; m 0745 863817; e kokonishotel@hotmail.com. In the Kokoni area between Malindi St and Creek Rd, a short walk behind the BP petrol station, this is the former Hotel Karwan Sarai. It's a big old house and has a range of rooms; some are large and airy with old wooden shutters leading onto a small balcony overlooking the square, while others are small and dark with no view. Most rooms have en-suite bathroom, all have fans, and some also have TV, while the rooftop lounge has great views across Stone Town. It's a quiet place and good value, but veering towards the soulless. *US$15/25 sgl/dbl (negotiable).*

🏠 **Malindi Lodge** (8 rooms) ☎ 024 2232359. In a handy position if you're coming by boat, near the port gates and next to the Ciné Afrique on Malawi Rd, the Malindi Lodge (not to be confused with the Malindi Guesthouse, see above in *Budget* section) is a good choice in this range. There are just 8 rooms, which are all very simple but clean, light and absolutely spotless. There are no fans, just noisy AC. The shared bathrooms are also basic but clean. This place has links with Sunset Bungalows in Kendwa in northern Zanzibar and can arrange bargain transport there and back. *Room with shared facilities US$15 pp; en-suite room US$20/35 sgl/dbl.*

🏠 **Manch Lodge** (22 rooms) ☎ 024 2231918; f 024 223 7925; email kashamanch@axcitl.com. Just up the street from the Haven Hotel, this is another friendly budget place, although their penchant for heavy brown furniture makes things a bit cramped. Phone in advance for a pick-up from the port (free), or from the airport (US$2.50). Sgl, dbl and tpl rooms are available, all with en-suite bathroom. *US$10 pp.*

🏠 **Mzuri Guesthouse** (11 rooms) ☎ 024 2230463; m 0748 740300. In the Malindi area near the port, on Malawi Rd opposite the Passing Show Restaurant, this is a definite budget place, used mainly by locals and a few backpackers. Rooms are quite small and have a fridge, TV and AC (noisy), and bathroom (small and a bit tired), but seem fair value. *US$18/25 sgl/dbl.*

🏠 **Pyramid Hotel** (11 rooms) PO Box 254, Zanzibar; ☎ 024 2233000; m 0777 461451/0748 255525; f 024 2230045; e pyramidhotel@yahoo.com. On Kokoni St, between the Malindi and Kiponda areas, this long-standing hotel is just behind the Ijumaa Mosque, a short walk back from the seafront. A budget travellers' favourite for many years, and deservedly so, it gets it name from the very steep and narrow staircases (almost ladders) that lead to the upper floors. The rooms have netting, fan and hot water, yet vary in atmosphere: some are large and bright, others small and dark, so choose carefully. The staff are very friendly, and the rooftop restaurant does good cheap food. Overall, it's a good budget choice, offering a free pick-up from the airport or port as well as a book-swap service. *US$15/25 sgl/dbl.*

🏠 **Riverman Hotel** (12 rooms) ☎ 024 2233188; e rivermanhotel@hotmail.com. Located at the back of the Anglican Cathedral, well signposted off Tharia St, this basic guesthouse is a fair budget option. Rooms have seen better days but are adequate. This hotel is an agent for the Tazara train on the Tanzanian mainland, and you can buy tickets here. *US$10 pp.*

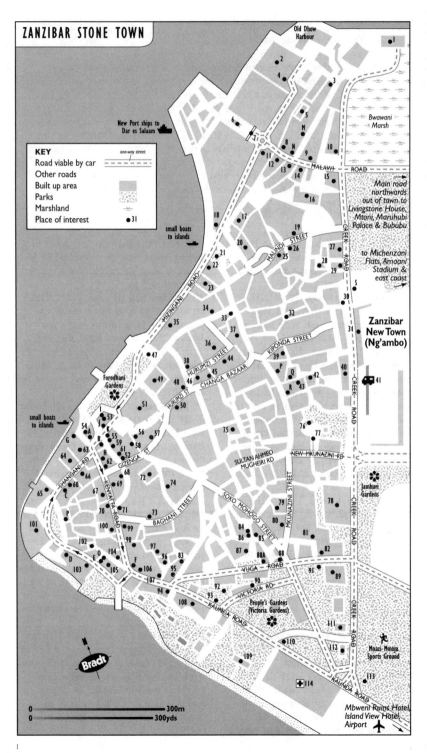

# ZANZIBAR STONE TOWN

**KEY**

one-way street -----

Road viable by car ---

Other roads

Built up area

Parks

Marshland

Place of interest ● 31

Old Dhow Harbour

New Port ships to Dar es Salaam

small boats to islands

small boats to islands

*Bwawani Marsh*

MALAWI ROAD

*Main road northwards out of town to Livingstone House, Mtoni, Maruhubi Palace & Bububu*

*to Michenzani Flats, Amaani Stadium & east coast*

**Zanzibar New Town (Ng'ambo)**

MALINDI STREET

KIPONDA STREET

HURUMZI STREET

CHANGA BAZAAR

HURUMZI ST

Forodhani Gardens

SHANGANI RD

KENYATTA ROAD

GIZENGA ST

SULTAN AHMEO MUGHEIRI RD

NEW MKUNAZINI RD

Jamhuri Gardens

BAGHANI STREET

SOKO MOHOGO STREET

MKUNAZINI STREET

CREEK ROAD

CREEK ROAD

CREEK ROAD

VUGA ROAD

VICTORIA RD

People's Gardens (Victoria Gardens)

KAUNDA ROAD

KAUNDA ROAD

Mnazi Mmoja Sports Ground

*Mbweni Ruins Hotel, Island View Hotel, Airport*

**Bradt**

0 ———————— 300m

0 ———————— 300yds

128

# Numerical key to Zanzibar Stone Town map opposite

1 Bwawani Hotel
2 Clove Distillery
3 Malindi Guesthouse
4 Fish market
5 Warere House
6 Shipping company ticket offices
7 Port gates
8 Ciné Afrique
9 Mzuri Guesthouse
10 Petrol station Gapco
11 Hotel Marine
12 Malindi Bureau de Change
13 Star Bureau de Change
14 Passing Show Restaurant
15 Police station (main)
16 Zan Tours & Zan Air
17 Old Dispensary (Stone Town Cultural Centre)
18 Mercury's Restaurant
19 Safari Lodge
20 Ijumaa Mosque
21 The Big Tree
22 Sea View Indian Restaurant, Seafront Internet, Sun N'Fun Tours
23 Old Customs House
25 Pyramid Hotel
26 Narrow Street Hotel
27 Zanzibar Tourism Corporation
28 Kokoni Hotel
29 BP petrol station
30 Taxi rank
31 Container shops
32 Narrow Street Annexe Hotel
33 Palace Restaurant (closed 2005)
34 Hotel Kiponda
35 Palace Museum
36 Hindu Temple
37 Aga Khan Mosque
38 Mandogo Café (shady, open air)
39 Hotel International, Bureau de change
40 Market
41 Bus & dala-dala station
42 Masumo Bookshop
43 Shamshuddin Cash & Carry Supermarket
44 Emerson's & Green Hotel
45 Bottoms Up Guesthouse
46 Clove Inn
47 Taxi rank
48 Microwaves Internet
49 House of Wonders
50 Sama Tours, Nassor curio shop
51 Old Arab Fort
52 Supermarket
53 Orphanage
54 Sweet Easy Restaurant
55 Radha Food House
56 People's Bank of Zanzibar
57 The Zanzibar Gallery
58 People's Bank of Zanzibar (Foreign Exchange)
59 Karibu Inn
60 Garage Club
61 Coco de Mer Hotel
62 The Zanzibar Gallery
63 Old British Embassy, Archipelago Restaurant, Too Short Internet Café
64 Tembo Hotel
65 Starehe Club
66 Fisherman Restaurant
67 Shangani Hotel & Shangani Internet Café

68 Namaste Indian Restaurant
69 Post office & telephone office
70 Memories of Zanzibar
71 Barracuda Restaurant & Fanny's Green Restaurant
72 St Joseph's Catholic Cathedral
73 Chavda Hotel
74 Chit-Chat Restaurant
75 Hamamni Baths
76 Anglican Cathedral
77 St Monica's Hostel
78 Haile Selassie School
79 Jambo Guesthouse
80 Flamingo Guesthouse
81 Zanzibar Medical & Diagnostic Centre
82 Kiswahili Language Institute
83 Mauwani Inn
84 Manch Lodge (guesthouse)
85 Nyumbani Restaurant
86 Haven Hotel
87 Florida Guesthouse
88 Fisherman Tours, Fernandes Tours
88A Maha Travel & Tours
89 Ben Bella School
90 Victoria House (guesthouse)
91 State University of Zanzibar
92 Two Tables Restaurant
93 Garden Lodge
94 Zanzibar Medical Group
95 Dr Mehta's Hospital
96 Afya Medical Hospital
97 Zanzibar Hotel (closed for renovation 2005)
98 Dhow Palace Hotel, Baghani House Hotel
99 Sunrise Restaurant & Pub
100 Mazsons Hotel, Precision Air, Kenya Airline, Cross Road Internet
101 Serena Inn
102 Tippu Tip's House
103 Amore Mio Restaurant
104 Pagoda Chinese Restaurant
105 Africa House Hotel
106 Camlur's Restaurant
107 Rendezvous Les Spices Restaurant
108 High Court
109 State House
110 Zanzibar Milestone
111 Museum Annexe
112 Peace Memorial Museum
113 Old Cricket Pavilion
114 Mnazi Moja Hospital
A Zanzibar Dive Centre
B National Bank of Commerce
C Wings Fast Food, Abuso Inn, Air Tanzania
D Jojoba Tours
E La Fenice
F Casablanca Restaurant
G Livingstone Beach Restaurant
H Dolly's Patisserie
I Monsoon Restaurant
J Buni Café
K Bahari Dive Centre
L Bamdari Lodge, Nalindi Lodge Annexe
M Mitu Tours
N Malindi Lodge
O New Happy Club 2000
P Zanzibar Coffee House, Beyt Al Char Hotel
Q CD shop
R Kaya Tea Room
S Vodacom shop

# Alphabetical key to Zanzibar Stone Town map (see page 128)

105 Africa House Hotel
96 Afya Medical Hospital
37 Aga Khan Mosque
103 Amore Mio Restaurant
76 Anglican Cathedral
K Bahari Dive Centre
L Bamdari Lodge, Nalindi Lodge Annexe
71 Barracuda Restaurant & Fanny's Green Restaurant
89 Ben Bella School
45 Bottoms Up Guesthouse
29 BP petrol station
J Buni Café
41 Bus & dala-dala station
I Bwawani Hotel
106 Camlur's Restaurant
F Casablanca Restaurant
Q CD shop
73 Chavda Hotel
74 Chit-Chat Restaurant
8 Ciné Afrique
2 Clove Distillery
46 Clove Inn
61 Coco de Mer Hotel
31 Container shops
98 Dhow Palace Hotel, Baghani House Hotel
H Dolly's Patisserie
95 Dr Mehta's Hospital
44 Emerson's & Green Hotel
4 Fish market
66 Fisherman Restaurant
88 Fisherman Tours, Fernandes Tours
80 Flamingo Guesthouse
87 Florida Guesthouse
60 Garage Club
93 Garden Lodge
78 Haile Selassie School
75 Hamamni Baths
86 Haven Hotel
108 High Court
36 Hindu Temple
39 Hotel International, Bureau de change
34 Hotel Kiponda
11 Hotel Marine
49 House of Wonders
20 Ijumaa Mosque
79 Jambo Guesthouse
D Jojoba Tours
59 Karibu Inn
R Kaya Tea Room
82 Kiswahili Language Institute
28 Kokoni Hotel
E La Fenice
G Livingstone Beach Restaurant
88A Maha Travel & Tours
12 Malindi Bureau de Change
3 Malindi Guesthouse
N Malindi Lodge
84 Manch Lodge (guesthouse)
38 Mandogo Café (shady, open air)
40 Market
42 Masumo Bookshop
83 Mauwani Inn
100 Mazsons Hotel, Precision Air, Kenya Airline, Cross Road Internet
70 Memories of Zanzibar
18 Mercury's Restaurant
48 Microwaves Internet
M Mitu Tours

114 Mnazi Moja Hospital
1 Monsoon Restaurant
111 Museum Annexe
9 Mzuri Guesthouse
68 Namaste Indian Restaurant
32 Narrow Street Annexe Hotel
26 Narrow Street Hotel
B National Bank of Commerce
O New Happy Club 2000
85 Nyumbani Restaurant
51 Old Arab Fort
63 Old British Embassy, Archipelago Restaurant, Too Short Internet Café
113 Old Cricket Pavilion
23 Old Customs House
17 Old Dispensary (Stone Town Cultural Centre)
53 Orphanage
104 Pagoda Chinese Restaurant
35 Palace Museum
33 Palace Restaurant (closed 2005)
14 Passing Show Restaurant
112 Peace Memorial Museum
56 People's Bank of Zanzibar
58 People's Bank of Zanzibar (Foreign Exchange)
10 Petrol station Gapco
15 Police station (main)
7 Port gates
69 Post office & telephone office
25 Pyramid Hotel
55 Radha Food House
107 Rendezvous Les Spices Restaurant
19 Safari Lodge
50 Sama Tours, Nassor curio shop
22 Sea View Indian Restaurant, Seafront Internet, Sun N'Fun Tours
101 Serena Inn
43 Shamshuddin Cash & Carry Supermarket
67 Shangani Hotel & Shangani Internet Café
6 Shipping company ticket offices
72 St Joseph's Catholic Cathedral
77 St Monica's Hostel
13 Star Bureau de Change
65 Starehe Club
109 State House
91 State University of Zanzibar
99 Sunrise Restaurant & Pub
52 Supermarket
54 Sweet Easy Restaurant
30 Taxi rank
47 Taxi rank
64 Tembo Hotel
21 The Big Tree
57 The Zanzibar Gallery
62 The Zanzibar Gallery
102 Tippu Tip's House
92 Two Tables Restaurant
90 Victoria House (guesthouse)
S Vodacom shop
5 Warere House
C Wings Fast Food, Abuso Inn, Air Tanzania
16 Zan Tours & Zan Air
P Zanzibar Coffee House, Beyt Al Char Hotel
A Zanzibar Dive Centre
97 Zanzibar Hotel (closed for renovation 2005)
81 Zanzibar Medical & Diagnostic Centre
94 Zanzibar Medical Group
110 Zanzibar Milestone
27 Zanzibar Tourism Corporation

☖ **Victoria House** PO Box 4137, Zanzibar; ✆ 024 2232861. Near the People's Gardens, this place on Vuga St is old (in fact, back in the early 1980s it was just about the only budget option on the whole island) and is nothing special. Though located in a fairly modern but dilapidated building, it's in a nice position and the spacious rooms all come with fan or AC. Some rooms have shared bathrooms, others are en-suite. *US$14 pp (negotiable).*

## ✕ WHERE TO EAT AND DRINK IN ZANZIBAR TOWN

This section lists restaurants, cafés, snack bars, eating-houses and all other places that serve primarily food – or food and drink in equal measures. Bars, and other places which serve primarily drinks, are listed along with music venues in the *Bars, clubs and entertainment* section on pages 136–7.

Some restaurants and cafés in Zanzibar Town are simple and aimed at locals; see page 135 for these. Others are smarter and cater specifically for tourists, expatriates and more well-off residents. The following list, arranged very loosely into categories of quality and price, cannot hope to be complete, but it indicates the type and range of places available. Nearly all those included are open in the evenings for dinner, and most also open for lunch; some are open all day. At busy times reservations may be necessary in some of the smarter restaurants.

### Top end (average main course US$10 upwards)

✕ **Baharia Restaurant** Serena Hotel, Shangani Rd; ✆ 024 2233587. Not quite as flamboyant as the restaurants at Emerson & Green, but this is a good-quality place nonetheless. The food is a mix of Asian, African and European. Starters like salads or mini kebabs are US$5, while main courses include curries for around US$10, fish in garlic and ginger for US$12.50, chicken in coconut for US$15, and lobster for US$25. In the coffee shop and patisserie, snacks and light meals start from around US$5, and you can have coffee and cakes for US$4.

✕ **Fisherman Restaurant** Shangani Rd; ✆ 024 2233658/0777 414254. Opposite the Tembo Hotel, a small old Zanzibari door leads into a dark building with thick white walls and blue tables, decorated in hybrid Zanzibari–Mediterranean style with fishing nets, crab boxes and other aquatic paraphernalia on the walls. Naturally, the menu is dominated by seafood. Starters such as fish kebabs are US$2.50, simple dishes around US$4–6, and larger dishes such as crab masala or grilled lobster around US$12, with specials around US$20, and a 3-course menu du jour (prawns or crab starter, lobster, prawns, crayfish and rice, plus dessert) for US$19. Open 11.00–midnight.

✕ **Kidude Restaurant** Emerson & Green Hotel, Hurumzi St; ✆ 024 2230171/0777 423266. Attached to the Emerson & Green Hotel, this place was originally set up as a café, but it is now also a more elaborate, and very impressive, restaurant. The ambience is delightful; the room has massive high ceilings, wall-hangings of rich fabrics, oil paintings, brass urns, antique furniture and ornaments. During the day, you can enjoy great cakes and coffees, order from the à la carte menu (from around US$5) or take lunch (the US$12 fixed menu changes every day). In the evenings there's also a fixed menu (US$25), with a vast and impressive range of dishes similar to those offered in Emerson & Green's Tower Top Restaurant (see below). On Friday evenings, a buffet is served (US$15). Reservations are usually required at busy times.

✕ **Livingstone Beach Restaurant** ✆ 0748 694803. The newest restaurant in Stone Town (it opened in Aug 2005) consists of a large, uncluttered and attractively decorated dining room leading out to a private beach where you can dine with your toe trailing in the sand if you so choose. Situated opposite Sweet Eazy, the restaurant has a decidedly upmarket ambience and the (mostly seafood) menu is priced accordingly, with most main courses falling into the US$10–18 range.

✕ **Tower Top Restaurant** Emerson & Green Hotel, Hurumzi St; ✆ 024 2230171/0777 423266. Up on the roof of the Emerson & Green Hotel, this restaurant has a superb view, which the management modestly claims to be the 'best on the island'. Most visitors seem to agree that it is. The hotel is in a house built in the 19th century by Tharia Topan, financial advisor to Sultan Barghash. As the second-wealthiest man on Zanzibar at the time, he built his home as the second-highest in town, lower only than the sultan's House of Wonders palace. A century later, he would be impressed by the feast still enjoyed by guests every evening. Meals here are relaxed affairs, starting with sunset drinks and cocktails, listening to the sound of the muezzins calling from the minarets around town. Guests sit local style on cushions and carpets, working slowly through starters and several courses of a top-quality Arabic-Swahili meal and ending with Arabic coffee. Numbers are limited, so that guests can stay for the whole evening, and reservations are essential. The cost is US$25 on weekdays. At weekends it's US$30, and includes performances by local dancers and musicians.

## Mid range (average main course US$5–8)

✗ **Amore Mio** Shangani Rd; tel 024 2233666; e e_walzl2yahoo.it. Rated by many as the best Italian eatery on the island, this unfussy new 'Cafeteria Italiano' also has an attractively breezy waterfront location and offers the alternatives of eating in or outdoors. Pasta dishes and pizzas cost around US$5, sandwiches are in the US$3–4 range, and it serves a good strong coffee as well as a range of ice creams.

✗ **La Fenice** Shangani Rd; ☎ 0777 411868; e fenice@zanzinet.com. Very near the seafront in the Shangani area, close to the Africa House Hotel, this is a smart new place with a big open courtyard, serving Italian and Swahili food. As well as the restaurant, it's a cocktail bar and ice-cream parlour. It's not cheap but you get excellent food and a warm welcome here. Starters are US$3–4, and main courses (such as lobster risotto) are US$4–7.

✗ **Mercury's Bar & Rest** Mizingani Rd; ☎ 024 2233076; m 0777 416666; e mercury's@zanlink.com. Named after Zanzibar's most famous son (see the *Freddie Mercury* box, page 135), this place has a fine setting on the seafront, overlooking a small beach, the bay, and part of the new port. It's popular, and has a good atmosphere. Wooden tables, director's chairs, and big sunshades are set out on the large wooden deck, and you can enjoy choosing from the menu which unashamedly cashes in on the former Queen singer's apparent dietary preferences – Freddie's Favourite Salad (US$3.50), Mercury's Special Pizza (US$5.20) etc; but despite this corniness the food is very good. Other options include pizzas (margaritas from US$5 up to prawn, beef, tuna and mushroom for US$7), a mixed plate of grilled seafood (US$10), smaller dishes of octopus, grilled fish, pastas (all for around US$5) and a huge range of cocktails around US$2.50–3. It's open daily (with happy hour 17.00–20.00) and there's live traditional music or other entertainment 3 evenings a week.

✗ **Monsoon Restaurant** Forodhani Gardens; ☎ 0777 411362; e monsoon@zanzinet.com. Near the Fort and the seafront, this is a smart French-run place serving a good and interesting selection of Mediterranean and Zanzibari food, accompanied by live taraab music on Wednesday and Saturday nights.

There are two parts to Monsoon: one is a bar, while the other is a massive open space covered in rugs and cushions. You leave your shoes at the door and lounge around kasbah-style. Thick walls and good ventilation mean it's always cool, and so are most of the clients. If you want to relax even more, you can enjoy a hubble-bubble pipe with your Arabic coffee or cocktail. There is also a very pleasant and shady terrace with about 10 tables facing Forodhani Gardens. Main courses cost US$4 upwards, while 4-course dinners cost US$8–10.

✗ **Mtoni Marine Restaurant** ☎ 024 2250117. At Mtoni Marine Centre, just a few kilometres north of Zanzibar Town, this restaurant is too far to reach by foot (and not a pleasant walk anyway) but worth the taxi ride. The food is an imaginative mix of European and Swahili techniques and ingredients, with sushi being something of a speciality. It gets many good reports for being good value. More details are given in the hotel listings: see page 168 in *Chapter 7*.

✗ **Pagoda Chinese Restaurant** off Kenyatta Rd; ☎ 024 2234688; e pagoda888@hotmail.com. The Pagoda, just off Kenyatta Rd near the Africa House Hotel, is run by Mr Chung, who has lived on Zanzibar for many years and used to run a diving outfit with his son George and other members of the family. They proudly and justifiably claim to serve the only genuine Chinese food in Zanzibar. The restaurant is open for lunch and dinner, and is highly rated, with good service, immaculate tables, nice surrounds, generous servings and excellent food. Chinese agricultural technicians from projects around the island often come here – so it must be good! Starters range from 5 spring rolls for US$1 to crispy deep fried squid for US$1.50, and main courses include sweet and sour fish, prawns piripiri, chicken in oyster sauce and satay beef, all around US$5. Roast duck is US$9, and the menu also includes a few specialities, such as Chinese curried crab, for US$6. There are also a lot of vegetarian options, and meals inc crisp, fresh vegetables specially flown in from Kenya. Rice and noodles are around US$2. Open daily 11.30–14.30 and 18.00–11.00.

✗ **Rendezvous Les Spices** Kenyatta Rd; ☎ 0777 410707. This French-owned restaurant, formerly

## DAFU

Young coconuts, known locally as *dafu*, are a delicious Zanzibari snack. When in season, piles of these rough, light brown 'footballs' can be found adorning street stalls and markets all over the island. Simply choose a coconut, watch the salesman chop off its top with a knife, and sit back to drink the refreshing milk inside, while the purveyor carves a makeshift spoon from the coconut shell, allowing you to scoop out the tender 'meat'.

known as the Maharaja, still serves what is arguably the best Indian food on the island. It's reasonably priced too, with starters around US$2–3, and main courses such as crab masala, chicken tikka, lamb biriyani or various tandooris for US$5–6. Vegetarian dishes are available, and specials, such as prawn curry, are US$7–8. Credit cards are accepted.

✗ **Sambusa Two Tables Restaurant** Victoria St; ☏ 024 231979/0777 416601. Usually called Two Tables, this place is particularly worthy of mention, because it's good and because for a long time there was nothing else quite like it on Zanzibar. This is a small place (it really does have only 2 tables – although one seats about 8 people), on the balcony of a private house. It's set back off Victoria St, near the junction with Kaunda Rd, but is clearly signposted. The entrance is round the back. Food is cooked by husband-and-wife team Salim and Hidaya, with help from the rest of the family. It's best to phone or call in the afternoon to tell Salim you'll be coming in the evening. A full meal with a variety of local dishes costs US$7. It's highly rated by all who go here, although we heard from some travellers who said pacing themselves was tricky – not knowing how many courses to expect, they filled up on snacks and starters and couldn't do justice to the main course when it arrived!

✗ **Sea View Indian Restaurant** Mzingani Rd; ☏ 024 2232132. On the seafront near the People's Palace, this is one of the oldest tourist-orientated restaurants in Zanzibar Town, founded back in the 1980s and still going strong. With tables on an upstairs balcony and a beautiful view across the bay, it's ideal for b/fasts, lunches and evening meals. During the day (until 18.00) you can enjoy spicy

snacks with your drinks – a plate of spring rolls, samosas and bhajis is about US$2 – plus toasted sandwiches for US$2.50, and omelette and chips from US$4. For larger lunches or evening meals the choice is very small, but the quality consistently good. Vegetarian *thalis* (a mixture of dishes) cost US$7.50, and fish, chicken, squid or octopus in coconut sauce with popadums, plus snacks for starter, a fruit dessert and tea or coffee costs US$7. Open all day from 07.00 until 22.00 or later.

✗ **Sweet Eazy Restaurant & Lounge** Shangani Rd; ☏ 0777 416736; e sweeteazy@retom.com. At the east end of Shangani Rd, between the Tembo Hotel and Forodhani Gardens, this is a cool, relaxed and trendy retreat. There are 2 big rooms with rough-hewn walls, electric-blue floor, tinga-tinga decorations, copious pot plants and wooden chairs with painted covers. One of these rooms is a bar, with a pool table: a very popular hang-out. The other room is the main restaurant, and there's also a small palm-filled garden outside. The bar has a good range of drinks, inc cocktails for US$2–3. In the restaurant, the food is mostly Thai (thanks to the specialist chef from Dar) but there is also an imaginative pan-African menu featuring dishes from Tanzania, Uganda, Ethiopia and elsewhere, and there are some good veggie options. Starters cost US$3–3.50, main courses are US$5–7.50. The waiters are friendly, and though a fun place to chill out, the food here is variable in flavour. However, on Fri there's live music or a disco, and on Sun the all-you-can-eat buffets (US$8) are very good indeed. Later in the evening this is where it's at for locals and visitors alike, and in the relaxed atmosphere, single men need not be lonely. Open 11.00 to midnight at least.

### Budget (average main course less than US$5)

✗ **Archipelago Restaurant** ☏ 025 223 5668. Opposite the NBC, this excellent new first-floor restaurant has rapidly established itself as one of the most popular lunch spots in Stone Town, thanks in large part to its bright décor and elevated balcony overlooking the beach. The other chief

ingredient responsible for its success is that the food – curries, fish dishes, burgers – is excellent and very reasonably priced, with most dishes falling in the US$4–5 range.

✗ **Buni Café** With a prime central location opposite the NBC, this small café serves great fresh coffee along with cakes and a selection of sandwiches and other snacks for around US$2 — the raised balcony is an excellent spot for a late b/fast or light lunch.

✘ **Camlur's** Kenyatta Rd; ✆ 024 2231919. A very long-standing favourite, this small and friendly place serves delicious Goan specialities, such as fish and coconut curry, starting from about US$3. (See *Freddie Mercury* box opposite) Open every evening, except Sun.

✘ **Clove Restaurant** Hurumzi St. Run by a friendly group of Swahili women, this is a nice, local, open-air place in a small and shady garden square opposite the Clove Hotel. Their busy times seem to be b/fast and lunch, and you should check in advance if you plan eating here in the evening. Local dishes such as meat and *ugali* (maize meal), rice and fish, or curry and chapatti cost US$1–2.

✘ **Dolphin Restaurant** Kenyatta Rd. The staff at the Dolphin have been serving tasty, unfussy Zanzibari, vegetarian and seafood meals for many years. It remains popular, and is open for lunch and dinner, with meals from US$2–3, and specials for around US$3.50. It's also a good spot for an inexpensive open-air drink before or after you eat elsewhere.

✘ **Fany's Green Restaurant** Kenyatta Rd; ✆ 2233918. Next to the long-standing Dolphin, this relative newcomer offers a very different atmosphere, with tables inside or outside overlooking busy Kenyatta Rd. Open from 06.30, you can get b/fast (traditional English or traditional Zanzibari) here until 10.00. Lunches and dinners are mainly fish and pizza, with main course US$3.50–4.50.

✘ **Green Garden Restaurant** off Mkunazini St. In the southern part of town, near the Jambo and Flamingo guesthouses, this nice, little open-air place offers snacks (around US$3) and meals (US$4–6), served by friendly staff in peaceful and unpretentious surroundings.

✘ **Nyumbani** between Soko Muhugo St and Vuga Rd; ℮ amir@artlover.com. Nyumbani is similar to Two Tables (described above), in that you eat in someone's house, although the dining room here is a bit larger. Nyumbani means 'at home', and it's most appropriate here, as you're welcomed into the home of Amir, a local artist, and his wife Khadija. They do the cooking, helped by Amir's sister Moulid. We think this place is wonderful, but if you need any more persuading, have a look at the visitors' book. For US$5 you get a set menu of Swahili specialities, with soup and spicy snacks as starters, a main course with local styles of rice, fish and vegetables, and a dessert of dates, fruit and numerous sweets made from nuts, sugar and spices. (Don't forget to

check out the works of art while you're there too.) This place is opposite the Haven Hotel, in the southern part of Stone Town between Soko Muhugo St and Vuga Rd. It's open in the evenings only from 19.30, and you need to make arrangements by around noon if you want to eat later that day. You can also book a few days in advance. Unfortunately in the past some people have made reservations then not turned up, so Amir very apologetically asks for a deposit. For more details or reservations it's easiest to visit the house. Alternatively, speak to Amir on the phone (✆ 024 2238170, office — he has a day job!) or leave a message via Manch Lodge (✆ 024 2231918/0777 413622).

✘ **Old Fort Restaurant** Mzingani Rd; ✆ 0744 278737/0741 630206. Opposite the Forodhani Gardens, Zanzibar's old Arab Fort (known locally as *Ngome Kongwe*) has been here for centuries, but was renovated in the early 1990s. As well as a historical landmark it's now a very impressive cultural centre, with a semi-circular open-air theatre, several smart souvenir shops, and this shady outdoor café-restaurant — a very good place to meet friends or take a break from sightseeing in the heat of the day, especially as it keeps the unusually long hours of 08.00 to 20.00 daily. There's a good selection of snacks for around US$2, local dishes such as chicken and ugali (maize meal) or octopus and chips for around US$3, plus coffees, beers and chilled wine. Open for lunch and dinner daily. Every Tue, Thu and Sat, there's an evening of entertainment (taarab music, African dance, etc) and a barbecue, which costs US$9 — you may need to book ahead.

✘ **Passing Show Hotel** Malindi Rd. Despite the name, this is not a hotel, but a Zanzibar institution nonetheless, serving bowls of rice and vegetable sauce or beans for around US$1, or larger plates of rice and meat or chicken for up to US$2. The food is good and the service quick. This place caters mainly for local people, although visitors are always welcomed. Open lunchtime only.

✘ **Radha Food House** off Kenyatta Rd; ✆ 024 2234808. Tucked away up the narrow street which runs parallel to Kenyatta Rd near the Karibu Inn, Radha Food House is a small, simple and very reasonably priced place, proudly serving pure vegetarian Indian food. This place is deservedly popular and at busy times it's wise to book a table in advance. A thali consisting of dal, rice, lentil and vegetable curries, okra, roti, popadum and lassi costs US$4. You can also get savoury snacks (US$1 for 4 pieces), cakes and sweets, fresh juices and beers.

The late Freddie Mercury, former lead singer and front man for the rock band Queen, was born on Zanzibar on 5 September 1946. His name then was Farouk Bulsara, and his father was an accountant working for the British government in the House of Wonders. His family had emigrated to Zanzibar from India but were originally of Persian extraction. When he was nine, Farouk was sent to boarding school in India, and never returned to Zanzibar. He later went to a college in London, and in the 1970s formed Queen with three other former students.

The current inhabitants of various houses around Zanzibar Town will tell visitors 'Freddie lived here'; his father moved house several times so the claims could all be genuine. Local historians confirm that the Bulsara family lived in the house now occupied by Camlur's Restaurant, and in at least one other house near the post office, either on Kenyatta Road or the small square just behind the post office.

✗ **Sunrise Restaurant and Pub** Kenyatta Rd; ☎ 2239142. Almost opposite Mazson's Hotel, the Sunrise is a simple, friendly, locally owned place serving cheap meals, snacks and drinks in an open-air courtyard above the road. It opens in time for coffee or b/fast and in the daytime it has more of a café feel, while in the evening it's more of a bar, open until late every night. Fish dishes are around US$4–6, chicken and chips is US$2.50. Open 09.00–late.

### Hotel restaurants

Several smart hotels in Zanzibar Town, such as those at Emerson & Green and the Serena, deserve a mention in their own right, and are listed above. Among the mid-range hotels, the restaurant at **Mazsons Hotel** has good main courses in the US$4–10 range. The rooftop restaurant at the **Shangani Hotel**, on Kenyatta Rd, has also been recommended, with simple main courses around US$4 and fine views. More recommendations come for the rooftop restaurant at

### Local restaurants

For a real local flavour, the **Tropicana Restaurant**, next to the High Court on Kaunda Rd, caters for office workers, serving cheap meals of fish and rice for around US$1. Similar is **Café Kelele** on Shangani Rd – a tiny place run by two nice old ladies. At both, only Swahili is spoken. Near the Masumo Bookshop in the Mkunazini area, just back from the market, are several local tea shops, also selling snacks and cakes, inc the **Sinai Restaurant**, the **Utamanduni Restaurant**, the **SB Café**, the **Baobab**

✗ **Wings Fast Food** Shangani. Opposite Tembo Hotel, this is the KFC or McDonalds of Zanzibar, complete with plastic tables, staff in red caps, burgers for US$2.50 and other take-away favourites.

✗ **Zanzibar Coffee House** This friendly new place on Mkunazini St, near the main market, is an excellent place to break the sightseeing with a cold soda, fresh juice, milkshake or strong cup of coffee accompanied by a light snack – cakes, pies, pastries, croissants and sandwiches.

the **Chavda Hotel**, just off Kenyatta Rd, where good Indian meals are in the US$5–9 bracket. Cheaper, but very good value, the restaurant at the **Hotel Kiponda** serves speciality Zanzibari and seafood dishes for US$3–5, but you may need to order some time in advance. The restaurant at the **Coco de Mer Hotel** is friendly and offers good food: beef escalope, masala jeera and chicken Chinese are all US$4.50, and vegetarian options go for US$3.

**Restaurant** and **Bakan's Restaurant**. There are many other, seemingly nameless, basic eating houses which you may just stumble across as you walk around the streets of Zanzibar Town. Menus are rare in these simple establishments, and some of the very small places may only have one meal available (sometimes called *chakula leo* – food of the day): you'll have to ask what they've got. If you're leaving Zanzibar by air, the airport restaurant does surprisingly good snacks and meals.

**FOOD STALLS** For very cheap eats, and a wonderful taste of the local atmosphere, by far the best place to eat in the evening is at Forodhani Gardens, on the seafront opposite the House of Wonders. This is a gathering place for local people and

6

tourists, and as the sun goes down, a long line of stalls fire up their braziers and hurricane lamps, and serve food such as fish and meat kebabs (*mishkaki*), grilled squid and octopus, chips, fishcakes, samosas, chapattis and 'Zanzibar pizzas' – more like a filled savoury pancake. Or try *chipsi mai yai*: an omelette filled with chips, sometimes served with shredded cabbage. Most of the food is grilled on hot coals in front of you, and served on a paper plate. Prices are very reasonable, and a filling plate will cost between US$1 and US$2. You can simply stroll along the line of stalls, seeing what takes your fancy, asking the price and buying a few items at each, or get a whole plate put together at one stall. Other stalls sell water, sugar-cane juice, ice cream and cold drinks – look for the refreshing local pineapple drink named Zed. The sweet-toothed could seek out *haluwa*, made from tamarind, oil and sugar: it's so sweet and sticky that a little goes a long way. Also there are lots of souvenir sellers, all touting their wares. All in all, an evening at Forodhani Gardens is one of the highlights of a trip to Zanzibar. Another place for snacks is the street outside the Ciné Afrique cinema in the Malindi area, or outside the Majestic cinema on Vuga Road. As crowds gather for the evening films, stalls do a brisk trade in peanuts, crisps, chips, cakes, chapattis and samosas.

**FOOD SHOPPING** If you are self-catering, or just going on a picnic for the day, Zanzibar Town has a large market selling many types of fruit and vegetables, plus fresh fish and meat. You can also buy fresh bread in the market from the salesmen who ride in from the bakeries in the suburbs with large baskets on the backs of their bicycles. Dotted around the town are many small shops with a supply of basics, such as bread, biscuits, some fruit and vegetables, and maybe a few tinned items. As these foods are mainly for local people, prices are low. For more choice go to the 'container stores' (they're built in converted shipping containers) along Creek Road or to the shops in the street near the Ciné Afrique, where you'll find a good range of food in tins and packets, imported mainly from Kenya, but also from other parts of the Indian Ocean. Most items are reasonably priced, only slightly more than if bought in Dar or Mombasa. The best supermarket with the widest stock in Stone Town is the **Shamshuddin Cash & Carry Supermarket**, off Creek Road, near the market.

## BARS, CLUBS AND ENTERTAINMENT

The number of bars in Zanzibar Town grows steadily each year as visitors continue to come in ever-increasing numbers. Some bars cater almost exclusively to tourists, others mainly to local Tanzanians who have migrated to Zanzibar from the mainland, as indigenous Zanzibaris are generally Muslim and so don't drink. Usually available are Tanzanian, Kenyan, South African and international beers and soft drinks, plus local and imported spirits. Wines are mostly South African.

Many of the larger hotels have separate bars, open to non-guests, and many of the restaurants and cafés mentioned in the section above also serve drinks.

### BARS AND CLUBS

☆ **Africa House Hotel** Shangani. No visit to Zanzibar is complete without a visit to the terrace bar at the Africa House Hotel (page 121), where people have been meeting up for drinks at sunset since colonial days. You can order snacks and meals (US$2–5) to enjoy on the terrace, and a smarter inside restaurant is promised. Especially popular among locals and the more adventurous visitors are the traditional pipes (also known as hubble-bubble pipes, water pipes or, correctly, *shisha* pipes).

☆ **Bwawani Disco** Bwawani Hotel. There is a disco most nights at the dire Bwawani Hotel (page 125), in a dark and equally seedy room under the swimming pool. Weekends are the most popular, entry is US$1.25 and evenings don't usually warm up until about midnight. If this hotel is renovated, the disco might also get a lick of paint and some decent furniture too, but don't hold your breath. Or rather, do, if you visit the loos!

☆ **Garage Club** Shangani. Almost opposite the Starehe (below) is the vastly different Garage Club, a fully air-conditioned and (fortunately) fully soundproofed disco. Here, the music is a loud, eclectic mix of house, hip-hop, reggae, and African and European pop. You can't miss this place – with outside walls painted in black-and-white zebra stripes. Entry is US$2, although often free for women. It rocks till dawn at weekends.

☆ **Mercury's** Mizingani Rd. As well as the Africa House Hotel (page 121), Mercury's is also good for sundowners, and serves drinks and food all day and long into the evening. This place is noted for its happy hour – out of high season running generously from 17.00 to 20.00 – and its excellent range of cocktails. Shisha pipes are also available (and popular). If you're here for the scenery more than the beer, in the May–Sep period the angle of the sun means the sunsets are easier to appreciate at Mercury's than at the Africa House (which is better Oct–Apr).

☆ **New Happy Bar** Shangani. Next to the Africa House Hotel, this joint has a very strong local flavour, which lurches dangerously towards the dire and disreputable. Frequented mainly by off-duty hookers and tour touts rapidly spending their ill-gotten gains, the attached New Happy Lodge seems to cater for the same clientele, and is best avoided.

☆ **Starehe Club** Shangani. Just 50m down Shangani Rd from the Tembo Hotel, the Starehe is a low-key and peaceful place with a terrace overlooking the bay. The staff are friendly and the beer (reasonably priced) is nearly always cold. Don't be put off by the wire mesh between the customers, the barman and the sea, nor by the souvenir stall at the entrance. This is the sort of place where you'll almost certainly end up chatting with the locals – and we don't mean fishermen! This place is due for renovation soon which might alter things, as a restaurant, ice cream parlour and marine sports centre are planned.

**LIVE MUSIC** There is live taarab music at the Monsoon Restaurant on Wednesday and Saturday nights. Otherwise, there is no one particular venue in Zanzibar Town for live music, but local artists – from traditional taarab to Afro-pop and rap – often perform at bars such as Sweet Eazy, Mercury's or the Starehe Club. To find out what's going on, ask at your hotel or look for posters around town advertising special events. The Arab Fort is another good venue for live music – mostly traditional musicians and dancers, but sometimes contemporary performances, too. A couple of times each week a 'Night at the Fort' evening is organised, which includes at least two performances plus a barbecue dinner. There are often performances on other nights, too. The best thing to do is call in at the Fort during the day, and ask the staff at the desk what's happening in the evening.

**CINEMAS** The main cinema in Zanzibar Town is the Ciné Afrique on Malawi Road, in the Malindi area, near the port gates. There is also the Majestic Cinema on Vuga Road. Tickets are around US$0.25. Films are almost exclusively kung fu or action flicks, or Hindi melodramas, but mainstream Hollywood movies are also shown a few times a week.

## SHOPPING

Zanzibar Town is something of an Aladdin's Cave for visiting shoppers, with a vast array of shops, large and small, catering for the ever-growing tourist influx. Even die-hard deal-hunters will be hard pushed to visit them all, and there are bound to be more by the time you visit. A selection of favourites is listed here.

**TOURIST SHOPS** One of the best places to start any shopping trip is the **Zanzibar Gallery** on Kenyatta Avenue. This shop sells an excellent range of carvings, paintings, jewellery, materials, maps, clothes, rugs, postcards, antiques and real pieces of art from all over Africa. You can also buy local spices, herbs, pickles and honey, and locally made oils such as pineapple bath oil or banana-scented bubble bath – all made naturally from Zanzibar fruit. It also has a very good selection of books (see opposite). The Zanzibar Gallery is run by local photographer and publisher Javed Jafferji; his own books (signed) are also for sale here, including some beautiful large-format photo books, plus illustrated diaries and address books featuring photos from Zanzibar and Tanzania.

Another good place on Kenyatta Road is **Memories of Zanzibar**, opposite the post office. This shop sells everything from beaded flip-flops and silver bracelets to carpets and gourd-lamps, as well as a good selection of books about Zanzibar, and African music CDs.

There are many more shops on Kenyatta Road and along Gizenga Street, as well as its continuations Hurumzi Street and Changa Bazaar, all the way to the Spice Inn. As well as shops, these streets are lined with pavement traders offering carvings and paintings. Most of the shops and stalls stock contemporary carvings and older traditional statues and artefacts from mainland Tanzania and elsewhere in Africa: tinga-tinga paintings on canvas or wooden trays, assorted gold, silver and stone jewellery, packets of spices, and mobiles made from coconut shells in the shapes of dolphins, dhows or tropical fish.

Some of the paintings and craftwork stocked in the souvenir and craft shops is bashed out and of very poor quality, but occasionally, if you search hard enough, you'll find real works of art which have been more carefully made. It's worth spending a bit more money (if indeed the stallholder charges more for better quality – some don't seem to) to get something that will still look good when you get it home, away from the glaring sunlight of Zanzibar which sometimes seems to cloud judgement!

Another place for good-quality crafts is **Hurumzi Art & Craft Gallery** next to the Emerson & Green Hotel on Hurumzi Street. The same owner has another fine shop called **Kibriti** on Gizenga Street, just off Kenyatta Road, near the post office, selling arts and crafts and a good selection of antiques and curios.

Around Zanzibar Town there are also several shops selling antiques from Arabia and India, dating from Omani and British colonial times. **Coast Antique Shop** on Gizenga Street has a particularly good selection of Zanzibar clocks. There are several more antique shops on the street between St Joseph's Cathedral and Soko Muhogo crossroads.

Other places to buy paintings and pieces of art include **Paul's Gallery** at St Monica's Hostel near the Anglican Cathedral (where you can also buy hand-painted T-shirts) and the **Tower Workshop** at the Old Fort, where the resident artists deliberately don't stock tinga-tinga stuff and concentrate on watercolours and some beautiful batik-like works 'painted' with different-coloured candle wax. In the main part of the Fort is another cluster of spice and craft shops, including **Namaan Art Gallery**, which has tinga-tinga works, some watercolours and some some superb oil paintings.

Outside the Fort, in **Forodhani Gardens**, are several more stalls selling carvings and jewellery – especially in the evening when nearby food stalls attract the crowds. Nearby, beside the House of Wonders, tinga-tinga painting salesmen hang their works on the railings, and you can also watch some of the artists (all men) working here. In the same area, local weavers (all women) make mats and baskets from grass and palm leaves. This area is also a good place to find local colourful fabrics and clothing.

For a different medium, visit the **Capital Art Studio** on Kenyatta Road, near the Dolphin Restaurant, which has a good selection of old photographic prints, most from the 1950s and 1960s, and a few earlier ones. (The shop itself seems unchanged since colonial times.) They also sell camera film and batteries, and offer a one-day developing service.

A *kanga*, the traditional coloured wrap worn by local women, makes an ideal souvenir. You can wear it, use it as a beach mat on the coast or a sheet to cover bare mattresses in cheap hotels, and then hang it on your wall, throw it over your sofa or turn it into cushion covers when you get home. A *kanga* normally comes as a large rectangle which the women then cut into two pieces, each about a metre square. One half is worn as a wrap-over skirt and the other is worn as a headscarf (a knot is usually tied in one corner and used for keeping money in). Prices for a *kanga*, from the market or a local cloth shop, start at about US$5.

On Zanzibar, and elsewhere on the coast, men traditionally wear a *kikoi*, a wrap-around 'kilt' of woven cotton, usually striped and thicker than a *kanga*. Once again, a kikoi also has many practical travel uses before you take it home to use as a seat cover. Prices start at US$8.

If you want to combine African and Western clothing, you could even have a local tailor make up a shirt or pair of baggy shorts from a kikoi. For more ideas see the excellent little book *101 Uses for a Kanga*, by David Bygott, available in Zanzibar bookshops.

Local craftwork can also be found in the **Orphanage Shop**, near the Fort. The orphanage is a large building on the main seafront road (Mizingani Road) with a tunnel passing right through the middle of it. The shop is on the side nearest the sea. Here, blind craft-workers weave a good range of baskets, rugs and other items.

At **Sasik Shop** on Gizenga Street, you can buy very beautiful and intricate patchwork cushion-covers and wall-hangings, made on the spot by a local women's co-operative. Also on Gizenga Street, the tailor at **Mnazi Boutique** can copy any shirt, skirt or trousers you like, from material you buy in the shop or elsewhere in town. Prices start at US$8, and go up to US$25 for a complicated dress. If you prefer traditional African clothing, consider a *kanga* or a *kikoi* (see box, above). On Kenyatta Road, the smart **One Way** boutique also sells piles and piles of T-shirts embroidered with giraffes and elephants or emblazoned with Kenyan and Tanzanian slogans and logos. If you want a T-shirt, this is the place. If not, it's a bit limited.

For postcards you can't go wrong at **Angi's Postcards & Maps**, on Mizingani Road, near the Big Tree; there's a truly massive selection here, all at good prices.

**NEWSPAPER AND BOOKSHOPS** Newspapers from Kenya and mainland Tanzania, some international magazines and a reasonable range of books, are available from the **Masumo Bookshop**, off Creek Road, near the market, and from some of the souvenir shops along Kenyatta Road near the old post office.

One of the best bookshops is the **Zanzibar Gallery** on Kenyatta Road. Although primarily a souvenir shop, it has a very good selection of guidebooks and coffee-table books on Zanzibar and other parts of Africa, animal and bird field guides, maps, histories and general novels.

**FILM AND CAMERA SUPPLIES** Slide and print film for cameras is available in several souvenir shops in Zanzibar Town (the ones along Kenyatta Road have the best stock). The Shamshuddin Cash & Carry Supermarket, near the Musoma Bookshop, also has a good stock. The best place to buy film is **Majestic Quick Foto**, on the east side of Creek Road, opposite the BP petrol station. Also see Capital Art Studio, above. Be sure to check the expiry dates if you buy film from more offbeat establishments.

This section covers local services that visitors may require during their time in Zanzibar Town. For more general matters covering Pemba and Mafia, see pages 268–9 and 303 respectively.

**TOURIST INFORMATION** The Zanzibar Tourist Corporation (ZTC) is the state travel service. It has offices in Livingstone House, on the northeast side of town on the main road towards Bububu, where you can make reservations for the ZTC bungalows on the east coast. For general tourist enquiries, you're better off asking at the ZTC office on Creek Road, where the members of staff are a bit more helpful, and there are postcards and maps for sale.

For general information, hotel staff and some tour companies are happy to help, even if you don't end up buying a tour from them. Try Sun N Fun Safaris, Sama Tours and Suna Tours, listed on pages 111–14. Also worth visiting is the information desk at the Arab Fort, which has details of local musical, cultural and sporting events.

For less formalised (but equally useful) information, check the noticeboard at the open-air restaurant inside the Fort. Local events are advertised here, alongside details of companies selling tours, spare seats on charter flights and local residents selling cars or motorbikes. This is also a good place to leave messages for those people you last saw in Cairo or Cape Town and are trying to contact again, as is the famous message board at the Africa House Hotel.

**AIRLINES** For details of international and domestic flights to and from Zanzibar, see the *Getting there* section on page 71. If you do need to book or reconfirm a ticket while you are on Zanzibar, this is most easily done through one of the tour operators recommended earlier in this chapter. Airlines represented on Zanzibar are:

✈ **Air Tanzania** Vuga Rd, near junction with Creek Rd; PO Box 773; ✆ 0242230213/0297; e bookings@airtanzania.com; www.airtanzania.com
✈ **Coastal Travel** Zanzibar airport; ✆ 024 2233112; e aviation@coastal.cc; www.coastal.cc
✈ **Precision Air Flight Services** Kenyatta Rd (next to Mazson's Hotel); ✆ 024 223 0029/4521; f 024 2234520; e pwznz@africaonline.co.tz; www.precisionairtz.com.
✈ **ZanAir** PO Box 2113; main office, Malawi Rd, Malindi; ✆ 024 223 3670/3788; f 233768; branch office, Zanzibar airport; ✆ 024 232993, 0777 413240; e reservations@zanair.com; www.zanair.com

**BANKS AND MONEY-CHANGING** Some general points on banks and change bureaux are given in *Chapter 4*, pages 88–9.

Hard-currency cash can be changed into local currency at most banks as well as at a number of private bureaux de change dotted around the Stone Town. These days, there isn't much to choose between the rates offered by banks and the private 'forex bureaux', indeed some of the private bureaux offer an inferior rate to the banks, but you'll generally find the transaction takes a minute or two at a private bureau whereas changing money at banks often involves long queues and plenty of paperwork. Good private bureaux de change include the Shangani bureau de change (at the northern end of Kenyatta Road, near the Tembo Hotel), and Malindi bureau de change (next to the ZanAir office, east of the port gates). Most large hotels will also change money, although some deal only with their own guests, and they often offer poor rates. There are also change bureaux at the port and airport. The only place that exchanges travellers' cheques is the first-floor 'Foreign Trade Dept' at the National Bank of Commerce on Kenyatta Road. The rate here is pretty good and the commission (0.5%) is negligible. You can draw cash against Visa cards at the ATM outside the same bank, but the only place where you can draw against MasterCard is the Barclays ATM a couple of kilometres out of town along the road towards the north coast.

Elsewhere, getting cash on a debit or credit card is virtually impossible, although most upmarket hotels will accept major credit cards.

## COMMUNICATIONS

**Post** Some general points on postal services and costs are given on page 99. Although letters can be sent from other post offices around Zanzibar Island, it's best to send all your mail from Zanzibar Town. The service is reliable, with letters taking about a week to ten days to reach destinations in Europe and North America (Australia takes a bit longer).

**General post office** (GPO) Zanzibar Town's main post office is a large building in the new part of town on the road towards the Amaani Stadium. Open Mon–Sat 08.00–12.30, 14.00–16.30, Sun 08.00–12.30. **Old post office** The old post office on Kenyatta Rd, in the Shangani area, is much more convenient for tourists. It's possible to buy stamps here, and this is also the place to collect letters sent by poste restante (although some items may get sent to the main post office by mistake – so make sure anyone writing to you addresses the envelope: 'Old Post Office, Kenyatta Road, Shangani'). Open Mon–Thu 08.00–13.00, 14.00–16.30, Fri 08.00–12.00, 14.00–17.00, Sat 09.00–12.00.

**Telephone and fax** Zanzibar Town has a very wide choice of places where you can make calls or send faxes. Some are properly equipped bureaux, others are just a dusty phone in the corner of someone's shop which is nevertheless proudly touted as an 'international communication centre'.

One of the best phone centres is **Tanzanian Telecommunications** international telephone office, next to the old post office on Kenyatta Road. Calls cost US$1 for ten minutes inside Zanzibar, US$1 for three minutes elsewhere in Tanzania, US$1 for about one-and-a-half minutes to other parts of Africa, and US$2.50–3 for one minute to Europe, the USA and other international destinations. This office is open 08.00 to 21.00 daily. The office is large, cool and quiet, and the staff members are very friendly and helpful – so much better than some of the privately owned booths, where they put a stopwatch in your face and there's no privacy at all.

Another option for international calls is to buy a **phonecard** from the international telephone office (they are also sold at some shops and hotels) and use this in the direct-dial phone booth outside. A 150-unit card costs US$7.50 and gives you two minutes to Europe or the USA. A 500-unit card costs US$20. For local calls a 10-unit card is US$1.25, and a 100-unit card is US$5.

If the international telephone office is closed, local boys loiter by the phone booths outside with cards and will charge you per unit to use them. There's even one young entrepreneur with a mobile phone who allows international calls at negotiable rates. It makes you wonder who is really paying the bill.

At the private phone bureaux around Zanzibar Town, international calls are about the same price as those charged by the Tanzanian Telecommunications office, although a few places manage to undercut this rate, and some can be considerably more, so it's worth checking, if you've got a lot of calls to make. For example, at Asko Tours, next to the old post office, local calls are US$0.40 per minute, calls to Africa are US$1.50 per minute, and international calls cost US$3 per full minute. Opposite the international phone office a souvenir shop offers international calls to Europe for US$2.60 per minute. At Next Step Services on Hurumzi Street, international calls cost US$5 per minute. For cheap international calls, worth seeking out is Asad Secretarial Services, near the Clove Hotel, which offers phone calls via the internet for US$2 per minute. There's a delay of a second or two while you're speaking, but once you're used to that, it's fine.

For current codes, see page 100 in *Chapter 4*.

**Mobile phones** If you bring a mobile phone with you from home, it's emphatically worth the minor investment in a Tanzanian SIM card (which costs around US$0.30 and gives you a local number) and airtime cards (available in units of Tsh 1,000 to 5,000). International text messages and calls out of Tanzania are seriously cheap: at the time of writing, US$1 will buy you around 20 text messages to anywhere in the world, and international calls work out at around US$1 for three to four minutes.

By contrast, you can expect to rack up a hefty bill using your home phone number for calls and/or messages, since in most instances these are charged at international rates out of your home country, even when you are phoning home. SIM and airtime cards can be bought at a specialist Vodacom outlet (there's one opposite the taxi rank on Creek Road) or at numerous other small shops displaying the ubiquitous Vodacom sticker.

**Email and internet** Since 2001, internet bureaux have sprung up everywhere in Zanzibar Town. Like the phone offices (indeed, many are also phone offices), some internet bureaux are large and air conditioned with several terminals, while others are in the corner of someone's shop and you connect to the outside world crammed between boxes of soap. In general, most hotels do not offer public email services.

There's a pretty standardised cost across town of US$1 per hour, and several dozen cafés to chose from. Most charge per 30-minute increment, starting at US$0.50, and if you go over this by a few seconds you'll be charged for the next 30 minutes.

Internet bureaux include:

⊜ **Shangani Internet Café** Kenyatta Rd; ✆ 024 2232925. This is one of the best places in Zanzibar Town. It has long opening hours, fast connections, about 15 computers, a fridge full of ice cream and cold drinks, and charges US$1/hr.
⊜ **Sanjay Internet Café** Just off Gizenga St, behind the House of Wonders, this small place has about 5 terminals, and normally charges US$1/hr, but

sometimes offers special rates of half this price.
⊜ **Asad Secretarial Services** Near the Clove Hotel, is this small place with good connections, charging US$1/hr.
⊜ **Too Short Internet** Opposite National Bank of Commerce, this is centrally located with long hours (08.00–23.00) around 8 quick machines at the standard rate of US$0.50/30 mins.

**HOSPITALS, DOCTORS AND PHARMACIES** Zanzibar Island's main public hospital is **Mnazi Moja General Hospital**, on the south side of Stone Town. During the island's revolutionary heyday it was called the Lenin Hospital, but this title has now been dropped. Like many hospitals in developing countries, the staff are dedicated but the wards are badly under-funded, under-supplied and in very poor condition. Equally distressing is the pile of rubbish (including drip-feeds and needles) simply dumped on the beach behind the hospital.

In case of real emergency, the nearest major hospital, fully staffed and equipped, is the Aga Khan Hospital in Mombasa. You may even need to fly there (by charter plane if necessary) if things are really serious, but this should be covered by your insurance.

Most tourists go to one of the private medical clinics where staff speak English and the service is usually better. Of course, this has to be paid for, and costs around

US$50 per consultation, but all fees should be covered by your travel insurance. The medical centres also have pharmacies selling medicines and other supplies.

## Main clinics

✚ **Zanzibar Medical and Diagnostic Centre** PO Box 1043; ☎ 024 223 1071, 24hr emergency no: 0777 750040/413714. Just off Vuga Rd, near the Majestic Cinema, this clinic is recommend by most expatriates. It's a fully equipped facility, run to European standards, and the staff members speak several European languages.

✚ **Zanzibar Medical Group** ☎ 024 2233134. Another good-quality private clinic on Kenyatta Rd, charging US$30 per consultation.

**Other medical centres** If your insurance covers only major medical problems, and you want to keep costs down for something minor, you could go to one of Zanzibar's other medical centres:

✚ **Afya Medical Hospital** ☎ 024 223 1228; m 0777 411934. Off Vuga Rd at the southern end of Stone Town, Afya is large and well stocked, with friendly staff. Consultations cost US$2, blood or urine tests are available, and there's also a pharmacy.

✚ **Dr Mehta's Hospital** ☎ 024 2230194/0741

612889. Also on Vuga Rd.

✚ **Fahaud Health Centre** Near St Joseph's Cathedral, this very basic centre offers consultations for US$1 whilst a malaria blood test is US$0.50. Should your test prove positive, they also sell Fansidar at US$0.50 per tablet.

**Pharmacies** If you need to buy medicines, Zanzibar Town has several pharmacies stocking drugs which are mostly imported from Europe and India, and other items such as toiletries and tampons. Stocks are not always reliable, so if you know you're likely to need a specific drug during your visit, it's best to bring a sufficient supply with you. There are pharmacies near the Musoma Bookshop, next to the Emerson & Green Hotel, and another on Creek Road near the market. Straightforward medicines, toiletries and tampons are also available at the 'container stores' on Creek Road.

**POLICE** In case of emergency in Zanzibar Town, the main police station is in the Malindi area, on the north side of Stone Town (☎ *999 or 024 223 0772*). This is also the central police station for the whole of Zanzibar. Robberies can be reported here (travel insurance companies usually require you, if you are making a claim, to prove you have notified the local police), but you should not expect any real action to be taken as the police are not particularly well motivated.

Zanzibar also has a platoon of Tourist Police, supposedly to assist and protect Zanzibar's foreign visitors, although many people question their effectiveness. They are mostly seen driving around town in fancy new patrol cars, while touts continue to hassle tourists unimpeded.

**SWIMMING** The swimming pool at the Tembo Hotel is open to non-guests for US$3, all day. At the Bwawani Hotel, swimming costs less than US$1, but the pool is only half full, of green and slimy water, so this is not at all recommended. There's also a pool at the Serena Hotel though this is reserved for hotel guests only.

**SWAHILI LESSONS** If you would like to learn a few words (or even more) of the local language, the Taasisi Kiswahili Institute (*PO Box 146;* ☎ *024 2230724*) inside the State University on Vuga Road offers lessons. Classes are normally 08.00 to noon and cost US$4 per hour, or US$80 for a week's course.

Single lessons away from the institute, and longer courses, which include lodgings in the house of a teacher or local family, are also available.

One writer has compared the old Stone Town of Zanzibar to a tropical forest where tall houses stretch to the sky instead of trees, and the sun filters through a fretwork of overhanging balconies instead of foliage. Its labyrinth of twisting streets and alleys is a stroller's paradise, with new sights, sounds or smells to catch the imagination at every turn: massive carved doors, ancient walls, tiny tempting shops with colourful wares and bustling shoppers, old men chatting on a stone bench or hunched over a traditional board game, kids with battered homemade toys, ghetto-blasters at full volume, thin cats curled in patches of sunlight, little boys hawking cashews or postcards or fresh bread, bright flowers in pots and window-boxes, golden-orb spiders weaving their giant webs on a stunted tree, the sound of the muezzin calling from the mosque and the scent of cloves or ginger or lemongrass – and everywhere the echoes of Zanzibar's rich and fascinating history, the sultans, shipbuilders, explorers, slave markets, merchants and exotic spice trade.

Stone Town was originally built on a peninsula which has probably been inhabited since the first people arrived on Zanzibar (although the creek that separated its eastern edge from the rest of the island has now been reclaimed). Ras Shangani, at the western tip of the peninsula, is thought to have been the site of a fishing village for many centuries, and at least one of Zanzibar's early Swahili rulers, the Mwinyi Mkuu, had a palace here.

In the 16th century, Portuguese navigators built a church and trading station on the peninsula as it had a good harbour and was easy to defend. When the Omani Arabs began to settle on the island in the 18th century, they built a fort on the site of the church, and today's Stone Town grew up around the Fort.

Most of the houses you see today were built in the 19th century, when Zanzibar was one of the most important trading centres in the Indian Ocean region. The coralline rock of Zanzibar Island was easy to quarry for use as a construction material, so that many of the houses were built in grand style with three or four storeys. Previously most of the houses on Zanzibar had been much smaller, built of mangrove poles and palm thatch, making the fine white buildings in Stone Town even more exceptional.

Today, nearly all of these old houses are still inhabited, although many are in a very bad state of repair. The coralline rock was a good building material but it is also soft, and easily eroded if not maintained. Crumbling masonry, along with dilapidated woodwork, is sadly an all too familiar sight in Stone Town – and in some places where the surface has disintegrated it reveals the rough blocks of ancient coral beneath.

However, since the end of the 1980s and through the 1990s, several buildings in Stone Town have been renovated. The Zanzibar government, with assistance from the United Nations Centre for Human Settlements (the Habitat Fund), plans to preserve many more, eventually restoring the whole Stone Town to something like its original magnificence. The Stone Town Conservation and Development Authority has been established to co-ordinate this work, although it is sometimes hampered by a lack of co-ordination with the local government authorities.

During the 19th century, many of Stone Town's inhabitants were wealthy Arabs and Indians. Consequently the houses were built in two main styles: the Arab style, with plain outer walls and a large front door leading to an inner courtyard; and the Indian style, with a more open façade and large balconies decorated with ornate railings and balustrades, designed to catch sea breezes and dispel the humid atmosphere.

Many of the buildings have doors with elaborately carved frames and panels, decorated with brass studs and heavy locks. The size of the door and the intricacies

Although the narrow streets of Zanzibar are like a labyrinth, Stone Town is not very large, and getting seriously lost is unlikely. (If you don't know where you are, just keep walking and you'll soon come out onto Creek Road or one of the streets alongside the sea.) In fact, for many visitors getting lost in the maze of narrow streets and alleys is all part of the fun.

However, if your time is limited, you prefer not to become disorientated, or you want to find some specific sites of interest, it's possible to hire a knowledgeable guide from most local tour companies.

If you don't want a formal tour, but would still like to be accompanied by a local, you could engage the services of the *papaasi* (see box, page 118), although generally they will be more interested in taking you to souvenir shops than museums. It might be wiser to ask your hotel or a reputable tour company to put you in touch with someone who will happily walk with you through the streets, and show you the way if you get lost. We have heard from readers who employed a local schoolboy, who was also very happy to practise his English, and this seems an excellent idea. About US$5 (in Tanzanian shillings) for a day's work would be a suitable fee.

If you are seriously interested in the history of Zanzibar, a local artist and historian, John da Silva, is very occasionally available for private guided tours around Stone Town. John knows the history of every public building and every house (and literally every balcony and door) in the town. His rates are US$20 for a tour lasting two to three hours. You can contact John through Sama Tours (page 112).

of its decoration were signs of the family's wealth and status. Today the Zanzibar door has become a well-recognised symbol of the town and island's historic and cultural background, and many new buildings incorporate one into their design – either a genuine one removed from an old building, or a reproduction. (For more on doors see box on page 40.)

Among the houses and tucked away in the narrow streets you will come across mosques, churches and other public buildings, almost hidden in the maze. Stone Town also has a few streets of shops, some of them still called bazaars. Some shops are very small, no more than a kiosk, with a few dusty food tins or a couple of jars of sweets on the shelf; others are larger, catering for locals and visitors, with a wider range of foods, books, fabrics, furniture and electrical goods. There are also antique and curio shops (bargain hard here!), and an increasing number of places selling a wide and inventive selection of locally produced arts and crafts, aimed specifically at the growing tourist market.

As you explore the narrow streets with all their historic links, remember that Zanzibar Town today is very much a real community, where people live and work. It is not a museum piece created for tourists. You should not enter any private house or courtyard unless expressly invited to do so, and before you peer through a window or doorway, stop and ask yourself – would you appreciate a stranger doing the same in your home? You should also show respect for local sensibilities (see *Clothing*, page 85). Mosques are not usually open to non-Muslim visitors. Taking photos of buildings is generally acceptable, but you should never photograph people without their permission. (See also *Mosques* on page 156.)

**THE MARKET** The market is about halfway along Creek Road and a good place to visit even if you don't want to buy anything. The long market-hall is surrounded by traders selling from stalls, or with their wares simply spread out on the ground.

It's a very vibrant place where everything, from fish and bread to sewing machines and second-hand car spares, is bought and sold. People bring their produce here from all over the island, and others come to buy things they can't get in their own villages. You could spot dog-eared schoolbooks, anonymous tangles of metal being soldered into usefulness, rough wooden chairs, suitcases, shoes, baskets, kitchenware, clocks and watches, CDs, mobile phones and doubtless the occasional kitchen sink. Some food displays may be best avoided by the squeamish: the massive deep-sea fish heads, jaws agape; dark haunches of beef and slabs of less identifiable meat; pearly squid tentacles; grubby recycled bottles and jars containing oil, honey, pickle and goodness knows what else … and the inevitable accompanying buzz of flies. Don't miss the swathes of multi-patterned cotton fabrics, the fragrant spices and mound after mound of exotic fruit and vegetables – and just enjoy people-watching and being part of a Zanzibar experience which, at the time of writing, hasn't yet become touristy.

Towards the end of the 19th century, the town's marketplace was inside the Old Fort. Today's market-hall was built in 1904, and some very early photographs of the market displayed in the museum show that very little has changed since then.

On occasional evenings, a public auction is held in the street behind the market where furniture, household goods, old bikes, and all sorts of junk are sold. It is very entertaining to watch, but make sure you don't bid for anything by mistake: keep your hands still!

**LIVINGSTONE HOUSE** On the northeast side of the town, this old building is now the main office of the Zanzibar Tourist Corporation (ZTC). It was built around 1860 for Sultan Majid (sultan from 1856 to 1870). At this time Zanzibar was used as a starting point by many of the European missionaries and pioneers who explored eastern and central Africa during the second half of the 19th century. David Livingstone, probably the most famous explorer of them all (see box, page 153), stayed in this house before sailing to the mainland to begin his last expedition in 1866. Other explorers, such as Burton, Speke, Cameron and Stanley, also stayed here while preparing for their own expeditions. The house was later used by members of the island's Indian community, and in 1947 it was bought by the colonial government for use as a scientific laboratory for research into clove diseases. After independence and the revolution it became the Zanzibar headquarters of the Tanzania Friendship Tourist Bureau, the forerunner of today's ZTC.

**THE OLD DISPENSARY** Opposite the new port buildings, on Mizingani Road, this is a grand four-storey building with a set of particularly decorative balconies. It is also called the Ithnasheri Dispensary, and lettering at the top of the front wall reads 'Khoja Haji Nasser Nur Mohammed Charitable Dispensary'. It was originally built in the 1890s as a private house for a prominent Ismaili Indian merchant called Tharia Topan, who was a customs advisor to the sultans, and one of the wealthiest individuals on Zanzibar at the time. In 1899 he gave the house up to be used as a dispensary, also funding the medicine and other services. Topan also provided money (with the Aga Khan and Sultan Ali) for a non-denominational school which opened in Zanzibar in 1891. The dispensary fell into disrepair during the 1970s and 1980s, but was renovated in 1995 with funding from the Aga Khan Charitable Trust. A few years later it opened as the Stone Town Cultural Centre. There is a small exhibition (free) of historical photographs, but most of the building is now used as offices. More businesses are due to open here in the future.

**THE OLD CUSTOMS HOUSE** On Mizingani Road (the main seafront), overlooking the sea, this large building has a plain façade and is fairly featureless apart from the beautiful set of carved wooden doors. These have been decorated in the Arab style with fish, lotus and anchor chain motifs. Hamoud, grandson of Sultan Said, was proclaimed sultan here in 1896. In 1995 the Customs House was renovated with funds provided by Unesco, the United Nations cultural organisation.

The equally large building next door to the Customs House was formerly Le Grand Hotel and then became a private house before being abandoned. A group of developers have long-term plans to convert it into a hotel once again.

**THE PALACE MUSEUM** This is a large white building with castellated battlements situated on Mizingani Road, where the latter runs very close to the sea. Originally called the Sultan's Palace, it was built in the late 1890s for members of the sultan's family. From 1911, it was used as the Sultan of Zanzibar's official residence, but was renamed the People's Palace after the 1964 Revolution, when Sultan Jamshid was overthrown. It continued to be used as government offices until 1994 when the palace was turned into a museum dedicated to the history of the sultans of Zanzibar.

Remarkably, much of their furniture and other possessions survived the revolutionary years and can now be seen by the public for the first time. The museum is well organised and informative: the ground floor is dedicated to the early years of the sultanate (1828 to 1870), while the upper floors contain exhibits from the later, more affluent period of 1870 to 1896. These include thrones, banqueting tables and ceremonial furniture, and also more personal items such as beds and the sultan's personal water-closet. There is also a room devoted to Princess Salme, the daughter of Sultan Said who eloped to Hamburg with a German merchant in 1866. It's a fascinating story, told by the princess herself in her book *Memoirs of an Arabian Princess from Zanzibar*, which you can buy in the museum. See also the *Princess Salme* box on pages 164–5. Outside in the palace garden are the graves of Sultans Said, Barghash, Majid, Khaled, Khalifa and Abdullah.

An excellent little leaflet is available containing a clear, concise historical background with plans and descriptions of all the palace rooms. Guides are also available to show you around and describe the exhibits in detail; their fee is open to negotiation, but should be agreed beforehand (approx US$5 is fair).

*US$3 entrance; open Mon–Fri 09.00–18.00, Sat–Sun & holidays 09.00–15.00.*

**BEIT AL AJAIB (HOUSE OF WONDERS)** This large, white building dominates the waterfront area of Zanzibar Town, and is one of its best-known landmarks. A perfect rectangle, it is one of the largest buildings on the island even today, rising over several storeys, surrounded by tiers of pillars and balconies, and topped by a large clock tower. After more than a century of use as a palace and government offices, it opened in 2002 as the Museum of History and Culture and contains some fascinating exhibits and displays. It's a pity to rush your visit: allow yourself enough time to browse.

Built in 1883 as a ceremonial palace for Sultan Barghash, *Beit al Ajaib* was designed by a marine engineer, hence the great use of steel pillars and girders in the construction, and located on the site of an older palace used by Queen Fatuma, the Mwinyi Mkuu (ruler of Zanzibar) in the 17th century.

In its heyday, the interior of the new palace had fine marble floors and panelled walls. It was the first building on Zanzibar to be installed with electric lighting, and one of the first in east Africa to have an electric lift – which is why, not surprisingly, the local people called it 'Beit el Ajaib', meaning 'House of Wonders'.

In 1896, the building was slightly damaged by naval bombardment during an attempted palace coup, started when Sultan Hamad died suddenly and his cousin

Khaled tried to seize the throne (see *The shortest war in history* box on page 25). From 1911 it was used as offices by the British colonial government and after the 1964 Revolution it was used by the ASP, the ruling political party of Zanzibar. In 1977 it became the headquarters of the CCM (Chama Cha Mapinduzi, the Party of the Revolution), the sole political party of Tanzania at the time. In the early 1990s, Beit al Ajaib was virtually abandoned by the government and the party and stood empty for some years, slowly falling into disrepair, despite short-lived plans, which never materialised, to turn it into a hotel.

Four years after it originally opened to the public, the museum is still under development, with about half the planned displays now completed. Those already finished cover a variety of subjects relating to Zanzibari and Swahili culture and history, including dhow-building (one of the amazing traditional 'stitched dhows' is there, its timbers literally 'sewn' together), the maritime history of the Swahili coast, and the early history of Stone Town and the Swahili trading empire of the 19th century. Further displays covering the Portuguese period, and Omani and British colonial times are planned, as is a library and conference centre. Among the many items recently transferred here from the now closed Peace Memorial Museum, although they may not yet be in their final locations, you should be able to find Dr Livingstone's medical chest, a section of track from the short-lived Zanzibar Railroad, some old bicycle lamps customised to run on coconut oil, and the old lighthouse lamp.

As well as the items on show, the House of Wonders building itself is a fascinating exhibit, to which the museum allows public access for the first time in decades. The ground floor offers great views up through the central courtyard to the top of the building. On the next level, the floor is covered with marble tiles. On each floor are four massive carved wooden doors. On the next floor up from the exhibition room you can go out onto the upper balcony and walk all the way around the outside of the House of Wonders. Needless to say, the views over Stone Town and the bay are spectacular.

Outside the House of Wonders are two old bronze cannons which have Portuguese inscriptions. It is thought that these cannons were made in Portugal some time in the early 16th century, but the Omanis probably brought them to Zanzibar, after taking them from Persian forces who had originally captured the guns from the Portuguese in 1622.

*US$3 entrance; photography permitted*

**THE ARAB FORT** The Arab Fort (also called the Old Fort, and by its local name *Ngome Kongwe*) is next to the House of Wonders. It is a large building, with high, dark-brown walls topped by castellated battlements. It was built between 1698 and 1701 by the Busaidi group of Omani Arabs, who had gained control of Zanzibar in 1698, following almost two centuries of Portuguese occupation. The fort was used as a defence against the Portuguese and against a rival Omani group, the Mazrui, who occupied Mombasa at that time.

The fort was constructed by the Busaidi Omani Arabs on the site of a Portuguese church which had been built between 1598 and 1612. In the main courtyard, remnants of the old church can still be seen built into the inside wall. In the 19th century the fort was used as a prison, and criminals were executed or punished here, at a place just outside the east wall. The Swahili word *gereza*, meaning prison, is thought to be derived from the Portuguese word *ireja*, meaning church.

In the early 20th century, the fort was also used as a depot for the railway line which ran from Zanzibar Town to Bububu. In 1949 it was rebuilt and the main courtyard used as a ladies' tennis club, but after the 1964 Revolution it fell into disuse.

Today, the fort has been renovated, and is open to visitors. It is possible to reach the top of the battlements and go onto the towers on the western side. In 1994 a section was turned into an open-air theatre. The development was imaginative yet sympathetic to the overall design and feel of the original building: seating is in amphitheatre style, and the fort's outer walls and the House of Wonders form a natural backdrop. The theatre is used for performances of contemporary and traditional music, drama and dance. The fort also houses a tourist information desk, with details on performances in the amphitheatre and other events around town, plus a selection of books for sale and a range of tour company leaflets to browse. There are also several spice and craft shops, a pleasant café, and remarkably some very clean public toilets. And don't miss the Tower Workshop in the west tower, where local artists create and display their works (more details are given in the *Shopping* section on page 138). Even if historical ruins don't interest you, the Fort is well worth a visit. With so many attractions and facilities, it's easy to spend quite a few hours here.

**FORODHANI GARDENS** The Forodhani Gardens (Jamituri Gardens on some maps) are between the Arab Fort and the sea, overlooked by the House of Wonders. Forodhani means 'customs' and this is close to the site of the original Customs House. The gardens were first laid out in 1936 to commemorate the Silver Jubilee of Sultan Khalifa (sultan from 1911 to 1960), and were called Jubilee Gardens until the 1964 Revolution. This is a popular place for local people in the evenings and there are some stalls serving drinks and snacks. In the centre of the gardens is a podium where the band of the sultan's army used to play for the public. Nearer the sea is a white concrete arabesque arch which was built in 1956 for the visit of Princess Margaret (sister of Queen Elizabeth II of Britain), although this was never officially used, as the princess arrived at the dhow harbour instead. She did visit the gardens, however, and planted the large tree with creepers that can still be seen today.

**SAINT JOSEPH'S CATHOLIC CATHEDRAL** This large cathedral, with prominent twin spires, is off Kenyatta Road in the Baghani part of town. Although its spires are a major landmark from a distance, the cathedral can be surprisingly hard to find in the narrow streets. It was built between 1893 and 1897 by French missionaries and local converts, who had originally founded a mission here in 1860. The plans were drawn by the same French architect who designed the cathedral in Marseilles, France. The tiles and the stained-glass windows were imported from France, and the murals on the inside walls, painted just after the cathedral was completed, also show a clear French influence. Unfortunately, some of the murals have recently been badly restored.

The cathedral is in regular use by the town's Catholic community, a mixture of Zanzibaris, Tanzanians from the mainland, Goans and Europeans. There are several masses each Sunday, and one or two on weekdays too. Outside mass times, the main cathedral doors may be locked, and entrance is via the back door reached through the courtyard of the adjoining convent.

**THE HAMAMNI BATHS** In the centre of Stone Town, east of St Joseph's Cathedral and northwest of Sultan Ahmed Mugheiri Road (formerly New Mkunazini Road), are the Hamamni Baths. The area is called Hamamni, which means simply 'the place of the baths' from the Arabic *hammam* (bath-house).

This was the first public bath-house in Zanzibar, commissioned by Sultan Barghash and built by an architect called Haji Gulam Hussein. It is one of the most elaborate on Zanzibar, and is constructed in the Persian style. (Such baths are found

From the earliest times, slaves were one of the many 'commodities' exported from Africa to Arabia, Persia, India and beyond. In the 18th century the demand increased considerably and Arab trading caravans from Zanzibar penetrated mainland Africa in search of suitable slaves. Various contemporary accounts describe all aspects of the trade, from the initial capture of the slaves to their sale in the infamous market of Zanzibar Town.

In the interior, the Arab traders would often take advantage of local rivalries and encourage powerful African tribes to capture their enemies and sell them into slavery. In this way, men, women and children were exchanged for beads, corn or lengths of cloth.

When the Arab traders had gathered enough slaves, sometimes up to a thousand, they returned to the coast. Although the Koran forbade cruelty to slaves, this was frequently ignored on the long journey to Zanzibar: the slaves were tied together in long lines, with heavy wooden yokes at their necks or iron chains around their ankles which remained in place day and night until they reached the coast.

The trade in slaves was closely linked to the trade in ivory: the Arab traders also bought tusks from the Africans and some of the captured slaves may have had to carry these on their heads as they marched towards the coast. If a woman carrying a baby on her back became too weak to carry both child and ivory, the child would be killed or abandoned to make the ivory load easier to carry. Any slaves unable to march were also killed and left behind for the vultures and hyenas. The passage of a slave caravan was marked by a long line of decaying corpses.

After many weeks or months of marching, the slave caravans reached the coast at ports such as Kilwa and Bagamoyo. Here, the slaves were loaded onto dhows, seldom more than 30–35m long, and taken to Zanzibar. Each dhow carried between 200 and 600 slaves, all crammed below decks on specially constructed bamboo shelves with about 1m of headroom. There was not enough room to sit, or to kneel or squat, just a crippling combination of the three. Sometimes slaves were closely packed in open boats, their bodies exposed day and night to the sea and the rain. They were thirsty, hungry and seasick and many died of exhaustion. Meals consisted of a daily handful of rice and a cup

in many Arab and Islamic countries, and are commonly known by Europeans as 'Turkish baths'.) Today the baths are no longer functioning, but it is still possible to go in and look around. Inside, the bath-house is surprisingly large, with several sections including the steam room, the cool room and the cool water pool.

The caretaker lives opposite: he will unlock the door, make a small entrance charge, give you a guided tour and sell you an informative leaflet about the baths' history and function.

**TIPPU TIP'S HOUSE** Tippu Tip (also spelt Tippoo Tib and Toppu Tob) was a slave trader, whose real name was Hamed bin Mohammed el Marjebi. He was born in the 1840s and began to participate in the slave trade at the age of 18. His nickname is thought to come either from a local word meaning 'to blink', as he apparently had a nervous twitch affecting his eyes, or because his eyes resembled those of a type of bird called Tippu Tib locally because it had characteristic blinking eyes.

During the mid 19th century, Tippu Tip travelled for many years across the east African mainland, trading in slaves and ivory. He also helped some of the European explorers such as Livingstone and Stanley with their supplies and route-planning.

Contemporary records describe him as tall, bearded, fit and strong, with dark skin, an intelligent face and the air of a well-bred Arab. He reportedly visited his concubines twice a day, and is said to have argued with missionaries that Abraham of stagnant water. Sanitation was non-existent and disease spread rapidly. When any illness was discovered, infected slaves were simply thrown overboard.

By the time the slaves reached Zanzibar, they were suffering from starvation and the effects of torturously cramped conditions: it was sometimes a week after landing before they could straighten their legs. The slave traders paid customs duty on all slaves who landed, so any considered too weak to live were thrown overboard as the ship approached the port. Even so, many more slaves died in the Customs House or on the streets between the port and the market.

Before being put on sale, the slaves who did survive were cleaned so that they would fetch a better price. Men and boys had their skins oiled and were given a strip of material to put around their waist. Women and girls were draped in cloth, and sometimes even adorned with necklaces, earrings and bracelets. Generous layers of henna and kohl were smeared onto their foreheads and eyebrows.

The slaves were put on sale in the market in the late afternoon. They were arranged in lines, with the youngest and smallest at the front and the tallest at the rear, and paraded through the market by their owner, who would call out the selling prices. The owner would assure potential buyers that the slaves had no defects in speech or hearing, and that there was no disease present. Buyers would examine the arms, mouths, teeth and eyes of the slaves, and the slaves were often made to walk or run, to prove they were capable of work. Once their suitability had been established, they were sold to the highest bidder.

After being sold to a new owner, slaves were either put to work in the houses and plantations of Zanzibar or else transported again, on a much longer sea voyage, to Oman or elsewhere in the Indian Ocean. However, the slaves were relatively well treated when they arrived at their new homes. They were fed, housed and clothed, and given small plots of land, with time off to tend them. Young mothers were rarely separated from their children, and good slaves were often freed after a few years. Many took paid jobs, such as gardeners and farmers, for their previous masters: some even became leaders of slave caravans or masters of slave ships.
*Source: Charles Miller 'The Lunatic Express', Macmillan 1971*

and Jacob (men of God, who appear in the Bible and the Koran) had both been slave owners themselves. Tippu Tip became very wealthy and by 1895, after many years of trading on the mainland, he owned seven plantations on Zanzibar and 10,000 slaves. He died in 1905.

The house where Tippu Tip lived is near the Africa House Hotel, behind the offices of Jasfa Tours. Until the 1960s it was a private residence, but after the revolution it was turned into a block of flats and is now occupied by several families. The house has not been maintained since its transformation, and one writer has called it 'the most magnificent squat in all of Africa'. It is not open to visitors. However, the huge carved front door (a sign of Tippu Tip's great wealth) leading into the courtyard can still be seen.

**THE ANGLICAN CATHEDRAL** The Cathedral Church of Christ, also called the Cathedral of the Universities Mission in Central Africa (UMCA), is near the junction of Creek Road and Sultan Ahmed Mugheiri Road (formerly New Mkunazini Road) on the eastern side of Stone Town. It stands on the site of the slave market, used in the 18th and 19th centuries when Zanzibar was a large slaving centre.

A group of UMCA missionaries had originally come to east Africa in 1861, following the call of the explorer David Livingstone to oppose the slave trade and spread Christianity across Africa. In 1864 they settled in Zanzibar, after a number of earlier sites proved unsuccessful. When the slave market was closed by Sultan Barghash in 1873 the missionaries bought the site and almost immediately started building the cathedral. Some adjoining land was donated to the mission by a wealthy Indian merchant called Jairam Senji. Today, nothing of the old slave market remains (but see *St Monica's Hostel*, below).

When the first service was held in the cathedral, on Christmas Day 1877, the roof was not finished. It was finally completed in 1880. Tradition has it that the cathedral's altar stands on the site of a tree to which the slaves were tied and then whipped to show their strength and hardiness. Those who cried out the least during the whipping were considered the strongest, and sold for higher prices.

The man who was the force and inspiration behind the building of the cathedral was Bishop Edward Steere, who was Bishop of Zanzibar from 1874 to 1882. (He was also the first compiler of an English–Swahili dictionary, using the Roman alphabet; until then Swahili had been written using Arabic script.) He trained local people as masons and used coral stone and cement for building materials. Sultan Barghash is reputed to have asked Bishop Steere not to build the cathedral tower higher than the House of Wonders. When the bishop agreed, the sultan presented the cathedral with its clock. The tower was finished in 1883.

The legacy of David Livingstone lives on in the cathedral: a window is dedicated to his memory, and the church's crucifix is made from the tree that marked the place where his heart was buried at the village of Chitambo, Zambia.

The mosaic decorations on the altar were given to the cathedral by Miss Caroline Thackeray (a cousin of the English novelist William Makepeace Thackeray), who was a teacher at the mission here from 1877 to 1902.

Behind the altar is the bishop's throne and 12 other seats for the canons. They are decorated with copper panels and show the names of several biblical figures, written in Swahili. The window behind the altar has been decorated with pictures of African saints, from Egypt, Carthage and Ethiopia.

Around the church are many plaques, dedicated to the memory of missionaries who died here, and to the sailors and airmen who were killed in action during the East Africa Campaign of World War I.

Today, services are held every Sunday (in Swahili), and an English service is held on the first Sunday of the month. The cathedral is also open to visitors.

Outside the cathedral, in a small garden next to the school, is a sculpture of four slaves chained in a pit – an understated yet powerfully emotive work of art that is well worth seeing.

*During the day (except at service times) there is an entry fee of US$10, payable at a small kiosk, to the cathedral and surrounding area (which includes the slave sculpture).*

**ST MONICA'S HOSTEL** This is an impressive old stone building in its own right. Apart from its hostel accommodation (see page 126) and its gallery and craft shop (see page 138), its basement provides one of Zanzibar's simplest, but arguably most moving and evocative, reminders of the dehumanising horrors of the slave trade. A stone staircase leads down from the entrance hallway to what is reputed to be the dungeon where slaves were kept before being taken to market.

Try to go there with a local person or competent guide who can set the scene and recount the history while you are *in situ*. It's chilling. The dank rooms – more like tombs – are cramped and airless, with low doorways and tiny windows. Even today it's a sombre place – but imagine it crowded with slaves in their hundreds, men, women and children together, sick and exhausted after their gruelling sea voyage (see *The east African slave trade* box on pages 150–1), crammed five deep on the narrow stone slabs and shackled with chains which still lie there today. Imagine the pain, terror, bewilderment, desolation – and death.

David Livingstone is the best-known of all the European explorers who travelled in 19th-century Africa, and many of his journeys began and ended in Zanzibar.

He was born on 19 March 1813 in the village of Blantyre, near Glasgow, in Scotland. In 1841, at the age of 28, he went to South Africa as a missionary doctor. There he married Mary Moffat, a missionary's daughter. On his early expeditions in southern Africa he crossed the Kalahari Desert and, in November 1855, became the first European to see *Mosi oa Tunya* ('the smoke that thunders'), which he renamed the Victoria Falls. Livingstone made his fourth major expedition from 1858 to 1864 in the area around the Lower Zambezi and Lake Nyasa (present-day Lake Malawi). He was accompanied by Dr John Kirk, another Scot, who joined the expedition as a medical officer and naturalist. After the expedition, in April 1864, Livingstone spent a week in Zanzibar before travelling back to Britain.

Livingstone returned to Zanzibar in January 1866 as he had been asked by the Royal Geographical Society to explore the country between Lake Nyasa and Lake Tanganyika, to solve the dispute over the location of the source of the Nile. He left for the mainland on 19 March 1866 and travelled around the southern end of Lake Nyasa.

After several years of exploring the region, during which time little news of his travels had reached the outside world, Livingstone met with journalist Henry Stanley at Ujiji on Lake Tanganyika on 10 November 1871 – the famous 'Dr Livingstone, I presume' incident described in more detail in the *Henry Morton Stanley* box on page 19. At this meeting, Livingstone was suffering terribly from foot ulcers, fever and dysentery, and had only a few days' supply of cotton with which to buy food. But two weeks later his strength had returned sufficiently for him to set out on a small expedition with Stanley. They explored the northern shores of Lake Tanganyika, establishing that the River Ruzizi flowed into (not out of) the lake, and could not therefore be a headwater of the Nile.

Livingstone and Stanley left Ujiji on 27 December 1871 and reached Kazeh, halfway to the coast, in February the following year. Livingstone was in good health, so Stanley continued on alone and arrived in Zanzibar in May 1872.

Livingstone stayed at Kazeh until August 1872, then set out on a short expedition around the southern shores of Lake Tanganyika. He was still looking for the source of the Nile when he became ill again with dysentery. He died at the village of Chitambo, a few miles south of Lake Bangweulu (Zambia) on 2 May 1873. Two of his loyal companions, Susi and Chumah, removed his heart and buried it under a tree at the spot where he died. They dried his body in the sun for two weeks, then carried it to Zanzibar, wrapped in bark and cloth, where it was identified by a broken bone in the left arm, once crushed in the jaws of a lion. Livingstone's body rested at the British consulate before being taken to London for burial. Stanley and Kirk were among the pall bearers at his funeral in Westminster Abbey on 18 April 1874.

The tree under which Livingstone's heart was buried eventually fell down, and a stone monument now stands in its place. However, some of the wood from the tree was made into a cross, and this now hangs in the Anglican Cathedral in Zanzibar Town.

**THE PEACE MEMORIAL MUSEUM** This is at the southern end of Stone Town, near the junction of Creek Road and Kaunda Road in the area called Mnazi Moja. It is also known by its local title: *Beit el Amani* (House of Peace). With its distinctive dome, arabesque windows and whitewashed walls, the building looks like a mosque or basilica church. It was designed by the British architect J H Sinclair, who also designed the High Court, the British Residency and several other public buildings around Zanzibar Town.

'Museum' is a misnomer nowadays, as virtually all its viewable exhibits have been shifted to the rapidly developing museum in the House of Wonders and the place now serves as a library. Its well-known giant tortoises have been transferred to Prison Island.

**THE ZANZIBAR ARCHIVES** For real aficionados, the Zanzibar Archives (*Nyaraka za Taifa* in Swahili) contain some fascinating material. This includes many books and manuscripts in Arabic dating from the 17th century, when the Omani sultans took control of Zanzibar; consular and protectorate records from the British colonial times; papers and documents relating to the various European expeditions that started from Zanzibar in the second half of the 19th century; plus a lot of contemporary material such as stamps, newspapers, maps and photographs. If there is something of special interest, the staff on duty can help you search through the collections. If you just want to browse there is an exhibition room, where some selected items of interest are on display. The archives are situated outside the main town, about 2km along Nyerere Road from the Mnazi Moja Hospital, in an area called Kilimani. To get there take a *dala-dala* on Route U and asked to be dropped at Nyaraka za Taifa, or at the prison. The *dala-dala* will stop at the bottom of Kinuamiguu Hill (the only hill on this road); turn left (north) off Nyerere Road, then take the first road on the right.

More information is available from the head of the national archives, or have a look at the (not directly related) website (*www.zanzibar-archives.com*).

*PO Box 116, Zanzibar;* \ *024 230342; entrance free; open Mon–Fri 07.30–15.30, Sat 07.30–2.00.*

**OTHER PLACES OF INTEREST IN ZANZIBAR TOWN** Although the following places aren't major sights in themselves, you'll probably find yourself walking nearby as you visit some of the more important palaces and museums, and the following background information will be useful.

**Mnazi Moja sports field** Opposite the museum, on the other side of Creek Road, is Mnazi Moja sports field. (*Mnazi Moja* means 'one coconut tree'.) This area used to be a swamp at the end of the creek that separated the Stone Town peninsula from the rest of the island. The land was reclaimed and converted to a sports field during the colonial period, hence the English-style cricket pavilion in the corner. In the 1920s, part of the sports ground was set aside for exclusive use by members of the English Club; it contained tennis courts, a croquet lawn and the only golf course on the island. Today, *Mnazi Moja* is used mainly for football matches and, although the creek itself has been reclaimed, the sports field is still prone to flooding in the rainy season.

The road leading southeast out of the town (now called Nyerere Road) was originally built by Bishop Steere of the Universities Mission in Central Africa as a causeway across the swamp. Today it is a pleasant avenue lined with giant casuarina trees.

**The People's Gardens** The People's Gardens are on Kaunda Road, at the southern end of Stone Town, near the main hospital. They were originally laid out by Sultan Barghash for use by his harem. Many of the trees and bushes in the garden, including eucalyptus, coffee, tea and cocoa, were added by Sir John Kirk, the British consul on Zanzibar from 1873 to 1887. The gardens were given to the people of Zanzibar by Sultan Hamoud on the occasion of Queen Victoria's Jubilee

The Palace Museum (formerly the People's Palace, and before that the Sultan's Palace) was constructed on part of the site of an even older palace called *Beit el Sahel*, the House of the Coast, which was originally built for Sultan Said between 1827 and 1834. Contemporary accounts describe *Beit el Sahel* as a two-storey whitewashed palace, with a roof of green and red tiles, separated from the beach by a high wall, with a grove of pomegranates behind. The accounts go on to describe how Sultan Said spent three days of each week at *Beit el Sahel*, and the rest of the time at his country palace at Mtoni, about 5km north of Zanzibar Town. He often walked from the town to Mtoni even though his stables were full of Arabian horses. Every morning, the best horses were brought out from the stables and fastened to the seaward side of the wall with long ropes, to roam about and wade in the soft sand at low tide.

Another palace, called *Beit el Hukm* (the House of Government), was built later behind *Beit el Sahel*. Then, in 1883, *Beit el Ajaib* (the House of Wonders) was also built. These three adjoining palaces were connected by a series of covered ways and passages. A lighthouse in front of the palaces was nicknamed the 'Sultan's Christmas tree' by British navy officers, on account of its many rows of lamps.

*Beit el Sahel*, *Beit el Hukm* and the lighthouse were all destroyed in the bombardment of 1896 (see *The shortest war in history* box on page 25). The palace that exists today (now the museum) was constructed partly on the site of *Beit el Sahel*. On the site of *Beit el Hukm* a private house was built, which is now the offices of Stone Town Conservation and Development Authority, easily seen between the Palace Museum and the House of Wonders, set back from the road. The building has a well-maintained garden with palm trees and shrubs. Outside the main entrance is a pair of cannons, made in Boston, Massachusetts, in 1868.

in 1899 and they were renamed Victoria Gardens. The building in the centre of the gardens was called Victoria Hall. It was built over the baths of the harem and used as the Chamber of the Legislative Council from 1926 to 1964. After the revolution, the hall and gardens fell into disrepair. They were renovated in 1996, with help from the German government, and Victoria Hall is now rather ignominiously the offices of the Zanzibar Sewerage and Sanitation Project.

The large house opposite the gardens, on the south side of Kaunda Road, was built in 1903 as the official British Residency. After the 1964 Revolution, when the Victoria Gardens were renamed the People's Gardens, the old British Residency became the State House – the official residence of the president. The building next door to the State House was the embassy of the Soviet Union, but is now the offices of the Zanzibar Investment Promotions Agency (ZIPA), a government agency set up to attract foreign business capital to Zanzibar.

**The big tree** Just west of the Old Dispensary, about 100m along Mizingani Road, is a large tree originally planted by Sultan Khalifa in 1911. Known simply as the Big Tree (or in Swahili as *Mtini* – the place of the tree), it has been a major landmark for many years. It can be seen on numerous old photos and etchings of Zanzibar Town viewed from the sea, and is still clearly visible on the seafront from ships approaching the port. Today, traditional dhow builders use the tree as a shady 'roof' for their open-air workshop.

**The orphanage** Next to the Fort, the road runs through a tunnel under a large building that is the island's orphanage. Built in the late 19th century, the

Most of Zanzibar's population is Muslim, consequently Zanzibar Town has several mosques. The oldest is Malindi Mosque, a small, inconspicuous building near the port, with a minaret which is thought to be several hundred years old. Three of the larger mosques are in the northern part of Stone Town: the Ijumaa Mosque (Sunni); the Ithnasheri Mosque (Shia); and the Aga Khan Mosque (Ismaili). These were all built in the 19th century. Compared with the large mosques of other Islamic cities, often decorated with domes and tall minarets, the mosques of Zanzibar are relatively plain and unpretentious. However, in 1994 the Ijumaa Mosque (near the Big Tree) was completely renovated in a modern arabesque style, and the other large mosques may follow this trend.

Non-Muslims are not normally allowed to enter any mosque in Zanzibar Town although, if you have a genuine interest, a good local guide might be able to speak to the mosque's elders on your behalf and arrange an invitation. Men will find this easier than women. There are usually no restrictions on non-Muslims (men or women) visiting the area around a mosque, although photos of local people praying or simply congregating should not be taken without permission.

building was used as a club for English residents until 1896, and then as an Indian school until 1950. There is a small craft shop on the ground floor opposite the gardens selling pictures and curios made by the orphans and other local artisans.

**The Upimaji building** Between the orphanage and the People's Bank of Zanzibar, this building is now the Commission for Lands and Environment. In the 1860s it was the offices and home of Heinrich Ruete, the German merchant who eloped with Princess Salme (see the *Princess Salme* box on pages 164–5).

**The old British Consulate** This fine old house was used as the British consulate from 1841 to 1874, after which the consulate was moved to the Mambo Msiige building (see below). The first consul was Lieutenant-Colonel Atkins Hamerton, posted here to represent the interests of Britain after Sultan Said moved his capital from Oman to Zanzibar.

Later consuls here played host to several of the well-known British explorers, including Speke, Burton, Grant and Stanley (see page 15), before they set out for their expeditions on the east African mainland. In 1874, the body of David Livingstone was brought here before being taken back to Britain for burial at Westminster Abbey.

From 1874 to 1974 the building was used as offices by the trading company Smith Mackenzie, but it was taken over by the government in the late 1970s. It is still used as government offices today, and visitors are not allowed to enter, but there is not much to see on the inside; most of the building's interest lies in its grand exterior.

**The Mambo Msiige building** Its name meaning 'look but do not imitate', this grand house, incorporating a variety of architectural styles, overlooks the open 'square' at the far western end of Shangani Road. It was originally built around 1850 for a wealthy Arab, but the building was sold to the British Foreign Office in 1875 and used as the British consulate until 1913. From 1918 to 1924 it was used as the European hospital, after which it became government offices. Today, the Zanzibar Shipping Corporation is based here.

**The Zanzibar milestone** Near the People's Gardens is this octagonal pillar, built with marble taken from the palace at Chukwani, showing the distances from Zanzibar Town to other settlements on the island. For complete accuracy, the distances were measured from this exact point. The distance to London is also shown: 8,064 miles. This is the distance by sea. (By 1870, ships between Zanzibar and London travelled via the Suez Canal. Before this all voyages were much longer, via the Cape of Good Hope.)

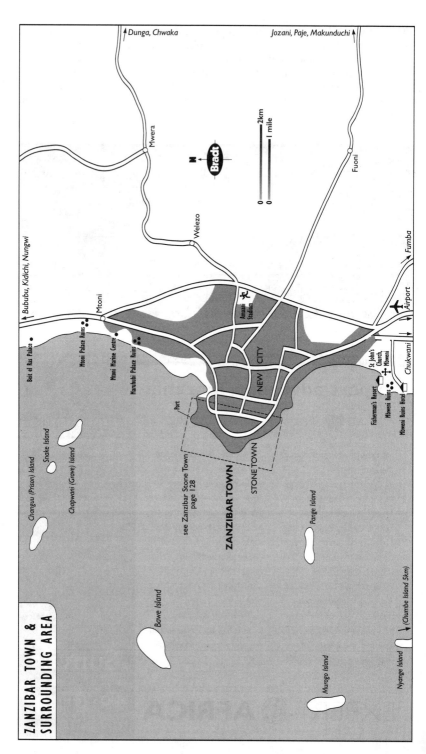

ZANZIBAR TOWN & SURROUNDING AREA

Dunga, Chwaka

Jozani, Paje, Makunduchi

Bububu, Kidichi, Nungwi

Mwera

Welezo

Mtoni

Fumba

Airport

Fuoni

Chukwani

Amaani Stadium

NEW CITY

St John's Church, Mbweni

Fisherman's Resort

Mbweni Ruins

Mbweni Ruins Hotel

Beit el Ras Palace

Mtoni Palace Ruins

Mtoni Marine Centre

Marahubi Palace Ruins

Port

ZANZIBAR TOWN

STONE TOWN

see Zanzibar Stone Town page 128

Changuu (Prison) Island

Snake Island

Chapwani (Grave) Island

Bawe Island

Pange Island

Murogo Island

Nyange Island

(Chumbe Island 5km)

N

Bradt

0 — 2km
0 — 1 mile

# 7

# Around Zanzibar Town

All the places listed in this chapter lie within about 20km of Zanzibar Town, and most can be reached from there easily (or at least without too much difficulty) as a day trip, whether by hired scooter, hired bike, or a combination of foot and public transport. If you prefer not to travel independently, visits to any of the places mentioned here can also be arranged with a tour company, often as part of a spice tour.

Of the places described, Mbweni lies south of Zanzibar Town, whilst the palaces of Maruhubi and Mtoni, and the Persian Baths of Kidichi and Kizimbani, lie to the north. Some of the palaces and bath-houses mentioned in this section are included in the spice tours arranged by tour companies and independent guides.

## SOUTH OF ZANZIBAR TOWN

The main attraction on the coast immediately south of Zanzibar is the Mbweni area, which lies some 3km from the town centre and hosts a number of ruined and extant buildings dating to the late 19th century. There are also several hotels dotted around these southern suburbs of Zanzibar Town, and while they are not so convenient for sightseeing, shopping or visiting restaurants as their more central counterparts, they lie close to the airport (useful for early departures or late arrivals) and most run free shuttle services for guests to/from the centre. The hotels outside town are generally quieter, and they are also handy for people on business trips, as some government and NGO offices are also in this area.

**MBWENI AND ENVIRONS** The area of Mbweni is on the coast, about 3km directly south of Zanzibar Town. It was originally a plantation bought by the Universities Mission in Central Africa (UMCA) in 1871. Bishop Tozer (Bishop of Zanzibar from 1863 to 1873) planned to build a mission station here. His successor Bishop Steere (Bishop of Zanzibar from 1874 to 1882) oversaw the building of a church and other mission buildings, several of which are still standing today, and also used the area as a colony for freed slaves.

At the Mbweni Ruins Hotel, and bookshops in town, you can find an informative book called *Zanzibar: History of the Ruins at Mbweni*, by Flo Liebst, which also touches on the general history of Zanzibar and the UMCA missionaries of east Africa.

**Getting there and away** To reach Mbweni, take the main road out of town going towards the airport. Go uphill through the area called Kinuamiguu ('lift your legs') and another area called Mazizini. After a few kilometres, at a signpost to Mbweni and Chukwani, fork right, then turn right again after 500m onto a smaller road. Continue down this road towards the sea to reach Mbweni. *Dala-dalas* on Route U run between the town and the airport and go past the main Mbweni and Chukwani junction.

## What to see and do

**St John's Church** At the heart of Mbweni (on the right side of the small road leading towards the sea) is the English-style St John's Church, complete with tower and surrounding cemetery. It was opened in 1882 by UMCA missionaries and converts, and consecrated in 1904. Descendants of freed slaves continued to live in the area. The church has a marble altar inlaid with mother-of-pearl (colourful shell pieces) and a wooden chair made for Bishop Tozer by sailors from the ship HMS *London*, famous for its slave-dhow captures. The nearby building, formerly the Inn by the Sea hotel, was originally the old clergy house. Today, the sexton at the church is Peter Sudi, a descendant of John Swedi, one of the first five freed slave boys taken in by the mission. There are Anglican church services at 09.00 every Sunday.

**St Mary's School for Girls** Past St John's Church towards the sea, a dirt road leads to Mbweni Ruins Hotel, whose grounds house the remains of the Victorian St Mary's School for Girls. This school was constructed by missionaries on a property known as Mbweni Point Shamba, bought for the church by Bishop Tozer in 1871, and it was completed in 1874 under the leadership of Bishop Steere. An old Arab house on the property was incorporated into the school entrance.

The school was a large square building, based around a central courtyard. The headmistress from 1877 until 1902 was Caroline Thackeray (a cousin of the English novelist William Thackeray). The school educated orphaned girls who had been freed from captured slave-dhows, and daughters of freed slaves who lived at the mission, each with their own house and small garden. Most of the girls were trained as teachers, and were taught reading, writing, arithmetic, geography and sewing. In 1877, Caroline Thackeray paid for the construction of an industrial wing, wherein her less academically inclined pupils were given vocational training in basketry, stitching, laundry and cooking. St Mary's had its own chapel which is still in good condition today, though without a roof. In 1906 the school became a convent and in 1920 the buildings were sold by the church to a consortium including the Bank of India. They slowly became ruins and were never used or lived in until the present time.

**Sir John Kirk's House** Along the road which passes northwards in front of St John's Church is the house of Sir John Kirk, British consul-general in Zanzibar from 1873 to 1887. Kirk first came to Africa in the 1850s as the medical officer and naturalist on Livingstone's Zambezi expedition. As consul-general he was very active in the suppression of the slave trade, and is often regarded as the 'power behind the throne' during the rule of his close friend Sultan Barghash. The house was built as a gift from the sultan and was used by Kirk and his family as a country retreat.

Kirk was an experienced botanist and established a large experimental garden here, which later provided the core species of all the botanical gardens of Zanzibar and mainland Tanzania. He imported many new plant species to the islands, and worked on improved varieties of useful and edible crops. Kirk also collected trees and flowers from the mainland of Africa which formed the basis of the then standard work, *Flora of Tropical Africa*.

In 1887 Kirk left Zanzibar, and sold his house to Miss Thackeray, who opened the grounds for an annual garden party. Although Thackeray retired as headmistress of St Mary's in 1902, she inhabited the house until her death aged 83 in 1926, when she was buried in the cemetery at St John's Church. The house was then sold by the church to a wealthy Arab, who used it until the early 1960s. It is now privately owned and not open to the public.

# Where to stay

🏠 **Mbweni Ruins Hotel** (13 rooms) ☎ 024 223 4578/9; f 024 223 0536; e hotel@mbweni.com; www.adventurecamps.co.tz. Situated in the grounds of the Mbweni Ruins, this small hotel is widely rated as one of the best of its type in and around Zanzibar Town. The rooms are spacious and very comfortable, each with large bathroom, AC, canopy beds, tasteful furniture and small private balcony. The hotel is set in extensive well-maintained grounds with a lush botanical garden and nature trail, and a swimming pool overlooking the beach. The food in the terrace restaurant overlooking the sea is recommended, with many visitors staying in Zanzibar Town coming here for lunch or dinner, combined with a swim or a walk in the grounds. Lunches are between US$5 and US$10, and a full evening meal is US$10–25. There is a free shuttle service to and from town, and transfers to/from the port or airport cost US$10 for 4 people. The ruins are open to visitors, and sometimes the hotel arranges atmospheric open-air dinners amongst the pillars and arches of the school chapel. Nearby mangroves provide good birding, and the hotel has its own list of birds and butterflies seen in the grounds and further afield. The staff are keen naturalists, and can advise visitors on all aspects of local natural history. *US$100/180 sgl/dbl, b&b; US$15/25 pp, HB/FB suppt.*

🏠 **Zanzibar Beach Resort** (60 rooms) PO Box 2586; ☎ 024 2230208; f 024 2230556; e znzbeachresort@zanlink.com. This hotel (formerly the Fisherman's Resort, and before that the Zanzibar Reef) is about 7km from Zanzibar Town and 3km from the airport, between the areas of Mazizini and Mbweni. The hotel is set in landscaped grounds overlooking the sea, with 60 en-suite rooms, and aimed more at groups (discounts are available), although individual tourists stay here as well. The rooms are in large 2-storey chalets with whitewashed walls and thatched roofs. There are 4 rooms in each chalet, 2 larger ones at the front with sea views, and 2 smaller ones at the back. All rooms have canopy beds, big bathrooms and a nice veranda, although the furniture seems unnecessarily heavy and dark. The hotel has a restaurant, bar and disco, squash court, gym, swimming pool, conference room, and facilities for fishing and watersports. *US$100/130 sgl/dbl; US$20 pp sea view suppt. US$10/18 pp HB/FB suppt.*

# NORTH OF ZANZIBAR TOWN

Along the coast from Zanzibar Town, stretching over a distance of about 5km, are several palaces dating from the 19th century built for the various sultans who ruled Zanzibar during this period. Some are in good condition and worth a visit; others will appeal only to keen fans of historical ruins. The entrance price (for the palaces that are open) is very low, and the ticket you buy at the first place you visit also allows you to visit many other historical sites on the same day. This includes the baths at Kidichi, the caves at Mangapwani, and several other sites around the island. The main settlement in this area, Bububu, some 10km north of the Stone Town, is known for the attractive Fuji Beach. A number of small hotels catering to most budgets are strung along the coast towards Bububu.

**GETTING THERE AND AWAY** Many of this area's historical sites are included in spice tours, and all are easily accessed with a hire car or private vehicle. On public transport, there is a bus (number 2) which heads north to Mangapwani village, and with a little persuasion the driver will often continue to the coast and Coral Cave. For Bububu (✦ *BUBUBU 6°6.291'S; 39°13.05'E*), Fuji Beach and Mtoni (✦ *MTONIM 6°8.191'S; 39°12.801'E*), take *dala-dala* Route B from Zanzibar Town; it's also best to take this route for the Persian Baths at Kidichi, alighting at Bububu and continuing on foot in a westerly direction for 3km.

## WHAT TO SEE AND DO
## Palaces
*Maruhubi Palace* The Maruhubi Palace is on the coast, about 4km north of Zanzibar Town. It was built in 1882 for Sultan Barghash (sultan from 1870 to 1888) and at one time he reputedly kept 100 women here: one official wife and 99

concubines. (The sultan himself lived at the palace in Zanzibar Town.) The palace's name comes from the original owner of the estate who sold the land to Sultan Barghash.

The palace was built with coral stone and wood, and was reported to have been one of the most ornate on the island. Large walls were built around the palace grounds, thought to have been inspired by the park walls seen by Sultan Barghash on his visit to England in 1875. Unfortunately, the palace was destroyed by a fire in 1899. All that remains today is the great pillars which supported the upper storey, and the Persian-style bath-house. The separate bathrooms for the women, and the large bath for the sultan's own use, can still be seen. The original water tanks, now overgrown with lilies, also remain in the grounds of the palace. To the north of the pillars, at the back of the beach, is a small set of arches and steps; this was part of the palace's reception area. (The House of Wonders in Zanzibar Town contains a photo of the palace taken at the end of the 19th century when it was still in use.)

To reach the palace, take the main road north out of Zanzibar Town towards Bububu. Pass Livingstone House on your right and, after a few kilometres, the Maruhubi Palace is signposted on your left. *Dala-dalas* on Route B run between the town and Bububu village, past the palace entrance gate.

**Mtoni Palace** Just north of Maruhubi is the ruined Mtoni Palace, which was built for Sultan Said (sultan from 1804 to 1856) on the site of an older house believed to have belonged to Saleh bin Haramil, the Arab trader who imported the first cloves to Zanzibar (see *Chapter 1*, page 12). Mtoni, which means 'place by the river', is the oldest palace on Zanzibar.

One of Sultan Said's daughters, Salme, later eloped with a German trader who lived and worked in Zanzibar in the 1860s. In her book about her life on Zanzibar (see *Princess Salme* box, pages 164–5). Salme describes Mtoni Palace in the 1850s: it had a large courtyard where gazelles, peacocks, ostriches and flamingos wandered around, a large bath-house at one end and the sultan's quarters at the other, where he lived with his principal wife, an Omani princess whose name was Azze.

Salme records that over 1,000 people were attached to the sultan's court in the palace. She describes how the sultan would pace up and down on a large round tower overlooking the sea, where he could see his fleet anchored off the shore. If visitors came by boat, he would greet them on the steps of his palace as there was no landing pier. Salme and the other princesses were carried out to their boats on chairs.

Salme goes on to describe her own return visit to Zanzibar in 1885. The palace at Mtoni had been abandoned and was already in ruins. Today, only the main walls and parts of the roof remain. The palace was turned into a warehouse during World War I, and evidence of the alterations can still be seen.

To reach the palace, turn left off the main road onto a dirt track, about 2km north of Maruhubi. There is a small signpost.

**Beit el Ras Palace** Further north along the coast, this palace was built for Sultan Said as an 'overflow' house for his children and their servants, when Mtoni Palace became too crowded (see the *Wives and Children of Sultan Said* box opposite). Building started in 1847 but was not completed by the time of Said's death in 1856. Sultan Majid (Said's successor) did not continue the project and much of the stone from the palace was used during the construction of the Zanzibar railroad (described below). The remaining ruins were abandoned and finally demolished in 1947 to make room for a school and teacher-training centre. Today, only the giant porch of the original palace remains, with high arches and steps leading up one side. The palace is in the grounds of the training centre, now called the Nkrumah Teacher Training College (Chuo Cha Ualimu Nkrumah), and is reached by turning off the main road a few kilometres beyond Mtoni. Beit el Ras means 'the palace on the headland' and from the porch you get good views over this part of the coast and out towards the group of small islands off Zanzibar Town.

**Kibweni Palace** North of Beit el Ras, this 'palace' was built in Arabic style by the British authorities in 1915. In the village of Kibweni, its official title was Beit el Kassrusaada (Palace of Happiness), although this name seems to have been forgotten. Sultan Khalifa II (sultan from 1911 to 1960) used the palace as a country residence. After the revolution it was taken over by the government and is still used as an official residence. It is not open to the public.

**Chuini Palace** About 10km north of Zanzibar Town, on the coast near the village of Chuini, lie the ruins of Chuini Palace. (Chuini means 'place of the leopard'.) It was built for Sultan Barghash, added to by Sultan Ali bin Said, and destroyed by fire in 1914. The ruins are on private land and cannot be visited.

**The Zanzibar railroad** In the early 1900s a light railway (36-inch gauge) was built and operated by an American company from a point outside the Arab Fort in Zanzibar Town, along the seafront and up the coast to the village of Bububu. Construction began in 1904 and ended in 1905, and the service was used mainly by local people, but a special first-class coach was joined to the train so that passengers from the steamers that put in to Zanzibar could get a brief glimpse of the island. The line was closed in 1928, but railway buffs can still see the remains of bridges and embankments, as today's main road between Zanzibar Town and Bububu runs parallel to the line (and in some cases over it). Bits of the original track can be seen at Bububu.

Salme was a daughter of Sultan Said. She was born at the Mtoni Palace in August 1844. Her mother was a *surie* (secondary wife) from Circassia, in southern Russia. Salme later wrote *Memoirs of an Arabian Princess*, from which we learn many interesting details about life at court and the events of the time (see *Appendix 2*, page 331).

In her book Salme describes her early childhood at the Mtoni Palace, where she lived until she was seven years old. Here she learnt sewing, embroidery and lace-making from her mother. She and her brothers and sisters had a private teacher and lessons were conducted in an open gallery containing just a single large mat and a Koran on a stand. The royal children were taught the Arabic alphabet, reading and a little arithmetic. The boys were also taught to write, using home-made ink, and the well-bleached shoulder blade of a camel for a slate. But Salme was rebellious and taught herself to write in secret.

Twice a day, early in the morning and in the evening, all children above five years old had riding lessons. When they had made sufficient progress, the boys received Arabian horses, while the girls received white donkeys from Muscat. When the princesses rode their donkeys to the clove plantations, slaves ran by the side of each animal with a large parasol to protect the riders from the sun. The children also learnt to swim in the sea at an early age.

Salme was given her own African slaves as personal attendants. At bedtime, one slave would massage her, while another fanned gently, until the princess fell asleep, still fully dressed. Slaves fanned the princess all night. In the morning, her slaves massaged her gently until she awoke. Her bath was filled with fresh spring water. Slaves laid out the day's clothes, on which jasmine and orange blossoms had been strewn overnight, and which were scented with amber and musk before they were worn. Windows and doors were left open throughout the year, even in colder, wetter weather when a charcoal fire was burning. The fresh air helped to disperse the strong scents. Slaves washed the linen daily. It dried in little more than half an hour, was smoothed flat (not ironed) and put away.

As a child, Salme was allowed to mix freely with boys of her own age. After she was nine years old, the only men allowed to see her were her father, close male relatives, and her slaves. She wore trousers, a shirt reaching to her ankles, and a handkerchief for the head. The shirt and trousers were always of a different pattern. On her walks, she wore a *schele*, a large shawl of black silk. When she appeared before a stranger, the law required her to be veiled; part of the face, the neck and chin, and above all, the ankles, had to be completely covered.

In October 1859 Salme became involved in family intrigue between her older brothers, Barghash and Majid. She helped Barghash escape to the Marseilles clove plantation, after his attempt to overthrow Majid failed. (See *The Escape to Marseilles* box on pages 16–17.) Majid never punished Salme for her part in the plot but by siding with Barghash she lost the friendship of many of her other brothers and sisters. When she renewed her friendship with Majid, she isolated herself from her fellow conspirators.

By 1866 Salme was living in Zanzibar Town. Although 22 years old, she was still unmarried. Rejected by her family, she began socialising regularly with many of the foreigners on the island. She became friendly with a young German merchant from Hamburg, called Heinrich Ruete, who was living in a house next to hers. They began a covert relationship, speaking to each other from their balconies across the narrow street, and meeting secretly in the countryside beyond the town.

In his book *Sketches in Mafeking and East Africa* (published in 1907), Lord Robert Baden-Powell quotes from a description of the Zanzibar train by an American writer called Miss Kirkland. 'Have you ever been to Bu Bu Bu? If not, do not call yourself a travelled person,' she wrote. 'Bu Bu Bu is a settlement in a shady grove

In July 1866 Salme discovered she was pregnant. Some historians have suggested that she was forced to leave Zanzibar in a hurry, as an illegitimate pregnancy would have brought disgrace to her family and the whole Busaidi dynasty and could have resulted in her death. Others have described her romantic 'elopement' with Heinrich Ruete. However, an analysis by Said el-Gheithy of the Princess Salme Institute presents events in a slightly different light: 'No doubt, her pregnancy sent shock waves through her clan and threatened the position of the European traders, reliant on the goodwill of the sultan. Yet following extensive research, and through a knowledge of her personality from at least one person who knew her, it seems Salme was a very organised and stable individual, with a strength of personality which made her adverse to irrational movements. We must not overlook or underestimate her ability to choose rationally from the options available. The concept of an "elopement" represents her as somewhat flighty. Rather, the move to Germany should be understood as a planned emigration and her departure could be described, to use a Swahili phrase, as "leaving without saying goodbye".'

Salme left Zanzibar on a British warship, and for several months after her departure a wave of anti-European feeling spread through Zanzibar Town. Another British warship was sent to suppress any possible reprisals against Europeans. When Salme reached Aden, she stayed with some European friends, renounced Islam and was baptised into the Anglican Church, with the name Emily. In Zanzibar, Heinrich wound up his affairs, then joined Salme in Aden. They were married immediately and travelled to Heinrich's home in Hamburg.

In the following three years Salme and Heinrich had two daughters and a son. Tragically, in August 1871, Heinrich fell while jumping from a tram, and was run over; he died three days later. No longer welcome in Zanzibar, Salme remained in Germany, making one short visit to London in 1875, and two brief returns to Zanzibar in 1885 and 1888, but her attempts at reconciliation were unsuccessful. She lived in exile in Syria until 1914 and died in Germany in 1924. Among the possessions found after her death was a bag of sand from the beach at Zanzibar.

In Zanzibar Town, Princess Salme is remembered at the Palace Museum, which has a room devoted to her life and writings. This was set in place by Said el-Gheithy in collaboration with the Museums of Zanzibar. In London, the Princess Salme Institute was established in 1994 to raise awareness about the life and writings of this remarkable woman, and to promote training and research relevant to Zanzibar. The Institute is based at the Africa Centre (*38 King St, London WC2E 8JT, UK;* \ *020 7240 0199;* e *sayyidasalme@hotmail.com*). The director of the Princess Salme Institute is Said el-Gheithy, who kindly checked the accuracy of the *Escape to Marseilles* box on pages 16–17, and provided some of the information.

For cultural events in Zanzibar, such as the Zanzibar International Film Festival (ZIFF), the Princess Salme Institute acts as a contact point in Europe. The Institute also mounts an exhibition about Princess Salme at the Festival. Additionally, the Institute's modest resources keep up the enthusiasm for Salme's life, and also provides practical help to academics, researchers, visitors and professionals working on or around Zanzibar. In the future, the Institute hopes to establish a larger base in Zanzibar from where various projects will be administered. These include 'Sayyida Salme tours' where guides will take visitors to the places and palaces lived in and frequented by Princess Salme, while providing a background history of her remarkable story.

on the island of Zanzibar, and is the terminus of a new and important railroad – six and a half miles long.'

It has been suggested that the name Bububu comes from the sound made by the train's hooter, but maps dating from before the building of the railway show the village already had this title. It is more likely that the name was inspired by the sound of the freshwater springs which bubble to the surface just outside the village. Most of Zanzibar Town's water supply still comes from here.

**Bububu** Bububu (✪ *BUBUBU 6°6.291'S; 39°13.05'E*) is a small, rural village with a police station and checkpoint. The main road continues north from here towards Mahonda (✪ *MAHOND 5°59.388'S; 39°15.106'E*) and Nungwi (✪ *NUSHOP 5°43.673'S; 39°17.614'E*), and a new minor tar road branches off east to reach the agricultural area of Kidichi, where most visitors on spice tours arranged in Zanzibar Town are taken. If you stay on the main road for a few more kilometres, near the village of Chuini (about 10km north of Zanzibar Town) a wide dirt road forks off left (✪ *TUMANG 6°3.113'S; 39°13.52'E*), signposted to Bumbwini, and this leads to Mangapwani.

**Fuji Beach** Fuji Beach, near Bububu village, is a pleasant place to pause at during or after your energetic sightseeing. A small dirt road leads down to the beach from near the police station in the centre of Bububu. This is the nearest beach to the town where swimming is not inadvisable and it makes a good day-trip destination in its own right if you fancy just relaxing for a while.

Local legend has it that the beach's name was due to one Mr Honda, a Japanese engineer who came to Zanzibar to build roads, but fell in love with a local girl and decided to stay. He built a 'taverna' called Fuji Beach Bar, at the time the best on the island, and the name stuck. Even though Mr Honda is no longer around, his legacy remains. The bar still sells beers and snacks, and the staff will look after your gear while you are swimming. (There have been reports of robberies here, so this is worth arranging.) If you want to stay for more than a day, see the list of accommodation on pages 168–9.

**Kidichi Persian Baths** The Persian Baths at Kidichi lie to the northeast of Zanzibar Town, about 4km inland from the main coast road, in the island's main clove and coconut plantation area. The baths were built in 1850 for Sultan Said. He owned land in this part of the island, and he and his second wife, Binte Irich Mirza (also called Schesade, more often written Sherazade), would come here for hunting or to oversee the work being done on their plantations. The bath-house was constructed so that they could refresh themselves after the journey from town. Schesade was a granddaughter of the Shah of Persia, so the baths were built in the Persian style, with decorative stucco work. An underground furnace kept the water warm. A small resthouse was also built nearby, but none of this remains.

Today, you can enter the bath-house, and see the changing room, bathing pool and massage tables. Unfortunately, the bath-house has not been especially well maintained, and there is mould growing on much of the stucco. A colony of bats seems to have taken up residence here as well. At the top of the domed ceiling is a circle of small windows: these used to be stained glass, which cast patterns of coloured light over the white walls.

To reach Kidichi, continue up the main road northwards from Zanzibar Town to Bububu. At the police station, turn right onto a new tar road that leads through coconut palms and clove plantations, and past a long row of souvenir stalls selling spices and other goods. After about 4km the bath-house, a domed white building, is seen on the right, just a few metres off the dirt road. There are several more spice–souvenir stalls here, and in the surrounding area several houses where tour groups go for lunch.

**Kizimbani Persian Baths** Near Kidichi, these baths were also built in the Persian style for Sultan Said, at about the same time as the baths at Kidichi which they resemble, though there is no interior decoration. The surrounding plantations originally belonged to Saleh bin Haramil, the Arab trader who imported the first cloves to Zanzibar, but they were confiscated by Sultan Said on the grounds that Saleh was a slave smuggler (see *Chapter 1*, page 12). Today the experimental station is the island's centre for agricultural research.

To reach the baths from Kidichi, continue eastwards along the tar road. After about 2km, at a crossroads, there are roads left (north) to Mfenesini and Selem, and right (south) to Mwendo and Mwera. Go straight on, along a dirt road, passing through plantations, to reach the Kizimbani Experimental Station headquarters. The baths are on the right of the track.

## Mangapwani

**Mangapwani Coral Cave** Mangapwani (meaning 'Arab shore') lies on the coast, about 20km north of Zanzibar Town. The Coral Cave is a deep natural cavern in the coralline rock with a narrow entrance and a pool of fresh water at its lowest point. Water was probably collected from here by early inhabitants of this part of the island but at some time in the past vegetation grew across the entrance and the exact position of the cavern was forgotten.

Later, the area became the property of a wealthy Arab landowner called Hamed Salim el Hathy who had many slaves working on his plantations. During this time, the cavern was rediscovered by a young boy searching for a lost goat. Local people were able to use the water again, and Hamed Salim arranged for his slaves to collect the water regularly for his own use. It has been suggested by historians that the cave may have been used as a hiding place for slaves after the trade was officially abolished in 1873.

Most people come here on an organised tour, or by privately hired car or bike. Buses on Route 2 link Zanzibar Town and Mangapwani village, but services are not frequent. To reach the cavern from Zanzibar Town, take the main road through Bububu to Chuini, then fork left towards Bumbwini. After 6km, in Mangapwani village, fork left again and head westwards towards the coast (the Serena Restaurant and Watersports Centre, due to be the site of the new Serena Hotel, is also signposted this way). About 1km from the junction, a narrow dirt road leads off to the left (there's a small signpost). Follow this to reach the cavern. A flight of stone steps leads through the entrance down into the cave itself.

**Mangapwani Slave Chamber** The Mangapwani Slave Chamber is a few kilometres further up the coast from the Coral Cave. Although sometimes called the Slave Cave, it is a square-shaped cell that has been cut out of the coralline rock, with a roof on top. It was originally built for storing slaves, and its construction is attributed to one Mohammed bin Nassor Al-Alwi, an important slave trader. Boats from the mainland would unload their human cargo on the nearby beach, and the slaves would be kept here before being taken to Zanzibar Town for resale, or to plantations on the island. It is thought that some time after 1873, when Sultan Barghash signed the Anglo–Zanzibari treaty which officially abolished the slave trade, the cave was used as a place to hide slaves, as an illicit trade continued for many years.

To reach the Slave Chamber from Zanzibar Town, follow the directions above to the Mangapwani Coral Cave. Instead of turning into the Coral Cave, continue on the dirt road for another 1km to reach the entrance to the Serena Restaurant and Watersports Centre. Just before you reach the Serena a small dirt track branches off to the right. Follow this for 1km through palm trees and bushes to reach the Slave Chamber. With care, you can reach the steps that lead down onto the chamber floor. Nearby a small path leads to a secluded beach, separated from the main Mangapwani Beach (described below) by some coral-rock outcrops.

**Mangapwani Beach** Mangapwani Beach lies a few kilometres west of Mangapwani village. This is the planned site of a new Serena Hotel, but for now it's the location of the Serena Restaurant and Watersports Centre. You can come here for a slap-up seafood lunch (US$30 for three courses), or something less gargantuan like lobster or prawns for US$9, or a pasta dish for US$4. There's also a nice little bar beneath the trees. The beach is exceptionally beautiful at high tide, and a great place to swim or relax. For other activities, the 'watersports' tag is a bit optimistic, as there's only one boat for snorkelling etc (about US$10 per hour) and even that was out of order when we visited.

Transfers by boat and road are arranged by the Serena Hotel in Zanzibar Town (where you can also get more information), and by local tour companies.

**WHERE TO STAY** The hotels below all lie alongside (or within a few hundred metres of) the main road between Stone Town and Bububu/Fuji Beach. They are listed in the order you would pass them coming from the direction of Stone Town.

**Maruhubi Beach Villas** (10 rooms) m 0747 451188; e Maruhubi@zanlink.com; www.maruhubibeachvillas.com/ www.zanzibarmaruhubi.com. Situated close to the eponymous ruins some 3km north of Stone Town, this attractively low-key new resort has a superb location on a sandy beach offering views back to the House of Wonders on the Zanzibar waterfront as well as to Mtoni Beach. Accommodation is in airy and spacious semi-detached bungalows with AC, fan, large netted dbl bed, self-catering facilities, and balconies facing a mangrove-lined inlet. There is also a large *makuti* restaurant offering a selection of seafood and other dishes. *US$80/90 sgl, b&b, low/high season; US$110/130 dbl, b&b, low/high season.*

**Mtoni Marine Centre** (31 rooms) ☎ 024 2250140; m 0747 486214; f 024 2250496; e mtoni@zanzibar.cc; www.mtoni.com. Situated in Mtoni, on the north side of Zanzibar Town, about 4km from the port, this marine activities centre is also a very good hotel, set in extensive gardens overlooking the bay and a large stretch of beach. The management style is relaxed and efficient – a perfect combination. There's a range of en-suite rooms with AC, and the food is very highly rated, in particular the sushi, and many people come from Zanzibar Town to eat even if they're not staying. Snacks start at US$3–5, and you can enjoy an excellent meal for US$10–20. The twice-weekly beach buffet barbecues (US$12) are particularly popular. At the other end of the gardens, the Mcheza Bar is a more casual beachfront place, serving straightforward

items such as pizza, sandwiches and burgers for around US$3.50. Mtoni is also well known for its popular sunset dhow cruises, which offer great views of Stone Town in the evening light (US$10 pp, inc snacks and soft drinks). All-day dhow cruises are also arranged, at US$40 including lunch, drinks and snorkel gear, with discounts for hotel guests. If you want to stay nearer your room, the hotel also has a swimming pool. The staff can also arrange tours, car hire, boat trips and so on. Mtoni Marine is also the official Visa International assistance agent for Zanzibar. A taxi from town to the hotel is US$4, and from the hotel to the airport US$10. *US$60–95 sgl, b&b; US$80–120 dbl, b&b.*

**Via Via** (5 rooms) m 0744 286369; e zanzibar.tanzania@viaviacafe.com. Also known as Kalinge's Garden Bungalows, this affiliate of the well-known Belgian-run café in Arusha lies in shady green gardens about 7km from Stone Town along the Bububu Rd, within walking distance of Fuji Beach. It's a relaxed set-up, owned and managed by a friendly Belgian–Tanzanian couple, and it offers uncluttered accommodation in rustic four-bed en-suite bungalows suitable for budget travellers and families. Facilities include free airport pick-ups and transport to and from the Stone Town, as well as a home-cooked plat du jour for around US$3–5. *Rates: Bungalows US$15/30/40/45 sgl/dbl/tpl/qdr, b&b.*

**Imaani Beach Villa** (6 rooms) ☎ 024 2250050; m 0741 333731; e info@imani.it; www.imani.it. This small and delightful hotel sits right on the beach outside Bububu, about 9km from Stone Town. There are about 10 rooms, with huge beds and en-suite bathroom, all decorated in local style. Meals in the Arab-style restaurant, with low tables, cushions and carpets on the floor, are around US$20. A taxi to/from town is US$6.50, and the hotel also has bikes for hire which are free for guests. *Rates: US$55 pp, b&b.*

🏠 **Salme's Garden** (4 rooms) ☎ 024 2250050; 📱 0741 333731; 🖃 info@houseofwonders.com; www.houseofwonders.com. On the edge of the beach, this beautiful old house – once owned by the sultan and occupied by Princess Salme – is set in lush gardens surrounded by a high wall. It's a private and exclusive place, with just 4 airy bedrooms, wide verandas and shady balconies, and is a perfect place for hire by small groups (which means you get cheaper rates too). With the lovely old furniture and historical links it's amazing this place isn't a museum; staying is a unique and privileged experience. The only disadvantage is that, like the Imaani next door, the high wall doesn't stop the noise of music drifting over when there's a disco at Fuji Beach Bar, a short distance along the sand. You

can buy food for the cook to prepare, or use the restaurant at the Imaani next door. This hotel can be booked through Imaani Beach Villa or directly via the House of Wonders. *Rates: US$120–150 per room, inc the services of a cook and housekeeper.*

🏠 **Bububu Beach Guesthouse** (8 rooms) ☎ 024 2250110; 📱 0747 422747; 🖃 kilupyomar@hotmail.com; www.bububu-zanzibar.com. Set in Bububu village, this guesthouse is a simple place but clean, friendly and very relaxed, and the adequate en-suite rooms with nets and fan seem good value. Meals are available, and the guesthouse is very near Fuji Beach (see page 166), which has a bar and restaurant. The guesthouse can also arrange spice tours, rental cars and motorbikes. There's a free transfer service to/from town twice a day, or you can catch a *dala-dala*: those on Route B run regularly between Bububu village and Zanzibar Town. From the *dala-dala* stop on the main road in Bububu village, it's a short walk down a dirt track towards the beach to reach the hotel. *Rates: US$15 pp.*

## ISLANDS NEAR ZANZIBAR TOWN

A few kilometres from Zanzibar Town are several small islands, some of which are good destinations for a relaxing day's outing. Boat trips to the islands can be arranged with a tour company, or with one of the papaasi (touts) who look for business around town and along the seafront, or direct with one of the boat captains. Costs range from US$15 to US$60 for the boat, or from US$5 to US$20 per person, depending on who you deal with, the number of hours you want, the quality of the boat and whether you're prepared to share with other people or want a boat to yourself. Other factors might be lunch or snorkelling gear included in the price. You can hire a boat for yourself, or reduce costs by getting your own small group together. If you're alone, it's usually easy to link up with other travellers. Boats go across to the islands every morning from the beach by the Big Tree on Mizingani Road (the seafront), from the beach near the Tembo Hotel and the beach opposite the Africa House Hotel.

**CHANGUU ISLAND** This island is also called Prison Island, and was originally owned by a wealthy Arab who used it as a detention centre for disobedient slaves. After the abolition of slavery, in 1873, the island was bought by General Lloyd Mathews, commander of the sultan's army, who built a house here (see the *William Lloyd Mathews* box on page 170). In 1893 a prison was built on the island, but it was used instead as a quarantine station for the whole east African region. In the 1920s passengers arriving from India had to spend between one and two weeks on Changuu before proceeding to Zanzibar Town. On some old maps, Changuu is called Kibandiko Island, but this name now seems to be forgotten.

Today, the island is owned by the government and non-Tanzanian visitors must pay a US$4 entry fee (TSh are not acceptable). You can still see the quarantine station, and the house built by General Mathews which is now used as a restaurant. A path leads right round the island (about an hour's easy stroll), also passing some old pits where coral has been dug out to make building stone. Some of these pits

## WILLIAM LLOYD MATHEWS

The house on Changuu Island, a short distance offshore from Zanzibar Town, once belonged to William Lloyd Mathews, a military officer and later a government official in Zanzibar in the latter part of the 19th century.

Mathews was a Welshman born in Madeira in 1850. He entered the British navy in 1864, and from 1870 served in the slave-patrolling boats of HMS *London*. In August 1877 Mathews was seconded from the navy and appointed to command and organise a European-style army for Sultan Barghash, who wanted to enforce his sovereignty over the interior. Until then, the sultan's army had been composed of Arabs and Persians only, but the new army contained 500 Africans, with a uniform of red caps, short black jackets and white trousers. The Arab officers wore dark-blue frock coats and trousers, with gold or silver lace, possibly modelled on uniforms of the British Royal Navy. The British government donated 500 rifles, and by the beginning of the 1880s Mathews had about 1,300 men under his command.

One of the new army's first tasks was to stop the slave smuggling between Pemba and Pangani on the mainland and they were soon successful, capturing several slave smugglers and hindering the illicit trade. Mathews was released from the navy and became Brigadier-General Mathews, commander-in-chief of Zanzibar's army.

A leading slave trader at this time was called Hindi bin Hattam. His dhow was captured by a British navy ship, captained by one C J Brownrigg, between Zanzibar and Pemba. Brownrigg found about 100 slaves on board Hindi bin Hattam's dhow, but before any action could be taken Hindi's men killed Brownrigg, and most of the British crew, and sailed away. In another ship General Mathews pursued Hindi bin Hattam to Wete in Pemba, and took him prisoner after a battle. Hindi died later of gunshot wounds. Brownrigg was buried on Grave Island.

In 1891, when a constitutional government was established in Zanzibar, General Sir Lloyd Mathews was appointed as His Highness's First Minister, and he was awarded a knighthood on 3 March 1894. On 11 October 1901 Sir William Lloyd Mathews died in Zanzibar, of malaria, at the age of 51. He was buried with full naval and military honours in the English cemetery outside Zanzibar Town.

fill with water at high tide, and in colonial days they were kept clean and used as swimming pools.

The island's other highlight is the large number of giant tortoises (*Geochelone gigantea*). Four tortoises were brought from the island of Aldabra in the Seychelles in the 18th century, as a gift from the Seychelles governor to his opposite number in Zanzibar. They started to breed, and by 1955 there were 200, but after independence the numbers began to drop, partly because people started to steal them to sell abroad, either as exotic pets, or as food for 'exotic restaurants'. The numbers dropped to 100 in 1988, then 50 in 1990, until by late 1996 there were only seven left. In the same year a group of 80 hatchlings were moved to Zanzibar for protection – and 40 of them disappeared. Today the tortoises are protected in a large sanctuary compound provided by the Zanzibar government with help from the World Society for the Protection of Animals. In 2000 there were 17 adults, 50 juveniles and 90 hatchlings, all individually identified and protected by microchips injected under the skin. Since then, many more have been brought in, mostly juveniles. You can go into the sanctuary to see the tortoises close up. You can feed them (they delight in fresh mango peel), but please obey the signs and do not lift or sit on the tortoises.

Changuu Island has a small beach, and you can go snorkelling on the nearby reef. A rundown former government guesthouse on the island ceased functioning a couple of years back, but it has been privatised and is likely to re-open in a more upmarket incarnation in the near future.

**CHAPWANI ISLAND** This is also called Grave Island as a small section of it has been used as a Christian cemetery since 1879. Most of the graves belong to British sailors who were killed fighting against Arab slave ships, including Captain Brownrigg (see the *William Lloyd Mathews* box opposite); others date from World War I when the British ship *Pegasus* was bombarded and sunk by the German ship *Königsberg* in Zanzibar Town harbour. (This latter event is described in detail in the book *Königsberg – a German East African Raider* listed in *Appendix 2*.) There is a small beach on the island, and a lovely patch of indigenous forest, with a population of small duikers, some massive coconut crabs and a colony of fruit bats, which every evening do a few circuits of the island then zoom off to Zanzibar Town in a dark cloud. There are about 100 species of bird. The island's small exclusive hotel ceased operating in 2003 and it is uncertain when or indeed whether it will re-open.

**SNAKE ISLAND** This is the popular name for the very small island between Changuu and Chapwani islands. Boats do not usually land here as there is no beach.

**BAWE ISLAND** About 6km directly west of Zanzibar Town, this uninhabited island is not as frequently visited as Changuu, although the snorkelling is reported to be of good quality. The same people who run the boats to Changuu will also take you to Bawe, either as part of the same trip, or as a separate out-and-back voyage. Prices to Bawe are a bit higher than those to Changuu.

In the 1870s telegraph cables were brought ashore here, linking Zanzibar with the Seychelles, Aden and South Africa. Another line was run from Bawe Island to the External Telecommunications building in the Shangani area of Zanzibar Town. The old 'Extelcoms' building has now been converted into the Serena Inn, and another hotel is planned for Bawe Island itself. To stay in touch it is thought that they will not use the original phone line …

**Mtoni Marine**

*Sense the Spice in Style...*

Tel:+255(0)242250140or+255(0)777486214Fax:+255(0)242250496     mtoni@zanzibar.cc www .mtoni.com

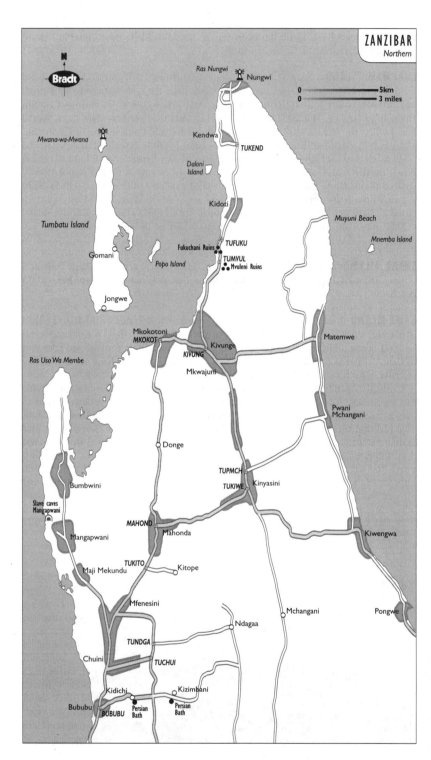

# 8

# Northern Zanzibar

Burgeoning guesthouses and vibrant nightlife are beginning to characterise northern Zanzibar, above its pleasant, white-sand beaches, warm sea, nautical heritage and good diving opportunities. A few hours' drive from Stone Town, past increasingly rural villages, this is the heart of the island's budget tourism industry. Focused around Nungwi village on the northernmost tip, and to a much lesser extent the golden sands of Kendwa, on the northwest coast, this bustling backpacker centre appears to offer every component of the perfect holiday to its sun-kissed guests: cheap accommodation, fresh seafood washed down with daily cocktails, and a lovely outlook. It is crowded though and the development not always attractive, so it's well worth escaping the 'Nungwi Strip' to seek out the quieter, more spectacular beaches of the northeast coast and Kendwa, the small turtle sanctuary, and the terrific local coral reefs. For a more cultural experience, head down the coast to the 16th-century Swahili ruins at Fukuchani and Mvuleni or the busy market at Mkokotoni, or venture across the water to Tumbatu Island.

## NUNGWI

Nungwi is traditionally the centre of Zanzibar's dhow-building industry, and, over the last decade, the coastline here has rocketed in popularity to become one of the island's busiest beach destinations. The ramshackle fishing village has been sidelined by an ever-increasing number of guesthouses, bars, shops, restaurants and bikini-clad backpackers. Ageing hippies, cool dudes, gap-year students and bright young things escaping European city jobs are all drawn to its white sand, stage-set palm trees, turquoise sea and sparkling sunshine. The setting is beautiful, but the number of people, constant noise and seemingly uncontrolled development, albeit low level, take the edge off its charm.

By day, the beach sees sunbathing tourists slumber, swim and indulge in lemongrass massages, whilst wandering local guys tout their 'tours' and sell a range of mediocre paintings, sunglasses and replica football shirts; then, as the sun sets, the visitors arise and the whole place buzzes with party spirit. Beach bonfires blaze, cocktails flow and the music rocks till dawn. This is not a location for those seeking peace and quiet.

Despite the influx of tourists, Nungwi is a traditional, conservative place. It was one of the last coastal settlements on Zanzibar to have a hotel, or any tourist facilities. As recently as the mid-1990s, proposals for large developments in the area were fiercely opposed by local people. Today, the proudly independent villagers give the impression that tourists are here on sufferance. However, they are not unfriendly and most visitors find that a little bit of cultural respect, politeness and a few words of Swahili go a long way.

Some visitors, particularly backpackers, find themselves torn between either coming to Nungwi and the north coast, or going to Paje, Bwejuu and Jambiani on

173

the east coast. For some thoughts on the differences between these two areas see page 219.

**GETTING THERE AND AWAY** Nungwi can be reached by bus, tourist minibus or hired vehicle. From Zanzibar Town the main road to Nungwi goes via Mtoni (✪ MTONIM 6°8.191'S; 39°12.801'E), Mahonda (✪ MAHOND 5°59.388'S; 39°15.106'E), Kinyasini (✪ KINYAS 5°58.088'S; 39°18.5'E) and Kivunge (✪ KIVUNG 5°52.895'S; 39°16.973'E). There is a more scenic road directly north of Mahonda to Mkokotoni (✪ MKOK0T 5°52.517'S; 39°15.308'E), but at the end of 2005 it was in extremely poor condition and the preserve of 4x4s only.

As you enter Nungwi, a conglomeration of signs advertising accommodation and activities marks a fork in the road. Head right for Nungwi's east coast hotels, or follow the road straight and then left around the football pitch to reach the village, and the north, south and west beaches.

If you arrive by *dala-dala* (number 16 from Stone Town), the main stop is opposite the football pitch, mentioned above, from where it's a 20-minute walk to the heart of the tourist throng. The shared tourist minibuses, a more popular option, will stop in the centre of the action beside Amaan Bungalows.

It has also been known for travellers to pay local fishermen to take them by boat to their next destination, even as far as Matemwe. Ask around to ensure reliability and safety, make sure people know where you're going, and check that there's a decent motor and safety equipment (like lifejackets) for longer trips.

**GETTING AROUND** Most places in and around Nungwi are within walking distance, but if you're staying on the more upmarket east side of the peninsula, and fancy letting your hair down on the lively west side, the local taxi service charges US$3 each way. Ask your hotel to put you in touch with a driver.

If you want to tour this part of the island, for example to visit Fukuchani and Mvuleni Ruins (see *Nungwi excursions* on pages 192–3), then it's possible to hire motorbikes, jeeps and bicycles. Ask your hotel to help you arrange this, and remember you must carry an International Driving Permit for a motorised vehicle: these are checked frequently by police, so don't be tempted to chance it. Drive with extra care, especially if you've rented a motorbike; traffic is unpredictable and pot-holes common, so accidents are frequent.

**WHERE TO STAY** The following hotels and guesthouses are listed roughly in clockwise order, from the southwest of the peninsula, round the headland and down the eastern coast.

**South Beach** The road into Nungwi from Zanzibar Town reaches a fork on the village outskirts. To reach places at the southern end of the west side of the peninsula, go left here, along a dusty track, towards the sea. This area has become unofficially known as South Beach, but it's a handy name, and might stick.

Just west of the village, South Beach is effectively the busiest beach. There is no reef in front of the shore here, so the water is deep enough for swimming, whatever the state of the tide. As the beach faces west, it is also a great spot for watching the sun go down. A number of the cheaper places to stay are located here, and it's certainly the liveliest part of Nungwi.

⌂ **Baobab Beach Bungalows** (69 rooms) PO Box 2632, Nungwi, Zanzibar; ☏ 024 2236315/0777 416964; f 024 2231199; e baobabnungwi@zanzinet.com/

baobabnungwi@yahoo.com; www.baobabbeachbungalows.com (✪ BAOBAB 5°43.927'S; 39°17.528'E). Although this is one of the largest establishments on this stretch of coast,

Baobab's location on a quiet, sandy cove at the southernmost end of Nungwi Beach holds great appeal. There are 4 categories of room, all spotlessly clean with en-suite bathrooms, hot and cold water, ceiling fans, mosquito nets, mains electricity, UK 3-pin sockets and a private balcony. Compact standard rooms are set back from the sea, amid neatly manicured gardens, but their small size makes them little more than a place to sleep. Unless your budget won't stretch the extra US$20, the best accommodation options are probably the lodges and deluxe rooms. Although they are set quite far back from the water's edge, the lodges do benefit from an unobstructed view of the sea, making their verandas a perfect spot to watch the sun set after a hard day on the beach. Alternatively, a row of comfortable deluxe rooms run perpendicular to the beach and offer a little extra space along with newly tiled floors, AC, Zanzibari coconut-wood furniture and incongruous fluffy pink bathmats. At the same price as the superior rooms, these are a far better bet. At the time of visiting, a swimming pool was being hand-cut out of the coral rock in front of these rooms. Opened in Jul 2005, the polygonal superior rooms, built in 2-storey structures at the back of the resort, again feature coconut furniture, a shower that would 'hold an entire football team', fabrics ranging from faux leopard-skin to pale-peach polyester, and a view across the rest of the bungalows. The Seaview Beach Restaurant & Bar enjoys the resort's premium position, right on the edge of a coral cliff, immediately above the sea. Local and international dishes feature on both the à la carte and buffet menus. Follow dinner with a game of pool or a table football match, or relax at the hands of the resident masseuse. The hotel has 24hr security and there is a safe at reception. *Standard room US$50/60 sgl/dbl; lodges US$70/90 sgl/dbl; deluxe and superior rooms US$90/130 sgl/dbl. All rates inc b/fast.*

⌂ **The Nungwi Inn Hotel** (18 rooms) PO Box 1496, Zanzibar; ☎ 024 2240091;
e thenungwi_inn@hotmail.com (✪ NUNINN 5°43.864'S; 39°17.517'E). Nungwi Inn Hotel is unusual in that its two categories of room and reception are all geographically detached; its seaview rooms are right on the beach, just behind Spanish Dancer's dive centre, whilst its non-seaview rooms are set in gardens, across the dirt road; and its reception is roughly between the two, in a parade of shops. However, if you can track down someone who works here, these rooms are a good bet. Bright and airy, they are spotlessly clean with starched white bedding, mosquito nets, fans (AC in the

seaview rooms), 24hr electricity, UK 3-pin sockets and hot water in the en-suite bathrooms. There is a basic restaurant and the hotel can arrange beach barbecues on the sand at night. Rooms here can also be booked though the Spanish Dancer dive centre website: www.spanishdancerdivers.com. *Seaview room US$50/80/105 sgl/dbl/tpl; non-seaview room US$30/50/75 sgl/dbl/tpl, inc b&b.*

⌂ **Safina Bungalows** (25 rooms) PO Box 3758, Zanzibar; ☎ 0748 717237;
e Luwamboi@yahoo.com (✪ SAFINA 5°43.839'S; 39°17.523'E). Under the enthusiastic new management of Aisha Oletei, Safina is slowly being renovated to a good standard. In spite of the lack of sea view, it's a comfortable and spotlessly clean bedtime retreat. All rooms have 24hr electricity, 3-pin UK sockets and hot water in en-suite bathrooms. Dbl rooms have duvets in addition to the standard sheets. *US$35/40/45/60 sgl/twin/dbl/tpl b&b.*

⌂ **H&H Beach Bungalows** (15 rooms) PO Box 114, Zanzibar; ☎ 024 2250630/0777 416937;
e info@hamimtour.com; http://hamimtour.com (✪ H-HBEA 5°43.829'S; 39°17.54'E). Tucked behind Safina, Hamim and Hamida Abdallah's bungalows are a basic but great-value option. Dbl, twin and tpl rooms are set out around a small, sandy quad, where fruit and cooked eggs are served each morning. Rooms are clean and the en-suite bathrooms have hot water and good quality fittings. Ceiling fans, mosquito nets, 24hr electricity and 3-pin UK sockets are standard. Hamim is a tour operator in Stone Town so arranging transfers and excursions can be done with ease. *US$15 pp b&b.*

⌂ **Amaan Bungalows** (53 rooms) PO Box 4769, Nungwi, Zanzibar; ☎ 024 2240026/0777 417390;
f 024 2240026; e amaannungwi@yahoo.com; www.amaanbungalows.com (✪ AMAANB 5°43.778'S; 39°17.497'E). Heralded by rows of fluttering international flags, Amaan Bungalows is a sprawling, whitewashed, castellated complex. The 53 rooms are divided into 3 broad categories, imaginatively named A, B and C, plus 5 more recent seaview rooms, perched on coral rock over the sea across the road. The rooms are all clean and cared for with en-suite tiled bathrooms, hot and cold water, ceiling fans, mosquito nets, mains electricity, UK 3-pin sockets and a private terrace. Safety deposit boxes are available at reception. Most rooms can be made up for sgl to tpl occupancy, and a couple are interconnecting for groups and families. This is an ever-expanding and developing complex popular with a young crowd seeking to be at the very centre of the action. Bordering the main track through town,

Amaan also has a parade of practical shops and a new café. The bureau de change will convert virtually any major currency into Tanzanian shillings or US dollars, the internet café offers reliable PCs and fast, satellite internet connection, and the travel agency is a good bet for arranging local excursions and onward travel in mainland Tanzania. The Souvenir Emporium is a great place to pick up a postcard before heading to Namaste, the new neighbourhood coffee house. Fat Fish restaurant and Upper Deck, immediately opposite on the sea front, are affiliated with Amaan and are the places to eat pizza and seafood, drink virtually anything and be merry at any hour of the day. *Seaview rooms are US$60/85 sgl/dbl. Room types A, B and C range in price from US$30–45 sgl to US$45–65 dbl. All room categories can be made up as a tpl for an extra US$20. Book directly with the hotel reception and receive a 10% discount. Credit cards are not accepted; travellers' cheques are subject to a 10% surcharge. Payment is preferred in US$.*

⌂ **Langi Langi Beach Bungalows** (19 rooms) PO Box 132, Nungwi, Zanzibar; ✆ 024 2240470; f 024 2240471; e langi_langi@hotmail.com (⊕ LANGIL 5°43.725'S; 39°17.491'E). The name Langi Langi is a

Swahili derivation of ylang ylang, the perfumed Asian tree (*Cananga odorata*) planted in the hotel's lush gardens. Essential oil from the flowers is often used in the aromatherapy treatment of stress: a condition rarely encountered on Zanzibar. The 19 en-suite rooms are compact and clean, each with AC, fans and constant hot water. Mosquito nets are available upon request and you can even borrow a hairdryer from reception. They are a walk from the beach, but they are of a good standard, and do sit right in the heart of Nungwi's tourist scene. At the end of 2005, construction was under way on an ambitious new bar, restaurant and lounge area, across the dirt road and next to the ocean. Set on a large cantilevered deck over the sea, with some innovative design features, there are plans to include a stylish massage spot on the upper deck and 2 luxury rooms with private seaview balconies. An internet café and small gift shop may follow. The owner, Mansour Saleh Said, is clearly investing heavily in this property and is keen to see it succeed; the quality he's providing make this a great option within the price bracket. *Rooms are US$50/75 tpl, US$40/60 dbl and US$35/45 sgl low/high season. All room rates include continental b/fast, service charges and VAT.*

## West Beach
Northwards from Paradise Beach Bungalows, still on the west side of the peninsula, is another stretch of beach, which for the purposes of this book we'll call West Beach. The places to stay here are described south to north.

⌂ **Paradise Beach Bungalows** (18 rooms) PO Box 2375, Nungwi, Zanzibar; ✆ 0777 418860/0777 416308; e shaabani_makame@hotmail.com. Accessed through a high gate at a sharp bend in the road, Paradise Beach Bungalows no longer has any bungalows. Following redevelopment in 2004, it now offers 18 virtually identical rooms in a 2-storey, concrete accommodation block. Whilst the building is aesthetically challenged and the landscaping sparse, the rooms are clean and all have fans, 24hr electricity and en-suite bathrooms. They also benefit from being positioned in front of a stepped access point to a small secluded cove: perfect for a quick dip in the heat of the afternoon sun. The affiliated sea-side restaurant serves pizza and daily curries. *US$35/40/60 sgl/dbl/tpl b&b. Sgl room rates reduce US$10 during low season.*

⌂ **Baraka Bungalows** (10 rooms) PO Box 3502, Zanzibar; ✆ 024 2240412/024 2240033/0777 415569; e barakabungalow@hotmail.com; www.geocities.com/barakabungalows (⊕ BARAKA 5°43.694'S; 39°17.511'E). In the shadow of Paradise Beach Bungalows's accommodation block, these

bungalows surround a small garden beside West Beach. The en-suite rooms here are dark but appear to be fairly clean and do have fans, electricity and hot water. At a mere coconut's throw from the pleasant West Beach, they're well placed for sun-worshippers. However, this proximity does also mean that the music from Cholo's is likely to prevent any sleep before dawn, at which time the villagers' radios will usually take over. *Rates: US$10/15 sgl low/high season; US$20/25 dbl low/high season; US$35/45 tpl low/high season. All rates are b&b.*

⌂ **Cholo's** (3 *bandas*) No contact details. Set at the back of a small beach, under towering makuti thatch, Cholo's is an idiosyncratic beach bar composed of 2 marooned dhows, suspended dugout canoes acting as seats and an array of bathroom sanitary ware serving as storage units. Immediately behind this curious establishment, there are 3 tiny backpacker *bandas* (or cottages). Of very basic timber and makuti construction, with only a cotton curtain across the entrance, these rooms offer simply a mattress on the floor and a mosquito net. One has a light, fan and flush toilet, whilst the others

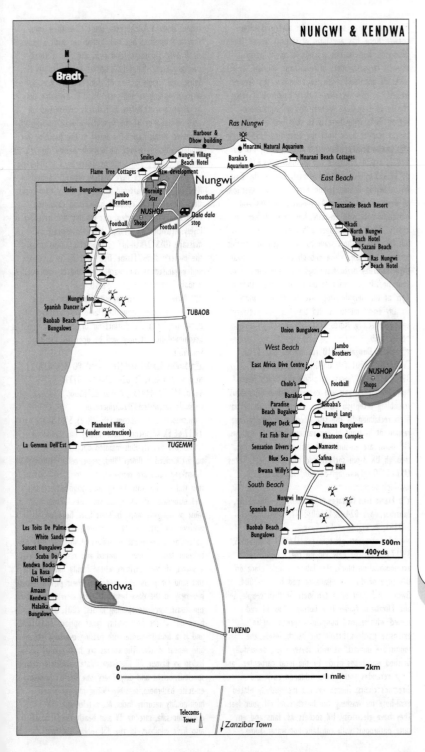

NUNGWI & KENDWA

*Ras Nungwi*

Harbour &
Dhow building

Mnarani Natural Aquarium

Smiles

Nungwi Village
Beach Hotel

Baraka's
Aquarium

Mnarani Beach Cottages

Flame Tree Cottages

New development

**Nungwi**

*East Beach*

Union Bungalows

Jambo
Brothers

Morning
Star

Football

**NUSHOP**

Dala dala
stop

Tanzanite Beach Resort

Football

Shops

Football

Mkadi
North Nungwi
Beach Hotel
Sazani Beach

Ras Nungwi
Beach Hotel

Nungwi Inn
Spanish Dancer

Baobab Beach
Bungalows

**TUBAOB**

Union Bungalows

*West Beach*

Jambo
Brothers

East Africa Dive Centre

**NUSHOP**

Cholo's

Football

Shops

Barakas

Paradise
Beach Bugalows

Alibaba's

Langi Langi

Upper Deck

Amaan Bungalows

Fat Fish Bar

Khatoom Complex

Sensation Divers

Namaste

Blue Sea

Safina

Bwana Willy's

H&H

*South Beach*

Nungwi Inn

Spanish Dancer

Baobab Beach
Bungalows

0     500m

0     400yds

Planhotel Villas
(under construction)

**TUGEMM**

La Gemma Dell'Est

Les Toits De Palme
White Sands
Sunset Bungalows
Scuba Do
Kendwa Rocks
La Rosa
Dei Venti
Amaan
Kendwa
Malaika
Bungalows

**Kendwa**

**TUKEND**

0     2km

0     1 mile

Telecoms
Tower

*Zanzibar Town*

177

have access to a separate toilet and cold-water shower. None has any form of security at all. Cholo's 'Non-stop, Rock it like it's hot, All night party' attracts large numbers of locals and tourists for its cocktails and loud music, so be aware that you're unlikely to get any sleep before daybreak if you choose to stay here. Anyway the only plausible reason for staying here is so that you won't have far to stagger back from the festivities. *US$10 pp.*

⌂ **Jambo Brothers Bungalows** (16 rooms) PO Box 1792; ☏ 024 2240002 (⊕ JAMBRO 5°43.615'S; 39°17.539'E). Located immediately behind the East Africa Diving Centre, Jambo Brothers is a collection of 8 simple bungalows. All rooms have fans and mosquito nets with en-suite, hot-water showers and toilets. There is no longer a bar or restaurant here, but it's only a short walk to the clutch of eateries further south, and close enough to Cholo's to hear their Saturday night festivities from the comfort of your bed. If you want to book in advance, Delene Kutz at the neighbouring dive centre will kindly pass on any email messages and translate as necessary: eadc@zitec.org. *Rates: US$10/15 low/high season pp for b&b.*

⌂ **Union Bungalows** (10 rooms) PO Box 1792; ☏ 0777 841901 (⊕ UNIONB 5°43.579'S; 39°17.558'E). A few steps along the beach from Jambo Brothers, you will come to Union Bungalows' crumbling reception building, whose foundations have been reclaimed by the sea. Check-in is now at the restaurant in front of the rather shabby bungalows. All rooms are en-suite with hot water, electricity through UK 3-pin sockets and mosquito nets. *Rates: US$15/20 sgl low/high season; US$25/40 dbl low/high season.*

⌂ **Flame Tree Cottages** (11 rooms) PO Box 1752, Zanzibar; ☏/f 024 2240100/0777 479429/0741 262151; e etgl@zanlink.com; www.flametreecottages.com (⊕ FLAMET 5°43.509'S; 39°17.611'E). The new kid on the Nungwi accommodation block, this fabulous little place on the edge of Nungwi village opened in mid-2004. Owned and built by a Zanzibari–Scottish couple, Seif and Elizabeth, Flame Tree Cottages has 11 red-roofed, whitewashed bungalows spread out in extensive gardens, beside the beach. Inside, the rooms are immaculate with lovely linen, beautifully finished wardrobes made by the local carpenters, and large verandas with white-cushioned easy and director's chairs. There's even a thoughtfully placed mini-hose for washing the beach sand off your feet. They have electricity, UK sockets, AC, fans and en-suite bathrooms with constant hot water. Some

rooms share a kitchenette, some have their own; they are compact but well kitted out with a hob, small oven (in some) and sink, and (for a small surcharge) the delightful head of housekeeping, Mr Salim, will supply a box of pans and crockery for anyone wishing to self-cater. Food is available only by arrangement. B/fast and snacks are served on your veranda or in the sunbathing area. Individually prepared meals can be ordered in the morning for dinner, which is served on a table beside the sea, lit only by candles and lanterns. There is a real feeling of space and peace here that is difficult to find in Nungwi; lounging around in one of many hammocks, slung between the coconut palms and casuarina trees around the garden, just reading and relaxing is lovely. Activities here range from lemongrass oil massage (US$12/half-hr) to snorkelling trips aboard the owner's dhow. Flame Tree's website is as clear and organised as the place itself, and is well worth a look. *US$80/105 sgl/dbl b&b.*

⌂ **New development opposite Flame Tree** In late 2005, construction opposite Flame Tree Cottages was under way with the distinct air of yet more tourist accommodation. It may well be open by the time you visit.

⌂ **Smiles Beach Hotel** (16 rooms) PO Box 4222, Nungwi, Zanzibar; ☏ 024 2240472/0777 417676/0777 444334; f 024 2238006; e smilesbeachhotel@zanzinet.com; www.smilesbeachhotel.com (⊕ SMILES 5°43.532'S; 39°17.66'E). An architectural medley has produced Smiles' DIY Beverly-Hills-mansion appearance. Spaced in an arc around a flower-filled, semicircular garden, the 4 striking villas are resplendent in fresh pale yellow and white paint, with neatly tiled pagoda-like roofs and elaborate exterior spiral staircases. (Given that most of Nungwi's hotel builders have been unable to achieve regularly spaced steps, these spirals are a particular achievement, regardless of whether they are to your taste.) Smiles is owned and run by Ibrahim, a smart, affable Zanzibari, whose family have owned this land for years and used it as their private beach hideaway in the days before tourism development hit this coast. Since its opening in Sep 2001, this has been one of the best-quality, quiet options in Nungwi, and is a firm favourite with passing overland groups and repeat visitors. The rooms are high quality and Indian in flavour. All are immaculate: spotlessly clean, spacious, bright and airy. Every one has a sparkling en-suite bathroom, sensibly sliding mosquito nets, high-quality security locks, AC, a telephone, an electronic safe, satellite TV and beach towels; some also have minibars. In the dbl rooms, the bed mattresses have been raised onto concrete plinths with painted moulding creating a headboard effect. The spacious tpl, which could fit 6 people, is made up with 3 large Zanzibari beds. The 'Honeymoon Sweet' (sic) features a giant corner bed as its centrepiece and, like the others, offers indulgent b/fasts in bed. For those who can drag themselves the few metres to the beach, there's a new fibreglass boat for snorkelling excursions. There is an on-site restaurant and regular beach barbecues, though the restaurant is not licensed to serve alcohol. *US$65/85/115 sgl/dbl/tpl b&b. Prices reduce by US$10–15 in low season.*

🏠 **Nungwi Village Beach Resort** (36 rooms) ☎ 022 2152187; f 022 2152072; e relax@nungwivillage.com; www.nungwivillage.com (✪ NUNVIL 5°43.488'S; 39°17.691'E). Opened in 1999, this mid-range resort is set in spacious grounds on the northernmost stretch of West Beach. The style of accommodation here varies tremendously between the standard and seafront rooms, though both are clean and tidy with en-suite bathrooms, AC, fans, mosquito nets and UK 3-pin electrical sockets. Standard rooms are laid out in single-storey blocks around a gravel courtyard, and are accessed through traditional Zanzibari carved doors, neatly flanked by narrow mirrors. Inside, the furniture is heavy and wooden and the décor Indian-influenced; dbl/twin beds are made up with fresh sheets and blankets, there's a small desk, seats and long mirror in each room, and an extra sgl bed can be added if necessary. In a diagonal line towards the beach, there are 20 seafront rooms in 5, 2-storey, whitewashed houses. At the front of each level is a narrow balcony, with red concrete floors and a neat balustrade, which leads to 2 rooms. Bright, airy and spotless with high ceilings, kingsize Zanzibari beds, good-quality wooden wardrobes and chests. The soft furnishings have a safari theme with herds of zebra migrating across the curtains and miscellaneous animal prints covering the lamp shades. The best of these rooms are numbers 129 to 132 for their immediate proximity to the beach and completely unobstructed views of the sea and bobbing dhows in the harbour. At the other end of the beach is the restaurant, where an old dugout has been mounted on the wall and an assortment of painted fish placed in its net. The usual array of surface-level water activities is available, along with table tennis, pool and volleyball. There a useful high-speed internet point and a satellite TV for the antisocial and sunburnt. *Rates: US$70 in standard or US$140 in seafront room b&b. Payment by VISA or MasterCard is preferred.*

**Nungwi Village** Away from the beaches, in Nungwi village itself there are a couple of options:

🏠 **Ruma Guesthouse** Located at the western edge of the village, close to the football pitch and shops, Ruma Guesthouse offers very basic, local-style rooms in a simple concrete building.

🏠 **Bagamoyo Spice Villa** (3 rooms) PO Box 3528, Zanzibar; ☎ 0746 442203; e sensationdivers@yahoo.com/ info@sensationdivers.com; www.sensationdivers.com (✪ BAGAMO 5°43.613'S; 39°17.61'E). Available exclusively to Sensations Divers' clients, and owned by the same person, Peter Minchin, Bagamoyo is a self-contained private house on the edge of the village. With a marked sub-aqua theme throughout, the 3 bedrooms in the main house are named after local dive sites — Leven Bank, Hunga and Kichafi. Each has 2 kingsize beds, solid furniture and an en-suite bathroom. Those who haven't had enough aquatic adventure during their day can happily wallow in the deep stone bath in Leven Bank. Bagamoyo can be booked on FB or HB basis, and has a barbecue area and fully equipped kitchen, known as Home Reef. There's a large tropical garden dotted with coconut palms and cerise bougainvillea, and for rainy afternoons, a lounge area with satellite TV, internet access and some interesting books and maps. *US$60/75 sgl/dbl b&b. Use of the Home Reef kitchen is an additional US$5 per day.*

**East Beach** At the tip of the Nungwi peninsula is the lighthouse; from here, the coast curves back sharply to the south. This eastern side of the peninsula is significantly less developed and quieter than South and West beaches, with some great choices of places to stay set on low cliffs of coral rock above sandy beaches.

🏠 **Mnarani Beach Cottages** (27 rooms) PO Box 3361, Nungwi, Zanzibar; ☎ 024 2240494/0777 415551; f 024 2240496; e mnarani@zanlink.com; www.lighthousezanzibar.com (✪ MNARAN 5°43.411'S; 39°18.252'E). Mnarani means 'at or near the lighthouse' in Swahili, and aptly describes this resort's situation. Close to the northernmost tip of the island, from where it is possible to see the sun rise and set, this is a delightful place. Neat sand paths, bordered by masses of established pink hibiscus, lead between the rooms and to the beachfront bar/restaurant area. Here, overlooking a stunning stretch of beach, a new cantilevered deck area provides a perfect spot for sunbathing, sundowners or simply chilling on one of the swings. Calm and shady, this is a very relaxed and civilised place to recharge your batteries. Rooms 1 to 8 have perfect sea views, interrupted only by an occasional coconut palm, whilst numbers 9 to 12 are set in lush, tropical gardens. The rooms are relatively small but spotlessly clean, tastefully decorated and with good en-suite facilities. Coconut-wood furniture sits on broad terraces at the front of each one, whilst beautiful loungers and inviting rope hammocks hang between coconut palms and shady fir trees. There is even a raised, manmade beach for relaxing during high tide. There are also 4 dbl-storey family cottages — Julie, Furaha, Huba and Maimuna — with large galleried interiors, a lounge, kitchen and useful information pack. Plus, at the end of 2005, a sizeable 3-storey accommodation building, Zanzibar House, was completed. Its 10 spacious en-suite rooms (all named after small Zanzibari islands) each offer good-quality furniture, AC, a telephone, fridge and large, seaview balcony. Alternatively, escape to the roof terrace for some of the best panoramic views of this area. It's possible to hire watersports equipt: hourly rental costs US$5/10 sgl/dbl kayak, US$10 surfboard and US$10 windsurf. The lagoon immediately in front of the hotel is also a great place for kite-surfers; here the reef offers some protection, the winds are perfect, the water warm and there's no risk of injury from the submerged canes of seaweed farmers. *Standard room US$84/108 dbl, b&b, mid/peak season; family cottage US$104/128 mid/peak season; Honeymoon cottage, 'Mahaba', US$200–224; Zanzibar House rooms US$170–190 dbl, mid/peak season. 'Mahaba' and 'Zanzibar House' are available only on HB or FB basis*

⌂ **Tanzanite Beach Resort** PO Box 4036, Zanzibar; ⌀ 024 2240255; e yankeestz@yahoo.com (⊕ TANZAN 5°43.599'S; 39°18.509'E). In late 2005, Tanzanite Beach Resort was under construction, on Nungwi's east coast, just south of Mnarani Beach Cottages. It has a stunning outlook from its raised location above the beach; let's hope the accommodation and facilities built here will do justice to the view!

⌂ **Mkadi** (⊕ MKADIG 5°43.686'S; 39°18.602'E). A barely functioning guesthouse, close to the road, above East Beach.

⌂ **North Nungwi Beach Hotel** (10 rooms) PO Box 3904, Zanzibar; ☏ vugahotel@yahoo.com; www.travelzanzibar.com (⊕ NTHNUN 5°43.712'S; 39°18.63'E). Framed by the main door as you approach this hotel, the picture-perfect view of sandy paths leading down to the Indian Ocean, with cerulean waves breaking on the distant reef, is as good as it gets. Step inside, and what may have been an idyllic retreat is now run-down and poorly managed. Once-neat flower beds are overgrown, rope handrails are frayed, rooms are tatty and staff are scarce. This hotel's fabulous outlook is currently the only possible reason to stay here. *US$25/30 sgl low/high season b&b, US$40/58 dbl low/high season and US$60/75 tpl low/high season.*

⌂ **Sazani Beach Hotel** (10 rooms) PO Box 4200, Zanzibar; ☏/f 024 2240014/0741 324744; e sazanibeach@aol.com; www.sazanibeach.com (⊕ SAZANI 5°43.775'S; 39°18.669'E). Adjacent to Ras Nungwi Beach Hotel, Sazani Beach opened in 1997 and has been in its current form since the new millennium. Part-owned and managed by an eccentric Englishman, Mike, who's been living and working in Tanzania for over 20 years, this is a slightly off-beat, thoroughly laid-back place to stay. Set high up on coral rock, there are 3 en-suite rooms in the main house, 2 large rooms suitable for dbl or tpl occupancy and 4 standard dbls in semi-detached bungalows, and a beach *banda*, currently occupied by Mike but also popular with single travellers. There are tentative plans to build an additional 2 rooms in 2006. All rooms have 24hr electricity, mosquito nets, fans, hot water, fabulous soft cotton sheets and a stunning sea view. Early-morning tea can be brought in your room, before b/fast is served on a new patio area under a trellis of passion fruit. Homemade jams and freshly brewed coffee feature alongside traditional eggs and bacon. Fish dinners are served by the beach and over a few sundowner drinks in the bar, Mike will tell you about his passion for cricket and writing short stories, and his latest development plans. There is an on-site dive centre, Divemaxx, but at the time of visiting no sub-aqua teaching was possible as there are no instructors on-site. However, Mike is a dive master and will rent out equipt and escort group trips for experienced divers, if desired. Sazani is also a hangout for kite-surfers keen to catch the shore trade winds (up to force 6) in the clear lagoon immediately in front of the hotel. Advice and back-up can be sought from Chris at the neighbouring Ras Nungwi Beach Hotel, even if the accommodation price there is over budget. Free internet is also available for all guests staying here: handy for anyone travelling with an overloaded memory card in their digital camera. *US$60/70 sgl, low/high season; US$80/90 dbl, low/high season. Children under 2 years stay free; age 2–12 US$30/35 low/high season. All rates are b&b.*

🏠 **Ras Nungwi Beach Hotel** (32 rooms) PO Box 1784, Zanzibar; ✆ 024 2233767/2232512; f 024 2233098; e info@rasnungwi.com; www.rasnungwi.com (✪ RASNUN 5°43.809'S; 39°18.691'E). A perennially popular choice for high-end honeymoon couples, Ras Nungwi Beach Hotel sits on the east coast, at the southern end of Nungwi's beach. It's by far the most upmarket place to stay in Nungwi but retains a calm, low-key atmosphere. Its 32 rooms are set in very compact, well-tended gardens. They were last renovated in 2000 to incorporate AC, electronic safes and neatly tiled bathrooms. The rooms are divided into 3 classes according to their location, view and finishing touches, from the inclusion of a minibar to branded toiletries. Broadly speaking, the higher the room category, the closer it is to the sea and the more it has to offer. The 13 lodge or garden rooms sit in a row above the central area and car park, some distance from the sea. Only a couple of these have sea views but each has a traditional Zanzibari bed with mosquito net, an en-suite bathroom and a veranda, and any can be made up for sgl, dbl or tpl occupancy. The 12 whitewashed rondavels of the superior chalets and 6 superior deluxe chalets all enjoy sea views, but only the latter offer dressing gowns and stereos. In addition, set slightly away from the rondavels, the Ocean Suite operates as a private, separate villa. With 200 square metres of space, inc a private plunge pool and sun deck, and access to a private chef, this is Ras Nungwi's premium accommodation offering. Alongside the large central bar and split-level dining room, there's an internet point, concealed satellite TV room and a games area with a pool table, table tennis, board games and darts, which is a popular post-dinner spot for younger visitors. In front of this area is a small, tiled, freshwater swimming pool and sun deck with paths radiating down to the beach and secluded reading areas. There's an excellent, efficient PADI dive centre with 4 dhows and 4 permanent instructors, offering courses and recreational dives to Mnemba, the east coast and around Kendwa. Snorkelling trips (US$30–65), kayaking (US$10/hr), water-skiing (US$50/15mins), windsurfing (US$10/hr) and a range of other watersports are often possible with top-of-the-range equipt on site. Big-game fishing has long been one of the manager's passions and the hotel has the only professional sport-fishing boat in Zanzibar, *Countdown*, along with professional tackle and international safety standards. 'Tag and release' fishing is generally encouraged, unless it's a record-breaking fish or fisherman's first-ever catch. The exceptional food and a great wine list are highlights of any stay here. Delicious fresh, often organic, dishes are the norm. With all guests staying on a HB basis there's an extensive b/fast buffet laid out every morning, an à la carte lunch menu and 5-course table d'hôte dinner. Occasionally tasty seafood BBQs with Swahili cuisine classics will feature for dinner, often accompanied by some gentle live music. *Lodge US$120–135 pp high/low season; superior chalet US$155–175 pp high/low season; superior deluxe chalet US$175–205 pp high/low season; Ocean Suite US$700–850 pp high/low season. All rates are HB and based on 2 people sharing. Sgl suppt is US$60/night. Children under 12 pay 75% of adult rate and those under 2 years stay free of charge. Road transfers from Zanzibar Town cost US$30 pp each way.*

🍴 **WHERE TO EAT** Nearly all the hotels and guesthouses in Nungwi have attached restaurants, many of which are open to guests and non-guests alike (see the *Where to stay* section for more details of these). Along South Beach a multitude of little local-style cafés and bars serve seafood dishes for around US$3, and snacks and burgers for around US$2, all washed down with fresh fruit juices, milkshakes, ubiquitous Coca-Cola and African beer. Between South and West beaches, a continuous band of more structured restaurants perch on the coral cliff above the sea. All have similar menus of fresh seafood, oven-fired pizzas and local curries, most are home to ever-hungry stray cats, and many do happy hours and backpacker meal-and-beer specials. For a more grassroots flavour, deep in the village you are likely to find cheap local fare from around US$1, though venues are highly changeable.

With little building regulation apparent, beachfront bars, restaurants and guesthouses tend to close and spring up again virtually overnight. Set up a barbecue beside a few chairs, tables or logs on the sand, and you're in business: only the names change. For this reason, we've only listed some of the more reliable, long-running eateries, notably between South and West beaches, and you should accept that you're quite likely to find many more newcomers on arrival.

✗ **Bwana Will's Bar** (⊕ WILBAR 5°43.825'S; 39°17.48'E). At the northern end of South Beach, raised up on the coral cliff, overlooking the sand and out to sea, Bwana Will's – named after its English owner William – attracts a trendy, young backpacker crowd. Drawn to fruit cocktails sipped at swinging bar seats and beer over leisurely games of bao, this they find a friendly, relaxed place to escape the afternoon sun.

✗ **Blue Sea Restaurant** (⊕ BLUESE 5°43.803'S; 39°17.48'E). Approached from South Beach, this is the first of this coast's clutch of raised seafront restaurants. Recommended by many for its seafood, its barbecued fish, octopus, barracuda and tuna are all popular (US$5.50–8), along with fresh fish kebabs with 'pineat butter' or hot sauce. Crab and lobster are reasonably priced at US$10 and US$19 respectively, whilst those tired of fish can sample delights from the pizza oven (US$4.50–6.00), or taste local curries (US$5.50–12.00). A high proportion of dishes boast 'Julian' vegetables. Cocktails (US$2.50–4.00) accompany most meals here with the 'Nungwi Mama' – dark rum, Kahlua and pineapple juice – a house special.

✗ **Fat Fish Restaurant & Bar** (⊕ FATFIS 5°43.773'S; 39°17.485'E). Fat Fish is a wonderfully relaxed hangout. The expansive mangrove-pole terrace is

cantilevered over the beach, affording diners uninterrupted views out to sea and a welcome breeze. The local fishermen's daily catch determines the extensive menu, and is served freshly grilled or in spicy curries. Sunset drinks are equally popular and there's also a satellite TV for catching up on international sporting events.

✗ **Upper Deck Restaurant and Bar** Next door to Fat Fish, Upper Deck serves similar fare and operates a well-stocked bar, so is worth popping into for after-dinner drinks.

🍺 **Namaste** (⊕ NAMAST 5°43.795'S; 39°17.489'E). Opposite Sensation Divers, this relaxed coffee shop is something of a haven. Run by the wife of Sandro from Fat Fish, this is a calm, restful escape from the music and games of the beach. In spite of bordering Amaan Bungalows car park and the village through-road, the outside terrace is perfectly pleasant. It is comfortable inside, and the coffee's pretty good too!

🍸 **Cholo's Bar** For all-day drinking and wild nights, Cholo's is a perennial favourite. Tucked under palms at the back of West Beach, this eccentric establishment is well known for its 24hr pumping music, cool crowd of local Rastas and backpackers, and free-flowing alcohol. Beach bonfires are an evening attraction along with ad hoc barbecues. See page 176 for very basic accommodation here.

## WHAT TO DO AND SEE

**Water activities** The sweeping cape on which Nungwi is sited is surrounded by sparkling, warm, turquoise seas, making it a perfect spot to engage in countless water activities. On the west side of the peninsula, especially on South Beach, locals offer simple boat rides, Mnemba picnic excursions, sunset booze cruises and snorkelling trips. Prices are all very similar; quality is variable. Take other travellers' word-of-mouth advice seriously when deciding who is currently offering the best trip.

**Diving** Diving is especially popular here and many of the hotels offer dives and dive courses: you can go on the local reef, or go further afield to reefs such as Leven Bank and Mnemba. Over recent years several dive operations have come, gone or changed their name or location; at the beginning of 2006, five serious dive operations were in operation in Nungwi.

✈ **Spanish Dancer Dive Centre** PO Box 3486, Stone Town, Zanzibar; ☎ 024 2240091/0777 417717/0777 430005; e spanishdancerznz@hotmail.com; www.spanishdancerdivers.com (⊕ SPANDA 5°43.891'S; 39°17.473'E). Taking its name from both an attractive marine creature and its owner's nationality, Spanish Dancer has been operational since 2001. Based in an open rondavel on South Beach, Spanish Dancer is run by Anna and Gregory, their daughter Sabina and her partner Carlos, 3 of whom are dive instructors. The team regularly dives 20 sites, inc Mnemba (1 hr 10min by boat) and Leven Bank (divers must have a min of 20 logged dives to participate). Equipt and steel tanks seem in good condition, and there are 2 boats: a large one capable of carrying 25 divers, and a smaller one for 15 divers on a 2-tank trip. Oxygen and first-aid kits are standard on all boats and Anna is a doctor, which should ensure good safety standards. By rule, only the instructors carry surface marker buoys, so you may want to consider taking your own. Though the instructors are all PADI-registered and can teach dive courses in Spanish, Italian and English, the centre itself is not a PADI resort. Sunset cruises in a local dhow can also be arranged here. *US$35/95/145/230 for 1/3/5/10 local dive packages (plus US$15 at Mnemba); US$60 PADI Discover Scuba Diving; US$350 PADI Open Water certification course; US$750 PADI Dive Master.*

✈ **Sensation Divers** PO Box 3528, Zanzibar; ☎ 0746 442203; e sensationdivers@yahoo.com/ info@sensationdivers.com; www.sensationdivers.com (⊕ SENSAT 5°43.795'S; 39°17.484'E). This dive outfit is based opposite Amaan Bungalows on the Nungwi restaurant strip, and its managers are firm fixtures on the Nungwi party circuit. Sensation appears to concentrate on some of the more adrenalin-influenced options for diving. They have 4 dhows, a fast new 12m RIB (rigid inflatable boat) that reaches Pemba in 90 mins, a raft of underwater toys from DPV motorised scooters to camera houses, and Nitrox tanks. The centre is a PADI Gold Palm 5-Star Instructor Development Centre and all boats carry oxygen, first aid and cell phones as standard. *US$35/90/150/225 for 1/3/6/10 dive packages (plus US$60/20 sgl/each multiple at Mnemba); US$60 PADI Discover Scuba Diving; US$300 PADI*

*Open Water certification course; US$600 PADI Dive Master; US$150 PADI Nitrox course. 10% discount for divers with own equipt.*

✈ **East Africa Diving & Watersport Centre** PO Box 2750, Nungwi, Zanzibar; ☎ 0777 416425/420588; e EADC@zitec.org; www.diving-zanzibar.com (⊕ EADIVE 5°43.602'S; 39°17.535'E). Owned and operated by an experienced, straight-talking German–South African couple, Michael and Delene Kutz, this is the oldest dive centre on north coast. On the beach in front of Jambo Brothers Guesthouse, this efficient PADI Resort Dive Centre offers courses to Dive Master and a host of scuba trips. Dive sites are reached by dhow (inc 2 engines for long trips) or zippy speedboat, and each boat has 2 experienced captains, with power of veto over any potentially unsafe dive. Safety appears to be taken seriously here, with all boats equipped with first aid and oxygen; dive leaders and every third diver carry inflatable marker buoys; with steel tanks Bauer serviced every quarter and air quality tested annually. Female divers also take note, the tanks here are all squat steel tanks, making them a much more comfortable shape on your back, and significantly easier to cart down the beach to the boat. A thankful Japanese diver created some stunning, accurate cartoon dive maps of the sites regularly visited by EADC, and these have been carefully laminated for dive briefings. Mnemba sites are visited every couple of days; Hunga is a frequent destination; Kichafi, Mbwangawa and Haji all feature on the east coast; Tumbatu is a weekly excursion and Big Wall at Mnemba is favoured over Leven Bank for safety and quality of marine life. *US$40/105/165/240 for 1/3/5/8 dive packages (plus US$25 to Mnemba Atoll). US$60 PADI Discover Scuba Diving instruction and 1 dive; US$350 PADI Open Water certification course inc 4 dives; US$270 PADI Advanced Open Water inc 5 dives.*

✈ **Divemaxx** PO Box 4200, Zanzibar; ☎/f 024 2240014/0741 324744; e info@sazanibeach.com; www.sazanibeach.com (⊕ SAZANI 5°43.775'S; 39°18.669'E). Based at Sazani Beach Hotel in Nungwi, Divemaxx does not currently have a resident dive instructor. The English lodge manager, Mike, is a dive master and will rent out equipt and escort group trips for experienced divers, but there are no scuba courses available here. *US$40/50 local dives/Leven Bank or Mnemba sites; Mnemba snorkelling trips US$35.*

**⚓ Ras Nungwi Beach Hotel Dive Centre** PO Box 1784, Zanzibar; ☎ 024 2233767/2232512; f 024 2233098; e watersports@rasnungwi.com; www.rasnungwi.com/diving/ (⊕ RASNUN 5°43.809'S; 39°18.691'E). A Gold Palm 5-Star PADI Instructor Development Centre, this centre offers all PADI qualifications to instructor level. It all appears to have the same high quality as the hotel in which it's based; equipt, service, safety and staff professionalism all seem top-notch here. For guests coming here to learn to dive, it's worth emailing in advance; there's a home-study option which allows all the Open Water course reading and paperwork to be done before you arrive. Beginners confined-water sessions are held in either the swimming pool or the adjacent lagoon in front of the hotel. A strict refresher policy means that all divers who have not donned scuba gear for 6 months must do a refresher course on arrival. New 3mm long and short Reef wetsuits, Aqualung masks and BCDs, Mares fins are neatly laid out pre-dive for individual collection. Watertight pelican boxes are available for cameras. Four permanent instructors, a local dive master and 8 local boat captains and snorkel crew keep everything shipshape on board the 4 large dhows. Two of these are capable of taking 10 divers on a 2-tank dive trip, whilst the other 2 sailing dhows are used for sunset cruises and snorkelling trips. Regular dive sites are predominantly on the west side of the island; though trips to Mnemba are also run regularly as clockwork. The 12 sites which they most frequently visit are chalked up on the centre's blackboard; they vary according to visibility and weather conditions. Trips to Leven Bank and Mnemba's Big Wall are strictly for Advanced Divers and above. Dive departure times vary by tide and sometimes depart from the village (*dala-dala* transfer) if the water in the lagoon is too shallow to allow their boat to pass through to the reef. *US$40/70/210/300 for 1/2/6/10 dive packages (Mnemba: US$30 suppt); US$30 Refresher course; US$475 PADI Open Water certification course; Snorkelling US$30–65.*

**Fishing** Nungwi's proximity to some of Africa's best deep-sea fishing grounds – Leven Bank and the deep Pemba Channel – offers serious anglers outstanding fishing opportunities (see *Natural environment* in *Chapter 3* for details on the fishing seasons). In addition to the weather-beaten local dhows which plough the coastal waters, two operators currently offer game fishing in fully kitted, custom boats.

**⚓ Ras Nungwi Fishing** PO Box 1784, Zanzibar; ☎ 024 2233767/2232512; f 024 2233098; e info@rasnungwi.com; www.rasnungwi.com (⊕ RASNUN 5°43.809'S; 39°18.691'E). One of the best game-fishing operations on Zanzibar is Ras Nungwi Fishing at the Ras Nungwi Beach Hotel. Using its own professional sport-fishing boat, *Countdown*, it runs a fully equipped deep-sea fishing operation in the rich waters between Zanzibar and Pemba. With a twin-screw shaft, and modern, purpose-built fittings, the boat is described as being equipped to the highest international safety standards. It has an experienced skipper and a raft of state-of-the-art technology, ⊕ navigational aids, colour echo-sounders and fish-finders. A full set of tackle is provided on board along with Shimano and Penn rod and reels, spooled with 30, 50 and 80lb mono lines, although clients can bring their own if preferred. Tag-and-release fishing is generally encouraged for all big fish unless it is the fisherman's first-ever catch, his biggest to date, or if it is likely to be an east African or All Africa record. *US$450 half day (6 hrs); US$650 full day (9 hrs); US$900 full night (Broadbill). Rates include charter of boat, skipper, bait, tackle equipt and lunch.*

**⚓ Fishing Zanzibar** e gerry@fishingzanzibar.com/ info@fishingzanzibar.com; www.fishingzanzibar.com. Operated by Gerry Hallam, *Unreel* is a 30-foot fly-bridge, sport-fishing boat based in Nungwi. Complete with a stand-up fishing chair, outriggers, downriggers, Shimano fishing gear (line classes 25–80lb) and a full selection of lures, it takes small charter groups (max 4 anglers) to Leven Bank and the Pemba Channel. Anglers are taken in search of black, blue and striped marlin, sailfish, yellowfin tuna, spearfish, dorado, trevally, king and queen mackerel, barracuda, and wahoo (travelling at 85km/hr, these are amongst the fastest fish in the sea). Night fishing for broadbills is an option. A catch-and-release approach is broadly encouraged, except when fish are injured or in the event of a possible record catch. *US$500 half day; US$800 full day, inc lunch.*

## Sailing

▲ **Dive 'n' Sail Zanzibar** ℡ 0777 420 770;
ℯ info@dive-n-sail.com/sales@gourmetzanzibar.com/
yachtjulia@hotmail.com; www.dive-n-sail.com. If
sailing appeals, Dive 'n' Sail operates a lovely 50ft
Admiral catamaran, *Julia*, specialising in live-aboard
dive trips to Pemba and Mafia. Available for charter
with its own professional skipper, chef, deckhand and
optional dive instructor, the boat is fully equipped
for diving and deep-sea fishing. On board are 4 en-
suite, dbl cabins, a large galley and saloon area
complete with stereo and DVD player, an outside
deck and sunbathing trampoline over the waves.
Complete with a Bauer 'Mariner' dive compressor for
refilling tanks, it has 8 full sets of dive equipt, inc
16 aluminium cylinders, BCDs, regulators, depth
gauges, weight-belts and weights. Certified divers
need carry little of their own equipt. With some
notice, PADI Advanced Open Water and speciality
courses can be taught on board. Dinner usually
comprises the daily catch so fishing is a frequent
activity. Day or overnight trips to the reefs around
Mnemba are possible, although the boat is more
likely to be used by serious divers for week long
ventures. *Private boat charter (1–5 guests)
US$1,320/day for min 4 days, exc dives; dives
US$42/dive for first 10 dives, then US$36. Mnemba
Island snorkelling day trip US$108pp (min 4 guests);
dive suppt US$66. Half-day fishing US$480
(07.00–12.00 or 13.00–17.00). All rates are subject
to periodic change!*

**Kite-surfing** In recent years, kiting has grown in general popularity and Nungwi is
no exception. Steady winds (approximately 15–20 knots) for most of the year, level
beaches, warm clear water and protected, shallow lagoons make it a great place for
both beginners and more experienced kite-surfers.

**Kite Zanzibar** c/o Ras Nungwi Beach Hotel, PO Box
1748, Zanzibar; ℡ 024 2240487/78 or 0777
415660; ℯ chris@kitezanzibar.com;
www.www.kitezanzibar.com/www.kitebeaches.com. Chris
Goodwin of Ras Nungwi Beach Hotel is a keen kite-
surfer and has a wealth of information on the local
conditions. He operates a dedicated website
(www.kitezanzibar.com) on the kite-surfing in this
area and can help secure accommodation and
storage facilities for equipt. The quiet, long, sandy
beach on the eastern side of Nungwi cape allows for
easy launching and landing, although, like all of
Zanzibar's east coast, the tidal change is significant
and this affects the exposed beach area. The fringe
reef here creates a calm and sheltered lagoon which
is ideal for kiting, and from May to Sep affords great
opportunities for wave-riding and surfing. There is no
seaweed farming here, and consequently no danger
from concealed underwater canes. The beach in front
of Sazani and Ras Nungwi Beach Hotel also benefits
from proximity to the staff and boats of the latter,
in the event of an emergency requiring recovery.

**Dhow-building and harbour activity** As well as being a tourist destination,
Nungwi is also the centre of Zanzibar's traditional dhow-building industry. A
number of hardwood trees, particularly good for boats, grow in this area (or at
least did grow here, until they were chopped down to make into boats).
Generations of skilled craftsmen have worked on the beach outside the village,
turning planks of wood into strong ocean-going vessels, using only the simplest
of tools.

It is a fascinating place to see dhows in various stages of construction, but do
show respect for the builders, who are generally indifferent towards visitors, and
keep out of the way. Most do not like having their photos taken (ask before you use
your camera), although a few have realised that being photogenic has a value, and
will reasonably ask for payment.

Fishing continues to employ many local men, and it's magical to watch the
local fishing boats bobbing in the sparkling waves of the morning, and then set
out to sea in the late afternoon. There can be as many as 40 going out at once, their
distinctive lateen sails silhouetted against the blush evening sky – it's probably
been unchanged for centuries. Early in the morning, around 06.00, they return
with their catch to the beach fish market. The spectacle is worth the early start,
but if you don't make it, there's a smaller re-run at around 15.00 each day.

Like the east coast, Nungwi's other key marine industry centres on its seaweed. Local women tend this newly introduced crop on the flat area between the beach and the low-tide mark. The seaweed is harvested, dried in the sun and sent to Zanzibar Town for export. (For more details, see *Sustainable seaweed farming* box, on page 225.)

## Turtle sanctuaries

**Mnarani Natural Aquarium** Hawksbill turtles have traditionally been hunted around Zanzibar for their attractive shells, and green turtles for their meat. In 1993, with encouragement and assistance from various conservation bodies and some dedicated marine biologists, the local community opened the Mnarani Natural Aquarium (*open 09.00–18.00 daily*).

In the shadow of the lighthouse ('Mnarani' meaning 'place of the lighthouse' in Swahili), at the northernmost tip of Zanzibar Island, the aquarium was created around a large, natural, tidal pool in the coral rock behind the beach. Originally set up to rehabilitate and study turtles that had been caught in fishing nets, the aquarium project expanded to ensure that local baby turtles were also protected.

Turtles frequently nest on Nungwi Beach, and village volunteers now mark and monitor new nests. The resulting hatchlings are carried to small plastic basins and small concrete tanks at the aquarium where they remain for ten months. By this time, they have grown to ten inches and their chances of survival at sea are dramatically increased. All bar one of these turtles are then released into the sea, along with the largest turtle from the aquarium pool. The one remaining baby turtle is then added to the pool ensuring a static population of 17 turtles.

In September 2005, this equated to four hawksbills (Swahili: *ng'amba*), identified by the jagged edge on their shell, sharper beak and sardine diet, and 13 seaweed-loving green turtles (Swahili: *kasakasa*). The aquarium manager, Mr Mataka Kasa, keeps a log book detailing all eggs, hatchlings and releases. On 5 June 2005, the sanctuary released its first tagged turtle, as part of a worldwide monitoring programme.

In spite of the aquarium being little more than a glorified rock pool, it's fascinating to see the turtles at close quarters. Further, the money raised secures the project's future, and goes towards local community schemes – in a bid to demonstrate the tangible value of turtle conservation to the local population. With luck, this will lessen the trade in souvenir shell products and ensure the species' survival.

On a practical note, when timing your visit, the water is clearest about two hours before high tide (Swahili: *maji kujaa*).

**Baraka's Turtle Aquarium** Owned by Mr Baraka, of Baraka's Bungalows on West Beach, this aquarium (⊕ AQUABA 5°43.443'S; 39°18.227'E; *rates: US$2 daily*) is signposted at a bend in the road, on the way to the East Beach area. It recently opened in direct competition with the long-established sanctuary scheme at neighbouring Mnarani Natural Aquarium. Although it has a lovely tidal pool, and the 15 resident green turtles appear to be well fed and healthy, this is fundamentally a business and not a conservation project. Given this, your support is probably better directed at the original rehabilitation and research scheme next door.

**Lighthouse** The lighthouse at Ras Nungwi is still in operation, although it is not open to visitors. As it is a designated strategic point, photographing the lighthouse is officially not allowed either, as the marines on guard may point out.

**Shopping** There are several small shops in Nungwi village (⊕ NUSHOP 5°43.673'S; 39°17.614'E), where you'll find an array of cheap souvenirs, such as carvings, paintings and jewellery, as well as essential items.

Head inland across the football pitch behind Cholo's, and you'll first come to a neat building on your right, one half of which is the well-equipped Nungwi School computer room where email and internet services are readily available, while the other half is Choices, a souvenir shop which also sells swimwear. A few steps further on, there is a small parade of shops. Here, the Pink Rose Salon advertises 'we prepare hair', Jambo Brother Shopping Centre offers a mixed bag of goods, an anonymous cosmetic shop does limited trade, and the Nungwi Supermarket is a veritable Aladdin's den of imported luxuries from toothpaste and toiletries to chocolate and Pringles.

Taking the road deeper into the village, there's another internet access point, the California Foto Store for film processing, the New Nungwi Salon where the brave can have a bikini wax, and the local-style Jambo Mixed Shop. Behind the last is the Ahsanna Dispensary for villagers.

South Beach has a smattering of small curio and snack shops, whilst beach traders parade the sand with boards covered in mirrored sunglasses, beaded jewellery and cold drinks. Amaan Bungalows Souvenir Emporium has a reasonable selection of knick-knacks whilst opposite Langi Langi, Mr Alibaba and his sons, Abdul and Suleiman, sell everything from *kangas* to cold drinks, postcards and tours. The post box outside their shop offers a twice-daily mail collection for those all-important postcards home.

**Henna tattoos and hair-braiding** Temporary henna tattoos are de rigueur in Nungwi. Painted onto your skin by friendly local ladies, as you lie under their makeshift palm shades on the beach, they seem to mark a rite of passage in the backpacker fraternity. As elsewhere on Zanzibar, the beach and bars are full of people with vaguely Arabic or Celtic-style rings round their biceps. Many clearly believe they look cool; but be warned, the henna can badly stain bed linen, which naturally annoys the hotel owners. For all-out African beach chic, hair-braiding services are also available by the same ladies, along with basic beach massages.

## KENDWA

On the west cost, about 4km south of Nungwi, is the tiny village and beautiful beach of Kendwa. What a relief after the noise and crowded development of Nungwi! It's a serene place (most of the time), with some well-spaced, simple places to stay, a clutch of beach bars, a dive school, and a glorious, wide, sandy beach, which doesn't suffer the vast tidal changes of the east coast.

Until the arrival of La Gemma dell'Est in late 2005, Kendwa catered almost exclusively for backpackers and those in search of simple, low-budget escapism. It remains a peaceful place to chill out and has a feeling of space not found in neighbouring Nungwi. It does liven up in the evening, with bonfires, barbecues and full-moon beach parties de rigueur, but apart from that it's an absolute haven of peace. Let's hope it stays this way.

**GETTING THERE AND AWAY** From Nungwi, you can simply walk along the beach at low tide. If you plan on doing this it's imperative that you are aware of tide times before setting off: with steep coral cliff bordering the beach, there is nowhere to escape the incoming tide. It is also worth noting that there have been a few incidents of robbery on the 1.5km stretch of beach between Baobab Beach Bungalows and La Gemma dell'Est.

A good option is to travel by boat from Nungwi. Several places in Kendwa run a free transfer service, or it's easy to find a local boatman who will take you for a few dollars, but do check their reliability with others first.

If you're driving, turn off the main road about 4km south of Nungwi (⊕ TUKEND 5°45.403'S; 39°18.065'E), and follow the very rough, undulating track for about another 2km. A high-clearance vehicle is essential.

**WHERE TO STAY** Looking at Kendwa's beach retreats from south to north (see *Nungwi & Kendwa* map, page 177):

**Malaika Bungalows** (5 rooms)
e khalfanpenot@hotmail.com. Although it officially opened in 2002, Malaika, meaning 'angel' in Swahili, has only recently been fully operational. Owned and managed by Mr Khalfani, who goes by the nickname 'Alfonso' and appears to be something of a wheeler-dealer on Kendwa Beach, there are currently 5 Spartan bungalows with plans to build 2 more and a restaurant on the beach in 2006. The rooms are basic but light and airy; concrete floors, 2-tone baby-pink painted walls with matching curtains and a dbl bed with mosquito net. All the rooms are en-suite with European flush toilets and cold water showers. There is no fan or AC, but the windows are only mesh and burglar bars so allow a cooling breeze into the rooms. Like many budget places, the electricity, we're informed, 'is coming' but this may still be the case for some considerable time. *UUS$15 pp, b&b.*

**Amaan Kendwa Beach Resort** (39 rooms) PO Box 4769, Kendwa, Zanzibar; ☎ 0777 492552/417127; e amaankendwa@hotmail.com (⊕ AMAANK 5°45.23'S; 39°17.436'E). Built on the site of the demolished Amaan Annex, this neat little resort has been fully operational since Aug 2005. The petite sibling of Amaan Bungalows in Nungwi, this place is run by the same management team, has the same whitewashed, castellated buildings and lies under the same fluttering, international flags, but it is an altogether quieter option. It's a reliable and consequently popular retreat, so it's worth booking in advance during peak season. Its 39 rooms run from the coral-rock cliff beside the beach, through sloping, densely planted gardens to reception and the bumpy track behind the village. Of the 3 categories, the furthest from the beach are the 11 garden rooms. A little Spartan inside with an uninspiring décor, these are clean and have sparkling white bathrooms, fans and mosquito nets. There are 21 seaview rooms set in 2 rows, those closest to the water commanding a worthwhile premium. These rooms are freshly painted in a suitably aquatic blue, with higher ceilings, tall glass windows — the burglar bars carefully missed off the seaward window so as not to spoil the view — and luxuries like mirrors and luggage racks. Set on the edge of a low

coral cliff, the cool verandas in front of these rooms overlook the local children's beach football pitch, and sea beyond.

The large beach restaurant and bar, the Titanic, serves food and drink all day, under a huge makuti shade with the sand still underfoot. Although Kendwa Beach is beautiful, the small section immediately north of Amaan is where the village fisherfolk pull ashore and 'park' their dugouts and nets, and can get a little messy. Email and internet facilities are available at reception (US$2/hr, min half-hr slots), along with currency exchange. *Garden view US$35/60/90 sgl/dbl/tpl; premium seaview US$40/75/110 sgl/dbl/tpl; front-line seaview US$50/90/120 sgl/dbl/tpl. All rates are b&b. Book directly with the hotel reception and receive a 10% discount. Payment must be in US$; no credit cards; 10% surcharge on travellers' cheques.*

**La Rosa Dei Venti** (8 rooms) PO Box 1543, Kendwa, Zanzibar; ☎ 0777 411314/414957; e info@rosazanzibar.com/ RosaZanzibar@hotmail.com; www.rosazanzibar.com (⊕ LAROSA 5°45.207'S; 39°17.429'E). In spite of opening only in 2003, La Rosa Dei Venti already feels tired and unkempt. Owned by an Italian, Franceso, and his Tanzanian wife, Esta, it all appears a little thrown together — the central areas are covered in salmon pink, yellow and orange paint; the rough-hewn coral-stone paths are dangerously uneven; the restaurant chairs sport particularly tasteless Mickey Mouse cushion covers; and rips in the window mesh are patched with plasters from the first-aid box. There are 2 bungalows and 6 rooms available. Each bungalow contains a dbl and a sgl bed, AC, fans, a small safe and a fridge. There are a couple of basic easy chairs, but no cushions; similarly, in the tiny kitchen area, there are cupboards with no internal shelves. The large shuttered patio doors open onto a wide terrace from where you can just see the sea through the feathery pines. Of the rooms, 5 are dbls and one's a tpl made up of sgl beds. All feel grubby thanks to chipped painted floors, dusty curtains and dim lighting, but they do offer mosquito nets, electricity, fans and en-suite bathrooms. The restaurant, though appearing bare, is actually able to offer most of the dishes on the menu: a novelty at many of the budget beach options. *US$75 in the bungalow based on dbl or tpl occupancy b&b. A room in the guesthouse is US$30/45 sgl/dbl.*

⌂ **Kendwa Rocks Resort** (20 rooms) PO Box 15, Mahonda, Zanzibar; ☎ 0777 415475/415527/415528; e kendwarocks@hotmail.com; www.kendwarocks.com (◈ KENROC 5°45.146'S; 39°17.403'E). The first property to open on this stretch of beach, Kendwa Rocks celebrated its 10th birthday in 2005. It's owned and run by Ally Kilupy, a worldly Zanzibari Rastafarian who grew up welcoming tourists at his mother's guesthouse in Stone Town before studying in Germany, taking a motorbike round Africa and living in south London. Returning to Zanzibar, Ally put his tourism skills to use and now runs a successful operation here. There are bungalows, *bandas* and a dormitory available, and they get booked up in that order. The coral-stone bungalows are all named after African countries with suitably themed interiors. They are all en-suite, though not all have hot water yet, with large Zanzibari beds and a veranda; each has mains electricity with UK 3-pin sockets, fans and mosquito nets. Most of these rooms can be used for dbl or tpl occupancy. The *bandas* are spread out in a semi-circle on a clean and lovely stretch of beach. They are simple makuti structures, with little more than a couple of traditional beds and a small table inside, but their location is excellent. The shared ablution block is set up on the coral rock and has 6 clean but bleak toilet/shower cubicles. They do have clever, energy-efficient electric heaters on the shower heads to ensure hot water though. There are also a couple of coconut-wood bungalows on the beach and these are probably the nicest option here. Above the bungalows and beach area, towards the road, is an 11-bed dormitory. It's usually taken by groups of off-duty VSO workers, or people waiting to upgrade to *bandas*. There are 2 rows of sgl, net-covered beds and a bank of lockers with a functional, if not pretty, shower and toilet block immediately behind. On the beach, the 2-storey Mermaid Bar is the epitome of backpacker drinking dens: a hip DJ messes on decks in the corner, smiling staff in blue branded tops stand behind a well-stocked, dhow bar festooned with laminated lists of cocktails, while batik-clad, sun-bleached blond girls recline writing diaries and drinking. That ubiquitous icon of a traveller's rebellion, Che Guevara, presides over events from a row of T-shirts pinned above the bar. This place is totally chilled, so don't expect anything to happen fast. Instead, pick one of the many green

and blue hammocks which radiate from the structure, lie back and enjoy the sea views. Also on the beach, there's a genuine Finnish steam bath, testament to Ally's time in Finland, and a huge dhow sheltering under makuti, which he's contemplating converting into floating accommodation. Every evening at 17.30, the US$15 Sunset Booze Cruise departs with a dhow full of tanned travellers and jugs of island punch, whilst at full moon there's a lively beach party here where revellers can enjoy bonfires, music, acrobatic shows, fire eating, a buffet and cocktails. The feel at The Rocks is accurately reflected by its promotional flyer: 'You've found paradise; now take time to enjoy it'. *From US$35/50/60 sgl/dbl/tpl b&b in a bungalow, whilst bandas are from US$12 pp. The dormitory is US$10 pp. All rates include b/fast.*

⌂ **Sunset Bungalows** (31 rooms) PO Box 3546, Kendwa, Zanzibar; ☎ 0777 414647/413 818; e sunsetbungalows@hotmail.com; www.sunsetbungalows.com. A faded upturned surfboard stuck into the beach marks Sunset Bungalows' location. The board is in fact the sign for a sizeable beachside structure known as the Bikini Bar, where the staff's T-shirts proclaim 'No bikini; No party'. Here, underneath the huge mukuti roof, circus-style swathes of blue and white fabric are draped. Outside, on wooden decking, large, white, Embassy-branded umbrellas shade diners indulging in US$6 lunches, featuring everything from fresh fish to egg and chips. On the adjacent stretch of beach, a bonfire pit is surrounded by wooden benches making it a popular after-dinner drinks spot, while the permanent volleyball net keeps the energetic entertained. Set back from the sea, on the beach behind the restaurant and bar, 2 widely separated rows of bungalows have been built perpendicular to the sea. These are extremely pleasant with solid furniture, bold-coloured fabrics (turquoise bed linen with white and cerise mosquito nets), white en-suite bathrooms, mains electricity, an electronic safe and AC. A shady terrace in front of each looks out onto white sand and feathery casuarinas. Higher up, on the coral cliff above the beach, 31 standard rooms are dotted around a pretty garden, overflowing with colourful hibiscus and bougainvillea. Suitable for dbl or tpl occupancy, these rooms are large with a bold Yin Yang symbol engraved in the concrete floor. Comfortable beds, white en-suite bathrooms, proper wardrobes, maroon-cushioned chairs, a coffee table and even a kitchen sink come as standard in these rooms. Open since 1999, Sunset remains a reliably good choice on this stretch of beach. *Standard room*

*US$40 dbl or tpl; beach bungalow US$60/65 dbl/tpl. Prices go up US$5 in high season.*

⌂ **White Sands Beach Hotel** (18 rooms) PO Box 732, Kendwa, Zanzibar; ☎ 0777 480987; e info@zanzibar-white-sands-hotel.com; www.zanzibar-white-sands-hotel.com (⊕ WHITES 5°45.054'S; 39°17.373'E). Laid-back Belgian, Jan, took over White Sands in 2002, and has spent the past few years renovating and rebuilding rooms and creating a fun, split-level bar and restaurant on the beach. The reception and all of the accommodation is perched on a coral cliff above the beach, and is surrounded by neatly planted gardens filled with aloes, papaya and bougainvillea. The cosy standard rooms have had little more than a lick of paint since Jan took over, but they are clean and functional. The bright red floor, neat bed, fabric-screened wardrobe, wall-mounted fan, cheerful paintings and Zanzibari concrete corner bench with cushions and table are all perfectly adequate. A little larger and with a beach-view terrace are the midclass rooms; whilst, significantly larger in size, the kingsize rooms have a large dbl bed, with plenty of room for another to be added, a bigger terrace and an en-suite bathroom. The red-painted concrete floors in these rooms are covered with dyed makuti mats, whilst the walls are awash with overwhelming African murals: the artwork of local talent, Moses. The mock rock art and swaying Masai dancers may be a little crude for some, and the African textiles are definitely hectic in design, but the rooms are certainly bright and individual. All have en-suite bathrooms, but the standard class does not yet have hot water. There are no safes in the rooms, but a deposit box is available at reception and accessible between 07.30 and 14.00. If you're accessing White Sands from the beach, look out for the old oil barrel suspended under a small makuti shade and the lodge's red and white, sun and sail logo. The drum is the restaurant's outside advertisement reading: 'Lobster tomorrow? Ask today! Kitchen open all day.' The large circular bar and restaurant is a fun hangout. Built on the beach with the sand still making the floor, it has swings to rival stools at the bar and a sunken central lounge filled with cushion-covered coir-rope sofas. A surrounding semicircular raised platform of tables for two creates a feeling of enclosure, and a couple of kingsize beds are laid out for those whose every effort has gone into dragging themselves away from their neighbouring lounger. *Standard US$30/40 low/high season; midclass US$45–55 low/high season; kingsize US$60/70 low/high season. All rates are based on*

*dbl occupancy; US$10 reduction for sgl. 10% discount on stays over 5 days during low season.*

⌂ **Les Toits de Palme** (10 rooms) PO Box 2728, Zanzibar; ☎ 0777 418548. Under joint French–Zanzibari ownership, Les Toits de Palme has 6 separate rooms in 3 bungalows raised above the beach on coral rock. All have dbl/twin beds and en-suite, cold water facilities. In addition, there are also 4 beach *bandas*, each of which has woven palm sides, a makuti roof and twin coir-rope beds. These are about as simple as you can get. That said, the sand is clean and soft underfoot, the bedding is fresh and the shared bathroom immediately behind has a European-style flush toilet and cold-water shower. There's generator electricity available from 18.00 to 24.00, when the atmospheric light of storm lanterns takes over. *US$15/20 sgl low/high season and US$20/35 dbl low/high season, b&b.*

⌂ **La Gemma Dell'Est** (138 rooms) ☎ 024 2240087; f 024 2240089; e info.gemma@planhotel.com; www.planhotel.com (⊕ LAGEMM 5°44.631'S; 39°17.369'E). La Gemma Dell'Est fully opened in Jul 2005 at the northern end of Kendwa Beach. It's about 800m north of White Sands Beach Hotel, and barely 1.5km south of Nungwi's Baobab Beach Bungalows. It's a large hotel, managed by the Swiss-based firm PlanHotel SA, and is certainly the most stylish of Zanzibar's large resorts. Sensitive architecture and stunning landscaping create a feeling of tremendous space, while minimal tidal changes allow for swimming in the sea all day. The hotel's 138 rooms have been cleverly built along the natural contours of the landscape, making them appear lower-density and fairly unobtrusive, while also allowing each one a seaview veranda. Inside, there are contemporary and comfortable, each having a kingsize bed or twin beds with mosquito net, a ceiling fan and AC, satellite TV, minibar, electronic safe, and an en-suite marble bathroom; everything you'd expect from a good, modern hotel. Thoughtfully planted screens offer privacy on each terrace and the emerald lawns and swathes of established exotic vegetation (all neatly labelled) make a beautiful foreground to the setting sun over the Indian Ocean. A walk around the sloping grounds to see the likes of lemongrass (*Cymbopogon citrates*) the size of pampas grass, the stunning russet flowers of the African tulip tree (*Spathodea campanulata*) or the crimson coral tree (*Erythrina variegate*) is highly recommended. The beach here is wide and beautiful, with nice loungers and makuti umbrellas dotted around the raked sand. The enormous, floodlit swimming pool is also set right on the beach, with a children's area, jacuzzi, waterfall, and swim-up cocktail bar. There is hotel security on the beach to ensure no hassle for sunbathers yet Kendwa's clutch of beach bungalows and their associated bars and restaurants are an easy 10-min walk south, past the proliferation of beach huts selling colourful local artwork. La Gemma has several bars and restaurants, from the sleek Pavilion serving tasty Mediterranean buffets to the Coral Cove alfresco pizzeria by the pool, and the intimate, à la carte seafood restaurant, Sea Breeze, at the end of the jetty. With the exception of the last, all food and drink is on a totally flexible, all-inclusive basis, and the Italian influence ensures that the food is invariably very good. By day, there's a PADI diving centre, outdoor gym, countless watersports, beach volleyball, sailing and even snorkelling over the artificial reef – created when the jetty was built – to keep everyone occupied, then the selection of optional evening entertainment kicks off with everything from quizzes to musical

Swahili beach BBQs. Children are well catered for at La Gemma, with cots, highchairs and babysitting all available. The staff's attitude is extremely positive towards families, and with a children's pool, easy access to food and drink all day, a good beach with easy swimming, and on-site doctor in case of accidents, La Gemma makes one of Zanzibar's best choices for families. *Deluxe US$168–324 pp dbl; villa US$192–348 pp, dbl; suite US$228–384; presidential villa US$2,622–5,760. When sharing with parents, children up to 6 stay free; age 7–12 50% discount on pp, dbl rate.*

⌂ **New PlanHotel Villas** On the plot of land bordering La Gemma dell'Est, immediately to the north, we understand that Swiss hotel company PlanHotel, are developing 25 plush private villas, complete with individual pools and chefs. No further information was available at the time of going to press but we understand that development will be relatively slow to avoid disturbing the guests at La Gemma.

**WHERE TO EAT** Virtually all the accommodations on Kendwa Beach have an affiliated beach bar and restaurant offering cold drinks, casual dining, and uninterrupted sea views. The menus and quality are close to identical, relying heavily on the day's catch for fresh seafood, with a number of Swahili curry and fresh pizza options. They are all open to anyone who cares to wander by and, as with many places on Zanzibar, this includes a number of friendly (and hungry) neighbourhood cats.

**WHAT TO DO AND SEE** Sunbathing, beach volleyball, diving and snorkelling are the main activities in Kendwa – it's a terribly laid-back beach hangout. The vast majority of the hotels and guesthouses will hire out basic snorkelling gear, organise day trips by boat to Tumbatu Island, and offer sunset dhow cruises; some will rent out kayaks too.

**Watersports** For fun below the water line, Kendwa's only dive operator is currently:

⚓ **Scuba Do Diving** PO Box 3546, Stone Town, Zanzibar; ☎ 0777 417157/0748 415179/UK +44 (0)1326 250773; e info@scubado.demon.co.uk/do-scuba@scuba-do-zanzibar.com; www.scubado.demon.co.uk/www.scuba-do-zanzibar.com (⊕ SCUBAD 5°45.071'S; 39°17.387'E). Owned and operated by a British couple, Christian and Tammy, Scuba Do appears to be a highly professional and well-equipped dive centre, based on the beach in front of Sunset Bungalows. The 4 permanent dive leaders take a max of 6 divers each to one of their repertoire of 15 reef sites, chosen according to conditions and diver experience. Diving is done from 2 high-powered RIBs (rigid inflatable boats), allowing

fast access to dive sites (Mnemba is reached in 30 mins, as opposed to nearly 2 hrs by dhow), and ⊕ navigation pinpoints precise dive entry points. There's plenty of good equipt – 'Buddy Explorer' BCDs, Mares regulators, masks and fins, and Reef wetsuits – and they have a code of stringent safety procedures. We were impressed to be told that all divers are issued with surface marker buoys and marine radios maintain contact between boats and base. Their on-site Bauer air compressor is regularly tested, and there's an emergency oxygen re-breather and a full medical kit. As part of this adherence to safety, Scuba Do will not take any divers below water without proof of their qualification. When out of the water, the team here are also involved in community work. Sep 2005 saw the first event of their annual Beach and Underwater Cleanup project. As part of the International Coastal Cleanup (ICC), the dive team galvanised 82 people (75% from the local community) into clearing Kendwa Beach: 108 bags of rubbish were collected. Plans are now under way to educate local school children about the effects of rubbish on the environment.

✂ **Scuba Shack** Scuba Shack's name is a little misleading as it no longer offers diving activities. It has changed ownership and is now part of the Kendwa Rocks empire, offering only basic snorkelling equipt and boat trips.

## MKOKOTONI

On the west coast of the island, about 21km south of Nungwi, Mkokotoni is a lively fishing village. Although there's no accommodation here that we could find, it's worth a short detour to soak up some rural atmosphere and vibrant village life. The bustling market, where Tumbatuans and local Zanzibaris buy and sell all manner of fresh seafood, is crowded, noisy and full of energy. Around this an abundance of tumbledown stalls display piles of coconuts, fruits, vegetables and spices whilst in the harbour behind, age-old techniques are used to repair and build the next generation of dhows.

In 1984, a major hoard of Chinese coins was discovered on the beach north of the village, indicating that this was once a prosperous trading port between the East, Arabia and Zanzibar, long before the arrival of the Europeans. Colonial rule brought the few grand administration buildings glimpsed along the central avenue of sweet almond trees, but today village life is still centred on simple trade with neighbours.

**GETTING THERE AND AWAY** Few tourists visit Mkokotoni (✪ *MKOK0T 5º52.517'S; 39º15.308'E*), and those who do are usually part of a tour en-route to Tumbatu Island. If you plan to drive here yourself or come by taxi, be aware that the road heading south of the village to Mahonda (✪ *MAHOND 5º59.388'S; 39º15.106'E*) was in a diabolical state of disrepair in late 2005. Access is far easier from the junction at Kivunge (✪ *KIVUNG 5º52.895'S; 39º16.973'E*), marked by a police post, on the island's main north–south artery.

## REGIONAL EXCURSIONS

About 12km south of Nungwi, on the main road to/from Zanzibar Town, are the ruins at Fukuchani and Mvuleni. These are the remains of large houses dating from the 16th century. They're worth a short stop if you're driving this way, and a possible excursion from Nungwi if lying on the beach gets all too much.

**FUKUCHANI RUINS** Fukuchani Ruins (✪ *TUFUKU 5º49.365'S; 39º17.479'E*) are on the edge of the village of the same name. Beside a large school on the western side of the road, there's a small signpost under a baobab tree which will point you in the right direction, along a track that bisects the local football pitch. The ruin is known locally as the 'Portuguese House', but although some Portuguese settlers may have built houses on Zanzibar during this period, this structure is considered by archaeologists to be of Swahili and not foreign origin. The ruins are well maintained and the surrounding land has been mostly cleared of vegetation.

Built in the 16th century, Fukuchani is a fortified dwelling that may have belonged to a wealthy merchant or farmer. It is constructed of coral bricks, with arched doorways and rectangular niches in the walls of the main room, and surrounded by a stone wall in which small holes have been inserted. It has been suggested that these are gun slits for the purposes of defence, but a more recent

Tumbatu is one of the largest of Zanzibar's offshore islands, measuring about 8km long by 2–3km across. The people of the island, the Watumbatu, speak their own dialect of Swahili. They have a reputation for pride and aloofness, and are reputed not to welcome visitors on their island. The Watumbatu men are traditionally known as the best sailors on Zanzibar, or even on the whole east African coast.

On the southern end of Tumbatu Island are a group of Shirazi ruins, thought to date from the 12th century. An Arab geographer writing in the 13th century recorded that the Muslim people of Zanzibar Island were attacked (by whom is not clear) and retreated to Tumbatu Island where they were welcomed by the local inhabitants, who were also Muslim, and it is assumed that these people were responsible for the Shirazi ruins.

The ruins were probably abandoned in the early 16th century, but the Watumbatu still claim to be descended from Shirazi immigrants.

theory suggests they may have been to hold projecting beams which supported a raised walkway, so that anyone inside the enclosure could see over the wall. The ruins are in good condition, compared with many others on Zanzibar of a similar age, and quite impressive. Buildings of a similar style have been found at other sites along the east African coast, though, alongside the ruins at Mvuleni, Fukuchani represents the finest domestic stone house architecture of this period.

Behind the ruin, a path leads to a small beach. Across the channel you can see Tumbatu Island, with the lighthouse at its northern tip clearly visible. At the southern end of the island are the remains of a large town, dating from around the 12th century (for more details see the *Tumbatu Island* box above).

**MVULENI RUINS** Mvuleni Ruins (✪ *TUMVUL 5°49.77'S; 39°17.496'E*) lie just to the south of Fukuchani, on the other side of the road (east), where you'll see a small signpost. Next to a few huts and a small shop, a path leads through banana and palm plantations to reach the site. Like Fukuchani, this structure was probably once a fortified house that would have belonged to a powerful member of the community. It, too, was thought to be the work of Portuguese invaders until recent research suggested that it is more likely to be Swahili in origin. The house was once larger than the one at Fukuchani, with thicker walls, but the ruins are in poor condition, and are partly overgrown with vegetation, obscuring some of the architectural features. Substantial sections of the walls remain standing, though, complete with carved door arches, conveying something of the impressive building that this once was. One of the most interesting features of this house is the large natural cavern just northeast of the house, outside the main wall. Crystal clear, salt water flows through the cave, collecting in a pool visible beyond an entrance fringed by vegetation: this was probably a source of water when the house was occupied.

Northern Zanzibar REGIONAL EXCURSIONS 8

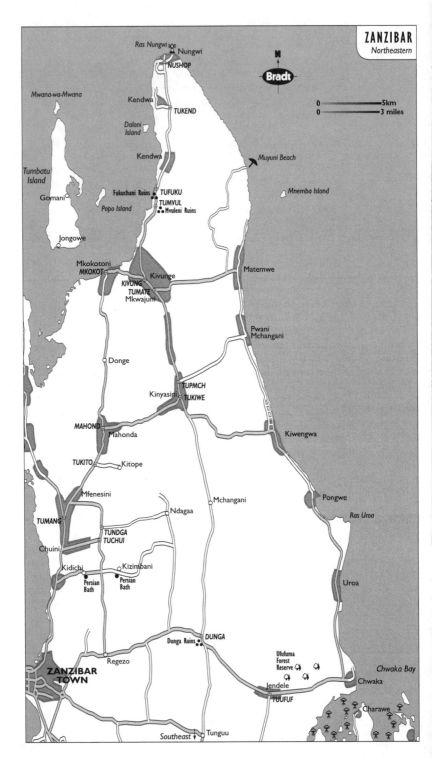

# 9

# Northeastern Zanzibar

The east coast of Zanzibar boasts the near continuous expanse of picture-perfect beaches which first attract most visitors to the island. Stretching from Nungwi on the northernmost tip of the island to the mangrove swamps of Chwaka Bay, the superb, powder-white sand beaches of the northeastern coastline are breathtaking in length and beauty. Less than a kilometre offshore, waves break along the fringe reef which runs the length of the island, and the warm, turquoise waters of the Indian Ocean attract divers, swimmers and fishermen alike. Bordering the sand, an almost unbroken strip of picturesque coconut palms provides shade for traditional fishing villages and sunbathing honeymooners, and completes many people's vision of paradise.

The beaches here slope very little, like those all along Zanzibar's east coast. Consequently, when the tide is out, the water retreats a long way, making swimming from the beach difficult. It does, however, allow for fascinating exploration along the top of the exposed reef. Seaweed can also negatively affect the powder-white beach expectations of uninformed visitors: between December and the rains in mid-February, it's common for many of the beaches to have a band of wind-washed brown seaweed. The rest of the year, the sand remains idyllic and clear.

Compared with those found in Nungwi to the north, the accommodation choices in the northeast tend to have more space, both in their private grounds and between properties. However, most are still within an easy walking distance along the seashore, and make useful refreshment stops on long beach walks. The central stretch of the coast, around Kiwengwa, is the busiest, with its cluster of large, Italian, package-holiday resorts, but there has been less tourism development to the north and south of this area, and it's still possible to find some lovely, individual places that seem to be virtually on their own.

Access from Zanzibar Town to the east coast is easy, on both private and public transport. However, there is currently little more than a narrow, bumpy track connecting the villages from Pongwe to Matemwe, necessitating very slow progress and either a 4x4 vehicle, or the hastening of the end for your vehicle's suspension!

## MATEMWE

A long, linear village, Matemwe is the most northerly of the east coast settlements. Although less than 20km south of Nungwi, it marks the end of the coastal road heading north. It's perhaps the classic Swahili fishing village, with little houses set among masses of elegant coconut palms. The sand is so white and smooth here that the wind blows it into mounds that look like snow drifts. A quieter section of coast, it has some good, small accommodation options and relatively close access to Mnemba's reefs for divers.

Matemwe is very much a working beach, especially close to the village centre, and this is part of its attraction for visitors looking for just a bit more than sea and sunshine. The main employment here is fishing, and the dhows and *ngalawa* (dugout canoes) go out most evenings, delivering their catch onto the beach each morning. There's also some seaweed farming here: look out for the makeshift racks of purple fronds drying in the sun. The local people are friendly and don't seem to mind tourists watching the scene, but this isn't a spot to be intrusive with in-your-face photography.

Sadly, like many villages on the island, Matemwe has a litter problem. In spite of Matemwe Bungalows arranging regular rubbish collections, blue plastic bags and general household garbage can be seen caught in bushes and strewn on the ground. With consistent assistance and education from local hotels, this will hopefully improve.

**GETTING THERE AND AWAY** If you are driving, there is a direct road to Matemwe from Mkwajuni (✪ MKWAJU 5°53.319'S; 39°17.293'E), on the island's central north–south road. Alternatively, turn east after Kinyasini (✪ KINYAS 5°58.088'S; 39°18.5'E) to Pwani Mchangani (✪ PWANIM 5°55.453'S; 39°21.466'E), and head north along the narrow, bumpy coastal track. A 4x4 vehicle is highly recommended for the latter route.

If you're staying at one of Matemwe's smarter accommodation options, transfers to/from Zanzibar Town can be arranged by them. Alternatively, a private taxi or minibus can be organised by a Zanzibar Town tour company or hotel.

By public transport, there's a daily *dala-dala* service (number 18) from Zanzibar Town to Matemwe village, which then continues up the coast to within about 2km of Matemwe Bungalows. The nearest regular bus service arrives and departs from Pwani Mchangani, 6km south, but there is no connecting transportation.

**WHERE TO STAY** Looking from north to south along the beach, your options for accommodation are:

**Zi Villa** (4 rooms) ☎ 0777 420710 or South African m 082 8233347;
e allan@starlight.co.za; www.zivilla.co.za (✪ ZIVILL 5°50.513'S; 39°21.458'E). Zi Villa is a private villa owned and let by a South African couple. North of Matemwe village, in a bay called Fisherman's Cove, the large, well-equipped, 4-bedroomed house is an excellent base for groups who are comfortable with being relatively remote and self-sufficient. Stylish, spacious interiors, packed with interesting objects d'art, a rogues' gallery of Zanzibari images, all mod-cons and a superb view out to Mnemba Island are all guaranteed. The eloquent Zanzibari manager, Seif, and the housekeeping team, inc a night watchman and resident chef, do their utmost to accommodate requests. There are 4 bedrooms, 3 dbls and a twin, 3 of which have direct access on to a large wrap-around outside deck and an en-suite bathroom. The fourth room has a separate, private bathroom. The upstairs master bedroom, or Sultan's Suite, has an enormous bed, large TV with video player, private sun deck and indoor jacuzzi. The 24hr mains electricity, hot water, AC and fans are standard throughout the house. The bright, light and airy lounge has 4 comfortable white sofas, a satellite TV and DVD player, a library of English books, and access to the pool deck through large glass French doors. Here, there's a deep swimming pool, with great sea views, and a sunbathing area of hammocks and loungers. The Fifo Bar, complete with fully stocked bar, pool table, music centre and dartboard, also accesses the deck and beach, and completes the package. *Exclusive use, all-inc, daily rental is US$536–714 for 4; US$670–878 for 6; US$804–1,041 for 8.*

**Matemwe Bungalows** (12 rooms) PO Box 3275, Zanzibar; ☎ 0777 475788/0774 414834; f 0777 429788; e info@asilialodges.com/ matemwebungalows@zanzinet.com; www.matemwe.com/www.asilialodges.com (✪ MATBUN 5°50.791'S; 39°21.434'E). Just past the northern edge of Matemwe village, occupying a windswept spot beside a sweeping sandy beach, Matemwe Bungalows is a very good, smart and informal place. Popular with well-travelled, unpretentious couples, it's relaxed and quiet. Being understated and calm, it's not really the place for families seeking action-packed adventures. Perched on the edge of a low coral cliff, lapped by the waves, each of the 12 thatched, whitewashed cottages has a superb view across the water to Mnemba Island. Following a 3-month closure in 2005, all the rooms have been upgraded into impressively stylish, split-level suites with private, curved verandas. Each is individual, though all are variations on a similar design, intent on providing a spacious, comfortable interior and maximising the sea view. Coconut-wood dbl beds are covered in bright appliqué throws; polished concrete floors are strewn with cheerful woven mats; and wooden lattice shutters conceal built-in wardrobe space. In the 6 new suites, the spacious en-suite bathrooms have a European toilet, twin sinks, a shower and large, decadent bath, whilst those in the older style have sgl sinks and only a large shower. Glass bottles filled with bathing condiments and tall candles are all welcome finishing touches. Constant mains electricity, 3-pin UK-style sockets, a solar-powered hot-water system, retractable mosquito nets, freestanding fan (available upon request), large Zanzibari safe box and a relaxing day bed (sgl in the older rooms; queensize in the new) are standard throughout the accommodation. For relaxing, the new rooms feature a sunken, cushioned *baraza* which looks through wide corner shutters to the terrace and sea beyond. On the terrace, a dbl hammock and turquoise director's chairs make the perfect seaside retreat. The older-style rooms have a small lounge area inside, while the veranda tempts with a dbl sofa as well as a dbl hammock. Below and behind the suites, a blush-coloured stone path meanders through lush tropical gardens to the pools, the main dining area and onwards to the sandy beach. Significant garden developments, planting and tending frangipani, bougainvillea, sweet almonds and carpets of flowering ground cover, make this a really lovely lodge to wander around. The beach ends where Matemwe Bungalows begin, resulting in virtually no passing foot traffic from the village and very little hassle. Some locals have set up curio stalls along the beach, but few approach guests and it's relatively low-key compared with other stretches of this coast. There are 2 new swimming pools, one infinity pool atop the coral cliff with a clear view across to Mnemba, and another below it, connected by a gently tumbling waterfall, offering protection when the coastal wind blows. The adjacent bar is a beautifully polished old dhow, set on powdery beach

sand and flanked by an impressively enormous sperm whale skeleton. Tasty buffets and plated dinners are served by friendly, uniformed staff in an open-sided dining room overlooking the end of the beach and sea. All guests stay on a FB basis and, space permitting, visitors will be welcomed for dinner with 24 hrs notice. Two day-rooms, complete with shower area, have also been added for people leaving late in the afternoon who have enjoyed their final hours on the beach or sunbathing by the pool. Two dhows are based at the lodge for snorkelling and sailing excursions, escorted reef walks can be arranged at low tide (local villagers, who already work as the lodge's boatmen, are being trained to guide these), and a large wooden chess set (complete with prawns as pawns!) is set up en route to the beach. Fishing and diving trips are now arranged through Urchin Watersports at Zanzibar Beach Hotel & Resort or Ras Nungwi, further up the coast. For the more sedentary, there's in-room massage, a library, or Scrabble, Boggle, Yatzy and a host of other games. There is complimentary internet access with the facility to download digital pictures from cameras and burn them to CD or DVD: this is especially useful for post-safari guests arriving with full memory cards. With close proximity to the local community and a desire to contribute to development, the company and guests have given time and money to supply the local villagers with fresh water and to build a school; now plans are afoot to try to arrange a much-needed rubbish collection for the village and to teach English. *US$260/315 sgl, low/high season; US$210/240pp dbl, low/high season. Children under 3 free; 3–12 50% discount sharing with parents. All rates are FB. Local and international currencies accepted and credit cards are not subject to any surcharge. Open Jun–Mar.*

⌂ **Mohamed's Restaurant and Bungalows** (4 rooms) ☎ 0777 431881 (⊕ MOHAME 5°51.451'S; 39°21.305'E). Follow the clear sign from the main road and you'll find these 4 small whitewashed cottages: they're hidden behind a high wall in the heart of Matemwe village. Owned and managed by Mohamed, ably assisted by his sparky girlfriend Juliana, this compact little complex offers 2 twin and 2 tpl rooms, each with mosquito nets and an en-suite bathroom with a cold water shower and flush toilet. The rooms here are basic but fairly clean and although the beds don't always have linen, this can usually be arranged. There are sandy paths and some plants leading down to an open-sided restaurant where simple meals can be organised with

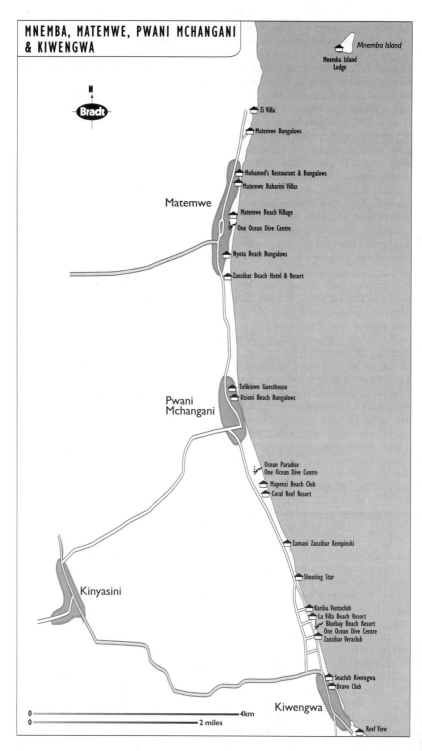

# MNEMBA, MATEMWE, PWANI MCHANGANI & KIWENGWA

Mnemba Island

Mnemba Island Lodge

Zi Villa

Matemwe Bungalows

Matemwe

Mohamed's Restaurant & Bungalows

Matemwe Baharini Villas

Matemwe Beach Village

One Ocean Dive Centre

Nyota Beach Bungalows

Zanzibar Beach Hotel & Resort

Pwani Mchangani

Tufikinwe Guesthouse

Uzioni Beach Bungalows

Ocean Paradise

One Ocean Dive Centre

Mapenzi Beach Club

Coral Reef Resort

Zamani Zanzibar Kempinski

Kinyasini

Shooting Star

Karibu Ventaclub

La Villa Beach Resort

Bluebay Beach Resort

One Ocean Dive Centre

Zanzibar Veraclub

Seaclub Kiwengwa

Bravo Club

Kiwengwa

0       4km

0       2 miles

Reef View

a little notice. The beachfront location and budget price make this a great backpacker option. *US$10 pp, b&b*.

⌂ **Matemwe Baharini Villas** (12 rooms) ☎ 0777 417768/0777 429642; f 255 2250092; e info@matemwevillas.com/ kibwenibeachvilla@zitec.org; www.matemwevillas.com (✣ MATBAH 5°51.501'S; 39°21.261'E). This place was opened in 2001, but its outside now feels distinctly rundown and tatty. The coral-stone paths are in need of repair, the gardens parched and the 2 villa buildings soulless and littered with burglar bars. At the time of visiting, the 2-bedroom villa had been newly decorated and was bright and airy, though the peeling lino flooring was already a trip hazard. Located on the ground floor of the building, it has 2 en-suite dbl bedrooms, which could be made into tpls for families or groups, and an open-plan, self-catering kitchen and lounge area. Generator electricity (18.00–22.00), hot water, fans, mosquito nets and deckchairs on the terrace all come as standard. Although we were assured it is for rent, the second villa has not been redecorated and in late 2005 appeared to be being used by staff. If you do want to stay in this building, there are 4 en-suite dbl rooms spread over 2 floors, with a small TV room but no kitchen. In addition to the villas, there are 8 rooms in traditional bungalows, one of which has an interconnecting door for family use. Set back from the beach behind a garden and low wall, each room has a Zanzibari dbl bed with mosquito net, fan, emergency light, radio/clock and an en-suite shower and toilet. There are ocean views and the rooms are cooled by the sea breeze through gauze windows. Facilities and activities here are quite limited, but there is a beachfront restaurant, drooping volleyball net, Swahili massage, and local fishing excursions on request. The very limited extent of the snorkelling equipt – 3 fins and a couple of masks – makes plans to create a dive centre questionable at best. For self-drivers, there is the advantage of secure parking behind the metal gate. *Bungalows US$40/70/90 sgl/dbl/tpl, b&b. Villas US$30/50/70 sgl/dbl/tpl, b&b*.

⌂ **Union Trust Resorts** At the end of 2005, a smart stone wall was erected to mark a beachside plot between Matemwe Beach Village and Matemwe Baharini Vilas. It has a sign reading only 'Union Trust Resorts' and as yet no apparent sign of development. This may be worth checking out in the future.

⌂ **Matemwe Beach Village** (22 rooms) PO Box 3481, Zanzibar; ☎ 024 2238374/0777 417250; e matemwebeachvillage@zitec.org; web: www.matemwebeach.com (✣ MATVIL 5°52.113'S; 39°21.2'E). Operating a strict 'no shoes; no news' policy, Matemwe Beach Village is a place to relax on the beach, read a book and indulge in the occasional dive or massage (US$15/hr). TVs and organised team games are not what this place is about: instead it is a simple, unassuming beach resort. The 16 compact standard rooms are in simple cottages a mere hop, skip and a jump from the beach. All are functional rather than particularly stylish or luxurious. With a mixture of kingsize, sgl and twin bed combinations, all have mains electricity, fans, mosquito nets, candles and handy torches. The en-suite bathrooms are moulded red concrete with hot-water showers, a toilet and sink. Outside, rattan chairs sit on a small terrace and the sound of the sea beckons. Forming a neat cul de sac of dbl-storey, whitewashed rondavels with steep pitched thatch are the 5 new shamba suites. Crossing the threshold, note the Swahili quotation inscribed above the door, 'Penzi la maana ni kuridhiana' (The real love is to love each other), and enter the highly stylised interior of designer Ivan Sutila. Matching hats, *kangas* and beach bags greet every guest at the door. The spacious central lounge area has built-in seating filled with blue and lilac cushions, and the bedroom is airy with a large dbl bed and pastel lilac linen. The en-suite shower is a stand-alone circular feature, whilst the very separate toilet is dressed to look like a throne with swathes of blue and purple circus-style fabrics streaming up towards the roof. On the galleried upper level, these suites have large navy mattresses covered in cushions, and a suspended dbl bed. Fun as these rooms are, their real disadvantage is that they are set at the back of the complex and, even from the upper level, their views are limited. Mains electricity, 3-pin UK-style sockets, a fan, minibar and tea/coffee-making facilities are standard throughout. The one-off asali suite is most frequently used by honeymooning couples keen to take advantage of its private plunge pool and dedicated chef. The resort's raised lounge area, overlooking the beach, encourages lazy afternoons and evenings, with metres of navy mattresses covered in assorted white and turquoise cushions, low wooden tables and a welcome sea breeze. The area is thatched but the walls are made of billowing cream canvas, with ribbons of aqua and royal-blue fabric hung between the ceiling supports to create a cool, intimate den. The adjoining restaurant offers a set menu at individual tables set with neat batik tablecloths. The on-site One Ocean PADI dive centre operates daily diving and snorkelling trips to Mnemba. Dive trips depart from Muyuni Beach, a 30-minute *dala-dala* trip away, except at the bi-monthly high tide. Bundles of dives can purchased at a discounted rate and PADI courses are taught (see *What to do and see* for more details). *Standard room US$50/70 sgl, b&b; US$80/120 dbl, b&b; shamba suite US$200, b&b; asali suite US$250/270 dbl, HB. Children under 2 stay free; age 2–12 years 50% discount. International and local currencies accepted; VISA and MasterCard 10% surcharge. Open Jun to Mar.*

🏠 **Nyota Beach Bungalows** (5 rooms) PO Box 93, Mahonda, Zanzibar; ☎ 0777 484303/0777 439059; e nyota@zanzinet.com; www.nyotabeachbungalows.com (✪ NYOTAB 5°52.985'S; 39°21.177'E). Opened in Dec 2004 by Italian Patrizia and Edi from Pemba, Nyota's 5 simple, stylish rooms are already receiving praise from guests. Set on a lovely stretch of beach, in the centre of Matemwe village, great care has been taken in decorating these 2-storey, stone-and-thatch cottages with bright fabrics, nice furniture and natural ornaments. There are 2 dbls, a twin, a family room and a tpl available, with plans to expand slowly. Each room has a fan, mosquito net, mains electricity, and an en-suite bathroom with constant hot water for showers and a flush toilet. There's a small but very relaxed dbl-storey lounge and bar area overlooking the ocean, which is used by residents and guests alike. Patrizia's background in Italian restaurants ensures

that the food is pretty good. Alternatively, the cushioned benches outside each room make a comfortable spot to chill, overlooking the banana and papaya trees in the garden. Diving and snorkelling trips can be arranged through one of the larger resorts nearby, and a central phone and email access readily available. *Sgl US$30; dbl US$60/50 upstairs/downstairs; tpl US$75. All rates are b&b. Accommodation must be paid for in US$; incidentals can be covered with TSh. Open Jul–May.*

🏠 **Zanzibar Beach Hotel and Resort** PO Box 4058, Kempton Park 1620, South Africa; ☎ 0777 417782–4; f 0777 417785; e enquiries@zanzibarbeachresort.com; www.zanzibarbeachresort.com (✪ ZANBEA 5°53.595'S; 39°21.168'E). As part of the Protea group, Zanzibar Beach Hotel & Resort was a stronghold for South African families, but it has recently been sold to a Kuwait-based company, IFA Hotels & Resorts, known for its considerable investment in Dubai's booming hotel scene. In late 2005, this resort closed for renovation, redevelopment and expansion. It is scheduled to re-open in Jul 2006, when it will be operated by the Swiss premium hotel chain, Mövenpick Hotels & Resorts. At the time of writing no details of the new property were confirmed, though there was talk of ambitious plans to upgrade the entire property, increase the number of rooms from 66 to 200, open the first east African decompression chamber outside Mombasa, and in the long term, build a golf course.

## WHAT TO DO AND SEE

Apart from lazing on the beach, or going for long walks along it, there are the usual diving and snorkelling possibilities which can be arranged through One Ocean:

✔ **One Ocean – Matemwe Beach Village** (✪ MATVIL 5°52.113'S; 39°21.2'E). Spanish instructor Xavier manages the One Ocean dive centre at Matemwe Beach Village. It's a 5-star PADI dive school offering a range of certification courses, Mnemba dive trips and snorkelling excursions. The staff are happy to accept referral certificates from guests who've completed dive-course classroom work before arriving in Zanzibar. Using a purpose-built dhow, MV *Henya*, dive

trips depart from Muyuni Beach (a 30-min *dala-dala* ride) at 08.00 each morning. Only twice a month do high tides allow for departures from the resort's own beach. 12 divers are accompanied by 2 guides, and it is not necessary to stay at the resort to use the dive centre. *US$65/95/180/255/390 for 1/2/4/6/10 dive packages; PADI Open Water US$450; Dive Master US$750. Snorkelling trips US$35. Prices include all equipt.*

## MNEMBA ISLAND

Lying approximately 2.5km off the northeast coast of Zanzibar, Mnemba Island is a picture-perfect, coral atoll. Previously uninhabited, it is now privately owned and one of Africa's ultimate beach retreats.

At its centre is a tropical forest, home to nothing more dangerous than cute suni antelope, a population of cooing white doves, butterflies and an ancient well. The island's circular perimeter is a kilometre and a half of soft, brilliant white, coral sand: perfect for romantic evening strolls, migrating wading birds, scuttling ghost crabs and nesting turtles. In the turquoise sea around, some of east Africa's best coral reefs hide in an unspoilt aquatic wonderland. There are virtually no insects on the island, making it a very low-risk malarial area.

Officially titled Mnemba Island Marine Conservation Area (MIMCA), the island is part of a coral formation supporting a staggering number and variety of marine life. Over-fishing and general disregard for the fragility of the environment began to threaten the marine environment, but sustained lobbying by Conservation Corporation Africa (CC Africa) and the government resulted in the area being declared a Marine Conservation Area in November 2002 and its future being secured.

A US$3 levy is now charged on all watersports, notably snorkelling and diving, within the protected zone. This revenue is paid into a community conservation fund, the primary purpose of which is to show local fishermen and their communities the very real economic value in protecting rather than exploiting these exceptional reefs. In addition to the money generated from MIMCA park levies, the Africa Foundation (the non-profit development organisation working in the areas around CC Africa's conservation areas) contributed US$46,000 to community projects close to Mnemba between 1999 and 2005.

**GETTING THERE AND AWAY** Guests for Mnemba Island (✪ *MNEMBA 5º49.2'S; 39º22.978'E*) are driven in air-conditioned minibuses to Muyuni Beach, north of Matemwe, along a bumpy road. From here, it's a pleasant, 20-minute motorboat trip to the island. It is not possible to visit the island unless you have a booking.

## WHERE TO STAY

🏠 **Mnemba Island Lodge** (10 *bandas*) ✆ +27 (11) 809 4300; f +27 (11) 809 4400; e information@ccafrica.com; www.ccafrica.com (✪ MNEMBA 5º49.2'S; 39º22.978'E). The crème de la crème of CC Africa's impressive portfolio, Mnemba Island Lodge is the height of rustic exclusivity: a place where the term 'barefoot luxury' is reality. Overlooking the beach from the forest's edge, its 10 secluded, split-level *bandas* are constructed entirely of local timber and hand-woven palm fronds, beautifully finished in a herringbone pattern. These are large, airy and open-plan, and the favoured retreat of both the rich and the famous, together with a few harmless hermit crabs who periodically scuttle across the immaculate *mkeka*-mat floors. Furnished simply but tastefully, each *banda* has a huge bed and solid wooden furniture, softened with natural, ivory-coloured fabrics and plenty of forest-view windows. As a place to escape the trappings of the modern world, in-room facilities only stretch to electricity, a simple fan to enhance the sea breeze, a padlocked wooden box for valuables, a couple of cotton bathrobes and a torch to ease evening ventures to the beach or bar. A palm-covered corridor leads to a stylish timber-and-glass en-suite bathroom. The purpose of showers may be to moderate the island's fresh-water consumption, but behind the stylishly curved glass-bead curtain the shower rose remains the size of the dinner plate, the pressure is high, and the desire to linger lathered becomes overwhelming. The spacious, beach-facing thatched terrace, with its built-in, cushioned *barazas*, director's chairs and table for lazy b/fasts, leads into a small forest clearing. Here, a day-bed swings in dappled light, suspended between weeping casuarinas, overlooking the beach yet hidden from view. The uncluttered, indulgent luxury, peaceful isolation and stunning situation make this a blissfully romantic haven: a place to curl up and count blessings. Mnemba's cuisine is predictably excellent, with plenty of fresh seafood, fruit and vegetables, and the flexibility to cater for individual needs exceedingly well. Guests can choose what, when and where to eat at any meal, from leisurely b/fasts in bed to candlelit, lobster dinners on the beach. An engaging 'butler' is assigned to each room, and from arrival will subtly go about tailoring each guest's stay, predicting requirements, to ensure everyone is content and carefree. A Belgian couple, Jan and Leen, run a first-class, professional dive centre on the island and, for qualified PADI divers, up to 2 dives per day are included in the rates. PADI courses are naturally available and one-on-one tuition may be expensive but the quality instruction and warm, shallow waters in front of the lodge make for excellent training. Once divers are qualified, a number of superb dive sites are within 15 minutes of the lodge, from gentle coral gardens dancing with colourful reef fish and gentle turtles to steep drop-offs: the haunt of huge, deep-water game fish. Over a delicious hot chocolate on the boat back to camp, sightings of dolphin pods are not uncommon, and even humpbacks can be spotted in season. For the non-diver, there's snorkelling, sgl and dbl kayaks, windsurfing, power kiting, sailing, and fly or deep-sea fishing. Hot stone, aromatherapy, deep tissue massage and reiki are all available, too. In line with its environmentally aware beginnings, the lodge strives to be eco-friendly. Water is desalinated, the beaches are rid of any manmade debris, organic waste is recycled and the rest is shipped off the island. Solar power is

used wherever possible, inc to heat the water, and guests are encouraged to do their bit through the eco guide left in each room. The lodge is also involved in marine and turtle conservation projects: watch out for the beach signs heralding new hatchlings. Although children are accepted at the lodge, it's probably not the best place for them. Only 2 children are allowed in the camp at any time, they aren't allowed in the bar after 18.00 and every child over 5 must have his/her own room, making it an extremely costly holiday for a 6 year old, who probably doesn't want their own room anyway! Mnemba is unquestionably expensive, but its flexibility and service levels are second to none, and its idyllic location and proximity to outstanding marine experiences are very hard to match. *US$585–880 pp, FB, low/high season. Payment in local or major foreign currencies; no suppt for credit cards, inc AmEx. Open Jun to Mar.*

## PWANI MCHANGANI

Pwani means beach in Swahili and this is certainly the focus of village life. This area is particularly noted for its seaweed collection and the dramatic low tides see women and children take to the beach to harvest and dry their marine quarry. The men, like most on Zanzibar's coast, concentrate on fishing, and the village boasts one of the island's main seafood markets.

Mass-market tourism is less developed than on the coastline around Kiwengwa (9km south), and Pwani Mchangani retains a more traditional air as a result. It's a sizeable village in the seaside coconut belt, where children and poultry run riot, colourful washing is strung between thatched houses, and conservative attitudes dominate.

**GETTING THERE AND AWAY** From Zanzibar Town to Pwani Mchangani (✛ PWANIM 5°55.453'S; 39°21.466'E) on public transport, take the number 18 *dala-dala* towards Matemwe, or the number 17 local bus to Kiwengwa. Those with a hire car approaching from the north coast or west coast should take the right turn about 1km north of Kinyasini (✛ KINYAS 5°58.088'S; 39°18.5'E) at Kikobweni, straight into the village. The coastal track north and south is passable, but is often narrow and uneven: 4x4 recommended.

### WHERE TO STAY

**🏠 Uzioni Beach Bungalows** (10 rooms) PO Box 1496, Zanzibar; 🕾 0777 417701/416269; ⓔ uzionipm@hotmail.com (✛ UZIONI 5°54.747'S; 39°21.29'E). Behind a wire gate, Uzioni's 5 cottages house 8 twin and 2 dbl rooms. Owned by Hon Mussa Silima, head of the Ministry of Industry, Trade, Marketing and Tourism, this is a pleasant, if slightly deserted, place used mainly by self-drive visitors. Entered through wide, divided doorways, each room has a fan, standard mosquito net, 3-pin UK-style sockets, and an en-suite bathroom with flush toilet

and hot-water shower. The whole complex has mains electricity and a back-up generator. There is a basic restaurant and, with enough notice, dinner can be arranged. *US$30/50 room low/high season. Payment in local currency or US$.*

**🏠 Tufikiniwe Guesthouse** (✛ TUFIKI 5°54.708'S; 39°21.281'E). Right in the centre of Pwani Mchangani village, this is an exceedingly basic local guesthouse. It was being rented to some young, local men during our last visit, and was not taking visitors. It is still owned and run by the local women's co-operative though; so if you are keen to stay here, ask around the village for the group's representative and enquire about the current situation.

⌂ **Ocean Paradise Resort** (92 rooms) PO Box 106, Kijangwani, Zanzibar; ✆ 0777 439990–3; f 0777 419991; e info@oceanparadisezanzibar.com; www.oceanparadisezanzibar.com (⊕ OCEANP 5°56.231'S; 39°21.635'E). Ocean Paradise is a big hit with UK honeymooners enticed to the resort by the bottle of bubbly, fruit basket and private beach dinner offered to newly weds. The imposing reception is a huge semi-circular area, with a high, vaulted makuti roof. From here, sweeping stairs curve round what should be an impressive waterfall, into manicured gardens, the beautiful central pool area, and beach-level accommodation. There are 92 rooms – 84 superior and 8 junior suites – all in neat, whitewashed rondavels. The rooms are stylishly understated and all have mains electricity, 3-pin UK-style sockets, AC, satellite TV, a hairdryer and a minibar. Each has an en-suite bathroom with a toilet and black shower, and an outside seated terrace area accessed through French doors. The 8 junior suite rooms are exactly the same in design as the superior, but with 2 separate rooms are twice the size. Half of these have a kingsize bed and sitting room, whilst the others have I kingsize and a twin room, which can be used by families. Transfers around the complex by golf cart can be arranged for disabled guests. If splashing in the tiled, seaside pool or reclining on the beach isn't stimulating enough, there's a daily schedule of hosted activities announced on a chalkboard by the pool: typically inc coconut weaving, Swahili lessons and beach soccer. Alternatively, there's a One Ocean dive centre for scuba and snorkelling, canoeing, windsurfing, snorkelling, fishing, volleyball, table tennis, billiards and a small fitness centre. Beach bikes can be rented (US$7.50) for outside exploration. For families, there's a children's pool and 'animators' to engage children in Butlins-style activities; cots are available and babysitting services are provided at a standard US$5/hr. Every night musicians perform from the bridge over the swimming pool, treating guests to traditional Swahili Ngoma drumming or Maasai acrobatics by the Taarabu Culture group. Evening meals at the Jahazi Restaurant overlook the performers and are usually themed, with any week incorporating 'surf n turf', Far-Eastern and BBQ dinners. Non-residents are also welcome to eat here. When the cabaret entertainment is over, the Jungle Disco and bar can

get lively. *Superior US$264 dbl, HB; junior suite US$350 ste, HB. Payment by local and major international currencies; VISA, MasterCard and AmEx subject to surcharge.*

⌂ **Mapenzi Beach Club** (87 rooms) PO Box 100, Mahonda, Zanzibar; ✆ 0741 325985; f 0741 333739; e gen@mapenziplanhotel.com/ planhotel@planhotel.ch; www.planhotel.com (⊕ MAPENZ 5°56.471'S; 39°21.741'E). Owned and managed by Swiss–Italian hoteliers, PlanHotel (who are also behind the new La Gemma, in Kendwa), Mapenzi is a large, comfortable resort, on a nice stretch of coast, with many facilities and activities. In spite of its size, this is a relatively serene place, catering mainly for large groups of Italian package holidaymakers. Increasingly though, British and South African families are staying here, enticed by the positive attitude towards children: easy availability of cots, highchairs and babysitting, and the Kids' Club during school holidays. The quiet reception area is shaded by an impressive makuti thatch supported by a tremendous network of poles. From here, wide corridor fingers lead to a pool table and mezzanine-level day-bed, a curio shop and stylish boutique selling pretty beaded sandals, swimwear and cotton clothing, a 'business centre' offering internet and fax services, and the pool. Raised above the beach, the long swimming pool, with children's area and jacuzzi, is surrounded with loungers and sun umbrellas, and affords views across the entire complex. The other outside public areas are dotted with palms and largely covered in white beach sand, the glare from which is quite bright – a touch more greenery would make the place feel cooler and be gentler on the eye. There are 87 cottages divided into 3 categories, fundamentally differentiated by location. Naturally those closest to the sea fetch the premium rate. All the rooms offer 24hr mains electricity, sockets (for plugs with 3 round pins), AC, fans, mosquito nets, an internal telephone, hairdryer, safe deposit (US$50 deposit for key), tea/coffee-making facilities, en-suite bathroom with European toilet, bidet and shower, and a veranda. In true European resort style, 'animators' do encourage active participation in games and activities, but at least there is a Swahili influence evident in their offerings. Tinga-tinga painting, village excursions and ngoma drumming lessons are just as likely to feature alongside archery and boules. There's a daily fitness programme of aqua aerobics and jogging, and catamarans, bicycles, windsurfs and snorkelling equipt can be hired. Football and volleyball matches benefit from properly marked pitches, and, for water-babes, diving is organised through One Ocean at Ocean Paradise. By night, entertainment ranges from live bands to acrobatic shows and quizzes. Mapenzi is all-inclusive and mealtimes and cuisine are set, though a seafood à la carte menu is also available. All meals are served in the spacious restaurant, though Sat night sees the weekly Swahili BBQ down on the sand of the volleyball court. There are 3 bars, inc one in the central area which opens at 22.00 for late-night revelling. Drinks are included in the room rates but long drinks are free only from 18.00 to midnight; it's a cash bar thereafter. *Garden room US$118–245 pp, dbl; standard room US$134–265 pp, dbl; seafront room US$151–290 pp, dbl. Children up to 6 years stay free; 7–16 years 50% discount. All rates are all-inclusive. Payment by local or major international currency; VISA and MasterCard accepted with no surcharge.*

⌂ **Coral Reef Resort** (43 rooms) PO Box 65, Mahonda, Zanzibar; ☏ 0777 415549/415254; e coralreef@zanzinet.com; www.zanzibar-coralreef.com (⊕ CORALR 5°56.645'S; 39°21.822'E). This was opened in 2000 by 3 Italians and virtually every guest here is a fellow compatriot. The sparse reception area is naturally raised above the beach area and decorated with simple murals showing acrobatic Maasai. It is enclosed on 3 sides, whilst the fourth is open and reveals a fine view of the sea. From here a central path steps down to the lovely swimming pool, complete with its own elegant palm island. Signs from the main path indicate the direction of various rooms, some of which are a fair stretch from the beach. The bungalow architecture is Arabic in style: brilliant white walls with arched windows and flat roofs. There are 32 standard rooms on the hillside, each either dbl or twin, plus 11 superior and seafront rooms on the beach. Every room has mains electricity, 2-pin European-style sockets, mosquito nets, and an en-suite bathroom with hot-water shower. The standard and some superior rooms have fans only, whilst 7 of the latter enjoy AC. There is a safe and left-luggage facility available at reception. Really a resort for young couples, children are accepted but specific provisions and activities for them are limited. There are a number of group sporting competitions, especially volleyball, whilst a couple of canoes and snorkelling equipt are available for individual use. Diving can be arranged with One Ocean, at the nearby Ocean Paradise Resort. Buffets are served for every meal in the enclosed restaurant area beside the sea. Inside it is dark and smoky with the feel of a school dining hall, though outside is a very pleasant deck with

large navy parasols and a lovely view along the beach. This is a great spot for an evening cocktail, or as a place to relax while the high-tide waves lap below deck. *Standard room: US$108/192 dbl, low/high season; seafront room: US$133/217 dbl, low/high season; superior room: US$142/227 dbl, low/high season. Local or major international currencies; no credit cards. Open Jul–Apr.*

⌂ **Zamani Zanzibar Kempinski** (110 rooms) PO Box 3140, Kiwengwa, Zanzibar; ☏ 0777 444477; f 0777 444488; e sales.zanzibar@kempinski.com; www.kempinski.com (⊕ ZAMANI 5°57.271'S; 39°21.979'E). In Dec 2005, luxury hotel group Kempinski, opened the stylish Zamani Zanzibar Kempinski. Set on 30 acres of immaculate landscaped gardens, each with a view over Kiwengwa's sandy beach to the sea, are 110 spacious guest rooms and suites, each with its own private terrace or balcony, and courtyard. In addition, there is a vast presidential villa and 6 smaller villas, each with a private pool. Rooms are all decorated in the cool blues and sandy tones of the surroundings, whilst the quality and number of in-room facilities reflect the resort's association with a serious European hotel group. Each offers satellite TV with movie channels, multilingual telephone voicemail, tea/coffee-making facilities, a minibar, an electronic safe, his and hers bathrobes, 24hr room service, and even a shoe-shine facility. All the rooms have en-suite bathrooms and, in safari style, also boast individual private courtyards with an outdoor shower. There are 2 restaurants: an all-day Mediterranean café, Cloves, and a smart Seafood grill, the Red Snapper. Drinks and snacks are on offer poolside and at the aptly named Zanzi Bar. For exercise and total relaxation, the Anantara Spa Zanzibar is one of the island's best well-being facilities. It is a calm, contemporary area with 6 private treatment rooms and professional Thai therapists, a large outdoor swimming pool with sun-deck and pool bar, a 23m lap pool and fully equipped fitness centre. If being outside is preferable, a number of watersports are available, from surfboarding to sailing. There is no dive centre at the resort, but this is easily arranged with a neighbouring property. A simple walk along the jetty offers terrific views, a cooling breeze and a touch of romance. Small conference groups are also welcomed at the resort and dedicated facilities are available: all fitted with the latest telecommunications and audio-visual equipt. *Garden room US$350/400 sgl/dbl; terrace room US$450/500 sgl/dbl; zamani suite US$600 sgl/dbl; all b&b.*

**WHAT TO DO AND SEE** Any lodge or resort will fix you up with one or more of the ubiquitous Zanzibar Island tours (see *Chapter 5*, pages 110–14). For diving, contact the One Ocean dive centre at the Ocean Paradise Resort.

⚓ **One Ocean – Ocean Paradise** PO Box 608, Zanzibar; ☎ 0777 453892/024 2238374; f 024 2234877; e oneocean@zanlink.com; www.zanzibaroneocean.com (✪ OCEANP 5°56.231'S; 39°21.635'E). The most recent of the One Ocean dive centres, this is a professional, PADI-accredited operation offering reliable equipt, custom-built dive-boats, knowledgeable staff and the usual array of certification courses. Most dive trips are dbl-

dives (perhaps because of the resort's distance from the better reefs), inc a light lunch in between, and it's possible for non-guests to dive from here. US$75/120/330/500 for 1/2/6/10 dive packages. PADI Open Water certification course US450; Dive Master certification course US$800. Snorkelling trips are US$45. All prices include equipt; 5% discount is given for using your own equipt.

## KIWENGWA

A small, traditional coastal village with a stunning beach, Kiwengwa is also the heart of Zanzibar's package-holiday industry. A glut of exclusively Italian, large, all-inclusive resorts cluster along the beach immediately around the village, with several other large hotels spaced along the coast to the north. That said, with continuous in-house entertainment and exhaustive facilities, the guests at all of these resorts are rarely seen outside of their chosen hotel's perimeter walls, so the area around is generally quite quiet. The contrast between the dusty Zanzibari fishing village and the lush, European hotel grounds is stark, and sadly the bigger developers and visitors have often displayed a lack of environmental and social consideration towards the local area and population. However, there are some who have made real efforts, notably Bluebay, La Villa and Shooting Star, and are good options on what is a truly beautiful beach.

**GETTING THERE AND AWAY** The easiest way to reach Kiwengwa from Zanzibar Town is along the good tar road, via Mahonda (✪ *MAHOND 5°59.388'S; 39°15.106'E*) and Kinyasini (✪ *KINYAS 5°58.088'S; 39°18.5'E*). The small coastal road, both north and south, is narrow, sandy and badly maintained, so 4x4 vehicles are advisable if you choose to travel it. You can come by taxi, rented car or motorbike, or arrange a minibus through a tour company. By public transport from Zanzibar Town, *dala-dalas* (number 17) run several times a day, until late afternoon. The 'official' *dala-dala* stop is in the village, though for a small fee the driver may well drop off at individual hotels. The major resorts and upmarket hotels all arrange transfers from the airport and Stone Town.

**WHERE TO STAY** Looking from north to south:

⌂ **Shooting Star** (14 rooms) PO Box 3076, Zanzibar; ☎ 0777 414166; f 0777 427560; e star@zanzibar.org; zanzibar.org/star (✪ SHSTAR 5°57.891'S; 39°22.237'E). Standing on a coral cliff above the stunning Kiwengwa Beach, Shooting Star is a firm favourite with young, well-travelled, independent Europeans. Built and run by the charismatic Eliamani 'Elly' Mlang'a, a charming and engaging Tanzanian, and his family, this small hotel is a delightfully social place, despite the high number of honeymooners who visit. There are

3 garden rooms bordering the lodge's central area. These all have a dbl/twin bed, mosquito net and en-suite bathroom, but are somewhat uninspiring. However, the new seaview cottages are lovely and all offer AC, fans, mosquito nets, en-suite bathrooms with a large shower, and a private terrace. All have comfortable Zanzibari beds, cool white walls, colourful tinga-tinga pictures and dyed makuti mats. In line with the lodge's child-friendly attitude, 4 of these cottages have been designed with families in mind and include a dbl bedroom and separate twin-

bedded upper room. New in 2005, a stunning horseshoe infinity pool and sun deck afford superb views over the ocean, barrier reef and beach below, as well as the opportunity for a cooling dip when the tide's out. Alongside, a small circular, powder-sand 'beach' area has been created complete with coir-rope loungers and blue deckchairs. A simple shower is secreted under a nearby palm for rinsing off before heading to the bar for a refreshing pineapple juice. Dining is split among 3 adjoining areas: 2 beneath makuti thatch and 1 under date palms, but all surrounded by tropical vegetation and featuring tables laid with batik tablecloths and red hibiscus flowers in individual vases. Meals here are simple and filling, but it's the lively bar and relaxed lounge area that is the true heart of Shooting Star. Drawn to the neon fridges, the bar-flies gather nightly to laugh and chat about the day's adventures. Elly's invariably on hand to offer friendly advice and help with planning, whilst card and board games are available for those content with a bottle of wine and a quiet seat in one of the cushioned, sweetheart booths. During full moon, Shooting Star opens its beach bar and hosts a bonfire and barbecue party on the beach for its guests. Diving and snorkelling trips can be organised through the PADI dive centre at nearby Bluebay, whilst trip fishing with locals on outboard boats will give a totally different take on life on the ocean wave. There's a central phone for guest use and with satellite connection, fast internet access is also available. *Seaview cottage US$210–235 dbl, low/high season; garden lodge US$130–160 dbl, low/high season. Child discounts available. Transfers to/from Stone Town US$50. Visa and MasterCard subject to 10% surcharge.*

⌂ **Karibu VentaClub** (135 rooms) PO Box 13, Mahonda, Zanzibar; ☏ 0777 417328; f 0741 323202; e direzione.karibu@zanzinet.com; www.ventaglio.com (✪ VENTAC 5°58.434'S; 39°22.32'E). One of several similar all-inclusive, all-Italian resorts on this coast, this is exclusively sold to Italians as a package holiday. All of its 135 rooms are classed as standard with little variation bar the number of beds they contain: dbls, twins, tpls and families all catered for. By the end of 2006, there will be an additional 20 dbl rooms. Two of the seaview rooms are completely wheelchair accessible but unfortunately there's no ramp network around the complex yet. Each room has mains electricity, a fan, AC, a reasonably sized safe, a telephone, mosquito nets, and an en-suite bathroom with hot-water shower. Local and satellite TV,

internet and phones are available centrally, along with an on-site doctor. Group activities are encouraged here and once a week a guest football team is assembled, supporters are furnished with flags and whistles, and a match is played against another Italian resort, Bravo Club. For those who want to get active without joining the team, there's canoeing, windsurfing, archery, aqua gym, volleyball, snorkelling and even yoga at sunset. Diving can be arranged through one of the neighbouring resorts. As one would expect at an Italian property, there's a very relaxed attitude towards children. Cots and highchairs are readily available and during school holidays there are separate kids' clubs. *All-inclusive and paid in advance. Additional charges in local or foreign currency: cash only up to €50, then travellers' cheques, VISA or MasterCard accepted. Open Jul–Apr.*

⌂ **La Villa Beach Resort** (14 rooms) PO Box 3156, Kiwengwa, Zanzibar; ☏ 0777 422137 (✪ LAVILL 5°58.604'S; 39°22.5'E). Owned by the man behind neighbouring Bluebay and Stone Town's Beyt al Chai, La Villa's lovely whitewashed rondavels, neatly tended gardens and smooth coral stone paths make this a delightful, quiet option on the beach. There are 10 dbls and 4 suites, all en-suite with flush toilets and hot-water showers, with 24hr mains electricity, 3-pin UK-style sockets, AC, a fan and mosquito nets. Interiors are simple, neat and clean, with quirky touches like concealing light bulbs behind large shells. Outside each room is a small terrace with 2 chairs. There's indoor and outdoor dining available at individual tables, and even an old dugout on the beach that's been converted into a table for card games, evening cocktails and bar snacks. No activities are available; this is a place to read books and soak up sunshine, not participate in volleyball tournaments, although guests can venture next door to Bluebay where facilities abound. Friendly, efficient, tidy and unpretentious: this is a great place for a reasonably priced beach break. *US$75–155pp, sgl, HB; US$75–120pp, dbl, HB. Christmas, New Year and Easter suppts US$40 adult/day and US$20 child/day. Children under 2 free; 2–12 50% discount.*

⌂ **Bluebay Beach Resort** (88 rooms) PO Box 3276, Zanzibar; ☏ 024 2240240–2; f 024 2240245; e mail@bluebayzanzibar.com; www.bluebayzanzibar.com (✪ BLUEBA 5°58.676'S; 39°22.48'E). Set on a lush, gently sloping site, there are currently 88 rooms in Bluebay's white, thatched, 2-storey villas: 80 superior, 6 deluxe and 2 sultans. All of the rooms have 2 large, 4-poster beds or 1 kingsize, a dressing area, en-suite bathroom and private balcony or terrace; the garden and deluxe rooms also have a lounge area. Fans, AC, minibars, hairdryers, satellite TV, electronic safes, tea/coffee-making facilities and mosquito nets are also standard. En-suite bathrooms all have European toilets and hot showers, though the deluxe rooms also enjoy a sunken bath and an indulgent outside dbl shower. Honeymooners are warmly welcomed with arches of fresh flowers adorning their doors, and families are equally well catered for with interconnecting rooms, a children's pool, playground, the possibility of babysitting and an on-site nurse for any illness or accidents. Disabled visitors are also encouraged with 2 rooms kitted out to include a shower shelf and ramp. There are oodles of activities from canoeing to catamaran sailing and waterskiing, a One Ocean centre on-site for diving and snorkelling trips, a large freshwater swimming pool with jacuzzi, a floodlit tennis court and beach volleyball. A proper, professional spa offers Vichy treatments inc a Vichy shower, massage tables with a sea view, a steam room, open-air whirlpool with loungers under shady palms, and an adjoining fitness centre. An 80-person conference room and business centre is also available, even if all that's required is internet access. The Makuti Restaurant, Bahari Grill and Pool Bar cover everything from extensive dinners to coffees and cocktails, with the majority of guests staying here on a HB basis. Bluebay is proud of being a Green Globe 21 organisation: companies satisfying a global benchmarking and certification programme for sustainable tourism. From its inception, it has recycled all room and laundry waste, purifying and using the water to keep its gardens green, incinerated all garden and kitchen rubbish, concealed its power generators in a soundproof structure, installed energy-efficient fittings in every room, and collected rainwater from its specially designed roofs to supplement the resort's supply. It addition, the gardens are planted only with indigenous species. *Garden room US$75–125pp; superior room US$100–160; suite US$130–190; sultan suite US$175–270. Christmas, New Year and Easter suppts US$40 adult/day and US$20 child/day.*

🏠 **Zanzibar Veraclub** (59 rooms) 📞 0777 466233/0741 320987/0777 414988;
e veraclubznz@zitec.org;
www.veratour.it/villaggi/zanzibar/zanzibar.html
(✪ VERACL 5°58.855'S; 39°22.529'E). 90% of Verclub's all-inclusive guests come on charter flights from Italy. Whilst simply lying on the shaded loungers, beside the sea or the lovely pool, clearly holds great appeal for most, the energetic Italian and Zanzibari 'animators' are keen to encourage participation in a variety of games, competitions and shows. Countless activities are available and there are formal courses in everything from diving to windsurfing. If it all gets too much, escape the midday sun and archery tournament by heading for a massage at the beauty centre, Ibiscus. Accommodation is in traditionally built bungalows with makuti thatch roofs and the 59 en-suite rooms, some suitable for families, are clean and comfortable. Each has AC, a safe, and a private, polished wood terrace with cane furniture. *No rack rates available at the resort; pre-booked packages only.*

🏠 **Sea Club Kiwengwa** (200 rooms) PO Box 4095, Zanzibar; 📞 0777 414351;
e sckiwengwa.recep@renthotel.org (✪ SEACLU 5°59.316'S; 39°22.548'E). Like its neighbouring resorts, Spanish and Italian package holidaymakers throng Sea Club's lush gardens and sandy stretch of beach. With 200 rooms divided amongst 25 villas, it's a sizeable place. Each of its en-suite rooms is decorated in pastel colours with light rattan furniture. Suitable for up to 3 adults or a family of 4, they have AC, a minibar, a safety deposit box (for which there's an extra change), telephone and a private balcony or veranda. In line with most all-inclusive resorts, there are buffets for every meal, with the welcome addition of the African 'Hakuna Matata' restaurant and an à-la-carte seafood establishment, 'Matunda'. The ever-present resident entertainers run an extensive programme of daytime events and evening shows, with a dedicated children's club for those aged 4 to 12. The hotel also boasts floodlit tennis courts and a basketball court, along with the usual assortment of beach and water sports at the Blue Diving centre. *Standard room US$110/180 sgl/dbl, all inclusive; Christmas and Aug suppt US$30/60 sgl/dbl, per night. Payment in local or major international currencies; VISA and MasterCard are accepted.*

🏠 **BravoClub** (107 rooms) PO Box 4095, Zanzibar; e bckiwengwa.recep@altamarea.it; www.bravoclub.it (✪ BRAVO 5°59.472'S; 39°22.712'E). Another big resort full of Mediterranean tourists. Here, even the resort signs and piped music are in Italian. With the mixture of whitewashed bungalows and dbl-storey blocks, the grounds feel quite built up, in spite of the profusion of flowers and tropical greenery. There are 107 rooms, some with a sea view, able to accommodate 2 to 3 people each. All rooms are en-suite with AC, a fridge, safe, telephone and individual terrace. The usual array of excursions and activities is available, and one of the resort's real assets is its lengthy pier, which allows easy, stepped access to swimming in the sea, even when the tide's out. By night there's a disco here, too. If you can read Italian and have good control over a computer mouse, a cartoon starfish will guide you around an interactive map of the village on the website, whilst 360° video images of your location spin in the corner. *No rack rates available at the resort; pre-booked packages only.*

🏠 **Reef View** (12 rooms) PO Box 3215, Zanzibar; ✆ 0777 413294 (✪ REEFVI 6°0.327'S; 39°23.117'E). Located on a dirt road south of Kiwengwa, Reef View is owned and run by a local man, Haroub Rashid, and his English wife: though Helen was not around during our recent·visit. The accommodation here is extremely basic, and at the end of 2005 had fallen into some disrepair. The lodge is literally right on the beach, with waves lapping only metres from some rooms, and the

views along the beach and out to the headland are lovely. There's a bar and restaurant, which reportedly offers a good range of vegetarian cuisine, and a large library and book exchange. The 2 en-suite brick and makuti-thatch rooms feature a mattress on the floor under a mosquito net, a rough rack for clothes, a freestanding fan, low-voltage lights and gauze-covered windows. There are also 10 *bandas* with shared facilities. Built entirely of makuti, these dbl/twin rooms are dark and dingy, with only a bicycle padlock to secure the door. The shared toilets are dirty and act as a very successful nursery for mosquitoes; and the shower water is cold. This place is not recommended for children or anyone who requires basic creature comforts. For self-drivers, there are parking bays on the opposite side of the road from the lodge. Although these are neatly marked by white painted pebbles, they are totally insecure being outside the property gate. *Bandas US$30 dbl, b&b; en-suite rooms US$50 dbl, b&b.*

**WHAT TO DO AND SEE** The major resorts and hotels can fix the normal range of tourist trips, as can tour operators in Zanzibar Town. For diving, there's a One Ocean centre at the Bluebay Beach Resort.

🤿 **One Ocean Bluebay** PO Box 607, Zanzibar; ✆ 024 2240244 or 0777 414332; e oneocean@zanlink.com; www.zanzibaroneocean.com (✪ BLUEBA 5°58.676'S; 39°22.48'E). A well-equipped and managed One Ocean operation, this PADI dive centre offers the usual array of courses and dive opportunities, inc pool-based training and refresher courses. The

3 custom-built dive boats — *Manta, Greta* and *Winnie* — are shared with One Ocean at Ocean Paradise, and concentrate on sites around Mnemba Island. The office is open 08.00–18.00, Mon–Sat. US$75/120/330/500 for 1/2/6/10 dive packages. *PADI Open Water certification course US$450; PADI Dive Master certification course US$800. Snorkelling trips US$45.*

## PONGWE

Northwest of the Ras Uroa headland, a series of idyllic, palm-fringed, sandy coves make up Pongwe. Bar a tiny fishing village and three small, individual accommodation options, there is very little else here: and that's its magic! Blissful beach relaxation, away from everything, is what's on offer.

**GETTING THERE AND AWAY** Pongwe Beach and Nature Safari Lodge can arrange minibus transfers from Stone Town, or these can be organised by local tour companies. By public transport, bus number 6 and *dala-dala* 14 from Stone Town to Uroa often continue to Pongwe village: ask the individual drivers.

Self-drivers should note that the tar road does not run from Pongwe to Kiwengwa: it's a bumpy mix of sand and coral rag, so a 4x4 is a good option for this route.

🏠 **WHERE TO STAY**

🏠 **Nature Safari Lodge** (9 rooms) PO Box 3671, Zanzibar; ✆ 0777 415613/414704; e info@pongwevillage.com; www.pongwevillage.com

(✪ NATURE 6°2.086'S; 39°24.411'E). This is a very rough and ready place, better suited to the self-sufficient. Surrounded by dense vegetation, on an

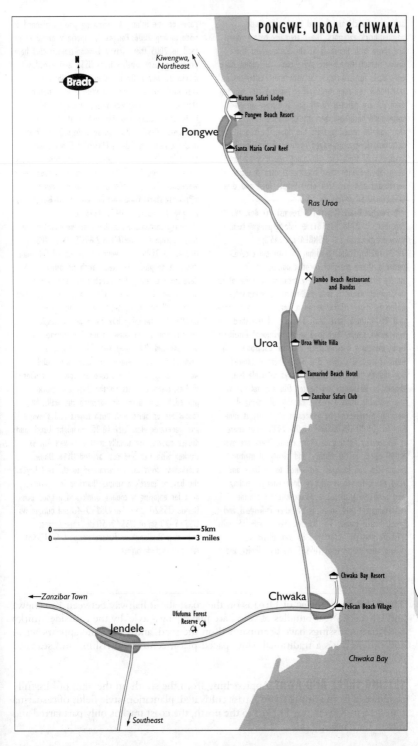

attractive beach, are 9 mud huts, with crude, painted-brick exteriors. The marginally better rooms are those with tin roofs at the back, whilst those under makuti thatch are more basic. All rooms have only basic furnishings, some with thin mattresses on traditional coir-rope beds, others with better wooden ones. All are painted candy pin and have an en-suite, tiled bathroom. Security is limited to a brick that can be rested against the door. The rooms are accessed along neat, edged paths and there's a 'nature trail' from the site, along which trees have been labelled with their traditional uses. A social restaurant and bar area offer simple food and drink. *US$20/40/50 sgl/dbl/tpl, b&b.*

🏠 **Pongwe Beach Resort** (13 rooms) PO Box 297, Zanzibar; ✆ 0748 336181; e info@pongwe.com; www.pongwe.com (✪ PONBEA 6°2.145'S; 39°24.392'E). Standing within its own quiet cove, under a shady oasis of coconut palms, this is a simple little lodge in a lovely location. In spite of its uninspiring name, it is a well-managed, good-value haven for pure relaxation on a beautiful beach. Since mid 2004, there have been 13 airy, whitewashed bungalows, simply furnished with traditional Zanzibari beds, mosquito nets, and an en-suite bathroom with flush toilet and shower. The water here is filtered but slightly brackish, though always available hot, thanks to an immersion heater. Dbl and tpl rooms are available, with 3 rooms capable of taking 4 beds at a squeeze. The generator electricity is time limited (06.00–15.00 and 18.00–24.00), but there is emergency lighting in every room. There are over 5,000 books in the library, and plenty of inviting hammocks and loungers on which to lie back and read them. For those who've done enough chilling and sunbathing, there's a power kite for seaside entertainment and an array of other individual and group beach games. The barrier reef is only 15 mins offshore and the resort has its own dhow for sailing, snorkelling trips (US$15, no time limit), and

game or line fishing. A swimming pool is planned to open in Aug 2006. Pongwe is especially proud of its food. In 2005 there was a London-trained chef here producing tasty lunches from US$4 and varied set menus at dinner. On occasion, beach BBQs and entertainment are arranged. With a little notice, children are warmly welcomed, with cots and highchairs readily available and great children's discounts. *US$75/120/150 sgl/dbl/tpl, b&b. Children under 2 years free; 3–7s US$30. HB additional US$15pp. Payment in local or international currency; credit card requires 24hr notice and isn't possible at weekends; 5% surcharge on travellers' cheques.*

🏠 **Santa Maria Coral Reef** (7 rooms) PO Box 4115, Pongwe, Zanzibar; ✆ 0777 432655; e info@santamaria-zanzibar.com; www.santamaria-zanzibar.com (✪ SANTAM 6°2.843'S; 39°24.408'E). Opened in 2005 by a young local named Suleiman, this is a delightful hideaway. With no other developments along the beach here, and very low-density population, this really is a place to get away from it all and relax. Set in a coconut grove, in the middle of a sweeping bay, there are 5 simple *bandas* and 2 bungalow rooms. The *bandas* are both sgl and dbl storey, with high thatch and suspended ceilings. Rooms are basic with solid wooden beds, fresh linen, coconut-rope and timber shelves, colourful mats on the floor and block-printed buxom mermaids adorning the walls. All rooms are en suite with flush toilets and showers, and generator electricity 18.00–midnight. Lunch and dinner options are usually freshly cooked fish or chicken with rice and cost around US$6. Dhow snorkelling trips can be arranged to the reef beyond the bay, or there's a simple thatched lounge/library area for enjoying a cooling drink and a good book. *Banda US$20–25 sgl or US$30–40 dbl; bungalows US$25–30 sgl or US$40–50 dbl; their largest bungalow 'Buckingham Palace' sleeps 6 for US$60. All rates include b/fast.*

# UROA

The small, neat village of Uroa is on the coast about halfway between Kiwengwa and Chwaka. Neat bundles of wood are piled 'jenga-style' by the roadside, quirky pedestrian crossings have been painted on the road, and village life appears active and ordered. It's a traditional, slow-paced place, centred on fishing and seaweed collection.

**GETTING THERE AND AWAY** Approaching from the south on the 9km of blissfully tarred road from Chwaka, you'll pass cultivated, plantation-style fields of casuarina pines; from Kiwengwa, 11.5km to the north, the coast track is only part tarred and makes for a bumpy ride.

From December to mid-February, some of the beaches on the east coast have large patches of brown seaweed washed ashore from the ocean by the wind. This can be quite a shock if you expect pristine, picture-postcard tropical beach conditions. The seaweed normally stays on the beaches until the start of the rainy season, when it is carried back out to sea. After March, and up until November, the beaches are mostly clear.

*Dala-dala* numbers 6 and 14 frequently ply the route from Stone Town to Uroa throughout the day. If you prefer, private minibuses and taxis can also be arranged by most reliable Zanzibar Town tour operators.

**WHERE TO STAY** Going from north to south, the accommodation options here are:

**Jambo Beach Restaurant & Bandas** (7 rooms) PO Box 3860, Uroa, Zanzibar; 0777 460446; e mail@p-web-marketing.de; www.jambo-beach.de/englisch (⊕ JAMBOB 6°5.225'S; 39°25.454'E). From a sizeable concrete roadside sign, advertising 'seafood, local food and continental food', a track leads down to the sea and this locally run restaurant. Once specialising in freshly cooked food, the building is now Spartan and very simple. However, 7 rooms have sprung up beside the quiet beach. There is one whitewashed bungalow right on the water's edge, with a dbl and 2 sgl beds, boasting psychedelic neon blankets, a fan, mosquito nets, and a small en-suite bathroom with flush toilet and shower. Alternatively, there are 6, tiny, round makuti *bandas* which each have 2 coir-rope beds, complete with lumpy mattresses, pillows and mosquito nets but no bed linen. In a nod towards the idea of security, a mini bolt has been fitted to the inside of each, and a large one to the outside; sadly, however, the door doesn't actually close. Outside each, perched on a miniscule curved deck, are 2 chairs. *Bandas US$15; bungalow US$25.*

**Uroa White Villa** (8 rooms) PO Box 2424, Zanzibar; 0741 488520/326874/436101; e mwadini@zitec.org; www.uroawhitevilla.net (⊕ WHITEV 6°6.03'S; 39°25.56'E). In the centre of the low-density village, with clear signposting to help with directions, this place sits on a fairly compact, walled plot, where bright white buildings stand on 3 sides of a quadrangle, and a row of beachfront fir trees makes up the fourth. Its 8 rooms are divided between the main villa and 2 thatched bungalows. The main villa, with its stark white blockwork walls, shiny metal window frames, tin roof and highly polished, red-paint floor, has all the character of a government administration building. The 4 rooms

inside are clean and cool but, much like the exterior, entirely soulless. Two of these rooms have en-suite bathrooms, whilst the others share facilities. There are 4 en-suite bungalow rooms. Again these are Spartan in appearance with little more than a bed, small coconut-wood table, and a 'fitted' wardrobe constructed from rough timber planks, but they are clean, quiet and functional. Outside there's a terrace area with chairs. There's a central lounge in the villa, with a selection of Italian and German books, and a separate open-sided restaurant. The food here is all freshly cooked and the seafood-dominated menu is all subject to availability. Snacks will usually cost US$1–5, with à-la-carte dinners ranging up to US$12. Although the central square is rather barren, a pleasant sandy beach is literally on the doorstep. Snorkelling equipt can be hired (US$15) and fishing trips with the locals are always possible. The villagers here are very relaxed around visitors so wandering into the community is also a possibility. The capable manager, Juma, will happily help organise anything; he's friendly and helpful and speaks English and Italian with ease. *Rooms in main villa US$25–40 sgl and US$40–60 dbl; bungalows US$35–50 sgl and US$60–70 dbl. All rates are b&b. Payment in local currency, US$ or euro. No credit cards, and travellers' cheques must be sent to Germany prior to arrival. Open May–Mar.*

**Tamarind Beach Hotel** (14 rooms) PO Box 2206, Uroa, Zanzibar; 0777 413709/411191; e tamarind@zanzinet.com; www.tamarind.nu (⊕ TAMARI 6°6.311'S; 39°25.574'E). Owned by 3 Norwegians and 3 Zanzibari locals, Tamarind was run by a German management company from its opening in 1992 until 2000. It is now managed by the very helpful Said Ali, and one of the Scandinavian owners, Trond. Minimal planting, parched grass and

9

low concrete walls lining the sand paths make Tamarind feel very dry in spite of its coconut palms and proximity to the sea. There are 7 semi-detached cottages built from coral-stone blocks and cement. Each is finished with neat moulded balustrades and white arches around the porch terrace. Traditional Zanzibari doors lead into the rooms and there are external stairs leading up to a 'terrace' formed by the roof of the porch: there is only a simple, open wooden barrier along the edge making this area unsuitable for children. All 14 rooms have a dbl bed, although extra beds are easily obtained for twin or tpl occupancy. Each has mains electricity, a fan and mosquito net, plus an en-suite bathroom with flush toilet and hot-water shower. A safe deposit box is kept at reception for valuables, along with a basic first-aid kit and telephone. There's a small local TV room and a curio shop selling the usual *kangas* and carvings. The restaurant offers indoor dining at individual tables and fresh produce, with an emphasis on seafood. Children are generally welcome at the hotel a cot is available and babysitting can be arranged with the staff, but, beyond playing in the sea, activities are limited. *US$40/60 sgl/dbl, b&b. Lunch and dinner each US$12pp. Payment in local or major international currencies; VISA and MasterCard accepted with no surcharge.*

⌂ **Zanzibar Safari Club** (50 rooms) PO Box 1282, Zanzibar; ✆ 0777 844481; f 0777 419998; e reservations@zanzibarsafariclub.com; www.zanzibarsafariclub.com (✆ ZSAFAR 6°6.642'S; 39°25.591'E). The mock cannons resting on painted, red-brick plinths scream of the idiosyncracies hidden behind the Safari Club's imposing gates. South of Uroa village, this is a themed, slightly kitsch, medley of Arabian and Indian styles, marketing primarily to large groups from Spain, Scandinavia and South Africa. Run by efficient staff, the resort has all the trappings of a large hotel (business centre, currency exchange, quality in-room facilities) but the feel of a hospitality training school. In the heart of the resort, the large central pool is lovely, and surrounded by tidy rows of sun loungers, and there's an idyllic, peaceful, palm-fringed beach for those who want to dip in the sea. The 48 standard rooms and

2 suites are a riot of colours and designs, both inside and out. We understand that a stream of different designers came and went during the development of this resort, which explains everything. The decoration would imply that each one simply carried on from where his predecessor left off, in a style of his choosing, and regardless of what had been done before. The neat, bright-orange cottages with forest-green tiled roofs sit in orderly rows around the complex. At the entrance to each, a Zanzibari bench, covered in multicoloured cushions, sits on a small terrace. Through the arched blue door, the décor is best described as distressed Van Gogh. Every piece of wooden furniture has been painted in bold colours and limed to reveal each brush stroke, and effect an aged, beach-hut quality. Yet, the rooms have all the essential hotel mod-cons: mains electricity with 3-pin UK-style sockets, AC, a fridge, satellite TV, a hairdryer and an electronic safe. The Zanzibari beds are covered in mosquito nets trimmed with bright, patterned fabrics, and all the rooms are en-suite with a flush toilet and hot shower, each with its own in-room boiler.

Reasonably sized but mediocre buffets are served in the circular, poolside Mwangaza Restaurant, or alternatively the quiet Ocean View Restaurant serves Swahili cuisine beside the beach. At the end of the jetty, which is lit like a runway by night, the Zinc Discotheque is a great place to boogie above the waves to classic disco and pop hits. Impressive, state-of-the-art sound and light systems, a good Kenyan DJ, and a free pool table for non-dancers make this an excellent, if noisy, after-dinner hangout. Even when no-one turns up, the music plays on until 02.00 every night. This hotel is very secure with a multi-gate security entry: good locks on room doors, safe deposit boxes at reception, fire alarms and extinguishers, and security guards on patrol. *Deluxe US$70–110 pp, dbl; suite US$100–130 pp, dbl. Sgl suppt US$30. All rates are HB; no credit cards accepted.*

⌂ **Uroa Beach Village Hotel** But for an overgrown perimeter wall, nothing remains of this once sizeable hotel. The land here has almost entirely reverted to bush.

# CHWAKA

Halfway down the east coast, directly due east of Zanzibar Town, Chwaka is a large fishing village overlooking a wide bay fringed with mangrove swamps, In the early 19th century, Chwaka was a major slave port, exporting human cargo across the Indian Ocean to Arabia. In more recent times, its sea breezes and lack of mosquitoes made it a popular holiday destination for British colonial administrators and affluent Zanzibari dignitaries: their grand, crumbling villas remain along the shoreline north of the village. Today, apart from some coastal researchers, there is not much in the way of facilities or activity, besides the large, lively seafood market: for the best atmosphere, arrive in the mornings when the fishing boats dock, laden with the day's catch.

Chwaka Bay itself supports the largest swathe of mangrove forest on Zanzibar and forms a significant part of the Jozani Chwaka Bay National Park: Zanzibar's only national park. The government is currently working with international charities, like CARE International, and conservation bodies, to develop and manage the forest as a conservation area and income-generating eco-tourism project. Some tours to explore the mangroves are possible, and do make an interesting diversion. There is little accommodation in Chwaka and few visitors, but it's possible to take a boat across Chwaka Bay to head further down the east coast, which may attract the adventurous.

**GETTING THERE AND AWAY** Chwaka can be reached by public bus (number 6, and occasionally number 14), or by hired car or bike. Tourist minibuses do not usually come here, although you could privately hire one through a tour company. However you choose to travel, if you approach from the west, the smooth, tarmac road through the island's lush interior is a pleasure.

If you are heading to or from the southeast coast, and don't want to go back to Zanzibar Town in between, you can get a ride on a boat (high tide only) across Chwaka Bay to Michamvi on the peninsula north of Bwejuu. Local people regularly travel this way, but only the occasional intrepid tourist is seen here. Boats from Michamvi come across to Chwaka's fish market most mornings, returning around noon, but there are no set schedules: you need to ask around on the beach. A ride will cost little more than a few dollars.

## WHERE TO STAY

🏠 **Chwaka Bay Resort** (30 rooms) PO Box 1480, Zanzibar; ☏ 024 2240289/0774 040400; e chwaka@zanlink.com; www.chwakaresort.com (⊕ CHWBAY 6°9.348'S; 39°26.204'E). North of Chwaka village on the coast road, past some near-derelict grand old colonial villas, Chwaka Bay Resort is under joint Tanzanian–Swedish ownership. Unsurprisingly, guests are primarily Scandinavian and German. The 10 original whitewashed rondavels, known as standard rooms, are light and airy thanks to 3 large windows in each. They are spacious, if a little Spartan. The simple, dark-wood furniture all matches and beds can be made up as dbls or twins. The ring mosquito nets can be tied up out of the way; there are fans, open wardrobes and sparkling en-suite bathrooms with hot water. Arguably, these rooms have more character than their more expensive new siblings. In a bid to expand and upgrade the resort, 5 villas (each with 4 independent rooms), were built on the far side of the resort in 2002. Referred to as 'deluxe', these large en-suite rooms have mains electricity with 3-pin UK-style sockets, AC, lockable drawers as safes, mosquito nets and constant hot water controlled by an in-room boiler. Each room has a terracotta tiled terrace or balcony with 2 coconut-wood director's chairs, a coffee table and a view through the palm grove to the beach. The ground-floor rooms in these buildings are a mix of dbls, twins and tpls, while upstairs all the rooms have a dbl bed. All the rooms, in both categories, are raised up away from the beach. The beach here isn't as good as many on the east coast, but boat trips to the other side of the peninsula can be arranged, and the inviting, kidney-shaped swimming pool, completed in 2002, is pleasant enough for a cooling dip. The swim-up bar stools are academic, however, given that the sunken pool bar has not been functional for some time. Coir-rope loungers and striped metal deckchairs sit on the surrounding triangular tiles, some shaded by makuti umbrellas, and all enjoying views of the band of palms along the coast. Like a giant board game, the resort's concrete paths are seemingly colour coded: green leads between the bungalows whilst azure blue takes you around the pool and gardens. Sunshine-yellow mushroom lights line all the routes, but sadly none hides any fairies! Gaudy green and patterned deep-pile velour sofas with safari print, faux-fur cushions give the bar and lounge a distinct '70s feel. Take your mind off the décor disaster with a game of pool or gaze outside at the large satellite dish and gardens beyond. Dinner is served in the restaurant, and, though most guests stay on a HB basis, there are really no other dining options in the area. For 2006, there are tentative plans to build a conference centre here. *Standard US$42/60 sgl/dbl, b&b; deluxe US$55/72/94 sgl/dbl/tpl, b&b. All major currencies accepted. No credit cards; travellers' cheques subject to 10% surcharge.*

🏠 **Pelican Beach Village** (16 rooms) PO Box 744, Zanzibar; 📞 024 2230862/0777 435623; e malik68@hotmail.com/ pelicanbeachvillage@hotmail.com (⊕ PELICA 6°9.907'S; 39°26.219'E). Opened in Sep 2005 on the outskirts of Chwaka village, Pelican Beach is a neat group of 7 large, whitewashed bungalows. Individually named after exotic spices, each houses an assortment of sgl and dbl rooms. Tiled throughout and with plenty of natural light, the interiors are bright, fresh and clean, if somewhat soulless, and with a curious number of sinks fitted in most rooms. There is a thatched bar and à la carte restaurant, complete with garish pink and yellow checkerboard flooring, on the water's edge, but there's no beach here. However, the adjoining lounge and games room offer pleasant views of the bobbing dugouts in Chwaka harbour. The manager here spent some time living in Birmingham and is keen to spend time with passing Brits. *US$40/60 sgl/dbl, b&b.*

## UFUFUMA FOREST HABITAT

The Ufufuma Forest conservation project was set up by the people of nearby Jendele village. It aims to protect the forest habitat and to educate the villagers in sustainable use. The 102 local volunteers, led by the dedicated and charismatic Mr Mustafa Makame, hope to make it a place for both locals and foreigners to visit, and to preserve the traditional worship of *shetani*, or spirits, which is performed here (see box *The Shetani of Zanzibar* on pages 36–7). The forest area is at present only 1km², but the villagers are leaving the surrounding 4km² area uncultivated to allow the forest habitat to expand in size. Tiny paths, marked with periodic, mid-blue arrows, wind through thick vegetation, while underfoot a tangle of roots clings to coral rag. A visit here is not a great wildlife experience, nor is it meant to be, although you might be fortunate enough to see skittish red colobus (early morning is best), island birdlife, snakes and lizards. Honey is also collected from the forest, so look out for the canopy-height hives. A few villagers act as guides, but they are not wildlife specialists and don't know a lot of the bird names. But they are trying to learn, and, meanwhile, they are very enthusiastic about Ufufuma's cultural importance – which is the primary reason for a visit here.

There are many underground caves hidden in the dense forest undergrowth: three are *shetani* caves being used by the local 'doctor', which tourists may also visit. It is a source of great joy and comfort to the local Zanzibari people who come to these cave to speak with the spirits. When local people are sick or troubled they come to these sites with the local witchdoctor and perform rituals and recitations to cure themselves. The cave entrances are adorned with tattered strips of red and white fabric and surrounded by piles of sweet offerings, often rotting, from sugar cane to Coca-Cola. Inside, the caves are dank and spooky, with the smell of smoke from recent fires and resident colonies of bats. It's a fascinating insight into a rarely seen aspect of Zanzibari culture.

Mr Mustafa and his small team believe wholeheartedly that in protecting the forest there is potential for the local communities to benefit financially from conservation tourism: they are simply unsure how to achieve their goal. Gaining support from all of the villagers is difficult – many want the timber for firewood and rocks for building, and perceive little monetary gain from conservation. But Mr Mustafa is determined, and, whilst searching for a solution, he travels to Ufufuma from Zanzibar Town every Sunday on his moped, keen to inspire and educate the villagers about protecting the forest. He even chairs the local NGO.

Mangroves are salt-tolerant, resilient, evergreen trees, anchored by stilt-like roots in the inter-tidal zone (eg: *Rhizophora mucronata*) or simply growing in sandy muddy bottoms (eg: *Avicennia marina*), or even perched on fossil coral pockets with minimum soil. They are found in low-energy or sheltered bays and river estuaries, and are vital components of the tropical marine environment: ensuring shoreline stability by protecting soft sediment from erosion, providing nutrients for sea organisms, and offering sanctuary to migratory birds, juvenile fish, shellfish and crustaceans.

Mangroves are nevertheless one of the most threatened habitats in the world. Environmental stress from changing tides and pollution takes its toll, but increasingly it's human interference that is the primary cause of irreparable damage. On Zanzibar, this is certainly the case: many people rely on the forests for fuel (firewood and charcoal), lime burning, boat repair and dugout manufacture, as well as material for house construction. Mangrove wood is dense and, because of its tannin content, it is termite-resistant, making it preferable for house construction. Income is also generated from trading in cut wood, poles and charcoal. The absence of alternative income-generating activities means heavy dependence on mangroves.

Ominously, as the rural population continues to grow, so does the demand for this fragile resource. It is therefore critical to fully understand and address the needs of the villagers in order to have any chance of developing successful conservation initiatives.

Chwaka Bay is fringed by Unguja's largest area of mangrove forest, approximately 3,000ha and accounting for 5% of the island's total forest cover. Here, fairly dense stands of diverse mangrove species, zoned by their tolerance to the conditions of the area (eg: volume of water and salt levels), are drained by a number of lovely creeks.

Over the last 60 years, assorted management plans have been drawn up with the communities bordering the forests, in a bid to control over-exploitation in the area. From issuing permits to control harvesting, imposing mangrove taxes and limiting creek access, each has successively failed to halt rapid deforestation. Ever-changing forestry policy, lack of serious patrolling, a decline in the authority of village elders to command community support, insufficient alternative income sources for villagers and minimal resources are all cited as reasons for the failure.

Conservation and development organisations continue to attempt to halt deforestation in the area, improve villager understanding of the forests' importance and lobby local and national government for support; but, without doubt, these valuable natural resources will be irretrievably ruined unless human activities are carefully controlled.

Six villages in the vicinity already benefit from the income of the forest. All of the money goes directly to the community leaders, who assess their village's primary needs, be it medicine for cows, wells, or school materials, and channel the money as appropriate. If more people visit the forest, accepting that it's not a slick tourism enterprise, the village coffers will slowly increase, and in turn the communities will begin to see the benefits of preserving rather than plundering their surroundings. We wish the Ufufuma Forest conservation project every success.

**ARRANGING YOUR VISIT** To visit Ufufuma Forest, it is best to make contact in advance, to ensure that an English-speaking guide is available at the time of your

As in most African societies, many of the trees and plants found in Ufufuma Forest play an important role in the daily lives of the local population. Be it for medicinal or practical use, religious or cultural significance, the flora is fascinatingly versatile when viewed through the eyes of a resident guide: though naturally we don't recommend that you attempt self-diagnosis and treatment on your journey through the vegetation. The trees below are a sample of what's to be seen and learnt. They are listed by their Swahili name, as the guides will not know them by anything else.

### MCHOFU
Across the island, the branches of this tree are commonly used as an all-purpose timber for firewood and furniture. Here, only its fruits are used as a cure for coughs, colds and flu.

**MDAA** (*Euclea natalensis*) Ufufuma's answer to Colgate: this is the local toothpaste. The villagers here chew on a piece of the tree's root to ensure a bright, white set of teeth and healthy gums. In 1991, research into this custom by the South African Medical Research Council at the University of Stellenbosch showed that oral bacterial growth was indeed suppressed by this chewing, giving this practice some scientific validity. Sadly, it also concluded that the daily exercise is too limited to have a truly beneficial effect: this is probably backed up by the smiles around you.

**MKOMWE** (*Caesalpinia bonducella*) Mkomwe's Latin name derives from the Arab word 'bonduc', meaning hazelnut. It's easy to see why when presented with the neat spherical seed kernels (Swahili: *komwe*) from within its fruit. These are the traditional pieces used in games of bao, but this dual-purpose tree can also be boiled with water to produce a drink for sufferers of stomach ache.

**MKUYU** The roots of this wild fig are boiled with water to form a drink. Given to pregnant women, the concoction is believed to have an abortive quality.

**MLALANGAO** Hunting for birds is a patient but ingenious process. Local men must first study the avian movements in the forest, watching flight paths and routines. To catch the birds, they cut the trunk of the *mlalangao* tree with a *panga*, collect the sap (Swahili: *utomvu*), and boil it to form a type of latex. Back in the forest, the chewing-gum-textured latex is smeared onto the branches where birds have been observed resting. Then the men wait … for when the birds do land, they simply stick to the latex from where they are easily collected and taken home to make soup.

**MUWAVIKALI** This sweet-smelling tree is boiled with water: the resulting liquid is drunk to combat symptoms of malaria.

**MKAAGA** Seek out the young leaves on this little bush: they'll provide you with the freshest tea!

visit (*Mr Mustafa Makame Ali, PO Box 1861, Zanzibar;* \ *255 7474 91069;* e *himauje@yahoo.com*).

The price of a visit is variable as a single tariff system has yet to be adopted. However, for a guided forest walk lasting a few hours, a visit to the caves, and usually a gift of fresh fruit or coconut refreshment, expect to pay US$5 per person/guide, and then volunteer to make a larger donation to the community fund. If you want to see a full *shetani* ceremony, consisting of about seven hours of singing, dancing and assorted rituals, this costs US$50 (for one or two people), and will have to be booked in advance and take place at a time convenient to the local 'doctor'. As the forest floor can be damp and rugged, be sure to take sturdy shoes, and, in the hot season, plenty of water to drink.

**GETTING THERE**  To reach Ufufuma (✪ *UFUFUM 6°10.419'S; 39°23.969'E*) from Zanzibar Town, take the road west towards Chwaka: the forest is on the left, about 5km before Chwaka. There is currently no sign or specific parking place, and only concealed paths lead into the forest. If you have contacted the Ufufuma volunteers in advance, then a welcoming party will likely be waiting for you. However, if your visit isn't scheduled, stop at Jendele village (✪ *JENDEL 6°10.676'S; 39°22.359'E*) and ask in the market area for an official forest guide. It has been suggested to the forest protection committee that a sign to the forest would be helpful, so one may have appeared by the time you visit.

To reach the forest on public transport, talk to the *dala-dala* drivers heading towards Chwaka on Route 6, and ask to be dropped in Jendele village: be aware this is a sprawling village with little tourism connection so it may not be an easy task.

## DUNGA RUINS

Equidistant from Chwaka and Zanzibar Town, in the lush centre of the island, lie Dunga Ruins. Close to the modern village of Dunga (✪ *DUNGA 6°8.047'S; 39°19.622'E*), these are the remains of the palace built for King Mohammed, the Mwinyi Mkuu (Swahili: great chief) of Zanzibar. Constructed between 1846 and 1856, the palace may have been built on the site of an earlier house. Prior to this, the residence of the Mwinyi Mkuu had been at Kizimkazi or Unguja Ukuu (see pages 243 and 253–4 respectively).

Local legend tells that when Dunga Palace was built, slaves were buried alive in the foundations, while others were killed and their blood mixed with the mortar. It was believed that this would bring strength and good fortune to the house. There may be some truth in this story as, in the 1920s, a nearby well was found to be half full of human bones. Today, in the centre of an overgrown garden, only the main walls of the palace remain, but it is still an imposing ruin and retains something of its original grandeur.

A few old passages, pillars and staircases can also be seen. The windows are empty and their decorative frames are now in the House of Wonders in Zanzibar Town, along with the Mwinyi Mkuu's sacred drums and horns. The latter were part of the royal regalia and both were kept at Dunga during King Mohammed's rule. The drums, carved from mango wood and inscribed with Arabic, were said to beat spontaneously to warn the king of impending trouble. The horns were kept in a secret hiding place, known only to the Mwinyi Mkuu. When he was near death, their location would be revealed to the heir apparent. Mohammed died in 1865 and was succeeded by his son Ahmed, but he died of smallpox in 1873, leaving no male heir. His two sisters had married into prominent families of Arab landowners, but the ruling dynasty came to an end.

A Swahili royal line is believed to have existed on Zanzibar prior to the first Shirazi immigrants arriving Persia in the 10th century AD. Leading figures among the Shirazis are thought to have married into the family of the then Swahili ruler, as the Mwinyi Mkuu later claimed to be descended from a Shirazi prince. In the following centuries, while the island was controlled by the Portuguese, and later by the Arabs and British, a Mwinyi Mkuu continued to be regarded as the traditional leader by the people of Zanzibar.

**GETTING THERE** About 14km from Stone Town on the road to the east coast, or 30 minutes' drive inland from Chwaka, the ruins sit in the centre of the island on the southern side of the road. It is also possible to reach Dunga (⊕ *DUNGA 6°8.047'S; 39°19.622'E*) from the south: along the dirt track from Tunguu, on the main road to the island's southeast: a 4x4 is necessary for this route. By *dala-dala* from Zanzibar Town, it's possible to reach the ruins on the Chwaka services, numbers 6 and 14.

# Southeast Zanzibar

From the finger of the Michamvi Peninsula to the coastal curve at Makunduchi, the southeast of Zanzibar, in many ways, offers a continuation of the stunning sandy beaches, fringe reef and traditional fishing villages found north of Chwaka Bay.

The area around the villages of Paje, Bwejuu and Jambiani used to be the busiest part of the east coast, especially for backpackers, as there was a good choice of cheap places to stay. However, over recent years, some middle-range and upmarket places have appeared, and the budget travellers have instead opted for the livelier environs of Nungwi and Kendwa, on the north coast.

The end result is that this area is probably a bit quieter than it used to be, which may just be a good thing. The beaches here are palm-fringed, longer and more windswept than their north coast counterparts. They also experience a much greater tidal range and offer fewer makuti-shaded cocktail bars. With the exception of a couple of larger properties, the southeast of the island generally presents itself as a more low-key, low-impact beach retreat.

## MICHAMVI PENINSULA

Along the length of the Michamvi Peninsula's 10km east coast, the sand is the fine, powder-white stuff of tourism advertising, and the sea suitably sparkling cobalt. Few local people live here, concentrating instead in Bwejuu to the south or the village of Michamvi beside Chwaka Bay, and only six hotels exist. All of the accommodation in this area is high quality, though each place is individual in its style and customers. Come here for the pristine, palm-fringed beaches, good diving opportunities, and space.

**GETTING THERE AND AWAY** All of the accommodation on this stretch of coast will arrange transfers, although most guests will set this up in advance with their tour operator. For those with a hired car, north of Bwejuu there is only one road so getting lost is difficult, even if the track becomes increasingly bumpy as you travel north. There is little in the way of public transport on the peninsula, but the number 9 *dala-dala* from Zanzibar Town will sometimes continue from Bwejuu towards Michamvi village. If your luggage is not prohibitive, it's probably easier to cycle or embark on the long beach walk from Bwejuu.

**WHERE TO STAY** This peninsula is the location for some of the island's most luxurious hotels. These are described in this section from north to south.

⌂ **Kichanga** (10 rooms) e info@athomehotels.com; www.athomehotels.com. Opened in Dec 2005, on the northernmost tip of the Michamvi Peninsula,

Kichanga is a pretty, flower-filled lodge on a lovely sandy beach. Its 10 stone-and-thatch cottages are all beach-facing and benefit from large wooden terraces

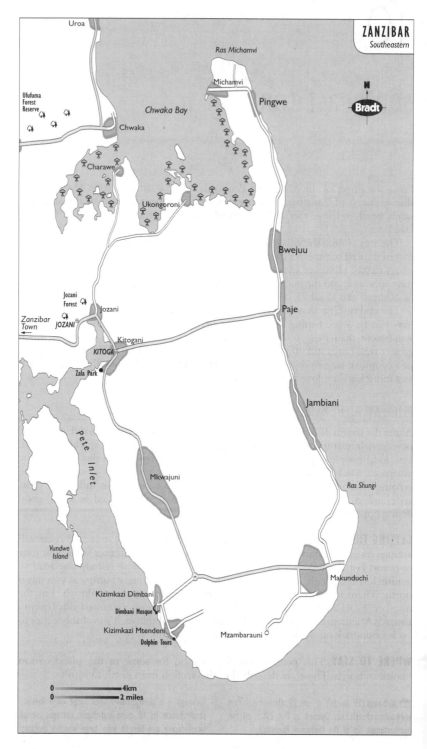

for enjoying the panoramic sea views. The rooms are all spacious and tastefully furnished: 7 are dbls, 2 are interconnecting for families and include a dbl bed and 2 sgls, whilst 1 bungalow has 2 bedrooms, a dbl and a twin. Mosquito nets, fans, safes, minibars, hairdryers and en-suite bathrooms are standard throughout. In the main building, there's an internet point, telephone facilities, a lounge bar and an Italian-influenced restaurant, though you may prefer a cocktail and the fresh grilled fish prepared on the beach. Watersports are well catered for here with an on-site dive centre, organised snorkelling trips, canoe rental and boat trips; even the beach towels are provided. *FB US$84/180 sgl, low/high season; US$144/240 dbl, low/high season. Payment by local or international currencies, VISA and MasterCard.*

🏠 **Karafuu Hotel and Beach Resort** (89 rooms) PO Box 71, Zanzibar; ☎ 0777 413647–8; f 0777 419915; e karafuuhotel@zanzinet.com; www.karafuuhotel.com. Owned by an Italian and currently managed by a charming Frenchman, Karafuu is the friendly and stylish place one would expect. Beautifully carved chaises longues sit on polished granite floors in reception, antique clocks adorn the walls, cosmopolitan young couples sip margaritas around the swim-up pool bar, and all around an air of cool confidence and sophistication pervades. Its 89 en-suite rooms are all terrific: smart and newly painted. They're divided into 3 categories, based solely on proximity to the beach, with only the junior suite having a sea view. The rooms all have big beds with neat wrought-iron seats at the end of each, a day bed, fan, AC, minibar, telephone and spacious en-suite bathroom. Outside each, a wide terrace with tasteful wooden furniture looks out on to gardens filled with beautiful white lilies and coconut palms: a perfect place to catch the evening breeze. Children are warmly welcomed and well catered for. There's a children's playground, sectioned-off baby area within the main swimming pool, and the general manager's own child's nanny is available for reliable babysitting. For older children and the young at heart, there's a large, brightly coloured diving and watersports base beside the pool: the Kaskazi Sports Centre (see *What to do and see*). *Superior US$74–US$192 dbl; cottage US$96–US$214 dbl; junior suite US$111–US$244 dbl. Children under 5 free; 6–13 years 50% discount.*

🏠 **The Sultan Palace** (15 rooms) PO Box 714, Village Market 00612, Nairobi, Kenya; ☎ +254 20 7123156; f +254 20 7122638; e sultanzanzibar@zanlink.com; www.sultanzanzibar.com (⊕ SULTAN 6°10.648'S; 39°31.766'E). High on a coral cliff, at the northern end of a pristine beach, the Sultan Palace is a sedate, elegant lodge, with beautiful rooms and a welcome feeling of space. Designed and built by Roberto Merlo, an Italian underwater photographer who sadly died in Dec 2004, the lodge remains privately owned and very professionally run. The British managers, Lara and Jamie, have a wealth of experience in east African beach destinations and make friendly, entertaining hosts over an evening cocktail and tasty nibbles at the bar. The main building has a huge white hexagonal interior, into which the sunlight casts a rainbow across the floor as it shines through multi-coloured glass windows. A small bar has neatly arranged bottles in individual recesses, silk-covered Zanzibari beds, and cushioned wooden furniture is set out in civilised clusters. Outside, a series of terraces offer glimpses of the sea from sumptuous sofas. Internet and email access, local and satellite TV and guest telephone are also available in this building, as is a curio shop. The lodge has 15 stunning, stone-and-thatch cottage suites – ocean, garden and imperial – spread through gardens of citronella, frangipani and bougainvillea. The large ocean and garden suites are identical in design, with dbl beds, en-suite bathrooms and wide, decked terraces complete with hammocks, loungers and a b/fast table. The only difference is their location, with the ocean suites, as their name suggests, being closer to the cliff edge and consequently enjoying a sea view through the garden vegetation. The 5 imperial suites are simply vast, curving round from a heavy wooden door to reveal an entrance hall and bedroom, complete with 2 dbl beds. A dressing room and enormous bathroom with twin shower and separate toilet complete the interior. Venture outside and there's a huge private terrace with its own access to the beach path. All the rooms have mains electricity (sockets with 3 round pins), mosquito nets, fans, AC, new electronic safes, a hairdryer and telephone. They are individually furnished with fabulous fabrics, tasteful antiques, hand-painted tiles, carved Omani wooden doors, and concealed lighting to highlight the stylised alcoves. A minibar, fluffy bathrobes and high-quality toiletries are all part of the package. The beach here is lovely, and being at the end of the sandy stretch there is little, if any, passing foot traffic. It's a pleasant 30-min stroll south to the dive centre at Breezes, or simply to burn up some excess calories. The food is beautifully presented and all guests stay on a FB basis (excluding bar drinks).

Southeast Zanzibar **MICHAMVI PENINSULA**

10

221

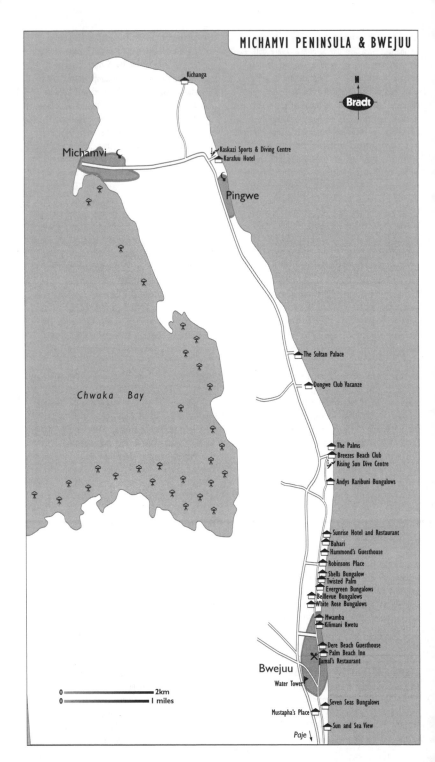

MICHAMVI PENINSULA & BWEJUU

Bradt

Kichanga

Michamvi

Kaskazi Sports & Diving Centre
Karafuu Hotel

Pingwe

Chwaka Bay

The Sultan Palace

Dongwe Club Vacanze

The Palms
Breezes Beach Club
Rising Sun Dive Centre

Andys Karibuni Bungalows

Sunrise Hotel and Restaurant
Bahari
Hammond's Guesthouse
Robinsons Place
Shells Bungalow
Twisted Palm
Evergreen Bungalows
Belllevue Bungalows
White Rose Bungalows

Mwamba
Kilimani Kwetu

Dere Beach Guesthouse
Palm Beach Inn
Jamal's Restaurant

Bwejuu

Water Tower

Seven Seas Bungalows

Mustapha's Place

Sun and Sea View

Paje

0 ——————— 2km
0 ——————— 1 miles

B/fast is served on the main terrace or in the comfort of your bed; delicious lunches of barbecued fish, curries and salads are then served on a cool, shaded platform by the beach, whilst dinner is a more formal candlelit affair on the upper floor of the main building. The atmosphere here is quiet and sophisticated, but not stuffy. Its rooms and setting are deeply romantic making it an excellent honeymoon spot, though pre-dinner drinks at the bar are invariably social, giving Sultan's a friendly but not overpowering atmosphere. Popular with Italian visitors, Sultan's is busy around Christmas and Aug, but away from these peak seasons it's very good value for the quality it offers. *Ocean/Garden Suite US$165/290 pp, dbl, low/high season; Imperial Suite US$200/380 pp, dbl, low/high season. Children under 2 free; under 12 50% of adult rate. All rates are FB. Payment in local or major currencies. VISA and MasterCard accepted without surcharge. Open Jul–Mar.*

🏠 **Dongwe Club Vacanze** (76 rooms) PO Box 1283, Zanzibar; ☎ 024 2240251; f 024 2250253; e dongwe.dir@zanzinet.com (⊕ CLUBVA 6°10.971'S; 39°31.682'E). If the name Club Vacanze doesn't give away this resort's origins, entering the vast makuti structure of the rectangular reception area will. Noticeboards in Italian display the 'Dongwe Club Programma', listing numerous timed activities throughout the day. At the time of researching, an exuberant Italian could be heard over the tannoy cheering on a kayak-racing competition in the nautilus-shaped pool. This is an all-action, family-friendly, unquestionably Mediterranean, holiday spot. Mountain biking and beach volleyball are available on the beach, whilst diving, snorkelling and countless other watersports are arranged for the seafaring. A DVD 'cinema' offers an escape from the sun. Aside from the emphasis on activities, this is a smart complex. Luxurious red and white fabrics cover the traditional Zanzibari beds standing on the cool tiled floor of the reception; welcome drinks are enjoyed on groups of green-cushioned, wooden sofas looking out across the resort's gardens; walking around the resort it is impossible not to notice the beautifully tended walkways and carefully planted kitchen garden borders. There are 74 rooms here, of which 4 are suites. The spacious standards have good-quality, solid wood furniture with huge wardrobes and cheerful turquoise soft furnishings. Each has a twin/dbl bed with mosquito nets, AC, a minibar, safe, telephone, hairdryer and, naturally in a resort of this size, 24hr electricity and hot water. Close by, but perpendicular to, the beach, the suites are accessed

along neat paths lined with bougainvillea being trained into low colourful hedges. Surrounded by established hibiscus bushes and with inviting rocking chairs on their terraces, these are tastefully decorated bungalows. The cream and orange interior includes a large bedroom with a huge bed and satellite TV, a separate lounge and a bathroom. The only (debatable) negative is the red light chosen to light the jacuzzi room. The all-inclusive restaurant offers international food with an Italian twist and usually hosts a weekly Swahili theme night. Soft drinks and beer are included in the rates. *Standard US$164–190 sgl or US$204–257 dbl; suite US$329–382. Children up to 2: free; 2–12 up to 50% discount.*

🏠 **The Palms** (6 rooms) PO Box 1298, Zanzibar; ☎ 0777 437007; f 0748 203093; e info@palms-zanzibar.com; www.palms-zanzibar.com. Immediately adjacent to Breezes and owned by the same family, The Palms is significantly more exclusive and expensive. With just 6 large, luxurious villas, Palms attracts young, affluent, honeymooners lured by privacy, image and intimacy. This is certainly a small, stylish option, but although the resort area is private, it's important to remember that it sits immediately next door to a family-friendly, 70-room resort, and everyone shares the same beach: romantic dinners for 2 on the sand may be subject to intrusion. Palms set out to achieve 'understated elegance', and this has broadly been achieved. The colonnaded Plantation House is the main resort building, housing its bar/lounge, dining room and mezzanine library. Here, antique cabinets, carved dark-wood sofas and natural palm mats rest on highly polished floors, while heavy old-fashioned fans spin in the high makuti thatch. The cappuccino and cream cushions, billowing organza curtains and afternoon tea on the deck complete the colonial feel. At the ocean end of the building, tarnished mirrors and candles fill a dining room set with ever-changing colours of linen, sparkling crystal glasses and simple flower arrangements. Individually named after exotic spices, the whitewashed villas sport shaggy thatch roofs and a large curved front terrace. Through the wide French doors, there is a lounge area with picture windows revealing the bedroom beyond. Decorated in chocolate brown, cream and apricot, with Arabian brass lanterns and wooden furniture, the huge rooms are classically elegant but feature all mod-cons: AC, minibar, safe, satellite TV and DVD player. There's an en-suite bathroom with a bath and even a private outdoor jacuzzi. The villas share a small, split-level, tiled swimming pool, and each is also allocated a private *banda* overlooking the beach. Makuti shades draped with panels of indigo fabric make these a good place to escape the heat of the day and survey the beach beyond. For most activities, head to the bigger facilities at neighbouring Breezes, though Palms does have a tiny spa, The Sanctuary. *US$615–695 sgl; US$830–990 dbl; Easter and Christmas suppt US$40 pp/day. All rates FB. Min age 16.*

⌂ **Breezes Beach Club & Spa** (70 rooms) PO Box 1361, Zanzibar; ☏ 0777 440883–5; f 024 2240450; e info@breezes-zanzibar.com; www.breezes-zanzibar.com (⊕ BREEZE 6°11.717'S; 39°31.968'E). A perennial favourite with honeymooners and families, Breezes is a large, efficient, family-run beach resort. Amid extensive, colourful gardens, there are 70 rooms in whitewashed villas virtually identical in size and interior, decorated in muted neutral colours, and with all the amenities of a good hotel. The rooms are comfortably furnished with large beds, and all have AC, en-suite bathroom, hairdryer, safe, fridge, and sofa-bed, but deliberately no telephones and TVs. The suite and deluxe categories are closer to the sea, and are upstairs and downstairs respectively. The suite also features a walk-in dressing room, slightly larger bathroom and wrap-around balcony with sun loungers. There is a large swimming pool at the centre of the resort, surrounded by verdant green grass, and a great stretch of sandy beach. Tall palms and makuti umbrellas offer shade at both, and wooden loungers are comfortable for reading and relaxing. The Rising Sun Dive Centre is based between the beach and pool. Independently owned and run, it's a fully kitted out, friendly PADI dive centre. Watersports from windsurfing to pedalos are easily arranged here, alongside an array of dive courses and trips. Or escape the sun to watch one of the daily DVD cinema shows on a big screen, or play pool, darts, cards or one of the available board games. The newly opened Frangipani Spa is another great retreat. Modern treatment rooms, a calm candlelit relaxation room, a deep private jacuzzi, a steam room, and a team of Thai and Balinese professional masseuses ensure you leave purified and pampered. Entertaining, and appropriate, treatments, inc the 'Kili Foot Treatment' and the 'Après Safari Treatment', allude to most guests' pre-beach safari. For indulgent couples, there's an enchanting private spa for 2. The yoga studio (which had a genuine yogi when we visited), fitness centre and floodlit tennis court complete the spiritual and physical well-being offered. There's a baffling number of restaurants: the Salama Dining Room for b/fast and the evening table d'hôte; the Makuti Restaurant offering à la carte seafood, and Breakers on the beach for those in need of lunchtime sustenance. The intimate Sultan's Table offers Indian cuisine in a wood-panelled tower filled with red velvet cushions and brass lanterns; or there's private dining for 2 in a carved beach hut, The Tides, complete with its own chandelier. Note that dinner at the smaller restaurants is charged as an extra, and not included in the HB rates. For a cocktail and bar snack, the shady Pool Bar is a fun spot, with soft sand on the floor, coir-rope sofas and smiling staff in funky indigo-blue batik shirts. By night, the sophisticated and atmospheric Baraza Bar is a cool drinking den: shrouded in cream and apricot silk and organza, it offers whisky, liqueurs and cigars. Beach weddings, which must be arranged in advance, are increasingly popular here. An altar shaded by fresh palm fronds and white bougainvillea will be erected for such ceremonies. *All rates are HB. Sgl occupancy only available in deluxe class at US$130–190. Standard US$160–250dbl, deluxe US$200–320dbl, suite US$250–370dbl. Easter and Christmas suppt US$40 adult/day and US$20 child/day. Children under 2 stay free.*

**WHAT TO DO AND SEE** With many of the hotels on this stretch offering a gamut of activities in idyllic grounds, few visitors need step outside their own resort in search of entertainment. Divers, however, may need to head to a neighbouring property for use of a dive centre. Although these are aimed mostly at hotel guests, it's commonplace for visitors to arrange dives in this manner, and any hotel will be able to assist. Excluding the one at the Italian-speaking, all-inclusive Club Vacanze, the dive schools on the peninsula follow.

↙ **Rising Sun Dive Centre** PO Box 479, Zanzibar; ☏ 0777 440883–5/88; fax 0741 333151; e bookings@risingsun-zanzibar.com; www.risingsun-zanzibar.com (⊕ BREEZE 6°11.717'S; 39°31.968'E). This smart, efficient company is based on the edge of the beach at Breezes Beach Club, but is independently owned and operated. The enthusiastic English manager, Paul Shepherd, is a great east coast fan with a passion for underwater photography. The dive school is geared

Seaweed has been harvested by coastal dwellers for centuries. This practice led to the export of red seaweed from Zanzibar to Europe in the 1950s, and continued until the wild stocks became exhausted. However, since the late 1980s, several development organisations and private companies have been working with Zanzibar's north and east coastal communities to develop and promote the commercial cultivation of seaweed. Providing initial funding, seedlings and technical skills, the aim is to encourage sustainable resource management, an essential prerequisite for long-term economic growth and employment, particularly for women. Currently 10,000 people are engaged in seaweed farming which provides much needed household income for many coastal workers. The revenue from this trade is also a great foreign-exchange earner for Zanzibar's economy.

Seaweed is used commercially as a source of carrageenan, a natural gelling agent produced from it by alkaline extraction. Used in the manufacture of toothpaste, cosmetics, medicine and also as a thickening agent in many food products, particularly some which are milk-based, this is a valuable, natural product.

With real market demand, several species of seaweed are now farmed, though the most common are the reliable, profitable strains of *Eucheuma cottonii, E. denticulatum* and *E. spinosum*. By hammering stakes into the sandy inter-tidal zone, and stretching lines of coir rope or nylon monoline a foot above the sea bed, cultivation lines are prepared and small seaweed stems are attached. Each plot can have up to 50 rows of strings 30cm apart, each line carrying 10 to 15 cuttings. The seaweed grows at a rate of 7% per day, increasing to tenfold its original weight in a fortnight. This rapid growth allows farmers to harvest their crop every two months; a total of 697kg of seaweed is harvested annually per farmer, earning them an average US$36.42 each in 2005.

The seaweed is then dried in the sun for a few days, bagged, and sold to seaweed brokers who transport it to Zanzibar Town and onwards to Europe. Replanting of seedlings can be done immediately, using fragments from the old crop, ensuring sustained farming and income. The Tanzania Coastal Management Partnership hopes that, by 2007, the country's export will leap to more than eight thousand tons.

The personal income generated from seaweed farming has significantly helped to improve many villagers' standard of living. In many parts of Africa, farming has been traditionally regarded as women's work, and this remains the case with seaweed farming on Zanzibar. Consequently, much of the money earned stays in the hands of these rural women, who would not normally have their own source of income. The advent of seaweed farming has resulted in many having a degree of freedom and empowerment previously impossible. Money is often used for school fees, house improvements, kitchenware or even luxuries like radios and cassette players. The villagers of Paje have collectively built two day-care centres for their children with their profits. Thus, sustained trade in these fast-growing marine algae may just be a viable way out of poverty for many Zanzibari families.

to taking both beginners and experienced divers looking for PADI speciality courses. Using ⊕ and Echosounder technology, several brand-new sites have been discovered, and the team are always keen to show experienced divers some underwater treasures very rarely visited by other companies. Snorkelling and fishing trips can also be arranged here, along with skippered boat rental and speedboat trips to the mangrove forests. *US$55/110/300/450 for 1/2/6/10 dive packages; night dive US$70; PADI Open Water certification course inc equipt US$480; PADI Digital Photography certification course inc equipt US$310; daily equipt rental (regulator, BCD, wet* suit, mask & fins) US$30; underwater digital camera rental (inc CD of images) US$40.

**Kaskazi Sports Centre** PO Box 71, Pingwe, Zanzibar; ☏ 0777 415447; f 0741 325670; e zanzibarsurf@yahoo.com; www.kaskazi.net. Kaskazi Sports Centre is within the Karafuu Hotel complex. Run by the enthusiastic Franco and Andrea, it has all the latest branded equipt, and offers everything from PADI diving to windsurf courses, kite-surfing, canoeing and mountain biking. Diving US$60/100 sgl/dbl; US$220/310/590 for 4/6/12 dive packages; PADI Open Water certification course is US$500 inc textbook. Windsurf hire US$30/70 for 1/3 hrs; kite-surfing US$190 for 6hrs.

# BWEJUU

Bwejuu is about 4km north of Paje. Sitting just back from the beach, the village itself is a dense network of dusty alleys and houses, interspersed with towering palm trees. This is a quiet area, excellent for escapism, where the only sound you'll hear outside the village is the wind rustling in the trees. The tide goes out for miles, and there's a great feeling of space. The local people do some fishing, and the women make rope from coconut husks, but seaweed farming is the major industry here. Unlike some of the other coastal villages, the hotels in Bwejuu seem comfortable within the village, and don't dominate it, so there's a still very traditional atmosphere.

North of the village, towards Michamvi, there are still a few huts and houses dotted among the palms, but generally speaking the local population thins out and, in their place, you'll find a wide choice of places to stay. The beach here is beautiful, and the water its customary deep turquoise, making this an ideal place to relax for anything from a day to a week.

**GETTING THERE AND AWAY** From Paje by car, there are two possible routes north to Bwejuu (✪ *PALMBE 6°14.087'S; 39°32.007'E*): a narrow, bumpy, dusty coastal track that wanders between village huts and palm trees until just south of Breezes Beach Club (✪ *BREEZE 6°11.717'S; 39°31.968'E*) and a wider, gravel road that runs parallel, less than 100m inland. The sandy coastal track is certainly more interesting, and a good bet if you're looking speculatively for somewhere to stay, but it's not for faint-hearted drivers: children and chickens regularly dart across the road, and navigation through Bwejuu village's dusty tracks is tricky and often without room for a three-point turn! If you're on foot or bicycle, hit the beach and enjoy the sea breeze as you travel.

*Dala-dala* number 9 leaves Zanzibar Town for Paje three times a day, and often travels onwards to Bwejuu: check with the individual drivers as some will turn south at Paje for Jambiani.

From Bwejuu and the beaches north, for independent and adventurous travellers who want to avoid back-tracking around Chwaka Bay yet continue north up the coast, it's possible to take a local fishing boat from Michamvi across to Chwaka.

 **WHERE TO STAY** Spanning several kilometres, this area has something to cater to almost every taste and budget. The accommodation options below have been divided between those in the immediate vicinity of the village, and those strung out along the coast to the north of the main settlement.

## Bwejuu village

**Sun and Sea View Resort** (8 rooms) PO Box 3881, Zanzibar; ☏ 0777 420774/0748 470628; e ssvresort@hotmail.com (✪ SUNSEA 6°14.876'S; 39°32.059'E). Covering a large, open plot beside the beach, this is a quiet corner. At the end of the entrance path, a rough-hewn, pink coral-stone building houses the reception and restaurant area. It's a relaxed place with cheerful African music playing at the bar and neat tables set with green tablecloths and fresh bougainvillea in vases. The large whitewashed rondavels contain 2, independent en-suite rooms. Simple and clean, they have white tiled floors, fresh linen on the beds, nets, mains electricity with UK-style 3-pin sockets and, curiously, a freestanding fan mounted to the ceiling. A desk and wicker-style chair covered in hide complete the look. Unusually for many budget rooms, there's plenty of natural light from 3 large windows, and a bath as well as shower in the en-suite bathroom. As there is no gate to the property, self-drivers may prefer to opt for a more physically secure option. *US$25/40 sgl/dbl.*

🏠 **Mustapha's Nest** (7 rooms) PO Box 3414, Zanzibar; ✆ 024 220069; ℮ mustaphas @ africamail.com; www.fatflatfish.co.uk/mustaphas (✪ MUSTAP 6°14.76'S; 39°32.053'E). Set back from beach, across the sandy road, Mustapha's Nest is long-established as a totally chilled, slightly eccentric hangout. Its name bears reference to both its Rastafarian owner Mustapha, and the site's overwhelming population of bright yellow weaver birds. Carefully constructed nests belonging to the latter drip from every available branch and these chirping little birds have become so iconic that they now adorn the signpost and staff T-shirts. Set around a neat, sandy circle (complete with bonfire and miscellaneous pieces of coir-rope and wood furniture) are 6 small, uniquely decorated *bandas*, with an additional room set further back. Inside, the white adobe walls are decorated with brightly painted patterns or pictures, and colourful *kangas* are used to cover the solid beds and as curtains. The floors and surfaces of the en-suite bathroom are a mosaic of different tile sizes, shapes and colours, with miscellaneous plants sprouting from soil-filled bottles and deliberately placed holes in the floor. This crude back-to-nature feel will not suit everyone. The 2-storey bar and restaurant area is as laid back as the reggae tunes it plays, and is repeatedly praised for its food. *Camping (illegal on the island) US$5; rooms US$15 sgl and US$30–50 dbl.*

🏠 **Seven Seas Bungalows** (9 rooms) PO Box 2330, Zanzibar (✪ SEVENS 6°14.706'S; 39°32.045'E). Once acceptable, this place is now in some disrepair. Local people are still willing to rent out rooms, but they are increasingly basic. Seven Seas' only asset is its location right on the beach, although not a particularly pleasant bit of it.

🏠 **Palm Beach Inn** (13 rooms) PO Box 704, Zanzibar; ✆ 024 2240221/0777 411155/0777 414666; f 024 2233597; ℮ mahfudh28 @ hotmail.com (✪ PALMBE 6°14.087'S; 39°32.007'E). In the heart of Bwejuu, sandwiched between the dusty village track and the beach, Palm Beach Inn sits behind a high, secure gate. Opened in 1990 by Niala Jadawi, a local girl and influential former MP, this is a real hotchpotch of a place. The management make an admirable effort to employ Bwejuu residents, particularly single mothers and the disadvantaged. The key employees are friendly and helpful, but there are also a high number of women wandering around – gardening, cleaning, or seemingly just ambling through – which adds to the distinctly local feel of the place. Separate cottages as well as rooms in a central building house 8 dbls, 2 twins, 1 tpl and a family room. Each is individually named after a marine animal or fish and doors are marked with carefully hand-painted signs of the corresponding creature. All the rooms have 24hr mains electricity, sockets with a universal adapter, mosquito nets over the beds, fans and efficient AC, a fridge and an en-suite toilet with a hot-water shower. Wooden boxes, painted with red and yellow flames, tidy fire extinguishers neatly away outside each room. Kamilo's suite, with its sea view and tiny lounge area, is viewed as the best room, but this depends upon your taste. Its interior has the décor of a budget Indian restaurant: heavy claret and gold sofas, a large brass, mock-Victorian kettle on the dresser, plastic beaded curtains separating the wardrobe area, floral velour-covered chairs, a large clock, and curiously, a Constable-esque picture of haystacks in Kent. If you subscribe to minimalist design, angle the freestanding fan, lie on the semadari bed and close your eyes, or alternatively hit the bar! The split-level, circular dining room is capable of seating 40, and there are easy chairs in a lounge area where games and cards are available. Although there are windows facing the sea, the restaurant is enclosed on all sides to give shelter from the evening wind. Most guests stay here on a b&b basis, but other basic meals are available: the staple fish, vegetable and rice dishes of the island (special fried prawns with rice and vegetables US$10). There is a large menu but, as is often the case, it's invariably only the 'specials' menu that shows what's available that day. Order food as early as possible to increase chances of it being available, and accept that service is slow. There's a well-stocked bar of beer and spirits to ease the wait. The nursery planting is striking all around this little complex: low timber trellis fencing is adorned with white bottles, each sprouting young climbing plants. Clearly the aim is to create lush hedging; it has a long way to grow. The rest of the area is divided into beds filled with miscellaneous cacti, frangipani and large-leafed climbers. The gardens are also home to two very old tortoises, a sizeable pigeon coop, and a few wooden tables with blue and yellow wrought-iron chairs. Like the bottled plants, Palm Beach has the general appearance of trying to cram too much into too small an area, making it feel cluttered and a little oppressive. Although it's located beside the ocean, there is a fence between the lodge area and the beach. Loungers are above the beach, not on it, and the staff are keen to warn guests not to take valuables onto the beach. As well as potential issues of theft, the beach immediately outside the property is strewn with sharp coral rock,

and litter caused by its proximity to dense village settlement. Think twice about a night-time stroll on the beach too, as high-speed motorbikes are known to bypass the bumpy village lanes, by taking to the sand. *US$40/50 sgl low/high season, US$60/70 dbl low/high season and US$75/95 tpl, low/high season, b&b. Kamilo's suite US$100/120 b&b, low/high.*

⌂ **Dere Beach Guesthouse** PO Box 270; ↘ 024 2240197 (⊕ DEREBE 6°14.038'S; 39°31.999'E). Once a reasonable backpacker haunt, this place has now completely degenerated. In the centre of the village, the beach immediately in front of the guesthouse is covered in litter, far from the east coast's pristine image, and the whole place has a generally unkempt look and an unpleasant air.

## North of Bwejuu village

⌂ **Kilimani Kwetu Restaurant & Bungalows** (4 rooms) PO Box 2647, Zanzibar; ↘ 0777 465243 (⊕ KILIMA 6°13.786'S; 39°31.92'E). Opened in 1994 as a partnership between 5 Germans, led by Dirk Rabien, and the village of Bwejuu, Kilimani Kwetu is rooted in community development. Built by local people, from local materials, on a gentle hill to the north of the village, overlooking the sea, this is a relaxed, hassle-free spot, with a positive impact on those who live in the area. Wadi and a delightfully friendly local team manage Kilimani Kwetu and are happy to help any visitors. There are 4 rooms — 2 dbls and 2 twins — in 2 white, thatched bungalows. Surrounded by palms and sweet almond trees, the rooms are basic and uninspiring, and in need of some care and attention. They have concrete floors, simple furniture, 2 deckchairs, mosquito nets, and en-suite bathrooms with a cold-water shower and clean squat, flush toilet. Electricity is available and there's a traditional well on-site. The neat restaurant serves fresh fish and vegetarian dishes on request, and b/fast boasts homemade tropical fruit jams and locally produced honey. Take any one of several zigzag paths, 50m to the sea, and there's a private beach area for guests, with makuti umbrellas and deckchairs. Development projects centred at Kilimani Kwetu have successfully financed the construction of an adult education centre and library, and, until its recent move to Bellevue Bungalows, this place was the centre for the local women's sewing co-operative. *US$15/35 sgl/dbl, b&b.*

⌂ **Mwamba Bungalows Village** (4 rooms) PO Box 1238, Zanzibar; ↘ 0777 840804; e dmwambal @yahoo.com (⊕ MWAMBA 6°13.746'S; 39°31.928'E). Opened in Feb 2005 by Khamis and Daniella, a Zanzibari–Slovakian Rastafarian couple,

Mwamba straddles the main village road. In time, it is hoped that the track will move behind the accommodation and unite the property but, at the time of writing, its 2 simple bungalows sit to the west and a couple of smaller *bandas* to the east. The bungalows are basic but clean and colourfully decorated with paintings and fabrics. Each has a Zanzibari bed, mains electricity, and a small en-suite bathroom with flush toilet and shower. Open the makuti shutters and it's instantly apparent that most of the effort going into establishing Mwamba is being directed at the garden, where large, lush plants are being introduced and cultivated. On-site activities are limited to a few cement-filled cans that have been turned into dumb-bells. *Banda US$10 pp, b&b; bungalows US$30 dbl, b&b.*

⌂ **White Rose Bungalows** (6 rooms) ↘ 0777 469824 (⊕ WHITER 6°13.574'S; 39°31.941'E). White Rose Bungalows re-opened in 2006 after a complete refurbishment. Its 3 white stone bungalows are set on a slope, above the coconut line, and benefit from tremendous sea views from their elevated position. Each of the 6 spacious rooms has a newly tiled entrance, sparkling green painted concrete floor, 2 ³/₄ beds and an en-suite bathroom with European flush toilet and hot-water shower. It's a peaceful place set back from the beach but with pleasant landscaping, inc sapling sweet almonds and poinsettia, several makuti sun umbrellas and coir-rope chairs dotted around. During the refurbishment and closure, the central bar, the 'First and Last bar and restaurant', was furnished with a stack of amplifiers and being used as a temporary local disco. Hopefully, these public areas will soon come to match the standard seen in the new rooms. There's a secure parking area making this a great option for self-drivers. *Rates not yet available at the time of writing.*

⌂ **Bellevue Bungalows** (4 rooms) PO Box 364, Zanzibar; ✆ 0777 465271; e bellevue01@hotmail.com/ christian.rask@kabelnettet.dk; www.geocities.com/bellevue_zan2 (✪ BELLEV 6°13.476'S; 39°31.949'E). Up steep steps from the road, on the top of coral rock, this is a thoroughly relaxed, gentle place. Over the last 2 years, a great deal of work has gone into establishing pretty gardens and in Oct 2005, a Danish couple, Iben and Christian, began renting the guesthouse. Working closely with the charming local owners, Mussa and Chulla, they plan to renovate and redesign the buildings and interiors by mid 2006. They plan for the 4 clean and spacious, dbl rooms to retain their fabulous outlook, cooling breeze, dbl beds and en-suite bathrooms but to gain new, bright Swahili fabrics and possibly electricity (the sockets are already wired in place) and hot water. Having previously spent 3 years working with local NGOs in the area, the new management team rate community development and inclusion as important. Christian trained as a chef in Copenhagen and has plans to work with the existing local chef, Chulla, to combine European and Swahili cuisine in meals (they're aiming at US$5–7). Scrumptious b/fasts are planned with spice-infused juices, fresh bread bought from the villagers, locally produced honey and homemade jams. There are also plans to build a fair-trade shop selling local crafts and 'Malkia' creations (www.malkia.dk). Founded by Iben, Malkia is a co-operative where women learn to design and sew children's clothes. These are currently being sold in upmarket Danish boutiques with a significant percentage of profits being invested back into the local school. *US$17/22 sgl low/high season; US$30/35 dbl low/high season. All rates are b&b.*

⌂ **Evergreen Bungalows** (11 rooms) PO Box 483, Bwejuu, Zanzibar; ✆ 024 2240273; e zanzievergreen@yahoo.com; www.evergreen-bungalows.com (✪ EVERGR 6°13.327'S; 39°31.956'E). There are 11 rooms in 2-storey beach bungalows here: those upstairs are in the apex of the makuti thatch and are accessed by steps at the front of the chalet. These rooms are extremely simple with a distant shared toilet. There are no real windows, though the open-weave palm mesh of the front does allow some light and air to penetrate. Downstairs, the rooms are much lighter and better, with solid walls, simple wooden furniture, clean bedding, mosquito nets and a cold-water en-suite bathroom.

There is no mains electricity here, but some solar powered lighting is provided at night. The central bar and restaurant is airy and spacious, and snacks and meals are available throughout the day. African Blue Divers is based here, although at the time of visiting the tanks were baking out in the sun with their valve caps off, and no dive instructors were on site. PADI courses (Open Water US$350) can apparently be arranged, but are currently being taught at Big Ocean Diver's classroom in Paje. There is a 5–10% discount for diving with your own equipt, though you may feel more comfortable simply going elsewhere. *Beach bungalow (en-suite) US$32/45/60 sgl/dbl/tpl; beach bungalow (shared bathroom) US$20/30 sgl/dbl; palm grove bungalow US$30/40/55 sgl/dbl/tpl; 4-bed banda US$15 pp. All rates are b&b.*

⌂ **Twisted Palm** (11 rooms) ✆ 024 2240060 (✪ TWISTE 6°13.292'S; 39°31.959'E). Currently being run by the Rasta couple from Mwamba Bungalows (above), this former backpacker stronghold is now distinctly tired and dreary. Six dbl rooms sit in stone-and-thatch bungalows on the beach, whilst another 5 rooms (2 tpls and 3 dbls) are set back on a small hill. There are no fans or AC here but the rooms do have mosquito nets, electricity (from a generator) between 18.00 and midnight, and en-suite bathrooms with European flush toilets and cold-water showers. The upstairs restaurant in the rundown main house closed in late 2005 and now sits on stilts above the sea instead. There is a daily set menu and, in theory, alternatives may be possible with enough notice. There is no safe deposit, the first-aid kit is lost and the fire extinguisher is kept down the road in the village, so this is probably not the place for those who are very safety conscious. *Beach bungalows US$20–40 low/high season; hill bungalows US20–30 low/high season.*

⌂ **Shells Bungalow** (4 rooms) PO Box 4663; ✆ 0748 310980 (✪ SHELLS 6°13.268'S; 39°31.967'E). All 4 rooms here are named after Tanzanian places — Arusha, Manyara, Serengeti and Kilimanjaro. Although they're a little rough on the outside, each is in fact large and clean, with a big dbl bed, some basic furniture and an adequate en-suite bathroom with flush toilet and cold-water shower. Hand-painted flowers around the windows and tinga-tinga pictures show thoughtful decorating attempts, and a generator providing electricity at night does make getting around easier. There's a good stretch of white-sand beach here, where hammocks under shady palms and no hassle make for a relaxed atmosphere. There's an extensive menu but don't be fooled as only fish and vegetables are actually available, and it's probably best to order in the morning if you want to eat dinner. *US$15/30 sgl/dbl, b&b.*

⌂ **Robinson's Place** (5 rooms) PO Box 3999, Zanzibar; ☎ 0777 413479; e robinsonsplace@hotmail.com; www.robinsonsplace.com (✪ ROBINS 6°13.162'S; 39°31.965'E). This is a delightfully off-beat family home set in lovely mature gardens, beside a superb beach. To Ann and Ahmed, the fascinating European–Zanzibari couple who own and run the place, being here is about a particular lifestyle choice rather than business, hence you can expect a very friendly welcome, a gentle and relaxed pace, but none of the trappings of a commercial lodge. Robinson's does its best to be fairly self-sufficient – keeping chickens across the road and growing tropical fruit. Simple meals are served either under the trees or on rugs and cushions on the floor in the main lounge area. There is no electricity here, so all cooking is done on open fires. In an effort to conserve wood, the only hot meal of the day is dinner. (For lunch, guests often wander along the beach to Sunrise or Breezes where for a fee they can also enjoy a dip in their pools.) Its 5 rooms cater for a max of 12 people so advance booking is invariably necessary. All rooms are very different in style and are divided amongst 2 small houses and a Robinson-Crusoe-esque, 2-storey treehouse. The master bedroom in the main house is a huge room with a dbl and a ³/₄ bed, bright fabrics, and vases filled with flowers. It is the only room with an en-suite bathroom, and this is spotless. Attached, but not interconnected, the main house 'guest bedroom' is a small but pretty room with a ³/₄ bed, a day-bed and vibrant orange linen. The proximity and contained feel of these 2 rooms make the house perfect for a family with older children. House Bondeni, literally meaning 'house in the corner', is a lovely, airy, 'L'-shaped room with white walls, cheerful *kangas* on both the European and Zanzibari dbl beds, and brightly coloured, woven palm mats on the floor. The pièce de résistance is Robinson's House, a rough-hewn, wattle-and-daub, 2-storey affair under a large tree on the edge of the beach. Upstairs is a basic but fun 'honeymoon suite' where the dbl bed looks out through the trees to the ocean and rainbow-coloured fabrics billow along the open sides. Downstairs is a small, clean sgl room with its own sea view. All rooms, except the master, share immaculate bathroom facilities. There are 2 cold-water showers and 2 toilets (1 European style and 1 squat), each separated by stylish cream curtains, and a large open-ended central area with mirrors and sinks. These are cleaner and more pleasant than many of the en-suite facilities offered by Zanzibar's more mid-range properties! Several resident dogs roam the property as effective security guards. *Master room US$50/60 low/high season; guest bedroom US$30; House Bondeni and Robinson's 'Honeymoon suite' US$40/45 low/high season; sgl room US$20. All rates b&b. High season 20 Dec–7 Jan, plus Jul and Aug. Dinner US$7. Payment in local or international currency. Open Jun–Apr.*

⌂ **Hammond's Guesthouse** (4 rooms) No contact details. (✪ HAMMON 6°13.019'S; 39°31.971'E). In a dilapidated house by the beach, there is an assortment of sgl and dbl rooms; some en-suite, some with shared facilities. At the time of visiting, Hammond's had ceased to take guests, though this may change in the future. In any case, there are plenty more pleasant and reliable options in the area.

⌂ **Gomani Bungalows** (2 rooms) No contact details. Neighbouring Hammond's Guesthouse to the south, Gomani has 2 basic bungalows. With inadequate staffing, no electricity and only cold water available, this is a pretty primitive option. *US$8–15 pp, room only.*

⌂ **Bahari Beach Village** (6 rooms) PO Box 4245, Zanzibar; ☎ 0777 858934; e sandrawelsing@hotmail.com (✪ BAHARI 6°12.832'S; 39°31.993'E). Opened in 2003 by a local from Bwejuu, Bahari is now being managed by a German lady, Sandra. There are 4 rooms in 2 bungalows, each with dbl bed, en-suite facilities and good sea views, plus a sgl and a dbl room inside the main house where Sandra lives which are also en-suite. There's no electricity or hot water, but the latter can be arranged if needed. The hexagonal bar/restaurant area opens onto a pleasant beach area which slopes down to the sea. There's a selection of good rope hammocks and a dbl swinging chair hung between 2 substantial palms; both provide unobstructed views of sea, or a place to study the communal German–Swahili dictionary. *Bungalows US$30 dbl, b&b; villa rooms US$20 b&b.*

⌂ **Sunrise Hotel and Restaurant** (13 rooms) PO Box 3967; ☎ 024 2240270/0777 415240; f 024 2240170; e sunrise@zanlink.com; www.sunrise-zanzibar.com (✪ SUNRIS 6°12.819'S; 39°31.998'E). Opened on 1 Jan 1994 by a Belgian chef, Georges Noël, Sunrise is an understated, relaxed old-style beach hotel, offering excellent-value accommodation on a good stretch of beach, and fabulous food. Hop over the decorative, canary-yellow hump-back bridge into the large thatched central bar and dining area, pull out one of the neatly arranged bar stools, place an order with the professional staff and enjoy some good old-fashioned customer service. There are 13 rooms, 8 pleasant bungalows facing the sea and 5 standard rooms in a row at the back of the main building. None is fancy, but they are all comfortable, clean, en-suite and reasonably priced. Both the standard rooms and bungalows are available with Zanzibari beds or European twin/dbls. Additional sgl beds are available for families using the bungalows. All the en-suite bathrooms were retiled in 2004, and all rooms have 24hr national-grid electricity, 3-pin UK-style sockets, a fan and mosquito nets. There is a back-up generator and emergency security lanterns in case of power failure. The water is slightly brackish but free bottled water is provided. A new safe is available at reception for valuables. The food here is reason enough to check in, and do so on a room-only basis to indulge in the à la carte menu. Head chef Richard Kicongwe and his excellent team prepare outstanding gourmet food on site; this is certainly some of the best food on Zanzibar, and sure to woo even the most jaded diners (see *Where to eat* section). There is a fairly large sheltered swimming pool, bikes to rent for beach cycling, local massage for US$10/hr, and free internet and WiFi access. Diving and snorkelling excursions can easily be arranged through Karafuu Hotel or Breezes Beach Club, the latter being only a 20-min stroll along the beach. Sunrise is highly recommended for children: an increasing number of families are staying here because of its price and pool. Babysitting is also easily arranged as most of the friendly staff are happy to make the extra money. *Standard room US$65/75/95 sgl/dbl/tpl,*

*b&b; bungalow US$80/90/110 sgl/dbl/tpl, b&b. Children under 2 free; 2–12 US$10/night sharing with parents. HB suppt US$25/15 adult/child. Local and foreign currency accepted; 10% surcharge credit cards; 5% surcharge travellers' cheques. Open Jun–Apr.*

🏠 **Andy's Karibuni Bungalows & Romantic Garden** (2 rooms) PO Box 650, Zanzibar; ✆ 0748 430942; e romantic-garden@web.de/nussera@web.de; www.eastzanzibar.com (✪ ANDYSK 6°12.194'S; 39°32.059'E). Away from the village, this tranquil place is owned and run by a well-travelled Hungarian, Andrea, with help from a friendly team of locals and 7 obedient dogs. There is currently only one bungalow here, divided into 2 independent en-suite dbl rooms. These are light, bright and airy with neatly painted ceiling beams, sparkling terracotta floor tiles, and cheerful orange café curtains. Each room has a large, low, kingsize bed, shrouded in a powder-blue mosquito net, and onto which blankets and towels are neatly piled. There is a spotless en-suite toilet and cold-water shower. Carefully woven tabletops make great rests for reading books, while coat stands act as space-saving wardrobes. Outside, a small terrace area looks over the pretty, shaded gardens towards the beach. Beautiful bougainvillea, hibiscus and other blossoming tropical plants surround the compound, attracting small birds and butterflies, and making for a pleasantly green setting. Andy's is simply a place to relax by the beach, read, walk and enjoy the peaceful setting; don't come here for a multitude of activities. There is a generator for electricity, though this is only occasionally used to power lights in the evening. The restaurant is a casual affair offering local produce, best ordered in advance, cooked simply but well. *US$40/60/75 sgl/dbl/tpl, b&b. Payment preferred in US$.*

🍴 **WHERE TO EAT** Nearly all of the hotels cater for guests and non-residents alike (see individual listings). In addition, there are a few small shops and local-style eating houses in the village itself. One of each category particularly worth noting are:

✗ **Jamal's Restaurant** No contact details. (✪ PALMBE 6°14.087'S; 39°32.007'E). Immediately opposite Palm Beach Inn, this has been recommended by several travellers. In spite of a sign implying that it's operational from 07.00 to 24.00, Jamal's opening is erratic at best and seemingly only in high season. No-one was around during our lunchtime visit, though an inside desk advertised Jamal Tours and Travels Ltd in addition to simple, local cuisine at around US$4.

✗ **Sunrise Restaurant** PO Box 3967; ✆ 024 2240270/0777 415240; f 024 2240170; e sunrise@zanlink.com; www.sunrise-zanzibar.com (✪ SUNRIS 6°12.819'S; 39°31.998'E). Located at the Sunrise Hotel, French classics mix with local flavours at this outstanding restaurant. Excellent crab pancakes are crisp on the outside and succulent inside; tasty *poisson cru* uses bluefin tuna; large juicy tiger prawns feature in Swahili-influenced curries; and the Belgian chocolate mousse is to die for! The waiters are polite and well-trained, seating guests in the bar to peruse the menu and sip cocktails before memorising orders and escorting diners to neatly laid tables. Open 07.30–09.30 for b/fast, 12.00–14.30 for lunch, 19.00–20.00 for dinner (last orders 21.00). Non-residents are always welcome and this is a must-visit for anyone staying in the area. (It's barely 2km along the beach south from Breezes, and not quite 700m north of Robinson's Place.) *Mains US$6.50–15.*

**WHAT TO DO AND SEE** Most visitors to this area are kept occupied by resort activities and sun-worshipping. If you're staying somewhere small or simply fancy a change, you can explore the offshore reef with snorkelling gear hired from Palm Beach Inn in the village (around US$4 per day for mask, snorkel and flippers) or Rising Sun Dive Centre at Breezes, although this means walking out at low tide. You can also hire bikes (US$5) or scooters (US$40) from local villagers, with a little help from your hotel, and ride a few kilometres north up the beach to the 'lagoon' at Dongwe, near the big Club Vacanze resort. There's a break in the reef here and it's possible to snorkel off the beach at low tide.

## PAJE

Paje is a small, straggling fishing village, where the main road from Zanzibar Town meets the coast, and from where minor roads go north to Bwejuu and south to Jambiani. Its road access makes it the easiest place on the coast to reach by public transport and contributed to its early success as the backpackers' choice location. With the rise in Nungwi's dominance over the livelier side of the budget scene, the number of travellers heading to Paje has reduced. By and large, the village remains a quiet spot for an idyllic beach break.

**GETTING THERE AND AWAY** To reach Paje, the main tar road from Zanzibar Town leads though Tunguu, Jozani (✪ *JOZANI 6°16.343'S; 39°25.167'E*) and Kitogani (✪ *KITOGA 6°17.34'S; 39°26.306'E*) before reaching the coast. From Paje, a dirt track then leads north to Bwejuu and Michamvi, while another heads south to Jambiani and Makunduchi, in the far southeast corner of the island.

Paje can be reached by public transport (*dala-dala 9*), tourist minibus or self-drive rental car, motorbike or bicycle. If you want to go north beyond Bwejuu or south past Jambiani, there's no public transport, so you'll need to have your own wheels, be willing to hitch on a local ngarawa, or enjoy a really good walk.

If you come to the Bwejuu–Paje–Jambiani area by tourist minibus, the drivers get commission from some of the hotels and will try to take you to these, unless you have a reservation or specifically explain that you want to go to one of the other places.

**WHERE TO STAY** There are several places to stay in Paje, most of them closely clustered at the southern edge of the village. All the accommodation here is small scale, individual and relatively cheap; most places are owner-run. Not all are on the beach, so choose carefully if it's a sea view you're after. Beside the main group of guesthouses is a private house, 'Paje Palace', which aside from being a pink-and-mint-green architectural monstrosity has brought floodlighting and security to its immediate surroundings, including the beach, which it's generally felt has helped to increase evening safety.

**Paje Ndame Village** (24 rooms) PO Box 4164, Zanzibar; ☎ 0777 865501; e booking@ndame.info; www.ndame.info (✪ PNDAME 6°15.635'S; 39°32.116'E). Managed by a pleasant Swedish couple, Lisbeth and Jan Kastner, since 2004 (they formerly ran Kitete Guesthouse down the road), Paje Ndame caters mainly to Scandinavian families, and is consequently at its busiest during the Nordic school

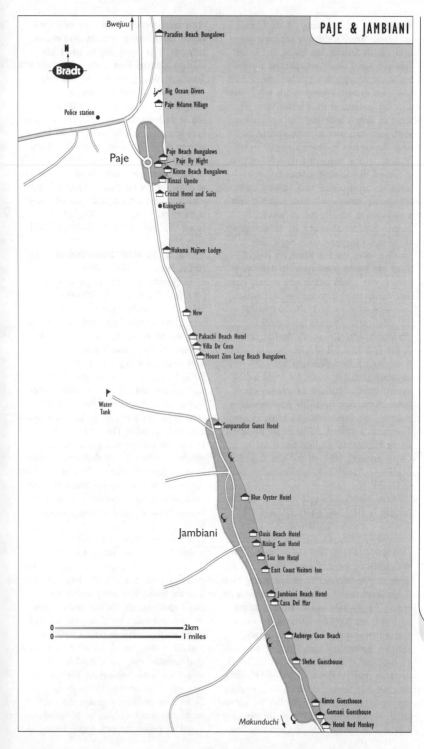

Paradise Beach Bungalows

Big Ocean Divers
Paje Ndame Village

Paje Beach Bungalows
Paje By Night
Kitete Beach Bungalows
Kinazi Upedo
Cristal Hotel and Suits
Kizingitini

Hakuna Majiwe Lodge

New

Pakachi Beach Hotel
Villa De Coco
Mount Zion Long Beach Bungalows

Water Tank

Sunparadise Guest Hotel

Blue Oyster Hotel

Jambiani

Oasis Beach Hotel
Rising Sun Hotel
Sau Inn Hotel
East Coast Visitors Inn

Jambiani Beach Hotel
Casa Del Mar

Auberge Coco Beach

Shehe Guesthouse

Kimte Guesthouse
Gomani Guesthouse
Hotel Red Monkey

*Bwejuu*

N

**Bradt**

Police station

Paje

0 ————————— 2km
0 ————————— 1 miles

*Makunduchi*

**PAJE & JAMBIANI**

holidays in Jul and Dec. Rooms (10 dbl, 9 twin, 3 sgl, 1 family house) are all light and bright and clean with checkerboard lino flooring, tiled en-suite bathrooms with a shower and toilet, and a shared semicircular balcony with a good sea view. All rooms have mains electricity (through sockets with 3 round pins), fans, mosquito nets and bedside lights. The resort sits along a lovely long stretch of beach on which guests laze, enjoy an African massage and watch the world go by. There's a pleasant seafront restaurant, a curio shop with a reasonable selection of colourful local paintings, a beach bar for sundowners and a popular beach volleyball court. Activities are relatively limited but snorkelling from a local ngarawa, bicycle rental and 'romantic moonrise tours' are all possible. On the opposite side of the road, 4 bungalows and a reggae bar, sometimes called New Paje Ndame, are used by Danish and Swedish school groups for 4 months of the year. With 2 bunk beds in each of the 8 rooms, these can be rented to backpackers on a room-only basis when not in use. US$30/40/50 sgl/dbl/tpl, b&b. Child and student reductions available.

🏠 **Arabian Nights** (8 rooms) PO Box 791, Zanzibar; ☎ 024 2240190; f 024 419172; e anights@zanzibararabiannights.com; www.zanzibararabiannights.com. The newest and smartest option in Paje, and the only one with AC, Arabian Nights offers immaculate accommodation in modern en-suite rooms with a sea or garden view. A restaurant is attached, and the on-site dive school charges US$50/80 for a sgl/dbl dive as well as offering snorkelling excursions and other activities. Ocean view US$80/90/120 sgl/dbl/tpl; garden view US$70/80/110.

🏠 **Kitete Beach Bungalows** (18 rooms) PO Box 183, Zanzibar; ☎ 024 2240226/0777 475104; f 024 2250365; e kitetebeach@hotmail.com/ ashuramahfoudh@hotmail.com; www.kitetebeach.com (✪ KITETE 6°16.104'S; 39°32.136'E). Owned and run by a determined Zanzibari woman, Ashura, Kitete has moved on from being just an old villa offering basic rooms. Guests are still welcome at the original house opposite Paje By Night, with its 6 simple dbl and twin rooms and cold-water bathrooms, but walk a little further along the beach and you'll reach Kitete's 3 sparkling new villas. Here there are 12 immaculate rooms with much better facilities. The downstairs rooms all have a dbl and sgl bed, whilst the upper floor has only dbl rooms. Mains electricity, fans, mosquito nets, serious burglar bars and a small outside terrace/balcony feature in all. The rooms are brilliant white and spotlessly clean, with crisp linen,

neatly folded towels in a star shape on the beds, modern clip-on bedside lights and clean en-suite bathrooms. To be critical, they are also a little lacking in character. There is also a family villa with 3 bedrooms, sleeping a total of 12, with fans, 1 shared and 1 en-suite bathroom, and a central dining area. The restaurant occupies the prime spot next to the beach but sadly makes little of this by being fully enclosed. Buffet b/fasts and the usual selection of fish and curries are available all day. Beyond the band of beach palms, there is absolutely no planted vegetation around the villas, making this place feel dry and hot. However, Ashura is keen to respond to guest-feedback, so this may well change in the future. Old villa US$25/40 sgl/dbl, b&b; new houses US$35/60 sgl/dbl, b&b; family villa US$60 room, b&b.

🏠 **Paje By Night or PBN Bizzare Hotel** (23 rooms) PO Box, Zanzibar; ☎ 0777 460710; e info@pajebynight.net; www.pajebynight.net (✪ PAJEBY 6°16.102'S; 39°32.117'E). Opened in 1984, this is a totally unpretentious joint where jovial Italian manager Marco warmly welcomes 'the young and the not so young any more'. The row of hammocks at the entrance hint at the pervading mood before you even get inside, for this is a slightly hippy, take-it-as-it-comes place. Come here for the relaxed vibe and social atmosphere rather than for chic style, modern facilities or endless activities. Set 50m back from the beach, and without a sea view, the hub of PBN is the bar. Chunky coconut-wood sofas are dotted all around, as are moulded concrete tables and chairs, and tall plastic sunflowers. Tiger-stripe faux-fur chairs and white shell chandeliers furnish the adjoining makuti TV Lounge, which plays satellite international news and sport virtually all day. An open-sided makuti structure, screened with panels of pastel fabrics, is used as a simple massage area, whilst the neighbouring rondavel with its spider's-web rope pattern across the window frames is a quiet reading spot. A small curio shop, games area with table football, a pool table and (unusually) a sewing machine are all in a shaded garden building. The food quality is good with a definite Italian bent: fresh pasta and pizza always available. Spur-of-the-moment lunches are prepared by Marco himself who will knock up some great homemade ravioli if the mood takes him. Seafood and Swahili barbecues are a weekly occurrence whilst the social cocktail bar is open 24 hrs a day. Herbs and vegetables that aren't bought from local spice farms can be spotted around the gardens: tomatoes, peppers, lemongrass and very hot chillies. Amusingly, 80% of the papaya crop is used as Marco's miracle cure for sunburn. The gardens attract a number of small birds and butterflies and for one month a year, Marco guarantees that twittering yellow weaver birds 'have a big party in the eucalyptus tree'. Around the garden area are 10 spacious standard rooms each with a dbl/twin bed, and 11 kingsize rooms. The latter refer to the larger size of the room not the bed, for only 9 of the rooms have a kingsize bed while the other 2 are tpls. All of the kingsize rooms have hot water, unlike their standard neighbours. There is mains electricity available throughout the complex, and every room has polished concrete floors with colourful mats, cheerful batik pictures, lockable wardrobes, a fan, and a clean, tiled en-suite bathroom. There is 1 family bungalow with 2 bedrooms, a shared bathroom and a spacious, square entrance hall decorated in slightly aboriginal tinga-tinga murals. Each of these rooms has 2 sgl beds with mosquito nets, sponge-painted walls, stripy palm mats on the floor and burglar bars wrapped in coconut rope. Inside each is only a wardrobe and ceiling fan. The large bathroom is Spartan but clean, and comes complete with a coconut-covered shower head; it appears to be angled to flood the room when in use. Designed and proudly built by Marco, the 2-storey jungle bungalows are very rustic. Within the downstairs coral-stone walls are twin beds and a small, hot-water bathroom; fumble upstairs in the dark and there's an additional dbl bed in the makuti roof space. Although a baby's cot was once borrowed from the village for a visiting child, the basic facilities and party spirit here are not really conducive to holidaying with infants. Primary guest activities seem to be sleeping and sunbathing on the beach by day, then chilling over cocktails and fresh juices before building up to serious parties by night. On a practical note, there's free internet access, a safety deposit box in the office, night-time security and a doctor in the village. *Standard US$40 dbl; kingsize US$60 dbl; jungle bungalow US$70 dbl. Local and major currencies accepted.Visa, MasterCard and Amex all subject to 5% surcharge.*

🏠 **Paje Beach Bungalows** (16 rooms) PO Box 1471, Zanzibar; 📞 0777 461917; e pajebeach@hotmail.com (✪ PAJEBB 6°16.111'S; 39°32.136'E). Opposite Paje By Night, but better located in a beachfront plot, is Paje Beach Bungalows. The 16 rooms, predominantly twin bedded, are arranged around a central quad of red and cream hexagonal tiles. Its rooms are simple but functional with en-suite bathrooms, mains electricity,

3-pin UK-style sockets and fans. The vibrant orange, polygonal restaurant is right on the beach but enclosed by glass windows so missing out on the cooling breeze. Minimal activities are arranged here, but it's right on the beach for swimming and sunbathing, and there's a dive centre only a few minutes away. *US$35 pp sgl/tpl; US$75 dbl.*

🏠 **Paradise Beach Bungalows** (10 rooms) PO Box 2346, Zanzibar; 📞 024 2231387/0777 414129; e paradisebb@zanlink.com/saori@cats-net.com; www.geocities.jp/paradisebeachbungalows/ (✪ PARADI 6°15.295'S; 39°32.133'E). Opened 13 years ago by a gentle, diminutive Japanese lady, Saori Miura, who abandoned her high-powered communications job to travel in east Africa, learn Swahili and avoid the corporate rat race, this is a cheap beach retreat offering basic facilities and great sushi. There are 10 rooms, 3 of which are dbl storey and newly completed in Jun 2005. The original rooms are in semi-detached cottages with 2 $^3/_4$ size traditional Zanzibari beds with mosquito nets. Some of these have interconnecting doors for groups of friends or families. The en-suite bathrooms are basic concrete rooms with squat toilets and cold-water showers. Hot water can be boiled on request though this does take some time (we're still waiting!). The new chalets are a better bet with a simple but spacious, ground-floor bedroom with a dbl and a $^3/_4$-length bed, neat coconut-wood shelves and a Zanzibari chest for storing valuables. The en-suite pink bathroom has a European toilet and shower, while outside, polished coconut-wood stairs lead from the veranda to a pleasant, private roof terrace with a picnic table, chairs, washing line and view into the surrounding palms and frangipani trees. There is no electricity here; storm lanterns are used sparingly at night but a good torch is absolutely essential. The split-level central restaurant houses 7 wooden tables, neatly covered in blue batik tablecloths adorned with white giraffes and glasses of fresh flowers, some simple dining chairs and a small multilingual library. The evenings see guests come here to read, play cards, chat and eat, all sheltered from the sea breeze by retractable wooden shutters. The home-cooked food is all good quality, especially the Japanese options of fresh sushi and tempura, but supplies are limited so order dinner well in advance to ensure your choice is available. B/fasts are simple affairs of fruit, fresh bread and a selection of local preserves. Next to the restaurant, an open-sided, 2-storey, hexagonal lounge area offers cushioned seating, good sea views and some shade during the heat of the afternoon. In spite of its very basic amenities, Paradise's quiet beach location, pleasant gardens, Japanese food and inexpensive rates do mean that it can get very busy: advance booking is advisable. In spite of the lack of power supply, Saori does have good email access (not for guest use) via a solar antenna, so reservations can be made electronically. *Standard US$15/30 sgl/dbl, low season; new bungalow: US$40 dbl, low season. Rates increase US$5 in high season. Local or major international currencies accepted. No credit cards; travellers' cheques 7% surcharge.*

🏠 **Hotel Kinazi Upepo** (13 rooms) PO Box 450, Zanzibar; ⤥ 0777 497495; www.kinaziupepo.com (⊕ KINAZI 6°16.161'S; 39°32.085'E). In a shady grove of beachside coconut palms, Kinazi Upepo has 8 bungalows and 5 more simple *makuti bandas*. Seven of the thatched bungalows have en-suite facilities, whilst one shares its facilities with the *bandas*. Three of the bungalows can accommodate up to 4 people and all have fans, mosquito nets and reading lamps. The hotel also has 5 very simple

*bandas* on the beach. These are small, raised off the sand on stilts, and almost entirely made of makuti – complete with small veranda at the front. There's a rustic beach bar serving the usual array of cocktails and fresh juices, and a recommended restaurant serving Swahili cuisine and grilled seafood. Hammocks and loungers seem to be enough to occupy guests here, and on a beautiful stretch of beach it's easy to see why. *Bungalows US$40–50 dbl; US$45–60 tpl; US$50–65 quad. Bandas US$28–38 dbl. Extra child bed in dbl US$5; free for under 5s. Snorkelling US$10 pp.*

🏠 **Cristal Resorts Hotel and Suits** ⤥ 0777 875515 (⊕ CRISTA 6°16.306'S; 39°32.086'E). Just south of Paje village, a substantial magnolia wall with neat wrought-iron railings atop heralds a new resort. Under construction in Sep 2005, Cristal Resorts, Hotel & Suits (sic) looks as if it will be an orderly, spacious place with concrete and makuti thatch bungalows running down to the sea.

✗ **WHERE TO EAT** All of the hotels above welcome non-guests to eat and drink. For some local flavour, try:

✗ **Kizingitini** (⊕ KIZING 6°16.413'S; 39°32.084'E). South of Cristal Resorts, this gated complex is a large local disco with music, dancing and food

available, along with an amount of sculpture and paintings for sale to visitors.

**WHAT TO DO AND SEE** The primary activities in Paje are sunbathing on the beautiful beach and swimming in the sparkling sea. If staring out at the waves breaking along the fringe reef pricks your curiosity, there are two dive schools in the vicinity for underwater adventures.

⤸ **Paje Dive Centre** Based in the village, close to its affiliated hotel, Arabian Nights.
⤸ **Big Ocean Divers** PO Box 1520, Zanzibar; ⤥ 0777 875515; e bigoceandivers@yahoo.com (⊕ BIGOCE 6°15.571'S; 39°32.148'E). Owned by a local Stone Town businessman, Big Ocean Divers is currently being run by a young Irish couple who arrived in Zanzibar in May 2005. With plans to travel

Africa, they are probably not a long-term fixture on the island. The concrete dive classroom is the northerly neighbour of Paje Ndame, and it's here that all courses are taught. The outfit has a 10-person boat and new equipt as of June 2005. From their seaside location, the fringe reef is only 800m off the coast. Six sites are regularly dived from here, 4 of which are unique to Big Ocean.

If you fancy something different, there is an old mausoleum nearby: a low rectangular edifice with a castellated wall, inset with antique plates and dishes. This design is thought to have originated in Persia, and may indicate that this part of the island was settled by Shirazi immigrants prior to the western side of the island, near present-day Zanzibar Town.

## JAMBIANI

Straddling the provinces of Kibigija and Kikadini, Jambiani village is a sprawling, linear coastal village. Beginning 4km south of Paje, it spreads for about 6km down the coast towards Ras Shungi. With around 4,000 permanent residents, it has a high population density, but also benefits from having nursery, primary and secondary schools (inviting visitors to donate money to improve facilities), a medical centre, several basic food stores, a local craft shop (selling delicious natural honey), a friendly post office and a bakery.

The village's name comes from the Arabic word 'jambiya': a dagger with a markedly curved blade. Local legend holds that early settlers found such a knife here; proof that others had been in the area before them. It now offers a wide choice of places to stay, mostly low-budget, but with a couple of mid-range places as well.

**GETTING THERE AND AWAY** The road both north and south of the village is an uneven, meandering track; however, it's possible to reach Jambiani by private vehicle or tourist minibus. In addition, *dala-dala* number 9 runs from Zanzibar Town to/from Paje four times a day, and often continues on to Jambiani village: it's important to check each individual bus's destination. It's also worth noting that most public transport from Paje heads only as far south as Auberge Coco Beach (⊕ *AUBCOC 6°20.014'S; 39°33.13'E*). To get to the more southerly resorts, you will have to either make a special plan with the driver, walk, or wait for one of the few daily *dala-dalas* that continue on to Makunduchi.

At the end of Jambiani village, the beach fizzles out and low coral cliffs, covered in vegetation, come right down to the sea. The dirt road heads inland and cuts through the scrub for 10km to Makunduchi. There are no hotels along this stretch of road, and public transport is limited. If you want to keep heading south to Makunduchi, you may be lucky and find a lift on one of the occasional vehicles passing this way. Otherwise, if you decide to walk, it takes three to four hours.

**WHERE TO STAY** Nothing on this stretch of coast qualifies as upmarket, but the pick of the mid-range options are Blue Oyster, Sau Inn and Casa del Mar. The best

## JAMBIANI MARINE AND BEACH CONSERVATION

The Jambiani Marine and Beach Conservation (JAMABECO) organisation was founded in Jambiani village in 2001, receiving official recognition in February 2005. It aims to eradicate beach pollution and destruction in the area by providing villagers of all ages with environmental education. It hopes ultimately to improve villagers' incomes by promoting sustainable, long-term use of the local marine resources.

Jambiani village life revolves around the sea – fishing, seaweed farming, coir-rope manufacture and beach tourism – so the quality of the sea life and coastal environment has the ability to impact directly upon the vast majority of villagers. Well-managed resource use and protection is important in maintaining and developing all of these industries and incomes.

The 30 JAMABECO committee members operate a year-round education programme to advocate environmental conservation, plant trees along the beaches and regularly patrol and clean the beaches and village, removing the broken glass, bottles, batteries, iron materials and huge number of plastic bags that litter many of Zanzibar's coastal villages. Since 2003, they have also organised annual clean-up days to mark International Environment Day on 25 June.

With support and sustained education, we must hope that their efforts pay off in Jambiani and that the message spreads to other coastal settlements.

*More information is available from Abdu M Vuai or Abdul Simai, PO Box 3874, Zanzibar; e jamabeco@yahoo.co.uk. To visit the organisation in Jambiani, follow the clear signs in the village or ask for directions to the JAMABECO office.*

10

budget options are probably the two most southerly lodges: Gomani Guesthouse and Red Monkey Bungalows. In between those mentioned below, new places are constantly popping up, so expect a few more names by the time you arrive. Places to stay are described from north to south.

🏠 **Hakuna Majiwe Lodge** (20 rooms) PO Box 3, Jambiani, Zanzibar; ☎ 0777 454505; f 0777 419975; e booking@hakunamajiwe.net; www.hakunamajiwe.net (⊕ HAKMAJ 6°16.973'S; 39°32.178'E). Situated about 2km south of Paje along the sandy road towards Jambiani, this excellent owner-managed lodge, which opened in late 2004, means 'place without stones' — a reference to the superb sandy beach and expansive inter-tidal flats. Isolated from any other lodge, it consists of 20 simple but airy and organically constructed beach houses with fan (no AC), and is designed to be a place to chill out in aesthetically pleasing surrounds rather than a base for activities and excursions. It has a good seafood and pasta restaurant, as well as a 27m swimming pool set a bit back from the beach. *US$90/120 sgl/dbl, b&b, dropping to US$70/100 Apr–Jun. HB an additional US$13 pp.*

🏠 **Unnamed new lodge** (⊕ NEW001 6°17.545'S; 39°32.367'E). Some 1,100m south of Mount Zion, there's a place with about 12 whitewashed, thatched bungalows and planted gardens. When last visited, it wasn't in use. The bumpy coral-rock road south of here is raised a few metres off the beach on a coral cliff.

🏠 **Pakachi Beach Hotel** (4 rooms) PO Box 3200, East Coast, Zanzibar; ☎ 024 224 0001/0777 423331; e pakachi@hotmail.com; www.pakachi.com (⊕ PAKACH 6°17.733'S; 39°32.418'E). Situated on an attractive secluded beach about 1km before you enter Jambiani from Paje, this pleasantly rustic small lodge offers simple bungalows with en-suite hot shower and a dbl bed with netting. Pizzas and other meals are available at around US$5. *US$50 dbl, b&b.*

🏠 **Villa de Coco** (9 rooms) ☎ 0777 844413; e villadecoco@hotmail.com; www.villadecocozanzibar.com (⊕ VILCOC 6°17.841'S; 39°32.445'E). Also set a short way out of town along the Paje road, this isolated and organic-looking, Italian-run lodge comprises a row of en-suite coconut-wood bungalows with fans and hot water. The restaurant serves Italian cuisine with an emphasis on seafood. *US$55 dbl, b&b.*

🏠 **Mount Zion Long Beach Bungalows** (11 rooms) ☎ 0777 439001/034; e znzmountzion@hotmail.com; www.mountzion-zanzibar.com (⊕ MOUZIO 6°17.924'S; 39°32.467'E). The last resort you pass before you

enter Jambiani from the north, Mount Zion is an adequate and attractively situated set-up but it feels overpriced for a rather gloomy beachfront bungalow or honeymoon suite. *Bungalow US$50/70 sgl/dbl; honeymoon suite US$90.*

🏠 **Sunparadise Guest House & ZTC** (turn at ⊕ SUNPAR 6°18.479'S; 39°32.581'E). With a basic signpost pointing off the main track through the village, about 1km south of Mount Zion, these were closed when visited and seemed very basic judging from the outside.

🏠 **Blue Oyster Hotel** (20 rooms) PO Box 007, Zanzibar. ☎ 024 224 0163; m 0741 33312; e blueoysterhotel@gmx.de; www.zanzibar.de (⊕ BLUEOY 6°18.985'S; 39°32.714'E). This is the first 'proper' hotel you come to in Jambiani, and arguably the best value in the lower-to-middle range. The main 2-storey building consists of budget rooms (using common showers) on the ground floor, as well as a breezy first-floor restaurant with a beautiful veranda overlooking the beach and ocean. En-suite accommodation is available in a trio of smaller 2-storey buildings. With friendly staff, clean rooms, good beds and furniture, running water and electricity, this is a fine deal for the price. In the restaurant, snacks and sandwiches cost around US$2–3, pizzas up to US$5, and good evening meals like octopus in coconut with rice around US$4–5. *Room with shared facilities US$20/30/40 sgl/dbl/tpl; en-suite room US$45/50/60 sgl/dbl/tpl. Visa cards are accepted.*

🏠 **Oasis Beach Hotel** (6 rooms) ☎ 024 224 0259; m 0777 858720 (⊕ OASISB 6°19.344'S; 39°32.837'E). This rather rundown but cheap resort lies about 750m south of the Blue Oyster, just along the beach. The en-suite rooms with fan are literally 20m from the beach, and there's a bar and restaurant, with meals costing US$2–5 and an elaborate-looking menu, which boasts crab-claw masala and banana flambé. Snorkel trips can be arranged from US$4 pp. *US$30 dbl.*

🏠 **Rising Sun Hotel** (5 rooms) PO Box 20, Jambiani, Zanzibar; ☎ 0777 497488 (⊕ RISING 6°19.421'S; 39°32.894'E). Next to the new primary health care unit, about 50m south of the Oasis Beach and similar in price and standard, this is a rather cramped set-up and can only be recommended if other resorts and hotels are full.

🏠 **The Sau Inn Hotel** (33 rooms) PO Box 1656, East Coast, Zanzibar; 🌑 024 224 0169/0205; e sauinn@zanlink.com; www.sauinn.net (✪ SAUINN 6°19.536'S; 39°32.981'E). The smartest hotel in Jambiani, the long-serving Sau Inn is often recommended by readers for its cool and comfortable en-suite rooms and cottages set in pleasant gardens. The swimming pool is a definite plus (although watch out for the surrounding wall — just low enough to trip over), as is the on-site diving centre, which charges US$45/75 for a sgl/dbl dive or US$20 to snorkel. There's a good restaurant overlooking the beach, and a bar with a TV. The hotel is used by some tour groups and often has a lively, friendly atmosphere. *US$60/70/80 sgl/dbl/tpl, b&b. HB/FB rates US$10/US$20 extra respectively.*

🏠 **East Coast Visitors Inn** (40 rooms) 🌑 024 224 0150; m 0777 438640/417312; e visitorsinn@zitec.org; www.visitorsinn-zanzibar.com (✪ VISITO 6°19.589'S; 39°33.015'E). Situated about 150m south of the Sau Inn along the village main street, past the health centre and the school, this is quite large for a budget place, clean and pleasant with friendly staff, and often gets good reports — although there's nothing exactly special about it either. Older en-suite rooms in the 'guesthouse' are available as well as larger en-suite bungalows with a fridge and sea view. Meals in the restaurant start at around US$3. *Guesthouse US$17/30 sgl/dbl, b&b; en-suite bungalows US$30/50 sgl/dbl, b&b.*

🏠 **Jambiani Beach Hotel Restaurant & Bar** (✪ JAMBIA 6°19.688'S; 39°33.031'E). Sandwiched in the few hundred metres between the East Coast Visitors Inn and Casa Del Mar, is the Jambiani Beach Hotel. When we last visited it was closed with no sign of it opening up again; the latest news from more recent travellers would be welcome!

🏠 **Casa Del Mar** (12 rooms) 🌑 024 224 0401; m 0777 455446; e infocasa-delmar@hotmail.com; www.casa-delmar-zanzibar.com (✪ CASADE 6°19.731'S; 39°33.04'E). Opened in 2005, this is among the more aesthetically pleasing beach lodges in this part of Zanzibar, consisting of 6 dbl-storey houses made almost entirely of organic material. It's owned and managed by an enthusiastic, environmentally conscious Lebanese couple who made all the furniture on site and have successfully replanted all the palms that were uprooted to make way for the lodge buildings. Ground-floor rooms are en-suite dbls with net and fan, while first-floor honeymoon suites with beds are set up in the makuti roof. A good restaurant is attached, and facilities include free internet access for hotel residents. *Rates: US$50/70 dbl/suite.*

🏠 **Auberge Coco Beach** (8 rooms) 🌑 0777 414254/413125; e cocobeach@zitec.org (✪ AUBCOC 6°20.014'S; 39°33.13'E). Affiliated to the Fisherman Restaurant in Stone Town (through which bookings can be made), this small lodge offers adequate en-suite dbl rooms. It's about 500m south of Case Del Mar, and 400m north of Shehe Guesthouse. Several travellers have recommended the restaurant here, which has an extensive menu. *US$30 dbl, b&b. Visa and MasterCard are accepted.*

🏠 **Shehe Guesthouse** (42 rooms) 🌑 024 224 0149; e shehebungalows@hotmail.com; www.shehebungalows.com (✪ SHEHEB 6°20.186'S; 39°33.194'E). Along the beach about 1,300m south of the centre of Jambiani, this friendly place has been popular on the backpacker trail for many years, although it has lost some of its once-legendary laid-back atmosphere. There are compact but bright older en-suite rooms, set round a sandy courtyard, and a newer annexe with slightly more comfortable en-suite bungalows. The guesthouse also has a small shop selling biscuits, soft drinks and a few items of tinned food, and an upstairs bar/restaurant (with TV) serving snacks and a cheap fixed-menu lunch and dinner (from US$3), plus other meals around US$5, but everything must be ordered several hours in advance. *US$20/35 sgl/dbl, b&b; annex bungalows US$50 dbl, b&b.*

🏠 **Kimte Guesthouse** (7 rooms) PO Box 3200, Zanzibar. 🌑 024 224 0212; m 0777 430992; e kimte@lycos.com. About 500m beyond the Shehe, at the quieter southern end of the village, this Rasta-managed lodge offers a warm welcome and fabulous location on a great stretch of beach. The cool and airy, but otherwise rather basic, en-suite rooms with fan seem a touch overpriced, but then there's always the dormitory. *Rooms US$30/45 dbl/tpl; dormitory US$15 pp.*

🏠 **Gomani Guesthouse** (13 rooms) 🌑 024 224 0154; m 0777 455957 (✪ GOMANI 6°20.482'S; 39°33.381'E). Two hundred metres further south, this is a clean and friendly place with a memorable location on a low coral cliff offering excellent views over the ocean. The rooms with fan, net and bathroom are good value for what they offer. *US$30 dbl, b&b.*

🏠 **Hotel Red Monkey & Restaurant** (7 rooms) 🌑 024 224 0207; m 0777 419635; e kassidipandu@hotmail.com (✪ REDMON 6°20.573'S; 39°33.401'E). This is the most southerly lodge in Jambiani, about 2km from the centre. It is also set on the low coral cliffs, and named after the Kirk's red colobus monkeys that live in the adjacent forest and pass through the grounds most days. Everything is clean and tidy, there's a nice view of the beach (which is reached by a short flight of steps), and the management and staff are very friendly. Rooms here represent one of the best budget deals in this part of Zanzibar. The skilful chef prepares fresh fish and other good meals for about US$2.50 to US$4. *US$20/30 sgl/dbl.*

✖ **WHERE TO EAT** All the places to stay listed above have restaurants, most of which serve a good range of seafood and other dishes. The Blue Oyster and Sau Inn are both recommended for food, but the best place to eat is probably Auberge Coco Beach, which is affiliated to the French-owned Fisherman Restaurant in Zanzibar Town. Good-quality meals, naturally with a seafood emphasis, cost US$4–9, drinks, snacks and lunches are also available, and if your taste buds get the better of your wallet, you can pay with a credit card.

The nearby Karibu Restaurant claims rather optimistically to be 'the most happening place in Jambiani', but was pretty quiet whenever we looked in. Still, the food is pretty good, though ordering long in advance is advisable. Also worth seeking out is the Women's Restaurant, close to the village football field, which serves good local fare. If you want supplies, the Jambiani Post Office & Mini-market near the Auberge Coco Beach doesn't quite warrant its prominent signposting throughout the village, but it does supplement the usual local fare with a selection of tinned foods and a few imported goodies (sweets and potato crisps), as well as selling stamps.

**SERVICES** If you need money, there's a bureau de change at the East Coast Visitors Inn, or Coco Beach Café might be able to give you cash from a bank card (although you'll need to have a meal there first).

**WHAT TO DO AND SEE** As with most of Zanzibar's coastal villages, the main focus of the tourist agenda is swimming and sunbathing. Diving and snorkelling can be arranged through the dive centre in the Sau Inn, which also allows non-residents use of its swimming pool for US$3 per person per day, but if you want a change from the beach, try the following:

### COIR ROPE PRODUCTION

The fruit of the evocative coconut palm does not look as many imagine: it has a smooth, leathery, green skin. The brown nuts sold in supermarkets worldwide are simply the central element of the fruit. Between the well-known shiny shell and green exterior is a coarse fibrous husk known as coir; it is from this that rope is made.

The patient process begins when the husk is separated from the nut. The fibres are then buried in the sandy inter-tidal zone and covered with a cairn of coral rock. Over the coming six to ten months, micro-organisms in the surrounding sand cause the husk tissues to begin biodegrading, in a process known as retting, loosening the fibre strands. The remains are then uncovered, beaten and sun-dried. When dry and clean, the long fibres are simply rubbed together to form strands which can be twined to the required thickness of rope.

According to the Royal Botanical Gardens at Kew, the total of world coir-fibre production is about 250,000 tonnes, with over 50% of the coir fibre produced annually consumed in its countries of origin. This bears out on Zanzibar where the relatively waterproof nature of the coir and its resistance to saltwater damage make it an invaluable material for boat rigging, fishing nets and seaweed-farming lines. As a tourist, you are likely to benefit from its more recent application in the manufacture of sun loungers, hammocks and the beds used by budget hotels.

If you happen to be visiting Zanzibar during the last week of July, try to reach Makunduchi. Every year there's a large festival here called the Mwaka Kogwa when local people come from all over the island for a great get-together of singing, dancing, drumming, making new friends and meeting old ones. It's no problem for tourists to see the festival, and when it's running several of the tour companies listed in *Chapter 5* run day trips to Makunduchi.

The festival is also called Mwaka Nairuz and it originates from Persia, marking the start of the New Year in the Shirazi calendar (for more details on the Shirazis in Zanzibar, see *History*, page 5) and involves several rituals, including a mock fight where men from different parts of the village beat each other with banana stems. It is believed that this fight gives each combatant a chance to vent his feelings, and in this way the disagreements and arguments of the past year are exorcised so that the new year can be started peacefully. (Although this is a mock fight, it can still get pretty serious. Fortunately the men are only fighting with banana stems – they used to do it with real clubs and cudgels!)

While the men are beating each other, the women have a far more pleasant way of celebrating: dressed in their finest clothes, they parade around the village singing. The songs contain comments about love, families and village life.

The next stage of the festival is the ritual burning of a traditional hut, which has been built especially for the purpose. A local healer goes inside before the fire is lit and runs out again when the hut is burning strongly. It is thought that the burning of the hut symbolises the passing of the old year and also ensures that, during the coming year, should any house in the village catch fire its inhabitants will escape unharmed.

After the fighting and the hut-burning, a large feast is held with all the villagers bringing food and eating together. People from other parts of Zanzibar are welcomed, as a local tradition holds that any villager without a guest must be unhappy.

After the eating, the music starts – traditional *ngomas* and *taarab* (see the section on *Music and dance* on pages 35–40), but these days may include some more modern amplified sounds as well. The locals dance into the night and die-hard party animals move on to the beach to continue singing and dancing until dawn.

**Kumbi Cavern** About two hours' walk outside Jambiani is a large underground cavern called Kumbi, which contains a natural spring. According to local legend, it was lived in at one time but today it is a traditional shrine: local people go there to pray and make offerings. You'll need a local guide to show you the way and it's an interesting trip: even if the cave doesn't awe you, the walk is pleasant. Around the village, you can also see several old tombs decorated with plates and dishes, similar to the mausoleum at Paje.

**Jambiani Village Tours** Day trips to local sites of interest can be booked a day in advance through Jambiani Village Tours (✆ *024 223 6806*) which is found in Mande's Gift Store between the East Coast Visitors Inn and Casa Del Mar. For US$10 per person you can arrange to visit an *mganga* (traditional herbalist), a plantation on coral rock, a seaweed farm and various local shrines, including Kumbi Cavern.

**Jambiani Wellness Centre** Opened in 2003 by a joint Canadian-Zanzibari NGO, Hands Across Borders, the Jambiani Wellness Centre primarily offers

Southeast Zanzibar JAMBIANI

10

homeopathic and other therapy to locals, but tourists are welcome to visit for massage, acupuncture, breema or homeopathic therapy. The centre is open 09.00–14.00 Monday, Tuesday, Thursday and Friday. A donation of at least US$10 is asked in lieu of a fee.

## MAKUNDUCHI

The ill-defined settlement of Makunduchi lies at the southeastern end of Zanzibar Island, and is divided into two distinct parts. On the coast is the small fishing village of 'old' Makunduchi, with some local huts and houses, a few holiday cottages, and a small beach from where you can sometimes spot dolphins. Then, about 2km inland is 'Makunduchi New Town', complete with one main road, some dusty side-streets, a bank, post and telephone office, police station, small shop and a few incongruous blocks of austere flats, built as part of a 1970s East German aid scheme.

With the exception of July's Mwaka Kogwa festival (see the box on page 241), Makunduchi hardly receives any visitors. It is significantly quieter than Bwejuu or Jambiani – not that they are particularly noisy – and its community focus on seaweed farming and fishing, not tourism.

**GETTING THERE AND AWAY** From Zanzibar Town, Makunduchi can be reached by public bus (number 10), or by rented car, scooter or bike. There are no tourist minibuses working regularly on this route, although you could always hire one for exclusive use through a tour company. You can also reach Makunduchi from Jambiani; see the *Getting there and away* section above.

 **WHERE TO STAY** There is a ZTC bungalow in the old village, but it seems to be permanently closed. In theory, if you really wanted to stay here, you could make enquires at the ZTC office in Zanzibar Town. There used to be another guesthouse near the beach, Kigaeni Reef Lodge, but this is also closed, although it's quite possible that it, or something similar, might reopen in the future.

# Southwestern Zanzibar

For most of Zanzibar's overseas visitors, the island's southwest corner holds little more than day-trip opportunities to see dolphins from Kizimkazi and troops of red colobus monkeys in Jozani Forest. Yet from Chukwani 10km south of Stone Town, around the Fumba Peninsula to the ruins at Unguju Ukuu, and the reefs around Chumbe Island and the Menai Bay Conservation Area are some of the best marine, animal and historical conservation projects on the island. Few people stay in this area, most opting instead for the endless beaches of the east coast or the buzz of Zanzibar Stone Town, but, away from the main tourist attractions, the villagers in these parts rarely encounter visitors, and their welcome is one of genuine friendliness and interest. It's a refreshing contrast to the more visitor-centric areas.

## KIZIMKAZI

The village of Kizimkazi lies at the southwestern tip of the island, about 12km west of Makunduchi. In a beautiful bay, it is one of the island's oldest settlements, being the former home of the Mwinyi Mkuu (the traditional king of Zanzibar). It is steeped in history, though there is little evidence of this today.

Kizimkazi has a sizeable population, a school, a dispensary, a couple of places to stay, and a burgeoning tourist industry based on dolphin-watching. Bottlenose and humpback dolphins are regularly seen off the coast here, and Kizimkazi has become a launch point for boats taking visitors out on viewing trips.

Technically, Kizimkazi consists of two villages: *Kizimkazi Mkunguni* and *Kizimkazi Dimbani*. Most boats go out to see the dolphins from Kizimkazi Mkunguni, and this is generally just called Kizimkazi. As an increasing number of tourists have arrived over the last few years, so an increasing number of 'guides', touts and hustlers have taken to the streets as well – some of them can be quite unpleasant. If you're driving, watch out for the squad that wait for custom on the roadside by the entrance to the village.

Kizimkazi Dimbani is 2km north along the coast from 'main' Kizimkazi (3km by road); it's smaller, much quieter and certainly prettier, and a few boats do depart from here as well. There are no touts, probably because it's mainly groups who come here, and the whole scene is monopolised by two large restaurant-and-boat operations. Dimbani is also the site of East Africa's oldest mosque.

**GETTING THERE AND AWAY** Most people come to Kizimkazi by tourist minibus or as part of a day tour; the alternative is to come by hired car, scooter or bike. To reach Kizimkazi Dimbani, turn off the main road between Zanzibar Town and Makunduchi at Kufile junction, and follow this small road to a fork: right goes to Kizimkazi Dimbani and the ancient Shirazi mosque; left goes to the main part of Kizimkazi (Kizimkazi Mkunguni), from where most of the boats are launched.

It is also possible to get here independently by public bus (number 10) or

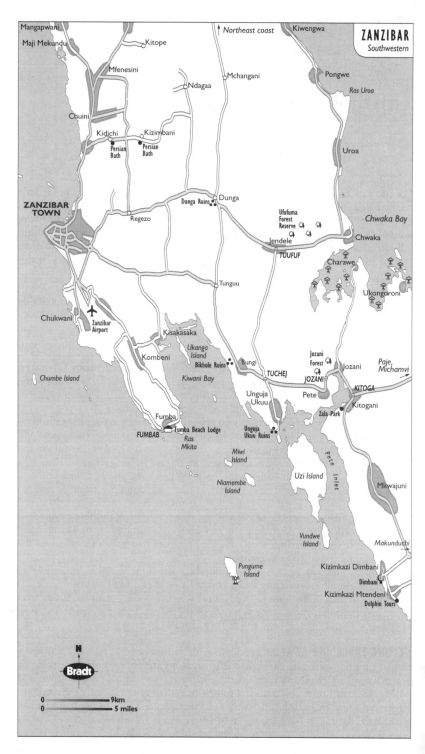

ZANZIBAR
*Southwestern*

Mangapwani

Maji Mekundu

Kitope

↑ *Northeast coast*

Kiwengwa

Mfenesini

Mchangani

Pongwe

Ndagaa

*Ras Uroa*

Chuini

Uroa

Kidichi

Kizimbani

Persian Bath

Persian Bath

Dunga Ruins

Dunga

*Chwaka Bay*

ZANZIBAR TOWN

Regezo

Ufufuma Forest Reserve

Jendele

*TUUFUF*

Chwaka

Charawe

Tunguu

Ukongoroni

Chukwani

Zanzibar Airport

Kisakasaka

*Ukanga Island*

Bikhole Ruins

Bungi

Jozani Forest

Jozani

*Paje, Michamvi*

Kombeni

*TUCHEJ*

*JOZANI*

*KITOGA*

*Chumbe Island*

*Kiwani Bay*

Unguja Ukuu

Pete

Kitogani

Zala Park

Fumba

Fumba Beach Lodge

*FUMBAB*

*Ras Mkita*

Unguja Ukuu Ruins

*Miwi Island*

*Uzi Island*

*Pete Inlet*

Mkwajuni

*Niamembe Island*

*Vundwe Island*

*Makunduchi*

Kizimkazi Dimbani

Dimbani

*Pungume Island*

Kizimkazi Mtendeni

Dolphin Tours

N

Bradt

0 ——————— 9km
0 ——————— 5 miles

minibus: some buses running between Zanzibar Town and Makunduchi divert down to Kizimkazi Mkunguni. Otherwise you'll have to get off the bus at Kufile junction and walk to Kizimkazi Dimbani (3km) or Kizimkazi Mkunguni (6km).

## WHERE TO STAY
### Kizimkazi Dimbani

**Kizidi Restaurant and Bungalows** (14 rooms)
⤷ 024 223 0081; m 0777 417053/418452;
e kizidi@hotmail.com; www.kidizibungalows.com.
This attractive cliff-top lodge started life as a large restaurant, aimed almost exclusively at dolphin-viewing tour groups from town and coast hotels. Now, it also offers accommodation in smart little en-suite bungalows. The tour groups still come, but once they head home in the afternoon it's very quiet and peaceful here. Kizidi also runs a fleet of 6 10-seater wooden boats for dolphin trips, charging US$35 per group of up to 8 people for a 3-hr dolphin-viewing and snorkelling trip out of the lodge. *Bungalows US$25/40 sgl/dbl, b&b.*

**Funky Shamba** (3 rooms)
e funkyshamba@hotmail.com; www.funkyshamba.com.
Situated about 1km south of town, along the sandy track that runs parallel to the coast, this small but attractive backpacker lodge consists of 3 bungalows, all built from local materials. It was closed at the time of research and its future looks uncertain.

**Coral Reef Village** (6 rooms) ⤷ 0777 479615/415374; e mkazi_coreevi@yahoo.com. Next door to Funky Shamba, this rather rundown, sleepy and isolated lodge has a great location. However, an undistinguished and rather basic en-suite, it seems below par in the value-for-money stakes. *US$30/45 sgl/dbl.*

### Kizimkazi Mkunguni

**Dolphin View Village** (7 rooms) ⤷ 024 2236577; m 0777 464738;
e rukiandame@yahoo.com. Situated about 500m further along the same track as Coral Reef Village, this place has friendly staff and large comfortable dbl bungalows with private bathrooms and lounge. Its finest feature is the small secluded beach, in a cove between 2 coral-rock outcrops, where swimming and sunbathing are possible out of sight from the locals. *US$30 dbl.*

**WHERE TO EAT** In the main part of Kizimkazi, near where the boats are launched, is the Jichane Restaurant, serving mainly lunches for the tour groups from Zanzibar Town.

In Kizimkazi Dimbani, there are two places – both geared mainly around feeding large groups. Kizidi Restaurant and Bungalows is mentioned above, and serves mainly seafood from around US$4–5. Cabs Restaurant (⤷ 0777 415554) has meals like chicken and chips or grilled seafood for around US$3–4. This place also has a fleet of six boats for dolphin-viewing, which again caters mainly for the big groups, but it's reckoned by local operators to be one of the safest and best-organised outfits based here.

**WHAT TO SEE AND DO** The main reason people visit Kizimkazi is to see the dolphins, but if you're keen on history you might also want to stop off at the ancient Shirazi mosque in Kizimkazi Dimbani.

**Kizimkazi Mosque** Hidden behind its new plain walls and protective corrugated iron roof, the mosque at Kizimkazi Dimbani is believed to be the oldest Islamic building on the east African coast. The floriate Kufic inscription to the left of the *mihrab* (the interior niche indicating the direction of Mecca) dates the original mosque construction to AD1107 and identifies it as the work of Persian settlers, working under the orders of Sheikh Said bin Abi Amran Mfaume al Hassan bin Muhammad. The silver pillars on either side of the niche are decorated with pounded mullet shells from the island of Mafia, and the two decorative clocks, which show Swahili time (six hours different to European time), were presented by local dignitaries. However, though the fine-quality coral detailing and columns

11

date from this time, most of the building actually dates from an 18th century reconstruction, testified to by a further inscription, to the right of the mihrab. The more recent additions of electrical sockets and flex have not been installed with a comparable degree of style or decoration.

Outside the mosque are some old tombs, a few decorated with pillars and one covered by a small makuti roof. The pieces of cloth tied to the edge of the tomb are prayer flags. The raised aqueduct which carried water from the well to the basin where hands and feet were washed is no longer used: running water is piped straight into a more recently built ablution area at the back of the mosque.

Archaeological evidence suggests that when the mosque was built Kizimkazi was a large walled city. Tradition holds that it was founded and ruled by a king, Kizi, and that the architect of the mosque itself was called Kazi. Legend has it that when the city was once attacked by invaders, Kizi prayed for divine intervention and the enemies were driven away by a swarm of bees. Later the enemies returned, but this time Kizi evaded them by disappearing into a cave on the shore. The cave entrance closed behind him and the enemies were thwarted once again.

Today, very little of the old city remains, but non-Muslims, both men and women, are welcome to visit the mosque and its surrounding tombs. It's normally locked, and you'll probably have to find the caretaker with the key (he lives nearby, but is usually under the trees near the beach a few hundred metres further down the road). Show respect by removing your shoes and covering bare arms and legs (this part of the island is very traditional so, out of politeness, your arms and legs should be covered anyway – see *Clothing* on page 85). On leaving you'll be shown the collection box and be able to make a donation.

**Dolphin tours** Most visitors come on all-inclusive 'dolphin tours' which include road transport, the boat, snorkelling gear and lunch. If you don't take an all-in tour, or want to spend the night at Kizimkazi, you can make your own way here, then hire a boat on the spot or arrange to join a group.

Generally, dolphin-viewing trips last for about two to three hours – usually enough time to locate the dolphins – although some captains trim the time down to about 90 minutes. Sometimes tourists become bored if they don't get quick and easy sightings, and decide to go back even sooner.

Dolphin tours are often promoted in a misleading light. It is important to realise that sightings cannot be guaranteed, and swimming with the dolphins is a rare occurrence. This is not a Florida-style dolphinarium; these are wild animals and their whereabouts cannot be predicted. It is they who choose to interact with people, not the other way around.

Observing dolphins in their natural environment, as with any other animals, requires time and patience. Shouting and excessive movement will not encourage them to approach your boat. Be satisfied with passive observation – do not force the boat-driver to chase the dolphins, cross their path, or approach too close, especially when they are resting. If you decide to swim, slip quietly into the water and avoid splashing. Never jump in. Stay close to the boat and let the dolphins come to you instead of you trying to catch up with them. You could try attempting to excite their curiosity by diving frequently and swimming below the surface, maintaining your arms alongside your body to imitate their own streamlined shape.

In reality, unless you charter your own boat and go out early in the morning, so as not to be disturbed, you're unlikely to be able to put any of these theories into practice. On some days it's not unusual to see 20 or more boats, carrying at least ten people each, all chasing the dolphins and desperate for a sighting. When the dolphins are seen, big groups of people jumping in does little to entice them any

## THE KIZIMKAZI DOLPHINS

The shallow coastal waters around Kizimkazi have been favoured by dolphins for many years (quite possibly for millennia) because the area offers a reliable food supply and is a good place to nurse calves or simply to rest and socialise. Two species of dolphin are resident all year round, the Indo-Pacific **bottlenose dolphin** (*Tursiops aduncus*) and the Indo-Pacific **humpback dolphin** (*Sousa chinensis*). The bottlenose dolphin is more sociable, and more readily observed, whereas the humpback dolphin is a shyer creature.

Studies conducted have revealed that there are about 150 bottlenose and 60 humpback dolphins inhabiting the area. A catalogue of all the individual dolphins has been compiled based on the shape, nicks and marks of their dorsal fins and most of the animals have been given names. (Look closely if you see the dolphins and you'll notice that they all look different.)

Tourists first started coming to see dolphins at Kizimkazi in the early 1990s. The continued presence of these popular creatures has attracted growing numbers of visitors, such that tourism has now created new job opportunities for the local villagers. Contrary to the practices of other fishing communities in the Indian Ocean, the fishermen of Kizimkazi are very protective of the dolphins and no longer hunt them, seeing instead the economic rewards from conservation.

In 1997, villagers from Kizimkazi also helped to arrest dynamite fishermen from Dar es Salaam, knowing their methods destroyed the coral reefs and important habitats for the dolphins. Today, other fishing methods such as drift nets pose the greatest threat to the dolphins as they are liable to get tangled up in the nets and drown.

Over the years there have been a number of studies carried out at Kizimkazi, to monitor the interaction between dolphins and tourists. It's widely believed that the overall effect is detrimental. However, on a positive note, in 2005 all the stakeholders involved in dolphin tourism formed an association, the Kizimkazi Dolphin Tourism Operators Association (KIDOTOA), and they are working towards getting a management plan in place. Training courses have also been initiated where boat operators are taught how to conduct their tourism activities in a responsible, sustainable way. Further, a system of certifying those that have taken the course is also being considered.

On the whole, the creation of KIDOTOA is very promising for the conservation and management of both the dolphins and the tourism. It is still early days and many boats continue to compete for the best views of the dolphins. But it is now up to everyone to make sure that this new strategy is put in practice. As a tourist you should ask for a copy of the existing dolphin tourism guidelines (see below) and ask the boat operators to follow them strictly. This should minimise the impact on the dolphins and ensure that they remain in the area for many years to come.

*This section is based on information from the Marine Mammal Education & Research group at the Institute of Marine Sciences, Zanzibar, and Dr Per Berggren, Department of Zoology, Stockholm University, Sweden.*

closer. One visitor commented: 'it's billed as "swimming with dolphins" but it's actually "jumping into the water a long way from the dolphins"'; another called it a 'shambolic turkey-hunt'.

It's little wonder that the dolphins are beginning to head for somewhere more peaceful. In recent years, the number of sightings has definitely gone down. They used to be almost guaranteed, but it's not unusual now for groups to return without having seen a single dolphin. Sadly, as the disturbances from too many boats and people increasingly outweigh the benefits of food and shelter, this trend is likely to continue, with fewer and fewer dolphins appearing in Kizmikazi's waters in the future.

**When to visit** The best time of year to see the dolphins is between October and February. From June to September, the southerly winds can make the seas rough, while during the rainy season (March to May) conditions in the boat can be unpleasant. However, out at sea you're likely to get wet anyway. You should also protect yourself against the sun.

**Organised tours** Most people who visit Kizimkazi come on a fully organised tour. These are easily arranged before you arrive, in Zanzibar Town, or by one of the hotels elsewhere on Zanzibar. Costs for these tours vary between US$25 and US$100 per person from Zanzibar Town, including transport to/from Kizimkazi, the boat, all snorkelling gear and lunch.

These prices vary considerably depending on the season, the quality of the vehicle, the standard of driver and guide, the number of passengers, and whether you want a private tour or are happy to share with others. Obviously they also depend upon where you are coming from: if you're taking a day-trip from Zanzibar Town, then it's going to be cheaper than driving here from Nungwi.

**Private boat charter** Excursions can be arranged with local fishermen through any of the guesthouses and restaurants in Kizimkazi Mkunguni and Kizimkazi Dimbani. (The latter is more group orientated; it might be harder finding spare seats here unless you can muster a group together.) Traditional wooden fishing boats are most commonly used, although several fishermen have upgraded to modern fibreglass boats. Chartering a boat costs about US$30–35 for the whole boat. If you're in a small group, you can of course share these costs, although you'll probably find that for groups of five or six the price for a boat may go up to about US$40, or you'll be charged US$10–12 per person. You can also hire snorkels, masks and flippers (around US$2–5 per person) from the souvenir stalls beside Jichane Restaurant: essential if you want to get in the water and observe the dolphins below the surface – which is highly recommended. As competition between the boatmen is stiff, some include free snorkel gear in the price of the boat, so it's always worth asking about this.

## JOZANI FOREST AND SURROUNDINGS

**JOZANI FOREST RESERVE** Jozani (✪ JOZANI 6°16.343'S; 39°25.167'E; *open daily 07.30–17.00)* is the largest area of mature indigenous forest remaining on Zanzibar Island, although today it is a tiny remnant of the forest that once covered much of the central part of the island. It stands on the isthmus of low-lying land which links the northern and southern parts of the island, to the south of Chwaka Bay. The water table is very high and the area is prone to flooding in the rainy season, giving rise to this unique 'swamp-forest' environment. The large moisture-loving trees, the stands of palm and fern, and the high water table and humid air give the forest a very 'tropical' feel.

Historically, local people have cut trees and harvested other forest products for many centuries, but commercial use started in the 1930s when the forest was bought by an Arab landowner and a sawmill was built here. In the late 1940s the forest came under the control of the colonial government and some replanting took place. Jozani has been protected since 1952 and, as the forest areas in other parts of the island have been cleared, much of the island's wildlife has congregated here. The forest was declared a nature reserve in the 1960s, but despite this the trees and animals were inadequately protected. Local people cut wood for building and fuel, and some animals were hunted for food or because they could damage crops in nearby fields.

Nevertheless, Jozani Forest retained much of its original natural character and now forms the core of the Jozani-Chwaka Conservation Area, a partnership between the Zanzibar government's Commission for Natural Resources and the charity CARE International, with funding from various sources including the government of Austria, the Ford Foundation and the Global Environment Facility. The objective is to protect natural resources which in turn should improve conditions for local people and wildlife in the area.

**Getting there and away** The entrance to Jozani Forest Reserve is on the main road between Zanzibar Town and the southern part of the east coast, north of the village of Pete. You can visit at most times of the year, but in the rainy season the water table rises considerably and the forest paths can be under more than a metre of water. The reserve is clearly signposted, and entrance costs US$8, inclusive of the services of a guide and the mangrove boardwalk.

Many tour companies include Jozani on their east coast tours or dolphin tours, but you can easily get here by bus, *dala-dala* (number 9), hired bike or car. Alternatively, take a tourist minibus heading for the east coast, and alight here. This road is well used by tourist minibuses and other traffic throughout the day, so after your visit to the forest you could flag something down and continue to the coast or return to Zanzibar Town.

**When to visit** Keen naturalists who want to watch wildlife undisturbed, or those who just like a bit of peace and quiet, should try to visit the reserve either very early or in the middle of the day, as most groups come at about 09.00–10.00 on their way to the coast, or 15.00–16.00 on their way back. The monkeys and birds seem subdued in the midday heat, so from about 14.00–15.00 seems to be the best time.

**Getting around the forest** A network of nature trails has been established. The main one takes about an hour to follow at a leisurely pace, with numbered points of interest which relate to a well-written information sheet which you can buy for a nominal cost at the reception desk. There are also several shorter loops. Some other information leaflets and species lists are also available, and there are a few very good display boards and other exhibits.

As you walk around the nature trails, it's possible to see lots of birds and probably a few colobus and Sykes monkeys, but these animals are shy, and will leap through the trees as soon as they hear people approaching. On the south side of the main road live two groups of monkeys who are more used to humans and with a guide you can come and watch these at close quarters. This is ideal animal viewing – the monkeys are aware of your presence but not disturbed. They are not tame at all, and don't come close, but just get on with their usual feeding, playing, grooming or resting. As the colobus monkeys look so cute, some visitors have been tempted to try to stroke them or give sweets to them. This is bad for the monkeys, but can be bad for tourists too – several people have been given a nasty nip or scratch. Read the rules in the box on page 253, and look but don't touch.

South of the forest, a long thin creek juts in from the sea, and is lined with mangrove trees. A fascinating boardwalk has been constructed, the only one of its type in east Africa, so you can easily and harmlessly go deep into the mangrove to experience this unique ecosystem. This is also a community project, and revenue from visitors coming to the boardwalk helps fund local development projects.

**Jozani's flora** Several distinct habitats exist within Jozani's borders – evergreen bushland to the west; dense groundwater forest of laurel wood (*Callophyllum inophyllum*), screw palm (*Pandanus rabaiensis*) and untidy oil palms (*Elaeis guineensis*) in its heart; thickets of flowering *Macphersonia gracilis*, cloves (*Eugenia*), and cabbage trees (*Cussonia zimmermannii*) to the north; and mangrove forest forming the eastern border along Chwaka Bay, dominated by the common red mangrove (*Rhizophora mucronata*), yellow mangrove (*Ceriops tagal*) and grey mangrove (*Avicennia marina*).

Other trees in the reserve include moisture-loving palms (five species, of which three are true palms), figs (two species) and red mahogany, plus some introduced species such as Sydney blue gum. Red mahogany was formerly regarded as an introduced exotic, but the weight of evidence is that it is native or anciently naturalised; this tree is found on other Indian Ocean islands and, like the mangrove, its seeds can float and survive in sea water. Although the size of the trees in Jozani is impressive, few trees become truly huge as the soils are too shallow to allow deep roots to penetrate, and they get blown over by strong monsoon winds. With several diverse habitat types, each brings its associated and equally varied wildlife to the reserve.

**Jozani's mammals** Several rare and endemic animal species occur in Jozani, making it a major attraction for wildlife fans. Even if you've got only a passing interest, a visit can be fascinating. The main reason most visitors come here to is to see some of the resident red colobus monkeys – their full name is Zanzibar red colobus or Kirk's red colobus (*Procolobus kirkii*); their local name is *kima punga* meaning poison monkey – which are unique to the Zanzibar archipelago. Many wildlife fans rate the red colobus of Jozani as one of the best monkey-viewing

Kirk's red colobus (*Procolobus kirkii*) are named after Sir John Kirk, the 19th-century British consul-general in Zanzibar, who first identified these attractive island primates. They are endemic to the archipelago and one of Africa's rarest monkeys. Easily identified by their reddish coat, pale underside, small dark faces framed with tufts of long white hairs, and distinctive pink lips and nose, the monkeys are a wildlife highlight for many visitors to Zanzibar.

Kirk's red colobus live in gregarious troops of 5–50 individuals, headed by a dominant male and comprising his harem of loyal females and several young (single births occur year round). They spend most of the day hanging out in the forest canopy, sunbathing, grooming and occasionally breaking away in small numbers to forage for tasty leaves, flowers and fruit. Their arboreal hideouts can make them hard to spot, but a roadside band at the entrance to Jozani Chwaka Bay National Park allow for close observation and photography.

Timber felling, population expansion and a rise in agriculture have resulted in the rapid destruction of the tropical evergreen forests in which the Kirk's red colobus live, thus dramatically reducing population numbers. Researchers estimate that fewer than 1,500 of these monkeys currently exist, a fact verified by their classification as 'endangered' on the IUCN Red List (2004) and their inclusion in Appendix II of CITES.

Human behaviour has undoubtedly caused the decline in Kirk's red colobus population numbers, yet now tourism may help to save the species. With national park status now protecting their habitat in Jozani Forest, and visitor numbers increasing, the local communities are beginning to benefit from the tangible economic rewards (see *Jozani Community Fund* box, page 252) that come from preserving these striking monkeys. If this continues, the future survival of the species should be secured.

experiences in Africa. Nowhere else can you get so close to a monkey in the wild that is not aggressive or likely to bite, as well as being attractive, endearing and very rare.

Brochures produced in the mid-1990s said there were 1,500 individual colobus monkeys in Zanzibar, but this was an estimate, and more accurate surveys in 1997 put the figure at around 2,300. The red colobus population of Jozani is growing, which is partly a result of conservation efforts. However, recent research shows that this is most likely caused by monkeys from elsewhere fleeing ongoing destruction of the small patches of forest elsewhere on the island into the safety of the Jozani area, rather than their numbers increasing as the result of breeding. Researchers think that Zanzibar's total population of red colobus is probably stable, but emphasise that habitat destruction is still a major threat.

Other residents of Jozani include a population of blue or Sykes monkey (*Cercopithecus mitis albgularis*), which you are also quite likely to see. The forest is also home to Ader's duiker (*Cephalophus adersi*), a species of small antelope found only on Zanzibar and some parts of the Kenyan coast, and suni (*Nesotragus moschatu moschatus*), another antelope which is even smaller than the duiker, but both of these are extremely shy and unlikely to be seen. The Ader's duiker is virtually extinct in Kenya now and is one of the two rarest antelopes in the world. Its only chance of survival is on Unguja. Its population is between 400 and 1,000 and efforts have been under way over recent years to ensure its survival, including protecting Jozani, working with local communities to establish sanctuaries and the proposed translocation of some individuals to Chumbe Island Coral Park.

Southwestern Zanzibar **JOZANI FOREST AND SURROUNDINGS**

11

There are even reports of leopards (*Pathera pardus adersi*) in Jozani. If present they would be a local subspecies, smaller than the mainland version, although the veracity of these claims is very questionable. (For more details of wildlife in Jozani and Zanzibar, see the *Wildlife* section on pages 49–56.)

**Jozani's birds** Jozani has a fairly good bird population, with over 40 species recorded, although many of the forest birds are shy and therefore hard to spot. Species occurring here include Kenya crested guineafowl (*Guttera pucherani*), emerald-spotted wood dove (*Turtur chalcospilos*), little greenbul (*Andropadus virens*), sombre greenbul (*Andropadus importunus*), cardinal woodpecker (*Dendropicos fuscescens*), red-capped robin-chat (*Cossypha natalensis*), dark-backed weaver (*Ploceus bicolour*), golden weaver (*Ploceus xanthops*), olive sunbird (*Nectarinia olivacea*) and crowned hornbill (*Tockus alboterminatus*). An interesting speciality is an endemic race of Fischer's turaco (*Turaco fischeri*), which is slightly larger than the mainland race, with blue-purple on the wings instead of green. In the mangroves you'll see various kingfishers (including the localised mangrove kingfisher – *Halcyon senegaloides*), sunbirds and coucals.

If you're especially keen on birds, it is well worth engaging the services of a bird guide. Jozani has two bird specialists on the staff: Ali Addurahim is an ecologist and chief bird guide; Ali Khamis Mohammed was trained by the other Ali, and also knows his stuff. They have a bird checklist and a copy of the big fat Zimmerman *Birds of Kenya and Northern Tanzania* book, which includes most species which occur on Zanzibar.

**ZALA PARK** The Zanzibar Land Animals Park (Zala Park for short) is in the village of Muungoni, just south of Kitogani (✪ *KITOGA 6°17.34'S; 39°26.306'E*), where the main road from Zanzibar Town divides into roads towards Paje and Makunduchi.

At first glance it's just a zoo, with various pens and compounds to hold the animals (mostly reptiles). However, this private project, run by the tireless and enthusiastic Mohammed Ayoub, has a more important purpose. It's primarily an education centre for groups of Zanzibari schoolchildren to come and learn about their island's natural heritage.

For tourists this is one of the few places in Zanzibar where you can observe snakes and lizards at close quarters; the chameleons are particularly endearing. Also look out for the geometric tortoises which are not native, but were brought to the park by customs officials who confiscated them at the airport from a smuggler of exotic pets. There are a few other species on display, most notably the small group of tree hyrax who spend some time in their pen and some time in the nearby forest. These part-time zoo animals come back mostly at feeding time, then seem quite content to rest or play in their pen before returning to the trees at nightfall.

Zala Park is only about 3km down the road from Jozani Forest Reserve, and can be combined with a visit there. If you have an overwhelming interest in wildlife, conservation or education, it is sometimes possible to stay in the small one-roomed guesthouse, although this is often used by visiting volunteers. Mohammed plans a nature trail in the nearby forest and mangrove stands, and can organise guided walks if you are interested in seeing more of this area: ideally, this should be arranged in advance.

*Contact:* ✆ *0741 329357;* e *mohdayoub@hotmail.com. Entrance is US$5 adults; free for children. Open daily 08.00–17.30.*

**ZANZIBAR HERITAGE CONSERVATION PARK** This rather grand-sounding place is actually a fairly low-key project run by some local people. Located to the north of the main road from Zanzibar Town to the east coast, west of the village of Tunguu, the park has some game birds on display (which are not that interesting), and a vast garden (which is more interesting) full of spices, herbs, fruit trees and medicinal plants. Everything is labelled, and sometimes a guide is available to show you round and explain the uses of the different plants. There's a small entry charge and it might be worth visiting on the way to Jozani Forest.

## UNGUJA UKUU AND BI KHOLE RUINS

For keen fans of history and archaeology, there are two places of interest in the southwest of the island. Both are just off the main road between Zanzibar Town and Jozani Forest, Paje and Kizimkazi, so make convenient stop-offs en route to there or the southwest coasts.

**UNGUJA UKUU** This is the site of the oldest known settlement on Zanzibar, dating from the end of the 8th century AD. It was believed to have been founded by early Shirazi immigrants from Persia, but recent archaeological evidence from here and other sites on the east coast of Africa suggests that it was Swahili in origin. Research at Unguja Ukuu is still taking place and more evidence may yet come to light.

*Unguja* is the local name for Zanzibar Island today, and *Ukuu* means 'great'. It is believed that the settlement may have been quite large, but was probably

---

**RULES FOR RESPONSIBLE MONKEY-WATCHING**

Jozani Forest asks all visitors to observe the following rules. They apply to watching primates anywhere in Zanzibar, or elsewhere in Africa:

- You must be accompanied by an official guide.
- Do not approach monkeys closer than 3m, and preferably remain at a distance of 5m. This is for your own safety – the monkeys are wild animals and can bite or pass diseases to you.
- Do not invite any interaction with the monkeys or try to feed them. If they come close, avoid eye contact and move away. Do not make noises to attract their attention.
- You are one of the major threats to the monkeys, as primates are susceptible to human diseases. Do not visit the monkeys if you are suffering from any illness, particularly a cold or flu.
- Observe the speed limits if driving through Jozani, and ask your driver to slow down if you're in a minibus. Even though speed-humps have been introduced, monkeys are regularly killed by cars.

11

abandoned in the 10th century when the local Muslim population came under attack. An Arab geographer, writing in the 13th century, recorded that the people of 'Lenguja' had taken refuge from their enemies on the island of Tumbatu, off the northwest shore of Zanzibar Island (see the *Tumbutu Island* box on page 193).

Despite this site's fascinating history, today there is very little remaining that would be of any interest to anyone except the keenest archaeologist: just some shallow earth pits and the remnants of a few crumbling walls.

**Getting there and away** To reach this site, you need to pass through the modern village of Unguja Ukuu, reached by turning south off the main road between Zanzibar Town and the southern part of the east coast, at a junction about halfway between the villages of Tunguu and Pete. South of the village, a small track branches off the dirt road that leads to Uzi Island (reached by tidal causeway; follow this to reach the remains of old Unguja Ukuu.

**BI KHOLE RUINS** Situated about 20km to the southeast of Zanzibar Town, the Bi Khole Ruins are the remains of a large house dating from the 19th century. Khole was a daughter of Sultan Said (*Bi* is a title meaning 'Lady') who came to Zanzibar in the 1840s, after Said moved his court and capital from Oman. With her sister Salme she helped their brother Barghash escape after his plans to seize the throne from Majid were discovered (see *History* and *Economy* sections, pages 16–17).

Khole had this house built for her to use as a private residence away from the town; she is recorded as being a keen hunter and a lover of beautiful things. The house had a Persian-style bath-house where she could relax after travelling or hunting, and was surrounded by a garden decorated with flowering trees and fountains. The house was used until the 1920s but is now ruined, with only the main walls standing, often overgrown,

The main front door has collapsed, but this is still the way into the ruin, over a pile of rubble. Directly in front of the door is a wide pillar, designed so that any visitor coming to the door would not be able to see into the inner courtyard, in case Khole or other ladies of the court were unveiled. In this room are alcoves and niches with arabesque arches, although the windows are rectangular.

**Getting there and away** The Bi Khole Ruins lie a few kilometres to the west of the main road from Zanzibar Town to the southern part of the east coast, about 6km south of the village of Tunguu. The road passes down a splendid boulevard of gnarled old mango trees, supposed to have been planted for Khole (although they may date from before this period): about halfway along is the track to the ruins.

## FUMBA

Fumba is a village at the end of the peninsula, about 15km southeast of Zanzibar Town. From the beach south of the village, local fishermen take their boats out to the islands of Chumbe, Kwale and Pungume, and to the fishing grounds around the smaller islands in Menai Bay. It's a quiet scenic place, but very few tourists come here. If you want to get a deeper insight, ask around for a local villager called Issa Kibwana, who conducts small tours of the nearby fruit and spice plantations. In Zanzibar Town, the people at Sama Tours can help put you in touch, or arrange a trip to Fumba for you.

**GETTING THERE AND AWAY** To get here, take the road from Zanzibar Town towards the airport. Then fork left (east) down a main road just after a petrol station. This will lead you northeast, before turning east and heading south, along the airport runway's eastern boundary fence. Leaving the airport behind you, you'll continue southeast.

After around 5km there is a right turn from the main road, signposted to the Menai Bay Conservation Area. You can continue or turn right to get to Fumba, as these roads join up at the southern end of the peninsula.

Alternatively, take a local bus or *dala-dala* (number 7) from Stone Town.

## WHERE TO STAY There's only one lodge in this area:

⌂ **Fumba Beach Lodge** (26 rooms) PO Box 3075, Stone Town, Zanzibar; ☏ 0777 860504/878025; e reservations@fumbabeachlodge.co.tz/info@fumbabeac hlodge.co.tz; www.fumbabeachlodge.com (⊕ FUMBAB 6°18.898'S; 39°16.501'E). Built on 40 acres of private land, inc 3 separate sandy coves, Fumba Beach Lodge opened its doors in Jun 2005 after only 8 months of construction. Just half an hour from the airport, and currently the only lodge in the WWF's Menai Bay Conservation Area, this is unquestionably one of the islands most stylish places to stay. Designed and built by Edwin and Annemarie, a Dutch couple with a solid African background, Fumba was built in line with contemporary, upmarket safari camps, and they've done a superb job. The result is a fabulously original place that oozes style and has been beautifully crafted with clean, crisp lines and bold colour. There are 20 well-spaced, deluxe rooms with canopied dbl beds, mains electricity, en-suite showers, fans and a sea view; 3 can become family rooms using inter-connecting doors. There are also 6 special suites with huge dbl beds, fabulous sunshine-yellow details, beautifully carved, built-in wooden wardrobes with safes, and tremendous views. Beautiful finishing touches abound, from sweet-smelling cinnamon sticks on the desk to a lovely, natural mobile above the bath, complete with sand dollars, corals and sun-bleached shells. There's a stylish outside shower and a magnificent dbl bath with a view. Large, shuttered terrace doors open onto a private deck and the beach beyond, or there's a delightful rooftop terrace with views out to Kwala Island. Two of these suites are built on the edge of a low coral cliff, around a beautiful baobab tree, into which an additional large outdoor bath has been set. Beside the large, infinity swimming pool is a comfortable cushioned lounge and a sophisticated, open-sided restaurant, specialising in seafood. Nearby the outside bar, 'Dhow FumBar', is constructed from an old dhow and sits under an enormous baobab on the edge of a coral cliff, its west-facing perspective making it a stunning spot for sundowners. The full-day 'Safari Blue' trip (see below) to explore nearby islands and the lagoon departs from the next bay so makes for a very convenient excursion. Following some interesting dives on the surrounding reefs, a dive centre is being built and equipped, with a view to being fully operational in Jun 2006. *Deluxe US$100/142 pp, low/high season; suite US$125/167 pp, low/high season; baobab suite US$140/182 pp, low/high season. All rates are b&b. Children under 2 years free; 2–12 years 50% discount.*

**WHAT TO DO AND SEE** The Menai Bay Conservation Area has a number of picturesque, uninhabited islands and sandbanks to explore as well as some fascinating marine life, and it's well worth taking one of the full-day sailing and snorkelling excursions that Safari Blue (see below) operate in the bay. The experience has been highly recommended by other travellers.

The trip departs at 09.00 from close to Fumba Beach, pausing at the islands and sandbanks for exploration, tasty lunches and relaxation, in between guided snorkelling forays in the turquoise waters and spotting for humpback and bottlenose dolphins.

The first stop of the day is usually Kwale sandbank, an idyllic spot for gentle snorkelling (equipment provided) and sipping fresh coconut milk. Sailing on further, barbecued seafood lunches await on Kwale Island, where tamarind trees offer a shady spot to enjoy a cold beer, or to sample fresh calamari, lobster and fish (vegetarian/non-fish options must be ordered in advance), and a platter of up to a dozen different tropical fruits. It's worth noting that there's a field toilet on the island. A visit to a mangrove lagoon, where swimming is possible during high tide, a walk across the island, and a chance to try your hand at sailing an *ngalawa* follow,

11

Tremendous effort is being made by the government, research institutions and NGOs to increase the returns from seaweed production (see *Seaweed farming*, page 225). At the beginning of 2006, a pilot scheme began to integrate seaweed and shellfish farming. Funded and supported by the Institute of Marine Sciences in Dar es Salaam, Woods Hole Oceanographic Institute in Massachusetts and the McKnight Foundation, the scheme aims to maximise workers' time by engaging them in the farming of both seaweed and shellfish, particularly oysters. Some 200 women from Fumba, Bweleo, Nyamanzi and Unguja Ukuu are already involved in the project and it's hoped that the benefits of a dual income will considerably improve their independence and standard of living. If the scheme proves successful it will be a model easily transferred to other island communities.

To complement this work, the Institute of Marine Science is also working with the Western Indian Ocean Marine Sciences Association (WIOMSA), the Coastal Resource Center (CRC) at the University of Rhode Island and USAID on a programme called Sustainable Coastal Communities and Ecosystems (SUCCESS). Operating as a local NGO, they aim to promote the inclusion of shellfish on tourist hotel menus so as to increase its overall consumption. It is hoped that this raised demand for shellfish will drive market prices up, and ultimately improve the incomes of the shellfish collectors and farmers. In addition, SUCCESS has built a kiosk in Fumba which by mid-2006 will sell shellfish meals made by the women to the tourists who are passing though on their way to islands in the Zanzibar Channel. The organisation is also researching an alternative method of seaweed farming in deeper water.

before the dhow's lanteen sail is hoisted and the boat heads back to Fumba, returning around 18.00.

There is an element of forward thinking needed for this trip. Fumba Beach is a remote beach with no formal changing facilities, so wear any swimwear under your clothes. Shade is available on the boats and beaches but remember to apply sunscreen and preferably wear a T-shirt for snorkelling. Towels and waterproof shoes are also recommended as you'll most likely have to wade out to the boat across coral rock.

*Rates: US$45 adult, US$22 child aged 6–14 years. Children under 6 years free. The excursion is fully inclusive of guided snorkelling, use of snorkelling equipment, all food and drinks, activities and the entrance fee of US$3pp to the Menai Bay. Transfers from Stone Town to Fumba cost an additional US$50/vehicle and must be privately arranged.*

**Safari Blue** Safari Blue *(PO Box 4056, Zanzibar;* ✆ *0777 423162;* e *adventure@zanlink.com; www.safariblue.net;* ✆ *SAFBLU 6°19.163'S; 39°16.832'E)* has been operating in Zanzibar since 1996 and many of the local crew have worked with the company since its inception. The trips are made on board locally made, traditional sailing dhows 8–10m in length, which have been kitted out with Yamaha outboard engines, marine VHF radios, life jackets, sunshades, boarding ladders, first-aid kits, fire blankets, and waterproof bags for cameras and valuables. Public liability and marine insurance complete the adherence to safety.

## CHUKWANI

The small village of Chukwani, to the south of Zanzibar Town, is about 5km beyond Ras Mbweni. Southwest of the village, on the coast, is the Chukwani Palace. It was built by Sultan Barghash in 1872 and used mainly as a place to recuperate after illness, as the air here was supposed to be particularly healthy. The palace was built as a smaller version of the House of Wonders, without the tower. During the reign of Sultan Ali bin Hamoud (sultan from 1902 to 1911) the palace was used by government officers.

Today, most of the palace has been demolished, leaving only the bath-house. The new buildings around the ruins are used by the army, so visitors are not allowed to enter, but you can get a good view from the air if you fly out of Zanzibar as the palace lies only a few kilometres southwest of the airport.

## WHERE TO STAY

**Coconut Beach Inn** (6 rooms) PO Box 3587; 024 2235897, 0742 740030; e coconutbeachinn@hotmail.com. This quiet and simple place is about 9km south of Zanzibar Town, on the road towards Chukwani, about 4km from where the road to Mbweni turns off the main airport road. The owner-managers are relaxed and friendly, and the setting is perfect. Six little cottages surround a swimming pool overlooking the beach, with views straight out to Chumbe Island. Evening meals (lots of seafood, around US$4) and lunches are available. US$30 pp.

**Mawimbini Club Village** (85 rooms) 024 2231163. Near the village of Chuini, about 20km outside Stone Town, this is an international-style resort complex, part of the Italian VentaClub chain, catering almost exclusively for fly-in package tourists. The hotel consists of bungalows set in a large garden around a central area with a swimming pool, restaurant and bar. A theatre has regular dancing and cabaret shows. To stay here, it is perhaps easier to make arrangements through one of the tour companies in Zanzibar Town. US$100–200 pp, FB.

## CHUMBE ISLAND

Chumbe lies about 10km south of Zanzibar Town, and is one of the largest of the offshore islands in this area. The coral reef surrounding Chumbe Island is in very good condition because until recently the island was inside a military area and public access was not allowed. Consequently, it has not been damaged by high volumes of tourists, transfer boats, or destructive fishing techniques employed by local fishermen. The reefs around Chumbe were officially gazetted as a Marine National Park (the first in Tanzania) in 1994, and the island has since been declared a Forest Reserve. Together, the island and reef are known as Chumbe Island Nature Reserve or Chumbe Island Coral Park (CHICOP).

CHICOP's own information publicity states: 'Chumbe Island is a rare example of a still pristine coral island eco-system in an otherwise heavily over-fished and overexploited area. It includes a reef sanctuary and a forest and bird sanctuary of exceptional biodiversity.' This has been verified by various global conservation and scientific bodies, including IUCN, WWF and Unesco. A specialist from the Australian Institute of Marine Sciences called Chumbe 'one of the most spectacular coral gardens to be found anywhere in the world'.

Over 350 species of fish have been identified in the reef and surrounding area. Other marine wildlife frequently seen includes turtles, sharks and dolphins. On the island, 60 species of bird have been recorded, including breeding pairs of the rare roseate tern (*Sterna dougallii*). The island is also home to various lizards and a population of rare giant coconut crabs (*Birgus latro*) – see box on page 258. Ader's duiker (*Cephalophus adersi*), an endangered small antelope whose range is restricted to a handful of coastal forests in and around Zanzibar, was recently reintroduced to Chumbe and appears to be thriving.

Buildings of historical and cultural interest on Chumbe include a lighthouse built by the British in 1904 (still clearly visible from ships approaching Zanzibar from Dar es Salaam), now converted into an observation tower, and an old mosque built in an Indian style unique to Tanzania. A cottage originally built for the lighthouse-keepers has been converted into a visitor information centre, including an education room

Common on Chumbe Island, yet endangered elsewhere in the South Pacific and Indian Ocean, the rare and remarkable 'coconut crab' (*Birgus latro*) is the world's largest land invertebrate.

A member of the *Coenobitidae* family, it is one of only a few hermit crabs that is wholly adapted to spending most of its life away from the sea. In some areas coconut crabs are known to move several kilometres inland; however, they do begin life in the sea, with the female depositing hatched eggs in the water as planktonic larvae (*zoea*). Over a matter of a few weeks, the larvae develop claws to become *megalopa*, and sink to the sea bed as tiny crabs, in search of a protective shell. They retain these shells when they reach land, discarding them only when their carapace is fully hardened. Unlike other hermit crabs, these creatures develop a dual-purpose shell over their abdomen, similar in appearance to a lobster. This guards against water loss and saves on 'house-hunting'. And without the need to fit inside abandoned shells, the coconut crab is free to grow indefinitely, accounting for its serious size (adults have been recorded with a 3ft leg span!).

Nocturnal by nature, the crabs are most active at night, scavenging and feeding on decaying vegetation, fruit, small animals, and naturally coconuts. Although adept at climbing palms to reach the coconuts, these crabs do not actually have any special adaptations for scaling tree trunks. The crab will use its powerful claws to heave itself up to the coconut snip it off the palm using its sharp pincers, descend the tree backwards (facing up), gather its prize and feast. With its razor-sharp claws, the crab attacks the coconut, ripping away the husk, cracking its shiny nut and devouring the flesh inside.

The coconut crab is listed on the IUCN endangered species list, with no record of the number in existence. Habitat destruction, human hunting and introduced predators continue to threaten their global survival. Happily, Chumbe Island reports a healthy population and is working to gain international support for the protection of this amazing species. Guided by one of the island's staff, you are likely to be able to watch them forage by night (especially in the salubrious surroundings of the camp's compost heap!) – but keep still and quiet; the crabs have poor eyesight and so detect predators and threats by vibrations.

for local schoolchildren who are brought here by the Chumbe management and other conservation organisations to learn about local environmental issues.

Tourism is being developed on Chumbe in a very sensitive manner. In conjunction with an environmental organisation called Green Ocean, trails have been established through the forest, along the inter-tidal section of the beach, and across the reefs. Permanent moorings have been built to allow visitors in boats to reach the coral without needing to drop anchor, and local fishermen have been employed as marine park rangers. Profits from tourists visiting the island are channelled back into local education and conservation projects.

Chumbe Island's unique situation has been recognised by an almost unparalleled string of awards for its responsible approach to tourism, and its ecologically sensitive approach to the environment. Meanwhile Chumbe seems effortlessly to combine a tourist attraction with a centre for ongoing education projects for the local people. It is an exceptional place.

For tourists, day trips to the island are available (these cost US$70 including all transfers, snorkelling equipment, guides and lunch) when the island isn't full, but visitors are encouraged to spend at least one night here – and two or three would be perfect.

## WHERE TO STAY

**Chumbe Island Lodge** (6 rooms) PO Box 3203; 0777 413 582; f 024 231040; e chumbe@zitec.org; www.chumbeisland.com. Run as part of the Chumbe Island Coral Park (CHICOP), this superb, trail-blazing lodge is an example of truly eco-friendly accommodation. Its 6 bungalows are simple but clean, very comfortable, ingeniously designed and genuinely ecologically sensitive. Each bungalow has 2 storeys and is made mostly from local materials using traditional construction techniques, and yet employing cutting-edge eco-architectural systems. Downstairs there's an open-fronted, lounge-terrace, complete with dbl seaview hammock, animal mosaics inlaid in the floor, and a bathroom at the rear. Upstairs, the bedroom comprises a comfortable mattress laid on the floor, shrouded in a mosquito net, and a stunning view through the ocean or stars, for the triangular front wall can be entirely lowered using a pulley system. The chalets are completely self-sufficient with solar panels to provide electricity, funnel-shaped roofs to catch, filter and store rainwater (there is no good groundwater on the island), and even 'compost toilets' to avoid septic tanks and the pollutants they often produce. Used water from the showers goes onto flowerbeds where specially chosen plants absorb salts and minerals before the water drains into the ground. This accommodation is unique in Zanzibar, and very unusual in the whole of Africa. The central area is a huge, star-shaped makuti structure – perfect for catching the sea breeze in the heat of the day. Simple, fresh meals and drinks are served on the terrace (on the sounding of a large gong), and there's a lovely upper deck of hammocks and chairs for chilling and counting blessings. The reference library and education centre are also here. Activities focus on learning about the surrounding environment and ecology, and include escorted snorkelling (scuba diving is prohibited) on the nearby reefs, escorted forest walks along the nature trail, and walks conducted across the inter-tidal zone on the beach. The coconut crab is a nocturnal creature and seldom seen in daylight, but if you ask the staff to take you into the woodland at dusk or after dark, you are virtually guaranteed to see several!

The lodge is a non-profit organisation and ploughs its proceeds back into great community education and conservation initiatives, making it not only a stunning holiday spot, but a cause worthy of great support. *US$230/400 sgl/dbl inc of FB, soft drinks, guides, transfers and all activities; rates are lower Apr–Jun.*

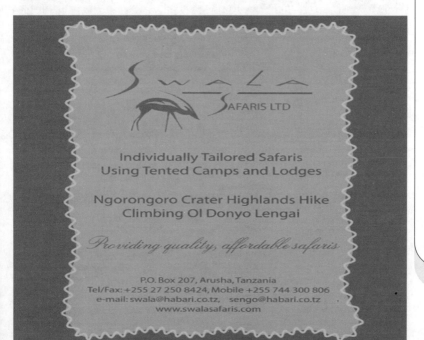
259

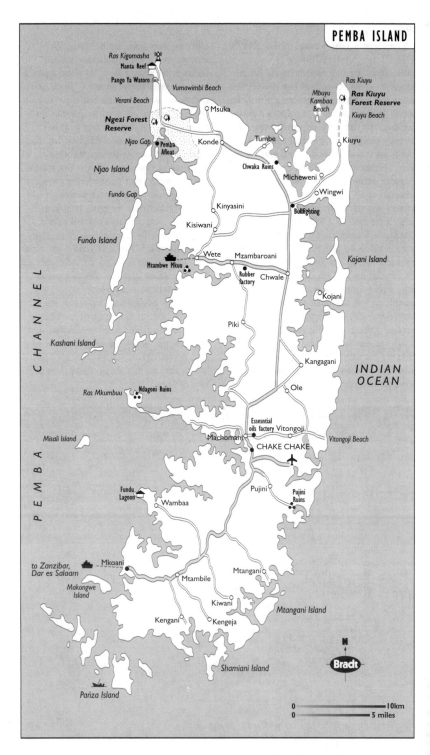

PEMBA ISLAND

Ras Kigomasha
Manta Reef
Pango Ya Watoro
Vumawimbi Beach
Verani Beach
Msuka

Ras Kiuyu
Mbuyu Kambaa Beach
**Ras Kiuyu Forest Reserve**
Kiuyu Beach

**Ngezi Forest Reserve**
Njao Gap
Pemba Afloat
Konde
Tumbe
Kiuyu

Njao Island
Chwaka Ruins
Micheweni
Wingwi

Fundo Gap
Kinyasini
Bullfighting

Fundo Island
Kisiwani

Kojani Island

Wete
Mzambaroani
Mtambwe Mkuu
Chwale
Rubber factory
Kojani

Piki

Kashani Island

Kangagani

INDIAN OCEAN

Ras Mkumbuu
Ndagoni Ruins
Ole

Essential oils factory
Vitongoji

Misali Island
Machomani
CHAKE CHAKE
Vitongoji Beach

Fundu Lagoon
Wambaa
Pujini
Pujini Ruins

to Zanzibar, Dar es Salaam
Mkoani
Mtangani

Makongwe Island
Mtambile
Kiwani
Mtangani Island

Kengani
Kengeja

Shamiani Island

Panza Island

PEMBA CHANNEL

Bradt

N

0          10km
0          5 miles

# 12

# Pemba

Pemba Island lies about 80km to the northeast of Zanzibar Island (Unguja), and about the same distance from the Tanzanian mainland, directly east of the port of Tanga. Smaller than Zanzibar Island, at just 67km long, it covers an area of 985km² and has a more undulating landscape, even though its highest point is only about 95m above sea level. But one of the first things that most strikes the visitor is how green it is. More densely vegetated than Zanzibar (with both natural forest and plantation), Pemba has always been seen as a more fertile place. The early Arab sailors called it *El Huthera*, meaning 'The Green'. Today, as always, far more cloves are grown here than on Zanzibar Island.

With 362,168 inhabitants at the last census, in 2002, Pemba is – like Zanzibar Island – one of the most densely populated areas of Tanzania, although this is no urban jungle. Most of the population lives in traditional square houses, with a wooden frame and mud walls, the thatched roofs occasionally upgraded to corrugated iron. The largest town on Pemba is Chake Chake, the island's capital and administrative centre, about halfway down the western side of the island. The island's other main towns are Wete, in the northern part of the island, and Mkoani, in the south, which is the main port.

As in Zanzibar as a whole, the people are predominantly Muslim. Right across the island, women wear the veil, most in bright colours but some in sombre black, while schoolgirls look immaculate in the uniform dark skirts and cream veils. Typically it's a subsistence economy, with cloves the only real revenue earner, and few jobs available, so the nascent tourist industry brings much-needed employment. Although English is spoken in the larger hotels, and by most of those who regularly come into contact with tourists, few villagers speak anything other than Swahili, so it's advisable to learn at least a few words of the language.

## HIGHLIGHTS

For today's visitor, Pemba's greatest attractions include long, empty beaches, some excellent diving and snorkelling, particularly around Misali Island, and the unspoilt forest reserve at Ngezi. There are several small historical sites which, although not 'must sees', certainly repay a visit if you use just a little imagination. Perhaps more important, though, with relatively few visitors, and little in the way of tourist facilities, Pemba is still a place where travel for its own sake (by car, bus, bike or on foot) remains a prime reason for visiting.

## NATURAL HISTORY AND ENVIRONMENT

Verdant and very fertile, Pemba was once densely forested, although all that remains now is Ngezi Forest, on the northwestern tip of the island. Nevertheless, numerous spice and fruit trees dominate the rest of the landscape. Cloves represent

For the people of east Africa, the island of Pemba is particularly known as a centre for traditional medicine and witchcraft. The British writer Evelyn Waugh, in his classic travel book *Remote People* (1931), described Pemba as a centre of 'black art' learning, and went on to record how '... novices would come from as far as the great lakes [of central Africa] to graduate there. Even from Haiti, it is said, witchdoctors will come to probe the deepest mysteries of voodoo. Nowadays everything is kept hidden from the Europeans, and even those who have spent most of their lives in the country have only now and then discovered hints of the wide, infinitely ramified cult which still flourishes below the surface.'

Sixty years later, little had changed. A 1995 travel story in a British newspaper reported that the village of Vitongoji, in the centre of the island, was 'the capital of Pemban sorcery ... a place of dark secrets. Some years ago a witchdoctor was arrested for eating children in the course of his duties.' This report may have been tongue-in-cheek, but it's an inescapable fact that local people seeking cures for spiritual or physical afflictions still come to the local doctors of Pemba from Zanzibar Island, mainland Tanzania, Kenya, and even as far as Uganda and Congo.

As a visitor to Pemba from the West, you shouldn't expect to be taken to see any cures or ceremonies. This type of thing is strictly for the locals. Even the most innocent of questions about witchcraft from tourists here will be met with nothing more than embarrassed smiles or polite denials. For more details on traditional religion and witchcraft, see pages 36–7.

---

the biggest cash crop, with Pemba responsible for the vast majority of cloves exported from Zanzibar, and sales monopolised by the government (see page 48). For several months each year, cloves are left to dry in the sun on mats by the side of the road. Consumption of almost all other fruit and spices, however, is restricted to domestic use. Mango, banana, avocado, coconut, citrus fruits, pineapple and papaya grow almost side by side with less familiar fruits: breadfruit, custardfruit, plantain, tamarind, bungo and jack fruit – this last a huge and hard sponge-looking thing that yields an improbably sweet flesh. Spices such as ginger, vanilla, cinnamon and pepper also grow in abundance.

Of the three primates that inhabit the island, the most visible is the Pemba vervet monkey (tumbili au kima, *Cercopithecus aethiops nesiotes*), while the small-eared galago or bushbaby (komba, *Otolemur garnettii garnettii*) is more likely to be heard than seen, its human-sounding cry disturbing many an otherwise peaceful night. A small population of Kirk's red colobus is also present in Ngezi Forest. Relatively easy to spot is the Pemba flying fox (popo wa Pemba, *Pteropus voeltzkowi*), a large fruit bat which is the only fully endemic mammal on Pemba, and is classified as a globally endangered species. Its name comes from its orange fur and dog-like snout and ears. This animal seeks out the high canopies of undisturbed forest with a ready supply of fruit and tree blossoms. Pemba flying foxes roost throughout Pemba, particularly along the west coast and on islands off the west coast, but are readily seen at Ngezi Forest where the forest rangers monitor their whereabouts, and at Kidike. They feed on soft fruits and weigh up to 1.5kg. Local people consider their flesh a delicacy, tasting like an oily chicken.

The Zanzibar tree hyrax (pelele, *Dendrohyrax validus neumannii*) is present not only at Ngezi but also on Njao and Fundo islands, whereas the rare and threatened Pemba blue duiker (paa wa pemba, *Cephalophus monticola pembae*) and marsh mongoose (chonjwe, *Atilax paludinosus rubescens*) are to be found only in Ngezi Forest.

Bird species on the island include three endemics: the russet or Pemba scops owl, which is fairly common in the clove plantations and at Ngezi, the Pemba white-eye, and the Pemba violet-breasted sunbird. A number of sub-endemic species include the Pemba green pigeon, the African paradise flycatcher, and the Pemba African goshawk. Without doubt, the best place to see birds on Pemba is in the Ngezi Forest. For more details, see pages 286–7.

## GETTING THERE AND AWAY

### TO/FROM THE MAINLAND

**By air** Daily services between Dar es Salaam and Pemba are run by ZanAir and Coastal Aviation (for contact details, see page 104), although all flights go via Zanzibar, and some may involve a change of plane. The duration of the flight is just over an hour. At the time of research, ZanAir flights depart Dar es Salaam at 09.00 Monday, Tuesday, Friday, Saturday and Sunday, returning at 10.15; there's also a daily flight leaving Dar at 15.15, and returning at 16.45. Coastal's flights are at 14.00, returning at 16.40. The one-way fare for non-residents is US$85, plus any fuel surcharge which may be operational (currently US$5).

Coastal also has a daily half-hour flight between Pemba and Tanga (on the Tanzania mainland) for US$55, leaving Pemba at 15.15; return flights leave for Tanga at 16.00. If you're coming from any other part of Tanzania or Kenya and want a direct flight, your only option is to charter a plane. In Dar, Nairobi or Mombasa, a travel agent will be able to help you. Spare seats on charter flights are sometimes sold to individuals. Once again, the best thing to do is contact a travel agent, who will probably phone the airport or one of the local charter companies to see if anything is going your way.

On leaving Pemba, don't forget that there is a US$6 departure tax (made up of US$5 'safety' tax, and a further US$1 airport tax), and be prepared to hand this over in cash. The modern terminal has few facilities – just a small bar serving drinks, a couple of toilets, and that's it.

**By sea** For some time, the only scheduled ship from the mainland to Pemba has been the *Sepideh*, which plies daily between Dar and Zanzibar Island, continuing on to Pemba (Mkoani) three times a week. The fare between Dar and Pemba is US$55. Recently, however, a new service – the *SES II* – has started up on the same route, with similar timing and the same fares. In addition, the *Aziza* operates a weekly service connecting Tanga with Zanzibar Island and Wete on Pemba. For details of all these, see under *To/from Zanzibar Island*, below.

In theory, there is a once-a-week service on the *New Happy* between Tanga and Wete, leaving Wete on Sundays at 09.00 and returning on Tuesday mornings. In practice, though, this service is none too reliable; for the current state of play, and for details of any other boats on this route, contact the tourist office in Chake Chake.

Similarly, you can in theory reach Pemba by dhow from Tanga or from Mombasa, in Kenya, although police at the port are unwilling to let tourists board, with good reason – the safety record on these boats is pretty dire (see page 75), and it's worth remembering, too, that services are irregular and far from idyllic. Most dhows from Tanga or Mombasa go to Wete, but a few go to Mkoani.

**Immigration formalities** Whichever type of boat you use to reach Pemba from the mainland (Kenya or Tanzania), you need to show your passport to the immigration officials at the port. This is a very relaxed and low-key affair. So low key in fact that sometimes the office is empty, and you have to go to the police station in town to present your credentials, or get redirected to wherever the immigration staff might be.

## TO/FROM ZANZIBAR ISLAND

**By air** Scheduled flights run by ZanAir and Coastal Aviation between Pemba and Dar es Salaam (see above) all touch down in Zanzibar Island in both directions. On all flights, the one-way fare for non-residents is US$70, plus the departure tax of TSh6,000.

Your other option for reaching Pemba from Zanzibar Island is to fly with one of the local air-charter companies based in Zanzibar Town. If you can get a group together and charter a whole plane, it can sometimes be cheaper per person than buying a ticket on a regular flight. Alternatively, these companies will often sell spare seats on charter flights to Pemba for US$50–100. In high season there are flights at least every other day, so it's worth contacting the companies direct, or getting a travel agency to do it for you, to see if there's anything going. For contact details, see *Scheduled flights* in *Chapter 5* (pages 103–4).

To book scheduled or charter flights to the mainland from Pemba, contact Pemba Aviation & Airport Services (the Coastal agent) opposite the National Microfinance Bank in Chake Chake, or the ZanAir agent on the other side of the road. Alternatively you can phone the airport control tower (✆ *024 245 2238*) and enquire yourself. This is a fairly standard procedure – the charter companies often tell the tower if they're looking for passengers to fill spare seats.

**By sea** Nearly all passenger ships, and some cargo ships, coming into Pemba arrive at the town of Mkoani (at the southern end of Pemba Island), while it's mostly cargo ships and dhows that go to/from Wete (at the northern end of Pemba Island). Very few ships or dhows, other than local fishing boats, go to/from Chake Chake. (In fact the old harbour of Chake Chake is silted up and only canoes can get here; the town's port is now at Wesha, about 10km west along the coast.) Schedules given below were correct at the time of research, but are notoriously unreliable and subject to change.

For more details on buying tickets to Pemba on one of the ships listed below, see under *Passenger ships and ferries* in *Chapter 5*, pages 105–6. To buy tickets on Pemba, contact the relevant local agent in Chake Chake, Mkoani or Wete (see pages 275, 278 and 282–3).

🚢 **Sepideh** Operated by Mega Speed Liners, the Sepideh runs between Dar es Salaam and Zanzibar Island once a day, with a service to Pemba (Mkoani) 3 times a week in each direction (currently Mon, Thu, Sat). It leaves Pemba at 13.30, and takes about 2hrs. Pemba–Dar US$55 1-way; Pemba–Zanzibar US$35.

🚢 **Aziza** This leisurely weekly service connects Pemba (Wete) with Zanzibar Is and Tanga. It leaves Zanzibar on Fri at 22.00, arriving 06.00 in Wete; dep Wete for Tanga Sun 10.00, taking 4hrs, returning Tue at 10.00 to arrive in Wete at 14.00, and finally leaves Wete for Zanzibar on Wed at 06.30, arriving 14.30. US$20 1-way.

🚢 **Mapinduzi** Between Zanzibar Island and Pemba, this old government-run Zanzibar Shipping Corporation ship plies between Zanzibar Town and Mkoani, carrying both cargo and passengers; in season, the smell of cloves being loaded on board is highly pervasive. Departs Zanzibar Is on Mon and Fri at 22.00, returning from Pemba on Tue and Sat at around 10.00, with the journey taking about 6hrs. US$15 1-way on deck; cabin bed: US$20 2nd class, US$25 1st class.

🚢 **Serengeti** Much more reliable than the old ZSC vessel is the passenger ship Serengeti, operated by Azam Marine Ltd. The 6–8hr crossing between Zanzibar Town and Mkoani runs 3 times a week (currently Tue, Thu, Sat), returning the following day. US$20 1-way.

**SES II** A new speedboat owned by Fast Ferries Ltd commenced operations between Dar, Zanzibar Island and Mkoani on Pemba in Nov 2005. Like the *Sepideh*, it serves Pemba 3 times a week in each direction (Wed, Fri, Sun), leaving Pemba at 13.00, and taking around 1½hrs – 30 minutes faster than the *Sepideh*. The sole agent on Pemba is Bachaa in Wete (see page 282). *Pemba–Dar US$55 1-way; Pemba–Zanzibar US$35.*

Most of Pemba's **dhow** traffic goes to/from Tanga on the mainland, and only occasionally do dhows go between Zanzibar Town and Pemba. Of those that do, most land at Mkoani. Although it is illegal in Tanzania for tourists to travel by dhow, and not especially safe, some intrepid travellers still report finding captains willing to take them on board. If you're determined to consider this, read the section on travel by dhow under *Getting to Zanzibar by sea* in *Chapter 5*.

## GETTING AROUND

Pemba's road system was given a boost in 2005 with the completion of the tarred road across the island from Mkoani to Konde, paid for by the World Bank. North of Konde, and elsewhere, however, most of the roads are pretty poor, with access to some of the outlying villages requiring 4x4 vehicles, particularly in the rainy season. From Chake Chake to Wete, a bumpy alternative to the main road is the 'old' – and more direct – road via Mzambaraoni, which goes through some beautiful scenery. Timewise, though, the new road is considerably quicker, despite the apparent diversion.

Options for getting around on Pemba are limited, although public transport allows independent travellers to see at least some parts of the island. To get further afield independently you'll have to hire a bike, motorbike, car or boat. It is also possible to arrange a car with driver, or an organised excursion, through hotels and guesthouses, a local tour company, or direct with the drivers.

For many travellers, the easiest way to set up an excursion or a tour of the island is to contact a driver, either direct (see below) or through your hotel or guesthouse. Alternatively, there are a number of companies in Chake Chake and Wete that can organise this for you (see pages 275 and 282–3).

**TAXIS AND CAR HIRE** It's pretty straightforward to rent a car with a driver for around US$70 a day, including petrol, depending on the distance you want to travel. Most of the hotels can organise this for you, as can tour companies. Alternatively, try contacting one of the following, both of whom offer tours to various places of interest around the island. They are reliable, interesting guides, and both speak excellent English:

🚗 **Said Mohammed Said** ℡ 0747 430201. Known to everyone as Saidi. Offers city tours, spice tours, transport to the north and east (inc 4x4 by arrangement), and visits to all Pemba's places of interest.

🚗 **Suleiman Seif** ℡ 0747 431793. The driver for Fundu Lagoon also offers a range of tours. He is a mine of information and is particularly knowledgeable about the island's spice and fruit trees.

In Chake Chake, vehicles and drivers wait for business outside the ZTC Hotel. In Mkoani and Wete they can be found near the market. Rates vary according to the vehicle: pick-ups, saloon cars, minibuses, Land Rovers and small Suzuki 'jeeps' are often available. Rates are also negotiable and should be discussed fully (and agreed) in advance. To give you an idea, a trip from Chake Chake to Wete or Mkoani costs about US$40 return. If you're planning a tour, a newish vehicle covering a round trip from Chake to Wete, Ngezi Forest and Manta Reef Lodge and back would cost about US$70. All rates include petrol. Whatever you hire, part payment in advance is usually required, and the first stop is likely to be the petrol station.

Although in theory it's possible to self drive, in practice this is less easy to set up. Some of the tour companies may be able to help, or perhaps North Lodge in Wete (see page 281), though unless you strike lucky you'll need to speak Swahili. Do check the insurance details, and see page 106 for further information.

**MOTORBIKE AND BICYCLE HIRE** There is no official establishment in Pemba for hiring bikes, although it's perfectly possible to hire both motorbikes and pedal bikes in each of the four main towns. The system seems to involve simply finding somebody who is not using their bike and doesn't mind making some extra shillings lending it out to tourists. Rates start at about US$2 a day for a bicycle, and US$20 for a motorbike. Be warned, however: motorbikes or scooters – locally known as *piki piki* – can be extremely dangerous, both on pot-holed side roads and on the main north–south road, where erratic driving, sharp bends and numerous chickens or goats are just some of the hazards. If you're determined to go this route, check that your vehicle is in reasonable condition, particularly the tyres and the rims.

Alternatively, you can sometimes arrange to hire a bike or motorbike through your hotel. Tell the staff what you want to do, and they may well know someone who can help you out – prices will be the same as mentioned above. If you're staying at Swahili Divers in Chake Chake, single-gear mountain bikes are in theory available for guests, though they're not in the greatest condition. Both Sharook Guesthouse and North Lodge in Wete also rent bikes for around US$5 a day – see page 281.

**BUS, MINIBUS AND DALA-DALA** Pemba's main form of transport is by *dala-dala* (see pages 108–9). Pemba used to be served by quaint old buses (actually converted trucks with wooden benches and canopies on the back), but these days they've been replaced by more modern *dala-dalas* (converted pick-ups) or the occasional minibus. Routes and numbers are listed below. On the main routes, of which the number 606 seems to have the most frequent service, there are several buses each day (at least one an hour after 06.00, or after 04.00 during Ramadan), but on the minor routes buses might operate only a few times – or just once – per day, and that'll be in the morning. Services to/from Mkoani are tied in closely with ship (especially *Sepideh*) arrival and departure times. In fact, it seems that Pemba Island's entire public transport system revolves around ship timetables. The fare on the longer routes (eg: Chake Chake to Mkoani) is about Tsh1,000/US$1. For shorter trips it's half that. The most useful routes for visitors are as follows, though it's worth noting that *dala-dalas* will stop to collect or drop off passengers at any point along their route:

## Route

| | | | |
|---|---|---|---|
| 602 | Chake Chake to Konde | 319 | Chake Chake to Pujini |
| 603 | Chake Chake to Mkoani | 330 | Chake Chake to Wambaa |
| 606 | Chake Chake to Wete | 10 | Wete to Wingwi/Micheweni |
| 305 | Chake Chake to Wesha (Chake's port) | 24 | Wete to Konde |
| 316 | Chake Chake to Vitongoji, about 5km east of Chake Chake | | |

Other buses connect Chake Chake and, to a lesser extent, Wete with outlying villages; for details, check with the station manager at the bus depot in each town.

Power cuts are more frequent on Pemba than they are on Zanzibar Island, and last much longer. According to one local, the power cuts out every third day, and sometimes is unavailable for two or three weeks when the generators run out of fuel and more has to be ordered. Despite plenty of rumours to the contrary, plans to improve reliability have yet to materialise.

Although the power is more reliable at night, some hotels have their own generators. Nevertheless, it's worth bearing in mind when choosing a room that having an electric fan or air conditioning is not nearly as important as having some sort of natural breeze.

**BOAT HIRE** Aside from booking through one of the hotels, there's no organised means of getting from Pemba across to the individual islands. That said, it's worth asking at Wacom in Chake Chake (see page 275), who sometimes have a boat called *Victoria 2* for hire. Alternatively, some of the local fishermen are prepared to carry passengers for a fee, which is fine for short distances, but do remember that the longer crossings – especially to Misali Island – could take a considerable period of time, and be pretty uncomfortable, especially in rough seas.

## ACCOMMODATION

Pemba has a very small number of places to stay compared with Zanzibar Island, from rock-bottom basic hotels and small local guesthouses through to a good backpackers-cum-dive lodge. More exclusively, the coastal areas boast just one mid-range hotel and a highly exclusive tourist hideaway. While rumours of further options have been mooted for some time, little has changed in recent years. For divers, though, there is the added bonus of a permanently moored live-aboard, as well as a number of more conventional live-aboards (see page 271).

As on Zanzibar Island, all accommodation on Pemba must officially be paid for with hard currency: cash US dollars are preferred, and anything else (pounds, euros) may not be accepted, unless otherwise quoted. If you have only Tanzanian shillings, these are usually accepted at the current rate of exchange. Breakfast is normally included in the room price unless stated otherwise. Other meals are payable in Tanzanian shillings. Also as on Zanzibar Island, during quiet times many of the lodges and guesthouses on Pemba lower their rates. Even if reductions aren't advertised, it's often worth asking about this. At the cheaper places, rates are often negotiable at any time of year.

## FOOD AND DRINK

All the hotels on Pemba serve food, although at the cheaper places it has to be ordered, even by residents – sometimes quite a long time in advance. Additionally, the island's main towns have simple restaurants where you can get local dishes, and Chake Chake has a couple of places with more elaborate options. Alongside the basics, featuring varying combinations of chicken, fish, chips and rice, many of the restaurants sell Indian-influenced dishes such as pilau and biryani.

Roadside stalls proliferate during market hours, most selling variations on meat kebabs (*mishkaki*) and omelettes. For a nutritious and cheap meal, try *chipsi mai yai* – an omelette filled with chips, sometimes served with shredded cabbage, for around TSh400. On the drinks front, it's easy enough to get branded fizzy drinks such as Coke and Fanta, but more refreshing is the local pineapple soft drink, brand-named Zed. And if you fancy a snack (or a simple souvenir), seek out the tamarind sweetmeat sold in small, hand-woven palm-leaf baskets. Called *haluwa*, it's made from oil and sugar, costs just a few shillings, and is so sweet that one packet will happily serve a whole group. Open it with caution, though – *haluwa* is very sticky. The best on the island is said to come from Wete.

For lunches or picnics, you can buy fruit at the markets and roadside stalls in Chake Chake, Mkoani, Wete or Konde. You can also buy bread – either from the occasional stall, or from men on bikes with baskets of fresh loaves on the back. Shops in the towns sell a reasonable range of food in tins and packets, imported from the mainland or elsewhere in the Indian Ocean, but in the smaller villages this kind of stuff is more difficult to find.

## LOCAL SERVICES

**BANKS AND BUREAUX DE CHANGE** Banking is limited to Chake Chake, which has branches of the People's Bank of Zanzibar and the National Microfinance Bank (*open 08.30–15.00, Sat to 12.30*). The banks will change money – US dollars are best, though expect a wait of 30 minutes or so – but travellers' cheques are another story, and likely to be refused. Financially, you may do slightly better at a bureau de change. The only one on Pemba is at the Zanzibar Tourist Corporation (see page 275), but be warned: it takes only US dollars cash, and tends to run out of shillings. An alternative is to ask at a local shop or seek advice from staff at your hotel who may be able to direct you to a local trader who could change cash dollars. Rates may well be higher than at the banks. If you're travelling to Pemba from Dar es Salaam, you'd be well advised to change money at one of the bureaux de change at the airport, or in Dar itself.

**CINEMA** Chake Chake's cinema, located on the main road coming into the town from the south, offers a nightly diet of Hindi melodrama and cheap action movies, with Hollywood films once a week or so. There's more of the same at Wete's inappropriately named Novelty Cinema.

**COMMUNICATIONS** Although there are communications centres in each of the main towns, the introduction of yellow public phone booths has made these somewhat redundant for the visitor. Phones take TTCL phonecards which cost US$10 and are available from the Tanzanian Telecommunications office and numerous other outlets – just look for the TTCL sign outside. International calls cost US$1 a minute. For more general information on telephone services into and out of Zanzibar, see page 99.

There are post offices in Chake, Wete and Mkoani and Konde (*usually open Mon–Thu 08.00–13.00 and 14.00–16.00, Fri 08.00–12.00 and 14.00–17.00*), but public email services are confined to two internet bureaux in Chake Chake (see pages 275–6).

**HOSPITALS AND PHARMACIES** The island's main hospital in Mkoani is a modern place, built with overseas aid. Although it is staffed by dedicated Chinese and Tanzanian doctors, the hospital suffers from shortages of drugs and other essential supplies. There's also a smaller hospital in Chake Chake, which has Western doctors and the island's only obstetrics unit, while X-ray facilities are based at the hospital in Wete, near the ferry port.

There are several pharmacies, including near the hospital in Chake Chake (close to the museum), where reportedly most things are available – if you know what you're looking for, that is.

**TOURIST INFORMATION** The Pemba office of the **Zanzibar Tourist Corporation** (ZTC), the state travel service, is in Chake Chake (see page 275). The manager and members of staff are helpful, and happy to give advice and information about the area, within reason. For their range of services, see pages 140 and 275.

## ACTIVITIES

**DIVING** Recreational diving off Pemba is for the most part confined to the Pemba Channel on the more sheltered west of the island. Misali Island in particular provides a wonderful array of corals and fishlife. Unlike the reefs around Zanzibar Island, many of the reefs off Pemba fall away into steep walls, offering opportunities for some exciting drift dives and the chance to see creatures such as the spotted eagle ray, with its 3m wingspan. Despite Pemba's undoubted reputation for the big pelagics, such as barracuda, trevally, giant groupers and the endangered Napoleon wrasse, sightings of shark are extremely rare on the west of the island, and even to the south. If it's sharks that you're after, you need to dive on the east of the island, where the steep walls and fast currents attract hammerheads. Discuss the options with one of the live-aboard outfits (see page 271), some of whom will visit the east of the island if sea conditions are favourable.

Most of the operators use either speedboats or motorised dhows to get to the dive sites. While the former are undoubtedly faster, there's a lot to be said for the leisurely pace of a dhow, giving the opportunity to take in the beauty of the islands or to watch large teams of fishermen working with their nets from narrow wooden boats. On the way to the dive sites, particularly further north, you may be joined by schools of common or spinner dolphins, just tagging along for the ride.

Diving on Pemba, as on Zanzibar Island, is good all year round, with visibility ranging from 10m to 30m or even more. Between December and March, the water is warm – around 30°C, but even quite early in the season the water temperature is a reasonable 25°C or so, and most operators have good wetsuits if you didn't bring anything suitable. For more details, see the box on page 95. Visibility, current and thus the choice of dive sites is strongly affected by the state of the tide: not just the level, but also whether it is spring or neap. Be guided by your dive instructor on this – it's important. On almost all boats, entry is a backward roll into the water.

**Dive sites** Although much of the reef around Pemba was adversely affected by the El Niño of 1998 (see pages 58–9), and the situation hasn't been improved by dynamite fishing (which sadly continues, despite being illegal), the diver is still spoilt for choice. Dive sites on Pemba tend to have been given different names by the individual dive outfits, so the following is an overview of what to expect.

Particularly popular is the protected area to the west of **Misali Island** (see pages 280–1), with its calm waters and spectacular coral gardens, where most (but not all) of the dives are suitable for novice or relatively inexperienced divers. Improbable giant clams hug the reef, as do numerous smaller creatures such as the exquisitely coloured nudibranchs: keep an eye out for the 30cm Spanish dancer. At one dive to the northwest of the island, though, currents can be strong, so this is more suitable for advanced divers with considerable experience. The rewards can be great however, with eagle rays and some of the big pelagics.

Dives around the southwestern tip of Pemba are for the most part around **Panza Island**, and are normally recommended for advanced divers. Sites here are relatively spread out, with 'blue dives' offering good opportunities to see pelagics. There's also the wreck of a 1950s freighter in 12m of water.

North of Misali, some excellent sites around **Ovinje Gap**, **Fundo Gap** and **Njao Gap** with their steep walls are usually better explored by more advanced divers with plenty of experience, able to cope with strong and sometimes unpredictable currents. Diving through the 'gaps' between the islands can be seriously exciting, earning plenty of comparison with fairground rides and express trains. Even the more leisurely drift dives may not be suitable for a just-certified novice, so do be sure to tell your dive leader if you have any doubts. **Manta Point**, just off Fundo Gap, is a great circular dive, as its name would suggest, with huge mushroom and cabbage corals; even if you don't get to see the manta ray, there are plenty of ocean-going fish in the vicinity, and all sorts of nudibranchs. Out of the currents, gentler dives offer plenty to see, while sheltered lagoons to the east of the islands are good locations to learn to dive and hone your skills. North of Njao Gap, however, the quality of the reef is poor, and dive operators rarely visit.

**Dive companies** There are several dive operators in Pemba, each with its own style, so be sure to check out what is available and choose the right operator for you. Equipment is available to hire from all companies, with standards generally pretty high. All apart from Bahari Divers offer PADI certified courses, including the popular Discover Scuba and Open Water. Night dives can usually be organised with advance notice, except with Swahili Divers. For those interested in underwater photography, cameras can be rented from Manta Reef for US$20 per dive, or from Swahili Divers, who run a photography course for €99.

On a practical note, some of the operators do not carry water on their boats, so check this before you leave and take your own if necessary, particularly in hot weather. For other practical advice, see page 94.

For comparison purposes, prices below have usually been given for a single or two-tank dive, the PADI Open Water course, and dive packages, plus rental of dive equipment. Inevitably, though, options vary considerably, so do check these out.

**✓ Bahari Divers** ☏ 245 2976, Zantel 856678, Pemba 0748 797749; e baharidivers@hotmail.com; www.zanzibar-diving.com. Bahari Divers at Wete is a satellite of the company's main base on Zanzibar Island. Their dive boat departs at 08.00 from Wete harbour, visiting sites to the west of Pemba. Dives are conducted by a PADI divemaster, with trips geared to small groups of experienced divers. Packages are available on request, with accommodation at Sharook or Bomani guesthouses (see page 281) for US$10–15pp, sharing a dbl room. *Sgl dive US$70, 2 tanks US$110, inc equipt; Misali Is extra; dbl dive on each of Zanzibar and Pemba US$175.*

**✓ Fundu Lagoon** ☏ 024 223 2926 (Zanzibar Stone Town), m 0747 438668; f 0747 419906; e fundu@africaonline.co.tz; www.fundulagoon.com. Dive 710, the professional yet friendly dive centre at Fundu Lagoon (see page 279), is exclusive to the resort's guests. Its location, just 20 mins or so by speedboat from the dive sites of Misali Island, makes it possible to leave at a civilised hour for the morning dive and be back in time for lunch. A more leisurely day allows for 2 dives, with a picnic lunch on the island. *Sgl dive Misali Is US$70, 2 tanks (inc picnic) US$140 (further afield additional US$15 per dive); Open Water US$620. Equipt included.*

**✓ Swahili Divers** ☏ 024 2452786; f 024 2452768; e swahilidivers@intafrica.com, www.swahilidivers.com. The longest-established dive operator on Pemba is a relaxed and friendly outfit run by Raf Jah, a well-travelled Brit of Turkish origin. From the company's base at Old Mission Lodge in Chake Chake (see pages 273–4), divers take a short ride by dala-dala-style vehicle to Chake Chake's port at Wesha, then it's a trip of 1½hrs or so in one of 2 traditional wooden boats, *Java Sparrow* or *Kiboko Kidogo* (the name means 'small hippo'), to the dive site, sometimes via Misali Island. But if you want to be on the water all the time, a live-aboard dhow, the *Sahil Reis*, should be ready by the end of 2006. Snorkelling is also on offer, and dhow sailing can be arranged with a day's notice. And if that's not enough, how about a 3-night camping trip on Kashani Island, to the west of Chake Chake, for €495, inc 2 dives per day, and fishing. *Rates (all quoted in euro): 2 tanks €85 (inc* lunch); Open Water €580, inc FB accommodation & PADI materials; 6 nights' FB accommodation & 10 dives €499–599. Equipt €25 per day. Fuel surcharge US$4 per day.

ᵥ✓ **Manta Reef Lodge** PO Box 82234, Mombasa, Kenya; ◥ 0741 320025; f +254 41 471771–2/ 473969/+254 733 619965; e info@oneearthsafaris.com;

www.mantareeflodge.com, www.onearthsafaris.com. On the northwestern tip of the island, Manta Reef was originally set up for divers and runs an efficient dive school with good access to most of Pemba's west coast dive sites. Sgl dive US$40 each, 2 tanks US$80, then on sliding scale; Open Water US$465; equipt US$15 per day.

**Live-aboards** Three live-aboards that cover the area around Pemba, the Aristos, the *Jambo* and the *Kisiwani*, run one-week trips out of Kenya. In addition, Swahili Divers expect their long-awaited live-aboard, *Sahil Reis*, to be operational at some time in 2006, or there's the unique experience of a live-aboard that's firmly anchored in calm waters. Finally, the Floating Beach Resort falls somewhere between a live-aboard and a floating hotel. For details of dive operators who include live-aboards in their itineraries, see page 96.

◤◢ **SY Aristos** ◥ +254 (0)720 441487, (0)733 825718, (0)723 110031; e info@divingsailing.com; www.divingsailing.com. This 17m ketch operates diving and sailing trips out of Kalifi in Kenya. Owned by a former British army officer, Tony Allport, and his Kenyan-born wife, Ali, it regularly visits Pemba and Zanzibar Island, and sometimes Mafia Island. Deep-sea fishing and canoeing are also on the agenda. Max 6 passengers. 7-night cruise about US$1,800 FB, inc unlimited diving; check website for special offers. Courses and equipt extra, by arrangement. Operates Sep–Apr.

◤◢ **Floating Beach Resort** ◥ 0747 414177; book through Italian agents such as Albatros (www.albatros.com) or Viaggiland (www.viaggiland.it). On Pemba, the booking office is in Mkoani, just as you leave the port. The Italian-owned and -run 32m *Relax* forms the basis of a floating hotel, moored off the south coast near Mkoani. Once a hydrofoil, it now features 15 en-suite dbl rooms with fans, a restaurant and bar, with a second, 18m, vessel alongside housing the kitchen and dive centre. Smaller boats take guests diving or on land to laze on the beach or explore further afield. Rates on application.

◤◢ **SY Jambo** Under the same ownership as Manta Reef Lodge (see above), the twin-masted 23m *Jambo* operates out of Shimoni. Impressive under full sail, the boat cruises down the west coast of Pemba, sometimes as far as Ras Nungwi at the northern tip of Zanzibar, with 6 nights on board and the last on land. 5 AC cabins; 2 tender boats. €1,250pp sharing FB, inc land transfers, 3 dives a day & night

dives; dive equipt & some drinks extra; charters available for groups of 5 or more.

◤◢ **MV Kisiwani** Book through one of the specialist dive operators (see opposite). Also based at Shimoni, the 22m motor yacht *Kisiwani* cruises the waters of Pemba for a week at a time. 6 AC cabins. Around US$1,550/£850pp per week FB, inc diving, tanks & weights.

◤◢ **Pemba Afloat** ◥ 0748 400748/0748 341459; e pembaafloat@zanlink.com/ pembaafloat@pembaisland.com; www.pembaisland.com. Bookings on the island can be made through Wacom in Chake Chake. Pemba Afloat consists of 3 20m ketches permanently moored in the calm waters of Njao Lagoon, with just enough breeze to keep the mosis and sandflies away. From the nearby village, fishermen sail or canoe past – it's a scene unchanged for centuries. One of the boats is mainly for daytime use, with a dining area under shade on the deck, while another has cabins for 12 people. Near the mooring is a small reef where beginners learn to dive, and 2 ribs take experienced divers to various sites in the area. Visitors also have use of a canoe and an *ngarlawa* (outrigger sailing dhow). For a spot of dry land, there are regular trips at no extra cost to the surrounding beaches and Ngezi Forest. To reach the boats from Wete is usually a 45-min drive and a 10-min boat ride. US$100 pp per day, all inclusive, plus US$40 per dive, inc equipt. Night dive US$60; PADI tuition on application.

◤◢ **Sahil Reis** Book through Swahili Divers (see opposite). Their new live-aboard should be ready around the end of 2006.

**SNORKELLING** While there is no shortage of places to swim and snorkel off Pemba, most are viable only at high water. One of the best places for snorkelling lies in front of the visitor centre on Misali Island, where – in just a few feet of water, and regardless of the tide – countless fish and other underwater life can be seen in almost perfect visibility. As you drift through the water, keep an eye out among many others for unicornfish, sea goldies, cleaner wrasse, deep red and blue parrotfish, and the startling Moorish idol. Giant clams hug the reef, and sea cucumbers edge along the sandy bottom; you may even spot a grouper. Other possibilities include areas around the sandbanks that dry out at low tide along the west coast. Snorkelling trips can be organised through all the hotels and lodges; expect to pay US$20–40, depending on the distance to the site.

**FISHING AND OTHER WATERSPORTS** The waters of the Pemba Channel are well known for their abundance of fish, including blue marlin, sailfish, barracuda, trevally and kingfish. **Fishing** can be organised from a traditional wooden *mashua* with Swahili Divers, using handlines under the guidance of a local fisherman (US$200 a day, plus approx US$50 fuel costs). Three-hour fishing trips can also be arranged for their own guests with Fundu Lagoon on their 10m catamaran, the *Solkattan* (US$85pp for 2–4 people). At the other end of the scale, Manta Reef Lodge offers three days of game fishing for up to four people at US$2,100–2,300, depending on the season, including lunch, beer and soft drinks. All conventional gear from 6lb to 80lb is provided, but guests should bring their own fly-fishing and spinning equipment. Rather more accessible is a 3–4hr trip at US$150. On a less organised basis, try visiting the harbour at Wete, Wesha or Mkoani. If you ask around, you'll almost certainly find a local fishermen who would be prepared to take you out for a small fee.

All the larger tourist lodges and hotels have **kayaks**, with guided trips offered by Fundu Lagoon for their guests. Manta Reef charges US$25 for up to two hours, US$40 for half a day. At Swahili Divers, marine anthropologist Cisca Jah runs kayak tours under the name Kasa Kayaks. A half-day guided mangrove tour with snacks and support boat costs €40. **Sailing**, too, is available, either in traditional *mashuas*, or – in the case of Fundu Lagoon – in the *Solkattan*. For contact details, see *Diving* above.

## CHAKE CHAKE

Chake Chake is the largest town on Pemba, just over halfway down the western side of the island. The island's capital and administrative centre, it forms the hub of the bus and *dala-dala* network. Although Chake Chake has been settled for as long as Zanzibar Town, it has never achieved the same degree of importance, and thus has little in the way of grand palaces or the winding narrow streets of the old Stone Town, although part of the Omani fort, near the hospital, has recently been opened to the public as a museum.

When the first edition of this guide was researched in the early 1990s, Chake Chake – and Pemba itself – was a real sleepy backwater. Today, it's a bustling community with more than a hint of modernity: there are a couple of video rental shops, and many of the tin-roofed houses have sprouted satellite dishes. In other ways, though, it's still very quiet and traditional, with ox-carts still trundling up the high street (although there are even more scooters). The market, around the bus station, is lively, and the old port, down the hill from the town centre, is also worth a walk. Down the back streets, particularly on the road opposite the market, are countless shops selling everything from foodstuffs and car parts to plastic mops and all types of clothing. In tiny booths tailors will knock you up a suit or skirt on an ancient treadle sewing machine. The whole place is much more peaceful than Zanzibar Town, with a very laid-back atmosphere, and tourists get no hassle at all, so it's great just to stroll around.

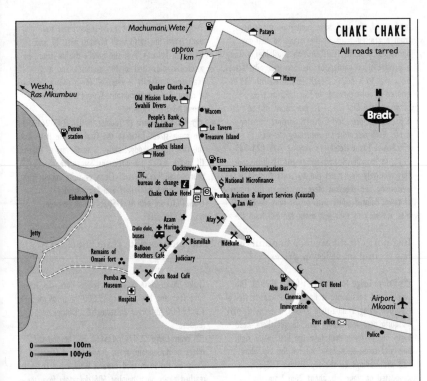

**WHERE TO STAY** You'd have to be pretty desperate to stay at the government-run Chake Chake Hotel ( *245 4301, US$10 per room*) in the centre of town, where bathrooms don't look as though they've been touched for years. The rundown GT Hotel ( *024 452823*) looked even worse when we visited, but fortunately there are some good alternatives in the centre of town, without paying too much more:

**Old Mission Lodge** (7 rooms, 10 dorm beds) *024 2452786;* e *swahilidivers@intafrica.com/ swahilidivers@zanlink.com; www.swahilidivers.com/ www.www.nottheredsea.com.* With the atmosphere of a first-rate backpackers' hostel, Old Mission Lodge is nevertheless popular with a wider range of visitors, particularly the diving fraternity. Owned and run by Raf and Cisca Jah, with the competing attention of Mr Dog and Spook, it's an idiosyncratic place with plenty of character, but it's not for everyone. Rooms are pretty basic (and pretty expensive, even those with AC), although beds in the 2 dorm rooms work out very cost effective since rates include FB, and dive packages can also be extremely good value. The former Quaker mission lodge was built to catch the breeze, with an airy upstairs veranda where comfortable chairs are set looking out over the trees towards the harbour. On the landing are

monochrome prints of photographs taken by Raf on his travels – many of them in Turkey. Outside, a shaded terrace hosts an informal cushioned area that is popular for after-dive chilling out, and a long table for communal dining. A new pool built for dive training is equally popular for those idle cooling-off sessions. While the location of Old Mission Lodge in the centre of Chake Chake has considerable charm, Swahili Divers now have permission to build a second resort at Makangale, right on the coast to the north of the island. To be called Kervansaray, it will have 15 bungalows, and will aim for the same atmosphere as Old Mission Lodge. One to watch from 2007. In the mean time, the company remains popular for its main *raison d'être* – diving. It also runs boat trips to Misali Island for swimming, snorkelling and picnics, and has recently taken delivery of a couple of kayaks for rent. If you'd prefer to stay land based, the staff have numerous suggestions, from organised tours of the island to half-day photography walks (€30, tuition available), visiting a private spice garden or the essential oils factory, or a trip to Vitongoji Beach (€20 return). *Prices quoted in euro; payable in TSh, US$ or £ by arrangement. Dbl €45–70 per room, dbl en-suite €80, b&b. Dorm bed €20 FB. Airport transfer €10. 40% discount for returning clients.*

⌂ **Pemba Island Hotel** (15 rooms) `\/f` 024 245 2215; e islandhotelpembaevergreen@hotmail.com. This relatively new hotel run by strict Muslims is a welcoming and pleasant place to stay in the centre of town. Painted white with bright pink decorative tiles, it's easy to spot just down the hill from the

People's Bank of Zanzibar. En-suite rooms have dbl beds (even the 'sgls') with AC/fans, nets, TV and fridge. In keeping with the hotel's Muslim ethos, no alcohol is permitted on the premises, and a marriage certificate is required for a couple to share a room. Rooftop restaurant. *Sgl/dbl US$35/55 per room, b&b, inc laundry.*

⌂ **Hotel Le Tavern** (9 rooms) `\` 024 245 2660. On the main street, between the Chake Chake Hotel and the Old Mission Lodge, above a small row of shops. (If you're asking for directions, forget French; it's pronounced 'Lay' Tavern.) Clean, en-suite rooms with sgl beds have mosi nets and fans. *Sgl/dbl US$20/30, sgl with AC US$25. Meals to order around TSh5,000.*

Just north of the town, a handful of small guesthouses with basic but clean rooms has sprung up at lower prices:

⌂ **Pataya Lodge** (6 rooms) `\` 0747 852970. This simple local guesthouse is fine if you want a feel of suburban living, Pemba-style. Rooms, 1 en suite, have mosquito nets and ceiling fans. To get there, head north out of town, then take the first major right turn you come to – look out for the big white wall with railings on the top. Pataya Lodge is signposted on your left, about 20m from the junction. *Dbl US$20. Meals TSh3,000 pp, with advance notice.*

⌂ **Mamy Hotel** (4 rooms) `\` 0747 432789. This new, whitewashed building with wooden louvred shutters is tucked away in the back streets north of

Chake Chake, close to Pataya Lodge. Here, too, rooms have fans and bed nets. *TSh8,000 for small room, TSh12,000 for larger en suite, b&b. Dinner on request.*

⌂ **Venus Lodge** `\` 0747 475164. Just beyond the village of Machumani, about 3km north of Chake Chake on the main road towards Wete, Venus Lodge is reached easily on a number 606 *dala-dala* from the centre of town. Re-opened in 2005, it's simple and looks reasonably clean, although when we visited there was no-one available to show us round. Prices are unlikely to have changed much in the last few years. *Dbl (some en suite) US$25pp. Meals on request.*

## ✗ WHERE TO EAT AND DRINK

All the hotels and guesthouses listed above will serve meals to non-residents, although normally food has to be ordered several hours in advance. Elsewhere, most of the town's street restaurants open from around 07.00 until 15.00, when the market closes. There's also no shortage of street stalls around the market or on the main road near Le Tavern selling simple hot food during these hours, with *chipsi mai yai* at US$0.50, beans and rice for around US$1, or chicken and rice at US$2.50. In the same area around the road junction, more small stalls open up in the evening, selling food such as fried fish and chapattis.

✗ **Abu Bus** Opposite the cinema, and open from 19.30, this place serving street food comes highly recommended. Try the *rojo* (a sauce made of green mango) with *mishkaki* for less than US$1, and there's fruit juice and chapattis as well. Despite the inevitable queue, it's worth the wait.

✗ **Afay Restaurant** Popular with local people, the more central Afay is often open till around 22.00, depending on trade and whether there's any food left. Serves good tea; pleasant service.

✗ **Balloon Brothers Café** Close to the market, there's quite a choice of snacks here – samosas, cake, popcorn, and *chiahoro* (like Bombay mix), as well as more substantial dishes such as *mishkaki*, or *chipsi kasava.*

✗ **Bismillah** One of the better small places around the market, good for a no-frills lunch.

✗ **Chake Chake Hotel** The hotel has a restaurant serving b/fast, lunch and evening meals, with advance notice only, until 22.00 for around US$6.

The hotel also dbls as the town 'pub', with a bar at the front that serves beer (usually cold). Stocks are decidedly erratic, but it remains one of the very few places in this predominantly Muslim community to sell alcohol.

✕ **Cross Road Café** Also near the market, and well frequented with traders, this café serves a range of local dishes.

✕ **Ndekule Restaurant** Set among the shops in the town centre, this is a good, local-style place, clean and tidy with plastic tables. There's usually only a few choices, such as chicken and chips or fish and rice (or vice versa) for about TSh600. If you stroll in at lunchtime you should find something ready.

✕ **Old Mission Lodge** On the informal terrace at Swahili Divers' base, non-residents may join in meals at the friendly communal table by prior arrangement — you'll need to phone in the morning for dinner, which is served at around 19.30. Light lunches of the salad and sandwiches variety cost US$5–8 and a 3-course evening meal at US$10 usually includes some vegetarian options, as well as local dishes. The management are serious coffee fans (having spent many years in Istanbul) and their copious flasks of strong black brew never seem to run dry. A big cup is US$0.50 (free to residents), with a jug of fresh creamy milk to top it off.

✕ **Pemba Island Hotel** A large TV dominates this hotel's pleasant rooftop restaurant with views across the town to the trees beyond. For evening meals, you'll need to order ahead. Vegetable dishes (mashed potato TSh2,500) as well as curries at TSh5,000–7,000. Soft drinks only. *Open 07.00–10.00, 19.00–22.00.*

## TRAVEL AND TOUR COMPANIES

**Azam Marine** Down the hill from the Chake Chake Hotel, next to the market, this is the main agent for the *Serengeti*. (For the *Aziza*, the agent is in a general trading shop opposite the Chake Chake Hotel.)

**Coastal Travels Ltd** ☎ 024 245 2162, 0747 420702. This helpful bureau, almost opposite the National Microfinance Bank, is set up to handle bookings of Coastal Aviation flights between Pemba and Zanzibar, Tanga and Dar. *Open 07.30–17.00.*

**Modern Travelling Agency** On the other side of the main street behind the Chake Chake Hotel, this is the main agent for the *Sepideh* ship to/from Zanzibar and Dar.

**Treasure Island Travel & Tours** ☎ 024 245 2045/ 0747 862131/0747 437397; e treasurecompany2005@yahoo.com. Next to Le Tavern, this company offers a range of tours at prices that vary according to the number of passengers. A full-day trip to Ngezi Forest and Vumawimbi Beach, for example, would cost US$70 for 1 person, dropping to US$25 pp with 6 passengers. Prices include all entry fees and a light lunch.

Others tours include boat trips to Shamiani Island (US$70–20), visits of Chake Chake and Wete, bullfights (US$100–40), Pemba traditional dancing (US$100–40), and the Pemba flying fox. On a practical note, the company can organise motorbike and bicycle hire, and will book both accommodation and flights.

**Wacom** ☎ 024 245 2976. Opposite Swahili Divers to the north of town, Wacom offers numerous trips on the island, inc fishing and — sometimes — boat hire. The owner, Ali, speaks excellent English though if he's out you'll need a few words of Swahili.

**ZanAir** ☎ 024 245 4990. The booking office for ZanAir flights is just down the hill from the National Microfinance Bank.

**Zanzibar Tourist Corporation** ☎ 0747 4218364. The state travel service runs trips for a min of 4 people to Ngezi Forest (US$30 pp), and Misali Island (US$35 pp) and spice tours (US$25 pp), inc entrance fees, lunch and soft drinks. They can also book train and ferry tickets (inc the *Sepideh*), and change money. *Open 07.00–15.30 Mon–Fri.*

**SHOPPING** Chake Chake's market is in the centre of town, around the bus station. In the narrow streets leading away from the market, small shops sell an almost infinite variety of goods. If you're craving *mzungu* ('white person's') food, look no further than the shop next to Wacom, opposite Swahili Divers, where the likes of chocolate, cereal, biscuits, cheese triangles, and even Pringles may be in stock, as well as good fruit juice for TSh100. There's often music here in the evenings.

## OTHER PRACTICALITIES

**Post and internet** The post office is on the way into town from Mkoani, on the left-hand side. For internet users, Chake Chake's Adult Training Centre (*open*

*07.30–22.00; TSh1,000/hr*), opposite the National Microfinance Bank, has five computers. In front of the Chake Chake Hotel, the ZCF internet café (*open 07.00–21.00; TSh1,000/hr*), with several computers, is located on an upper storey, up a flight of outside steps. Set up by the Zanzibar Children's Fund, it is run as a fundraising venture by the Muslim community in order to help children in orphanages in the fight against HIV/Aids. Note that in both places you are expected to remove your shoes before entering.

**WHAT TO SEE** Chake Chake itself has a dusty charm that repays a walk through its small market and around its narrow streets and alleys crowded with shops selling a wide range of goods. Definitely worth a visit is the new **Pemba Museum** (*open Mon–Fri 08.30–16.30, Sat/Sun 09.00–16.00; admission US$2*), opened in 2005. Located in part of the town's 18th-century Arab fort, it retains the original wooden door, but other features were lost during restoration, and the cannons at the entrance came from Wete. Exhibits are clearly laid out on five broad themes, covering every aspect of Pemba's history, economy and culture. Of particular interest are the display on the ruins of Pemba, and the room on the island's maritime history and boatbuilding, complete with a model of a *mtepe* – a boat made of coconut rope with sticks for nails and sail of palm leaves that was in use until the 1930s; the original is in the House of Wonders in Zanzibar Town. In addition to exhibitions on politics, fishing and farming, and a jailhouse (the fort was at one time Pemba's prison), there is also a considerable amount of space devoted to Swahili society. Several rooms are set out like the interior of a Swahili house, complete with relevant furniture and implements for cooking, while related displays focus on individual aspects of Swahili culture, from initiation and burial rituals to the use of herbal plants and traditional musical instruments. In the final archives room, researchers will delight in papers that have been painstakingly boxed and labelled.

Visitors to the museum will be accompanied around the exhibitions by a guide. Ask for Hamis Ali Juma, who speaks English and is particularly knowledgeable.

**AROUND CHAKE CHAKE** While most places in Pemba are within easy reach of Chake Chake, there are a few places of interest that are particularly well placed for those staying in the town. Of these, the easiest to get to is the flying fox centre at Kidike (see below). It is also possible to visit the **essential oils factory** (*admission TSh2,000*). To get there, head north out of Chake Chake to the village of Machumani, then turn right towards Vitongoji; it's a 10–15-minute drive from the town centre, or you could take the number 316 *dala-dala*. Oils are extracted from a variety of plants – cloves, of course, but others include citronella and eucalyptus. Interestingly, spent cloves are used to power the burners. You could combine this with a trip to **Vitongoji Beach**, another 10km or so to the east.

There are also a couple of archaeological sites relatively close to the town that give a glimpse into Pemba's past and provide a great reason for a day out in the country. The route to Pujini Ruins, for example, goes through scenic fields and farmland and a few small villages, while a visit to Ras Mkumbuu usually involves a beautiful boat ride down the bay, and a walk through a grove of massive palms.

**Kidike** Home to more than half of Pemba's flying foxes, Kidike (*open daily 08.00–18.00; admission TSh4,000*) is a shared initiative between villagers and the government. Located about 7km north of Chake Chake, it is clearly signposted from the main road. Several tour operators run trips here, and individual drivers charge around US$25 from Chake Chake, including entrance. Alternatively you can take a *dala-dala* from Chake Chake, then walk the 45 minutes or so along the 3.5km track to the reserve.

**Pujini Ruins** The Pujini Ruins (✥ 5°30.566'S, 39°81.118'E), the remains of a fortified palace built around the 15th century by Swahili people, lie about 10km to the southeast of Chake Chake, near the village of Pujini. Locally the place is called Mkame Ndume, meaning 'milker of men', derived from the name of a reputedly despotic king who ordered the palace walls to be built by local inhabitants who were forced to carry large stones while shuffling on their buttocks.

Today, the ruins of the palace cover an area of about 1.5ha, and the remains of the defensive ramparts and surrounding ditches can still be seen, although much of the area is overgrown. The ditch was once connected to the sea by a 1km-long channel. Inside the walls, a team of archaeologists working here since the mid-1990s have found remnants of three large buildings, and an underground shrine with plaster bas reliefs on the walls, and several other features. It is also possible to see some wide stairways that presumably allowed access to the defensive ramparts, the remains of a walkway that joined the town to the shore, and the site of the well. Legend tells of a wall that was built across the well so that the ruler's two wives, who lived in separate parts of the palace, would never meet if they came to get water at the same time.

The ramparts are the most interesting feature of the Pujini Ruins, in that they can be seen and appreciated by any visitor, and also because there is nothing else like them at any other Swahili site along the east African coast. They were built when the Swahili civilisation was at its zenith (see *History*, pages 5–6), and when the presence of Portuguese ships in the area posed a very real threat. It seems, however, that the walls may not have been strong enough to withstand the invaders: some Portuguese records dating from the 1520s mention the sacking of a fortified 'treasury' on the east coast of Pemba.

Archaeological evidence suggests that, although the palace may have fallen on hard times after this invasion, it remained occupied (or was possibly re-occupied) and only finally abandoned in the 19th century. Remains of other buildings, including a mosque, have been found in the area around the palace, suggesting that it did not stand alone, and that a town or larger settlement also existed here – possibly for many centuries.

**Getting there** You can walk the 8km or so from Chake Chake to the Pujini Ruins and back in a day, or take the number 319 bus as far as Pujini village, but it is easier to travel by hired bike or car. To get there, leave Chake Chake on the road south, and turn left onto a dirt road just after the tar road turns off to the airport. Follow the dirt road to a fork near a small dispensary, where you go left. At the next junction, go right to reach a flat grassy area which is usually wet. The ruins are amongst the trees and bushes on the far side of the grassy area. (If you get lost, ask for directions to Mkame Ndume.)

**Ras Mkumbuu Ruins** The headland of Ras Mkumbuu is at the end of a long peninsula about 14km to the west of Chake Chake (✥ 5°19.618'S, 39°66.272'E). The relatively well-preserved ruins are at the tip of the peninsula and also seem to be called Ndagoni (although Mkumbuu and Ndagoni may have been different places). This is the site of a Swahili settlement, thought to have been one of the largest towns on the coast (and in east Africa) during the 11th century. It is also considered to be the site of the earlier port of Qanbalu, where Omani sailors traded in slaves and timber.

Today, the remains of a large, 13th-century mosque can still be seen here, although this is becoming very overgrown, and also several 14th-century pillar tombs, graves with a tall 'chimney' at one end, used to mark the burial place of prominent Muslims. Pillar tombs are found in other parts of east Africa and are held to be one of the most distinctive forms of monument built by the Swahili people. The tombs here are in poor condition, although an inscription on one states that they were restored in 1916.

**Getting there** The easiest and most enjoyable way to reach the ruins is by hired boat, or on an organised tour – which may also visit Misali Island on the same day. Near the ruins is a small fishing village, and to reach the mosque and tombs you walk through maize fields and a plantation of tall palms with smooth white trunks. A road from Chake Chake leads westwards along the peninsula towards Ras Mkumbuu, but it becomes impassable and turns into a track for the final 5km, which is negotiable only on foot or by bike.

## SOUTH OF CHAKE CHAKE

The main road from Chake Chake south to Mkoani follows a winding route through hilly terrain clothed by an abundance of fruit trees, interspersed by villages at every turn. Bananas grow freely, with jack fruit, passion fruit, breadfruit, mango, papaya all very much in evidence. In season, cloves lie drying on mats by the side of the road, their scent pervading the air. Look out in particular for the trees to the east of the road that are home to the Pemba flying fox.

**MKOANI** Mkoani is the smallest of Pemba's three main towns, but the passenger boat services linking it to Zanzibar Town and the mainland make the port the busiest and most important on the island. Any time a boat is docking or leaving there's a buzz in the air, and perhaps the opportunity to watch boats being loaded with cloves for Zanzibar, but for the rest of the time Mkoani is very quiet and sleepy. Although a few businesses are located near the port, and the market is just along the coast, the main town of Mkoani is up the hill towards Chake Chake. A footpath leads up some steps from opposite the port towards the town, cutting out the bends in the road and bringing you out by the old petrol station.

**Where to stay** For some visitors, Mkoani remains the main gateway to Pemba, and a couple of local guesthouses cater for this, but the closure of some in recent years reflects the increasing reliance by visitors on air travel.

**Jondeni Guesthouse** (8 rooms) ☎ 024 2456042, e pembablue@hotmail.com. By far the best place to stay in Mkoani itself, Jondeni is to the north of town, a dusty 10–15-min walk uphill from the port. The clean, white-painted bungalow is set in lush gardens, complete with hammock, and the friendly staff make staying here a pleasure. Clean, simple rooms – some en suite – have fans and mosi nets. Drinks and meals (around US$5) are available, taken on the shady terrace overlooking the sea – a perfect place for whiling away a hot afternoon. If you're feeling more active, the guesthouse can also arrange snorkelling, sailing and fishing trips, and island tours. Sgl US$15 (US$20 en ste), dbl US$20/30, dorm bed US$8.

**Mkoani Hotel** This ZTC-run hotel is a clone of the ZTC hotel in Chake Chake, with the same prices, and is equally uninspiring.

**Where to eat** Apart from the hotels above, both of which serve food (the Jondeni is by far the better bet), places to eat in Mkoani are very limited. There's a small restaurant close to the hospital, at the eastern end of town, but that's pretty well it. A couple of stalls sell fruit, sweets and biscuits for the passing boat-passenger trade.

**Travel agents and tour companies** Almost next to the quay, Mkoani's port office is open daily from 08.00 to 15.30. Tickets can be bought here for the *Mapinduzi*, *Serengeti* and *Sepideh* ferries that run between Pemba and Zanzibar Island (see page 264).

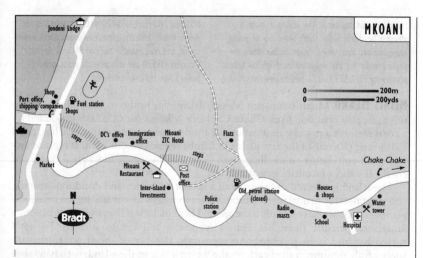

Jondeni Lodge

Shop
Port office,
shipping companies
Shops
Fuel station

steps

DC's office
Immigration
office
Mkoani
ZTC Hotel
Flats

Market

Mkoani
Restaurant
steps
Post
office

Inter-island
Investments
Police
station
Old petrol station
(closed)
Houses
& shops

Chake Chake

Radio
masts
School
Hospital
Water
tower

Bradt

0 ——————— 200m
0 ——————— 200yds

**Other practicalities** Aside from the hospital, towards the eastern end of town, Mkoani has very little to offer the visitor. A couple of communications centres lie on the road near the port, but more usefully there's a yellow telephone kiosk by the port office. In the centre of Mkoani, close to the Mkoani Hotel, is the post office, and there's a small shop in the hotel's car park selling groceries and general stores.

**WAMBAA** The small village of Wambaa is to the north of Mkoani. Nearby is the long and idyllic Wambaa Beach (⊕ 5°30.705'S, 39°66.885'E), facing southwest overlooking Mkoani Bay and out towards the Pemba Channel. At its northern end lies Pemba's most exclusive hotel, Fundu Lagoon.

## Where to stay

⌂ **Fundu Lagoon** (16 rooms) PO Box 3945, Zanzibar; ☎ 024 223 2926 (Zanzibar Stone Town); m 0747 438668; f 0747 419906; e fundu@africaonline.co.tz; www.fundulagoon.com. It's not difficult to see why young honeymooners flock to this secluded, lodge-style place tucked away 15 mins by boat from Mkoani. Combining the flexibility of a hotel with the individuality of a smaller lodge, it's a relaxed hideaway on the beach with attentive service, and a lively atmosphere of bright young things. Linked to the central area by sandy walkways, tented rooms nestle among the trees to form the core of each carefully designed, thatched bungalow. Inside are polished wooden floors, furniture of wicker and wood, and a ceiling fan above the bed. At the back, a small en-suite bathroom showcases the hotel's own range of handmade aromatherapy toiletries (available to purchase from the shop). Each bungalow has its own veranda, facing out to sea. Suites expand on the theme to offer a private plunge pool, and – in superior suites – a 2-storey lounge area to sit and watch the birds with a cool drink or simply to chill.

The restaurant serves 3-course meals with 3 or 4 options for each course; fish dishes are a speciality. The tables are individual, some overlooking the beach, while less formal bites may be taken in the breezy jetty bar, a perfect spot to watch the sun go down (eased by the availability of a free 'cocktail of the evening'!). There are also regular barbecue and Swahili nights. Researchers for this book, visiting separately, disagreed over the quality of the food; one noted 'first-class – some of the best fish I've ever had' whilst another regarded the food as 'mediocre and way below the standard expected for a lodge of this cost level'. When it comes to activities, snorkelling, kayaking and fishing are on offer, as well as a fully equipped dive centre (see page 270). Rather less strenuous are sunset dhow cruises, and boat trips to Misali Island. Off the water, there's a popular treatment room with a wide range of massages and beauty treatments at US$15–60, and a games room with satellite TV. Excursions to the village of Wambaa can be arranged with members of the resort's staff, as can hair braiding. Fundu Lagoon's marketing and prices

12

are glossy and top-notch. The reality is quite a pleasant beachside lodge that's often top of young honeymooners' lists, whilst rather further down the pecking order for the well-travelled. High/low season pp sharing, FB US$335/275 (ocean view/beachside),

US$440/380 (ste), US$470/410 (superior ste), inc meals, drinks, laundry, unguided kayaks, dhow sunset cruise, and boat transfer to/from Mkoani. Airport transfers US$70 per vehicle each way. Open 15 Jun–15 Apr. No children under 12.

**MISALI ISLAND** Misali (also spelt Mesali) Island lies to the west of Chake Chake town, an easy boat ride from Chake Chake or Mkoani *(fee US$5)*. Surrounded by a coral reef, it's a popular destination for tourists, with some idyllic beaches, good swimming (it's one of the few places in Pemba where you can swim at high or low tide), and even better snorkelling, with clear shallow water, and a good display of corals. It's also a favourite spot for divers.

The island is covered in forest, with a mix of evergreen and deciduous species, and most notably many large baobabs. Vervet monkeys cavort among the branches, peering down at visitors. Birds to be spotted here include red-eyed dove, mangrove kingfisher, paradise flycatcher, Pemba white-eye and Pemba sunbird. Fischer's turaco has also been recorded. An increasing number of green sea turtles are successfully nesting on the beach on the western side of the island, with hawksbill turtles also present.

Locally, Misali has 'holy island' status. When the prophet Hadhara found himself without a prayer mat, it is said that he made use instead of the teardrop-shaped island which faces Mecca; the word *msala* means 'prayer mat'. The strong Islamic environmental stewardship ethic is being used to support management and environmental education, and the island was a 'sacred gift for a living planet' from the Islamic faith as part of a millennium celebration organised by WWF in 2000.

The notorious pirate Captain Kidd is reputed to have had a hideout on the island in the 17th century, and even to have buried treasure here. Today, the island and the surrounding reef are incorporated in the Misali Island Marine Conservation Area, under the auspices of the Misali Island Management Committee. Formed as a partnership between the Zanzibar government, the local fishermen's association and the Misali Island Conservation Association (MICA), with support from CARE International, the committee is dominated by fishermen, while the rangers are employed by MICA. It's not entirely satisfactory, with considerable concerns locally about infringements of the no-take zone to the west of the island, and armed soldiers have recently been introduced to support the rangers. Almost two-thirds of the revenue from visitors goes towards managing the island, with the rest earmarked for community development. Conservation measures involve the input of local fishermen, who can continue working here in a managed environment. As just one example of how the scheme is working, local fishermen are prevented from camping on the beach itself (they camp among the trees), so as not to disturb turtles nesting. Additionally, the nests are monitored and protected, along with the rest of the island, by the rangers.

Just 1.4km long, and covering a total area of 90ha, the island consists of 15,000-year-old uplifted coral, with a surrounding coral reef to a maximum depth of 64m. Mangroves fringe much of the island, making a fascinating place for snorkelling during spring high tides. A series of walking trails has been established through the forest, where there are three caves that are considered sacred. In time of need, local people would come to one of the caves with a witchdoctor to pray for help, making payment in the form of a chicken, a goat or even a cow. It takes about 2½ hours to walk round the island (at low tide only), taking in an inter-tidal trail to the west of the island. At the landing point for visitors, there is a shaded information centre, with benches for picnics, and displays on what to see with a good map showing the various trails. On the beach in front, a few sunbeds have been set out, but banish all thoughts of commercialism – it remains a tranquil spot visited by just a few people at any one time.

**Getting there** Misali Island can be reached by hired boat from Chake Chake or Mkoani (see the *Boat hire* and *Travel and tour companies* sections), or through Swahili Divers in Chake Chake (*€33, plus park fee*). There are also organised excursions run by various local tour operators, as well as by individual hotels for their guests. In addition, several of the dive centres based in the northern part of Zanzibar Island, and the boat-based operators such as Cat-Diving, run trips here. The island is also visited by groups from passing cruise ships and live-aboards.

**SHAMIANI ISLAND** Shamiani Island, also called Kiweni Island, is a remote and beautiful spot east of Mkoani, off the far southeastern tip of Pemba Island. A hotel has been planned here for several years, but by 2005 the plans had been shelved.

**Getting there** To reach Shamiani you'll probably have to arrange private transport from Chake Chake to the village of Kengeja, reached by branching off the main Mkoani to Chake Chake road at Mtambile. The vehicle will cost a minimum of US$20 return. South of Kengeja is a small beach, and from here you have to sail across to Shamiani Island. This will cost about US$10.

## WETE

The second-largest town on Pemba, Wete is at the head of a large inlet on the west coast, in the northern part of the island. Spread out down a long central street, it's quieter than Chake Chake, with more ox-carts and fewer mopeds. For most travellers Wete is a good base for exploring northern Pemba: from here Tumbe, the Chwaka Ruins, Konde and Ngezi Forest can all be easily reached.

Wete has a large harbour, mainly used by cargo ships and dhows. It can sometime be busy here, with vessels from Tanga off-loading cement or timber, and loading up with cloves, coconuts or other Pemban commodities. Local ferries also sail across the inlet to Mtambwe Island, where you can get to the ruins of Mtambwe Mkuu, and to Fundo Island.

**GETTING THERE** North of Chake Chake, the dense vegetation of the south gives way to open pasture and scrubland. The new main road bypasses Wete entirely as it hugs the eastern side of the island, but it is still the quickest route between the two towns. The turning off to Wete is about 20km from Chake Chake at the village of Chwale. From here it's a reasonable road to Mzambaroani, past the rubber plantation where what look like old flannels are hung out on racks to dry in the sun, before winding the last few kilometres to Wete.

### WHERE TO STAY

▲ **Bomani Guesthouse** (6 rooms) ✆ 024 245 4384. Rather less attractive than the Sharook, but on the same street, the Bomani is owned by the port in Wete, and sometimes used by Bahari Divers. *US$10 pp, dbl en-suite US$25.*

▲ **North Lodge** (4 rooms) ✆ 0747 427459. Not far from the ZTC hotel, behind a block of flats on the other side of the road, this converted house has basic rooms of sometimes dubious cleanliness, with fans and nets; 2 are en suite. The owner, Mr Abouey, is something of a Mr Fixit, prepared to arrange tours, and cars or bikes for rent. *Dbl US$20. Dinner on request TSh4,000.*

▲ **Sharook Guesthouse** (5 rooms) ✆ 024 245 4386. Wete's best accommodation bet is in the lower part of town, on a quiet side street near the market and bus station. It's a small, clean, family-run place, peaceful and friendly. With its own generator, the

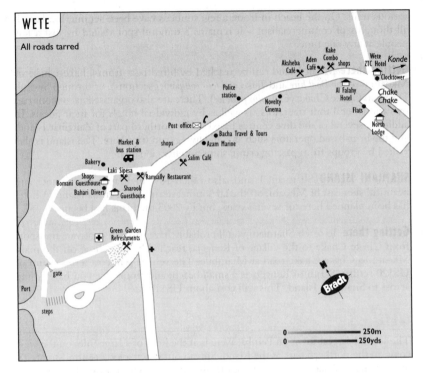

**WETE**

All roads tarred

guesthouse offers constant running water and functioning TV. Dinner, with local dishes, must be ordered well in advance. Bike hire (US$5 per day) can be arranged, as can a range of tours around the island. *US$10 pp, dbl en-suite US$25. Dinner US$5.*

**Wete Hotel** (6 rooms) ☎ 245 4301. This is the third in the series of cloned ZTC-run hotels on Pemba, and its en-suite rooms afford no pleasant surprises. *Dbl US$15 b&b.*

✗ **WHERE TO EAT** All the hotels and guesthouses serve food with advance notice, and Wete also has a choice of local eating houses, most open until the last buses have left at 16.00. Several are located to the west of town, close to the port and bus station. Of these, the best is **Green Garden Refreshments**, a pleasant open-air café. Omelette and chips or beans and rice are less than US$1, and other meals, based on beef and chicken, are also available. It's open all day, but not always at weekends. Opposite the market and bus station, **Laki Sipesa** (which means '100,000 has no value') serves pilau rice and meat, plus bread, chapattis and tea, while next door is the similar **Ramsally** restaurant. There's also a good bakery next to the market.

Further up the main street away from the port is the **Salim Café**, a large place with loud TV popular with locals, who recommend the biryani and pilau at TSh1,500 each. Unusually, it's open all day, 07.00–22.00. Up towards the ZTC Hotel, a number of small local cafés vie with street stalls selling the usual range of fare, including – we've heard – very good octopus and chapattis, with sugarcane juice to drink at TSh100.

## TRAVEL AND TOUR COMPANIES

**Bachaa Travel & Tours** ☎ 0747 423429/427658; e samhamx@yahoo.com. Opposite the post office,

Bachaa handles everything from tourist information, tickets and accommodation reservations to various

tours. Sole agent for Fast Ferries' new *SES II* ferry, it also handles tickets for the *Aziza*. Various trips include visits to Ngezi Forest (US$110 for 1–3 people; US$150 4–9, inc fees and lunch, or US$85/115 without lunch). *Open 07.30–15.00.*
**Raha Travel Agency** On the main street, sells tickets for the *Sepideh* (although this ship goes to/from Mkoani).
**Azam Marine** Opposite the post office. Sells tickets for the *Serengeti*.
**ZSC office** Opposite Green Garden Refreshments. Sells tickets for the *Mapinduzi*.

For additional services, including organised tours, try the Sharook Guesthouse or North Lodge (see *Where to stay*, above). **Sharook Guesthouse** offers a good range of tours: a boat ride to Mtambwe Mkuu Ruins costs US$5 per person; a minibus to Ngezi Forest costs US$35. Highly recommended all-day trips to Fundo Island cost US$30 for the whole motorboat (seating up to ten) or US$27 for a dhow; or you can go to Misali Island for US$70.

**CAR AND BIKE RENTAL** If you want to reach the places of interest around Wete independently, North Lodge (see *Where to stay*) can arrange small Suzuki 'jeeps' for US$50 per day, motorbikes for US$20 per day, and bikes for US$5 per day. The Sharook, too, can hire out bikes for the same price.

**OTHER PRACTICALITIES** The **post office** (*open Mon–Thu 08.00–13.00, 14.00–16.00; Fri 08.00–12.00/14.00–17.00*) is on the right of the main street about halfway towards the port. The so-called **Novelty Cinema**, on the left nearer the entrance to the town, opens in the evenings, with an entrance fee of TSh600.

### WHAT TO SEE
**Mtambwe Mkuu** The ruins of Mtambwe Mkuu are on the small island of Mtambwe, which is joined to the mainland at low tide, directly south of Wete. For over a thousand years, it was one of the most prosperous ports of east Africa. The 'Mtambwe hoard', a collection of coins found near the beach in 1984, included gold coins dating from 11th-century Egypt, and one of very few examples of pre-colonial minted silver currency anywhere in east Africa. Despite its rich past, there's little to see at Mtambwe Mkuu these days, although a trip there from Wete is a very pleasant way to pass the day.

*Getting there* From Wete harbour you go by small dhow or canoe to Mtambwe village, then walk south, west and north around a creek and through mangrove swamps to reach the ruins. Apparently, when the water is high, you can get cut off at the ruins, or be forced to wade back to Mtambwe village through the mangroves, so careful checking of the tides is recommended. Sharook Guesthouse in Wete can arrange tours or give you advice.

## NORTH OF WETE

Although there are more direct routes from Wete to the north of the island, it is quicker to head east to Chwale, then take the main tarred road north. This also has the advantage of passing close to many of Pemba's places of interest, so makes for an interesting journey in its own right.

From Chwale, the landscape is mainly farmland, dotted with coconut palms as it heads up the east coast. Just before the turn off to Micheweni, in an area generally known as **Wingwi**, is a rather unprepossessing stretch of green which, come the end of the year and at times of government celebration, plays host to the island's **bullfights** (see box, overleaf).

Somewhat surprisingly, the island of Pemba is a place where you might see bullfighting in Iberian style. The origins of this sport are uncertain although it is thought to have been introduced here by the Portuguese during the 16th century. Bullfights take place close to Wingwe, in the northeast of the island, during holiday times, mostly between August and November, after the harvest and before the short rains, but also between December and February after the short rains. Local 'matadors' put on a brave display, posing in front of the bull, goading him into a charge and then standing aside at the last moment, much to the appreciation of watching villagers. At the end of the fight, the bull is not killed but praised by the fighter, and sometimes decorated with flowers and leaves, then paraded around the village.

If you happen to be in Pemba when a bullfight is planned, it's worth going to see, but, although sometimes it can be a lively and fascinating spectacle, a few visitors have reported that in reality some bullfights can be fairly uneventful, and seem to involve a group of local wide-boys annoying an apathetic cow by beating her with sticks, while the local girls shriek loudly.

Exactly when a bullfight is about to take place is hard to find out. Ask at your hotel or a reliable tour company for more details.

**KIUYU PENINSULA** To the east of the main north–south road, a narrow isthmus separates the rest of Pemba from the Kiuyu Peninsula. A rough road, north of the 'bullring', leads after about 5km to the village of Micheweni, which has a school, a hospital and a few shops, but no place to stay. (Confusingly, Micheweni is also sometimes called Wingwi, the name not only of the area but also of another village a few kilometres to the south.) The road deteriorates from here passing through the village of Kiuyu, and becoming a deep-red dirt track, reminiscent of mainland Africa, before it reaches **Ras Kiuyu Forest Reserve**, almost at the tip of the peninsula. It's a remote and somewhat inaccessible place, smaller than the forest at Ngezi (see pages 286–7) and with a less impressive range of vegetation and wildlife. Nevertheless, it has been highly recommended as a day trip from Wete or even Chake Chake, as much for the interesting journey through the fields and villages as for the forest itself. The unspoilt Kiuyu Beach, to the east of the forest, is an added attraction.

**Getting there** By public transport, you can catch an early *dala-dala* from Wete to Micheweni. From here, it's a 5km walk to the village of Kiuyu and another 5km into the forest itself. About 3km beyond Kiuyu village, a narrow track branches right (east) to Kiuyu Beach. Nearby, another track branches left to another small beach on the west of the peninsula called Mbuyu Kambaa. The only alternative is to hire a driver with a 4x4, since the road beyond Micheweni is unsuitable for other vehicles.

**CHWAKA RUINS** Continuing north from the bullring, near the coast, are the ruins of the town of Chwaka (✪ 04°96.864'S, 39°80.471'E). Dating from as early as the 9th century, the town was active as a port in the 15th century, probably linked to a network of villages trading with the east African coast and beyond. The ruins are sometimes referred to as Harouni, a reflection of the town's association with a local king called Harouni, who was the son of Mkama Ndume, builder of Pujini (see page 277).

The most easily recognised buildings are two small mosques, standing well apart. The larger and better-preserved Friday mosque is also the site of the king's tomb. Local legend has it that the two mosques were built because the king's two wives were constantly at loggerheads, and that the town was eventually destroyed by the second wife's family.

There are also remains of houses and tombs. Nearby stood another group of tombs and an 18th-century fort built by the Mazrui group of Omanis, and on the other side of the road are some more remains called Old Tumbe. As with most of Pemba's ruins, don't go expecting a major archaeological find, but it's an interesting place and offers free rein to the imagination.

**Getting there** Chwaka is signposted to the east of the main road between Wete and Tumbe, just north of where it crosses a swampy area on an embankment with metal crash barriers on either side. The ten-minute walk takes you through cassava fields and past lofty palms, with a splendid view over the bay towards Micheweni as you approach the ruins themselves.

**TUMBE** The village of Tumbe, not far from the Chwaka Ruins, has the largest fish market on Pemba. Particularly busy in the mornings, it attracts people from all over the island to buy fish, which they carry away in plaited baskets strapped to the back of bicycles. It's an interesting place for visitors to watch the boats come in with fish of all sizes to be offered for sale.

Tumbe lies off the main tar road about 5km east of Konde, and can be reached by bus or bike from Wete, or with a hired car. A *dala-dala* stops at the junction, from where it's a pleasant walk through the long, narrow village to the coast; by car, it's about a ten-minute drive from the main road.

**KONDE** Near the end of the tarred road, the small town of Konde is also the end of the road for the *dala-dala* network, and the last place to stock up for a picnic before venturing further north to Ngezi Forest and Vumawimbi Beach. Men on bicycles weave up and down the dusty main street, with palm-leaf baskets strapped to the back laden with produce. During market hours, until 14.00, fruit stalls line the road, and there's a bakery selling fresh bread. There's also a restaurant where dishes such as pilau and *chipsi maiyai* can be bought for around TSh550. And for those with a sweet tooth, Konde is said to be the only place on Pemba where fresh ice cream is sold.

## NGEZI PENINSULA

The Ngezi Peninsula is the northernmost point on Pemba, jutting out from the northwestern corner of the island. Beyond Konde, a significant area is taken up by Ngezi Forest, the last remains of a huge tract of indigenous forest which used to cover much of Pemba.

Curving round the eastern side of the peninsula is **Vumawimbi Beach**, one of the most beautiful on Pemba, with miles of dazzling white sand flanked by pristine forest (✦ 4°90.355'S, 39°69.609'E). Here and there fishermen sit and mend their nets, watching over their *ngalawas* as they wait for the tide, and occasionally an ox-cart rolls along the sand. Rumours have abounded for years about the construction of a hotel, but for now the beach remains remote and unspoilt. You can walk there across the fields from Ngezi Forest or Manta Reef Lodge, or go with a driver.

The west of the peninsula is flanked by the long expanse of **Verani Beach** (✦ 4°93.410'S, 39°68.806'E) with, at its northern end, a place called **Pango ya Watoro** ('the cave of the fugitives'). At low tide, sandbanks dry out offshore, and boat trips from the nearby Manta Reef Lodge take visitors out with a picnic to swim and snorkel. It's possible to walk along the beach to the **lighthouse** near Ras

Kigomasha, but only at low tide, so do check carefully before setting out; there's an alternative route through the fields if the water is up. Built by the British in the 1800s, the lighthouse offers some outstanding views out to sea and across the lush green landscape of northern Pemba. It costs US$2 per person to climb the 95 narrow steps to the top – just ask at the house nearby for the lighthouse keeper.

**GETTING THERE AND AWAY** You can get from Wete as far as Konde by *dala-dala*, but from there you'll need to walk the 5km along the road, bordered by farmland, to the Ngezi Forest entrance gate. If you make an early start this walk is a nice part of the day out. Alternatively, and especially if you want to go on to one of the beaches, you'll need to hire a car from Wete or Chake, for which you can expect to pay US$40–70 for the day, or travel as part of an organised tour (see pages 282–3 and 275). Beyond the entrance gate to Ngezi Forest the road is rough, and to get to the beach is sandy too, so unless it's dry a high-clearance 4x4 is recommended.

**WHERE TO STAY** It's possible to visit the forest and beaches around Ngezi for the day, and stay overnight in Wete or Chake Chake. Alternatively, there is one more upmarket place to stay nearby:

⌂ **Manta Reef Lodge** (12 cottages) PO Box 82234, Mombasa, Kenya; ☎ 0741 320025; f +254 41 471771/2, 473969/+254 733 619965; e info@oneearthsafaris.com; www.mantareeflodge.com/www.oneearthsafaris.com. Overlooking the northern end of Verani Beach, in a truly stunning location, Manta Reef was originally built as a dedicated diving place, but also caters very well for those looking for good but not luxury accommodation in natural surroundings. Spacious, individual wooden chalets built high on stilts have an open front to catch the sea breeze, affording a panoramic view across the Pemba Channel. A big dbl bed, sofa and table, plus en-suite bathroom, complete the picture; a larger honeymoon suite has its own jacuzzi. Cottages set behind the chalets are less open, with views across the gardens; there are plans to build more of these over the next few years. A barn-like central area serves as dining room, bar, lounge and lobby, with a couple of terraces looking out to sea and steps leading down to a powder-sand beach.

For entertainment, there's a TV in the entrance, a pool table by the bar, and a small selection of books to browse. It's a place that offers much, and delivers – most of the time; a bit more attention to detail wouldn't go amiss. Aside from diving (see page 271), guests benefit from a location that boasts a wide range of birdlife (birdwatching trips US$25), and some interesting walks to the lighthouse, Vumawimbi Beach and Ngezi Forest, 5km away. Other options include kayaking, boat trips and fishing (advance notice required for big-game fishing), as well as village tours, and several beauty options at US$20/hr. An on-site shop sells the basics. Internet access US$5/¹/₂hr. *High/low season US$120/88pp sharing FB (seafront), US$160/110 (garden view); honeymoon ste per room US$320, inc fruit, sparkling wine, personal dinner, sandbank trip. Christmas/Easter suppt US$30pp per night. Airport transfer US$25pp. Transfers from Shimoni in Kenya US$120 1-way (min 2 people), either by speedboat in 90mins or on MV Jambo in 3hrs. Open all year.*

**NGEZI FOREST RESERVE** Ngezi Forest Reserve (*open daily 07.30–15.30; entrance TSh4,000/US$4; transit fee US$2; night walks by prior arrangement*) is a protected area of forest, virtually all that remains of a vast area of indigenous forest that used to cover much of the island. One of the highlights of Pemba, especially if you have an interest in wildlife, it offers the opportunity to discover Pemba as it once was. It's advisable not to arrive too early because mosquitoes remain active in the morning. A 2km nature trail takes in sections of moist forest, and several large ponds. A guided walk with the rangers takes about an hour, and is a must if you want to have a brief insight into the forest's different habitats and to spot some of the animals and birds that live among the trees. The fee is negotiable, but it's reasonable to give around US$5 for a small group. Birdwatching trips can be organised, too, as can walks in the late evening, or at night, when you have a much better chance of seeing the Pemba flying fox and the russet scops owl. To set up a trip of this ilk, contact the rangers' office in advance, during opening hours.

**History** Historically, the forest was used by local people, as it provided timber, fuelwood, edible plants, medicinal plants, and material for baskets and ropes, but at the same time areas of forest were being cleared for small-scale agriculture, and since the early 19th century for large plantations – especially for cloves. Although the first forest inventory was carried out in the 1920s, it wasn't until 30 years later that the reserve was established. Even then, a commercial sawmill owned by one Vi Arnjosh continued to extract timber until the mid-1960s, when the government officially took control. The rude hut in which he lived and the rusting remnants of his sawmill can be seen on the nature trail.

Through the 1970s and 1980s Ngezi was virtually ignored by the government, while encroachment and over-use by local people endangered the forest and its wildlife. Then, in 1995, funds were received from the Forest and Park Service of Finland, and a management plan was drawn up to preserve the remaining forest by strengthening conservation efforts and improving management. In this way, people from the ten villages within the reserve could still utilise the forest, but at a sustainable rate, and wildlife could also benefit. It is hoped that the forest can be developed to attract tourists as a way of raising revenue – which would in turn ensure its future protection.

**Ecology** The reserve covers just 1,476ha but the variety of soil types has resulted in a wide range of vegetation. Dominant are 943ha of tropical moist forest, which once covered most of the island. Found mainly in the central and eastern parts of the reserve (the part most easily reached by visitors) it has some trees reaching over 40m in height – most notably the *Odyendea zimmermanii*, known locally as mbanko. Also to be found is the endemic Pemba palm (mpapindi), *Dypsis pembanus*, an ornamental tree whose red seeds are attractive to birds.

Other vegetation types include swamp forest, coastal thicket, heathland, pockets of mangroves and palms, and raphia stands. The mix is unique in east Africa, with several species more usually found in lowland mountain regions, as well as those more often found in coastal areas, plus eastern Indian and Malagasy species, and even a southeast Asian wild banana. There are also several introduced tree species.

The forest is home to several animal species, most notably the Pemba flying fox. Other animals found in Ngezi include the Pemba vervet monkey, the greater bushbaby, Zanzibar tree hyrax (pelele, *Dendrohyrax validus neumannii*), blue duiker (paa wa pemba) and marsh mongoose (chonjwe, *Atilax paludinosus*). A band of wild European pigs, descended from domestic animals introduced by the Portuguese centuries ago, also lives in the forest. As most people on Pemba are Muslims and abstain from pork, these animals are not hunted.

For birdwatchers, Ngezi Forest is undoubtedly the best place on Pemba, with all the endemics and sub-endemics present here. Visitors could also see palm-nut vultures, crowned hornbills, red-billed hornbills, and kingfishers, as well as turacos and starlings. For more details, see *Natural history*, page 56.

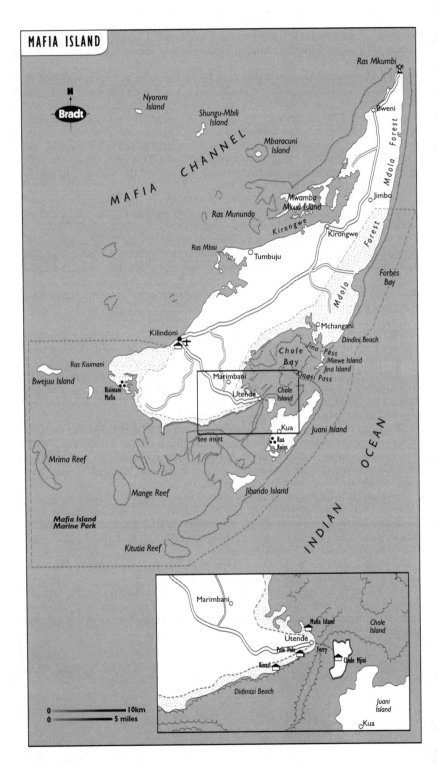

# 13

# Mafia Archipelago

While Zanzibar is entrenched as probably the most popular ocean resort in east Africa, the small archipelago around Mafia Island, 160km to its south, remains virtually unknown. Poor communications with the mainland and a rather unfortunate name have not served Mafia well, but a growing trickle of visitors over recent years has been unanimous in singing the island's praises. A few interesting Swahili ruins notwithstanding, Mafia lacks for an equivalent to Zanzibar's atmospheric Stone Town, so that it cannot be recommended as an alternative destination for those whose primary interest in Tanzania's islands is cultural or historical.

By contrast, the combination of a clutch of small, high-quality lodges, offshore diving and snorkelling that ranks with the very best in the Indian Ocean, and a conspicuous absence of hassle and crime, make it the ideal destination for those seeking an exclusive but low-key Indian Ocean retreat. Paradoxically, perhaps, Mafia also has considerable potential for budget travellers seeking a truly off-the-beaten-track and adventurous experience.

The Mafia Archipelago, which lies in the Indian Ocean some 20km east of the Rufiji River Delta in central Tanzania, probably became isolated from the mainland some 20,000 years ago. The archipelago consists of about 15 sandstone and coral rag islands and numerous smaller atolls and sandbars, none of which reaches an elevation above 80m, and all but two of which are little more than 1km² in extent. The central island, known today as Mafia (though it seems that this name applied to the archipelago rather than any specific island prior to the 20th century), is by far the largest, approximately 50km long by 15km across. The second-largest island is Juani, about 8km long and up to 4km wide, which lies to the southeast of the main island and was the centre of local political activity in medieval times. Sandwiched between these two larger islands, the tiny Chole Island superseded Juani as the local centre of trade in the Omani era.

The archipelago's estimated population of nearly 41,000 lives in rustic fishing communities and farming villages dotted all over Mafia and the smaller islands, although many of the islands are theoretically uninhabited. The largest town and port on Mafia Island is Kilindoni in the southeast, the site of the airstrip, and the main landing point for dhows from the mainland. Although several local guesthouses can be found in Kilindoni, the centre of upmarket tourist development is Chole Bay on the southeastern side of the island. Three established tourist lodges lie within 1km of each other near the village of Utende, roughly 10km from Kilindoni by road, with a fourth situated on Chole Island within the bay. Utende is the only area other than Kilindoni that has electricity.

## HISTORY

Little is known about the early history of the Mafia Archipelago, but presumably it has been settled for millennia, and it may well have participated in the ancient

There are a number of suggestions for the source of the archipelago's name, but it isn't derived from the Sicilian crime syndicate. It may have origins in the Arabic word *Morfiyeh* meaning 'group', describing the archipelago of Mafia, or be named after the Ma'afir, an Arab tribe from Merku (Mocha) in present-day Yemen. An unlikely suggestion is that the name derives from the Arabic *mafi* meaning 'waste' or 'rubbish', or perhaps from the Swahili *mahali pa afya* meaning 'a healthy place to live'. The authors would be grateful for any further suggestions!

coastal trade with Arabia. The eminent archaeologist Neville Chittick regarded Mafia as a strong candidate for the 'low and wooded' island of Menouthesias, described in the 1st-century *Periplus of the Erythrian Sea* as being two days' sail or 300 stadia (roughly 50km) from the river port of Rhapta (which, according to this theory, was situated in the Rufiji Delta). Although the anonymous writer of the *Periplus* also mentions the sewn boats and hollowed-out tree canoes that are still used widely on Mafia today (as they are elsewhere on the coast), several other aspects of the description count against Mafia. Two days rather exaggerates the sailing distance from the island to the Rufiji Delta; furthermore, either the *Periplus* was mistaken in its assertion that there are 'no wild beasts except crocodiles' on Menouthesias, or the crocs have subsequently vanished and the island's few hippos are a later arrival.

The earliest known settlement on the archipelago, Kisimani Mafia, was situated at Ras Kisimani in the far southwest of the main island. Archaeological evidence suggests that this town, which covered about three acres, was founded in the 11th century, possibly by a favoured son of the Sultan of Kilwa. Several coins minted at Kilwa have been unearthed at the site, as have coins from China, Mongolia, India and Arabia, all minted prior to 1340. A second important town, Kua, was probably founded in the 13th century, again as a dependency of Kilwa, and it must surely have usurped Kisimani as the islands' political and economic hub soon after that. In its prime, Kua was probably the second-largest city along what is now the southern coast of Tanzania, boasting seven mosques as well as a double-storey palace and numerous stone homesteads spread over an area of more than 30 acres.

Following the Portuguese occupation of the coast, Kua was chosen as the site of a Portuguese trade agency in 1515, when a fortified blockhouse was built at the town. The name Mafia (more accurately Morfiyeh) was well established by this time, and the islands are marked as such on the earliest Portuguese naval charts. Several explanations have been put forward for the origin of this name, (see box above). Because the archipelago lies 20km offshore, Mafia attracted a large influx of refugees from the mainland during the cannibalistic Zimba raids that dealt the final deathblow to so many coastal settlements during the late 16th century.

Control of Mafia changed hands frequently in the 17th century as Portugal's fortunes declined. An Omani naval raid in 1670 effectively terminated the Portuguese presence on the Mafia islands, and by 1598 the entire east African coast north of modern-day Mozambique was under Omani control. Little is known about events on the islands over the next two centuries. In about 1829, however, the archipelago was attacked by the cannibalistic Sakalafa of Madagascar, who succeeded in wreaking havoc at Kua, one of the few coastal towns left untouched by their Zomba forbears 250 years earlier. Kisimani, though also attacked by the Malagasy, stumbled on into the 1870s, when a devastating cyclone dealt it a final deathblow, but Kua was abandoned to go to ruin.

One reason why Kua was not resettled after 1820 is that a new seat of the Sultanate of Zanzibar had been founded on the north end of Chole Island barely ten years earlier. Known as Chole Mjini (Chole Town), this settlement was also attacked by the Sakalafa, but it was soon rebuilt to emerge as the most important town on the islands. Chole became the established home of a number of wealthy Omani traders and slave owners, while the main island of Mafia, known at the time as Chole Shamba (Chole Farm), was occupied by newly established coconut plantations and the slaves who worked on them. Although Chole was not so directly involved in the slave trade as Pangani, Bagamoyo or Kilwa Kivinje, it was an important stopover for slave ships heading between Kilwa and Zanzibar, and the ruined mansions that survive today indicate that it was a very wealthy settlement indeed.

Mafia was part of the Zanzibar Sultanate throughout the Omani era, and it should have remained a part of Zanzibar in the colonial era, according to a treaty that placed it under British protectorateship along with Zanzibar and Pemba islands. However, in the complex Anglo–German treaty of 1890 Mafia was ceded to Germany in exchange for a part of what is now Malawi, and it has been administered as part of mainland Tanzania ever since. In 1892, Germany sent a local administrator to Chole, who constructed the two-storey Customs House that can still be seen on the beach today.

In 1913, Germany relocated its administration from Chole to the deeper harbour at Kilindoni on the main island. Two years later, Mafia was the first part of German East Africa to be captured by British forces. The island was subsequently used as the base for a series of aerial assaults on the German cruiser *Königsberg* which, having evaded capture in the Rufiji Delta, was finally sunk on 11 August 1915. A six-cent German Tanganyika Territory stamp overprinted Mafia by the British and listed at £9,000 in the Stanley Gibbons catalogue makes philatelists one of the few groups of people aware of the existence of the islands.

## ECONOMY

Coconuts were the main source of income for the islands until the 1970s, when the price of coconut products dropped, and the fishing industry grew in importance. Cultivated since the 19th century, coconuts remain a secure income source and, although the trees are still climbed by hand, some 30 tonnes are exported to Dar daily in dhows. Coconut products have a number of local uses: leaves are used for roofing, coconut coir makes doormats and ropes, and even the ribs are used to make fishing traps and brooms. The wood can also be used to make furniture.

Other produce grown on Mafia is used for subsistence farming, particularly the primary crop, cassava. Rice, sweet potato, maize, pumpkin, okra, banana, pineapple, lime, mango and tomato are also seen growing on the islands, some of which are exported to Dar. Cashew nuts are either sold locally or exported, and the cashew fruit is used to make local beer. At subsistence level, mushrooms, raffia fibre, medicinal plants and game (monkey, bush-pig and duiker) play an important role. Mangrove trees provide many raw materials; their wood is used for building poles, and boatbuilding and repair. Dead mangrove branches are used for firewood; leaves, bark and fruit are all used for medicines and colour dyes. Firewood is collected to burn coral rag for lime, and also for charcoal, which is sold to locals, hotels, and at Kilindoni, as well as exported.

The sea is vital to the livelihood of many of Mafia's inhabitants. Seaweed farming exists on a small-scale basis, used for export and for processing food additives. It is grown on lines attached to wooden stakes across the seabed of

13

shallow lagoons, and is dried on palm leaves. Traditionally the inter-tidal area has been the women's domain, where they fish for octopus at spring tide. In the 1990s, however, men too began collecting octopus on the inter-tidal flats, as fish catches were declining yet prices increasing. Now 60% of octopus is caught by men, often through free-diving. Sea cucumbers are harvested for export to Zanzibar or Dar, then out to the Far East. Fish is also exported. Chole and Jibonde were well known for their boatbuilding in the past, but this now is in decline. You can still see people working in the shipyards, but more of the work is now repairing smaller dhows rather than building large cargo-carrying boats.

## RELIGION AND CULTURE

The majority of the islanders are Muslim, but there are also many Christians. Voodoo manifests itself in ritual dances linked to the lunar cycle. While traditionally reserved, the islanders are tolerant of visitors provided they dress discreetly and behave in a manner becoming to local customs. Mafia women wear the colourful patterned *kanga* of the Swahili coast (see box, page 139), and on weekends and religious holidays men exchange Western dress for the long, white *kanzu*. Older folk who remember the British era can speak some English, as can staff working at the tourist lodges, but it can help to know a little Swahili when talking to other islanders.

A word of caution: Mafia is a conservative society, and the passing visitor is unlikely to be asked for handouts. Children who beg from tourists are quickly reprimanded by their elders. Please make sure that you, and your travelling companions, keep it this way. For further information, see page 99.

## NATURAL ENVIRONMENT

**VEGETATION** Natural vegetation on Mafia ranges from tidal mangrove thickets (eight species of mangrove grow here), marshland, heath and scrubby coastal moorlands to palm-wooded grassland and lowland rainforest, although the evergreen forest was cleared for coconut plantations in the 1980s. Baobabs are prominent along with the native *Albinza*. A patch of coastal high forest, the Chunguruma Forest, is a dense tree canopy interlaced with lianas and having an abundant floor-covering of ferns.

### WILDLIFE

**Mammals** A large, reed-lined lake in central Mafia, probably a relic lagoon dating from when the island was joined to the mainland, harbours about 20 hippo that were washed out to sea during flooding in the Rufiji River system. Unpopular with locals, they eat from the rice farms at night and can cause considerable damage, but are hard to see. Other island fauna includes a colony of flying foxes (the lesser Cormoran fruit bat), while bush pigs are found in Mdola Forest and Juani Island. The pigs eat the cassava from farms on Juani, so are a menace to farmers, who try to trap the pigs where possible.

Mdola Forest stretches along the east coast of Mafia Island for about 30km, from Bweni to Chole Bay, and has a high level of diversity, as well as a number of endemic species, such as the blue duiker, a subspecies endemic to Pemba and Mafia. Other fauna includes at least one bushbaby species, the genet, and the black-and-rufous elephant shrew. Monkeys (Syke's and vervet) and squirrels were introduced for the pot by the Portuguese.

**Reptiles and insects** The leaf-litter toad has been recorded in Mdola Forest, and may be endemic to Mafia; the writhing gecko is found both in Mdola Forest and on the Tanzanian mainland. The monitor lizard is known locally as *kenge*. Butterflies (there are five endemics) are best in the wet season, particularly around Ras Mbizi and mangroves, which flower during the rains.

**Birds** More than 120 species of birds have been recorded on Mafia, including five different types of sunbird. The island is of particular interest for its concentrations of resident and migrant shorebirds, which have breeding grounds in northern Europe but come to Mafia in October to March for the nearby mangrove estuaries, where they feed on the mud flats. Waders include ringed plover, crab plover, grey plover, Mongolian plover, great sandplover, curlew, whimbrel and turnstone, and the island is also a nesting area for fish eagles and open-billed storks.

**Marine life** Of far greater ecological importance than Mafia's terrestrial habitats is the immensely rich marine environment, which provides some of the finest snorkelling and diving sites in the Indian Ocean. It may be surprising that the biodiversity of the Rufiji–Mafia complex has global significance, and of 21 sites in east Africa has been described as having 'one of the world's most interesting and diverse ecosystems'. The coral-reef habitats around Mafia have a diversity of species rivalled only by rainforests, with at least 380 species of fish and 48 of coral. The beds of seagrass (12 species of which are found here, the only flowering plants to have colonised the sea) and the deep open waters support some of the planet's most endangered marine life.

Four species of turtles live in Mafia's waters, and two of these use Mafia as a nesting ground. The hawksbill, *Cretmochelys imbricata,* lays eggs between December and January; the green turtle, *Chelonia mydas,* between April and June. The east African coast is one of the last strongholds for the critically endangered dugong, *Dugong dugon*, and during the 1960s and '70s these gentle seacows were regularly caught in the shark nets of Mafia's fishermen. Despite two separate sightings in 1999, there are fears that the dugong may now be extinct from Mafia's waters.

The lowland coastal forest of the eastern seaboard has been 'recognised as a critical site for biodiversity', and the inter-tidal flats are important for octopus, while in the open sea marine mammals like the humpback whale give birth and nurse their young in east Africa's warm waters. Sadly the demand for shark-fin soup in the Far East is one contributor to diminished populations of shark along the coastline. The large pelagics such as marlin, billfish and tuna also inhabit the deeper sea.

Oceanographers often talk of the Rufiji River Delta–Mafia–Kilwa area being one extended ecosystem. It's particularly exciting that a coelacanth was caught here in 2003. Archaeologists have found fossils of this very rare, bony fish which date back to the era of the dinosaurs, and today's specimens are almost identical.

From October to April, whalesharks are seen in the area. Chole Mjini on Chole Island is the headquarters for the newly formed Mafia Island Whaleshark Conservation Project and during the season offers regular dhow excursions for guests to visit these gentle giants.

## CLIMATE

The Mafia Archipelago experiences a tropical climate tempered by ocean breezes. Rainfall averaging 2,000mm a year occurs mainly between April and May, although November can also be wet. February and March are hot and humid, while a strong southerly wind, the *kusi*, blows during July. The best holiday period is from June until mid-October, when the islands enjoy blue skies with temperatures kept pleasant by light coastal breezes. The water temperature varies from 24° to 31°; the air temperature rarely exceeds 33°C or drops below 20°C.

Over the past two thousand years, turtle-shell, mangrove poles and seashells have been part of east Africa's trade to Arabia. By the 1960s, however, it had become clear that natural resources were not coping with human progress. In Tanzania, dried and salted fish, exported to the mainland, contributes more to the national protein consumption than meat and poultry combined. Dynamite fishing became very popular on Tanzania's coast, despite the destruction that it causes to fish populations and to coral. Small-mesh, beach-seine nets were catching all sizes of fish, again damaging populations. In some areas the only source of building materials has been coral, used as bricks and in the production of lime: this was the second-largest industry on Mafia at one time. Mangrove wood is very hard, insect-resistant, and makes excellent building material, so vast areas were cleared to provide timber, fuelwood, farmland and salt-pans for salt production.

In the 1970s four islands were declared marine reserves to slow the damage, but in the absence of facilities to police the park, fishermen ignored the rules and continued as usual. By 1995 it was clear that conservation had become an urgent priority, so the following year a partnership of investors, communities and the government set up the Board of Trustees of Marine Parks and Reserves of Tanzania, and on 6 September 1996 an area of Mafia extending across 822km$^2$ was gazetted as Tanzania's first marine park, to protect the ecosystems as well as the future livelihood of coastal people. The park embraces most of the southern and eastern shore of Mafia, including Chole Bay and associated reefs, a number of isolated atolls to the south of the main island, and the reefs enclosing Juani, Jibondo and Bwejuu islands.

The marine park now owns six boats and has one full-time park warden. The park authorities are aiming to co-operate and collaborate with local residents, using community-based projects to dispel conflict between groups. If the islands are to be protected, the success of the marine park is imperative. Mangroves trap river sediments that would be otherwise washed out to sea and, along with coral reefs, protect the shoreline from the erosion of rising sea levels. The natural forest shields the island's crops from storm damage from the ocean, and a healthy ecosystem helps in the recovery from natural disasters such as cyclones, hurricanes and floods. Significantly, wetlands have also been shown to provide clean water, perhaps the most significant issue in terms of sustainable development of the islands.

*For further details, contact the warden-in-charge, Mr George Msumi, Mafia Island Marine Park, PO Box 74, Mafia;* 023 240 2690; f 023 240 2526; e *mimpmafia@raha.com.*

## GETTING THERE AND AWAY

**BY AIR** The most efficient way of getting to Mafia is by light aircraft (Cessna) with Coastal Travel (see page 140), who run two scheduled flights from Dar es Salaam every day, costing US$270 for a single flight: the first leaves at 15.00, arriving in Mafia at 15.30, and the second at 17.45, arriving at 18.45. This is perfectly timed so that the sun sets behind the Rufiji Delta as you fly in. If one of these flights is not running, you can sometimes persuade Coastal to fly by paying for a minimum of two passengers.

Coastal also fly from Kilwa via Songo Songo to Mafia daily (16.30–16.45) for US$120 one-way and Zanzibar to Mafia daily, usually via Dar (14.00–16.20), costing US$140 single.

If you are staying at Kinasi Lodge on Mafia for three nights or more, ASF Kinasi (\ *Shaam 074 741 8256, operations 074 124 2977, Dar airport office at domestic terminal*

*074 143 3449; e kinasilodge@mafiaisland.com*) can fly you to Mafia from Dar for US$90 or from Zanzibar to Mafia for US$120. They try to be as accommodating as possible for their guests, looking after bags etc, but these flights are ad hoc, not scheduled. If you're not staying at Kinasi, it's worth giving them a call anyway: it's the same rate for non-guests if there's space on a flight already running.

You can also charter planes to Mafia with Zantas Air Charter and Tropical Air (**\** *Omar Hadj 074 745 0777 or Faruk 074 741 2278*). To charter a whole plane with Tropical costs around US$500.

The flight to Mafia crosses over the Rufiji River Delta: at 40km$^2$ the largest delta in east Africa with the region's greatest concentration of mangroves. The dhows look tiny as they go about their fishing unfeasibly far from shore. The white, stony landing strip that greets the visitor is not the best runway you'll ever see; in fact, most airlines refuse to fly to the island because the runway is so bad.

Note that an airport departure tax of US$6 per person, which includes a US$1 'safety fee', is payable in cash on leaving Mafia.

**Mafia Airport** Mafia's small airport (*open around 08.00–18.30, unless there's an early-morning flight*) is situated on the edge of the main town of Kilindoni, a 15km drive from Utende, where the tourist lodges are located. It's Mafia's centre of communication for visitors, and even if visitors arrive on Mafia by boat they tend to be directed the 14km from the harbour to the airport.

The airport has a simple waiting room with wooden benches and basic toilets. At the Chole Interbureau Change (*open 08.00–17.00*), you can change limited amounts of currency at market rates, as well as US dollar, euro and sterling travellers' cheques, but it's probably best not to rely on this tiny exchange for all your financial needs on Mafia.

Visitors holding a hotel reservation will be met at the airport; transfers to Pole Pole or Kinasi are included in their rates. If you don't have a reservation, most of the lodges have representatives who speak English, and can radio the lodges to organise your accommodation. They can also help individual travellers to find a Land-Rover taxi, costing US$25 to Utende one-way; note that you'll cross the border into the marine park en route, so have the fee (US$10 per person, per day) for the requisite number of days ready in US dollars cash, and remember to keep your receipt as proof of payment when you leave the island.

**BY BOAT** The options for budget travellers who wish to visit Mafia are limited to boats that connect Kilindoni to the mainland. Many of these dhows are uncomfortable and crowded and the trip can take anything from 10 to 24 hours. The safety record is none too inspiring: sailing dhows have a reputation for hitting reefs, as these are very dangerous waters that require an experienced captain. If you want to take a boat, make sure you check that they're properly licensed to carry passengers or vehicles, and at least that they have marine radios and lifejackets.

For the incorrigible, a tide table is incorporated in the free booklet, the *Dar Guide,* available from bars and hotels in Dar es Salaam. This is invaluable when trying to organise a boat trip to Mafia, as the boats have to arrive at high tide, and often leave on a high tide, too. There are, though, plans to build a jetty in Kilindoni, which would mean that boats no longer have to restrict their arrival to high tide. This should lead to a much more regular service in the future.

The closest mainland port to Mafia is Kisiju, 30km from Dar, and 45km southeast of Mkuranga on the Kilwa road. From the Kariakoo bus depot in Dar, you take a bus to Kisijuni and then a dhow to Mafia. Another possibility from Dar es Salaam is via Kimbiji, easily reached by catching the motor ferry from the city centre to Kigomboni (boats leave every ten minutes or so and take five minutes) then a *dala-dala* direct to Kimbiji (about one hour). There are also dhows connecting Mafia to Kilwa Kivinje.

## GETTING AROUND

The island infrastructure is basic. Hardly any villages are connected to mains water or electricity and at the time of writing there are no tarmac roads. Throughout the island the best you'll find is a bouncy sandy track. Vehicles are few, mainly Land-Rover pick-ups and 4x4s belonging to the hotels and other organisations. Most local people use bicycles to get around, although this is quite hard work on the sandy roads. Bicycles can be rented by arrangement with the Hotel Lizu in Kilindoni, or from any of the lodges.

A minibus runs every three hours or so between Kilindoni and Utende charging Tsh700 one way. It seats a minimum of 12, and has no fixed timetable – it departs when it's full. There are also two *dala-dalas*, one at Kilindoni and one at Utende, and these pick people up along the way. They're not the most comfortable way of getting around, but are a good way of meeting local people and really getting to understand life on Mafia. Hitchhiking is an accepted means of getting about, but it usually entails a long wait. Islanders also use *jahazis*, widely referred to in English as dhows, to commute between Kilindoni and outlying villages on Mafia, and for inter-island travel.

Maps of Mafia can be obtained from Mafia Island Tours at Mafia Island Lodge for Tsh5,500.

## WHERE TO STAY

Mafia isn't really the place for easy backpacking, but budget travellers who do come here may stop in Kilindoni itself. Meanwhile, the majority of Mafia's (very few) tourists head straight though town and over to one of three or four more upmarket small lodges on Chole Bay.

**CHOLE BAY** Chole's three upmarket lodges – Pole Pole, Kinasi and Chole Mjini – are all *totally* different in style and approach, and each has its advocates to claim that it is 'the best'. The truth is that they're all very good, given their different styles – and all offer really very good value for money given their relative isolation, and the quality of the marine experience to be had here. The trick is to choose the one that's right for you.

Mafia Lodge doesn't reach the standards of the other three, but you won't find a better-value spot for a quiet retreat with access to great diving.

**Pole Pole** (7 bungalows) ☏ 022 260 1530/022 260 0649; f 022 260 1531; e contact@polepole.com; www.polepole.com. Pole Pole, meaning 'slowly, slowly' in Swahili, is a superb destination for relaxation. This Italian-managed lodge is designed to be fairly luxurious whilst still a little rustic, and smart without being pretentious. Set in a garden of coconut palms, and connected by pathways of the softest sand, Pole Pole has a small beach in front of it, perhaps 100m wide, with mangroves on either side. A path through the mangroves leads in a short walk of a few mins to Kinasi Lodge (if you turn right) or to Mafia Island Lodge (if you turn left). Pole Pole's large bungalows, built almost entirely from organic materials, have modern en-suite bathrooms, inc twin washbasins, showers, a bidet and a flush toilet. The bedroom has a polished wooden floor, some stylishly simple furniture, a ceiling fan and 24hr electricity; its dbl or twin beds are surrounded by a walk-in mosquito net. Large dbl doors lead onto a very wide, shaded veranda overlooking the sea below, complete with some relaxing day-beds and chairs. Typical Italian 4-course dinners are served at private tables in the restaurant. Starters are usually light, eg: crab salad, followed by a sizeable pasta course (or soup), then a main dish (typically seafood with simple vegetables) followed by dessert. Service is attentive and helpful, and there are also 2 good local masseuses to relax your muscles after a hard day's exertions. Pole Pole has no swimming pool, but snorkelling, diving, game fishing and other excursions are offered. One dhow trip — usually inc some snorkelling and perhaps a picnic lunch — is normally offered every day on a complimentary basis, if guests wish to join in. If you're looking for somewhere small, comfortable and fairly remote with great diving and with some snorkelling, and involving but very low-key excursions, then Pole Pole offers very good value indeed. *US$260/US$200 pp sgl/dbl FB; US$299/US$230 Aug and Christmas period; inc dinner, airport transfers, laundry, excursions. Diving US$40; equipt US$30 per day.*

🏠 **Kinasi Lodge** (14 bungalows) ✆ 074 741 8256, operations 074 124 2977; e kinasi@intafrica.com; www.mafiaisland.com. A 5-min walk along the beach from Pole Pole brings you to the more formal Kinasi Lodge. This Indian Ocean hideaway is named for the indigo pass through the outer reef that frames Mafia. Large landscaped grounds, studded with coconut palms, slope down to a swimming pool area and small sandy beach. Either side of the beach, which perhaps extends for 100m, are mangroves — though which weaves the short sandy path to Pole Pole. Inset into the lawns, about halfway up, is a swimming pool area, complete with poolside bar and grill. Also dotted around are 14 solid, self-contained bungalows with makuti roofs and wooden verandas complete with armchairs and addictive hammocks. Inside, Zanzibar-style dbl beds are enveloped in vast mosquito nets, and each bungalow has an en-suite bathroom, inc a washbasin, a shower and a flush toilet. The lodge's large, open-sided main bar area contains a top-notch reference library as well as a book-swap service, while the adjacent dining area serves seafood. Meals can be either in a group or private, with 3-course dinners varying from tender barbecued seafood to meat, either served or in buffet style. Kinasi has its own fully equipped dive centre beside the beach, and the resident instructor can arrange dives in and around Chole Bay, as well as snorkelling trips, windsurfing and game fishing. An 'activity manager' in the lodge organises the various excursions, which include the usual range of dhow trips, village visits, and 4x4 excursions across the island, plus the unique option of hiring mountain bikes to explore local villages. These excursions all have individual costs. The lodge has constructed a 2hr nature trail for birdwatching along the coastal flats, which are rich in waders, and through patches of coastal scrub that harbour sunbirds, tinker-birds and bee-eaters. *US$140–205/120–180 pp sgl/dbl FB, inc airport transfers, laundry, windsurfing, kayaks, bicycles. Diving US$55/US$60 per dive in/outside the bay. Dbl day dive US$99/US$108 in/outside bay, inc equipt. Closed post-Easter–May.*

🏠 **Chole Mjini Lodge** (6 treehouses, 1 chalet) ✆ 0748 520799; e 2chole@bushmail.net (the lodge doesn't have its own website). This fabulously original lodge, situated on the northern side of Chole Island, consists mostly of large, wooden treehouse-style bedrooms perched high in the baobabs, amongst the crumbling 19th-century ruins of Chole Mjini. The owners, Jean and Anne de Villiers, who live on site, stress that they are emphatically not catering for people seeking Sheraton-style luxury or a conventional beach retreat — there is no electricity for starters (lighting is by paraffin lamps at night, so bring a good torch!), and the waterfront in front of the lodge is overgrown with mangroves. Nevertheless this must rank as one of the most original and aesthetically pleasing lodges on the east African coast. It's also an atmospheric base for exploring Chole Island and the surrounding waters. Lunch is usually served at group tables in a family atmosphere, with fresh seafood and vegetable dishes in a mixture of African and European styles, usually with tasty sauces. B/fast and dinner are served at individual tables dotted around the garden, jetty or ruins. Six of the bedrooms at Chole Mjini stand high on stilted platforms; 3 are in or beside their own huge baobab tree. Each is made almost entirely of wood, thatch and local materials by the local people of Chole — and the sheer quality of the carpentry says much of the islanders' reputation for building fine dhows. All the rooms are slightly different, but climb the stairs and inside you'll generally find a large dbl bed surrounded by a walk-in mosquito net, billowing fabrics, an open wardrobe and dressing area, and a large, padlocked wooden box for your valuables. Most also have an upper floor, with relaxing day-beds. Each of these treehouse rooms has private ablutions — but all are separate and down on the ground. The sit-down toilet is a long-drop, using ash to keep it dry and composting; they rank among the cleanest long-drops in Africa! Enclosed from view, behind a circular bamboo, the large open-air shower uses an 'intermediate technology'-type of design to heat the water. You light a small metal cup of paraffin, push it under a hollow waterpipe, and turn on the tap. Remarkably, these usually supply a very good, hot shower. Chole

Mjini has just one more conventional chalet which is on the ground level, next to the lodge's main lounge/dining area. This is very open-plan, with walls open to the breeze, and has a huge bed, a conventional en-suite flush toilet (the only one on the island) and large sunken bath. It's not quite as romantic as the treehouses, but might be just the place if stairs to the toilet don't appeal. Finally, a recent addition to the lodge's range of accommodation is a converted wooden dhow, allowing guests to spend a night or two on the water or fly-camping on a secluded beach. In keeping with the eco-friendly ethos, a community fee is included in the rates. The owners and their dive instructor have more than 50 years' experience of diving Mafia between them, can instruct in English, Italian, French or German, and know the dive sites intimately. Jean is also a research biologist who teaches coral-reef ecology to US college students twice a year, and can teach short PADI courses on this, and fish identification, on request. He has a fully equipped dive centre here, making Chole Mjini an excellent lodge both for experienced divers seeking adventure, and those learning to dive, or for finding out more about the marine environment. While there is no pool here, or any beach to lie on, guests can swim by the mangroves in a beautiful tidal inlet, with sunbeds set on wooden decking. There are usually one or two complimentary trips organised every day, with organised or self-guided walks, snorkel trips and excursions to nearby sandbars. Chole Mjini is somewhere that people either love or hate; they view it as either totally magical or quite uncomfortable. It's owned and run by a couple who have put their heart and soul into the lodge, and in helping the surrounding community to develop. Visitors need to accept the lodge, and its team, as they find them; and then a really enjoyable stay is almost guaranteed.

*US$180–300/240–480 sgl/dbl FB. Diving US$40 per dive; equipt US$15 per day. Transfers cost extra. No children under 2 years.*

⌂ **Mafia Island Lodge** (40 rooms) PO Box 2, Mafia; ☎ 022 260 1530/022 260 0649; e contact@mafiaislandinfo.com/ reservations@mafialodge.com; www.mafialodge.com. This very simple hotel, built by the government in 1971, is situated on one of the island's few open, palm-lined beaches; it's next to Pole Pole and about 10 mins' walk from Kinasi Lodge, directly opposite the ruins of Chole Mjini on Chole Island. The lodge consists of small, box-like rooms (inc 8 dbl and 2 family) laid out in short blocks, with French windows facing the sea, AC, Zanzibar beds and en-suite bathrooms with 24hr hot water. Despite the dated décor and equipt, and rather featureless lawn, it's a functional place offering access to Mafia's superb diving at bargain-basement rates. The bar/restaurant is a large and fairly pleasant spot, with a large airy terrace facing the ocean, and a small shop here contains a few essentials, from toothpaste to tampons. There's also an internet access point costing US$5/hr, a pool table and equipt for beach volleyball. Mafia's only real tour company, Mafia Island Tours, is based here, and makes an obvious choice from which to book dives and excursions if you're not staying at one of the upmarket lodges. For example, a short hop to Chole Island for a village tour, inc a visit to the flying foxes, costs US$10 pp; and a half-day trip to the Kua Ruins and Channel, or Jibondo Island, costs US$25 pp. A longer snorkelling trip with a picnic lunch to Marimbani or Kitutia costs US$35 or US$45 pp; and a full-day excursion to Ras Mkumbi or Bwejuu Island costs US$50 or US$60 pp. *US$75/52 dbl/sgl b&b, US$119/74 dbl/sgl FB. Diving US$40/70 sgl/dbl dive; equipt US$20 per day.*

**KILINDONI** The guesthouses in town are all pretty basic, with little to draw travellers to them; even Mafia Pwani Camp has relatively little to recommend it.

⌂ **New Lizu Hotel** (5 rooms) Bookings c/o Post office, Mafia; ☎ 023 240 2683. This is the most comfortable of 4 guesthouses in the centre of Kilindoni. Used by local traders, it is a min's walk from the market, and 10 mins from the dhow landing jetty. With 24hr electricity, mosquito nets and fans, it is fairly clean but extremely basic. All but 1 room (a sgl) share washing facilities, with water very limited (depending on who else is using it!). Toilets are flushed with a bucket; hot water can be boiled on request. The hotel also offers a laundry service, a stationery shop, a phone and a tailoring school. A simple bar/restaurant with fan sells beer, sodas and rice and seafood meals. Food can be delivered to other locations for an excursion, eg: the campsite at Bweni village. *Tsh10,000 twin. B/fast Tsh700–1,000, lunch/dinner Tsh1,500–5,000. Bike hire Tsh3,000 per day; motorbike (with helmet) Tsh20,000–30,000 per day.*

**Classic Visitor's House** (7 rooms) ✆ 0746 749176. The signpost to this local guesthouse is quite unhelpful. To get there from the Sports Bar on your left, take the first right, then left – it's behind the white wall. From the mosque on your right, take the first left at Sofia Soft Drinks, walk to the end of the road, then it's on your left. The owner speaks English, so the manager (who doesn't) will call him if needed. This is a very basic but pleasant guesthouse, with mosquito nets on the windows and the beds, and ceiling fans (24hr electricity). Existing rooms share 2 squat toilets with a tap and bucket, and 2 showers that weren't working when we visited. Three en-suite twin rooms were under construction in late 2005. Laundry service, but no restaurant. *Tsh5,000/6,000 sgl/dbl, Tsh8,000 en suite.*

**Harbour View Lodge** (10 rooms) ✆ 074 536 0314. Owned by an ex-MP, this lodge is right on the seafront: an interesting location as you have to walk through the timber yard to get here and the lodge itself overlooks the fishing boats. There is a large bar area with music and a dance floor, with small tables outside so you can sip your drinks by a view of the harbour. This is a good basic lodge with fans and AC, nets on the windows (not on the beds), and 24hr electricity. En-suite rooms have a shower, basin and flushing toilet, and hot water can be boiled for you. There's also a lockable cupboard. Harbour View also has a little restaurant with a fan. *Tsh8,000 dbl, Tsh10,000 sgl b&b en suite with AC, Tsh8,000/12,000 sgl/twin en suite with fan.*

**Mafia Pwani Camp** (4 *bandas*, camping) ✆ 023 240 2244/0745 696067; e carpho2003@yahoo.co.uk. Outside central Kilindoni, a 15-min walk from the airport, this camp is also known as Sunset Resort Camp. It's owned by one of the directors of Pole Pole, and is one of the only basic lodges that offers a relaxing atmosphere. It's also an excellent area for spotting the rufous elephant shrew, as well as vervet monkeys. To get there, turn right out of the airport, follow the road round to the right, and take the first left by the concrete wall. By the time you read this, the entrance should be here (currently it's behind the hospital: follow the sand road through the chicken wire). The camp is in a beautiful area overlooking the sea, and has considerable potential. Its individual *bandas* (3 twin, 1 dbl) are sizeable and clean, with nets on windows and beds and 24hr electricity; a laundry service is available. Despite the good standard of building, facilities are very basic, with no running water; buckets of water are provided in the shared bathroom facilities, and this can be heated on request. If you follow the steep pathway down to the beach, you'll come to the campsite. There are plans to build a platform, bar and lounge area. *US$12 twin/dbl b&b pp, US$7 camping.*

**Camping** There is a campsite at Mafia Pwani (see above). Otherwise, check with the marine park authorities before camping independently, as it's not legal to camp in Tanzania unless you're in a specified area. It has been known for innocent campers to be arrested, and thrown into prison, or worse. Don't take any chances.

## ACTIVITIES

### DIVING With Jean de Villiers

Many people visit Mafia purely for its diving, which is often considered the best anywhere in east Africa. It's easy to dive two sites outside the bay on a single outing; the trip out and back can also be great for fishing, sunbathing, sailing and dolphin-spotting. The marine park off Chole Bay is home to 48 species of coral, including giant table corals, delicate sea fans, whip corals and huge stands of blue- and pink-tipped staghorn coral.

As well as the spectacular variety of reef fish there are turtles and large predatory fish such as grouper, Napoleon wrasse and barracuda. Manta rays and several species of shark are encountered in Kinasi Pass. November to January is best for black-tip and white-tip reef sharks. The corals of Chole Bay, in the heart of the marine park, have recovered dramatically from damage caused by El Niño (of 1997–98) and the destructive fishing practices used before the establishment of the park.

Almost all Mafia's best diving is in depths of less than 30m. Between June and September you can dive only within Chole Bay, albeit in almost any weather. For

13

the more challenging dives outside the bay, you have to wait until the calmer conditions in mid-September. Outside the bay the average size of the fish is bigger, and you've a good chance of seeing a 2–3m grouper; these are friendly and let you come quite close. Visibility from June to September tends to be 10–15m, whereas in October to February it can be 25m. Mafia is good for beginner divers, as it's very safe inside the bay. However, diving outside the bay on an outgoing tide can be extremely dangerous, with strong currents that can sweep you out to sea: in this position, if you miss your rendezvous with a boat, the next stop is Mogadishu.

When diving in the open ocean, divers are advised always to carry two means of signalling: one audible (a whistle or air horn) and one visible (an inflatable surface marker, a flare, strobe light or mirror). In addition, always wear a full wetsuit as protection against exposure, and drink water before commencing a dive. Don't take any risks or push the safety boundary while diving here; it's a long way to the nearest decompression chamber in Nairobi. Note that you can't buy diving insurance in Tanzania – you *must* have this before you travel.

All of the lodges on Mafia offer diving excursions as well as full PADI courses. Chole Mjini, Pole Pole, Kinasi and Mafia Island lodges all offer specialist diving courses with every conceivable type of dive site – reefs and bommies, channels, walls, caves, drift, ocean and night dives. All these are accessible in a day, while diving safaris catering for 12 people can be arranged to destinations further afield such as Ras Mkumbi, Forbes Bay southeast of Mafia, and the spectacular reef complex around the Songo Songo Islands, which lie about 80km south of Mafia and about 50km north of Kilwa.

## Diving and snorkelling sites in Mafia Marine Park

There are at least half a dozen more scuba-diving sites in the park and numerous snorkelling sites. Wherever possible, names given are those used by local fishermen.

The first three sites are relatively close together and can be reached on a stronger drift dive starting near the Pinnacle in Kinasi Pass. These sites sometimes suffer from being in the mouth of a bay in that the visibility can be poor for a few days after stormy periods at sea and when tidal currents are very strong at full moon or new moon.

**Kinasi Pass: South Wall** *Dive depth: max 27m. Recommended for experienced divers or beginners under professional supervision.* Justifiably Mafia's most famous dive site, this has it all: wall with caverns, big critters and spectacular corals. At times huge volumes of water flow through the pass, creating an exhilarating drift dive, or dive at slack water to enjoy the 30m wall and its resident potato cod and giant grouper. Schools of snappers and sweetlips are often here, as are their predators: barracuda, giant trevally, jacks, cobia, wahoo and kingfish. Rays and morays are common, with whale sharks, eagle rays and manta rays seasonal visitors (late Dec–Mar is best.) Finish the dive in a splendid coral garden, and maybe catch up with a Napoleon wrasse or a feeding turtle.

**Utumbi (or Kinasi Wall)** *Dive depth: 5–25m. Recommended experience: all certified divers. (Outstanding snorkelling site nearby, mainly at low tide.)* If you don't tackle the pass right off then

this is the must-do dive in Mafia. About 300m before the pass, inside the bay, is a truly gorgeous reef: the ease of access and safe, sheltered location and the obliging currents all add up to a world-class dive. The corals rapidly change from soft corals (gorgonians and whip corals at the pass end), to more and more hard corals, until finally you find yourself in shallow gardens of tabular and staghorn acropora and gold-hued fire coral. The fish fauna is mostly typical reef inhabitants, with a huge variety of multi-coloured wrasses, parrotfish, damsels, surgeons, triggerfish and anthiases. Big wahoo and barracuda cruise off reef, and 2–3ft greasy cod and malabar grouper are abundant.

**Kinasi Pass – Pinnacle** *Dive depth: max 29m. Recommended for experienced divers or beginners under professional supervision.* In the entrance of the bay, 50m north of Kinasi Wall, this pinnacle rises sharply to within 8m of the surface, usually surrounded by a school or two of sweetlips or trevally and their attendant predators. When the visibility is good, this is the most likely place within the bay to meet a bull shark (or zambezi). We also occasionally come across a 3m guitar fish (shark that is half ray, with a flat, triangular head) and a huge, mottled green-black giant grouper accompanied by a bevy of attendant yellow-and-black-striped pilotfish. It's an excellent site at slack water.

**Dindini or Shangani Wall** *Dive depth: max 24m. Recommended for experienced divers only.* Dindini is only accessible seasonally: it's directly in front of surf-pounded cliffs. There are a lot of fish: big fish, small fish, sharks, rays and also turtles. In periods of good visibility, usually Nov–Mar, this is one of the better places in Mafia to see sharks (usually reef sharks). It's also good for large groupers and, very occasionally, big-game fish like tuna, sailfish and marlin. The wall has many caverns and U-shaped tunnels, and some deep, unexplored caves: there is the occasional appearance of a big shark or other large creature. The dive ends on the top of the wall, with really spectacular powder blue, purple and pink alcyonaria soft corals teeming with fish, especially red-toothed triggerfish, and a variety of surgeons.

**Mlila or Jina Wall** *Dive depth: max 24m. Recommended for experienced divers or beginners under professional supervision. Seasickness can be a problem.* Less than a mile away, the wall has formed a slight fold close to the cliffs. It starts out quite mediocre but rapidly changes as you get where fishing boats seldom penetrate. In the pocket there are more grouper than you'll probably ever see. There are also lots of other fish around and this is likely to be your best chance of seeing big Napoleons or getting close to a feeding turtle. At the base of the wall is a lot of coral, with many holes to investigate; look out for lobster and small stingrays as well as giant and ribbon-tailed rays.

**Milimani – 'mountain tops' in Swahili** *Dive depth: max 20m. Recommended experience: all skill levels; often used for courses and Discover Scuba experiences.* The most often-requested repeat dive in the park. This is a long reef inside the bay, characterised by spectacular coral turrets rising above corals to form mini mountains and alleys. A gentle entrance in just 6m of water over pure white sand makes this the easiest dive in the park, and the diversity of the coral is phenomenal: the topology of the reef is stunning and it just goes on and on. As you explore the twisting, turning reef interspersed with mounds of coral teeming

with fish you may become so absorbed that you suddenly find you're in 20m with a towering reef above. A small gap in the reef is an excellent place to view planktivores, usually swarms of counter-shaded fusiliers and schools of unicorns but occasionally (in the right season) a cruising manta, accompanied by a flotilla of remoras and pilotfish. You can end the dive by climbing over the reef crest to look for turtles or to join the millions of kasmira and blackspot snappers in the very shallow water among the magnificent fire corals.

**Miewe Shoulder – the 'Washing Machine'** *Dive depth: max 25m. Recommended experience: in slack water possible for all levels.* In deep water just outside the bay during spring tides, two hours before high tide, this is almost white-water diving and only for experienced and advanced divers who can control their buoyancy instinctively and know how to surf currents without fear of injury. Outside the bay, this is a sloping fringing reef north of the pass, with a fabulous diversity of fish, corals and topology. The reef is teeming with fish but you can't stop because the relentless current drags you over the top. The trick is to then drop down into one of the many deeper pools that lie just behind the jagged reef crest for a 'rinse and spin' cycle and watch the fish rush in and out. When you have been thoroughly wrung out you leave this lunar landscape of craters and spires and head south, across the current as much as possible, and will soon drift along the drop-off through Kinasi Pass for a very satisfying and relaxed end to an awesome experience.

**Mkadini** *Dive depth: max 25m. Recommended experience: all skill levels.* Outside the bay, off Miewe Island, there is a short vertical step in shallow water (12–14m maximum). This flattens out into a deeper shallow-sloping reef. There are many alcyonarea soft corals and diverse hard corals, lots of turtles (green and hawksbill), diverse groupers (back-saddled, lyretail, greasy cod, potato cod), schools of batfish and a good chance to see white-tip reef sharks and dolphins.

**Juani Reef** *Dive depth: max 30m. Recommended for experienced divers or beginners under professional supervision.* Outside the bay, a sloping fringing reef south of the pass extends for 12km. This is a good place to see turtles (green and hawksbill), guitar fish and white-tips, as well as stunning alcyonarea soft corals.

**Mange Reef** *Dive depth: max 24m. Recommended experience: all skill levels.* 12 nautical miles south-southeast of Chole Island, this is another beautiful coral-encrusted sandbar, once feared by local fishermen because of the many sharks. There is a good variety of reef fish and this is easily combined with Kitutia (see below) for an excellent day trip.

**Chole Wall** Dive depth: max 16m. Recommended experience: all certified divers; good training site. Reef inside the bay; gentle slope. About 1km in length with lots of coral and reef fishes. A grand skin-diving site when the weather is calm.

**Musambiji** Dive depth: max 16m. Recommended experience: Open Water or equivalent; good training site. This is a submerged island inside the bay, with diverse walls and sloping fringing coral reefs. It would be better if it were deeper and didn't suffer from poor visibility so often; but it can be a great snorkelling site.

**Kitutia** Dive depth: max 20m. Recommended experience: all skill levels. Once a fantastic dive site, Kitutia was badly degraded by El Niño some years ago, although it's recovering rapidly and regaining much of its former glory. It is a spectacular sandbar encrusted with corals, ideal for a day of mellow dives, snorkelling and swimming. Combined with a picnic and a fabulous sail home, it's the perfect day.

## AROUND MAFIA ISLAND

Although Mafia is predominantly visited for its waters, many choose to explore the islands, and see some of Mafia beyond the marine park. It's easiest to arrange this through one of the lodges. For a good English-speaking guide, ask for either Moussa from Chole Mjini, or Ali from Pole Pole. To go it alone, you could either hire a bike, or negotiate a price with the 4x4 drivers parked in Kilindoni to take you on an excursion.

**KILINDONI** All arrivals on Mafia pass through Kilindoni, the main town as well as the island's airport and sea port, but few visitors venture into Kilindoni for any length of time. New by east African standards, the town was established by the Germans in 1913 on discovering that Chole Island lacked a deep-water anchorage. While it has none of the Arab architecture of the Stone Town on Zanzibar, its coral and lime-mortar shop-houses with quaint signs and rusting corrugated-iron roofs exude an ambience of old Indian Ocean days.

At first, Kilindoni appears to have all the accoutrements of a small town: a district hospital, school (complete with science laboratories), police station, bank, post office, airport, mosque and churches. Then suddenly the sandy road opens into a square full of clothes for sale, music and activity. There are stands selling mobile phone chargers (continental two-pins), an unexpected but necessary slice of modern Africa.

Peaceful rather than bustling, the **market** is the centre of local life. Tomatoes, chillies, potatoes, onions, limes, dried prawns, bananas, cassava and whatever the trader can get his hands on are arranged in little piles. A large amount of food here is from Dar, grown elsewhere on the Tanzanian mainland. Spices are from Zanzibar, naturally, all wrapped up in little plastic packets. Baobab seeds for kids to chew are sold in piles and the fish stalls are pungently gathered together a little further off. Other stalls sell pottery, *kangas* and second-hand clothes, and if you're brave enough to buy a homemade snorkelling/diving mask, ingeniously made of pieces of metal stapled to thick black rubber, it'll set you back Tsh3,000.

A number of small shops are of interest to the visitor: the **Dubay Store**, next to Mapozi Haircutting Salon, sells cold Cokes and Fantas for Tsh350. For items such as sausage, orange juice, Sprite, water, chocolate, toilet paper, washing power and toothpaste, try **Mwishehe Shopping Centre**. On the road to the harbour (Bandani Road), by the little roundabout, you'll find **WTC** selling drinks, ice cream and chocolate, chicken and chips. **Kisoma Store** sells basic stationery; its proudly advertised 'computer' doesn't have internet access, but you can print from it at Tsh800 per sheet. Make a right turn from the petrol and diesel pumps (opposite the 4x4 parking area), and you'll find **Fantastic Hair Cutting** which can cut different grades using a proper shaver for Tsh500 a haircut, and Tsh300 for a wet shave.

There are more stores on the road descending to the dhow landing. The **Market General Supply Store** and the **Peace and Love** sell soft drinks, and off the main square, Utende Road has the rather vulgar monument presented by the fish factory. On the left is a grey weather-beaten **mosque** and further along the Roman Catholic **church**, one of at least six churches.

The **landing** in Kilindoni usually has 15–20 *jahazis* moored on the beach. Whether unloading fish or mending their nets, the fishermen object strongly to being photographed, as do the people frying cassava chips and cooking octopus on small stoves under the trees.

**Where to eat** With a burst of modernity, Kilindoni has recently gained the **Mafia Sports Bar**, complete with flat-screen TV and satellite. This big orange building is slap-bang in the middle of the town, providing a bar and restaurant for tourists and locals alike, and is part owned by Kinasi Lodge. A more African establishment, the tiny **Royal Pub Mafia**, may be rather surprised by visitors, but sells local beers: Kilimanjaro, Tusker, Serengeti, Bin Bingwa for Tsh1,000, and Konyagi (a local firewater with rather descriptive flames on the bottle) for Tsh2,000. This local bar also sells food: chips are Tsh500, egg and chips Tsh900, and a beef kebab Tsh200.

**Practicalities** A bank and a post office are located on the airport road. The bank is the National Microfinance Bank (*open 08.30–15.00 Mon–Fri, 08.30–12.30 Sat*). The post office (*open Mon–Fri 08.00–13.00 and 14.00–16.30, closed Sat*) is just past the bank, but be aware that your letter may take months to leave Mafia. A better option may be to ask your lodge to mail your post in Dar es Salaam.

**NORTH OF KILINDONI** One of the few places that travellers visit on Mafia is the lighthouse at Ras Mkumbi, via the charming village of Bweni. This is approximately 47km north of Kilindoni, and the drive there, over bouncy sand roads that follow or run parallel to the west coast of Mafia, takes about two hours direct, or all day if you want to include swimming and a picnic. Note, though, that while there are some stunning white-sand beaches along this coast, with excellent swimming opportunities, the sea on this side of the island is largely devoid of the underwater attractions around Chole Bay to the east. The excursion is best organised through one of the lodges; you'll find an English-speaking guide is invaluable. Alternatively, a full-day excursion to Ras Mkumbi with Mafia Island Tours costs US$50 per person. Bring everything you are likely to need from your hotel, not forgetting clothes to cover knees and shoulders, suncream, and insect repellent in case you return after dark.

Driving through Mafia is a good way of seeing the island, and finding out about everyday life here. As you drive through the villages, you'll see crops of mangoes, pineapples, bananas, cassava and cashew nuts, as well as sweet potatoes, which grow after the rainy season. About 8km from Kilindoni is a picturesque swamp covered in mauve lotus. Small tilapia and catfish dart among the reeds. Further on, the old agricultural village of **Kirongwe**, with a tradition of making clay pots, counts a score of houses, a handful of shops and a market selling the usual dried octopus, bananas and coconuts. Beyond here the countryside is intensively cultivated with beans, pigeon pea and cassava, and – rather less attractive – numerous indications of slash-and-burn agriculture. Syke's and vervet monkeys raiding the crops flee at the sound of any vehicle.

The north of Mafia is markedly different to the wetter southern part of the island, which is dominated by vast coconut plantations. After **Jimbo**, where you may see local blacksmiths working by the side of the road, the landscape suddenly becomes more undulating open grassland with outcrops of mia'a or palm, and baobabs similar to those on the mainland coastal plain. Birdlife is plentiful with bee-eaters and lilac-breasted rollers flashing amongst the trees and large flocks of guinea fowl scuttling off the road. While only about 30m above sea level, it is noticeably cooler here than on the coast.

**Bweni village**, built behind 2km of glistening white-sand beach, seems a likely spot for future tourism development. Its traditional Swahili-style houses of coral and lime plaster are dotted among slender coconut palms. You need to stop to collect the lighthouse key from a keeper in the village, and will be soon surrounded by excited and curious children, delighted at the chance to shout '*Mzungu!*' at the unexpected visitor. Their behaviour is polite, however, and their fascination mixed with a fear of the unknown. Bweni women are experts at weaving striped prayer mats from the palms on the plateau, and you only need to show interest for items to be shyly produced. The larger mats are square, 2.5m by 1.5m, and cost around Tsh3,000; smaller oval mats go for Tsh2,500 or so.

The **lighthouse** at Ras Mkumbi is a 3km drive on a good stretch of road from Bweni. Built on coral rag on the northern tip of Mafia, it is worth climbing the 15m up to the top of the red-and-white structure for a spectacular view of the Mafia Channel lying between the archipelago and the mainland. The stretch of deep blue water is reputed to offer some of the best big-game fishing in east Africa. This working lighthouse also has concrete outbuildings, now owned by Pole Pole, who organise trips to the area. One of the buildings has basic rooms with mosquito nets around basic beds, and flushing toilets. At present it is used for overnight fishing trips but is being developed into a small guesthouse.

The grassy area in front of the lighthouse leads towards a rocky beach which repays half an hour or so of exploration at low tide. Black kites swoop low over the cliffs, while further out fishermen search for octopus in their race against the tide. It's possible to rent a bike from the village, or to go on a forest walk to see birds and monkeys. Snorkelling, fishing and diving trips can also be organised in this area.

**KISIMANI MAFIA** Kisimani (KiSwahili for 'the place of the well') lies on Ras Kisimani, at the south end of the island 30 minutes' drive from Kilindoni, or a two-hour boat trip. The town was an important centre during the Shirazi domination of Kilwa between the 12th and 14th centuries (see page 290). The hands of the sultan's chief mason were cut off after he built the palace, so that he could never repeat the task. The story goes on to claim that this was why a few months later Kisimani was inundated by the sea. There is little left of the submerged medieval settlement, but you can see the well for which it is named on the beach. Wandering about, you might find a few coins and pottery shards.

The shady coconut palms are a nice spot for a picnic, and there's a lovely white beach here with good birding and snorkelling, but bring everything you want to eat or drink.

**UTENDE** The three main tourist lodges on Mafia Island all lie along the beach below this small village, at the end of the 15km road west from Kilindoni. Many of Utende's inhabitants are Makonde people from the mainland, who keep their fishing boats in Chole Bay. One or two shop-houses sell strings of dried octopus and fish. Like everywhere else on Mafia, the village is quite safe to explore, being only ten minutes' walk from any of the hotels. The beach in front of Utende (close to Mafia Island Lodge) is where local dhows leave for Chole Island every 30 minutes or so, costing Tsh500 on a local ferry oneway. Alternatively, it'll cost around US$10 to hire a boat.

Schools here are developing with aid from the lodges. A new primary school is being built on the site of the old school, offering standards 1–6, and nursery education for 31 pupils. Since 2000 this has been financed by Pole Pole. The government then helped them to build another school building for 7–14 year olds. Utende also has a couple of small shops, and you'll notice a number of buildings made with cement blocks and corrugated iron. Although not as picturesque, cement blocks are relatively cheap and an easy material for building, while corrugated-iron roofs last longer than a palm-leaf roof, which has to be replaced every three years or so.

**OTHER EXCURSIONS** Most other villages on Mafia are inaccessible by road and, like the offshore islands, may be visited only by boat. Given advance warning, the lodges can usually arrange trips to visit them.

However, the most popular excursions are probably those to isolated sand bars. You'll sail to these from your lodge, and then the boat crew will set up some shade on the beach, and cook lunch over a barbecue. Meanwhile, you can relax, sunbathe, swim and snorkel with nothing around you except miles and miles of deep blue ocean. Trips like these are included by some of the lodges, which others will charge you extra, depending on the destination (US$40–60 per person per trip is typical).

Destinations for excursions include Chole, Juani and Jibondo islands, described in the following pages, and several smaller spots including:

**Mchangani Village** is the end of an interesting excursion winding for nearly 3km up a creek on the north side of Chole Bay. Syke's monkeys can be seen in the mangrove forests and fish eagles are commonly observed. The village lies on the east bank of the creek, and takes about an hour to reach. Depart only on a high tide. If you would rather walk, it takes 90 minutes over sand and rock.

**Dindini Beach** is likewise accessible only at high tide. It faces the ocean from Mafia Island just north of Chole Bay, and from December to February can see big waves. Behind the beach is a large, sea-fed rock pool, which contains a variety of marine life. There are also low sand dunes and interesting vegetation on the coral rag.

**Didimizi Beach** is the lovely white beach seen from Chole Bay, around 4km from the main tourist lodges, or a 45-minute walk. You could arrange for a vehicle going to Kilindoni to drop you at the turn-off and walk back, not forgetting to take refreshments and a hat. Alternatively a short trip by dhow brings you straight to the beach dotted with little pyramids of sand caused by the white ghost crabs that scuttle around – they'll be all you share the sandbar with.

**Bwejuu Island**, off Ras Kisimani to the west of Mafia, has its own small village and makes a good day trip. Located between the Rufijji River Delta and Mafia's main island, it offers good snorkelling at Mange Reef, as well as diving and fishing. You can also camp on Bwejuu Island for a few nights. Further afield, the Rufiji River is close enough for trips which can go all the way to the Selous Game Reserve.

**Ras Mbisi**, only 90 minutes by road from Kilindoni, has an ideal beach for picnics, swimming and snorkelling.

**Mbaracuni Island**, lying 12km northwest of Mafia, can be visited by arrangement. Uninhabited, quiet and said to be very beautiful, it is used by fishing dhows. This is a good place to see black kites and occasionally two or three fish eagles.

**Miewe** is another small, uninhabited island, used by fishermen to clean and dry fish, and can be visited for picnics, as can the sandbank of **Marimbani**. If you're interested in sailing a little further, and for a good chance of seeing dolphins, you can take a day excursion to the island of **Kitutia**. After a couple of hours under sail, you'll be rewarded by some stunning snorkelling on a reef which surrounds a pure-white sandbank. This is all covered by the sea at high tide, so the trip needs to be timed carefully.

## CHOLE ISLAND

Chole is the lush, tropical island lying to the west of Kinasi Pass. With the adjacent islands of Juani and Jibondo, it forms a barrier between Mafia and the open ocean. The shallow reef in front is rich in soft corals, sea anemones and sponges, and, sloping to 15m, it is a good spot to practise drift diving. The bay itself is ideal for sailing and windsurfing. The town of Chole Mjini was the main urban centre on the archipelago for much of the 19th century, the home of wealthy merchants whose plantations lay on the main island of Mafia (see *History*, page 289, and *Recollections of Chole* box opposite). Ruins dating from this era include a reasonably preserved German Customs House on the waterfront, and several more ruined mansions dating to the Omani era. A path behind the new market leading to the village brings you to a prison, whose broken cells are invaded by tangled tree roots. Farther along and also in ruins is a Hindu temple.

Hanging upside down in a nearby baobab is a colony of fruit bats of the same family as the Comoros Islands' lesser flying fox, *Pteropus seychellenis comorensis*, found in the Comoros, the Seychelles and Mafia, but nowhere on mainland Africa. Each evening the bats fly across Chole Bay to feed on the cashew-nut and mango trees of Mafia, as well as marula fruit, figs, and mangrove flowers. Like the Comoros bats they dip over the surface of the water – an action which scientists believe may be an attempt to rid themselves of parasites. A more enchanting local explanation claims 'they are washing before evening prayers'. Bats are nocturnal, so it's imperative for the continuation of the Chole colony that visitors allow them to sleep in the day, ensuring that neither they nor their guide throw stones at them, or shake their tree, just to wake them up and take photos of the bats in flight. Remember that it is a bat sanctuary.

Chole's population was estimated at 5,000 during the early years of German rule, but today it is no more than 1,000. The islanders cultivate smallholdings of cassava, beans, mangoes, paw-paw, citrus (including very sweet oranges) and passion fruit. Encouraged by the lodges, these smallholdings have flourished and produce is now exported to Mafia, with the oranges also making their way to the mainland. Most of the menfolk fish, while many of the women are engaged in catching octopus beyond the mangroves at low tide. Winding past traditional houses, the path brings you to a beach where fishermen can be seen mending nets, or making sails and coconut-coir ropes. Chole was once a centre of boatbuilding, and boats are still repaired and occasionally built on the island. The boatyard is indicated on the circular walk available from Chole Mjini, about half an hour from the lodge.

The Norwegian Womens's Front and Chole Mjini Lodge have been instrumental in much of Chole's development. They have funded the building of a hospital and a free clinic for the under fives, a kindergarten, a market, and the Society for Women's Development (which runs savings and loan schemes). They

Factual histories of the east African coast tend to focus on the activities of the ruling classes – whether indigenous, Arabic or European – largely because such accounts are drawn from historical sources written by the powerful, and archaeological excavations of their mosques and palaces. The following quotes provide a rather different perspective, though it should be borne in mind that they are not first-hand accounts, but traditions passed from one generation to the next.

The woman quoted is the late Bi Hadija Mahommedi Bacha of Chole Island, and her stories are reproduced from the *Chole Handbook* (available from any of the lodge gift shops on Mafia) with the kind permission of its editors Chris Walley and Dudley Iles.

The wife of an Arab slave owner said, 'I don't understand how a child lies in the womb', so [her husband] cut open a pregnant slave woman to show his wife how the foetus lay inside. That young woman was cut open like a piece of dried fish so they could see how the child lay inside the womb of its mother... Next the wife asks the slave master, 'When a monkey is shot what happens?' So a person is found to climb up a tree, like that baobab over there. He sends a gun over there, he shoots, Pow! Down falls a human being. That slave master was called Masinda; he was the owner of Kaziwa... He was harsh! If you did anything at all, you would be made to climb a tree and shot – boom! – with a gun. You would fall down like an animal. You would already be dead and then you would be thrown away.

[Under the Germans,] if someone did something wrong, that person would be hanged at the Boma there on the beach, near the Casuarina tree at the spot along the beach where people today like to sit. It was an open spot and a box would be placed below and the person's neck would be placed in a rope. It was the Germans who arranged to use the place in this manner, and indeed they were the ones who did the hanging.

have also helped to set up a school, so that children no longer have to walk across to Juani Island at low tide, and a learning centre to help educate adults.

**GETTING THERE** The lodges at Utende operate boat trips to Chole, or you can visit it independently from Mafia, or on a 'bat and village tour' with Mafia Island Tours (*US$10*). A dhow dubbed the 'Chole taxi' leaves the beach in front of Mafia Island Lodge throughout the day – last sailing at 16.00 – a crossing of 10–15 minutes depending on the wind and tide, for a cost of Tsh500 one-way. It is also possible to charter a local boat across for a fee of about US$10. If you plan to stay more than a few hours on the island it is advisable to bring a picnic and refreshments from your hotel, and note that you'll have to wade a short distance from the boat. Make sure that you're wearing shoes, as there are stingrays in this area.

There is no motorised transport on Chole Island. In the early '90s there was only one bike, which now hangs from the rafters of Chole Mjini; today there are 150. Neither are there any budget hotels; the only place to stay is Chole Mjini Lodge (see *Where to stay*, pages 297–8), which does not cater to passing custom or serve meals to non-residents.

## JUANI ISLAND

The boat trip from Mafia to Juani, site of the ruined city of Kua, takes about ten minutes longer than the one to Chole, but the island can be approached only at high tide. The landing, in a small bay sheltered by dense mangroves, is covered in

The political relationship between Kisimani and Kua is unclear, but an intriguing if unverifiable oral tradition recounted by T M Revington in an essay in *Tanganyika Notes & Records* suggests that it was not always amicable:

The people of Ras Kisimani constructed a ship, and when it was finished and still on the stocks, they made a feast to which they invited the people of Kua. From amongst the guests they took by force several children, laid them on the sand, and launched the ship over their bodies. When the Kua people heard what had been done at Ras Kisimani, they were infuriated and thought out a scheme of revenge. Seven or eight years later, when they thought that the incident had been forgotten, an invitation was sent to the inhabitants of Ras Kisimani to attend a wedding at Kua. When the guests arrived in the evening they were ushered to a room that had been especially prepared beneath a house; the hosts one by one left their guests on the excuse of inquiring into the food, until only an old man remained to entertain them. This he did so well that the doors were bricked up without the guests perceiving it. The bodies are there to this day

So, too, is the sealed-off basement in which the bodies lie, according to the site's caretaker, who claims that it is situated below the ruins in front of his hut!

thousands of opened oyster-shells, so remember to wear good shoes, as you'll have to wade to shore. Seafood is the staple diet on Juani, but, unlike Chole, Juani has no well water, and locals practise rain-dependent cultivation.

Beneath three big baobabs near the landing, your shoes crunch on the rocky paths of a buried civilisation. Bits of blue-and-white pottery from Shirazi suggesting trade links with China are embedded in the dirt. In the past, people from the mainland came to Juani to bathe in a seawater cave reputed to have curative properties for rheumatism. It is a long, difficult walk across to the ocean side, where there are also said to be three turtle-nesting beaches. The Kua Channel slices a tiny chunk off Juani as it opens into Chole Bay. It makes a superb picnic excursion with birdwatching and swimming. A friendly grouper lives in one of the rock pools at the southern end.

The ruined city of **Kua** (see *History*, pages 290–1), spread across 15 acres on the west coast of Juani, was the Shirazi capital of Mafia. It was one of the few east African ports to be continuously inhabited from medieval times into the early 19th century, when it was sacked by raiders from Madagascar. A trail hacked out of the undergrowth leads up to a large building shedding masonry: the former palace, still revered locally as a 'spirit place' where offerings such as bits of glass are left. The ruins here have been defeated by the powerful strangler figs that dominate a number of the walls, and the tomb of the sultan himself has been destroyed by a tree growing in its centre. The path passes other ruined edifices, including two 14th-century mosques and a series of tombs.

The buildings are made from coral rock and lime cement, which does not survive well in this sea air. Looking at cracks in the walls you wonder how long they will remain standing, with the occasional monkey as the only inhabitant. If you see the caretaker, he expects and deserves a small gratuity; ask him to show you the foundations of the house referred to in the box *Kua's revenge* above.

You depart on a beautiful sail home between the islands, watched by the scores of ibis on the mangroves. There is a guide and map of the ruins, as well as the report on its archaeology, in the library at Kinasi Lodge.

Jibondo is a long, low-lying island another 20-minute sail from Juani. This traditional village community is rather different from the rest of Mafia, and the atmosphere is somehow more charged than in other villages. Coming ashore, a big *jahazi* dhow is one of the first things you see. Built 15 years ago, it has never been launched and is subsequently something of a museum piece, but the old men sitting under the quinine tree nearby have already learned its value to tourism, wanting to charge Tsh1,000 (or US$1) for a photo. Behind the boat is a rather plain white mosque, built in 1979.

Some of its furniture was taken from the queen's palace in the ruins at Kua, and it's worth wandering around the back to see the carved wooden door from Kua (by contrast, the window-frames were made of wood from India). This is all set off by the pungent smell from the row of long-drop loos that literally drop into the sea. Jibondo does not have a fresh water supply, so the islanders depend on rain which is collected in a primitive concrete catchment area.

The rainwater lasts only three months after the rains; after this, the islanders have to go to Mafia with drums to collect water. Jibondo people are well known as shipbuilders and, as on Chole, use only traditional tools. Even the nails are handmade and the holes are plugged with local kapok and shark fat. Local women play a prominent role in trading as well as fishing. They also sail boats, which is unusual in African society, and are more affable and confident than women elsewhere. Jibondo people also collect and dry seaweed to export.

Another unusual aspect of Jibondo is that cultivation is carried out at one end of the island while the people live in an urban community at the other. The village, which consists of traditional Swahili-style houses with makuti roofs, is laid out in a grid pattern. As on Chole and Juani, there is no transport other than boats which shelter on the western side of the narrow neck of the island.

The island has one school, easily identified by the football field in front. If the tide is good for fishing, the children – encouraged by their parents – go straight out on the water, ignoring lessons. In a year, only one child is likely to leave the island and go to secondary school on Mafia. There are, however, three *madrasas* on the island, where there is a strong Muslim faith. There are no other social services, and only a basic shop. On the other side of the island is Flamingo Beach, which makes an interesting two-hour trek. Village trail and sailing dhow with Mafia Island Tours costs US$25.

**FCO TRAVEL ADVICE**
know before you go
fco.gov.uk/travel

Mafia Archipelago  JIBONDO ISLAND

13

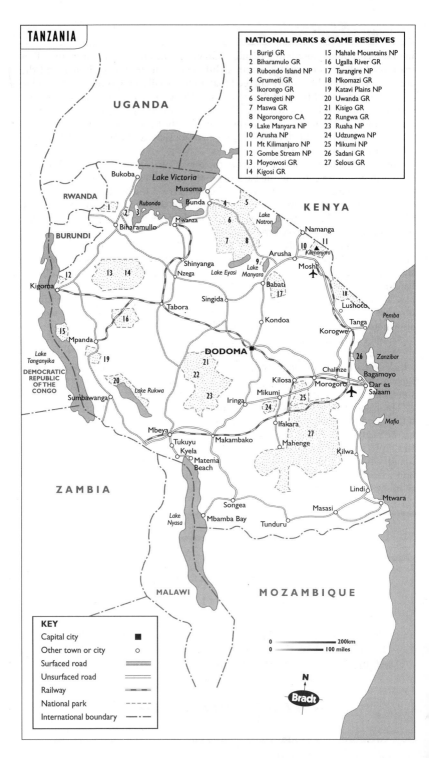

TANZANIA

**NATIONAL PARKS & GAME RESERVES**

| | |
|---|---|
| 1 Burigi GR | 15 Mahale Mountains NP |
| 2 Biharamulo GR | 16 Ugalla River GR |
| 3 Rubondo Island NP | 17 Tarangire NP |
| 4 Grumeti GR | 18 Mkomazi GR |
| 5 Ikorongo GR | 19 Katavi Plains NP |
| 6 Serengeti NP | 20 Uwanda GR |
| 7 Maswa GR | 21 Kisigo GR |
| 8 Ngorongoro CA | 22 Rungwa GR |
| 9 Lake Manyara NP | 23 Ruaha NP |
| 10 Arusha NP | 24 Udzungwa NP |
| 11 Mt Kilimanjaro NP | 25 Mikumi NP |
| 12 Gombe Stream NP | 26 Sadani NP |
| 13 Moyowosi GR | 27 Selous GR |
| 14 Kigosi GR | |

**KEY**

| | |
|---|---|
| Capital city | ■ |
| Other town or city | ○ |
| Surfaced road | |
| Unsurfaced road | |
| Railway | |
| National park | |
| International boundary | |

0        200km
0        100 miles

N

Bradt

# Southern Tanzania Safaris

*with Philip Briggs*

In recent years, there has been increasing interest in the national parks and reserves of southern Tanzania – especially the Selous and Ruaha, and to a lesser extent Sadaani. For decades these areas have been overshadowed by their more famous northern counterparts (Lake Manyara, Ngorongoro Crater and the Serengeti), but today the secret is out, and southern Tanzania is a favourite amongst safari aficionados as well as first-time visitors who are put off by the crowds which so often mar the northern parks.

Zanzibar is barely 200km from the Selous, the largest of all Tanzania's (and indeed Africa's) game reserves, and easily reached by air. Ruaha is further – about 400km from Zanzibar – while Sadaani is just a 25km hop away, directly across the channel separating Unguja (Zanzibar Island) from the mainland.

Gradually a 'southern circuit' has developed, with many individuals and small groups flying to Selous (and sometimes also Ruaha) before finishing their trip with time on the islands. These flight links are now daily, even to Ruaha, making this an increasingly straightforward option. If you want to include the parks of southern Tanzania in your travels, then this chapter aims to help you plan your trip, and enjoy it to the full.

## OVERVIEW OF YOUR TRIP

It's often difficult for first-time visitors to decide which reserves to visit – so an overview here might help.

If you're planning on a beach-and-safari trip then first be mindful that safari time will usually cost much more than beach time; it's often double the nightly cost. For example, a half-decent safari lodge will easily cost US$300 each per night, whilst you'll have to try hard to find equally comfortable beach lodges at more than US$150 each per night. (The reason for this is partly that most safari lodges include a full day of activities and all your meals, whereas a beach lodge often provides only a room and breakfast; and partly because the logistics at most safari lodges are that much more expensive.)

With this in mind, consider how long you want to spend on each part of your trip. A 50/50 split (a week on safari and a week by the beach) is typical for a two-week trip, but this depends on your priorities and budget.

If you decide on five nights or less on safari, then our advice is probably to stick to Selous – and spend all your time there. If you decide on eight nights or more on safari, then our advice is probably to combine time in Selous with time in Ruaha – as then the extra cost of flying between the parks is worth it for the change in scenery and environment. If you decide on six or seven nights on safari, then it's less clear if Ruaha is worth the extra travelling or not; you need to think about it.

Finally, if you're really looking for just two or three days of safari, perhaps beside a beach where you can lie back and forget safari activities completely if you wish, then consider Saadani. This small, coastal park allows you the flexibility to do just that.

## SELOUS GAME RESERVE

Covering more than 45,000km², the Selous (pronounced 'Seloo') is Africa's single largest game reserve, three times larger than the Serengeti, more than twice the size of South Africa's Kruger National Park, and roughly 50% bigger than either Belgium or Swaziland. It is, furthermore, the core sanctuary within the greater Selous-Niassa ecosystem, which extends over 155,000km² of practically uninhabited wilderness in southern Tanzania and northern Mozambique – the largest chunk of comparably untrammelled bush left in Africa.

The claim that the Selous lies at the core of the greatest surviving African wilderness is supported by the prodigiously large mammal populations protected within the reserve and the greater ecosystem. The elephant herd of 65,000 represents more than half of the Tanzanian population, and 5–10% of the African total. The buffalo, estimated at 120,000–150,000, and the reserve's 40,000 hippo and 4,000 lion are probably the largest such populations on the continent. The Selous also harbours an estimated 100,000 wildebeest, 35,000 zebra, 25,000 impala and significant herds of greater kudu, hartebeest and eland. It is also one of the most important sanctuaries in Africa for the endangered black rhinoceros, African wild dog, and sable and puku antelope.

**BACKGROUND INFORMATION** That the Selous ranks as one of east Africa's most alluring and satisfying safari destinations is not in dispute. However, given that much of the publicity surrounding the Selous bangs on and on about its vast area, prospective visitors should be aware that the extent of the reserve is in practice something of a red herring. The Selous is divided into two disproportionate parts by the Rufiji, Tanzania's largest river, which together with the Great Ruaha, a major tributary, runs through the reserve from west to east. About 90% of the Selous lies to the south of the river and has been divided into a number of privately leased hunting concessions, all of which are off-limits to casual tourism. A proportion of the northern sector has also been set aside for hunting concessions. The remainder – no more than 5% of the reserve's total area – forms what, to all intents and purposes, is the Selous Photographic Reserve. The five lodges (and most activities for visitors) are actually concentrated within an area of about 1,000km² immediately north of the Rufiji.

Fortunately, this photographic part of the Selous is wonderfully atmospheric, a dense tract of wild miombo woodland abutting the meandering Rufiji River, and an associated labyrinth of five pretty lakes connected to each other and the river by numerous narrow streams. Arriving by light aircraft, as most visitors do, it is exhilarating to sweep above the palm-fringed channels teeming with hippos and waterfowl, the swampy islets where immense herds of elephant and giraffe graze alongside each other, and exposed sandbanks where antelope drink and all manner of shorebirds scurry about.

No less exciting are the boat excursions along the Rufiji, which generally culminate with a brilliant red sun setting behind the tall borassus palms and baobabs that line the wide sandy watercourse. Gulp-inducing dentist-eye views of the Selous's trademark gigantic crocs can pretty much be guaranteed from the boat, as can conferences of grunting, harrumphing hippos – and you'd be unlucky not to be entertained by herds of elephant, buffalo or giraffe shuffling down to drink.

The most memorable aspect of the boat trips, however, is the profuse birdlife. Characteristic waterbirds along this stretch of the Rufiji include yellow-billed

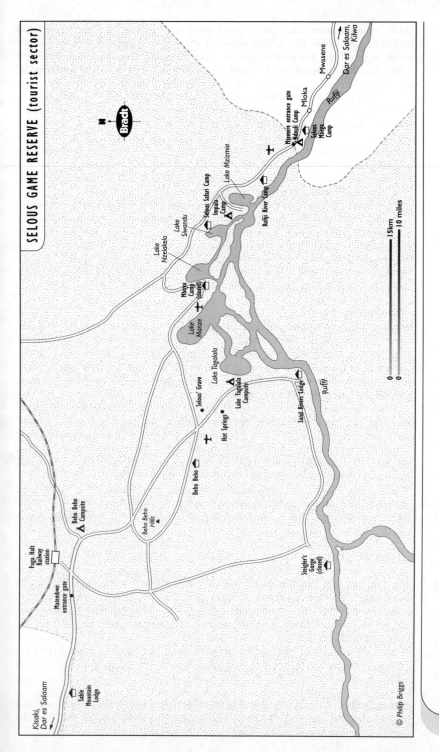

© Philip Briggs

stork, white-crowned and spur-winged plovers, various small waders, pied and malachite kingfishers, and African skimmer. Pairs of fish eagle and palmnut vulture perch high on the borassus palms, seasonal breeding colonies of carmine and white-throated bee-eater swirl around the mud cliffs that hem in some stretches of the river, and pairs of trumpeter hornbill and purple-crested turaco flap between the riparian trees. Worth looking out for among a catalogue of egrets and herons is the Malagasy squacco heron, a regular winter visitor, while the elusive Pel's fishing owl often emerges at dusk to hawk above the water.

Game drives along the network of rough roads to the north of the Rufiji are reliably rewarding, especially towards the end of the dry season, when large mammals concentrate around the five lakes. More frequently seen ungulates include impala, common waterbuck, bushbuck, white-bearded wildebeest, eland, greater kudu, buffalo and common zebra.

The northern sector of the park has been dubbed 'Giraffic Park', with some justification, as herds exceeding 50 individuals come down to drink in the heat of the afternoon. Giraffes seem exceedingly common here, which is odd as they are entirely absent south of the Rufiji. The river also forms a natural barrier between the ranges of the distinctive white-bearded and Niassa races of wildebeest. The endangered African wild dog is commonly observed, as is the spotted hyena, while leopards are common but elusive, but cheetah have not been recorded in this part of the reserve for about 20 years.

Much in evidence are Selous's lions, with two or three different prides' territories converging on each of the five large lakes. The lions typically have darker coats and less hirsute manes than their counterparts elsewhere in east Africa. During the dry season, the lions of Selous evidently rely on an unusual opportunistic diurnal hunting strategy, rarely straying far from the lakes, where they rest up in the shade to wait for whatever ungulate happens to venture within pouncing distance on its way to drink.

While the marketing line of 'only five small camps in a 50,000km² wilderness' does rather overstate the exclusivity of the Selous experience, it is true that a mere 5,000 foreigners annually – about 1% of tourist arrivals to Tanzania – ever make it to this excellent reserve. Particularly if you are based at one of the western lodges – Beho Beho, Sand Rivers and Sable Mountain – it is still possible to undertake a game drive in the Selous without coming across another vehicle.

Whereas the national parks of northern Tanzania are dominated by large impersonal hotels that evidently aim to shut out the bush the moment you enter them, the Selous boasts a select handful of low-key, eco-friendly, thatch-and-canvas lodges whose combined bed capacity amounts to little more than 100 visitors. Furthermore, because the Selous is a game reserve and not subject to the regulations that govern Tanzania's national parks, visitors are offered a more primal and integrated bush experience than the usual repetitive regime of one game drive after another. In addition to boat trips, all lodges offer guided game walks, which come with a real likelihood of encountering elephant or buffalo – even lion – on foot. Better still are the overnight fly-camping excursions offered by some of the camps, which entail sleeping beneath a glorified mosquito net in the middle of the bush. It's thrilling stuff!

Note that the roads within the Selous become impassable after heavy rain. Hence camps here close towards the end of the wet season, in April, and re-open in July.

**Entrance fees** An entrance fee of US$30 per person per day is charged, and payable in hard currency. On most organised trips this will be included in the overall price, but it's worth checking this when booking.

**Further information** Two useful booklets are *Selous Game Reserve: A Guide to the Northern Section* and the glossier *Selous: Africa's Largest & Wildest Game Reserve*. Most lodges stock both and they are similar textually. For details on the man behind the park's name, read *The Life of Frederick Courtney Selous* by J G Millais, published by Gallery Publications and available in Zanzibar.

**GETTING THERE AND AWAY** Many tour operators, both overseas and in Tanzania, offer a variety of trips to the Selous. These usually include flights to/from the reserve, accommodation and activities. Most use frequent daily flights between Dar es Salaam and Selous operated by Coastal Airlines and ZanAir. These generally connect very easily to/from Zanzibar. Some of the Coastal flights continue (daily from 2006) to connect with flights to/from Ruaha. Once inside the parks, these flights will all stop at any of the camp airstrips by prior arrangement.

If you are travelling in mainland Tanzania it's perfectly possible to reach the Selous by road, although that's generally more costly than flying. For full details of these options, *Tanzania: The Bradt Travel Guide* by Philip Briggs is, of course, highly recommended.

**WHERE TO STAY** Although there are ten entries listed below, the reality is that only six are currently fully operational camps inside the park.

**⌂ Beho Beho Camp** (8 units) ☎ 022 260 0352–4; f 022 260 0347; UK ☎ 020 8750 5655; e reservations@behobeho.com; www.behobeho.com. Beho Beho's site was used for a safari camp as early as 1972; one of the first such sites in the Selous. It still has an unusual location for this park, high on a hill in an area dotted with baobabs. In 2004 it was virtually rebuilt and completely refurbished, and is now widely regarded as the best lodge in the Selous. Accommodation is in one of 8 very large and attractively decorated en-suite *bandas* built of local stone on the footslopes of the Beho Beho Hills, on the west side of northern Selous. All have large bathrooms with great showers, flush toilets and dual washbasins. The bedrooms have canopied kingsize beds, ceiling fans and 24hr electricity (3-pin UK-style plugs). All are slightly different, and each has a separate area that is partly lounge, partly veranda. This lies under a high thatched roof, with almost a whole wall open at the front. The elegant dining area serves very high-quality food, with everyone usually sitting around the same table — even if the location of the table varies. Afterwards there are vast sofas to relax in around the bar area, and a full-size slate-bedded billiards table to keep the restless entertained. Slightly down the slope, the swimming pool and its sundeck also command a spectacular view. Beho Beho is the only lodge within Selous set away from the river, but a permanent pool in the valley below supports a resident pod of hippos and attracts plenty of game and birdlife. Although very comfortable, what has really gained such a top reputation for the camp in the past few years is the quality, and enthusiasm, of its guiding team — currently led by Spike Williamson and Sean Lues. Here lies the camp's real attraction, as both were guide-trainers in Zimbabwe (under what was certainly Africa's best system of safari guide accreditation), and thus offer a depth of knowledge and guiding experience that's very hard to match. Being in a relatively remote area of the park, you'll find few other visitors in Beho Beho's vicinity. The camp's activities include 4x4 game drives, boat trips on Lake Tagalala, and particularly good walking safaris. (It's not unknown for morning activities to last for 5 or 6hrs if you are enthusiastic and energetic!) Nearby sites of interest include some World War I trenches (complete with scattered artefacts), the grave of Frederick Courtney Selous and a group of hot springs set in a patch of riparian woodland. New for 2006 are Beho Beho's super-luxurious 'bush nights' — with a small fly-camp set up for just 2–4 guests. At a high cost, this must rate as some of Africa's most exclusive, and expensive, camping! As a relatively new camp which is rapidly gaining something of a revered status, it raised its rates substantially between 2005 and 2006; they may well continue to rise. *US$ pp sharing for FB, inc drinks and activities but exclusive of park fees. 'Bush nights' cost an extra US$350 pp, on top of the normal room cost.*

🏠 **Sand Rivers Selous** (8 rooms) 📞 022 286 5156; 📠 022 286 5731; e info@nomad.co.tz; www.sandrivers.com. Set above a wide, sandy bend in the Rufiji River, Sand Rivers has been regarded as the top camp in the Selous for many years, and still puts up very stiff competition to Beho Beho. Sand Rivers' pedigree is top-notch, it's run by Nomad Safaris and is the sister-camp of Chada, in Katavi National Park, and Greystoke, in Mahale Mountains National Park — both of which are top camps and names to conjure with in the safari world. Like Beho Beho, Sand Rivers is situated in an isolated area of the Selous, the wild southwest of the public part of the reserve, which is visited by vehicles from the other lodges infrequently. It is another very comfortable lodge with a large thatched boma dotted with large sofas sporting sumptuous heavy-cotton cushions, but in contrast Sand Rivers stands on a wide curve of the Rufiji River; being able to watch the life of the river adds greatly to the special feel of the lodge. For those who need to be closer still to the water, there is a stylish curved swimming pool under a large baobab tree. Meals are high-quality and eaten together, at the same table. The camp's 8 stone-and-makuti units are large and elegant, though a touch dark in places. Each has a large dbl bed, with walk-in mosquito net; an en-suite bathroom with flush toilet, shower and wash basin; and a private balcony overlooking the river. Sand Rivers' activities focus on 4x4 game drives (the plains around nearby Lake Tagalala are one obvious goal); boat trips along the river and up through the impressive Stiegler's Gorge; and walking safaris. The standard of guiding is exceptionally high, and in recent years Sand Rivers has often been the base for at least one top Zimbabwean professional guide. Sand Rivers also run very popular fly-camping trips, whereby a couple of guests sleep out on a dry riverbed with their guide — usually having had a lovely meal under the stars, complete with table-linen, crystal glasses and some fine food. Usually these are run for 1 or 2 nights as part of a longer stay at the lodge, although they do offer 5-night set walking trails (on fixed dates throughout the year) for die-hard walking-safari addicts. *From US$545/840 to US$660/970 sgl/dbl, inc FB and activities.*

🏠 **Selous Impala Camp** (7 units) 📞 022 245 2005–6; 📠 022 245 2004; e reservations@adventurecamps.co.tz; www.adventurecamps.co.tz. Set up with help from Coastal Aviation in 2004, this unpretentiously tasteful new camp boasts a magnificent location on a wooded stretch of the Rufiji. It's relatively small, with just 7 Meru-style tents, built on wooden platforms with a private balcony. These are very comfortably furnished, in an 'old Africa' style. The camp uses Maasai guards to escort guests to their rooms at night. Impala has one of the most scenic locations in the park and its thatched lounge and communal deck looks out over the river to mountains, although one's gaze is usually drawn back to the Rufiji River by the elephants and other wildlife which visits it. Activities are fairly flexible, inc game drives and boat trips, and the camp has a lovely swimming pool — allowing you to look out over the river and to the hills while you're in the pool. Impala is a very welcome addition to the Selous: a good camp that doesn't charge top prices. It seems likely to strengthen its reputation to become a firm favourite. In combination with its sister-camp in Ruaha (the rather more spartan Mdonya Old River Camp), safaris are varied and particularly excellent value. *US$375/630 sgl/dbl FB for drive-in clients (no activities); US$460/800 inc FB and activities.*

🏠 **Selous Safari Camp** (13 rooms) 📞 022 212 8485; m 0748 953551; 📠 022 211 2794; e info@selous.com; www.selous.com. This plush camp is set back slightly from the shores of Lake Siwando. Approaching across the lake, all you see of the camp over the treetops are the tall apexes of the main *bandas*, which have been built on stilts. The camp has recently been divided into a main camp with 9 rooms, known as 'Selous Safari Camp', and a smaller section with just 4 rooms called 'Selous Private Camp'. Both provide accommodation in spacious stilted en-suite tents, which are set far apart from each other and have fans, open-air showers and a private deck. The main camp's lounge and dining area is a fabulous stilted treehouse lit at night by dozens of gas lamps. The main camp has a separate swimming pool. The private camp's tents are rather larger than those at the main camp, and more luxuriously appointed, and these have their own dining area on decking near the swimming pool. Game drives, boat trips, guided walks and fly-camping are all offered here — although the camp is geared more for driving and boating than it is for walking. When last visited, activities commenced quite late in the morning, at 09.00; perfect for honeymooners who want a long lie-in and a safari. More recently we understand that they're starting these earlier, if requested. In short, Selous Safari Camp is a very high-quality, professional operation that pays great attention to detail — especially where comfort and food are concerned.

US$525/700 sgl/dbl for the main camp (US$600/800 for the private camp) inc FB and 2 activities daily; excludes park fees. Drinks are usually included at the private camp; they are charged as an extra at the main camp.

🏠 **Rufiji River Camp** (20 rooms) 🕿 +022 212 8663; **m** 0744 267706; **f** 022 212 8661; **e** info@hippotours.com; www.hippotours.com. One of the first lodges to be established in the Selous, the ever popular and reasonably priced Rufiji River Camp is situated at the eastern extremity of the photographic northern area of the reserve, overlooking an atmospheric stretch of the Rufiji River alive with hippos and crocs and regularly visited by elephants. The camp consists of 20 en-suite standing tents, shaded by thatch. Inside are simple twin beds and fairly basic furniture; everything is very clean and well maintained, though it's not luxurious. The en-suite bathrooms each have a flush toilet and solar-heated water for showers. These tents are spaced along the river in a lush stretch of woodland populated by monkeys and numerous birds — and occasionally visited by more exciting large mammals. A swimming pool has recently been constructed. The lodge has a refreshingly informal and unpretentious atmosphere; delicious home-cooked food reflects the nationality of the laid-back Italian owner-manager. Rufiji River Camp offers an excellent range of boat and foot activities, as well as half-day game drives encompassing the 3 nearby lakes, full-day excursions further afield and overnight fly-camping. Rufiji River's guides are generally highly experienced Tanzanians, most of whom have been guiding here for many years; many have worked as game scouts before joining the lodge. Rufiji River Camp offers a straightforward, very good-value safari in a great wilderness area. *US$365/530 sgl/dbl inc FB, activities and park fees.*

🏠 **Sable Mountain Lodge** (12 rooms) 🕿 022 211 0507; **m** 0741 323318; **e** tentview@cats-net.com; www.saadani.com. Situated 1km outside the park's western park boundary near the Matembwe Gate, Sable Mountain Lodge stands on some small hills, offering views into the surrounding dense brachystegia forest. It consists of 8 fairly simple stone *bandas*, and 4 more luxurious tented *bandas*. Two of the tents are honeymoon suites; these have the better views and each has a small, private plunge pool. All the rooms have en-suite hot shower and toilet, mosquito nets over the beds and 24hr electricity. Sable Mountain's dining area is open with good views, and there's a swimming pool nearby.

Activities include 4x4 safaris in the park, walks and boat trips — whilst the tireless can go on all-day trips, with a picnic lunch and a boat trip on Lake Tagalala. The surrounding woodland is very thick, and guided walks offer the opportunity to see forest-associated species such as blue monkey, black-and-white colobus and the amazing chequered elephant shrew, as well as a host of forest birds inc the exquisite Livingstone's turaco, a variety of hornbills and the vociferous forest weaver. Between Dec and May, sable antelope move into the area. Game drives concentrate on the plains north of the main cluster of lodges, which can be very worthwhile seasonally, with very few other vehicles around. fly-camping is also available, as are river trips during the wet season on the lushly forested Mbega River. Sable Mountain is very close to the train station at Kisaki, on the TAZARA line between Dar and Zambia. In the past there have been attempts to start a luxury train service; when successful, Sable Mountain will be an obvious first-stop for visitors to the reserve. It is one of very few camps which can be arranged on a FB basis, without activities — so is ideal for those on a tighter budget who just want to do nothing for a few days! *US$160/230 sgl/dbl for FB (or US$260/430 inc activities)*

🏠 **Mbuyu Tented Camp** (20 rooms) This attractively located camp lies on the shore of Lake Nzerakera, and its lounge and dining area are built around a large baobab tree. An attractive feature is the stilted hide overlooking the lake, which is visited by numerous animals. The camp had been closed for some time when this edition was researched, but rumour is that it will soon re-open under new ownership.

🏠 **Selous Mbega Camp** (13 rooms) 🕿 022 265 0250–1; **m** 0748 613335; **f** 0744 794110; **e** baobabvillage@raha.com; www.selous-mbega-camp.com. This small German-owned camp lies on the banks of the Rufiji immediately east of the park boundary some 5.5km outside Mtemere Gate. Most of the en-suite tents are set in the riparian woodland overlooking the river, but two stand alongside a small waterhole. Game drives, guided walks, and boat trips can be arranged at US$35 pp per activity. Standard non-resident rates are US$95 pp sharing, and substantial discounts are offered by prior arrangement to backpackers who are prepared to bus from Dar es Salaam to the village of Mloka, about 4km from the camp (a free transfer is provided).

🏠 **Ndovu Campsite** (5 units) 🕿 0744 782378; **e** hkibola@yahoo.co.uk. This new budget camp,

14

situated outside the reserve boundaries between Mbega Camp and the Mtemere Gate, consists of 5 dbl standing tents with thatched roofs, as well as a campsite, all of which use common toilets and showers. Accommodation in the standing tents costs US$20 pp while pitching your own tent costs US$10 pp. A restaurant should be operational by early

2006. The camp caters primarily to self-drive visitors, but boat trips are offered at US$30 pp.

**Lake Tagalala & Beho Beho Campsites** These little-used official campsites have no facilities worth talking about, but they both boast a great setting and bush feel. A camping fee of US$10 pp is levied.

# RUAHA NATIONAL PARK

Tanzania's second-largest national park extends over 10,300km² of wooded hills and open plains to the west of Iringa, and it lies at the core of a greater ecosystem that is five times larger, embracing six other protected areas including the contiguous Rungwa and Kizigo game reserves. Ruaha is widely regarded by Tanzania's safari cognoscenti to be the country's best-kept game-viewing secret, and it has unquestionably retained a compelling wilderness character that is increasingly savoury when compared with the package safaris and 100-room game lodges common in the parks of northern Tanzania.

**BACKGROUND INFORMATION** The dominant geographical feature of the park is the Great Ruaha River, which follows the southeast boundary for 160km, and is known to the local Hehe people as the Lyambangori (Ruaha being a corruption of the Hehe word *luhava*, which simply means 'river'). Only the small part of the park around the river is developed for tourism, but with just two small lodges currently operating – though more are likely to open over the next couple of years – even this limited 400km road circuit sees relatively few visitors, and has a reassuringly untrammelled mood.

Ruaha has a hot and rather dry climate, with an average annual rainfall of around 500mm falling almost exclusively between October and May, and peaking in February and March. Daytime temperatures in excess of 40°C are regularly recorded, particularly over October and November before the rains break, but a very low humidity level makes this less noticeable than might be expected, and it cools down reliably at night. The best game viewing is generally from May to November, but the bush is greener and prettier from January to June, and birding peaks during the European winter months of December to April. The vegetation of Ruaha is transitional to southern miombo and eastern savanna biomes, and a wide variety of habitats are protected within the park, including riparian forest along the watercourses, swamps, grassland, and acacia woodland. The dominant vegetation type is *brachystegia* woodland and several areas of the park support an impressive number of large baobab trees.

The floral variety of Ruaha is mirrored by the variety of wildlife likely to be seen over the course of a few days on safari. The most common ungulates, not unusually, are the widespread impala, waterbuck, bushbuck, buffalo, zebra and giraffe, all of which are likely to be encountered several times on any given game drive. The park lies at the most southerly extent of the range of several east African ungulate species, including lesser kudu and Grant's gazelle. Yet it also harbours a number of antelope that are rare or absent in northern Tanzania, most visibly the splendid greater kudu – some of the most handsomely horned males you'll come across anywhere in Africa – but also the more elusive roan and sable antelope. The elephant population is the largest of any Tanzanian national park, despite heavy losses due to poaching in the 1980s, with some 12,000 elephants migrating through the greater Ruaha ecosystem. The most impressive pair of tusks weighed in the 20th century – combined weight 201kg – were from an individual shot in Ruaha

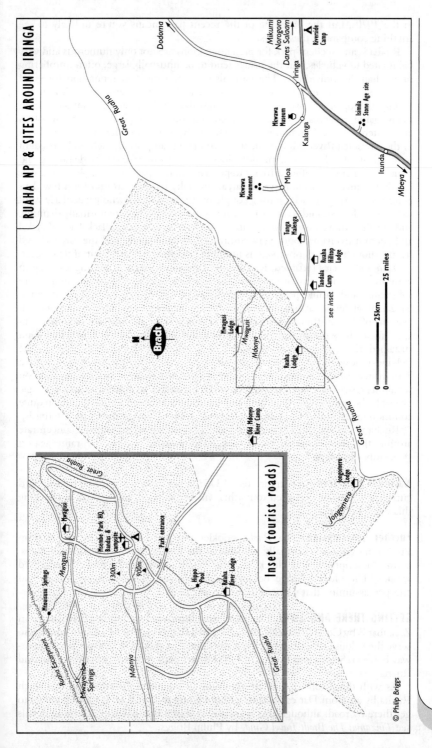

**Inset (tourist roads)**

25km

25 miles

0

0

© Philip Briggs

in the 1970s, but the poaching of the recent past means you're unlikely to see anything comparable these days.

Ruaha is an excellent park for predators. Lions are not only numerous and very habituated to vehicles, but the prides tend to be unusually large, often numbering more than 20 individuals. The park also boasts a justified reputation for good leopard sightings, and, while it's not as reliable as the Seronera Valley in the Serengeti, leopard are usually seen every few days and they are less skittish than in many game reserves. Cheetah, resident on the open plains, are quite often encountered in the Lundu area – known locally as the mini Serengeti – northeast of the Mwagusi River. More than 100 African wild dogs are thought to be resident in the greater Ruaha ecosystem. Wild dogs are known to have very wide ranges, and their movements are often difficult to predict, but one pack of about 40 individuals regularly moves into the Mwagusi area, generally hanging around for a few days before wandering elsewhere for a couple of weeks. Visitors who particularly want to see wild dogs should try to visit in June or July, when they are normally denning, and are thus more easy to locate than at other times of year. Black-backed jackal and spotted hyena are both very common and easily seen, and the rarer striped hyena, though seldom observed, is found here at the southern limit of its range.

With 450 species recorded, Ruaha also offers some excellent birding, once again with an interesting mix of southern and northern species. Of particular note are substantial and visible populations of black-collared lovebird and ashy starlings, Tanzanian endemics associated with the Maasai Steppes found here at the southern extreme of their distribution. By contrast, this is perhaps the only savanna reserve in east Africa where the crested barbet – a colourful yellow-and-black bird whose loud sustained trilling is a characteristic sound of the southern African bush – replaces the red-and-yellow barbet. Ruaha is also the type locality for the recently described Tanzanian red-billed hornbill *Tockus ruahae*, a Tanzanian endemic that is very common within its restricted range. Raptors are well represented, with bateleur and fish eagle probably the most visible large birds of prey, and the localised Eleanora's falcon quite common in December and January. The watercourses support the usual waterbirds.

Ruaha is best visited between July and November, when animals concentrate around the river. Internal roads may be impassable during the rainy season (December to May).

**National park fees** An entrance fee of US$25 per 24 hours must be paid in hard currency. On most organised tours this will be included, but it's worth checking this when booking.

**Further information** The *Ruaha* booklet published in 2000 by the African Publishing Group is normally available at the lodges, and contains useful maps, animal descriptions and checklists, and details of where to look for localised species. The older 64-page booklet *Ruaha National Park* is just as useful, and cheaper, assuming that you can locate a copy!

**GETTING THERE AND AWAY** The most straightforward way to reach Ruaha from Zanzibar is by Coastal Travel's daily scheduled flights via Dar es Salaam, which also serve the Selous Game Reserve. Typically these cost about US$280 per person one-way between Selous and Ruaha, or US$310 per person one-way between Dar and Ruaha.

As with the Selous, if you are travelling in mainland Tanzania you can reach Ruaha by air from Dar es Salaam, without going to Zanzibar. It's also possible to get there by road, although this is usually at least a two-day trip; for more details see *Tanzania: The Bradt Travel Guide* by Philip Briggs.

## WHERE TO STAY

**Jongomero Tented Camp** (8 tents) ✆ 022 212 8485; 📱 0748 953551; 🖷 022 211 2794; 📧 info@selous.com; www.selous.com. Sister-camp of Selous Safari Camp in the Selous, this is the most overtly luxurious of the lodges in Ruaha, and the only one with a swimming pool. Jongomero consists of 8 spacious tented rooms with private balconies carved into the dense riverine woodland bordering the eponymous seasonal river. It's about 500m upstream of its confluence with the Ruaha, where a semi-permanent pool hosts a resident pod of around 50 hippos. Jongomero has a very isolated feel, situated 60km southwest of the entrance gate, and the little-used road running back towards the entrance gate often yields good elephant and buffalo sightings. The area to the south of camp functions much as a private game reserve, because so few other vehicles head this way, but this area borders a hunting concession and so the wildlife tends to be rather skittish. The birdlife within camp can be excellent, with Livingstone's turaco topping the gaudiness stakes, while the localised Bohm's spinetail can be distinguished from the other swifts and swallows that soar above the camp by its distinctive bat-like fluttering. The catering is to an exceptionally high standard, but, unlike several other lodges in this price range elsewhere in Tanzania, drinks are not included. *US$495/660 sgl/dbl inc all activities and meals.*

**Mwagusi Safari Camp** (10 tents) ✆/🖷 (UK) 20 8846 9363; 📧 tropicalafrica.uk@virgin.net. This small and exclusive tented camp, situated on the north bank of the seasonal Mwagusi River, is one of the most alluring lodges anywhere in east Africa, immensely comfortable, yet with a real bush atmosphere. The accommodation, strung along the riparian woodland fringing the river, consists of spacious walk-in tents, enclosed in a wood, thatch and reed shelter, each of which has a vast shower and toilet area, and a private balcony. Because the lodge is owner managed, the service is top-notch, and includes some great touches — most memorably, starlit bush dinners around a campfire in a clearing above the camp or in the riverbed. Game viewing from the camp is superb, with elephant and greater kudu regularly putting in an appearance, and plenty of birds hopping around the trees. Wild dog are regularly sighted in the area, several lion prides are resident, and the closest game-viewing circuits are situated far enough from the larger Ruaha River Lodge and park headquarters to let you feel you have the whole park to yourself. Game walks with

an armed ranger are also offered, with a good chance of encountering elephants and other large animals on foot. *US$390/450 sgl/dbl inc all activities, meals and park fees; drinks are extra, and there is a charge of US$25 pp for an extra early-morning walk.*

**Ruaha River Lodge** (24 rooms) ✆ (UK) 01452 862288; ✆ 023 244 0194; 📱 0744 237422; 🖷 0741 327706; 📧 fox@safaricamps.info; www.tanzaniasafaris.info. This wonderfully scenic and comfortable camp is the oldest in Ruaha, situated on a rocky hillside above a set of rapids on the Ruaha River some 15km from the entrance gate. Game viewing is excellent from the camp, with rock hyrax scuttling around everywhere, hippos resident on the river, elephant passing through regularly, and many other animals coming down to drink. Accommodation is in unpretentious stone cottages or fixed tents — all quite simple and compact. It is divided into 2 camps of 12 rooms each, both of which have their own restaurant and bar. *US$295/540 sgl/dbl inc all activities, meals and park fees; drinks are extra. Reduced rates available for locals who drive themselves into the camp.*

**Mdonya Old River Camp** (10 tents) ✆ 022 245 2005–6; 🖷 022 245 2004; 📧 reservations@adventurecamps.co.tz; www.adventurecamps.co.tz. Like its sister-camp, Selous Impala Camp, Old Mdonya was set up with help from Coastal Aviation in 2004. It stands on the wooded banks of the 'old' Mdonyo River, which has not flowed in earnest since a newer path was carved by the river a couple of decades back. Comfortable rather than luxurious, the en-suite standing tents all have a private balcony, while the culinary emphasis is on tasty home-style cooking eaten beneath the stars. Old Mdonya makes no apologies for being a fairly simple camp; it's aiming for a fairly elemental experience of Africa, and not for the comforts and fripperies that so many camps seem to have been striving for in recent years. Isolated though it may be, the camp offers good access to the superb Mwagusi River game-viewing circuit. The old riverbed is an important wildlife passage, and plenty of animals pass through camp daily, most profusely impala, warthog and giraffe, but also the occasional lion or elephant, while the helpful staff will gladly show you nocturnal visitors such as honey badger, genet and bushpig. The birding is also superb, with the likes of purple-crested turaco, bearded woodpecker, crested barbet, black-necked weaver, orange-breasted bush-shrike and green-winged pytilia among the colourful and conspicuous residents. US$400 pp sharing, US$460 pp sgl; includes all meals and activities, house wine with dinner and soft drinks.

⌂ **Tandala Camp** (10 units)
e tandala@iwayafrica.com/ tandalacamp@yahoo.com. Situated some 13km outside Ruaha's entrance gate along the Tungamalenga road, this new lodge overlooks a seasonal river in private conservancy buffering the national park. Accommodation is in no-frills but comfortable en-suite tents set on a stilted wooden base, while facilities include an attractive makuti restaurant and bar area alongside a small swimming pool. The greater kudu for which the camp is named is evidently quite common in the surrounding woodland, while a waterhole fringing the camp attracts a steady stream of wildlife in the dry season, inc elephants on most days. Because it lies outside the national park, activities such as night drives, guided game walks and fly-camping are offered. US$150/180 sgl/dbl FB, or US$170/300 inc activities outside the national park. Game drives into the park are offered at US$55 pp (half-day) or US$75 pp (full day) inc park entrance fees.

⌂ **Ruaha Hilltop Lodge** (8 rooms) ☏ 026 270 1806; m 0748 726709;
e ruahahilltoplodge@yahoo.com; www.ruahahilltoplodge.com. Situated on a steep hillside some 20km from the park entrance gate

along the Tungamalenga road, this is another new lodge, and good value at US$80 pp for FB accommodation in a simple en-suite thatched *banda* with hot water, solar power and a private balcony. There's a great view from the restaurant/bar area, and the management can arrange transfers from Iringa as well as game drives into the park by prior arrangement.

⌂ **Msembe Camp** (11 rooms) This national park camp near the headquarters lies close to the river and some extensive open plains teeming with game. The accommodation isn't up to much – prefabricated en-suite dbl and family *bandas* that look like they must get seriously hot during the middle of the day – but it's the cheapest on offer within the park. Bedding, firewood and water are provided, and drinks can be bought at the nearby staff bar, but all food must be brought with you. US$20 pp.

⌂ **Tungamalenga Camp** ☏ 0744 983519/0745 469504; e tungcamp@yahoo.com. This new camp and curio shop is situated in the eponymous village about 27km before the park entrance gate on the left fork coming from Iringa. The small en-suite *bandas*, each with 2 beds and netting, would seem rather overpriced were it not for their proximity to the park. Camping, with access to a clean shower and toilet and a self-catering area, costs US$10 pp. Meals are available by arrangement. US$18 pp bed only, US$20 b&b or US$40 FB.

# SAADANI NATIONAL PARK

Protected as a game reserve since 1969 and recently gazetted as a national park, Sadaani is the only wildlife sanctuary in east Africa with an Indian Ocean beachfront. The original 200km² game reserve, centred on the small but ancient fishing village of Saadani, was expanded to cover 500km² in 1996, and it is likely to redouble in area with the proposed incorporation of a tract of former ranchland when the national park is gazetted.

As recently as ten years ago, despite its proximity to Dar es Salaam, Saadani was among the most obscure and inaccessible conservation areas in east Africa, lacking tourist facilities in any form. Inadequate protection and resultant poaching also meant that wildlife had been severely depleted, to the extent that Saadani's status as a game reserve seemed all but nominal. In recent years, however, Saadani has received renewed attention from conservationists and tourists alike. A top-notch private tented camp has been established, access has improved, there's been a concerted clampdown on poaching and an attempt to integrate adjacent villages into the conservation effort that was initiated by the Department of Wildlife with assistance from Germany's GTZ agency in 1998.

Viewed purely as a wildlife destination, Saadani cannot yet bear comparison to Tanzania's finest – though if present trends continue, it may well be up with them ten years hence. But even as things stand, Saadani is a thoroughly worthwhile and enjoyable retreat, allowing visitors to combine the hedonistic pleasures of a perfect sandy beach with guided bush walks, game drives, and boat trips up the Wami River. It is also the closest national park to Zanzibar – 15 minutes away by air, with scheduled flights likely to be introduced in the near future.

**BACKGROUND INFORMATION** Inland of its 20km coastline, Saadani supports a park-like cover of open grassland interspersed with stands of acacia trees and knotted coastal thicket. Along the coast, palm-lined beaches are separated by extensive mangrove stands, while the major watercourses are fringed by lush riparian woodland. The park supports a wide range of ungulates, with game densities generally highest in January and February, and from June to August, when the plains near the lodge hold more water. At all times of year, however, you can be reasonably confident of encountering giraffe, buffalo, warthog, common waterbuck, reedbuck, hartebeest and wildebeest, along with troops of yellow baboon and vervet monkey. Something of a Saadani special, likely to be seen a few times on any game drive, is the red duiker, a diminutive, beautiful and normally very shy antelope of coastal scrub and forest. Quite common, but less easily seen, are greater kudu and eland. Saadani also harbours a small population of Roosevelt's sable, an endangered race elsewhere found in the Selous Game Reserve.

The elephant population, though small, is on the increase, and herds of up to 30 are sighted with increasing frequency. Lion are also making something of a comeback, with at least three different prides observed during 2001, one of which actually came to drink at the lodge waterhole! Leopard, spotted hyena and black-backed jackal are also around, along with the usual small nocturnal predators. In addition to game drives, guided walks offer a good chance of seeing various antelope and representatives of Saadani's rich variety of woodland birds. Hippos and crocodiles are normally encountered on river trips, along with a good selection of marine and riverine birds. The beaches in and around Saadani form one of the last major breeding sites for green turtles on mainland Tanzania.

The lodge – and effectively the park – is often forced to close over April and May when the black cotton soil roads tend to become waterlogged.

**Entrance fees** Entrance to the game reserve costs US$20 per person per 24 hours.

**GETTING THERE AND AWAY** No scheduled flight currently lands at Saadani airstrip but air charters can be arranged in Zanzibar through reliable tour operators or agents, or through the lodges listed below. The lodges also operate road transfers to/from Dar es Salaam, so you could fly between Zanzibar and Dar and go the rest of the way to Saadani by road.

## WHERE TO STAY
### Upmarket

☖ **Saadani Safari Camp** ✆/f 022 277 3294; m 0748 585401; e info@saadanilodge.com; www.saadanilodge.com. This small and intimate tented camp, which runs attractively along a palm-fringed beach about 1km north of Saadani village, has undergone a major facelift over the last couple of years, most notably with the addition of a swimming pool. Accommodation is in comfortable framed canvas tents with a makuti roof, en-suite facilities, solar electricity and twin or dbl bed, as well as a second netted bed on the balcony should you want to sleep outside. The open wooden bar

and dining area is very peaceful, while a treehouse overlooks a waterhole regularly visited by waterbuck, bushbuck, buffalo and various waterbirds – and very occasionally by lion and elephant. Activities include game drives, guided walks with a ranger, and boat trips on the river. *US$290/500 sgl/dbl FB inc one activity per day. A honeymoon rate of US$300 pp includes a private candlelit dinner and wine.*
☖ **Tent With A View** (8 rooms) ✆ 022 211 0507; m 0741 323318; e tentview@cats-net.com; www.saadani.com. This is another small camp, built a couple of years ago along a pretty beach set about

30km north of Saadani village near Mkwaja, an area regarded to be the best in the park for elephant sightings. The camp consists of 8 standing tents on stilted wooden platforms spaced out in the coastal scrub immediately behind the beach. It offers a similar range of guided activities to Saadani Safari Camp, while several short self-guided walking trails emanate from the camp, and you can canoe in the nearby Mafuwe Creek. *FB US$255/350 sgl/dbl; inc all activities and park fees US$355/550.*

## Budget

🏠 **Saadani Resthouse** Though somewhat rundown, this 10-room government resthouse situated on the beach some 500m north of Saadani Safari Lodge is by far the most affordable option in the park at US$20 pp. Bookings are seldom necessary and although camping is permitted, it costs the same as a room.

# Appendix 1

**LANGUAGE** with thanks to Said el-Gheithy

**PRONUNCIATION** Pronunciation of Swahili is generally straightforward: every syllable is sounded and there are no 'silent endings'. In longer words the stress is on the penultimate syllable. The most confusing feature for learners is that many words have a prefix and suffix which change according to subject and tense. However, when speaking, beginners can ignore these additions, and still be understood.

Of course, the best way to learn is to listen to the people around you. For more detailed information, use a phrasebook (see *Appendix 2*, page 333), or visit the Kiswahili Institute (see page 143).

**USEFUL SWAHILI WORDS AND PHRASES** The following basics are necessarily very simplified, and may not be grammatically correct, but by using them you will be understood in most situations. Many Zanzibaris will be delighted to hear a visitor using a few Swahili words – even if they are mispronounced or put in the wrong order!

**Introductions and greetings** Introductions and salutations are very important in Swahili culture, particularly when speaking to adults or people older than yourself, even if the age difference is slight. (Children are not usually greeted by adults outside their family.)

The most common forms of address are the traditional Muslim greetings (in Arabic), regardless of the religion of the people being greeted, each with its own response:

| | |
|---|---|
| *Salama aleikum* | Peace be with you |
| *Aleikum salam* | And peace be with you (response) |

You can also use the following greetings when addressing older people:

| | |
|---|---|
| *Sblakheri* | Good morning |
| *Msalkheri* | Good afternoon/evening |
| *Shkamoo* | (a general greeting which can be used at any time of day) |
| *Marahaba* | (response to '*shkamoo*') |
| *Habari zako* or *hujambo* | How are you? |
| *Al humdul allah* | Everything is well (response: literally 'Thanks be to Allah') |

For people of the same age, and especially for friends, you can use *Habari*, which means 'Hello' (also meaning 'How are you?', literally 'what news?'). The reply might be *Al humdul allah*, or the more casual *Nzuri* ('good'), *Nzuri sana* ('very good') or *Safi* ('fine'). In areas where Swahili is not spoken as a first language the reply is often *Mzuri*, with an 'M', rather than 'Nzuri'. *Habari* can also be used for 'Excuse me' (when attracting somebody's attention), but it is still considered impolite to simply say '*Habari*' ('hello') to someone older than you.

*Mambo* is an even more casual way of greeting friends, meaning 'how's it going?' The response is *Poa* (something along the lines of 'neat', 'cool' or 'dandy').

Although *Jambo* also means 'Hello', Zanzibaris never use this word speaking to each other, and it tends only to be used by Zanzibaris talking to tourists. (In the same way, the oft-quoted '*Hakuna matata*' – 'no problem' – is mock-Swahili-for-tourists imported from Kenya, and not used by Zanzibaris. If you want to express this idea, a more correct alternative would be '*Hamna neno*' or '*Haidhuru*'.)

Children in Zanzibar greet adults with *Chechei*, usually followed by the title of the adult. The response is the same.

Even when speaking in English a Swahili acquaintance will ask 'How are you?', 'How are things today?', 'How is your husband/wife/friend?' You should do the same. Launching straight into any subject without the opening questions is rude. Traditional Zanzibaris expect women to be less forward than men, although in areas used to tourists this does not apply.

*Hodi* means 'Hello, anyone at home, can I come in?' used when knocking on somebody's door. *Karibu* is the response, meaning 'welcome' (literally 'come near').

You may hear the word *mzungu* ('white person') directed to you, particularly by children, but it is not disrespectful.

## The basics

| | |
|---|---|
| Goodbye | *Kwaheri* |
| Welcome | *Karibu* |
| Please | *Tafadali* |
| Thank you (very much) | *Asante (sana)* |
| yes | *ndiyo* |
| no | *hapana* |

## Conversation starters and enders

| | |
|---|---|
| What is your name? | *Jina lako nani?* |
| My name is Chris | *Jina langu Chris* |
| Where are you from? | *Unatoka wapi?* |
| I am from … | *Mimi ninatoka …* |
| | (the *mimi* is often dropped) |
| Where do you live? | *Unakaa wapi?* |
| Where are you staying? (ie: locally) | *Umefikia wapi?* |
| I am sorry, I don't understand | *Samahani sifahamu* |
| I don't speak Swahili | *Sijui Kiswahili* |
| I speak a very little Swahili | *Nazungumza Kiswahili kidogo tu* |

## Other useful words and phrases

| | |
|---|---|
| OK (agreement) | *sawa* |
| sorry (condolences) | *pole* (not used for apologies) |
| where? | *wapi?* |
| what | *nini* |
| here | *hapa* |
| there | *hapo* |
| there is | *ipo* |
| is there…? | *iko…?* |
| there isn't… | *hakuna…* |
| how much? | *bei gani?* (literally 'what price?') |
| how many shillings? | *shillingi ngapi?* |
| I want to go to Bububu | *Nataka kwenda Bububu* |
| Where is the bus for Makunduchi? | *Liko wapi basi la Makunduchi?* |

| | |
|---|---|
| Where is the ruin? | *Liko wapi gofu?* |
| I am ill | *Mimi mgonjwa* |
| Where is the hospital? | *Iko wapi hospitali?* |
| Where is the doctor? | *Yuko wapi daktari?* |
| I am lost | *Nimepotea* |
| left | *kushoto* |
| right | *kulia* |
| straight on | *moja kwa moja* |
| near | *karibu* |
| far | *mbali* |
| today | *leo* |
| tomorrow | *kesho* |
| yesterday | *jana* |
| | |
| bank | *benki* |
| shop | *duka* |
| market | *soko* |
| cafe, local eating-house | *hoteli ya chakula* |

## Food and drink

| | |
|---|---|
| beef | *nyama ya ngombe* |
| chicken | *kuku* |
| eggs | *yai* |
| fish | *samaki* |
| potato | *viazi* |
| rice | *mchele* |
| water | *maji* |
| tea | *chai* |
| coffee | *kahawa* |
| milk | *maziwa* |
| sugar | *sukari* |

The word *soda* means any fizzy drink in a bottle. In the smarter hotels in Zanzibar Town, if you want soda water try asking for a club soda.

## Numbers

| | | | |
|---|---|---|---|
| 1 | *moja* | 21 | *ishirini na moja* |
| 2 | *mbili* | 30 | *thelathini* |
| 3 | *tatu* | 40 | *arobaini* |
| 4 | *nne* | 50 | *hamsini* |
| 5 | *tano* | 60 | *sitini* |
| 6 | *sita* | 70 | *sabini* |
| 7 | *saba* | 80 | *themanini* |
| 8 | *nane* | 90 | *tisini* |
| 9 | *tisa* | 100 | *mia* |
| 10 | *kumi* | 101 | *mia na moja* |
| 11 | *kumi na moja* | 102 | *mia na mbili* |
| 12 | *kumi na mbili* | 200 | *mia mbili* |
| 20 | *ishirini* | 300 | *mia tatu* |

**Time** Swahili time starts at 00.00, the hour of sunrise, which is at 06.00 in Western time.

| | |
|---|---|
| What time is it? | *Saa ngapi?* |

| 07.00 | *saa moja* (literally one o'clock) |
|-------|------------------------------------|
| 08.00 | *saa mbili* |
| noon | *saa sita* |
| 13.00 | *saa saba* |

When finding out about bus or boat departures, check if the time you've been told is Swahili time or Western time. This can be complicated further by some buses leaving outlying villages very early in the morning.

# Appendix 2

## FURTHER INFORMATION

### BOOKS
### History and background

**General histories of Africa** The following books are general histories of Africa or the east African region, which include sections on Zanzibar. Some are old and now long out of print, but make interesting reading if you can find them – try a specialist historical bookshop. Pakenham's classic history of Africa from the 1870s onwards is particularly compulsive, and often reprinted in paperback. Taylor's book about the European settlers who 'stayed on' in east Africa after the countries gained independence, looks at the colonial past in the present context, and neatly combines history with contemporary travel writing.

Coupland, R *The Exploitation of East Africa 1856–1890: The Slave Trade and the Scramble* (Faber, London, 1939)

Davidson, B *The Story of Africa* (London, 1984)

Freeman-Grenville, G S P *The East African Coast: Select Documents* (Oxford University Press, 2nd edn, 1975)

*A History of East Africa* (Oxford University Press, London, 1963)

Pakenham, T *The Scramble for Africa* (Weidenfeld and Nicolson, London, 1991)

Prestage, E *Portuguese Pioneers* (A & C Black, London, 1933)

Taylor S *Livingstone's Tribe* (HarperCollins, London, 1999)

**Early histories of Zanzibar** The next five books cover Zanzibar specifically, but they are old guidebooks and histories from British colonial days, and all long out of print. Lyne's book was reprinted in 1987 and 2000 by Gallery Publications – a local Zanzibar publisher. Likewise Pearce's *Island Metropolis* and Ommanney's *Isle of Cloves* have also been reprinted or are due for reprint in 2003, by the same publisher.

Brode, H *Tippu Tip: His Career in Zanzibar and Central Africa* (Gallery Publications, Zanzibar, 2002). This is a reprint of the original 1903 study of the career of Tippu Tip, Zanzibar's most famous (or infamous) trader. A fascinating and highly readable account of life on Zanzibar and the east African mainland over a century ago.

Gray, J *History of Zanzibar from the Middle Ages to 1856* (Oxford University Press, London, 1962).

Ingrams, W H *Zanzibar: Its History and People* (Witherby, London, 1931).

Lyne, R N *Zanzibar in Contemporary Times* (Darf, London, 1905). Reprinted 1987.

Ommanney, F D *Isle of Cloves* (Longman, London, 1957)

Pearce, Major F B *Zanzibar: The Island Metropolis of Eastern Africa* (Fisher Unwin, London, 1920).

### General histories of Zanzibar and the Indian Ocean

Hall, R *Empires of the Monsoon* (HarperCollins, London, 1999). A fascinating history of the lands around the Indian Ocean, including good sections on Zanzibar.

Hamilton, G, *In the Wake of da Gama* (Abacus, London, 1951).

Hamilton, G, *Princes of Zinj* (Hutchinson, London, 1957). Comprehensive and accessible historical accounts, with an emphasis on readability, sometimes at the expense of accuracy.

## Modern histories of Zanzibar

Nurse, D and Spear, T *The Swahili: Reconstructing the History and Language of an African Society* (The Ethnohistory Series. University of Pennsylvania Press, Philadelphia, 1985). This is an excellent, short, readable book which argues convincingly that the Swahili culture is more of an African (and less an Arab) phenomenon than previously thought. Highly recommended.

Horton, M C 'The Swahili Corridor'. This article was published in *Scientific American* 255(9) 86–93 (1987). Horton has been one of the most influential archaeologists to work on the east African coast, and has done excavations and surveys on Pemba and Unguja (Zanzibar Island). This is an excellent short piece that touches on some of the Mediterranean connections with east Africa.

Mapuri, O *The 1964 Revolution* (published in 1996). This short, locally published book is a concise history of Zanzibari politics, covering the period from 1964 up to the 1995 elections.

These three books are modern, post-revolution, textbook-style histories:

Martin, E B *Zanzibar: Tradition and Revolution* (Hamish Hamilton, London, 1978)

Sheriff, A *Slaves, Spices and Ivory in Zanzibar* (James Currey, London, 1987)

Sheriff, A, and Ferguson E D *Zanzibar under Colonial Rule* (James Currey, London, 1991).

**Zanzibar and Oman** Four modern and very detailed books, with specific reference to the Oman-Zanzibar link:

Al-Maamiry, A H *Oman and East Africa* (Lancers Books, New Delhi, 1979).

Al-Maamiry, A H *Omani Sultans in Zanzibar* (Lancers Books, New Delhi, 1988).

Bennett, N R *A History of the Arab State of Zanzibar* (Methuen, London, 1978).

Bhacker, M R *Trade and Empire in Muscat and Zanzibar* (Routledge, London, 1992).

## Railways and ships

Hill, M H *The Permanent Way* (East African Literature Bureau, Nairobi, 1949) and Miller, C *The Lunatic Express* (Macmillan, Ballantine Books, Random House, 1971). These two books are histories of the East African railways, both with good sections on Zanzibar.

Patience K *Zanzibar and the Bububu Railway* (published by the author, 1995). A fascinating little booklet about the only railway on Zanzibar, which existed at the beginning of the 20th century.

Patience K *Zanzibar and the Loss of HMS Pegasus* (published by the author, 1995) and Patience K, *Zanzibar and the Shortest War in History* (published by the author, 1994). Two excellent booklets written and published by Zanzibar historian Kevin Patience. Well researched, they describe in full events which might otherwise be confined to the footnotes of history. The gunship *Pegasus* was sunk during World War I and this book also contains background information on British naval ships in east Africa, while *Shortest War* describes the 1896 bombardment of the sultan's palace, with several fascinating archive photos.

Patience K *Königsberg – A German East African Raider* (published by the author, 1997). The *Königsberg* was the German gunboat which sunk the British *Pegasus,* fully described in an earlier book by the same author. This painstakingly researched book covers historical events before and after the *Pegasus* incident, including the *Königsberg's* final sinking by another British ship in the Rufiji Delta, southwest of Zanzibar. The chapter describing the present-day position of the *Königsberg's* relics scattered all over East Africa is particularly interesting.

## Architecture and history

Mwalim, M A *Doors of Zanzibar* (Gallery Publications, Zanzibar, 2002). Using hundreds of photographs by Uwe Rau, this fascinating book catalogues the unique doors which have become an icon of Zanzibar Stone Town, and covers the various Indian, Arabic and Swahili influences.

Pitcher, G and Jafferji, J *Zanzibar Style* (Gallery Publications, Zanzibar, 2001). This celebration of Zanzibari architecture is listed under *Large-format photo books*.

Siravo, F, and Bianca, S *A Plan for the Historic Stone Town* (Gallery Publications in association with the Aga Khan Trust for Culture, Zanzibar, 1997). A large and detailed discussion document, full of fascinating photos, plans and drawings, which analyses the current situation then proposes a major and systematic plan for the repair, preservation and conservation of the many old buildings in Stone Town. This is a vital reference for anyone interested in the history and architecture of Zanzibar.

Sheriff, Prof A *Zanzibar Stone Town: An Architectural Exploration* (Gallery Publications, Zanzibar, 1998). With skilful photographs by Javed Jafferji and illuminating text by a leading Zanzibar historian, this handy little pocket-sized book is an ideal guide and companion for your strolls around the narrow streets of Stone Town. Highly recommended.

Sheriff, Prof A *The History and Conservation of Zanzibar Stone Town* (published by James Currey). This book is part of Currey's Eastern African Studies series, and although quite academic in tone, it has a lot of useful information for anyone keen on the history of Zanzibari architecture.

## Princess Salme

Ruete, E (born Salme binte Said Al-Busaidi), *Memoirs of an Arabian Princess from Zanzibar* (Gallery Publications, Zanzibar, 1998). This book is a translation of *Memoiren einer Arabischen Prinzessin*, which was first published in 1888. It was also reprinted by Markus Wiener Publishing (New York, 1989), but the latest translation is now easily available in Zanzibar bookshops. It is a very readable first-hand account by a unique figure in the history of Zanzibar, providing a good overview of the period and several fascinating personal insights. Highly recommended.

Ruete, E (born Salme binte Said Al-Busaidi), *An Arabian Princess Between Two Worlds: Memoirs, Letters, Sequels to the Memoirs*, ed E Van Donzel, (E J Brill Publishing, Leiden, Netherlands, 1993). Volume 3 in a series on Arab History and Culture. This is a very detailed and comprehensive account of Salme's life in Zanzibar, Germany and Syria. Includes a biography of her son, Said-Rudolph Ruete. Expensive and hard to obtain.

## Travel and exploration

Batchelor, J and J *In Stanley's Footsteps* (Blandford Press, London, 1990) and Wilson, C, and Irwin, A, *In Quest of Livingstone* (House of Lochar, Scotland, 1999). Two books in which British couples follow the routes of the great explorers in Africa. Livingstone started many of his travels in Zanzibar. The Batchelors mount a full expedition, while Colum Wilson and Aisling Irwin trace Livingstone's final journey through Tanzania and Zambia at a more grassroots level.

Burton, Richard Francis *Zanzibar: City, Island and Coast* (London, 1872). Many early European explorers in Africa mentioned Zanzibar in their journals, but Burton, perhaps the most 'colourful' of them all, is the only one to write a specific book on Zanzibar. Although published first over a century ago, reprints are sometimes available.

Hugon, A *The Exploration of Africa* (New Horizons, Thames and Hudson, 1999). This is a fascinating and beautifully illustrated little book, with good coverage on the journeys of Livingstone, Stanley and others in east Africa.

Moorehead, A *The White Nile* (Hamish Hamilton, London, 1960). A classic book on the history of European exploration in the east African region. Often reprinted. Readable and recommended.

Mountfield, D *A History of African Exploration* (Domus Books/Hamlyn, London, 1976) and Richards, C, and Place, J *East African Explorers* (Oxford University Press, London, 1960). Two books on exploration in Africa, although both out of print and hard to find, including some mentions of Zanzibar where many journeys began and ended.

Royal Geographical Society (ed John Keay), *History of World Exploration* (Paul Hamlyn, Reed International, London, 1991). Includes sections on exploration of east Africa

Teal, J *Livingstone* (Putnam, New York, 1973). A fine biography of the great explorer.

Waugh, E *Remote People* (Duckworth, 1931, republished 1985 by Penguin Books, UK, as part of their 20th Century Classics series). Waugh travelled to many parts of Africa, including Zanzibar, as a newspaper correspondent, and his dry observations are as engaging today as they were when first written.

## Large-format photo books

Jafferji, J, and Rees Jones B *Images of Zanzibar* (HSP Publications, London, 1996). Much of east Africa has been covered by publishers of lavishly illustrated 'coffee-table' books, but until recently Zanzibar seems to have escaped their notice. Local photographer Javed Jafferji has made up for this with a portfolio of his finest work, showing rich colours and an eye for detail perfectly capturing the spirit of the islands.

Jafferji, J, Jafferji, Z and Waterman, P *A Taste of Zanzibar: Chakula Kizuri* (Gallery Publications, Zanzibar, 2001). Not hungry? You will be if you read this bountiful cookbook which celebrates (and helps you create) Zanzibar's delicious cuisine, enhanced with 250 mouthwatering colour photos.

Pitcher, G and Jafferji, J *Zanzibar Style* (Gallery Publications, Zanzibar, 2001). This sumptuous and stimulating book combines evocative photos by Javed Jafferji and text by Gemma Pitcher to explore the themes that have inspired Zanzibar's unique architecture and interior design – from Europe, Oman and India, as well as of course the natural forms of Africa – and also covers related aspects such as crafts, textiles and furniture. Listed by *The Times* as one of the 'Top 20 travel books for Christmas' 2001.

Sheriff, A *Zanzibar – Romance of the Ages* (HSP Publications, London, 1996). Accomplished photographer Javed Jafferji compiled this fascinating collection of archive photos from the late 19th and early 20th centuries – the text and captions were provided by Abdul Sheriff, Professor of History at the University of Dar es Salaam and Principle Curator of the Zanzibar Museums.

## Fiction and autobiography

Bateman, G *Zanzibar Tales* (Gallery Publications, Zanzibar, 2002). Another reprint from the industrious Gallery house; a collection of amusing (and sometimes confusing) Zanzibari folktales originally recorded and translated into English by George Bateman almost a century ago, and enhanced by lively illustrations by Walter Bobbett.

Haji, M M *Sowing The Wind* (Gallery Publications, Zanzibar, 2002). This autobiographical novel explores life and politics on the islands of Zanzibar during the turbulent years which led to independence in 1963, and the revolution which followed.

Kaye, M M *Death in Zanzibar* (Penguin, London, 1984 – first published as *The House of Shadows*, Longman 1959) and Kaye, M M, *Trade Wind* (Longman, 1963, Penguin, 1982). Two historical romantic novels set in Zanzibar. *Death in Zanzibar* is also published with two other M M Kaye *Death in...* stories in a larger book called the *House of Shade*.

## Field guides
### Mammals and birds

Kingdon, J *The Kingdon Fieldguide to African Mammals* (Academic Press, USA and UK, 1997). For animals on Zanzibar, a field guide to the more common species of east Africa is of limited use. However, Kingdon's book is by far the best, as it covers every species in Africa in detail, including those on Zanzibar, with excellent illustrations and background notes.

van Perlo, B *Illustrated Checklist of the Birds of Eastern Africa* (Harper Collins, London, 1996) and Williams, J, and Arlott, N *A Field Guide to the Birds of East Africa* (Collins, London). For birds, the field guide you choose is determined by your level of interest. Of the books listed above, the van Perlo *Illustrated Checklist* is complete, with illustrations of every bird occurring in Africa, including those on Zanzibar, while the classic Williams & Arlott also has fairly good coverage. The large and comprehensive *Birds of Kenya & Northern Tanzania* by Zimmerman is used by keen birders, and it includes most species which occur on Zanzibar, but it's quite heavy to carry around.

### Marine wildlife

Richmond, M (ed), *A Guide to the Seashores of Eastern Africa and the Western Indian Ocean Islands* (Sida/SAREC, 1997). This excellent book contains around 450 pages, including over 150 of colour illustrations. More than 1,600 species of marine plants and animals are illustrated, plus notes on geology, climate, ecology and human activities. This is an essential tool for scientists, and a useful handbook for all visitors to the region. Proceeds from the sales of this book are put towards marine education purposes in the region, administered by the SEA Trust. Although hard to find overseas (only specialist stores stock it), this book is readily available in Zanzibar from all good bookshops.

Forstle, A, and Vierkotter, R *Marine Green Book* (Green Ocean, Zanzibar, 1997). This handy little pocket encyclopaedia covers everything you need to know about marine life (from algae to zooxanthellae) and marine activities (from anchor damage to the Zanzibar Sea Turtle Project) in and around the Zanzibar archipelago. It also covers snorkelling, diving, coral reefs, fish and marine habitats. It is available in Zanzibar bookshops at a very reasonable price, and all proceeds go to fund environmental education projects.

## Manuals, guidebooks and phrasebooks

Bogaert, P *The Krazy Kanga Book* (Gallery Publications, Zanzibar, 2002). An offbeat 'adult' study of the *kanga* or 'wrap', the ubiquitous and vital garment for the women of east Africa.

Dawood, R *How to Stay Healthy Abroad* (Oxford University Press)

Leonard, R *Swahili Phrasebook* (Lonely Planet)

Hatt, J *The Tropical Traveller* (Pan)

Koornhof, A *Dive Sites of Kenya & Tanzania, including Zanzibar, Pemba & Mafia* (New Holland)

Wilson-Howarth, Jane, and Ellis, Dr Matthew *Your Child Abroad: A Travel Health Guide* (Bradt Travel Guides, UK, 2004, with updates on www.bradtguides.com)

## BOOKSHOPS

**The Travel Bookshop** 13 Blenheim Cres, London W11 2EE, UK; ☏ 020 7229 5260; f 020 7243 1552; www.thetravelbookshop.co.uk. Stocks guidebooks, phrasebooks, history, fiction, maps, and anything else to do with travel publications. They can source old and out-of-print books, and operate a worldwide mail-order service.

**Risborough Books** 81 Manor Park Av, Princes Risborough, Bucks HP27 9AR, UK; ☏ 01844 343165. Specialises in second-hand books on east Africa, and offers mail order only. Contact them by post (no fax or email) for a list.

## WEBSITES
If you've got access to the internet, you can get further information on Zanzibar from the following websites. Most have links to other useful relevant sites.

**Africa Confidential** (*www.africa-confidential.com*) gives the inside story on political events across Africa, including Tanzania and Zanzibar.

**Africa Travel Association** (*www.africa-ata.org*) has close links with the US-based *Africa Travel* magazine and is an interesting source of information on the whole continent.

**African Travel and Tourism Association** (*www.atta.co.uk*) represents many tour operators covering Africa, and is an excellent directory of useful contacts.

**Internet Living Swahili Dictionary** (*www.yale.edu/swahili*) is a very handy on-line Swahili–English dictionary, with links to other Swahili-related sites.

**The Hunger Site** (*www.thehungersite.com*) is not directly related to Zanzibar, but if you visit this site (no more than once per day) and click on a 'donate' button, the site's sponsors will give two *free* cups of food to a developing country.

**Zanzibar Travel Network**, also called **Zanzibar Net** (*www.zanzibar.net*) has sections on history, diving, touring, beaches, history, travel tips and so on. It also has a good selection of links to other sites which cover Zanzibar.

**Zanzibar.org** (*www.zanzibar.org*) is a gateway site with pages on several hotels in Zanzibar Town and around Zanzibar Island, plus coverage of various aspects of Zanzibar such as culture, history and wildlife.

## Sites for general news and information

**www.allafrica.com** Huge pan-African news site with vast amounts of topical content.

**www.theexpress.com/** Weekly newspaper based in Dar es Salaam.

**www.tanserve.com** Interesting and slightly off-beat Dar-based portal with a mix of news and information.

**www-sul.stanford.edu/depts/ssrg/africa/tanzan.html** Extensive listing of links for Tanzania and Zanzibar.

**www.zanzibarwatch.org/** Human rights organisation listing abuses in the run-up to recent elections.

**www.zanzibargovernment.org/** Official site of the government of Zanzibar.

**http://home.globalfrontiers.com/Zanzibar/sights_to_see_in_zanzibar.htm** Historical site on Zanzibar, with pictures and illustrations.

**www.africa.upenn.edu/Country_Specific/Tanzania.html** University of Pennsylvania African studies course – links pages.

**www.zanzibar-travel-guide.com** Online site where you'll find much of the text of this guide, plus many additional useful links.

# WIN £100 CASH!
## READER QUESTIONNAIRE

**Send in your completed questionnaire for the chance to win £100 cash in our regular draw**

All respondents may order a Bradt guide at half the UK retail price – please complete the order form overleaf.

*(Entries may be posted or faxed to us, or scanned and emailed.)*

We are interested in getting feedback from our readers to help us plan future Bradt guides. Please answer ALL the questions below and return the form to us in order to qualify for an entry in our regular draw.

Have you used any other Bradt guides? If so, which titles? . . . . . . . . . . . . . . . . . .

. . . . . . . . . . . . . . . . . . . . . . . . . . . . . . . . . . . . . . . . . . . . . . . . . . . . . . . . . . . . . . . . . . .

What other publishers' travel guides do you use regularly? . . . . . . . . . . . . . . . . . .

. . . . . . . . . . . . . . . . . . . . . . . . . . . . . . . . . . . . . . . . . . . . . . . . . . . . . . . . . . . . . . . . . . .

Where did you buy this guidebook? . . . . . . . . . . . . . . . . . . . . . . . . . . . . . . . . . . . . . .

What was the main purpose of your trip to Zanzibar (or for what other reason did you read our guide)? eg: holiday/business/charity etc.. . . . . . . . . . . . . . . . . . . . . . .

. . . . . . . . . . . . . . . . . . . . . . . . . . . . . . . . . . . . . . . . . . . . . . . . . . . . . . . . . . . . . . . . . . .

What other destinations would you like to see covered by a Bradt guide?

. . . . . . . . . . . . . . . . . . . . . . . . . . . . . . . . . . . . . . . . . . . . . . . . . . . . . . . . . . . . . . . . . . .

Would you like to receive our catalogue/newsletters?

YES / NO (If yes, please complete details on reverse)

If yes – by post or email? . . . . . . . . . . . . . . . . . . . . . . . . . . . . . . . . . . . . . . . . . . . . .

Age (circle relevant category) 16–25     26–45     46–60     60+

Male/Female (delete as appropriate)

Home country . . . . . . . . . . . . . . . . . . . . . . . . . . . . . . . . . . . . . . . . . . . . . . . . . . . . . .

Please send us any comments about our guide to Zanzibar or other Bradt Travel Guides. . . . . . . . . . . . . . . . . . . . . . . . . . . . . . . . . . . . . . . . . . . . . . . . . . . . . . . . . . . .

. . . . . . . . . . . . . . . . . . . . . . . . . . . . . . . . . . . . . . . . . . . . . . . . . . . . . . . . . . . . . . . . . . .

. . . . . . . . . . . . . . . . . . . . . . . . . . . . . . . . . . . . . . . . . . . . . . . . . . . . . . . . . . . . . . . . . . .

. . . . . . . . . . . . . . . . . . . . . . . . . . . . . . . . . . . . . . . . . . . . . . . . . . . . . . . . . . . . . . . . . . .

## Bradt Travel Guides
23 High Street, Chalfont St Peter, Bucks SL9 9QE, UK
☎ +44 (0)1753 893444 f +44 (0)1753 892333
e info@bradtguides.com
www.bradtguides.com

# CLAIM YOUR HALF-PRICE BRADT GUIDE!

## Order Form

To order your half-price copy of a Bradt guide, and to enter our prize draw to win £100 (see overleaf), please fill in the order form below, complete the questionnaire overleaf, and send it to Bradt Travel Guides by post, fax or email.

Please send me one copy of the following guide at half the UK retail price

| *Title* | *Retail price* | *Half price* |
|---------|---------------|-------------|
| . . . . . . . . . . . . . . . . . . . . . . . . . . . . . . . . . . . . . . . . . . . . . | . . . . . . . . | . . . . . . . |

Please send the following additional guides at full UK retail price

| *No* | *Title* | *Retail price* | *Total* |
|------|---------|---------------|---------|
| . . . | . . . . . . . . . . . . . . . . . . . . . . . . . . . . . . . . . . . . . . . . . . . . . | . . . . . . . . | . . . . . . . |
| . . . | . . . . . . . . . . . . . . . . . . . . . . . . . . . . . . . . . . . . . . . . . . . . . | . . . . . . . . | . . . . . . . |
| . . . | . . . . . . . . . . . . . . . . . . . . . . . . . . . . . . . . . . . . . . . . . . . . . | . . . . . . . . | . . . . . . . |

| | | |
|---|---|---|
| | *Sub total* | . . . . . . . |
| | Post & packing | . . . . . . . |
| (£1 per book UK; £2 per book Europe; £3 per book rest of world) | | |
| | *Total* | . . . . . . . |

Name . . . . . . . . . . . . . . . . . . . . . . . . . . . . . . . . . . . . . . . . . . . . . . . . . . . . . . . . . . .

Address . . . . . . . . . . . . . . . . . . . . . . . . . . . . . . . . . . . . . . . . . . . . . . . . . . . . . . . . .

Tel . . . . . . . . . . . . . . . . . . . . . . . . . .    Email . . . . . . . . . . . . . . . . . . . . . . . . .

☐ I enclose a cheque for £ . . . . . . . . made payable to Bradt Travel Guides Ltd

☐ I would like to pay by credit card. Number: . . . . . . . . . . . . . . . . . . . . . . . . . .

  Expiry date: . . . / . . .    3-digit security code (on reverse of card) . . . . .

☐ Please add my name to your catalogue mailing list.

☐ I would be happy for you to use my name and comments in Bradt marketing material.

Send your order on this form, with the completed questionnaire, to:

**Bradt Travel Guides/ZAN6**
23 High Street, Chalfont St Peter, Bucks SL9 9QE
☏ +44 (0)1753 893444   **f** +44 (0)1753 892333
**e** info@bradtguides.com   www.bradtguides.com

# Bradt Travel Guides

www.bradtguides.com

**Africa**

| | |
|---|---|
| Africa Overland | £15.99 |
| Benin | £14.99 |
| Botswana: Okavango, Chobe, | £14.95 |
| Northern Kalahari | |
| Burkina Faso | £14.99 |
| Cape Verde Islands | £13.99 |
| Canary Islands | £13.95 |
| Cameroon | £13.95 |
| Eritrea | £12.95 |
| Ethiopia | £15.99 |
| Gabon, São Tomé, Príncipe | £13.95 |
| Gambia, The | £13.99 |
| Georgia | £13.95 |
| Ghana | £13.95 |
| Kenya | £14.95 |
| Madagascar | £14.95 |
| Malawi | £13.99 |
| Mali | £13.95 |
| Mauritius, Rodrigues & Réunion | £13.99 |
| Mozambique | £12.95 |
| Namibia | £14.95 |
| Niger | £14.99 |
| Nigeria | £15.99 |
| Rwanda | £13.95 |
| Seychelles | £14.99 |
| Sudan | £13.95 |
| Tanzania, Northern | £13.99 |
| Tanzania | £16.99 |
| Uganda | £13.95 |
| Zambia | £15.95 |
| Zanzibar | £12.99 |

**Britain and Europe**

| | |
|---|---|
| Albania | £13.99 |
| Armenia, Nagorno Karabagh | £13.99 |
| Azores | £12.99 |
| Baltic Capitals: Tallinn, Riga, | £12.99 |
| Vilnius, Kaliningrad | |
| Belgrade | £6.99 |
| Bosnia & Herzegovina | £13.95 |
| Bratislava | £6.99 |
| Budapest | £7.95 |
| Cork | £6.95 |
| Croatia | £12.95 |
| Cyprus see North Cyprus | |
| Czech Republic | £13.99 |
| Dubrovnik | £6.95 |
| Eccentric Britain | £13.99 |
| Eccentric Cambridge | £6.99 |
| Eccentric Edinburgh | £5.95 |
| Eccentric France | £12.95 |
| Eccentric London | £12.95 |
| Eccentric Oxford | £5.95 |
| Estonia | £12.95 |
| Faroe Islands | £13.95 |
| Hungary | £14.99 |
| Kiev | £7.95 |
| Latvia | £13.99 |
| Lille | £6.99 |

| | |
|---|---|
| Lithuania | £13.99 |
| Ljubljana | £6.99 |
| Macedonia | £13.95 |
| Montenegro | £13.99 |
| North Cyprus | £12.99 |
| Paris, Lille & Brussels | £11.95 |
| Riga | £6.95 |
| River Thames, | £10.95 |
| In the Footsteps of the Famous | |
| Serbia | £13.99 |
| Slovenia | £12.99 |
| Spitsbergen | £14.99 |
| Switzerland: Rail, Road, Lake | £13.99 |
| Tallinn | £6.95 |
| Ukraine | £13.95 |
| Vilnius | £6.99 |

**Middle East, Asia and Australasia**

| | |
|---|---|
| Great Wall of China | £13.99 |
| Iran | £14.99 |
| Iraq | £14.95 |
| Kabul | £9.95 |
| Maldives | £13.99 |
| Mongolia | £14.95 |
| North Korea | £13.95 |
| Oman | £13.99 |
| Palestine, Jerusalem | £12.95 |
| Sri Lanka | £13.99 |
| Syria | £13.99 |
| Tasmania | £12.95 |
| Tibet | £12.95 |
| Turkmenistan | £14.99 |

**The Americas and the Caribbean**

| | |
|---|---|
| Amazon, The | £14.95 |
| Argentina | £15.99 |
| Bolivia | £14.99 |
| Cayman Islands | £12.95 |
| Costa Rica | £13.99 |
| Chile | £16.95 |
| Chile & Argentina: Trekking | £12.95 |
| Eccentric America | £13.95 |
| Eccentric California | £13.99 |
| Falkland Islands | £13.95 |
| Peru & Bolivia: Backpacking and Trekking | £12.95 |
| Panama | £13.95 |
| St Helena, Ascension, Tristan da Cunha | £14.95 |
| USA by Rail | £13.99 |

**Wildlife**

| | |
|---|---|
| Antarctica: Guide to the Wildlife | £14.95 |
| Arctic: Guide to the Wildlife | £15.99 |
| British Isles: Wildlife of Coastal Waters | £14.95 |
| Galápagos Wildlife | £15.99 |
| Madagascar Wildlife | £14.95 |
| Southern African Wildlife | £18.95 |
| Sri Lankan Wildlife | £15.99 |

**Health**

| | |
|---|---|
| Your Child Abroad: A Travel Health Guide | £10.95 |

# Index

*Page numbers in bold indicate major entries; those in italic indicate maps*